Chorti (Mayan) Texts
1

The fifteenth publication in the Haney Foundation series, University of Pennsylvania. *A volume in the University of Pennsylvania Folklore and Folklife Series. Editor,* KENNETH S. GOLDSTEIN

Isidro González, New Haven, 1967

JOHN G. FOUGHT

Chorti (Mayan) Texts
1

Edited by SARAH S. FOUGHT

University of Pennsylvania Press · Philadelphia

Publication of this book has been made possible
by a grant from the Haney Foundation of the
University of Pennsylvania

Library of Congress Catalog Card Number 72–80380
ISBN 0–8122–7667–1
Printed in the United States of America

Contents

Acknowledgments

My work on Chorti has been supported by the National Science Foundation (Grants 516, 1175, 2867, IG 68-14) and was directed in its early stages by Floyd G. Lounsbury. The Haney Foundation has made publication of this book possible.

Sarah Fought has shared in the work from the first field season to the editing and typing of this manuscript. Many details of the analysis and translation were her suggestions, and many more took shape in discussions.

Many of the Chorti have helped me, always with courtesy and patience, even when their own work was interrupted. I am particularly indebted to Isidro González M., Pedro Ramírez R., Juan Quizar, and Ismael León.

I am grateful to Mr. and Mrs. Homer Sharpless, volunteers in agricultural and resettlement assistance to the Chorti, and to the Rev. and Mrs. John Astleford and the Rev. and Mrs. John McNichols, of the Friends Mission in Guatemala, for their assistance and hospitality in Jocotán and Chiquimula.

Francis Gall, of the Dirección General de Cartografía of Guatemala, generously made available copies of the official *Diccionario Geográfico de Guatemala,* and topographic maps of the Chorti area. Unless otherwise noted, geographical information is drawn from these sources.

Finally, I thank Gerald E. Parsons, Jr., and Margaret J. Bouslough for generously contributing the motif and type index to the texts; it appears as an appendix to this volume.

Preface

This book is the first in a series on Chorti now in active preparation. It begins with a brief report of the history and aims of the research program which brought it about, and an introduction to the structure of Chorti as illustrated by the texts.

My interest in Mayan studies began in a seminar on Maya hieroglyphic writing given by Floyd Lounsbury at Yale in 1963. In this work we naturally relied heavily on the available reference books on Mayan grammar and vocabulary. Although some of these were fairly useful, and though the main outlines of the Mayan group's linguistic history were known, there was a frustrating lack of information on many of the languages. In particular, there was (and is) a shortage of reliable descriptive studies of the lowland languages. Because of its geographical and linguistic position within this group, Chorti was especially interesting, and had received even less attention than the other languages.

With the support of the National Science Foundation (Grants GS 516, 1175), Professor Lounsbury, as principal investigator, undertook two projects over a three-year period (June 1964–June 1967) in which I was an assistant investigator and Mrs. Fought was a research assistant. Our primary objective was to collect a linguistic corpus adequate for a descriptive phonology and grammar, and for a preliminary dictionary. Thus, much of the early work was aimed at establishing phonological contrasts and morphological structures. We also wished to collect whatever information seemed immediately interesting from an ethnographic perspective, though the time and anthropological training of the field workers were severely limited.

In June 1964, Mrs. Fought and I went to Guatemala, first staying in Chiquimula, where we were very hospitably received at the Friends Mission. There were few informants available there, but arrangements were made with Sr. Isidro González, who became our principal informant, and soon, a valued friend.

Sr. González was born in 1926 in Pelillo Negro, and remained there until about 1962, when he lost the use of his right hand and was unable to perform the heavy work of farming. Some time before, he had been converted by the Friends Missionaries in Jocotán, and had served as a linguistic informant for Miss Helen Oakley and her successor, John McNichols. After his injury he moved to Jocotán and worked for the mission, taking charge of its reception center.

Working with Sr. González was an extraordinary privilege. He is sensitive to differences in the speech of individuals, and has a rare ability to supply examples pinpointing these differences. Moreover, he has what I take to be great skill in using the resources of Chorti to advantage in storytelling and conversation. A number of his relatives, including two grandparents, were well-known shamans, diviners, and curers. From his earliest childhood he was constantly exposed to their folklore, beliefs, and ceremonies, often serving as an assistant to one of his relatives. A few folk-tales, first used only as specimens of connected discourse, soon awakened our interest in their content. Finally, as we became more comfortable and grew to trust each other, González began to reveal his knowledge of religion. It became evident that this material was of more than linguistic relevance, and I made an effort to collect as much as I could. To Sr. González, it was important that these traditions be recorded and preserved. The curing ceremony and many other religious practices he describes represent a considerably earlier stratum of tradition than anything now practised in the region north of Jocotán, according to his reports and my own observation.

In August 1964, we returned to New Haven with Sr. González, who stayed until early December. During this period Prof. Lounsbury joined in the elicitation phase of the work. Most of the tape-recorded texts in this collection were recorded in New Haven between September and December 1964. Asked to tell all the stories he knew, González produced more than fifty, filling nearly six hours of tape.

In June 1965, I went back to Guatemala alone and worked in Jocotán for two months. In August, Mrs. Fought joined me in

Guatemala City, where collating and analysis could be done more comfortably. Then, in September and October, I worked in Jocotán again. During this period, González and I worked out a successful method for collecting texts. We would visit a village, if possible having first arranged and paid for a ritual meal for all comers. A dozen men could usually be gathered in this way, and sometimes a few women as well. After setting up the tape recorder in a friend's house or a vacant schoolhouse and demonstrating what it did, we would explain that we would pay 25 centavos for each story from any of them; usually González would then tell all or part of a story to get the session started. Invariably, others would follow, overcoming their initial nervous reluctance, and visibly enjoying the stories until the session had to be ended hours later. Offering an example was a practical necessity, since the lack of commonly known terms for tales had previously made it difficult to collect anything but translations or answers to questions. These examples seemed to have no inhibiting effect on the Chorti however; a variety of tales was collected, and some informants offered narratives of things they had seen on the same terms as tales and legends. Later, in New Haven, González and I indexed these tapes, noting more than 170 texts of folkloric value, and a smaller number of texts of interest as linguistic specimens only.

My research continued during the next academic year. I finished my dissertation, *Chorti (Mayan) phonology, morphophonemics, and morphology* (Yale University, 1967) and, in December 1966, went to Guatemala briefly, returning with Sr. González, who stayed in New Haven until June 1967. Most of the material on Chorti religion was collected during this period, after the material recorded on tape had been translated and checked. Because of the complexity of the language and my desire to have as much background information and vocabulary as required for understanding by an outsider, González preferred to write out a brief version in advance, and to dictate it to me phrase by phrase, with frequent pauses and digressions prompted by my questions. The dictated narratives were translated, and in many cases extensively reorganized and expanded during these interviews. Some passages were inserted to clarify obscure points; others were moved from their original position in an effort to make the sequence of events easier to follow.

The organization of the dictated narratives then, is the result of a collaboration between us, and should not be used uncritically as evidence in discussions of Chorti style. The language of these texts, however, is exactly as González dictated it in the final version.

All the texts in this collection were spoken by Sr. Isidro González. Most were tape-recorded:

Reel 07, 7 August 1964, Chiquimula.
Reel 15, October 1964, New Haven.
Reel 38, January 1967, New Haven.
Reel 39, 24 January 1967, New Haven.
Reel 42, 28 January 1967, New Haven.

There are three texts (and miscellaneous material) on reel 07, 21 on reel 15, three on reel 38, one on reel 39, and two on reel 42. Some of these texts were omitted from this collection: 15/04, the Basilisk, because it will appear in MLA/ERIC (Educational Resources Information Center, Clearinghouse on Languages and Linguistics), 15/15, a long anthology of etiological episodes, because it is too long and repetitive for inclusion here, and D 13, a cornfield ceremony, because it is incomplete.

Between January and June 1967, in New Haven, González dictated fourteen texts; later a fifteenth (D 15) was produced by combining related portions of the fifth and eleventh of the series.

In the following table, the position of a tape-recorded text on the reel is shown by the number following the solidus. The date of recording follows. In the case of dictations this date shows when *my* first transcription was completed; González used notes he had prepared in advance.

Text	*Source*	*Date*	*Text*	*Source*	*Date*
1	15/05	10/64	11	15/16	10/64
2	15/07	10/64	12	38/03	1/67
3	15/06	10/64	13	42/02	28/2/67
4	15/09	10/64	14	15/13	10/64
5	15/08	10/64	15	15/14	10/64
6	15/01	10/64	16	15/19	10/64
7	15/02	10/64	17	15/20	10/64
8	07/02	7/8/64	18	15/21	10/64
9	07/01	7/8/64	19	D5	28/2/67
10	15/03	10/64	20	D6	14/3/67

Text	*Source*	*Date*	*Text*	*Source*	*Date*
21	15/11	10/64	31	D1	31/1/67
22	15/12	10/64	32	D7	24/3/67
23	15/18	10/64	33	38/01	1/67
24	D14	13/6/67	34	D2	22/2/67
25	15/10	10/64	35	D4	25/2/67
26	42/01	28/2/67	36	D3	23/2/67
27	D11	30/5/67	37	D8	17/5/67
28	39/01	24/1/67	38	D9	17/5/67
29	D12	7/6/67	39	38/02	1/67
30	D15	30/5/67	40	D10	20/5/67

The tales and narratives published here are presented with two main objectives in view. First, they are to be an accurate, permanent record of the Chorti language of today. Second, they are a primary resource for studies of the Chorti culture and belief system, and for studies of the Mayan peoples as a group. The plan of this book reflects these priorities and my training. The language is the main focus of interest. Cultural points are taken up briefly when information is available. This collection includes only about one-fourth of the texts dealing with these matters, however, so it has been necessary to postpone discussion of many points until the remaining texts have been prepared for publication. At that time, texts by more than two dozen informants, from several of the villages north of Jocotán, will be added to the remaining texts recorded by Sr. González.

Besides a second collection of texts, a detailed descriptive grammar is in preparation, the first part dealing with the phonology, morphophonemics, morphology and lexicon, and the second part treating the syntax at length.

From the outset, I have sought the most accurate possible transcription of the tapes and field notes. No editing of 'errors' or hesitations has been done. The texts given here are, as nearly as possible, a faithful record of exactly what the informant said. The taped texts have been checked many times over a period of five years. From text to text, however, there is noticeable variation in the number of recorded syllable-initial prevocalic glottal stops. These are *not* always present, but they are more frequent than I once thought. It has been impossible to distinguish them in some sections of the tape recordings, and easy in others. I have not supplied them by rule, but I believe that texts like #4 and #11 are a more representative record than are #1 and #2, for instance. I can not be sure how much of this variation is due to the speech of the informant, how much to the condition and quality of the recording, and how much to variation in the accuracy of my transcriptions. It should be clear that there is free variation between the presence and absence of such glottal stops; the issue is the relative frequency of each variant. This variation is of no consequence within the grammatical system.

The dictated texts were transcribed and edited with the informant when long months of work had fully prepared us to make an accurate record of nearly natural speech. Moreover, the phonological notation used in all this work is entirely independent of grammatical or morphological categories or segmentation, so that it accurately and neutrally reflects all the details of morphophonemic and lexical alternation.

The texts and field notes were filed in a concordance system taught me by Professor Lounsbury, The forms and translations were typed on duplicator masters in blocks of file-slip size, about fifty copies of each master were made and cut into file slips, and these were filed together, item by item: each form was underlined, beginning with the first item on the first copy of a slip, then the second item on the second copy, and so on, until every item on a slip was represented by a copy of the slip showing the entire context. After underlining, the slips were sorted alphabetically and filed, thus bringing together all occurrences of each item in context. The method is laborious, but it permits extraordinary control of the details of the corpus, and gradual refinement of the analysis, up to the limits of the data and the patience of the analyst.

My refusal to remove or alter material in tape-recorded texts and the sensitive notation in which they have been painstakingly transcribed both reflect my belief that phonological and morphophonemic patterns are important aspects of linguistic structure, deserving careful study for their own sake, and that to do justice to the complexity of these patterns requires the very highest standards of completeness and accuracy in collecting and processing the corpus. I am further convinced that a permanent record should be as faithful to the data and as rich in information as possible, to allow at least a fair chance of finding in it answers to questions as yet unforeseen.

These attitudes, like the analysis reflected in the introduction and notes, were shaped in general, though not always in detail, by the teaching of Bernard Bloch and Floyd Lounsbury, and by their exacting standards of accuracy and explicitness, using componential analysis as a basic technique. The approach to phonology used here owes much to Bloch, while the morphological and semantic notes incorporate a number of Lounsbury's ideas.

Most of the introduction is devoted to a sketch of Chorti structure. This is not meant to be taken seriously by linguists, who in any case will insist on restating most of the material for themselves. It is offered instead as a guide for those who wish to follow the texts closely but who have little training in linguistic analysis, or too little time to carry it out.

Introduction

JOCOTAN AND VICINITY

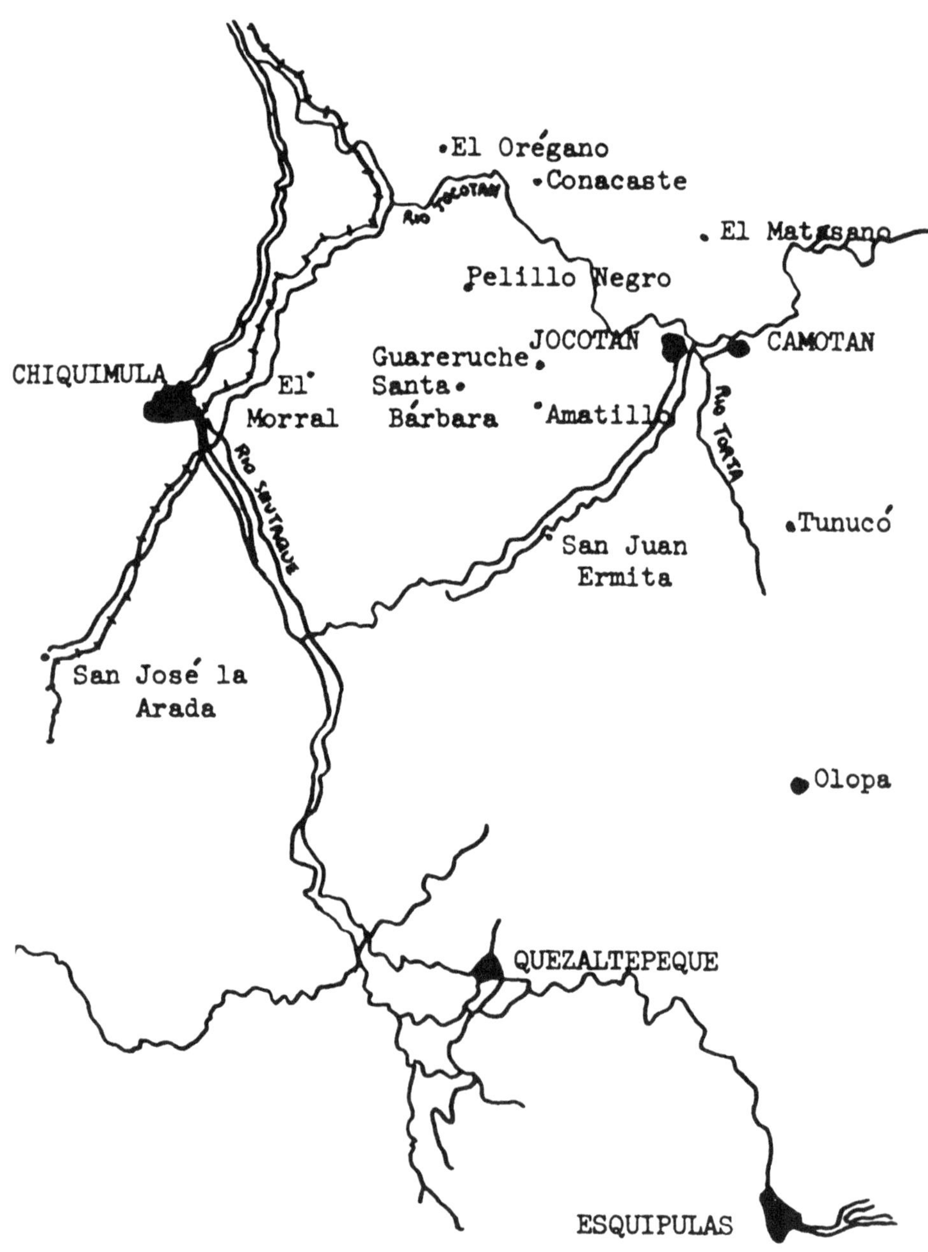

The Chorti

Most Chorti speakers live around three market towns in the Guatemalan state of Chiquimula. The towns -- Jocotán, La Unión, and Olopa -- are not economically interdependent to any significant degree, and their populations of Chorti speakers have little regular contact. There appears to be no geographical pattern of dialect differences within this zone, but there is considerable diversity among the idiolects. A few Chorti speakers live between Camotán and the Guatemala-Honduras border. Their dialect is notably different from the Jocotán dialect, but mutual intelligibility is not affected.

It is difficult to estimate the number of speakers with any accuracy. There has been steady population growth in recent years, due in part to somewhat better medical services becoming available. Wisdom (1940:17) reported the 1921 census figures for Jocotán as 894 (612 ladinos) in the town itself, and 14385 for the entire _municipio_. The 1950 census figures, as reported in the _Diccionario Geográfico de Guatemala_ (1961) are as shown for the area:

MUNICIPIO	TOTAL POPULATION	RURAL POPULATION	TOWN POPULATION	'INDIGENAS'	'LADINOS'
Jocotán	17,226	16,138	1,088	16,173	1,053
Camotán	12,408	12,101	307	10,888	1,520
Olopa	7,473	6,577	896	6,618	855
La Unión	6,451	5,417	1,034	4,743	1,708
Quezaltepeque	10,963	9,448	1,515	8,872	2,091
Esquipulas	11,930	9,087	2,843	4,312	7,618
Chiquimula	23,824	14,984	8,840	12,852	10,972
TOTAL	90,275	73,752	16,523	64,458	25,817

The census figures are not an accurate guide to the number of Chorti-speaking Indians, however. Material culture and other factors were as decisive as language in assigning inhabitants to the *indígena* or *ladino* category. The category *indígena* includes many monolingual Spanish speakers of mixed ancestry whom the Chorti-speaking Indians consider *ladinos*. There are rural settlements, in Jocotán at least, whose inhabitants are all *ladinos*, by Indian standards; these settlements are nucleated, in sharp contrast to the dispersed Indian settlements. It is obvious from the census figures that these settlements were counted as Indian. The total number of Chorti speakers is probably between twenty and thirty thousand. There are probably no adult Chorti monolinguals.

A number of sources of information on the geography and climate of the area are listed in the bibliography. Wisdom 1940 is a useful though dated guide. Wisdom spent three seasons in Guatemala, working in Tunucó (Jocotán) from May to October 1931, in Jocotán and nearby settlements from June to September 1932, and in Olopa from June to October 1933. He surveys the entire area; rather than focusing on the cultural and social system of a single settlement, he gives a mosaic of observations from a number of quite diverse communities, concentrating on material culture and social organization. He worked on the language also, collecting a number of texts and vocabularies on folkloric and religious subjects, besides his data on material culture.

Wisdom's linguistic material was never prepared for publication; it was microfilmed directly from file cards and manuscript (Wisdom 1950). The grammatical analysis was not carried very far, and the transcription is at times of uncertain accuracy. The texts and word-lists, on the other hand, are voluminous and of potentially great value.

In the summer of 1933, Ernest Noyes left for Guatemala to work on Chorti, after considerable work on the manuscript _Arte de la lengua Cholti_, some of which is preserved in his correspondence with Oliver LaFarge (Noyes-LaFarge 1932-33). Two rather brief vocabulary lists on file cards, with comparative notes, one set for Cholti and one for Chorti, were microfilmed after his death in 1942 (Noyes 1957).

Since that time, Rafael Girard has written extensively on the Chorti, their religion, and their place in his view of Middle American prehistory. The five volumes of _Los Chorti ante el problema Maya_ (1949, 1958) and other, briefer works (1962, 1966) contain a wealth of information based on observations over a period of many years of Chorti customs and beliefs. He has done little linguistic work however, and the transcription he uses is inadequate.

Miss Helen Oakley worked among the Chorti for a number of years on Bible translation, and published a very brief sketch (Oakley 1966). Her successor at this task, Rev. John McNichols of the Friends Mission, is presently at work in Jocotán; I believe at least one book, _Mark_, has been completed.

There is, then, a considerable body of ethnographic information on the Chorti, and some linguistic material, so far unorganized. Although none of this work is more than a starting point for detailed anthropological investigation the linguistic data have been scarcer and less reliable than any other. Chorti belongs to the Cholan subgroup of Mayan, with Chol and Chontal. The relationship of this subgroup to the Chiapas group (Tzeltal, Tzotzil, Tojolabal) and to Yucatecan is disputed (cf. McQuown 1956 for a survey.) There is convincing evidence that this group once stretched across the entire central zone of the Maya area, from the regions of Copán and Quiriguá through the southern Petén to the lowlands of Tabasco and Campeche (Scholes and Roys 1948: 17-19). It is thus quite possible that the Chorti occupy a portion of their ancestral territory, and likely that their position in the history of the Mayan peoples and languages makes them especially worthy of careful study.

Phonological and Morphophonemic Notations

The phonological features represented in the phonemic transcription are established independently of grammatical segmentation; they are based on contrast -- a relation of partial difference in sound and meaning between utterances -- and on phonetic qualities alone. Keeping the phonological transcription wholly independent of grammatical boundaries makes it sensitive to every variation of grammatical form, and so, the ideal medium for studying these alternations in detail. The morphophonemics of Chorti is relatively rich in fusion and free variation. Fusion is the overlapping or merging of morphs so that segmentation at any one of the possible points is either arbitrary or impossible. Free variation is the unpredictable occurrence of one of a set of variants in a given class of environments.

Both these traits are easily observed together in American speech, e.g. 'Did you eat yet?' as [džíi̯tšɛt↑] or [džə̆íi̯t͜?i̯ɛ́t͜?↑] or [di̯ə̆?íi̯tšɛ́t↑], etc. Some morphophonemic alternations, often called 'automatic', can be stated by reference to the presence of phonological features in some specified relation to any morphological boundary. The alternants in free variation in Chorti are nearly all of the 'automatic' type. It is possible to state by rules the range of possible phonological outcomes, but not the precise outcome for any particular occurrence. For these, a morphophonemic notation is especially advantageous, since rules or definitions applied to phoneme-sized elements allow a single, compact statement to cover all cases of an automatic alternation, and the morphophonemic spelling of each form tells which rules apply to it.

Other alternations, called 'regular', or in extreme cases, 'suppletive', can only be stated by reference to a small class of elements or to individual morphemes as conditioning or undergoing the alternation. Augmenting the morphophonemic notation to include such relatively rare alternations is unappealing, for a list of items by itself is more compact than a specialized apparatus of symbols and interpretive rules applying only to that same list of items. Here, as in Fought 1967, all three methods of presentation are used systematically to account for the sounds and forms of the textual material.

All the texts are given in a phonemic notation, explained in the next section. The first five texts are also transcribed in full in a morphophonemic notation which shows the morphological boundaries and whose interpretation shows how the attested forms of the texts are related to other automatic alternants. In the process, use is made of a technically interesting solution to the problem of free variation, employing unordered, optional rules. In the texts transcribed morphophonemically, those alternants conditioned by other morphemes are shown instead of the underlying or basic forms of the morphemes they belong to. Thus, both *uinik* and *uiŋk* are alternants of *uinik* 'man', the second occurring before the *-ir* 'intensive' suffix. In the texts, e.g. in 1.40, the form is transcribed morphophonemically as *uiŋk-ir*. The forms shown in morphophonemic transcription, then, are the ones undergoing *automatic* alternations. The patterns of morphemically conditioned alternation, in so far as they are clear, are discussed in the section on affixes, and in the notes on the texts.

Phonology

Chorti utterances are composed of one or more pause groups, each an uninterrupted sequence of one or more syllables bounded by intersyllabic pauses. Some pause groups are accompanied by a pitch contour. For reference purposes, pause groups are serially numbered through each text, with the number of the first group of each utterance appearing just before the group itself. These same numbers are used for the translation and notes on the groups. Thus, a number 1.47 refers to the forty-seventh pause group of the first text, and so on.

There are two distinct pauses: pause, /+/, a brief, stressless span of silence, and hesitation, /--/, a longer stressless span of silence, sometimes lasting a second or more, and usually preceded by progressively increasing drawling, laryngealization, or both, spanning the immediately preceding segment or segments. Note that these pauses are phonetically as well as functionally distinct. The usual hesitation pause filler is /'?e?e --/, probably the e prefix with drawling and laryngealization. One or more hesitations, filled or not, sometimes only postpone the completion of the construction they interrupt:

1.25 /+ "por 'ke?e -- 'txe?e"no?p
'ke?e -- ,'a"ian 'u'uiŋ"kir +
.'e"pe 'nia'ia"ha?a +/
'Because -- they say that --
it has a master, that rock.'

Others, of course, are used to postpone the start of a new construction. Most occurrences of loanwords are preceded by hesitations. In 1.3-8, for instance, there is an initial filled pause after the opening formula of the tale and before the beginning of the narration, and an unfilled pause between 5 and 6 which has no effect on the syntax, but which precedes a Spanish loan:

1.3 /'e?e -- ,'a"ian 'in"te?e --
'no"xi?i "pe 'nia + ,"ua?ar +
."ser 'ka'e'al"de 'ia'mor"ral +/
'Ah ... there is a big rock
standing near the village of
Morral.'

Some hesitations occur between the beginning of a construction which is never completed and a new construction. In 4.195-7, for example, Gonzalez mistakenly but grammatically notes that the serpent is a female, begins the next phrase, realizes his mistake, hesitates, scraps that phrase, and makes his correction:

4.195 /+ ."txe 'ke?e'?i'xik"txan +
196 + '?i?i'ui?i -- ."txe
'ke?e'ui'nik"txan +/
'It is said it was a female
snake, and the m -- it is said
it was a male snake.'

There are two pitch contours, rise, /,/, and fall, /./. In long pause groups, the rise or fall occurs during the last syllable or syllables; in shorter groups it sometimes spans the entire group. Some groups, especially those ending with a hesitation, do not have a pitch contour, being approximately level in pitch. At present, it does not appear that the amount of rise or fall is significant, only the direction of pitch change. The rising contour indicates a nonfinal pause in declaratives and a final pause in some interrogatives. Like stress and laryngealization, pitch contours are 'suprasegmental', i.e. they span one or more segments. The symbols for these three components are placed in linear order before the symbol for the segment where their onset occurs. Since the onset marks the end of a pause, and since each syllable has a stress span, the order of symbols at the beginning of a typical group is pause, contour, stress, and then the first segment. Segment symbols appear in order of onset.

A syllable is composed of a stress, a nucleus, and sometimes an onset, a coda, or both. Onsets and codas consist of one, two, or three consonant segments. A nucleus consists of one or two peak segments sometimes preceded or followed by one or two satellites. A satellite is an occurrence of a high vowel (/i, u/) as a glide vocoid allophone. There is no contrast calling for the recognition of */y/ and */w/. The distribution of satellites is: adjacent to a more open vowel (/e, a, o/) in the same syllable, last in a syllable made up of a consonantal onset and two high vowels, and first in a nucleus made up of two high vowels in all other environments. All other high vowel allophones are syllabic. In the following examples, the satellites are underscored.

The phonological notation assigns an alphabetic symbol to a bundle of phonological components, so that a linear notation represents a multidimensional array of these components. The alphabetic symbols are equivalent to the phonemes of some structuralist descriptions, but they are not the fundamental elements here. The ultimate phonological constituents are the distinctive (articulatory) components, the features of a phonetic space whose dimensions are the active articulators, the relative articulatory aperture left by each, special configurations of the front of the tongue, and contrastive manner and stress of articulation. The articulators are the lip (L), the front of the tongue (F), including the apex, the back of the tongue (B), including the root, the velum (N), and the vocal bands (G); the degrees of aperture are obstruent (0), close (1), mid (2), and open (3); the configurations are sibilant (S), retroflex (R), and lateral (%). The distinction between tense (T) and lax (X) manners is made on impressionistic rather than instrumental grounds, but it is thought to correspond to relatively high or low back pressure behind the point of articulation. Heavy (") and light (') stresses are also judged impressionistically.

Stress components span, and thereby delimit entire syllables. The combinations or bundles of the other distinctive components which define segmental transcription symbols are shown in Table 1.

Table 1

/	p	f	b	m	t	x	d	n	k	h	g	ŋ	?	s	r	l
L		O	O	O												
	T	X	X	X												
F						O	O	O								
					T	X	X	X								
B										O	O	O				
									T	X	X	X				
N																
		T	T	X		T	T	X		T	T	X				
G			O				O				O					
			X				X				X		T			
-														S	R	%

	a	a	e	e	i	i	o	o	u	u	'	"	/
L	3	3	3	3	3	3	2	2	1	1			
F	3	3	2	2	1	1	3	3	3	3			
B	2	2	3	3	3	3	2	2	1	1			
N													
	T	X	T	X	T	X	T	X	T	X			
-											'	"	

In Chorti, as in other Mayan languages, there are both plain and glottalized or 'ejective' obstruents, and both single (short) and geminate (long) vowels, as well as more complex nuclei. The second part of geminate nuclei is laryngealized. That is, there are rapid, periodic interruptions of the vibration of the vocal bands during such segments, so that corresponding portions of spectrograms show vertical bands of white cutting across the voice bar and other formants, and a characteristic 'creaky voice' is heard. Although the physiological details are not well understood, it may be that the glottal closure in glottalized obstruents and the laryngealized voicing in long nuclei are both due to the same articulation, probably a tensing of the vocal bands greater than the normal tension associated with ordinary voicing. In any case, the higher-than-normal air pressure within the oral cavity (in the obstruents) or the pulmonic cavity (in the vowels) allows both phenomena to be characterized by the feature GT.

The different manifestations of the glottal articulation are to be explained by reference to the different oral articulations they accompany. Because of the shapes and relative positions of the various articulators, high oral air pressure tends to force the nasal and glottal articulators more firmly closed and to push open the oral articulator. Conversely, a lowered, negative oral air pressure, produced by depressing the larynx with the glottis closed and expanding the oral cavity, tends to maintain complete closure of at least some oral articulators, while forcing the vocal bands into laryngealized voicing (perhaps of a different type from that described by Ladefoged 1967). Segments of this implosive glottalized type are common in other Mayan languages, but are found only in the Camotán dialect of Chorti. The appropriate notation is ?b for LOXNTGT, as against ?p for LOTNTGT.

The components GT are represented in the segmental notation by a /?/ <u>preceding</u> the symbol for the segment with tensed glottal articulator. Thus, /"?ka?ar/ 'remembering' consists of four segments, <u>?k-a-?a-r</u>, making up a heavy-stressed syllable. During the dorsal stop, the glottis is fully closed, while during the second /a/ segment, the glottis is producing laryngealized voice. In a form like /"?txa?ar/ 'lying', the glottal closure is maintained through the stop and spirant segments of the onset, and the next two segments are voiced and laryngealized, respectively. After the onset, the form is like /"?ka?ar/.

Each segment of an utterance, then, as shown in Table 1, is characterized by the aperture and state of the glottal, nasal and oral articulators as they interact to open and close the oral and pulmonic cavities and the nasal passage, producing relatively high or low air pressure within the cavities at various times. A segment is laryngealized (if GT) or plain (otherwise), nasalized (if NX) or oral (otherwise), and an obstruent (if LO, FO, or BO) or a vowel (otherwise). A summary of the principal segment types is given in Table 2.

Table 2

Segment Type	Articulator States:		
	Oral	Nasal	Glottal
Plain Voiceless Stop	OT	OT	3X
Laryngealized Stop	OT	OT	OT
Plain Voiced Stop	OX	OT	OX
Plain Voiceless Spirant	OX	OT	3X
Laryngealized Spirant	OX	OT	OT
Voiced Nasal Consonant	OX	3X	OX
Voiceless Nasal Consonant	OX	3X	3X
Voiced Oral Vowel	1 2 3X	OT	OX
Voiced Nasalized Vowel	1 2 3X	3X	OX
Voiceless Oral Vowel	1 2 3X	OT	3X
Laryngealized Oral Vowel	1 2 3X	OT	OT

Each segmental symbol, used in the transcription of a portion of discourse, may be interpreted as standing for a simultaneous bundle of components arranged in a column beneath it. The bundle consists of an aperture and manner value for every articulator, a stress value, and for some segments, a configuration. Table 3 is an unordered set of rules, each applying to a single column of components as given by Table 1, none applying across the syllable boundaries specified by stress spans, and each filling in some of the componential values, either unconditionally or conditionally. The rules are meant to apply repeatedly and in any order until all values have been supplied and further application to a given pause group is vacuous. They are not rewrite rules. Symbols separated by spaces should be considered in inclusive alternation.

The phonetic scheme which the rules execute holds that a syllable nucleus colors the syllable margins: the rules assimilate otherwise unspecified features to those of the syllable nucleus.

Table 3

	a = L F B N G
	o = L F B
Variables:	n = 0 1 2 3
	v = 1 2 3
	m = T X R S %

Rules:

All av are also aX.
All aT are also aONT.
All NX are also N3.
All S R % are also FOXNT.
All ' " GT . , are also anm before anm.
All anm are also ' " before and after ' ".
All oO are also GT after GT.
All oONT are also G3 if not after GT.
All LO are also FvBvNnm before and after FvBvNnm.
All FO are also LvBvNnm before and after LvBvNnm.
All LO FO are also B3 after BOXG3 if not before B1 B2.
All BO are also LvFvNnm before and after LvFvNnm.
All LvFvBv are also GT after GXGT.
All LXFXBX are also G3 after BnBnBOXG3.
All LvFvBv NX are also GOX if not after BnBnBOXG3 GXGT.

The effects of these rules are illustrated in Table 4, showing pause group 1.40. Part A shows the components supplied by Table 1 alone. In Part B, these same components are underscored and the components supplied by the rules of Table 3 are in roman.

Table 4 Part A

```
1.40 + ."ia?a "?txa?ar 'u'uiŋ"kir +

    L    33 3     3 3   1 13   3

    F    13 3    03 3   3 31   1
                TX
    B    32 2     2 2   1 130  3
                            X T
    N
         TT T    TT T   T TTX  T
    G
           T   T   T
    -   "      "        ' '    "
        .             R          R
```

Table 4 Part B

```
1.40 + ."ia?a "?txa?ar 'u'uiŋ"kir +

    L   333333 33333333 1111333333
        XXXXXX XXXXXXXX XXXXXXXXXX
    F   111333 00003330 3333111110
        XXXXXX TTTXXXXX XXXXXXXXXX
    B   333222 22222222 1111300033
        XXXXXX XXXXXXXX XXXXXXTTXX
    N   000000 00000000 0000030000
        TTTTTT TTTTTTTT TTTTTXTTTT
    G   000000 00000000 0000003303
        XXXXTT TTTTXTTT XXXXXXXXXX
    -    """""" """""""" ''''''""""

        .             R          R
```

Table 4 Part C

1.40 + ."ia?a "?txa?ar 'u'uiŋ"kir +

```
L  3               1   3
   X
F  1  3   0   3  0 3   1    0
   X      T  X
B  3  2            1   30  3
   X                     T X
N  0                    30
   T                    XT
G  0                     3 03
   X   T      XT    X
_  "      "         ' '   "
   .             R          R
```

Note that a segment, a minimum homogeneous span, often corresponds to more than one symbol and column in this linear notation, but that no symbol represents more than one segment. The values in Part B of Table 4 are sometimes specified redundantly by two or more rules, or indirectly by the joint effects of two or more rules, or both. Consider the /r/ in Table 4, for instance. According to Table 1, its distinctive component is just R (retroflexion). In Table 3, one rule specifies that all S R and % (Sibilants Retroflexes and Laterals) are FOXNT (Lax frontal obstruents with tensed velum) and another rule specifies that all aT (Tensed articulators -- L F B N or G) are aONT (whatever articulator is tensed is at aperture 0, and the velum is tensed). It follows immediately that if N is the tensed articulator, it is at aperture 0. These rules jointly and redundantly supply the 0 aperture for the R segment here. The aT rule also supplies the 0 aperture for the /?t/ segment later in the same group. Table 1 supplies the distinctive components GT for /?/ and FT for /t/. Since all aT are aONT, these additional features are added, giving NOTGOT in the first column and FOTNOT in the next, by two applications to each column. Since all oO are GT after GT, and since F is in o, the features GT are added to the /t/ column and the aT rule reapplies, giving GOT there. The remaining features are added by assimilations to either the syllable nucleus or the stress columns, as the reader may verify for himself. Part C of Table 4 shows the same pause group, this time in a fully componential notation derived from the other array of components by deleting redundant symbols to the right of any component, so as to leave only the starting state and subsequent change-points of each articulator.

Any pause group can be represented in these three ways by first looking up the distinctive components of each segmental symbol in Table 1, applying the rules of Table 3, and deleting the repetitions, as shown in parts A, B, and C here. Alternatively, a componential representation can be reduced to a string of segmental symbols by reversing these steps: the notation is biunique. If reduction to segmental symbols were contemplated, rather than expansion to a componential notation, Table 3 might be restated in order to make this task easier.

Pitch contours may be represented by simply substituting the appropriate componential symbol at the beginning of a group. Stress spans, on the other hand, must be observed or taken as given in applying the rules: these do not state, for instance, whether /?a?a/ falls into one syllable, /'?a?a/, or two, /'?a'?a/. They are stated so as to apply to either of these sequences.

Morphophonemics

Types of Alternation

One of the fundamental tasks of a descriptive grammar is to state the phonological form of each content-unit, or morpheme, in all of its environments: to describe the morphophonemics of the language, in the broadest sense.

When morphophonemic alternations are complex and frequent, as they are in Chorti, and when they are not the focus of attention, as they are not in discussions of syntax or semantics, then a strictly phonological notation becomes frustratingly clumsy and distracting to use. To accomplish more economically the task of morphophonemic description, linguists commonly resort to intervening variables of one of two types, morphophonemes or allomorphs. The allomorph, a 'morpheme-sized clump of phonemes' (Hockett 1961) has generally been preferred by structuralists since the Forties. The morphophoneme, 'a phoneme-sized piece of a morpheme' (Hockett 1961), affords many advantages in the description of phonologically conditioned alternation. After the introduction of the allomorph method, it was eclipsed for some years, but it has been revived lately by both structuralists and transformationalists.

This study takes up a suggestion first made by Floyd Lounsbury (1953:13) to use both phoneme sized and morpheme sized intervening variables so as to capitalize on the advantages of each. Here, a _morpheme alternant_ is a string of morphophonemes. A morpheme has one or more alternants, whether conditioned by other morphemes in its various environments, or by adjoining morphophonemes.

These two modes of alternation are described differently. The pattern of alternation conditioned by neighboring morphemes, called <u>morpholexical</u> alternation, is stated for a set of morpheme-sized units, the <u>morpholexical</u> or <u>basic</u> alternants (Bloomfield 1939:105). The Chorti texts in morphophonemic transcription are given as sequences of morpholexical alternants; it is to them that the rules for <u>automatic</u> alternation apply. These alternations are conditioned by the morphophonemic environment of particular morphophonemes. Since most automatic alternations in Chorti involve combinations of vowels, basic alternants are usually found in their directly corresponding phonological form between consonants or pauses. A system of alternation rules, each optional and unordered with respect to all the others, describes the pattern of automatic alternation and the range of free variation for each of the basic alternants.

The Problem of Free Variation

The descriptive problems raised by free variation have not been widely discussed. Instead, the notion has come to be accepted as a kind of residue of unaccountability in grammar. With a few very recent exceptions, current linguistic theory continues to view linguistic systems as having a single norm at each level or position. Given a selection of content units, the grammatical model is expected to specify what position and what form each shall have in the chain of utterance. At the same time, every linguist who does descriptive work encounters free variation in the form or position of elements. In a sense, this 'free variation' is an artifact of a conception of grammar as having a single norm.

The same considerations which have led to

the revolutionary improvements in syntactic description -- the recognition and transformational analysis of paraphrastic sets -- also apply to other aspects of language structure. What is proposed here is a description recognizing multiple norms, or in the phrase of Weinreich, Labov and Herzog (1968:187-88), an orderly differentiation of heterogeneous structures.

The technique used here for morphophonemics works by allowing the rules needed for certain clear and simple cases to interact and produce the sets of free variants as joint outputs.

Assimilation and Contraction

The 'reflexive' suffix has two basic alternants, p before the 'causative' (alternant es), and pa finally and before the plural, among other environments. Note the following pattern of alternants and their phonological representations:

Basic Alternants	Phonological Representations
p-es	"pes
pa-o?p	"po?p
	"po?o?p

There is free variation in the plural forms of the reflexive, but the causative is invariable. Two optional and contradictory alternation rules whose general form is based on many other cases, account for the case of free variation. The invariable case is counted as morpholexical alternation. It too appears to fit a larger pattern of alternation common to many but not all affixes, such that vowel sequences are contracted just as the contraction rule given below would specify for automatic cases. It is likely that continuing analysis will reveal more of these patterns of morpholexical alternants of affix morphemes, allowing further condensation of the description, but this phase of the work is not yet complete.

Both of the optional alternation rules mentioned above apply to the same sequences of basic alternants: those where an alternant-final vowel is followed by an alternant-initial vowel. One rule, of assimilation, states that the first vowel of the sequence becomes the same as the second. The other rule, of contraction, states that the first vowel of the sequence is lost.

Because there will be a number of other

rules, a notation will be used for all of them. In it, the _:_ stands for the one-way relation of alternation. The morphophoneme sequence to the left alternates with the sequence to the right. Variables _1_ and _2_ stand for any of the vowel morphophonemes, but both have a constant value within a rule, on either side of the alternation. Hyphens indicate the morphological boundaries; they are never represented by phonemes. The two rules just described may now be stated as follows:

Assimilation:	1-2 : 2-2
Contraction:	1-2 : -2

Other examples of assimilation and contraction follow:

Assimilation

ta-ka e-sapo 'ta'ke?e"sa 'po
'with the toad'

ket-pa-ix 'ket"pi?ix
'he stayed'

a-ohr-i 'o?o"hri
'he falls'

a&-num-se a&-?pa 'a'num"sa?a "?pa
'it happens to you'

u&-num-se u&-?pa 'u'num"su?u "?pa
'it happened to him'

kai-to ani 'kai"ta?a "ni
'as it began'

Contraction

u&-ir-a-et-o?p 'u'ui're"to?p
'they see you'
tu?ka-ix-to 'tu'?kix"to
'then what'
a-kor-ma-o?p 'a'kor"mo?p
'they hunt'
u&-txe auantar 'u'txa'uan"tar
'he endures'
u&-ah?k-u-en 'u'iah"?ke?en
'he gave to me'

The following table shows all the alternation rules together. In subsequent discussion, they will be mentioned by letter, e.g. Rb, Wc for Raising rule (b) and Weight rule (c).

Alternation Rules

Following is a table of alternation rules:

A	Assimilation:		1-2 : 2-2
B	Breaking:	(a)	i-1 : il-1
		(b)	u-1 : ul-1
		(c)	a&-i : ee-i : ee-
		(d)	a&-u : oo-i : oo-
C	Contraction:		1-2 : -2
H	H:	(a)	1h-2 : 1-2
		(b)	1-h2 : 1-2
O	Onset:	(a)	C-'1 : 'C-1
		(b)	C-"1 : "C-1
		(c)	hC-'1 : h'C-1 : 'hC-1
		(d)	hC-"1 : h"C-1 : "hC-1
R	Raising:	(a)	e-1 : ei-1
		(b)	e-1 : i-1
		(c)	o-1 : u-1
W	Weight:	(a)	'1-'2 : '1-2
		(b)	'1-"2 : "1-2
		(c)	"1-'2 : "1-2
3	Three Vowels:	(a)	1-1 1 : 1-1
		(b)	1 1-1 : 1-1
		(c)	1-1-1 : 1-1

Some of the possibilities of the rule system may be seen in the following graph, whose edges are labeled with the letters of the rules linking the outcomes:

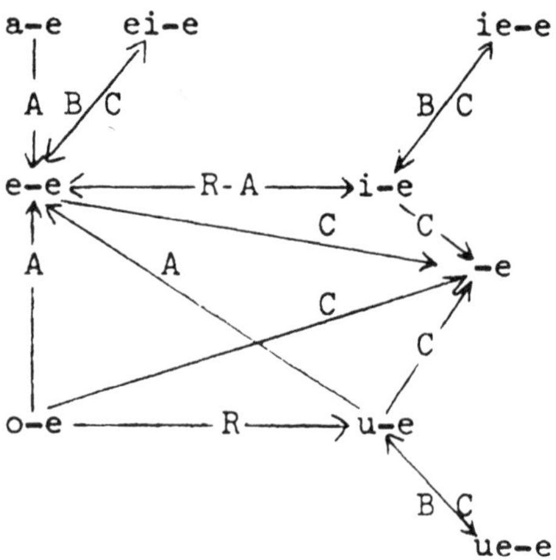

More concrete examples will be found in the remainder of this section.

Stress Onset

It is convenient to ignore differences of stress onset in discussions of morphology and syntax, so syllabication is accomplished by the onset rule shown in the table of alternation rules. The variable C stands for consonants or satellites. Parts (c) and (d) account for variation in such forms as 'o"hron and 'oh"ron 'He spoke', and part (b) places the final stress on 'o'hro"ner 'tale'. Part (a) places the second stress of 'u'ioh'ro"ner 'his tale'.

Alternations of h

Intervocalic h at a morphological boundary is frequently lost, as shown in the H rule:

ah-at-er	'a?a"ter	'bather'
a-?txih-i	'a"?txi?i	'it grows'
a-hi-h-?t-a	'e?eih"?ta	'it is tied'
a-hatx-pa	'a?atx"pa	'it rises'

Alternations of &

The u prefixes, whose functions are discussed below in the morphology section, end in a morphophonemic glide element, symbolized by &. The & element is represented by i between u and any vowel but i, by u between u and h followed by a vowel, by nothing between a or i and o or u or before a consonant, and by u (optionally gu after n = /n/) elsewhere. The 3 rule reduces uu-u to u-u.

The following lists of forms illustrate most of these combinations. In each list, the prefixes are vn& 'I', a& 'you (sg.)', i& 'you (pl.)', and u& 'he'. The combination of root and suffixes and its gloss are indicated at the top of each group of forms. There is no free variation in the third person forms. Here, the

H rule applies first, but the outcomes of & after u always distinguish basic h from basic vowels (except that hi and i are the same).

ah?k-u 'give'	er-p-es 'worsen'
'iŋ'guah"?ku	'iŋ'guer"pes
'a'uah"?ku	'a'uer"pes
'i'uah"?ku	'i'uer"pes
'u'iah"?ku	'u'ier"pes

ir-a 'see'	ohr-i 'fall'
'iŋ'gui"ra	'õ?õnh"ri
'a'ui"ra	'o?oh"ri
'i'ui"ra	'io?oh"ri
'u'ui"ra	'u'ioh"ri

u?tx-i 'drink'

'ũ?ũn"?txi
'o?oi"?txi
'iu?u"?txi
'u'iu"?txi

Alternations of v

The v morphophoneme is represented by the same vowel as the preceding nucleus of its stress group. If it is the first vowel in its stress group, v is represented by /i/. It occurs most frequently in the vi suffix, in the vn and vn& prefixes ('one' and 'first person') and in one very common root, vx 'go'. This root does not fit the usual pattern of assimilation. Compare these imperfective (a-prefix) forms with the corresponding perfectives (with no prefix):

'?a?a"xin	'he goes'	'?i"xin	'he went'
'?e?er"na	'being seen'	'?ir"na	'seen'

The mutual assimilation of the _ir_ root is the usual pattern -- either regressive or mutual assimilation, depending on the combination of vowels. 'Go', on the other hand, shows the _v_ pattern. The _vi_ suffix is attested with roots having _a_, _o_, and _u_ nuclei:

a-txam-vi	'a'txa"mai	'He dies.'
a-lo?k-vi	'a'lo"?koi	'He leaves.'
a-lum-vi	'a'lu"mui	'He passes.'

Interaction of _H_ and _&_ rules

The _H_ and _&_ rules apply independently; there are free variant forms with null (preconsonantal) representation of _&_, and others with the appropriate prevocalic representations. The most natural way to account for this is by rule applications _&_, _H_, and _H_, _&_, respectively. Fought 1967:161-62 missed this point completely, setting up a 'hybrid' set of morpholexical alternants with no _&_ (then written _+_) in first and second person forms, in free variation with the other, 'regular' set of _u_ prefixes.

The personal prefix paradigms of _hi?t-i_ 'tie' illustrate the two outcomes:

_H_, _&_		_&_, _H_	
'iŋ'gui"?ti	'ka'ui"?ti	'i?in"?ti	'ke?ei"?ti
'a'ui"?ti	'i'ui"?ti	'e?ei"?ti	'i?i"?ti
'u'ui"?ti		'u'ui"?ti	

When the two paradigms above were being elicited I asked González to repeat the second person plural after he had supplied it: _'i?i"?ti_. He responded with _'i'ui"?ti_. Unsophisticated informants rarely maintained either order through a paradigm; rather, the notes show much free variation even in such artificial situations as paradigm elicitation.

A further complication involves the first person singular prefix vn& (or vn in the a prefix paradigm) which optionally permutes with the initial vowel of the roots with initial h, as in the right-hand group of examples. The basic alternants and the outcome of this permutation are as shown here:

vn&-hi?t-i : i-vn-?t-i

and 'i?in"?ti or 'i?i"?ti or '?i?in"?ti are all attested as phonemic representations. If the first person prefix basic alternant were in&, the outcomes of roots with a vowels would sometimes be e?e nuclei; these are never attested. Only v allows the progressive assimilation.

H Set of Free Variants

Optional and independent alternation rules with overlapping or matching domains of application and different outputs interact to produce free variant sets of outputs. This may be understood most easily by using the rule system to account for a set of free variant forms. At a certain point in tabulating the data, there were twenty-one occurrences of the sequence e-otot 'the house', including forms with a plural suffix. There were six different representations of the sequence:

	Form	Number of Occurrences
(1)	'e'o"tot	1
(2)	'e'io"tot	3
(3)	'i'io"tot	3
(4)	'i'o"tot	1
(5)	'io"tot	4
(6)	'io?o"tot	9
		21

These alternants all fit the pattern of automatic alternations covered by the rules. In the first form, none of the optional rules applies. It corresponds point by point to the morphophonemic form. The second example illustrates the first part of the raising rule: e-l : e-il. Both parts of the raising rule apply to the third form: e-l : e-il : i-il. The fourth form shows the application of the second part alone. Weight rule (a) applies to the fifth form either before or after raising. Parts (b) and (c) are attested in the second and fourth examples of assimilation, given on page 25.

In accounting for Sr. González' speech, if the weight rule is applicable, it is almost always applied. Informants from the Ramírez family, however, rarely or never use it, so that the syllabication pattern of their speech is strikingly different from that of the majority. Compare their treatments of the same paradigm, at-i 'bathe', with a prefixes, where the only difference is application or omission of the weight rule:

Isidro González		Sebastián Ramírez	
'a?an"ti	'ka?a"ti	'a'?an"ti	'ka'?a"ti
'ia?a"ti	'i'xa"ti	'ia'?a"ti	'ix'a"ti
'a?a"ti	'a?a"tio?p	'a'?a"ti	'a'?a'ti"o?p

The result is what has been called syllable-timed speech in the Ramírez family, with each syllable nucleus receiving an equal weight and time, whereas the majority pattern, illustrated by González' usage, approaches the stress-timed pattern of English, with heavy-stressed syllables' nuclei tending to be evenly spaced, and weak-stressed syllables crowded or stretched between them. The Chorti are well aware of this difference. The Ramírez men are subjected to humorous imitation and joking by the others, who told me that Grandfather Ramírez had forcefully explained to his wife that nothing less than inheritance of his own style of speaking by his children would be acceptable proof of paternity.

The sixth and most frequent form shows raising, weight and breaking.

The use of a system of rules to generate multiple norms, of course, allows the description of overall patterns as well as the characterization of idiolects in terms of rule choice frequency, besides accounting quite naturally for the range of free variation. Some of the outputs of the rule system are not attested in the speech of a single informant, or indeed in the corpus as a whole; all the outputs are plausible, however, and there is no reason to guard against predictions which are not falsified by any data and which may be confirmed by future research.

Morphology

Chorti expressions are of two types, <u>substantive</u> and <u>active</u>. Active roots, with one or two exceptions, are bound forms; they occur with a suffix, either <u>thematic</u> or <u>derivational</u>. Substantive roots are free forms.

Personal Affixes

There are three sets of personal affixes in Chorti: the <u>u</u> prefixes, the <u>a</u> prefixes, and the suffixes.

U Prefixes			A Prefixes	
Sg.	Pl.	Person	Sg.	Pl.
vn&	ka&	1	vn	ka
a&	i&	2	i	ix
u&		3	a	

Suffixes

	Sg.	Pl.
1	en	on
2	et	ox

In familiar but inappropriate terms, their syntactic functions may be summarized as follows: the <u>u</u> prefixes are the possessives and the subjects of transitive verbs, the <u>a</u> prefixes are the subjects of imperfective intransitive verbs, and the suffixes are the subjects of perfective intransitive verbs and the objects of transitives. Each set can be shown to have a single function in the organization of discourse, although traditional descriptive categories tend to complicate their interpretation.

The *U* Prefixes

The ordinary sentence construction in Chorti is equational:

haax e-otot
"ha?ax 'io?o"tot
'That is the house.'

Using bracketing to indicate constituent boundaries and relations, the same example appears as

(haax) (e-otot).

In Weinreich's terms, this is a linking relation; it is symmetrical (Weinreich 1963/6:163).

The *u* prefixes have the same function in both 'possessive' and 'transitive' expressions: they organize the substantives they accompany into a *nesting* relationship (Weinreich 1963/6: 164).

Possessive Expressions

Possession may be simply construed as a relation between two substantives. The roles of possessor and possessed are not interchangeable, however; they are in a nesting relationship. In Chorti, this relation is indicated by a *u* prefix on the possessed element.

The constituents of a Chorti possessive expression are, then, a *u* prefix and two substantive expressions placed in a nesting relationship by the prefix.

(u&-otot (e-uinik))
'u'io"tot 'e'ui"nik
'the house of the man'

A possessive expression is not normally found as a free form; it must be linked in an equational construction with another constituent.

Transitive Expressions

A Chorti transitive expression typically has an active root with a u prefix and a thematic ('stem-forming') suffix, and two substantive expressions. The parallelism between the possessive and transitive expressions is shown in these examples:

(haax) (u&-otot (e-uinik))
"ha?ax 'u'io"tot 'e'ui"nik
'That is the house of the man.'

(haax) (u&-io?p-i (e-uinik))
"ha?ax 'u'io"?pi 'e'ui"nik
'His striking of the man.'

In both cases, the u prefix marks a nesting relation between its root and the following constituent. In other words, the u prefix forms complex constituents by nêsting simpler ones together. In both examples, the pronominal haax stands for (is linked with) a substantive. In the possessive example, it is linked with otot 'house'; in the second it is linked with a substantive in the larger context. The only differences between the examples, then, have to do with the active root and its thematic suffix. These indicate that the haax of the transitive example is an agent and the uinik a patient or object.

The Suffixes

The personal suffixes are the objects of transitive expressions and the subjects of perfective expressions, including the so-called stative verbs, which are merely substantives in apposition with the suffixes:

uinik-en
'ui'ni"ken
'I'm a man.'

The function of such 'statives' parallels that of active expressions like the following:

kan-o-en
'ka"nue?en
'I learned.'

In both types, the person designated by the suffix is in a state indicated by the preceding stem. States of manhood and learning, respectively, have been reached.

There is no third person suffix in the set, so that a bare substantive root, like the active form, must be considered perfective in the sense just outlined:

uinik
'ui"nik
'(He has become a) man.'

kan-o
'ka"no
'He learned.'

The perfective aspect, in other words, is unmarked. It is the imperfectives which are overtly and unambiguously marked as such in every occurrence, by an <u>a</u> prefix.

The A Prefixes

The <u>a</u> prefixes occur in imperfective intransitive expressions. They link the active root with a substantive agent, which usually follows:

a-kan-o e-uinik
'a'ka"no 'e'ui"nik
'The man is learning.'

It is characteristic of an aspect system that time is specified contextually and that the imperfective or perfective status of the action is relative to this shifting contextual time of reference, rather than to the time of speaking, as it commonly is in tense systems. The particle ani, for instance, designates an indefinite past period:

hente
"hen 'te
'(They're) people."

hente ani
"hen 'te'a"ni
'They used to be people.'

In the following examples, note the contrast between an explicitly past time of reference, indicated by ani, and an unspecified, and hence implicitly present time of reference. In both cases, the lo?k 'leave' root is in an imperfective construction.

a-ar-o?p-na e-txinam tuaa
a-lo?k-vi-o?p
'The town is told that
they should leave.'

ar-o?p-na e-txinam tuaa
a-lo?k-vi-o?p ani
'The town was told that
they should leave.'

Thematic Suffixes

Active roots occur before suffixes, with one or two exceptions. There are two types of suffixes, called _thematic_, or stem-forming, and _derivational_.

Thematic suffixes characterize active expressions. There are a few minimal contrasts:

u&-?paax	'his curse'
u&-?paax-e	'his cursing'

In the first form, the curse 'belongs to' the person designated by the prefix; in the second, it is an act he commits.

The suffixes _i_, _e_, _a_, _o_, and _u_ occur with either _a_ or _u_ prefix sets, and the _an_, _on_, _uan_, _vi_ and _vn_ suffixes with _a_ prefixes only. Most active roots occur with a _u_ prefix and a thematic suffix, and an _a_ prefix and a different thematic suffix, but never without any suffix at all. The derivational systems to which a given root belongs are predictable once its thematic suffix or suffixes are known.

It is frequently necessary to refer to both the prefix and suffix governed by a root. This is done by placing the suffix occurring with the root and a _u_ prefix _before_ a solidus, and the suffix coming after the root and an _a_ prefix _after_ a solidus. Thus, _io?p_ is an _i/on_ root, taking an _i_ suffix with _u_ prefixes and an _on_ suffix with _a_ prefixes. The following list shows some of the attested combinations.

Class	Root	Gloss	Examples	
a/on	ir	see	'u'ui"ra	'e?e"ron
e/o	aar	tell	'u'ia?a"re	'a?a"ro
e/uan	?paax	curse	'u'?pa?a"xe	'a'?pa?a"xuan
i/i	?kan	want	'u'?ka"ni	'a'?ka"ni
i/o	man	buy	'u'ma"ni	'a'ma"no
i/vn	uai	lay	'u'ua"ii	'a'ua"ian
i/an	xuh?tx	steal	'u'xuh"txi	'a'xuh"txan
i/on	xa?t	tear	'u'xa"?ti	'a'xa"?ton
i/uan	xa?p	scratch	'u'xa"?pi	'a'xa"?puan

Four different categories of active constructions must be distinguished in tracing the derivational patterns of Chorti. These are the *i*/ system, the other *u* prefix systems, the /*vi* system, and the other *a* prefix systems. Each of these four categories, for instance, figures in the statement of distribution of the imperative suffix alternants. It must be remembered that most roots belong to more than one of these categories, according to their thematic suffix classification. The outline given here covers only the major derivational systems, including those suffixes, like the causative, common to all the systems.

The *I*/ System

The *i*/ system is the most complex and most frequently encountered of the major derivational patterns. Roots taking the *i* and *e* thematic suffixes and *u* prefixes make up this system of shared derivational properties. The *h* infix and the suffixes occurring immediately after the root (primary suffixes) are briefly discussed here.

The *H* Infix

The infix occurs immediately after the syllabic nucleus of the root, and before a consonantal coda. Active forms take *a* prefixes and an *a* thematic suffix. There is one infix, the *h* 'potential'. It occurs with *i*/ system roots. Although its meaning is unusually elusive, it appears to designate an event presented as potential rather than actual. The infix also occurs in many of the numeral classifiers of Chorti.

u&-man-i	a-ma-h-n-a
'u'ma"ni	'a'mah"na
'He buys it.'	'It is for sale.'
vn&-hi?t-i	vn-hi-h-?t-a
iŋ'gui"?ti	'ĩ?ĩnh"?ta
'I tie it.'	'I can be tied.'

The Imperatives

There are three basic alternants of the imperative, each governed by roots belonging to one of the major derivational systems. Two of these occur with roots of u prefix classes, v with the i/ class, and n with other classes. The en alternant occurs with a prefix roots, including those bearing derivational suffixes. The imperative suffix occurs immediately after the root with i/ class and /vi class roots; with other root classes, the imperative suffix follows the thematic or derivational suffix. The last two examples are not thematic forms, but the translative and customary suffixes, respectively. They are included to show the consistency of the pattern.

Following is a table of imperatives:

Root	Gloss	Thematic Form		Imperative Form	
		Basic	Phonol.	Basic	Phonol.
xa?t	tear	u&-xa?t-i	'u'xa"?ti	xa?t-v	'xa"?ta
?kux	bite	u&-?kux-i	'u'?ku"xi	?kux-v	'?ku"xu
?ketx	carry	u&-?ketx-e	'u'?ke"txe	?ketx-v	'?ke"txe
?pihn	think	u&-?pihn-u	'u'?pih"nu	?pihn-u-n	'?pih"nun
xohx	poke	u&-xohx-o	'u'xoh"xo	xohx-o-n	'xoh"xon
ir	see	u&-ir-a	'u'ui"ra	ir-a-n	'i"ran
xan	walk	a-xan-a	'a'xa"na	xan-a-en	'xa"ne?en
?pahn	dig	a-?pahn-o	'a'?pah"no	?pahn-o-en	'?pah"nuen
?taa?p	climb	a-?taa?p-vi	'a'?ta?a"?pai	?taa?p-en	'?ta?a"?pen
?txa	lie	u&-?txa-?pu	'u'?txa"?pu	?txa-?pu-n	'?txa"?pun
xa?t	tear	a-xa?t-ma	'a'xa?t"ma	xa?t-ma-en	'xa?t"me?en

I/ System Derivational Suffixes

There are a number of suffixes which derive a prefix expressions with i/ system roots, so that the object of the u prefix form is the subject of the a prefix form. They are merely listed here, with a few suggestive examples, and a brief statement of their meanings.

'Customary' ma: the subject acts customarily, as part of his job, or the like:

u&-xur-i 'He cuts it.'	a-xur-ma 'He's a cutter.'
u&-?ketx-e 'He carries it.'	a-?ketx-ma 'He's a porter.'

'Middle' ?ka: the subject acts by or upon himself:

u&-?pu?t-i 'He fills it.'	a-?pu?t-?ka 'It fills up.'
u&-pus-i 'He drops it.'	a-pus-?ka 'It pours out.'

'Passive' ?tsa: the subject is acted upon. The agent may be specified or not:

u&-io?p-i 'He strikes it.'	a-io?p-?tsa 'It is struck.'
u&-man-i 'He buys it.'	a-man-?tsa 'It is bought.'

'Reflexive' pa: the subject acts upon himself:

u&-muk-i — 'He covers it.'
a-muk-pa — 'He submerges.'

u&-xa?t-i — 'He tears it.'
a-xa?t-pa — 'It tears apart.'

'Resultative' ta: the subject is in the state resulting from the action:

u&-?tsak-i — 'He adds to it.'
a-?tsak-ta — 'It accumulates.'

The 'Translative' Suffix

The 'translative' suffix occurs with u prefixes; it indicates that an object is placed in a certain position or attitude. It has three alternants: ?pa after root syllabics o and u, ?p after root syllabics a, e, i and before na, and ?pu elsewhere. All the roots in this class have /uan thematics, and all involve a handling act of some kind: ua 'stand upright', tur 'sit down', ?txa 'lay flat', etc.

The /VI System

Roots belonging to the /vi system do not have u type thematic formations. Most of these roots have to do with motion or a state transition, e.g. lum 'pass', ?taa?p 'climb', txam 'die', pur 'burn', otx 'enter', lo?k 'leave', etc. These roots govern the en alternant of the imperative, like the other a prefix systems, but as a primary suffix, like the i/ system; they govern the se alternant of the causative, again like the u type roots.

Other Affixes

Less extensive derivational patterns based on u/, a/, and o/ suffixes, and the various a prefix thematic forms, will be taken up in the notes as they occur in the texts.

Two suffixes occur with either a or u prefixes, offering alternative formations in many instances, one intransitive and marked for aspect and one transitive and neutral in aspect. These suffixes, the causative and the cursive, occur together in some constructions.

The Causative Suffix

The alternants of the causative suffix are s before an or ah , se with u class roots and vi class roots, and es with other a class roots.

a-txam-vi	u&-txam-se
'a'txa"mai	'u'txam"se
'He dies.'	'He kills it.'

a-txam-s-an
'a'txam"san
'He kills.'

u&-ir-a	u&-ir-se
'u'ui"ra	'u'uir"se
'He sees it.'	'He shows it.'

a-ir-s-an
'e?er"san
'He shows.'

The Cursive Suffix

Cursive suffixes designate an action or state in the course of its development or progress, without reference to a beginning or end. The cursive suffix might also be called an iterative-durative. With a personal affix, _a_ forms have alternant _r_ before a vowel, and _vr_ before a consonant; _u_ forms have alternant _rv_.

u&-io?p-rv	a-io?p-r-on
'u'io"?pro	'a'io?p"ron
'He beats it.'	'He beats.'

a-io?p-vr-s-an
'a'io'?por"san
'He is beaten.'

Substantives also occur with the cursive suffix and _an_ thematic:

sihk	'a nest'
'a'sihk"ran	'It is becoming a nest.'

Without a personal affix, the basic alternants are _vr_ after _u_ roots, _er_ after /_vi_ roots, and _ar_ with other _a_ formations. Such forms have been called gerundives in other Mayan languages.

a-kar-vi	kar-er
'a'ka"rai	'ka"rer
'He's drunk.'	'Drunkenness.'
u&-?txu-?pa	?txu-vr
'u'?txu"?pa	"?txu?ur
'He hangs it.'	'Hanging.'
u&-?ketx-e	?ketx-vr
'u'?ke"txe	'?ke"txer
'He carries it.'	'Carrying.'
u&-mak-i	mak-vr
'u'ma"ki	'ma"kar
'He covers it.'	'Covering.'
a-io?p-?tsa	io?p-?tsa-vr
'a'io?p"?tsa	'io?p"?tsa?ar
'He is struck.'	'Being struck.'

The Na Suffix and the Independent Pronominals

With an a prefix form, a following substantive is ordinarily the agent of the active form. This is not the role of tamal and chicha in the following examples of na suffix constructions. Rather, these substantives appear to be the objects of pseudo-passive expressions. The na suffix is in the subject position, however, and it has in its other environments, the independent personal pronominal forms, equally clear substantive functions.

u&-tur-?pa e-tamal
'u'tur"?pa 'e'ta"mal
'He sets down the tamale.'

a-tur-?pa-na e-tamal
'a'tur'?pa"na 'e'ta"mal
'The tamale is set down.'

u&-ah?k-u-on e-txitxa
'u'iah"?ko?on 'e"txi 'txa
'He gives us the rum.'

ah?k-u-na-on e-txitxa
'ah'?ku"no?on 'e"txi 'txa
'The rum was given to us.'

Although the phonemic form of the independent pronominals is invariant, only na- as a base satisfies the morphophonemic pattern.

na-en	"ne?en	'I'
na-et	"ne?et	'You (sg.)'
na-on	"no?on	'We'
na-ox	"no?ox	'You (pl.)'

Accordingly, it is reasonable to interpret the na suffix as a third-person subject in this specialized construction where both an agent and an object are ordinarily indicated, but in a passive relationship.

The 'Agentive' Prefix

The ah 'agentive' prefix occurs with most stem types, designating a person who performs an act, or has an attribute, or the like.

muak "muak 'Disease'	ah-muak 'ah"muak 'Diseased person'
u&-hu?tx-i 'u?u"?txi 'She mills it.'	ah-hu?tx 'ah"hu?tx 'Miller'
u?tx-er 'u"?txer 'Drunkenness'	ah-u?tx-er 'o?oi"?txer 'Drunkard'
u&-tar-es 'u'ta"res 'He brings it.'	ah-tar-es 'ah'ta"res 'Bringer'
a-txam-s-an 'a'txam"san 'He kills.'	ah-txam-s-ah 'ah'txam"sah 'Killer'
in-naht 'in"naht 'Distant'	ah-naht-ir 'ah'nah"tir 'Foreigner'

Substantives, Attributives and Classifiers

Chorti substantives are expressions sometimes occurring with the e prefix, the 'definite article.'

Of the following examples, the first has a plain substantive root, the second an attributive with the 'agentive' prefix, the third a compound base with attributive, substantive, and substantive-deriving suffix, the fourth a compound base with an active root (<u>mak</u> 'cover') and a substantive (<u>txan</u> 'sky'), and the last is a substantive phrase composed of an attributive and a substantive. All are marked as substantive elements of larger constructions by the <u>e</u> prefix, which frequently is bound to an entire phrase, as in the last example.

e-uinik	'the man'
e-ah-muak	'the diseased person'
e-nuk-ir-tee	'the big tree'
e-mak-txan	'the rainbow'
e-noxii uinik	'the big man'

Chorti attributives are impersonal <u>a</u> type constituents, since it seems best to recognize in them a feature of <u>aspect</u>, as in the intransitive active constructions. There is an affix deriving attributives from active and other bases which occurs in two positions. One is a suffix, <u>n</u> or <u>en</u>, as in these forms:

u&-?tsu?p-a	?tsu?p-a-n
'u'?tsu"?pa	'?tsu"?pan
'He stacks it.'	'Stacked'
txam-vi	txam-en
'txa"mai	'txa"men
'He died.'	'Dead'

The other is a prefix, <u>in</u>:

u&-xer-e	in-xe-h-r
'u'xe"re	'in"xehr
'He divides it.'	'Split'
a-sis-a	in-sis
'a'si"sa	'in"sis
'It cools.'	'Cold'

The aspectual relation of imperfective, marked by a prefix, and perfective, marked by a suffix, as in the personal active forms, is quite plausible.

Numerals and Classifiers

The in prefix is best treated synchronically (and historically) as the numeral 'one' in Chorti (though perhaps not in other Mayan languages). Numerals through four are in common use; five is remembered by a few informants. Each numeral prefix is followed by an appropriate classifier, and then by a substantive. Counting beyond four is done in Spanish, without classifiers. The other numeral prefixes are txaa 'two', ux 'three', txan 'four', and hoo 'five'.

Most classifiers are active roots with an h infix; the general classifier is apparently for stiff objects:

vn-tee-tee	vn-tee uinik
'in'te?e"te?e	'in"te?e 'ui"nik
'Stiff'	'One man'

Note that usually vn-tee tee 'one tree' would be 'in"te?e "te?e, showing minimal contrast of the stresses.

The commonly used classifiers, with a tentative indication of their roots' semantic features, are listed here.

go-h-r	enclosing, containing
ko-h-t	bent over, crouching
pe-h-t	sparse, scattered
ta-h-tx	turned face up, on back
xe-h-r	divided, cut apart
ahr	times, repetitions
?pii	days ago
?pih	days hence

Among the commonly encountered substantives with go-h-r are houses, jugs, smoking pipes, stones, and tamales; with ko-h-t, children, animals and poultry; with pe-h-t, corn stubble and, for comic effect, a rat's whiskers; with ta-h-tx, shallow vessels; with xe-h-r, lips, river banks, and forked tails; with ahr, acts of any kind. The last two forms in the list are not used with a substantive; they have the following alternants:

'txa?a"?pi?i 'two days ago'	'txa?a"?pih 'two days hence'
'u"xi?i 'three days ago'	'u"xih 'three days hence'
'txu"ni?i 'four days ago'	'txu"nih 'four days hence'

Texts

Translations

Notes

The Texts

The texts have been grouped by subject matter, as indicated in the table of contents, for those readers interested primarily in their content. Readers especially interested in the language will find full morphophonemic transcriptions and more complete morphophonemic and grammatical annotation in the first group of texts. Each text is accompanied by a translation and explanatory notes.

Instead of retelling the texts in English, I have chosen to follow the original as closely as possible, to the limits allowed by English, and perhaps at times beyond. The result is far from a natural English style. Some readers may depend on the translation for interpretations of the content, however, and for their sake I have stayed close to the Chorti. Others are welcome to smooth over the resulting oddities as they think best. Sometimes the order or subordination of the Chorti constituents can not be followed, however, and the English departs from it in the full translations. Some of these expressions are given one translation in the text and another in the introduction or notes; when this is the case, the isolated form has the closer translation.

The texts, translations, and notes are linked together by a system of pause-group numbers. Each text is numbered, and within a text, each pause group is numbered. A note on 1.25, for instance, refers to pause group 25 of text 1, and so on. A note begins with a reference number of this kind, and, if it has to do with morphophonemics only, the reference number ends with an asterisk.

The notes on morphophonemics are planned to show the important features of the rule system as it operates to account for the forms. Some obvious points are mentioned only once or twice, when they are first encountered, usually in the first group of texts. The Onset and Weight rules are mentioned in the notes only when they are of special importance or interest, or when they are not applied. In the absence of a special note, then, they may be taken for granted.

The texts collected and presented here are meant to serve the interests of linguists, anthropologists, folklorists, and others interested in the Chorti or in Mayan studies generally. As a record of linguistic usage in a previously little-documented language, a collection of texts on almost any subject would serve well, but these texts, thanks to Sr. González, considerably extend and reshape our knowledge of the language, folklore, and religion of the Chorti, and, perhaps more importantly, they suggest a number of promising lines of inquiry.

It is implicit in the work of both Wisdom and Girard that Chorti religion is sufficiently homogeneous to justify simply assembling observations from a number of communities, ordering the ceremonies chronologically, and perhaps noting a few minor differences in emphasis. To do this misses a point about Chorti life which seems to me to be vitally important: the Chorti are no more cohesive socially and culturally than residentially. Individual and family patterns assume as much importance as regional regularities.

The texts are divided into groups according to subject. The first group, texts 1-5, deals with the txih txan serpent; these texts have full morphophonemic transcriptions as well as the phonemic versions, translations, and notes. The second group, 6-13, is made up of etiological tales, although at least one, the Armadillo (text 10), takes on additional interest in relation to the beliefs about lightning as the missiles of the rain gods (in texts 25-28). Social themes, especially marital fidelity and the maintenance of authority, as well as some of the details of social roles, may be studied in the third group, texts 14-18. Text 14, and to some extent texts 16 and 17, are regarded as amusing.

The fourth group, 19-24, deals with the diagnosis, causes, and curing of diseases. The texts in this group represent an older stratum of usage than can easily be observed today. In all his reports on disease, González follows the practices of Damasio López (ca. 1880-1949) and his pupil Narciso Álvarez (ca. 1913-1953). The form of the chanted prayer in text 20, though not perfectly preserved, is especially noteworthy for its resemblance to passages in the Chilam Balam books.

The fifth group, 25-30, deals with the structure of the universe and the functions of its parts. A number of elements are manifestly of precolonial age, such as the colored seas at the corners of the world, the prayers to and the attributes of the sun, the moon, and Venus, and the astronomical observations used to predict the coming of the rainy season.

The sixth and last group of texts, 31-40, includes dictated and tape-recorded narratives of a number of ceremonies, including some not previously reported (texts 31-34).

Texts 19, 20, 24, 27, 29-32, 34-38, and 40 were dictated by Sr. González in New Haven, in the Spring of 1967. They differ from the other, tape-recorded texts in the length of pause groups, and in the relatively careful organization of explanatory and descriptive passages. They were dictated at nearly normal speed from

González' own notes, written in Chorti in an orthography of partly Spanish and partly missionary ancestry. Although the essential portions of each text are in the notes, the edited version is much more detailed, and in some cases, reorganized in collaboration with Gonzalez.

I have not made a point-by-point comparison of the details of the ceremonies reported with those reported by Wisdom and Girard. It is clear that there are considerable differences among the ceremonies as performed by the various prayer-sayers. Neither Girard nor Wisdom reports anything like the sequence of pilgrimages to Esquipulas, the return ceremony, and the Earth Spirit offerings, beginning early in January (texts 31-33). My informants, on the other hand, do not report anything resembling the ceremony of February 8 described by Girard (1966:7-42).

The consequences of this variation for the views of Rafael Girard on the calendrical system of the Chorti are quite serious. Briefly, he finds a 260 day cycle beginning with a New Year ceremony on February 8 or so, and ending on October 25 or so, varying slightly according to altitude and having a direct relationship to the agricultural cycle (Girard 1966:3-42). The evidence of the texts presented here points to a more complex picture, where some of the ceremonies are closely related to the agricultural cycle, and some are only indirectly concerned with it, asking for food, water, and health as gifts of the gods. These considerations, and the importance of the <u>tsikin</u> ceremony (November 1; text 22) which falls outside the period Girard speaks of, make it difficult to accept the notion of a fixed 260 day cycle.

That some elements of these ceremonies are survivals from precolonial times can hardly be doubted. There are, for instance, the planted crosses, the palo jiote trees which serve as household crosses and as the site of the 'altar' for the Earth Spirit offering in January. Wisdom (1940:422) describes these planted or living crosses, whose crossbar is inserted in a notch, and later enclosed by the tree as it grows. He does not explain their use.

Among the recurring elements whose significance should be investigated at length is the ritual confinement or enclosure which figures in nearly every ceremony and in many legends.

The coming of the rainy season, and the rainmaking ceremony, are predicted by a number of astronomical signs (texts 27, 29, 30), substantially as reported by Girard (1949:437-470).

The continued growth of theoretical and technical sublety in both anthropology and linguistics has made the editing of mere texts seem an old-fashioned procedure. Yet, to an amateur (and to at least some professional anthropologists) it does not seem that advances in theory and field work practices have always compensated for the depth and richness of material to be found in bodies of texts collected from expert informants. For example, a number of the ceremonies and beliefs recorded here have never been reported for the Chorti, despite the relatively extensive literature dealing with their culture, and their religion in particular. Even those which have been described before will be seen to differ in detail from the other reported versions, and, more importantly, to gain in ethnographic value from being told in Chorti, with the native system of associations and values intact.

I: Legends

1. *The Sesimite*
2. *The Serpent*
3. *The Landslide*
4. *Stuckhorn*
5. *The Man and the Serpent*

1. Sesimite

1 + ,'?ka"nin 'txe 'kon"tar + .'o'tron "te?e 'o'hro"ner + 3 + 'e?e -- ,'a"ian + 'in "te?e -- 'no"xi?i "pe 'nia + ,"ua?ar + ."ser 'ka 'e'al"de 'ia'mor"ral + 9 + 'i?i -- ,'i'ta'me?e "pe 'nia'ia"ha?a + ,'a'lo"?koi + .'in'te?e"kohn + 13 + ,'ie?e"kohn + ,'a?a'ro?p"na + .'ti'mu "xan + 16 + ,'i'?a"ian + ,'o'tron'te?e"kohn + 'a?a'ro?p"na + .'xu'kin"lih + 20 + 'i?i -- , 'ta'me?e"kohn 'ia"ha?a + 'e?e -- ,'e"kohn 'ti'mu "xan + .'a"ian "mei 'gra'e"hu 'te + 25 + "por 'ke?e -- 'txe?e"no?p 'ke?e -- ,'a"ian 'u'uiŋ"kir + .'e"pe 'nia'ia"ha?a +

29 + ,"no?on + ,"kai '?ko'to"ion + 'ka -- ,'ka'?ko"pi + .'ta'man"te?e "di 'ia + 34 + "pe 'ro?o -- 'u'?pah'?ku"sio?on -- ,'e"hen 'te'ta'me 'lu"gar 'ia"ha?a + ."ia?a "?txa?ar 'u'uiŋ"kir + 41 + "por 'ke?e'txe?e"no?p 'ke?e -- 'ta'ma?a -- 'u?u -- ,"su 'ie"pe 'nia'ia"ha?a + .'a"ian 'in 'te?e"?txen 'tu"ru + 46 + 'i?i -- ,'i'io"?pe?e "pe 'nia + ,"ua?ar + .'txa?a"te?e 'i'xik"tak + 50 + 'txe?e"no?p 'ke?e -- ."bir 'hen +

52 + 'i?i -- .'i"mei 'gra"u?ut 'a"nam + 54 + ,'tia?a'lo"?koi + .'e"ha?a 'ia"ha?a + 56 + "txe 'ke?e -- ,'me?e"rer + ,'o?o"txoi 'in"te?e 'ta"mar + "por 'ke?e -- ,"u?ut 'ia?a"nam 'ia "ha?a + ."mei 'gra + 62 + "txe 'ke?e -- ,'e'ua "kax + 'hai -- ,'o?o"txoi + ,'a?a'ua"no?p 'ta "mar + ,'a'?puh"?ko?p 'u"me 'nu?ut'ia?a"nam + .'i'ma?a"txi 'a'lo"?kuo?p +

69 + .'i"?pan 'e"hen 'te + 70 + 'tia?a -- ,'o?o"txoi + ,'a?a'ua"no?p 'ta"mar + ,'ma?a "txi?ix 'a'lo"?kuo?p + "por 'ke?e -- "en 'tre?e -- ,"mas + "ua 'ru?u -- 'u"txo?p 'e"huer 'sa 'ta?a -- ,'u'lo?k"se 'u'io"ko?p 'ma'kia?a"nam + "kon 'da?a -- ,'o?o"txoi 'u'io"ko?p 'ta'mia?a "nam + ,"mas + 'a?a -- ,'a'?puh"?ko?p 'u"me 'nia?a"nam + 85 + ,'uar"xix 'u'ui"ro?p + 'a?a

1. Sesimite

1 + , ?kan-i vn&-txe kontar + . otro vn-tee ohron-er + 3 + e -- , aian + vn-tee -- noxii penia + , ua-ar + . serka e-aldeia morral + 9 + i -- , i ta-ma e-penia ia-haa + , a-lo?k -vi + . in-tee kohn + 13 , i e-kohn + , a-ar-o?p-na + . timuxan + 16 + , i aian + , otro vn -tee kohn + a-ar-o?p-na + . xuk-inlih + 20 + i -- ta-ma e-kohn ia-haa + e -- , e-kohn timuxan + . aian meigra e-hute + 25 + por kee -- txe-e-na-o?p kee -- , aian u&-uink-ir + . e-penia ia-haa +

29 + , na-on + , kai ?kot-vi-on + ka -- ka&-?kop-i + . ta-ma vn-tee diia + 34 + pero -- u&-?pah?k-u-se-on -- , e-hente ta-ma e-lugar ia-haa + txe-e-na-o?p kee -- , kee t-iaa a-lo?k-vi + , e-haa + . iaa ?txa-ar u&-uink-ir + 41 + por kee txe-e-na-o?p kee -- ta-ma -- u& -- sui e-penia ia-haa + . aian vn-tee ?txen tur-u + 46 i -- , i io?p-i e-penia + , ua-ar + . txaa-tee ixik-tak + 50 txe-e-na-o?p kee -- . birhen +

52 + i -- . i meigra u&-hut anam + 54 + , t-iaa a-lo?k-vi + . e-haa ia-haa + 56 + txe kee -- , ma ir-er + , a-otx-vi vn-tee ta-ma-r + por kee -- , u&-hut e-anam ia-haa + . meigra + 62 + txe kee -- , e-uakax + hai -- , a-otx-vi + , a-au-an-o?p ta-ma-r + , a-?pu-h-?k-a-o?p u&-men u&-hut e-anam + . i ma atxi a-lo?k-vi-o?p +

69 + . i ?pan e-hente + 70 + t-iaa -- , a-otx-vi + , a-au-an-o?p ta-ma-r + , ma atxi-ix a-lo?k-vi-o?p + por kee -- entre -- , mas + ua-r u& -- u&-txe-o?p e-huersa ta -- , u&-lo?k-se u&-ok-o?p mak-uu e-anam + konda -- , a-otx-vi u&-ok -o?p ta-ma e-anam + , mas + a -- , a-?pu-h-?k-a-o?p u&-men e-anam + 85 + , ua-r-xix u&-ir-a-o?p + a

1. Sesimite

— 'a'?puh"?ko?p + .'in'iah"rer + 89 + ,'i'po
"re 'so + 'ma?a"txi 'a'?ko"toi 'ta'kix'e"hen 'te
'ta'me?e -- .'e"kohn 'ia"ha?a +

92 + ."pe 'ro"txe 'ke?e + ,'tia?a'lo"?koi
'e"ha?a + ,'di"al 'ma'e'ho"pop + 'pa"kar 'a?a
"xin 'ta'me?e -- .'u"ti?i 'e'?txe"no?p + 97 +
'i"ti?i 'na'?ko"toi + ,'u'txu"ki 'e'ho"pop 'ia
"ha?a + ,"txe 'ke?e"ia?a 'ta"kix + 'a?a -- 'a
'?txah"ma 'u"me 'ne?e -- ,'e'?ke"?txuh + "por
'ke?e -- ,'e"hu 'te + ,'e'ho"pop + ,"txe 'ke'a
'ra?k"?pir + "tua?a 'e?e -- .'e'men"ta 'do'?ke
"?txuh + 109 + ,'i'po"re 'so + 'ma?a --
,"no?on + ,'ma?a"txi 'ka'?ko"toi + ,"ehs 'to
'tia?a'lo"?koi 'u"nu?u?k 'e"haa + "por 'ke'ka
'?pa?a"kre?e -- 'e?e -- .'e'no"xi?i '?ke"?txuh +

117 + 'i?i -- "txe 'ke?e -- ,'a"ian 'in
'te?e"di 'ia + 'in"te?e -- ,"si?its '?ko"toi + ,
'ko'txa'ma?a"txu?u 'na?a"ta + ,'?ko"toi 'ta'me?e
"kohn + 'u'ui"ra 'ke?e + ,'di"al 'ma'e"hu 'te +
,'a"tsa?ai 'u'ui"ra + ,'i"xin + 'ta'me?e -- .'e
"kohn +

130 + 'i?i -- ,"kon 'da'?ko"toi + "ser 'ka
'e?e -- ,'u"nu?u '?ke"ha?a + ,"kai 'u'tah"ui 'e
'ho"pop + .'pa"kar 'a?a"xin + .'ta'me?e"ha?a +
137 + .'en"ton 'ses + ."txe 'pues + .'ko"ne?er
'in'kor"ma + 140 + 'i?i -- ,'i"xin + "as 'ta
'ke?e'?ko"toi + ,'ta"ma 'u"su 'ie"pe 'nia + ,'u
'ui"ra 'ke?e'di"al 'ma'e'ho"pop + ,'i'u'ui"ra
'ke?e'?ko'?pi"rik 'pa"kar + "ma?a -- "io '?pe?e
-- ,'e"?txen + ,'tia?a'lo"?koi 'e"ha?a + ,'u'uo
"?tsi 'u"?puhk + "txe 'ke?e -- .'tua?a'a'kor"ma
+ 153 + "u?ut -- ,'u'lo?k"se 'u"?puhk + ,'u
'tur"?pa 'nah"tir + ,'i"xin + ,'pa"kar 'pa"kar +
'io"?pe?e "?txen + ,'tia?a'lo"?koi 'e"ha?a + .
"por 'kiu'ui"ra 'ke?e"dial 'ma'e'ho"pop +

161 + "kon 'de"txa?a -- ,"kon 'de"txe 'u

1. Sesimite

— a-?pu-h-?k-a-o?p + . vn-iahr-er + 89 + , i por eso + ma atxi a-?kot-vi ta-k-ix e-hente ta-ma e -- . e-kohn ia-haa +

92 + . pero txe kee + , t-iaa lo?k-vi e-haa + , dialma e-hopop + pak-ar a-vx-in ta-ma e — . u&-tii e-?txen-o?p + 97 + i tiin a-?kot-vi + , u&-txuk-i e-hopop ia-haa + , txe kee iaa ta-k-ix + a -- a-?txa-h-m-a u&-men e -- , e-?ke?txuh + por kee — , e-hute + , e-hopop + , txe kee ara?k-?p-ir + tuaa e -- . e-mentado ?ke?txuh + 109 + , i por eso + ma -- , na-on + , ma atxi ka-?kot-vi + , ehsto t-iaa a-lo?k-vi u&-nuu?k e-haa + por kee ka&-?pa?k-r-e -- e -- e-noxii ?ke?txuh +

117 + i -- txe kee -- , aian vn-tee diia + vn-tee -- , siits ?kot-vi + , ko-txa ma atxi u&-naat-a + , ?kot-vi ta-ma e-kohn + u&-ir-a kee + , dialma e-hute + , a-tsaa-i u&-ir-a + , vx-in + ta-ma e — . e-kohn +

130 + i -- , konda ?kot-vi serka e -- u&-nuu?k e-haa + , kai u&-tahu-i e-hopop + . pak-ar a-vx-in + . ta-ma e-haa + 137 + . entonses + . txe pues + koneer vn-kor-ma + 140 + i -- , vx-in + asta kee ?kot-vi + , ta-ma u&-sui e-penia + , u&-ir-a kee dialma e-hopop + , i u&-ir-a kee ?ko?p-ir-ik pak-ar + ma -- io?p-e e -- e-?txen + , t-iaa a-lo?k-vi e-haa + , u&-ho?ts-i u&-?puhk + txe kee -- . tuaa a-kor-ma + 153 + u&-hut — , u&-lo?k-se u&-?puhk + , u&-tur-?pa naht-ir + , vx-in + , pak-ar pak-ar + io?p-e e-?txen + , t-iaa a-lo?k-vi e-haa + . por kee u&-ir-a kee dialma e-hopop +

161 + konde txaa -- , konde txe u&-

1. Sesimite

"txe 'sen"tir + ."iix "ua?ar + 'ta'mu?u -- .'u
'?txa'ri"?pir 'e'no"xi?i '?ke"?txuh + 166
+ 'a'ro?p"na 'u"me 'ne?e -- .'e'?ke"?txuh + 168
+ "ne?et 'ah"txi?i 'ma?a"txi 'a'uak"ta 'ni'gua
"ra?k + 169 + ,"ne?eŋ 'gua'rin'?to"xi + 'i?i
-- ,'i"kon 'da?a"xin 'e"tar 'de + ,'in'mo'roh
"sio?p + ,'i?iŋ'gui"ra + 'ke"mix "ha?ax 'tu
"no?or 'lo'ke?e -- .'a'lo"?koi 'a'xa"no?p + 176
+ ,"pe 'ro"ne?et + 'ah"txi?ix 'e"uar 'a?a -- .'a
'?ke"txi 'ni'gua"ra?k 'a?a"xin + 179 + .'tu
'?ka?a"non 'ua'ra"txe 'ta"kar +

180 + .'en"ton 'ses'txe?e"si?its + 'ko
'txa?a -- 'ma?a"txi 'na?a"ta 'hai -- ,'a'ua"ra?k
"no?on + 'de'por"si 'ua"to?oŋ 'ka?a -- ,'ka'kor
"ma + "por 'ke?e -- 'ka'na?a"ta 'ke'di"al 'me?e
-- ,'e'ko"rom + 'ta'me?e -- ,'e"kohn 'ia"ha?a +
.'i'po"re 'so'ua"to?on +

192 + 'a?a -- ,"ne?et + .'a'ua?a"re 'ko
"rom + 195 + 'ma?a"txa?a 'na?a"ta 'hai --
"txi?i 'u'ia"ra?k "uar 'a'?ka?a"pa?a -- .'a'txu
"ki + 198 + "pe 'ro?o -- ,'ko"ne?er + 'ke?e --
,'in'tah'uie"tix + "ua 'ra?a -- 'a'?ka?a"pa?a
'txu"ki 'ni'ua"ra?k + ,'ko"ne?er + 'i'ket"pa 'ta
'ka"ren +

206 + ,'en"ton 'ses + ,'e"si?its 'ia"ha?a
+ .'sa"kat 'a?a"ru + 209 + "kon 'de?e -- 'a
'ro?p"na 'ke?e -- .'ma?a"txi?ix 'tua?a'lo"?koi +
212 + ,'en"ton 'ses + ,'a'ro?p"na 'u"me 'ne'?ke
"?txuh + "ne?et 'ke?e -- ,'txu'txue?e"to + ,
'me?e"ra "ta?a '?ka?a"pa?a 'ui"ra + 'lo'ke?e'u
"txe?e -- ,'a'pia?a"ro?p + 'e?e -- ."to?or 'e
"rum + 221 + .'in'xi"toŋ 'uak"te?et 'i?i"xin +
222 + "pe 'ro -- 'i"ri?i 'sut"pa 'ua"te?et 'a?a
-- 'a'txu"ki 'ni'ua?a -- .'ni'ua"ra?k + 226 +
"por 'ke"hai -- ,'iŋ'gui"ro?oit 'o'tro"niahr + .
'ma?a'txix"to?on 'uak"te?et 'in'xin"ia?a +

1. Sesimite

txe sentir + . i-ix ua-ar ta-ma u& -- . u&-?txa-
r-i?p-ir e-noxii ?ke?txuh + 166 + a-ro?p-na
u&-men e -- e-?ke?txuh + 168 + na-et ah-txii
ma atxi a&-ak-ta ni&-ara?k + 169 + , na-en ua-
r vn&-?tox-i + i -- , i konda a-vx-in e-tarde +
, vn&-mor-oh-se-o?p + , i vn&-ir-a + kee m-ix
haax tunoor lo kee -- a-lo?k-vi a-xan-a-o?p +
176 + , pero na-et + ah-txii-ix e-ua-r a -- a&-
?ketx-i ni&-ara?k a-vx-in + 179 + . tu?ka anon
ua-r a&-txe ta-ka-r +

180 + . entonses txe e-siits + ko-txa --
ma atxi vn&-naat-a hai -- , a&-ara?k na-on + de
por si uat-a-on ka -- , ka-kor-ma + por kee --
ka&-naat-a kee dialma e -- , e-korom + ta-ma e
-- e-kohn ia-haa + . i por eso ua-ta-on +

192 + a -- , na-et + . a&-ar-e korom +
195 + ma atxi a-naat-a hai -- txii u&-ara?k ua-
r a-?kaap-a -- . a&-txuk-i + 198 + pero -- ,
koneer + kee -- , vn&-tahu-i-et-ix + ua-r a --
a-?kaap-a a&-txuk-i ni&-ara?k + , koneer + i-
ket-pa ta-ka-r-en +

206 + , entonses + , e-siits ia-haa + .
sak-at a-ar-u + 209 + konde -- ar-o?p-na kee
-- . ma atxi-ix tuaa a-lo?k-vi + 212 + ,
entonses + , ar-o?p-na u&-men e-?ke?txuh + na-et
kee -- , txu-txuu-et-to + , ma ir-a-to a-?kaap-
a a&-ir-a + lo kee u&-txe -- , a&-piaar-o?p + e
-- . ta-hor e-rum + 221 + . vn-vx-i-to vn&-ak-
ta-et i-vx-in + 222 + pero -- ir-a i-sut-pa
uat-a-et a -- a&-txuk-i ni&-a -- . ni&-ara?k +
226 + por kee hai -- , vn&-ir-a a&-hut otro vn-
iahr + . ma atxi-ix-to vn&-ak-ta-et vn-vx-in
iaa +

1. Sesimite

229 + 'i?i -- ,'i'po"re 'suix"to + 'a'?kah "na 'ke?e -- 'ke?e -- ,'tia?a"?txa?ar 'e'?ke "?txuh + ,'ga"lan 'io?o"tot + .'tia?a"?txa?ar + 236 + 'i?i -- ."mei 'gra + ,'a?a"?katx + ,'ma "kar 'u'me"ner + 'tia?a -- .'tu"ru + 242 + . 'por'ke'?ko"toi 'u'ui"ra + 243 + ,"pe 'ro"txe 'ke?e + ,'por'ke'txu'txu?u"to + ,'iaht'na"tu?ut + .'ak'ta'na"to 'lo"?koi + 247 + ,"pe 're'nuk 'ta"hen 'te + .'ma?a"txa?ak 'ta"na 'lo"?koi + 249 + ,'i'po"re 'suix"to + .'e"hen 'te'u'?pa?a "krio?p 'e"kohn 'ia"ha?a + "por 'ke?e -- ."ia?a "?txa?ar 'e'?ke"?txuh +

253 + ,'ie"kohn 'ia"ha?a + ,'in"so 'lo "u?ut '?ka'xi?p"ha?a + 'tia?a -- .'?ah"ni 'e "ha?a + 257 + ,"por 'ke"txe 'ke?e'?ke"?txuh + 'e?e -- ,'u"iok + ,'ma"ha?ax "?paŋ 'ko'txe?e + .'u'iok'e"hen 'te + 262 + "txe 'ke?e -- ,'a "tras + ,'a?a"xin + ,'u"pun 'tu"o?or 'u"iok + , 'iu?u"su 'iu"iok + .'u'?pa?a"xi 'de"lan 'te + 268 + 'po"re 'so"txe 'ke?e -- ,'tua?a'e?ek"mai + ,'ta"mu?ut 'e'?ka'xi?p"ha?a + .'ha?a"xir 'ga "lan 'e?ek"mai + 272 + "por 'ke?e -- "por 'ke?e -- ,'u"su 'iu"iok + 'e?e -- .'su"tur 'de "lan 'te +

277 + 'i?i -- ,'po"re 'so + ,'txe?e"no?p + .'e"hen 'te + 281 + 'i'po"re 'so'txe?e"hen 'te 'ke?e -- ,'e'?ke"?txuh + '?pa'?kax"?pa?k 'a'xa "na 'por'ke?e -- ,'ta"me?e + 'u'su'iu"iok + 'e?e -- .'su'tu"tuh + 288 + ,'i'po"re 'so + "txe 'ke?e -- ,'e'?ke"?txuh + ,'ma?a"txi 'a'xa"na + .'ko'txe'ka'xa"na "no?on + 'si"no 'ke?e -- ,'u "pat + ,'u'su"ti + ,'de"lan 'te + 'por'ke?e -- "?pan 'tu"ru?u "iok + 299 + ,'i'po"re 'so + 'e?e -- ,'ga"lan 'e?ek"mai + .'ta"mu?ut 'e'?ka "xi?p "ha?a + 303 + "por 'ke?e -- 'e"kohn 'ia "ha?a + ,'in"so 'lo"u?ut '?ka'xi?p"ha?a + .'e?e "kohn + 307 + ."por 'ke"txe 'ke?e'u"?pi?ir + 308 + ,'ga"lan + .'e?ek"mai 'ta"mar + 310 +

1. Sesimite

229 + i -- , i por eso-ix-to + a-?kah-na kee -- kee -- , t-iaa ?txa-ar e-?ke?txuh + , galan e-otot + . t-iaa ?txa-ar + 236 + i -- . meigra + , e-a?katx + , mak-ar u&-men-er + t-iaa -- . tur-u + 242 + . por kee ?kot-vi u&-ir-a + 243 + , pero txe kee + , por kee txu-txuu-to + , iaht-na ta-u&-hut + . ak-ta-na-to lo?k-vi + 247 + , pero e-nuk-ta hente + . ma atxi ak-ta-na lo?k-vi + 249 + , i por eso-ix-to + . e-hente u&-?pa?k-r-i-o?p e-kohn ia-haa + por kee -- . iaa ?txa-ar e-?ke?txuh +

253 + , i e-kohn ia-haa + , vn-solo u&-hut ?kax-i?p-haa + t-iaa -- . ahn-i e-haa + 257 + , por kee txe kee e-?ke?txuh + e -- , u&-ok + , ma haax ?pan ko-txa e + . u&-ok e-hente + 262 + txe kee -- , atras + , a-vx-in + , u&-puntu u&-hor u&-ok + , i u&-sui u&-ok + . u&-?pa a-vx-i delante + 268 + por eso txe kee -- , tuaa a-ekm-ai + , ta-ma u&-hut e-?kax-i?p-haa + . haax-ir galan a-ekm-ai + 272 + por kee -- por kee -- u&-sui u&-ok + e -- . sut-ur delante +

277 + i -- , por eso + , txe-e-na-o?p + . e-hente + 281 + i por eso txe e-hente kee -- , e-?ke?txuh + ?pa?k-ax-?pa?k a-xan-a por kee -- , ta-ma e + , u&-sui u&-ok + e -- . sut-ut-uh + 288 + , i por eso + txe kee -- , e-?ke?txuh + , ma atxi a-xan-a + . ko-txe ka-xan-a na-on + sino kee -- , u&-pat + , u&-sut-i + , delante + por kee -- ?pan tur-u u&-ok + 299 + , i por eso + e -- , galan a-ekm-ai + . ta-ma u&-hut e-?kax-i?p-haa + 303 + por kee -- e-kohn ia-haa + , vn-solo u&-hut ?kax-i?p-haa + . e-kohn + 307 + . por kee txe kee u&-?pi-ir + 308 + , galan + . a-ekm-ai ta-ma-r + 310 +

1. Sesimite

"por 'ke?e -- ,'u'su'iu"iok + ,'ma"ha?ax "?pan + 'ko'txe?e -- .'u"su 'iu"iok 'e"hen 'te +

315 + ,"pe 'ro + ,"no?on + ,'me?e'ra"to 'ka'ui"ra + 'ko'txa?a -- ,"ma 'tia?a'ka'tah"ui + .'ma?a"txi 'ka'na?a"ta 'tu"ru?u "su 'iu"iok +
321 + ."pe 'ro"?pa 'na'?kah"na 'u"me 'ne"hen 'te + ."ti?in 'u'ui'ro"?pix +

1. Sesimite

por kee -- , u&-sui u&-ok + , ma haax ?pan + ko-txa e -- . u&-sui u&-ok e-hente +

315 + , pero + , na-on + , ma ir-a-to ka&-ir-a + ko-txa -- , ma t-iaa ka&-tahu-i + . ma atxi ka&-naat-a tur-u u&-sui u&-ok + 321 + . pero ?pan a-?kah-na u&-men e-hente + . tiin u&-ir-a-o?p-ix +

1. Sesimite

1 I'm going to tell another story. There is a large rock standing near the aldea of Morral. 9 And at that rock a stream comes out. 13 And the stream is called Timuxan. 16 And there is another stream that is called Xukinlih. 20 And in the stream Timuxan there are many snails. 25 They say that that rock has a master.

29 We had just arrived there one day to gather snails. 34 But the people in that place frightened us, saying that where the water comes out, there lies its master. 41 Because they say that at the foot of that rock there lies a cave. 46 And under the rock there stand two women. 50 They say that they are virgins.

52 And there is much mud. 54 Where that water comes out. 56 They say that no one can go into it because there is so much mud. They say that cows, if they go in and stand on it, are swallowed up by the mud. And they don't come out.

69 And so it is with people. 70 When they enter, standing on it, they do not come out because the more they use their strength so as to withdraw their feet from the mud, the more they are swallowed up by the mud. 85 While they are looking, they are suddenly swallowed up. 89 And that is why the people do not go into that stream at all.

92 But they say that where that water comes out, there are lots of crabs scuttling around at the walls of the cave. 97 And there are some who go there to catch those crabs. They say that right then and there they are taken by the Sesimite, because snails and crabs are the poultry of the one called 'Sesimite'.

1. Sesimite

109 And therefore we do not go there, up to the source of the water, because we fear the big Sesimite.

117 And they say that one day a boy went — since he did not know -- he went into the stream, and saw that there were many snails. He was happy to see them and went into the stream.

130 And when he got near the source of the water, he began to find the crabs scuttling in the water. 137 Then, he said, "today I am a fisherman." 140 And he went until he came to the foot of the rock, and he saw that there were many crabs, and he saw there were big ones in the cave, where the water came out. He took off his clothes, they say, to go fishing. 153 He took off his clothes, and put them down at a distance, and went on all fours into the cave, where the water came out, because he saw there were many crabs.

161 Then, they say, he heard a noise, and the big Sesimite was right on top of him. 166 He was addressed by the Sesimite: 168 "So you are the one who won't leave my poultry alone. 169 I am raising them, and when evening comes I herd them together and I see that not all the ones that went out walking are there. 176 But you are the one who has been carrying off my poultry. 179 I don't know what you do with them."

180 Then the boy said, "Since I didn't know they were your poultry, we naturally kept coming, and catching them, because we thought that there would be a big catch in that stream. And that is why we came."

192 "Ah, you call it a catch. 195 Don't

you know whose poultry you kept taking? 198 But now I've just found you, and you're still taking my poultry. Now you will stay with me."

206 Then that boy let out a yell. 209 When he was told that he could not leave. 212 Then he was told by the Sesimite, "You, who are still a little one, you haven't seen everything that your friends do, all over the earth. 221 I am going to let you go. 222 But don't come back to catch my poultry. 226 Because if I see your face again, then I will not let you go."

229 And that is why it is said that where there is a Sesimite, there there is a beautiful house. 236 And lots of chickens kept by him where he lives. 242 Because he keeps an eye on them. 243 But they say that because the boy was little he was pitied for it, and he was let go. 247 But big people are not let go. 249 And therefore people are afraid of that stream, because that is where the Sesimite lives.

253 That stream is all waterfalls, where the water runs. 257 Because they say that the Sesimite's feet are not like people's feet. 262 They say that his toes point backward, and his heels go forward. 268 It is so, they say, so that he may go down waterfalls. He goes down very well. 272 Because his heels are turned forward.

277 And that is why, people say. 281 And that is why people say the Sesimite walks backwards, because his heels are all turned around. 288 And therefore they say that the Sesimite does not walk as we do, but rather, he turns his back frontward, because that's the way his feet are. 299 And so he comes down waterfalls very well. 303 Because that stream is all water-

falls. 307 Because, they say, it is his path. 308 He comes down it very well. 310 Because his heels are not like people's heels.

315 But we didn't see him; we haven't met him, and we don't know where his heels are. 321 But so it is said among the people who have seen him.

2. Serpent

1 + 'a"ian 'o'tron"te?e -- 'o'hro"ner + .'a'?kah"na + 'ta"ma 'e?e -- .'e"sier'po + .xe?e 'a'ro?p'na"txan + 7 + ,"txe 'ke?e + ,'a"ian 'in"te?e "tiem 'po + 'ta'ma'e?e -- 'e'xu"kur + ,'xe'a'lu"mui + 'ta'ma?a -- 'u"ti?i 'e'txi"nam 'ho'ko"tan + 14 + 'e?e"txe 'ke?e -- 'ta"ma re?e -- ,'e'xu"kur 'ia"ha?a + ,'a"ian 'in'te?e 'tiem 'po + ,'e"?txi?i + ,'i"xin + "ehs 'to 'ma "ku '?ko"pat + ,'e"ha?a + ,'?ka?a"pa + 'u'?ku "txi 'tu"no?or 'e?e -- ,'e"si '?ka"?po?p + ,'e 'ke"ne?e + ,'lo"ke?e '?pa?ak"?pir 'a"ni + "ser 'ka'e'o"ri 'ia'e?e -- .'e"ha?a +

29 + ,'?ka?a"pa + ,'u'?ku"txi 'ta"ri + 'i?i -- ,'?ka?a"pa 'u'?ku"txio?o 'to"to?p + 'lo 'ke?e -- ,'io'to"to?p + ,'lo'ke?e'u'tah"ui + "ser 'ka'e?e -- 'tia?a -- ,'a'lu"mui 'e"ha?a + ,'?ka?a"pa + 'u'?ku"txi 'ta"ri + ,'u'uah'pi"nik + 'e?e -- ,'txi"tam + ,'a"?katx + ,"txih + ,'ua "kax + 'tu"no?or 'lo'ke?e -- ,'u'tah"ui + ,"tia?a '?pu"?tur 'a?a"xin + "ser 'kio"ri 'ia?a "ne?e -- ,'e'xu"kur + 'tu"no?or '?ka?a"pa 'u?u -- .'u'?ke"txe + 54 + .'i'io'to"to?p + 55 + 'por"ke?e -- ,"txe 'ke?e + 'e?e -- ,'e"sier 'po 'lo"?koi + .'ta'man"te?e 'mon"ta 'nia + ,'u'?ka "?pa?a + .'se'sek"mil +

62 + ,'ma?a"txi 'ka'txe'ko'no"ser 'e'lu "gar + ,'pe"ro + '?pa'na'?kah"na 'ke?e -- "ha?ax -- "?pan 'u'?ka"?pa?a 'e'mon"ta 'nia + .'tia?a 'lo"?koi 'e"txan 'ia"ha?a + 68 + ,'ta'rix"to 'txe'?e"hen 'te + 'ke?e -- ,'e"txan + "kon 'da?a -- ,'a?a"?txi?i + ,'ma"kui?ir 'e'ui"tsir + .'a 'lo"?koi 'u"kaa "txuo?p +

75 + ,'i'kon'daix"to + ,'a?a"?txio?p + ,'en"ton 'ses + 'e?e -- 'e"txan + 'xe?e -- 'ma?a "to?o -- 'ma?a"to?o "ha?ax -- ,'o'nia?an"txan + ,'i'kon'da?a"?txi?i + "txe 'ke?e -- ,"?pan 'ko 'txe?e"hen 'te + ,'a'xa"na + ,'u'si?k"?pa 'u?u

2. Serpent

1 + aian otro vn-tee -- , ohron-er + . a-?kah-na + ta-ma e -- . e-sierpo + . xee a-ar-o?p na txan + 7 + , txe kee + , aian vn-tee tiempo + ta-ma e -- . e-xuk-ur + , xee a-lum-vi + ta-ma -- u&-tii e-txinam hokotan + 14 e txe kee -- ta-ma e -- , e-xuk-ur ia-haa + , aian vn-tee tiempo + , e-?txih-i + , vx-in + ehsto mak-uu ?kopat + , e-haa + , ?kaap-a + u&-?kutx-i tunoor e -- , e-si?ka?p-o?p + , e-kenee + , lo kee ?pa?k-?p-ir ani + serka e-oriia e -- . e-haa +

29 + , ?kaap-a + , u&-?kutx-i tar-i + i -- , ?kaap-a u&-?kutx-i e-otot-o?p + lo kee -- , e-otot-o?p + , lo kee , u&-tahu-i + serka e -- t-iaa -- , a-lum-vi e-haa + , ?kaap-a + u&-?kutx-i tar-i + , u&-hahp-i-nik + e -- , txitam + , a?katx + txih + , uakax + tunoor lo kee -- , u&-tahu-i + , t-iaa ?pu?t-ur a-vx-in + serka e-oriia ani e -- , e-xuk-ur + tunoor ?kaap-a u& -- u&-?ketx-e + 54 + . e-otot-o?p + 55 por kee -- , txe kee + e -- , e-sierpo lo?k-vi + . ta-ma vn-tee montania + , u&-?ka?paa + . sesekmil +

62 + , ma atxi ka&-txe konoser e-lugar + , pero + ?pan a-?kah-na kee -- haax -- ?pan u&-?ka?paa e-montania + . t-iaa lo?k-vi e-txan ia-haa + 68 + , tar-i-ix-to txe e-hente + kee -- , e-txan + konda a -- , a-?txih-i + , mak-uu-ir e-uitsir + . a-lo?k-vi u&-kaatxu-o?p +

75 + , i konda-ix-to + , a-?txih-i-o?p + , entonses + e -- e-txan + xee -- ma to -- ma to haax -- , oniaan txan + , i konda a-?txih-i + txe kee -- , ?pan ko-txa e-hente + , a-xan-a + , u&-si?k-?pa u&

2. Serpent

-- 'u?u -- ,'u'uix'ka?a"ro?p + .'tua?a'nuh "?pio?p 'ta"kar + 93 + ,"pues + "txe 'ke?e + ,'kon'da'lo"?koi 'e'?ki"?pi?ts + ,'ie?e"txan 'ia "ha?a + ,'a'lo'?ko"io?p + ,'txe"ke?e 'u?u -- 'u 'uix'ka?a"ro?p + ,'a?a"xin + ,'u'sah"ko?p + .'a 'nuh"pio?p 'ta"kar + 103 + ,'i'po"re 'so + ,'a 'lo"?kuo?p 'te?e'ui"tsir + ,'tia?a'?txa?a"ro?p + ,'a?a"xin 'a'?txa?a"no?p + .'ta"mo 'tron"te?e 'ui"tsir + 108 + ,"pe 'ro + 'tia?a'lo"?kuo?p + ,'u"txo?p "mei 'gra'e'?ki"?pi?ts + 'i?i -- .'u 'sa"tio?p 'e'lu"gar +

113 + 'i?i -- ,'i'ta'rix"to + 'txe'ke?e 'a?k -- ,'u'?kah"ti 'e"hen 'te'ko"ne?er + 'ke?e -- 'ke?e -- "ma 'tu"no?or + ,'a'lo"?kuo?p + 'e?e -- .'a?a'xi"no?p 'tia?a'?ka"na '?ko"tuo?p + 123 + "por 'ke?e -- ,"txe 'ke?e'e"txan 'ia"ha?a + 'e?e -- ,"ia "tah 'ui"na + ,"?txa?ar + 'ta'ma'?e -- ,'u'io'ri"iir 'e"ha?a + ,'i'ha?a"xir + ,'ket "pa "?txa?an + .'ma"kui?ir 'e"ha?a + 'ta'ma?a -- 'ta'mu?u"hor + ,'iŋ"gohr 'no"xi?i "tun + .'ia 'ket"pa "?txa?an + 137 + 'por'ke"txe 'ke?e'hah "?tsa 'u"me 'ne?e -- ,'e'dio"so?p + 'por"ke?e -- 'ir"na 'ke?e -- "mei 'gra -- "uar 'u'sa"ti 'e?e -- 'e'lu"gar + 'i"ua 'ra?a -- ,'u'?ku"txi 'i'io 'to"to?p + ,'ien"ton 'ses + .'hah"?tsa 'u"me 'ne 'dio"so?p + 148 + 'i?i -- ,'po"re 'so + 'u '?kah"ti 'e"hen 'te'ke?e -- ,'ke'?e"txan + ,'me?e"rer 'a'lo"?koi 'a?a"xin + .'hai'ma?a"txi 'ah'?ku"na 'per"mi 'su?u"me 'ne"dios +

154 + 'i"ti?i 'ne'a'lo"?koi + 'ma'tu"?ka?a -- 'e'ki"?pi?ts 'u"txe + ,'mo"tor 'u"txe + "pe 'ro?o -- 'ma'tu"?kio?o 'to"to?p 'u'sa"ti + 160 + ,'i'ha?ax"to + 'a?a"xin + ."es 'to"tia?a '?ka "na '?ko"toi + 163 + "pe 'ro"hai -- 'e?e -- ,"txan + 'e?e -- ,"uar + ,'u'sa"ti "mei 'gra + 'e?e -- ,'e'io'to"to?p + ,'tia?a"uar 'a'lo"?koi + ,'ma?a"txi 'a?ak'ta"na 'a?a"xin + ,"ehs 'to 'tia?a'a'?ko"toi 'u"me 'ne"dios + ,'a?ah"?tsa +

2. Serpent

-- u& -- , u&-ixka-ar-o?p + . tuaa a-nuh?p-i-o?p ta-k-ar + 93 + , pues + txe kee + , konda lo?k -vi e-?ki?p-i?ts + , i e-txan ia-haa + , a-lo?k-vi-o?p + , txe kee u& -- u&-ixka-ar-o?p + , a-vx-in + , u&-sahk-o?p + . a-nuh?p-i-o?p ta-k-ar + 103 + , i por eso , a-lo?k-vi-o?p ta e-uitsir + , t-iaa ?txa-ar-o?p + , a-vx-in a-?txa-an-o?p + . ta-ma otro vn-tee uitsir + 108 + , pero + t-iaa a-lo?k-vi-o?p + , u&-txe-o?p meigra e-?ki?p-i?ts + i -- . u&-sat-i-o?p e-lugar +

113 + i -- , i tar-i-ix-to + txe kee a?k -- , u&-?kah-ti e-hente koneer + kee -- kee -- . ma tunoor + , a-lo?k-vi-o?p + e -- . a-vx-in-o?p t-iaa a-?kan-i a-?kot-vi-o?p + 123 + por kee -- , txe kee e-txan ia-haa + e -- , ia tahu-i-na + , ?txa-ar + ta-ma e -- , u&-orii-ir e-haa + , i haax-ir + , ket-pa ?txa-an + . mak-uu-ir e-haa + ta-ma -- ta-ma u&-hor + , vn-go-h-r noxii tun + i a-ket-pa ?txa-an + 137 + por kee txe kee ha-h-?ts-a u&-men e -- , e-dios-o?p + por kee -- ir-na kee -- meigra -- ua-r u&-sat-i e -- e-lugar + i ua-r a -- , u&-?kutx-i e-otot-o?p + , i entonses + . ha-h-?ts-a u&-men e-dios-o?p + 148 + i -- , por eso + u&-?kah-ti e-hente kee -- , kee e-txan + , ma ir-er a-lo?k-vi a-vx-in + . hai ma atxi ah?k-u-na permiso u&-men e-dios +

154 + i tiin-e a-lo?k-vi + ma tu?ka e -- e-ki?p-i?ts u&-txe + , motor u&-txe + pero -- ma tu?ka e-otot-o?p u&-sat-i + 160 + , i haax-to + a-vx-in + . esto t-iaa a-?kan-i a-?kot-vi + 163 + pero hai -- e -- , txan + e -- , ua-r + , u&-sat-i meigra + e -- , e-otot-o?p + , t-iaa ua-r a-lo?k-vi + , ma atxi a-akt-a-na a-vx-in + , ehsto t-iaa a-?kot-vi u&-men e-dios + , a-ha-h-?ts-a +

2. Serpent

.'i"ia?a 'ket"pa 'txa"men + 176 + "por 'ke?e — ,"txe 'ke?e"txan 'ia"ha?a + ,'u"me 'ne?e'dio "so?p 'hah"?tsa + ,'i'ia?a'ta"kix + ,'ket'pa "?txa?an + 'ta'me?e -- .'e"ha?a 'ia"ha?a + 'tia?a -- ,'a'lo"?koi 'e"?pi?ir + ,'ua"tar + .'ta'me'al'dei"io?p +

187 + ,'a"kai + ,'a'?kah"na + ,'ke?e"txan 'ia"ha?a + "ia?a -- ,"ia 'kai"?txa?an -- 'e?e -- ,'?tsak"ta "o 'txo"di 'ia + ,"ia "?txa?ar + ."to?or 'iŋ'gohr"tun + 196 + 'por"ke?e -- 'ia "ha?a -- ,'ma'mah"txi 'u"men + ,'a'?ko"toi 'e?er "na 'tia?a"?txa?ar + .'por'ke'a'?pa'?kahr"na + 201 + ,'i"txe "ke?e "txan + ,'ta"ma '?u"neh + 'u?u -- ,'u'ku"txi + ,'txa?a"te?e 'ba"li 'ha'a 'xa"na + ,'txe"ke?e + ."ia '?pu"?tur 'e'tu"min 'ta"mar +

208 + ,'i'po"re 'so + ,'txe'ke?e'e"txan 'ia"ha?a + 'kuan'do'tah -- ,'tah'ui"na + ,"?txa?ar 'txa"men + ,'?pu?t"?ka 'e"hen 'te'ta 'me'o"ri 'ia'e"ha?a + ,'?ka"na?a "ni + 'a?a"xin 'u?u — ,'u'?txa"?kio?p 'u"neh 'a'lo"?koi + ,'?ka"nu?u -- .'u'lo?k"sio '?pe'tu"min + 219 + "pe 'ro'a'?pa?ak"to?p + "por 'ke?e -- ,"txe 'ke '?e"txan + ."mei 'gra'u'ui"?ka 'ri"ru?ut + 'i'ta "me?e -- ,'u'ui"?ka 'ri"ru?ut 'ia"ha?a + ,'ua?ak "txe 'ta"ka + 'u'ia"ri?in "te?e 'tam -- ,'ta'me "ha?a + 'i?i -- .'ma?a"txi?ix 'a'lo"?koi 'in "te?e + 230 + 'i'po"re 'so + .'a'?pa'?kahr"na 'e"txan +

232 + ."pues + ,'e"txan 'ia"ha?a + 'txe 'ke?e"ia "?txa?an + ,'e"o 'txo"di 'ia + 'ma'mah "txi 'a?a -- ,'a'?ko"?toi 'ta'?u'ieh"?tser + ,'por'ke"txe 'ke'mo'tor'txa"men + ."pe 'ro'a'ian "tu?u 'ui"?ka 'ri"ru?ut + 240 + ,'i'ma?a"txi 'u'iak"ta 'e"hen 'te + .'a'?ko"toi 'ta'u'ieh "?tser + 242 + "pe 'ro'e"hen 'te"ha?ax 'e?e -- ,'e'tu"min 'xe"?txu?ur 'ta"ma '?u"pun 'tu'u"neh +

2. Serpent

. i iaa ket-pa txam-en + 176 + por kee -- , txe kee e-txan ia-haa + , u&-men e-dios-o?p ha-h-?ts-a + , i iaa ta-ka-ix + , ket-pa ?txa-an + ta-ma e -- . e-haa ia-haa + t-iaa -- , a-lo?k-vi e-?pi-ir + , ua-ta-r + . ta-ma e-aldea-o?p +

187 + , a-kai + , a-?kah-na + , kee e-txan ia-haa + ia -- , ia kai ?txa-an -- e -- , ?tsak-ta otxo diia + , ia ?txa-ar + . ta-hor vn-go-h-r tun + 196 + por kee -- ia-haa -- , ma m-ah-txi u&-men + , a-?kot-vi a-ir-na t-iaa ?txa-ar + . por kee a-?pa?k-a-h-r-na + 201 + , i txe kee e-txan + , ta-ma u&-neh + u& -- , u&-?kutx-i + , txaa-tee baliha a-xan-a + , txe kee + . ia ?pu?t-ur e-tumin ta-ma-r +

208 + , i por eso + , txe kee e-txan ia-haa + kuando tah -- tahu-i-na + , ?txa-ar txam-en + , ?pu?t-?ka e-hente ta-ma e-oriia e-haa + , ?kan-i ani + a-vx-in u& -- , u&-?txa?k-i-o?p u&-neh a-lo?k-vi + , ?kan-i u& -- . u&-lo?k-se-o?p e-tumin + 219 + pero a-?pa?k-ta-o?p + por kee -- , txe kee e-txan + . meigra u&-hi?k-ar-ir u&-hut + i ta-ma e -- u&-hi?k-ar-ir u&-hut ia-haa + , ua-ak txe ta-ka + u&-ar-i vn-tee ta-m -- , ta-ma e-haa + i -- . ma atxi-ix a-lo?k-vi vn-tee + 230 + i por eso + . a-?pa?k-a-h-r-na e-txan +

232 + . pues + , e-txan ia-haa + txe kee ia ?txa-an + , e-otxo diia + ma m-ah-txi a -- , a-?kot-vi ta-u&-eh?ts-er + , por kee txe kee motor txam-en + . pero aian-to u&-hi?k-ar-ir u&-hut + 240 + , i ma atxi u&-akt-a e-hente + . a-?kot-vi ta-u&-eh?ts-er + 242 + pero e-hente haax e -- , e-tumin xee ?txu-ur ta-ma u&-puntu u&-neh +

2. Serpent

."ha?ax 'ua'ru'ui"ro?p + 'por'ke?e -- ."txe 'ke?e"mei 'gra'tu"min + 247 + ,'u'?ku"txa?a 'lo"?koi + "kuan 'do?o -- ,'a?a"xin + ,'tia?a '?ka"ni 'a'nuh"?pi + 'ta"ka 'o'tron'te?e'u"ieh 'txa"nir + ,'ta'mal"gun 'ui"tsir + .'u'?ke"txe 'tu"no?or 'u'tu"min 'a?a"xin + 254 + .'i"txe 'ke"mei 'gra +

255 + ,'i'ha?ax"to + 'e?e -- ,'?ka"ni 'a 'lo'?kes"na 'u'me'ne"hen 'te + "pe 'ro -- .'a '?pa'?kahr"na + 260 + 'i?i -- ,'i'ta'mu?u"ka 'txu + 'txe"ke?e -- .'in"so 'lo'tu"min '?pu"?tur + 264 + ,'u"ka 'txu + "txe 'ke?e"?paŋ 'ko'txa 'u"ka 'txu'e?e -- ,'u"ka 'txu'e'ua"kax̃ + ."pe 'ro"mei 'gra'noh"ta?a + 268 + 'i?i -- ,'?i'po "re 'so + .'e'txan'txe?e"no?p 'ke?e'a"ian 'u'tu "min +

271 + ,'kon'dix"to + ,"kai + ,'ta"ki 'e "ha?a + ,'ha?a"xir 'ket'pa"?txa?an 'ta'ta"kin + ,'en"ton 'ses + ,"txe 'ke"kai '?pu?t"?ka 'e"sia 'nu"sih + .'i"kai '?kuh"xa + 278 + ."pe 'ro '?ix"na "?txa?ar + 279 + ,'ua'ra'?kuh"xa 'u"me 'niu"sih + 'por'ke"txe 'ke?e -- ."mei 'gra + .'noh"ta?a 'e"txan 'ia"ha?a +

283 + 'i?i -- ,'i'po"re 'so + .'ix"na '?ka?a"?pa '?kuh"xa 'u'me'niu"sih + ,"pe 'ro "ne?en + 'ko'txa?a -- ,'ma?a"txi '?iŋ'gui"ra + ,'ma?a'txi?i"xe?en 'iŋ'gui"ra?a -- .'tia?a "?txa?ar 'txa"men + ,"ha?ax 'nik"iŋ 'gui"ra + .'ki"sas 'in'lo?k"se '?a"ni '?u'tu"min +

2. Serpent

. haax ua-r u&-ir-a-o?p + por kee -- . txe kee meigra tumin + 247 + , u&-?kutx-i a-lo?k-vi + kuando -- , a-vx-in + , t-iaa a-?kan-i a-nuh?p-i + ta-ka otro vn-tee u&-eh txan-ir + , ta-ma algun uitsir + . u&-?ketx-e tunoor u&-tumin a-vx-in + 254 + . i txe kee meigra +

255 + , i haax-to + e -- , ?kan-i a-lo?k-es-na u&-men e-hente + pero -- . a-?pa?k-a-h-r-na + 260 + i -- , i ta-ma u&-katxu + txe kee -- . vn-solo tumin ?pu?t-ur + 264 + , u&-katxu + txe kee ?pan ko-txa u&-katxu e -- , u&-katxu e-uakax + . pero meigra noh-taa + 268 + i -- , i por eso + . e-txan txe-e-na-o?p kee aian u&-tumin +

271 + , konda-ix-to + , kai + , tak-i e-haa + , haax-ir ket-pa ?txa-an ta-tak-in + , entonses + , txe kee kai ?pu?t-?ka e-sian usih + . i kai ?ku-h-x-a + 278 + . pero ix-na ?txa-ar + 279 + , ua-r a-?ku-h-x-a u&-men e-usih + por kee txe kee -- . meigra + . noh-taa e-txan ia-haa +

283 + i -- , i por eso + . ix-na ?kaa?p-a ?ku-h-x-a u&-men e-usih + , pero na-en + ko-txa -- , ma atxi vn&-ir-a + , ma atxi vx-i-en vn&-ir-a -- . t-iaa ?txa-ar txam-en + , haax-nik vn&-ir-a + . kisas vn&-lo?k-se ani u&-tumin +

2. Serpent

1 There is another story that is told about the serpent that is called Txan. 7 They say that at one time, about the river that passes by the edge of the town of Jocotan, 14 they say that that river, at one time, rose until it went into the brush. The water carried off absolutely everything, -- the cane, the bananas, whatever was planted near the banks of the water.

29 It carried off everything, and carried off the houses that -- the houses which were found near where the water passes. It carried everything off; it grabbed and carried off the pigs, the chickens, horses and cattle -- everything that it found where it was overflowing, near the banks of the river. It carried everything away. 54 And the houses. 55 Because they say that the serpent came out of a mountain named Sesekmil.

62 We don't know the place but so it is said, that that is what the mountain's name is, where the serpent came out. 68 And for that reason the people say of the serpents, when they grow within the mountains, that their horns come out.

75 And then when they grow, then the serpents which still aren't -- still aren't Great Serpents, when they grow, they say that they go like people; they look for their wives, to mate with them. 93 Well, they say that when there is a landslide, that that is the serpents coming out; they say that they go looking for their wives to mate with them. 103 And therefore they come out of the mountains where they live, and go crawling to another mountain. 108 But where they come out they make great landslides, and they destroy the place.

2. Serpent

113 And so they say that -- people today say that not all come out and go to where they want to go. 123 Because they say that that serpent was found lying there on the banks of the stream. And he remained lying in the water, on top of a big rock. And there he lay. 137 Because they say that he was smitten by the gods because it was seen that he was causing great destruction in that place. He carried off the houses, and then he was smitten by the gods. 148 And therefore the people say that the serpent may not come out, if he is not given permission by God.

154 There are some that come out without causing a landslide, or they do but do not destroy any houses. 160 And then they go wherever they want to go. 163 But if the serpent destroys many things, -- houses -- where he comes out, he is not allowed by God to go wherever he wants. He is smitten, and killed right there. 176 Because they say that that serpent was smitten by the gods; and there he lay in that stream where his path came out, passing by the villages.

187 It has come to be said that that serpent -- lay there for eight days, lying there, on top of a rock. 196 Because that -- nobody came by where he lay and saw him. Because they were frightened. 201 And they say that the serpent, in his tail -- went around carrying two bags. They say that they were filled with money.

208 And therefore they say of that serpent that when he was found, lying dead, people filled the banks of that stream. They wanted to go chop off his tail, and take out the money. 219 But they were afraid because they say that the wind of the serpent's passing is very great.

2. Serpent

And by — ... That wind suddenly throws one down into the river. And one can not get out. 230 And therefore the serpent is feared.

232 Well, that snake, they say it was lying there for eight days. No one came to its side, because they say that although dead, it still had the wind of its passing. 240 And that didn't let people come up beside it. 242 But people, they — the money which hangs from the end of its tail -- they watched it, because, they say, it was a great deal of money. 247 It came out carrying it when it emerged, when it wanted to go mate with its fellow serpent, in some other mountain. It took all its money along. 254 And they say it was a great deal.

255 And then the people wanted to take it out, but they were frightened. 260 And they say its horn was all full of money. 264 Its horn, they say, was like the horn of a bull, but very large. 268 And that is why they said the serpent had money.

271 When the water began to dry up, he remained lying on dry land. Then they say that many vultures began to gather, and he began to be eaten. 278 But he lay there a long time. 279 He was being eaten by the vultures, because they say that that serpent was very large.

283 And that is why it took a long time for the vultures to eat him all up. But I didn't see it, since I didn't go see where he was lying dead. If I had seen it, maybe I would have taken his money.

3. Landslide

1 + ,'?ka"nin 'txe'kon"tar + .'o'tron"te?e 'o'hro"ner + 3 + ,'a"ian 'in'te?e'txi"nam + ,'u'?ka"?pa?a 'o'ko'te"pe 'ke + 'e?e -- 'ta?a -- .'ta"ma '?e'on"du 'ras + 8 + ,'ia"ha?a 'e'txi "nam 'ia"ha?a + ,"txe 'ke?e'ta"rix 'e"tiem 'po + ,"mei 'gra'?a"ni 'e'txi"nam + ,'i"mei 'gra'a"ni '?e"hen 'te + .'?a"ian 'ta"mar + 13 + 'i'io'to "to?p -- 'e?e -- ,'ga"la 'ni'?ka"ni + .'u'uir "na?ar + 17 + ,"pe 'ro + ,'?ko"toi + ,'in'te?e "di 'ia + ,'sat"pa + ,'ke?e'txi"nam 'ia"ha?a + 'sat -- ,'sat"pa + 'ta"ma '?e?e -- ,'e"a 'nio + ,"mil 'no'be"sien 'tos + ."trein 'ti"dos +

28 + .'ma?a"te?eix "na + .'sat"pa 'e'txi "nam 'ia"ha?a + 'i'txe"ke?e -- 'kon'da?a -- ,'sat"pa 'e'txi"nam 'ia"ha?a + 'e?e -- 'kon'de?e -- ,'sa'koh"pa + .'kai'xa"na 'in"te?ei "la 'ma + 37 + ,'a'ro?p"na 'e'txi"nam + .'tua?a'lo"?ko?p 'a"ni + 39 + "txe?e -- .'txa?a"ii 'e'?i"la 'ma + ,'ke?e'lo'?ke"nik 'ko"ne?er + ,'por'ke?e'ko "ne?er + .'mix"ha?ax 'tua?a'e'kor"pa?ar 'e'txi "na 'mi"ra + 44 + ,'por'ke'?e'txi"nam 'i"ra + 'ko"ne?er 'tu"ru?u "di?i "ir + 'tua?a -- ,'a'sat "pa + ,'i'ti?i'ne'?a'lo"?koi + ,'a?ah"ni + ,'a 'kor'pa"to + ,'i"ti?i 'ne'ma?a"txi + .'ia'tua?a 'a'?ka?a"pa +

53 + "pe 'ro'?e"hen 'te + .'ma?a"txi 'u '?ku?up"sio?p + 55 + ,'txe?e"no?p 'ke'?i"la 'ma"ra + 'in'ta"ka?a -- 'ma'tu"?ku?u "hui 'sio + ."ua?ar 'uar'a'xa"na 'o?o"hron + 59 + 'por'ke "txe 'ke?e -- 'e?e -- ,'e'i"la 'ma'ia"ha?a + .'in"te 'ri'o'to"to?p + 'xa"na 'kai -- .'u"txe 'a'bi"sar 'e"hen 'te + 'i?i -- ,"pe 'ro'ha?a "xo?p + 'txe?e"no?p 'ke?e -- ,'ke?e'?i"la 'ma "ra + .'in'ta"ka 'lo'koh"ran + 70 + ,'ma?a"txi 'u'?ku?up"sio?p + .'lo'ke?e'u'?kah"ti 'e'i"la 'ma +

3. Landslide

1 + , ?kan-i vn&-txe kontar + . otro vn-
tee ohron-er + 3 , aian vn-tee txinam + , u&-
?ka?paa okotepeke + e -- ta -- . ta-ma e-onduras
+ 8 + , ia-haa e-txinam ia-haa + , txe kee tar
-ix e-tiempo + , meigra ani e-txinam + , i
meigra ani e-hente + . aian ta-ma-r + 13 + e-
otot-o?p -- e -- , galan i&-?kan-i u&-ir-na-ar +
17 + , pero + , ?kot-vi + , vn-tee diia + , sat
-pa + , kee e-txinam ia-haa + sat -- , sat-pa +
ta-ma e -- , e-anio + , mil nobesientos + .
treintidos +

28 + . ma to a-ix-na + . sat-pa e-txinam
ia-haa + i txe kee -- konda -- , sat-pa e-txinam
ia-haa + e -- konde -- , sak-oh-pa + . kai xan-a
vn-tee ilama + 37 + , ar-o?p-na e-txinam + .
tuaa lo?k-vi-o?p ani + 39 + txe -- . txe aii e
-ilama + , kee lo?k-en-ik koneer + , por kee
koneer + . m-ix haax tuaa e-kor-pa-ar e-txinam
ir-a + 44 + , por kee e-txinam ir-a + koneer
tur-u u&-dii-ir + tuaa -- , a-sat-pa + , i tiin-
e a-lo?k-vi + , a-ahn-i + , a-kor-pa-to + , i
tiin-e ma atxi + . ia tuaa a-?kaap-a +

53 + pero e-hente + . ma atxi u&-?ku?p-se-
o?p + 55 + , txe-e-na-o?p ke e-ilama ir-a + vn
-ta-ka -- ma tu?ka u&-huisio + . ua-ar ua-r a-
xan-a a-ohron + 59 + por kee txe kee -- e -- ,
e-ilama ia-haa + . interu e-otot-o?p + xan-a kai
-- . u&-txe abisar e-hente + i -- , pero haax-
o?p + txe-e-na-o?p kee -- , kee e-ilama ir-a + .
vn-ta-ka loko-h-r-an + 70 + , ma atxi u&-?ku?p
-se-o?p + . lo kee u&-?kah-ti e-ilama +

3. Landslide

72 + "pe 'ro"kuan 'do -- 'e?e -- ,"tar 'de "ran + ,"kai + '?ka"xi 'e'ha"ha?ar + 'e?e -- . "ua 'ra'?ka"xi 'ehs"to 'sa'koh"pa + 79 + 'e?e -- ,'sa'koh"pa 'o'tron"te?e "di 'ia + .'ma?a "txa?a 'nu"mui + 82 + 'i?i -- ,'ehs'to'ke?e "?pan 'nu"mui 'e"di 'ia + .'ma?a"txa?a 'nu"mui 'e'ha"ha?ar + 85 + ."i + ,'kon'dix"to + ,'sa 'koh"pa 'o'tro"di 'ia + ,'e're"uar 'a?an'?txak "na + ,"kuan 'do'hi?ik"na 'e'ui"tsir + .'ti"txan + 92 + "por 'ke?e -- ,"ha?ax + 93 + 'in'te?e 'ui"tsir + ."mei 'gra + 96 + ,"ha?ax + ,'ki?ip "?tsa 'ta"ri + .'u'ma"ki 'e'txi"nam + 'por'ke?e -- ,"no?on + ,'a"kai 'ka'?ko"toi + ,'i'ka'ui'ra "to + 'e?e -- 'e?e -- .'ki"?pi?ts 'xe'ta"ri + .'u'ma"ki 'e'txi"nam +

107 + ,'u'?kah"ti 'e"hen 'te'ko"ne?er + "ti?i 'ne -- ,'tu"ruo?p 'ia"ha?a + "txe 'ke"kuan 'do?o -- ,'sat"pa 'e'txi"nam + 'e?e -- ,'a'ian "to + .'e"hen 'te + ,'kai'lo"?koi 'ah"ni + 'e?e -- ,'ta'me?e'txi"nam 'ia"ha?a + ,'ta"ri + ,"kai 'tu'rua"no?p + 'ehs"to 'ta'man"te?e "plan + ."mei 'gra'u'nah"tir +

122 + ,'pe'ro'?a"ian 'in"te?e "kohn + 'a 'lu"mui + 'ta'me?e -- ,'u'io'ri"iir 'e'txi"nam + ,"tia?a 'sat"pa 'ia"ha?a + ,'i'txe"ke?e '?e"kohn 'ia"ha?a + 'ha?a -- ,"ia 'ta"ri + 'e?e -- 'e?e -- ,'e"sian 'a"nam + 'lo'ke?e -- .'ta"re?e 'ki "?pi?ts 'ti"txan + 135 + 'i"txe 'ke?e -- '?a "ian 'ti?i"ne?e -- ,'kai"to 'u'lo?k"se 'u'tu"min + .'ta"ri 'kai'u'?txa"?pu?u + ,'nah"tir + "tia?a 'u'na?a"ta 'ke'ma?a"txi 'tua?a'lu"mui 'e?e -- .'e'ki"?pi?ts + 142 + ,"por 'ke?e"txe 'ke?e'e 'ki"?pi?ts 'ia"ha?a + ,'im'?pihk'im"?pihk "kai 'ki?p"?tsa 'ta"ri + 'u?u -- 'u?u -- 'u'iu"?pio?p + .'a'hi?ik"na + 148 + "txe?en "ton 'ses -- 'txe?e"no?p 'ke?e -- ,'?pah"?kat 'ka'sat"pa 'ber "da + ,'por"ke?e "me 'ru'ki"?pi?ts + .'uar 'ua "tar 'ti"txan +

3. Landslide

72 + pero kuando -- e -- , tarde-r-an + , kai — ?kax-i e-ha-haa-r + e -- . ua-r a-?kax-i ehsto sak-oh-pa + 79 + e -- , sak-oh-pa otro vn-tee diia + . ma atxi a-num-vi + 82 + i -- , ehsto kee ?pan num-vi e-diia + . ma atxi a-num-vi e-ha-haa-r + 85 + . i + , konda-ix-to + sak-oh-pa otro diia + , er-e ua-r a-han?txak-na + , kuando hi?k-na e-uitsir + . ti-txan + 92 + por kee -- , haax + 93 + vn-tee uitsir + . meigra + 96 + , haax + , ki?p-?tsa tar-i + . u&-mak-i e-txinam + por kee -- , na-on + , a-kai ka-?kot-vi + , i ka&-ir-a-to + e -- e -- . ki?p-i?ts xee tar-i + . u&-mak-i e-txinam +

107 + , u&-?kah-ti e-hente koneer + tiin-e — , tur-u-o?p ia-haa + txe kee kuando , sat-pa e-txinam + e -- , aian-to + . e-hente + , kai lo?k-vi ahn-i + e -- , ta-ma e-txinam ia-haa + , tar-i + , kai tur-uan-o?p + ehsto ta-ma vn-tee plan + . meigra u&-naht-ir +

122 + , pero aian vn-tee kohn + a-lum-vi + ta-ma e -- , u&-orii-ir e-txinam + , t-iaa sat-pa ia-haa + , i txe kee e-kohn ia-haa + haa -- , ia tar-i + e -- e -- , e-sian anam + lo kee -- . tar-i e-ki?p-i?ts ti-txan + 135 + i txe kee -- aian tiin-e -- , kai-to u&-lo?k-se u&-tumin + . tar-i kai u&-?txa-?pu + , naht-ir + t-iaa u&-naat-a kee ma atxi tuaa a-lum-vi e -- . e-ki?p-i?ts + 142 + , por kee txe kee e-ki?p-i?ts ia-haa + , vn-?pi-h-k vn-?pi-h-k kai ki?p-?tsa tar-i + u& -- u& -- u&-u?p-i-o?p + . a-hi?k-na 148 + txe entonses -- txe-e-na-o?p kee -- , ?pah?k-at ka-sat-pa berda + , por kee meru ki?p-i?ts + . ua-r ua-ta-r ti-txan +

3. Landslide

153 + ,'en"ton 'ses + ,'tu"no?or 'e'siaŋ "hen 'te + ,'ta'me?e'txi"nam + "kai -- 'e?e -- ,'u'lo?k"se 'tu"no?or 'lo'ke'?a"ian 'ta'mu?u'io "tot + .'u'tu'ru"?pa 'nah"tir + 160 + 'i'ti?in 'e?e -- ,'u'iah"tu?ut 'u'tu"min + ,"kai + 'u'?ke "txe 'lo"?koi 'u?u -- ,'u'ba"li 'ha + .'kai'ta "ri 'u'?txa"?pu 'nah"tir + 166 + 'i"ti?i 'ne?e -- ,"kai + ,'ta"ri 'u'?txa"?po?p 'ia"ha?a + .'i "txe 'ke"tua?a 'a'sut"pa 'a?a"xin + ,'u'?txa"mi + "o 'tro?o -- "o 'tra"ko 'sa'lo'ke?e -- ,"ua 'ru'lo?k"se 'ta'?u'io"tot + ,'tia?a"uar + ,'ua "tar + ."ia "ua 'ra'mak"?tsa + "por 'ke?e -- ,"ia 'he'ki"?pi?ts + .'ua'ru'ua"tar 'ti"txan +

180 + 'i"tia?a -- ,'ua'ra'lu"muo?p 'ta 'me?e"kohn 'ia"ha?a + ."ia?a 'mak"?tso?p + 183 + 'i?i -- 'i"txe 'ke?e -- ,'e'tu"min 'ia"ha?a + 'lo'ke?e"kai -- ,'kai'lo"?kes "na '?txa?p"na 'nah"tir 'tia?a'ma?a"txi 'a'lo"?koi 'e'ki"?pi?ts +

188 + ,'iu?u'uiŋ"kir + ,'ia?a'mak"?tsa 'kon"da?a 'sut"pa?a "xin + 'u?u -- ,'tua?a"tan 'u'lo?k"se + ,"mas 'lo'ke?e'a"ian 'tu?u'io"tot + 'i?i -- ."ia?a 'mak"?tsa + 195 + "kon 'de?e -- "txu?u 'txe'sen"tir + ,'ua"tar 'e'sian"rum 'ta'?u"hor + ."ia?a '?ka?a"pa + 199 + 'i'ma?a "txi?ix + .'a'sut"pa?a 'io?o"pa '?u'ui"ra 'u'tu "min 'tia?a'?u'iak"ta +

201 + 'i?i -- ,"?i 'po"re 'so + ,'u'?kah "ti 'e"hen 'te'ta'me?e'txi"nam + ,'o'ko'te"pe 'ke + 'ke?e -- 'ia"ha?a + ."mei 'gra + ,"hen 'te + '?e?e -- "kai + ,'u'?ka"?pio?p 'e'tu"min 'ia "ha?a + ,'i'ta"mar + ,'ko"ne?er + .'a"ian 'u'tu 'mi"no?p + 215 + ,'por"ke?e + ."mei 'gra"hen 'te + ,"kai + ,'u'lo?ok"se 'u'tu"min 'u'?txa"?pu 'nah"tir 'tia?a'ma?a"txi 'a'lu"mui 'e'ki"?pi?ts + ,"pe 'ro'ha?a"xir + ,'ma?a"txi?ix 'kor"pa + "por 'ke?e -- "ha?ax 'e'tia?a -- ,'a'sut"pa

3. Landslide

153 + , entonses + , tunoor e-sian hente + , ta-ma e-txinam + kai -- e -- , u&-lo?k-se tunoor lo kee aian ta-ma u-otot + . u&-tur-u-?pa naht-ir + 160 + i tiin-e -- , u&-iaht-i u&-hut u&-tumin + , kai + u&-?ketx-e lo?k-vi u& -- , u& -baliha + kai tar-i u&-?txa-?pu naht-ir + 166 + i tiin-e -- , kai + , tar-i u&-?txa-?pu-o?p ia -haa + . i txe kee tuaa a-sut-pa a-vx-in + , u&- ?txam-i + otro -- otra kosa lo kee -- , ua-r u&- lo?k-se ta-u&-otot + , t-iaa ua-r + , ua-ta-r + . ia ua-r a-mak-?tsa + por kee -- , e-ah e-ki?p- i?ts + . ua-r a-ua-ta-r ti-txan +

180 + i t-iaa -- , ua-r a-lum-vi-o?p ta-ma e-kohn ia-haa + . iaa mak-?tsa-o?p + 183 + i -- i txe kee -- , e-tumin ia-haa + lo kee kai -- , kai lo?k-es-na ?txa-?p-na naht-ir t-iaa ma atxi a-lo?k-vi e-ki?p-i?ts +

188 + , i u&-uink-ir + , iaa mak-?tsa konda a-sut-pa a-vx-in + u& -- , tuaa tan u&- lo?k-se + , mas lo kee aian ta-u&-otot + i -- . iaa mak-?tsa + 195 + konde -- txe u&-txe sentir + , ua-ta-r e-sian rum ta-u&-hor + . iaa ?kaap-a + 199 + i ma atxi-ix + . a-sut-pa a- ioop-a u&-ir-a u&-tumin t-iaa u&-ak-ta +

201 + i -- , i por eso + , u&-?kah-ti e- hente ta-ma e-txinam + , okotepeke + kee -- ia- haa + . meigra + , hente + e -- kai + , u&-?ka?p -i-o?p e-tumin ia-haa + , i ta-ma-r + , koneer + . aian u&-tumin-o?p + 215 + , por kee + . meigra hente + , kai + , u&-lo?k-se u&-tumin u&- ?txa-?pu naht-ir t-iaa ma atxi a-lum-vi e-ki?p- i?ts + , pero haax-ir + , ma atxi-ix kor-pa + por kee -- haax e-t-iaa -- , a-sut-pa

3. Landslide

'?a?a"xin 'tu'io"tot + ,'u'ta"res 'an'o'tro "niahr + 'e?e -- ,'tu"?ka 'lo'ke'?ka"nu?u 'ta "res + 'i'ma?a"txi?ix 'a'lo"?koi 'por'ke?e -- , 'e'ki"?pi?ts + ,'ua'ra'ua"tar 'ti"txan + ."ua 'ra'mak"?tso?p +

231 + ,'en"ton 'ses + 'e?e -- 'u'ui"ro?p 'ke?e'ma?a'txix"tu 'iu"?pa 'a'lu'muo?p"ia?a 'ta 'me?e"kohn + 'por"ke?e -- ,'ket"pi?ix + ,"pu 'ru 'a"nam 'e"kohn + 237 + ,'en"ton 'ses + ,'lo"ke 'u"txo?p "ti?i 'ne'tu"ro?p + ,'ta'ta're'txi"nam + ,'u'mo'roh"se '?u"?po?p + 'tu'rua"no?p 'ta'man "te?e + ,'o"tot + "mei 'ra'e?e -- "mei 'gra -- , 'u"ial "tir + 246 + ,'a"ian "ti?i 'ne'kor"po?p "to + 'e?e -- ,"kai + .'kor"po?p +

250 + ,'pe'ro'ti?i'ne'kai"to + ."?peh "ruo?p + 252 + ,'tua?a"ta?a "ni + 'u'lo?k"se 'u?u -- ,'u"ko "so?p + ,'lo'ke'?a"ian 'tu?u'io 'to"to?p + ,'u'tu'mi"no?p + ,'u'?puh"ko?p + 'e?e -- ,'tu"no?or '?kan"tan 'u'lo?k"sio?p 'nah"tir + ,'i'ia"kai '?ka?a"po?p + 'e?e -- ,'ta'mu?ut'e "?pi?ir + 'tia?a -- "ua 'ra'ua"tar 'e'sian'ki "?pi?ts + 'i?i -- ,"ehs 'to'ke"?pan + '?pu?t"?ka -- ,'tu"no?or 'e'txi"nam + ,'ta'ke?e'?a"nam 'mah "ka 'tu"no?or 'e'o'to"to?p + 'e?e -- ,'ket"pa + ."pu 'ru'a"nam + 'e'txi"nam +

274 + ,"pe 'ro'iŋ"gohr 'ta'kix'o"tot + 'e?e -- ,'ket"pa 'ta'mu?u -- 'io'ri"ier 'e'txi "nam + ,'ta'me?ein"xehr + "tia?a -- ,'i"to?or 'in'te?e'san"tar + ."ha?ax 'ta"kix 'ket"pa + 282 + ."ia '?pu?t"?ka 'e"hen 'te + ."ti?i 'ne 'kor'po?p"to +

284 + 'i?i -- ,'kon'dix"to + ,"kai + 'nu "mui 'e'ki"?pi?ts 'ia"ha?a 'en"ton 'ses + ,'ta 'me?e'a"bion + ,'kai'?ko"toi + 'e'puh"sa 'e?e -- '?e"pan + 'e?e -- "to?or 'io"tot 'ia"ha?a + 'tia?a -- .'ma'ka"ro?p + 296 + 'i?i --

3. Landslide

a-vx-in ta-u&-otot + , u&-tar-es san otro vn-iahr + e -- , tu?ka lo kee ?kan-i u&-tar-es + i ma atxi-ix a-lo?k-vi por kee -- , e-ki?p-i?ts + , ua-r a-ua-ta-r ti-txan + . ua-r a-mak-?tsa-o?p +

231 + , entonses + e -- u&-ir-a-o?p kee ma atxi-ix-to u&-u?p-i a-lum-vi-o?p iaa ta-ma e-kohn + por kee -- , ket-pa-ix + , puru anam e-kohn + 237 + , entonses + , lo kee u&-txe-o?p tiin-e tur-u-o?p + , ta-ta-ma e-txinam + , u&-mor-oh-se u&-?pa-o?p + tur-uan-o?p ta-ma vn-tee + , otot + meira e -- meigra -- , u&-alt-ir + 246 + , aian tiin-e kor-pa-o?p-to + e -- , kai + . kor-pa-o?p +

250 + , pero tiin-e kai-to + . ?pehr-u-o?p + 252 + tuaa-to ani + u&-lo?k-se u& -- , u&-kosa-o?p + , lo kee aian ta-u&-otot-o?p + , u&-tumin-o?p + , u&-?puhk-o?p + e -- , tunoor ?kan-tan u&-lo?k-se-o?p naht-ir + , i ia kai ?kaap-a-o?p + e -- , ta-ma u&-hut e-?pi-ir + t-iaa -- ua -r a-ua-ta-r e-sian ki?p-i?ts + i -- , ehsto kee ?pan + ?pu?t-?ka -- , tunoor e-txinam + , ta-ka e-anam ma-h-k-a tunoor e-otot-o?p + e -- , ket-pa + . puru anam + e-txinam +

274 + , pero vn-go-h-r ta-k-ix otot + e -- , ket-pa ta-ma u& -- orii-er e-txinam + , ta-ma e-vn-xe-h-r + t-iaa -- , i ta-hor vn-tee santar + . haax ta-k-ix ket-pa + 282 + ia ?pu?t-?ka e -hente + . tiin-e kor-pa-o?p-to +

284 + i -- , konda-ix-to + , kai + num-vi e-ki?p-i?ts ia-haa entonses + , ta-ma e-abion + , kai ?kot-vi + e-pu-h-sa e -- e-pan + e -- ta-hor c-otot ia-haa + t-iaa -- . mak-ar-o?p + 296 + i --

3. Landslide

,'i'xin"na + ,"kai 'xa"na 'e'?a"bion + ,'kai'u 'pu"si 'e"pan + 'tia?a -- ,'ket'pa"to 'e?e -- , "mohr 'ia"ha?a + ,'ta'me'o"tot 'ia"ha?a + ."pe 'ro'tu"no?or 'e"hen 'te'?ka?a"pa 'mak"?tsa + . 'ta'mu?u'io'to"to?p + 306 + "por 'ke?e -- ,'in 'iah"rer + ,'mak"?tsa 'e'txi"nam + .'u"men 'ia?a "nam + 310 + 'ie?e -- 'e?e -- ,'e"ha?a + ."mei 'gra + ,"kai "?txi?i + 'i?i -- 'pues -- 'e'ia "ha?a 'si?i -- ,'ka'na?a"ta 'ke?e'ber"da + 'por "ke?e 'ka'?ko"toi 'ka'ui"ra 'ke?e -- ,'e'ki "?pi?ts 'tu'ru"to "es 'to'ko"ne?er + ."xe '?u'sa "ti '?e'txi"nam +

322 + ,'i'ko"ne?er + ,'e'txi"nam 'o'ko'te "pe 'ke + 'mix"ha?ax 'lo'ke?e -- ,'tu"ru '?a"ni 'ta"rix 'e"tiem 'po + 'si"no 'ke?e 'e?e -- 'e?e -- .'in"te?eix 'txi"nam + 329 + .'sut"pa 'o'ko 'te"pe 'ke + 330 + ,'i'po"re 'so'u'?ka"pa?a 'e 'txi"nam 'ia"ha?a + ."nue 'ba'o'ko'te"pe 'ke + 332 + 'por'ke?e'mix"ha?ax 'e'o'ko'te"pe 'ke 'xe?e -- .'tu"ra?a "ni 'ix"ni?ix +

334 + 'pe're?e"txe 'ke?e -- ,'xe?e'txi"nam 'ix"ni?ix + ,'txe'ke?e"mei 'gra'?a"ni 'e'txi"nam + 'i?i -- .'a"ian 'a"nu?u 'tu"min 'e"hen 'te'lo 'ke?e'tu"ro?p 'ta"mar + 339 + "pe 'ro -- , '?ka?a"pa + .'sat"po?p + 342 + .'ta'me?e"tiem 'po'ia"ha?a + 343 + .'u'?kah"ti 'e"hen 'te + 'ke?e -- ,'ke?e'e'txi"nam 'ia"ha?a 'sat"pa + . 'por"ke?e 'in"te?e "sier 'po + ,'lo"?koi 'ma"kue 'ui"tsir + .'i'ha?ax'u"txe 'sian'ki"?pi?ts "tia?a 'lo"?koi +

349 + ,'i'po"re 'so'ko"ne?er + ,'e"sier 'po + 'txe'?e"hen 'te'ke?e -- ,"sier 'po + "ha?ax 'e?e -- ,"txan + ,'e'nu'kir"txan "?txa?ar 'ma'kui?ir'e'ui"tsir + ,'i"kuan 'do'a'lo"?ko?p + ,'en"ton 'ses + ,'u"txo?p 'e'sian'ki"?pi?ts + ."ia?a 'sat"pa 'e'lu"gar 'u'me'ne"ro?p +

3. Landslide

, vx-in-na + , kai xan-a e-abion + , kai u-pus-i
e-pan + t-iaa -- , ket-pa-to e -- , mo-h-r ia-
haa + , ta-ma e-otot ia-haa + . pero tunoor e-
hente ?kaap-a mak-?tsa + . ta-ma u&-otot-o?p +
306 + por kee -- , vn-iahr-er + , mak-?tsa e-
txinam + , u&-men e-anam + 310 + i e -- e -- ,
e-haa + . meigra + , kai ?txih-i + i -- pues --
e-ia-haa si -- , ka&-naat-a kee berda + por kee
ka-?kot-vi ka&-ir-a kee -- , e-ki?p-i?ts tur-u-
to esto koneer + . xee u&-sat-i e-txinam +

322 + , i koneer + , e-txinam okotepeke +
m-ix haax lo kee -- , tur-u ani tar-i-x e-tiempo
+ sino kee e -- e -- . vn-tee-ix txinam + 329
+ . sut-pa okotepeke + 330 + , i por eso u&-
?ka?paa e-txinam ia-haa + . nueba okotepeke +
332 + por kee m-ix haax e-okotepeke xee -- .
tur-u ani ix-na-ix +

334 + pero txe kee -- , xee e-txinam ix-na
-ix + , txe kee meigra ani e-txinam + i -- .
aian ani u&-tumin e-hente lo kee e-tur-u-o?p ta-
ma-r + 339 + pero -- , ?kaap-a + . sat-pa-o?p
+ 342 + . ta-ma e-tiempo ia-haa + 343 + . u&
-?kah-ti e-hente + kee -- kee e-txinam ia-haa
sat-pa + . por kee vn-tee sierpo + , lo?k-vi mak
-uu e-uitsir + . i haax u&-txe e-sian ki?p-i?ts
t-iaa lo?k-vi +

349 + , i por eso koneer + , e-sierpo +
txe e-hente kee -- . sierpo + haax e -- , txan +
, e-nuk-ir txan ?txa-ar mak-uu-ir e-uitsir + , i
kuando a-lo?k-vi-o?p + , entonses + , u&-txe-o?p
e-sian ki?p-i?ts + . iaa sat-pa e-lugar u&-men-
er-o?p +

3. Landslide

1 I'm going to tell another story. 3 There is a town whose name is Ocotepeque ... in Honduras. 8 Of that town, they say, that once upon a time the town was large, and there were many people in it. 13 And the houses were very pretty to look at. 17 But there came a day it was destroyed, when that town was destroyed in the year 1932.

28 Not long ago that town was destroyed. And they say that when that town was destroyed, when -- day came, an old woman began to go around. 37 The whole town was told that it should leave. 39 They say that the old woman said, "Get out now! Because today this town no longer has any protection. 44 Because this town, ... today is the day that it will be destroyed, and those who leave running will still be saved, and those who do not, will be done for."

53 But the people did not obey. 55 They said, "This old woman, she's just out of her mind, going around talking." 59 Because they say that that old woman went to all the houses, and began to warn the people. And ... but they said that ... "This old woman has just gone crazy." 70 They did not believe what the old woman said.

72 But when ... evening came, the rain began to fall ... it fell until day came. 79 Another day dawned -- it didn't stop ... 82 And -- until the day was done, the rain did not end. 85 And then when the next day broke, at the moment day was breaking, the mountain thundered up above. 92 Because that was 93 a great mountain. 96 It all slid down and buried the town, because we went there and saw the landslide which had come and buried the town.

3. Landslide

107 The people say today, those who were there, they say that when the town was destroyed there were still people who began to flee, from that town; they went and stayed in a place far away.

122 But there was a stream that ran by the edge of the town, where it was destroyed. And they say that to that stream came a great deal of mud, which was brought by the landslide above. 135 And they say that -- there were those who began to get out their money then. They began to put it away, far away, where they thought that the landslide would not come. 142 Because they say that that landslide little by little began to slide down; they heard its thundering. 148 It is said then -- they said that -- "there is danger we may truly be destroyed, because that is a real landslide coming, up there."

153 Then all the many people of the town began -- they got out everything that was in their houses, and put it far away. 160 And some worried about their money, and began to take it away in their bags. They began to take it to put it away. 166 And some -- who began to carry it away, they say that they turned back to get other things they were getting out of their houses. The place where they were going was buried because that landslide came down from above.

180 And there where they were running down that ravine they were buried. 183 And -- they say that -- that money which was beginning to be taken out and put far away, where the landslide did not reach.

188 And its owners were buried when they

turned back, so they could get out more of what was in their houses. And there they were buried. 195 When, it is said, they heard all the earth coming down on their heads, there they were finished. 199 And they could not return to see their money where it was left.

201 And therefore the people of that town, Ocotepeque, say that there many people began to gather up that money, and because of that, today they have money. 215 Because many people began to get out their money to put it far away where the landslide did not come. But that was not a safe place, because that was where they came back to their houses, wanting to bring away again what they had been bringing, and they did not get out because the landslide coming down from above buried them.

231 Then they saw that they were not able to go down the ravine, because the ravine had completely filled with mud. 237 Then, what those who were still there, back in the town, did, was to gather together, in a house which was very high. 246 There were those who were safe -- they were safe.

250 But there were those who still began to move things. 252 So as to get their -- things out, that were in their houses; -- their money, their clothes, -- everything they still wanted to take far away. And there they were done for. On the path where the great landslide came down. And -- so until the whole town was filled, with mud that buried all the houses. The town was completely covered with mud.

274 But only one house remained at the edge of the town, on one side where -- on top of a high place it alone remained. 282 There it

was filled with people who were safe then.

284 And when that landslide was done, then a plane came and dropped bread on that house where they were shut up. 296 And -- it went on, the plane went on, dropping the bread where the others were still there, in that house. But all the people were buried in their houses. 306 Because -- the town was buried all at once by the mud. 310 And -- the water began to rise very high. And -- well -- and that if -- we know it is true, because we have been to see that -- the landslide which destroyed the town is there to this day.

322 And today the town of Ocotepeque is not where it was in the old days, but rather -- another town 329 has become Ocotepeque. 330 And therefore that town's name is New Ocotepeque. 332 Because it is not the Ocotepeque that used to be.

334 But they say that the town that used to be, they say, was a big town, and the people that lived in it had money. 339 But -- they were all destroyed. 342 At that time. 343 The people say that -- that town was destroyed because a serpent came out of the mountain.

349 And therefore today, the serpent, the people say that, -- the serpent is the Snake, the Great Snake lying inside the mountain. And when they come out, then they cause great avalanches. And places are destroyed by them then and there.

4. Stuckhorn

1 + '?a"ian 'o'tron"te?e -- .'?o'hro"ner
'u'?kah"tio?p + 'ta"mar 'ta'ke?e -- .'?e"txan +
5 + '?e?e -- ,'xu"kur 'xe'?a'lu"mui + ,"tia?a
'tu"ro?on 'ho'ko"tan + "txe 'ke?e -- ."kuan 'do
+ ,'txek"ta 'e'xu"kur 'ia"ha?a + '?e?e -- "ha?ax
-- .'?e"txan + .'ta"ri 'ta"kar + 15 + ."por
'ke?e"?pan 'u'?kah"ti '?e"hen 'te + .'ta"ri 'xe
"tiem 'po + 17 + 'ke?e -- ,'kon"da + ,'txek"ta
'e"ha?a 'ia"ha?a + .'ta"ri 'xe"tiem 'po'ma?a"ni
'tu"?ka?a +

21 + 'pe'ro'txe?e"no?p 'ke?e -- ."txan 'ta
"ri + 23 + ,'?i?i + ,'?u'?txa"?pu + '?e?e -- ,
'?e'xu"kur 'ia"ha?a 'ta"ri + '?i'txe?e"no?p
'ke?e -- ,'?e"txan 'ia"ha?a + .'?i'xik"txan +
30 + ,'por'ke?e'ta"ma '?e'xu"kur + '?e?e -- .
"mei 'gra'u'uam"?txen 'a"ian 'ta"mar + 33 +
'?i'po"re 'so'txe?e"no?p 'ke?e -- ,'?i'xik"txan
'ta"ri + 'por"ke?e -- .'ma?a"txu?u 'na?a"ta 'ko
"txa 'ta?a'pat"na + 37 + ,'por'ke?e'?in"so 'lo
'u'uam"?txen + '?a"ian 'ta'me?e -- .'?e'xu"kur
'ia"ha?a +

40 + '?i?i -- ,'?i'u'?kah"tio?p + 'ke?e --
,"kon 'da'ta"ri + ,'?e"txa 'nia"ha?a + ,'?u'?txa
"?pu + ,'?e?e'xu"kur 'ta"ri + ,"txe 'ke?e +
.'?in"te 'ru"no 'txe + .'?u'iu"?pio?o?p 'a'lah
"?pa + 'ko'txe?e -- .'?a'lah"?pa '?e'ma"rim 'ba
+ 52 + ,'?u'iu"?pio?o?p 'a'lah"?pa + ,'?i
'?pa?ak"ta 'tu"no?o 're"hen 'te + "txe 'pues --
'tu"?ka?a "non 'i"ra + 56 + ,'a'sa"ber 'ma?a
"txi '?ka"ni 'ka'sat"pa 'ko"ne?er + "por 'ke?e
-- .'?in"te 'ru"no 'txe + '?e?e -- ,'?e'lu"gar
"me 'ro'ta'ma"?a?a?p "?txu?ur + '?a?a -- ."ua
'ra'iuh"?ki + 63 + .'?i'?pa?ak"ta 'tu"no?o 're
"hen 'te +

64 + ,'kon'dix"to 'sa'koh"pa + ,'lo"?koi
'ka'ui"ro?o?p + "to?or '?e?e -- ,'?e'san'ta"ro?p
+ 'u'ui"ro?o?p 'ke?e -- "?txa?ar '?e?e --

4. Stuckhorn

1 + aian otro vn-tee -- . ohron-er u&-?kah
-ti-o?p + ta-ma-r ta-ka e -- . e-txan + 5 + e
— , xuk-ur xee a-lum-vi + , t-iaa tur-u-on
hokotan + txe kee -- . kuando + , txek-ta e-xuk-
ur ia-haa + e -- haax -- . e-txan + . tar-i ta-
ka-r + 15 + . por kee ?pan u&-?kah-ti e-hente
+ . tar-ix e-tiempo + 17 + kee -- , konda + ,
txek-ta e-haa ia-haa + . tar-ix e-tiempo ma ani
tu?ka +

21 + pero txe-e-na-o?p kee -- . txan tar-i
+ 23 + , i + , u&-?txa-?pu + e -- , e-xuk-ur
ia-haa tar-i + i txe-e-na-o?p kee -- , e-txan ia
-haa + . ixik txan + 30 + , por kee ta-ma e-
xuk-ur + e -- . meigra u&-ham ?txen aian ta-ma-r
+ 33 + i por eso txe-e-na-o?p kee ixik txan
tar-i + por kee -- . ma atxi u&-naat-a ko-txa ta
-a-pat-na + 37 + , por kee vn-solo u&-ham
?txen + aian ta-ma e -- . e-xuk-ur ia-haa +

40 + i -- , i u&-?kah-ti-o?p + kee -- ,
konda tar-i + , e-txan ia-haa + , u&-?txa-?pu +
, e-xuk-ur tar-i + , txe kee + . interu notxe +
. u&-u?p-i-o?p a-la-h-?p-a + ko-txa e -- . a-la-
h-?p-a e-marimba + 52 + , u&-u?p-i-o?p a-la-h-
?p-a + , i ?pa?k-ta tunoor e-hente + txe pues --
tu?ka anon ir-a + 56 + , a saber ma atxi ?kan-
i ka-sat-pa koneer + por kee -- . interu notxe +
e -- , e-lugar mero ta-ma e-a?p ?txu-ur + a -- .
ua-r a-iuh?k-i + 63 + . i ?pa?k-ta tunoor e-
hente +

64 + , konda-ix-to sak-oh-pa + , lo?k-vi
ka&-ir-a-o?p + ta-hor e -- , e-santar-o?p + u&-
ir-o?p kee -- ?txa-ar e --

4. Stuckhorn

.'e"ha?a 'ua"tar + 71 + .'?i'?ka?a"?pa '?pa?ak "ta 'e"hen 'te +

72 + .'txe?e"no?p 'ke'tu'?ke?e"ra + 73 + 'iu'ui"ro?o?p "?txa?ar 'e?e -- 'no"xi?i 'xu"kur 'ua"tar + '?i?i -- 'ta'ma?a -- ,'dos"di 'ia + , 'en"ton 'ses + .'txek"ta + 80 + 'na?a'taŋ"gua 'ke?e -- ,"txan 'ta"ri + ,"por 'ke?e'?a"ian + 'io?o'to"to?p 'xe?e -- "ser 'ka'?e?e -- '?e?e -- ,'tia?a'lu"mui 'e'xu"kur + ."txe 'ke?e -- 'u"ia 'ha?a -- ,'u"kuer 'pu'e"txa 'nia"ha?a + ,"mei 'gra'u"?txa 'u"tar + .'ko'txa'?iŋ"go 'hro"tot + ,"?i + ,'u"ka 'txo + 'm -- "mei 'gra +

96 + ,'?i'ta"mar + ,"uar 'u'hu?u"ru + '?e?e -- .'?e"rum 'a?a"xin + .'ie?e"siaŋ "ha?a 'ta"kar + 101 + "txe 'ke?e"kon 'da"?txu?ur '?a?a"xin 'ta'me?e"ha?a + ,"ua 'ra?a"xin 'ta 'ke?e'siaŋ"ha?a + ,"txe 'ke?e"?pan 'a'ki'rik"na + .'ko'txa?a'ki'rik"nu?ut 'e"?kin "kon 'da"ua 'ra'?ka"xi 'e'ha"ha?ar + 105 + .'?i'ha?a"xo?p '?pa?ak"to?o?p +

106 + '?i?i -- ,'kon'da'ix"to + ,'?ko"toi + 'ta"ma?a -- .'?in"te?e + ,'lu"gar + ,'?ka "?pa?a 'ko'na"kas 'te + .'i"ia?a "ua?ar 'in"te?e 'no"xi?i "pe 'nia + 114 + '?i?i -- ,'?i'kon'da '?ko"toi + ,'ia"ha?a + ,'ma?a"txi + ,'?u'iu"?pi 'tua?a'nu"mui + 'ta'ma'?e"pe 'nia'por"ke?e -- . 'por"ke?e "mei 'gra"pe 'nia +

121 + '?i?i -- '?i"txe 'ke?e -- 'ma"ha?ax 'por"ke?e -- ,'ma?a"txi 'u'iu"?pi '?a'nu"mui 'ta "mar + 'si"no 'ke?e -- .'?u'io"tot 'u"pia?ar + 127 + 'i'ko"txa?a -- ,'?u'io"tot 'u"pia?ar + ,"ma 'ko'txe?e"rer 'tua?a'?u'uin"txu + ,'in"ton 'ses + ,'lu"mui 'in'te?e"la 'do + '?e?e -- 'ta "ma '?e?e -- "ser 'ka'?e?e -- .'?e?e'?al"de 'ia 'u'?ka"?pa?a 'ko'na"kas 'te +

4. Stuckhorn

. e-haa ua-ta-r + 71 + . i ?kaa?p-a ?pa?k-ta e -hente +

72 + . txe-e-na-o?p kee tu?ka ir-a + 73 + i u&-ir-a-o?p ?txa-ar e -- noxii xuk-ur ua-ta-r + i -- ta-ma -- , dos diia + , entonses + . txek-ta + 80 + naat-a-n-ua kee -- , txan tar-i + , por kee aian + e-otot-o?p xee -- serka e -- e -- , t-iaa lum-vi e-xuk-ur + . txe kee -- u&-ah u& -- , u&-kuerpu e-txan ia-haa + , meigra u& -?txa-u-ta-r + . ko-txa vn-go-h-r otot + , i + , u&-katxo + m -- meigra +

96 + , i ta-ma-r + , ua-r u&-huur-u + e -- . e-rum a-vx-in + . i e-sian haa ta-ka-r + 101 + txe kee konda ?txu-ur a-vx-in ta-ma e-haa + , ua-r a-vx-in ta-ka e-sian haa + , txe kee ?pan a -kir-ik-na + . ko-txa a-kir-ik-na u&-hut e-?kin konda ua-r a-?kax-i e-ha-haa-r + 105 + . i haax-o?p ?pa?k-ta-o?p +

106 + i -- , konda-ix-to + , ?kot-vi + ta-ma -- . vn-tee + , lugar + , ?ka?paa konakaste + . i iaa ua-ar vn-tee noxii penia + 114 + i -- , i konda ?kot-vi + , ia-haa + , ma atxi + , u&-u?p-i tuaa num-vi + ta-ma e-penia por kee -- . por kee meigra penia +

121 + i -- i txe kee -- ma haax por kee -- , ma atxi u&-u?p-i a-num-vi ta-ma-r + sino kee -- . u&-otot u&-piaar + 127 + i ko-txa -- , u& -otot u&-piaar + , ma ko-txa ir-er tuaa u&-hin-tx-u + , intonses + , lum-vi vn-tee lado + e -- ta-ma e -- serka e -- . e-aldeia u&-?ka?paa konakaste +

4. Stuckhorn

136 + '?i"txe 'ke?e -- '?e?e -- '?e"hen 'tio?p'ia"ha?a + ,'?ka?a"pa 'lo"?koi '?ah"nio?p + ,'?i'xi"no?p "mas 'ti"txan + 141 + 'por'ke?e '?u'ui"ro?p 'ke?e -- ."uar '?e?ein"txa '?e"siaŋ 'gui"tsir 'ua"tar + 143 + ,'u"me 'ne"txan + '?i'ha?a"xo?p + 'lo"?koi '?ah"nio?p + ,'u'iak "tu?u 'io'to"to?p + .'i'xi"no?p 'ti"txan + 148 + ,'u'io'to"to?p 'kutx"pa + ,"pe 'ro'ha?a"xo?p 'ma?a"txi + ,'?i'kon'dix"to + ,'lu"mui + ."kai 'u"txu?u 'io'to"to?p 'o'tro"niahr +

153 + '?i?i -- '?i?i'?e"txan 'ia"ha?a + 'io?o"pa 'ta'ma?a -- 'in"te?e 'lu"gar + 'u'?ka "?pa?a -- '?e?e -- ,"san 'ta"bar 'ba + 160 + ,"pe 'ro'?e'lu"gar '?a'ro?p"na + .'?al'iŋ"kuen 'tro + 162 + "por 'ke?e"txe 'ke?e -- ,"ia '?u 'tah"uu?u "?po?p + '?e"txan 'ia"ha?a 'ta"ka?a -- ,"?o 'tron'te?e"txan 'ta"ri + ,'ta'ma'?e"par 'te '?i"pa 'la + '?e?e -- ,'lu"mui 'e"ha?a + ."ser 'ka'e'txi"nam 'txi'ki"mu 'la + 170 + ,"ia?a 'lu"mui 'e"ha?a + '?i"txe 'ke?e -- ,'?e"txa 'nia "ha?a + .'in'te?e"ra "di 'ia + .'ta"rio?p +

175 + '?i?i -- '?i'?ko"toi 'ta'me?e -- , '?e'lu"gar 'ia"ha?a + 'u'nu"?tu?u "?po?o?p 'ta 'ke?e -- ,'e"txan 'xe'ta"ri + '?e?e -- ,'xe?e'lu "mui + ,'tu?u'ti?i'txi"nam 'ho'ko"taŋ + ,"ia '?ko"toi + .'u'nu"?tu?u "?po?o?p + 185 + '?i 'kon'dix"to "txe 'ke?e -- '?u?u -- ,'?u'nu"?tu?u "?po?p 'ko"mun + ,'en"ton 'ses + ,"uar '?a?a "sio?p 'i'xi"no?p + 'por'ke?e -- ,'?e"txan 'xe?e 'ta"ri + '?e?e -- 'ta'me?e -- '?e"par 'te?e -- , '?i"pa 'la + ."txe 'ke?e'?i'xik"txan + 197 + '?i?i'ui?i -- ."txe 'ke?e'ui'nik"txan +

199 + ,'i'kon'dix"to + ,'u'tah'uu?u "?po?p + 'ta'ke?e -- '?e?e -- ,'?e"txan 'xe?e'ui"nik + '?i?i -- ,"kai + '?a"sio?p + .'u'me?e"kru?u "?po?o?p + '?i?i -- ,'?i'?ko'to"io?p + ,"mas '?eh"mar + .'en"ton 'ses"ua?ar 'in"te?e 'ni'xi?i

4. Stuckhorn

136 + i txe kee — e — e-hente-o?p ia-haa + , ?kaap-a lo?k-vi ahn-i-o?p + , vx-in-o?p mas ti-txan + 141 + por kee u&-ir-a-o?p kee -- . ua-r a-hin-tx-a e-sian uitsir ua-ta-r + 143 + , u&-men e-txan + i haax-o?p + lo?k-vi ahn-i-o?p + , u&-akt-a u&-otot-o?p + . vx-in-o?p ti-txan + 148 + , u&-otot-o?p kutx-pa + , pero haax-o?p ma atxi + , i konda-ix-to + , lum-vi + . kai u&-txe u&-otot-o?p otro vn-iahr +

153 + i -- i e-txan ia-haa + ioop-a ta-ma — vn-tee lugar + u&-?ka?paa -- e -- , santa barba + 160 + , pero e-lugar ar-o?p-na + . al inkuentro + 162 + por kee txe kee -- , ia u&-tahu-i u&-?pa-o?p + e-txan ia-haa ta-ka -- , otro vn-tee txan tar-i + , ta-ma e-parte ipala + e — , lum-vi e-haa + . serka e-txinam txikimula + 170 + , iaa lum-vi e-haa + i txe kee -- , e-txan ia-haa + . inteera diia + . tar-i-o?p +

175 + i -- i ?kot-vi ta-ma e -- , e-lugar ia-haa + u&-nu?t-i u&-?pa-o?p ta-ka e -- , e-txan xee tar-i + e -- , xee lum-vi + , ta-u&-tii txinam hokotan + , ia ?kot-vi + . u&-nu?t-i u&-?pa-o?p + 185 + i konda-ix-to txe kee — u& -- , u&-nu?t-i u&-?pa-o?p komun + , entonses + , ua -r a-as-i-o?p vx-in-o?p + por kee -- , e-txan xee tar-i + e -- ta-ma e -- e-parte -- , ipala + . txe kee ixik txan + 197 + i e-ui -- . txe kee uinik txan +

199 + , i konda-ix-to + , u&-tahu-i u&-?pa -o?p + ta-ka e -- e -- , e-txan xee uinik + i -- , kai + as-i-o?p + . u&-me?k-r-u u&-?pa-o?p + i -- , i ?kot-vi-o?p + , mas e-h-m-ar + . entonses ua-ar vn-tee nixii

4. Stuckhorn

"pe 'nia + 212 + ,'?i'ia"ha?a "txe 'ke?e'?ko "toi + '?kas"pa 'u"ka 'txo'?e'no'xi?i"txan 'xe?e — '?e?e -- .'?e'ui'nik"txan + 216 + "por 'ke?e -- 'ta"me?e -- 'ta"me?e -- ,"kai + '?a"si 'ta'ka'?e?e -- .'?e?ei'xik"txan + 222 + '?i'po "re 'so"txe 'ke?e -- .'?kas"pa 'u"ka 'txo +

224 + ,"?pan 'u'?kah"ti '?e"hen 'te'ko "ne?er + 'ke?e — '?e?ep -- ,"pe 'nia'ia"ha?a + ,'?a?a'ro?p"na + .'ta'?tsa'?pre"ka 'txo + 230 + ."por 'ke?e"txe 'ke?e"ia '?tsa"?par 'u"ka 'txo 'e'no"xi?i "txan 'xe?e'?kas"pa 'u"ka 'txo + 231 + ,"pe 'ro'u'?kah"ti 'e"hen 'te'ke'ma?a"txi "nik + ,'sut"pa 'u'ui"ra '?e'i"xik + ,'?i'ma?a"txi '?a"xi 'ta"kar + ,'?i'ma?a"txu?u 'iak"tu?u "?pa?a 'meh"?ka 'u"me 'ne?ei"xik + .'ma?a"txa?a "ni '?kas"pa 'u"ka 'txo +

236 + "pe 'ro?o -- "txe 'ke?e -- "por 'ke?e — ,'sut"pa '?u'ui"ra '?e'i"xik + '?i?i -- ,'?a'sa"ber 'tu"?ka '?o"hron 'tu?u"ial 'ma + '?u 'ui"ra '?e'i"xik + '?i'po"re 'so + '?kas"pa 'u "ka 'txo + 245 + '?i?i -- 'kon'dix"to + ,'?kas "pa 'u"ka 'txo + '?e?e -- ,'ma?a'txix"to + ,'?i "xin + ,"tia?a '?ka"na?a "na?a"xin + "por 'ke "txe 'ke?e -- ,'ha?a"xir + ,'xe'?ka"na?a "na?a "xin + '?e?e -- 'ta"ma '?e?e -- 'ta'me?e -- . '?ix'ner"?kin +

259 + "pe 'ro'ko'txa?a -- ,'?kas"pa 'u"ka 'txo + ,'ma?a'txix"to '?i"xin + ,"tia?a '?ka "na?a "na?a "xin + 'si"no 'ke?e -- .'?i"xin 'in "te?e "la 'do + 265 + ,'ma?a"txi '?ko"toi + . "tia?a "tua?a '?ko"toi 'a"ni + 267 + "pe 'ro "txe 'ke?e -- '?u?u -- ,'?u"txe 'per"der + 'ta 'me?e — ,'?u'iak"ta '?u"?pa + .'meh"?ka 'u'me 'ne?ei"xik +

273 + "pe 'ro -- "no?on + 'ma?a"txi 'ka'ui "ra "kai '?a?a"sio?p + 276 + ,"por 'ke?e'?e "mar + ,'?e"mar + ."txe 'ke?e'?in"so lo"txam

4. Stuckhorn

penia + 212 + , i ia-haa txe kee ?kot-vi + ?kas-pa u&-katxo e-noxii txan xee -- e -- . e-uinik txan + 216 + por kee -- ta-ma e -- ta-ma e -- , kai + as-i ta-ka e -- . e-ixik txan + 221 + i por eso txe kee -- . ?kas-pa u&-katxo +

224 + ,?pan u&-?kah-ti e-hente koneer + kee -- e-p -- penia ia-haa + , a-ar-o?p-na + . ta-?tsa?p-r-e-katxo + 230 + . por kee txe kee ia ?tsa?p-ar u&-katxo e-noxii txan xee ?kas-pa u&-katxo + 231 + , pero u&-?kah-ti e-hente kee ma atxi-nik + , sut-pa u&-ir-a e-ixik + , i ma atxi vx-i ta-ka-r + , i ma atxi u&-akt-a u&-?pa a-me-h-?k-a u&-men e-ixik + . ma atxi ani ?kas-pa u&-katxo +

236 + pero -- txe kee -- por kee -- , sut-pa u&-ir-a e-ixik + i -- , a saber tu?ka ohron ta-u&-alma + u&-ir-a e-ixik + i por eso + ?kas-pa u&-katxo + 245 + i -- konda-ix-to + , ?kas-pa u&-katxo + e -- , ma atxi-ix-to + , vx-in + , t-iaa ?kan-i ani a-vx-in + por kee txe kee -- , haax-ir + , xee ?kan-i ani a-vx-in + e -- ta-ma e -- ta-ma e -- . ix-n-er-?kin +

259 + pero ko-txa -- , ?kas-pa u&-katxo + , ma atxi-ix-to vx-in + , t-iaa ?kan-i ani a-vx-in + sino kee -- . vx-in vn-tee lado + 265 + , ma atxi ?kot-vi + . t-iaa tuaa ?kot-vi ani + 267 + pero txe kee -- u& -- , u&-txe perder + ta-ma e -- , u&-akt-a u&-?pa + . me-h-?k-a u&-men e-ixik +

273 + pero -- na-on + ma atxi ka&-ir-a kai a-as-i-o?p + 276 + , por kee e-mar + , e-mar + . txe kee vn-solo txan

4. Stuckhorn

'?pu"?tur 'ta"mar + 279 + ,'?i'po"re 'so + , '?e"txan 'xe'?a'lo"?koi 'ta'me?e'ui'tsi"ro?p + "ia?a '?a?a"xin + '?a'noh"?pio?o?p + "por 'ke?e "ia?a '?txah"mo?o?p + ,"ti?in '?a'?txah"ma 'de '?a'ri?p"?tsir + , "ti?in '?a'?txah"ma + .'de'ni '?ar"?tsir + 287 + '?i?i -- .'po"re 'so + ,"txe 'ke?e'?e"txan + ,"tie?e 'ne"ua 'ra?a "?txi?i + ,"uar '?a?a"xin '?u'sah"ka + '?u?u -- '?u'pi"xan 'tua?a -- '?a'nuh"?pi 'ta'ka?a -- . '?u'uix"ka?ar + 296 + ,'?i'po"re 'so'txe?e "no?p '?e"hen 'te + 'ke?e -- ,'?a"ian "ti?i 'ne '?a'ket"pa + ,'ta're"ra '?al"gun 'ui"tsir 'ta 'mu?u"ti?i 'e"ho?p + ,'ia?a"ian "ti?i 'ne'?a?a "xin + ."?ehs 'to'ta'me?e"mar +

302 + "pe 'ro?o -- .'lo'ke'?u'?kah"ti 'e "hen 'te + 'ke?e'?e"txan 'xe?e -- .'?u"txe "mei 'gra + '?e?e -- ,'per"hui 'sio + ,'ta'ke?e'ui 'tsi"ro?p 'u'sa'tio?p 'io?o"tot + 'ma?a"txi 'a '?ko"tuo?o?p 'tia?a'?ka"nia?a -- .'?ka"ni 'a'?ko "tuo?o?p + 311 + ,"pe 'ro"ti?i 'ne'ma?a"txi + ,'ha?ax"to '?ah'?ku"no?p 'lu"gar '?u"me 'ne"dios + .'?a?a'xi"no?p "?ehs 'to'tia?a'?ka"na?a '?ko "tuo?o?p + 314 + "pe 'ro"ti?i 'ne?e -- ,'?u "txo?p 'per"der "tu?ut 'e"dios + .'ma?a"txi '?a '?ko"tuo?p + "?pa 'nu'?kah"ti '?e"hen 'te'?ehs 'to?ok -- .'ko"ne?er 'i"ra +

319 + "pe 'ro?o -- "no?on 'ma?a"txi 'ka?a -- 'ka'na?a"ta 'hai -- ."?pam 'ber"da + 323 + ."pe 'ro'?e"hen 'te"?pa 'nu'?kah"tio?p + 324 + 'ke?e -- ,'?e"txan 'ia"ha?a + '?e?e -- 'ta'me?e -- "kai '?a?a"si + ,'ta'ke?e'?i'xik"txan + . '?kas"pa 'u"ka 'txo + 331 + "pe 'ro?o -- , "no?on 'ma?a"txi 'ka'ui"ra + ,'ha?ax"nik 'ka'ui "ra "ka 'ia?a"sio?p + .'ka'tse?e"nio?p '?a"ni +

4. Stuckhorn

?pu?t-ur ta-ma-r + 279 + , i por eso + , e-txan xee a-lo?k-vi ta-ma e-uitsir-o?p + iaa a-vx -in + a-noh?p-i-o?p + por kee iaa ?txa-h-m-a-o?p + , tiin a-?txa-h-m-a de ar-i?p-?ts-ir + , tiin a-?txa-h-ma + . de ni&-ar-?ts-ir + 287 + i -- . por eso + , txe kee e-txan + , tieen-e ua-r a-?txih-i + , ua-r a-vx-in u&-sahk-a + u& -- u&-pixam tuaa -- a-nuh?t-i ta-ka -- . u&-ixka-ar + 296 + , i por eso txe-e-na-o?p e-hente + xee -- , aian tiin-e a-ket-pa + , tar-er-ra algun uitsir ta-ma u&-tii e-haa-o?p + , iaa aian tiin-e a-vx-in + . ehsto ta-ma e-mar +

302 + pero -- . lo kee u&-?kah-ti e-hente + kee e-txan xee -- . u&-txe meigra + e -- , perhuisio + , ta-ka e-uitsir-o?p u&-sat-i-o?p e-otot + ma atxi a-?kot-vi-o?p t-iaa ?kan-i a -- . ?kan-i a-?kot-vi-o?p + 311 + , pero tiin-e ma atxi + , haax-to ah?k-u-na-o?p lugar u&-men e-dios + . ma atxi a-?kot-vi-o?p + ?pan u&-?kah-ti e-hente ehsto ok -- . koneer ir-a +

319 + pero -- na-on ma atxi ka& -- ka&-naat-a hai -- . ?pan berda + 323 + . pero e-hente ?pan u&-?kah-ti-o?p + 324 + kee -- , e-txan ia-haa + e -- ta-ma e -- kai a-as-i + , ta-ka e-ixik txan + . ?kas-pa u&-katxo + 331 + pero -- , na-on ma atxi ka&-ir-a + , haax-nik ka&-ir-a kai a-as-i-o?p + . ka-tseen-e-o?p ani +

4. Stuckhorn

1 There is another story they tell about the same Snake. 5 The river which runs by where we live, the Jocotan; ... it is said that when that river appeared -- that snake came with it. 15 Because so people said in the old days. 17 That when that water appeared, for a long time there had not been any.

21 But they say that the snake came. 23 And laid that river out here. And they say that that snake was a female. 30 Because at the river -- there are high, steep banks. 33 And that is why they say that a female snake was there, because she didn't know how to work. 37 Because there are just steep banks along that river.

40 And -- they say that when she came, that snake laid out the river here. They say that all night long they heard her playing, like the playing of a marimba. 52 They heard her playing and all the people were afraid. They said, "Well, what can this be? 56 I wonder if we aren't going to be destroyed now." Because all night long the place was lying in a hammock, swinging back and forth. 63 And all the people were afraid.

64 And then when day broke they came out and saw, on the high ground -- they saw that -- the river lay there. 71 And the people were scared to death.

72 They say that so it was. 73 They saw that the Great River lay there. And for two days then it happened that the news went out that the snake had come, because there were houses which were near where the river passed; they say that they saw that snake's body pass. It was as big around as a house. And its horn

was very large.

96 And with it she plowed the earth as she went, and all the water with it. 101 They say that when she went floating in the water, when she went through the great water, they say it was like a thunderbolt, as it thunders in the sky when rain falls. 105 And it crashed.

106 And then she came to a place named Conacaste where there stands a big rock. 114 And when she came there, she was not able to pass by the rock, because it was a big rock.

121 And they say that it wasn't because -- she could not pass by it, but rather -- it was her friend's house. 127 And since it was her friend's house, there was no way for her to knock it down. Then she passed to one side of it, and near the aldea named Conacaste.

136 It is said that those people all came out running, to go up higher. 141 Because they saw that many mountains were crumbling. 143 Because of the snake. And they came out running and left their houses and went high up. 148 Their houses were carried off but they were not. And when she had passed, they began to build their houses again.

153 And -- and that snake came to a place called Santa Barbara. 160 But the place is called El Encuentro. 162 Because they say that that snake and another snake which came by way of Ipala met one another. And the water passed near the town of Chiquimula. 170 There the water passed, and they say that -- those snakes had come for just one day.

175 And -- and she came to that place and

4. Stuckhorn

they joined themselves together -- the snake that came there and -- that passed by the edge of the town of Jocotan. She came there and they coupled. 185 And when they say that -- their -- they were joined together as one, then, they were playing, because -- the snake that came there by way of Ipala they say was a female. 197 Uh -- they say it was a _male_.

199 And when they met -- the snake that was a male -- they began to play, writhing together. And they came farther down. There stood a big rock. 212 And there, they say, they arrived. The horn of the big snake, which was the male, broke. 216 Because -- at -- at -- he began to play with the female snake. 222 And because of that it is said his horn broke.

224 So the people tell it today, that -- that rock is called Stuckhorn. 230 Because they say there the big snake whose horn broke stuck his horn. 231 But the people say that if he hadn't turned back to look at the female, and if he hadn't gone with her, and if he hadn't left off being embraced by the female, he wouldn't have broken his horn.

236 But they say that -- because -- he turned around to look at the female and -- I wonder what he said to himself when he saw the female ... And that's why his horn broke. 245 And then when his horn broke -- he could not go where he had wanted to go, because they say that he wanted to go -- to -- to the West.

259 But since his horn was broken he didn't go where he intended to go, but instead went to one side. 265 He didn't reach the place he had intended to reach. 267 But they say that -- he lost -- he let himself be embraced by the

female.

273 But we didn't see them start to play. 276 Because the sea, the sea they say is all full of snakes. 279 And that is why the snakes that come out of the mountains go there and mate because there they find each other. Some are taken for daughters-in-law. Some are taken for sons-in-law. 287 And -- that is why they say that the snakes, those which are growing, go looking for -- their fathers-in-law so as to -- take a wife. 296 And therefore, the people say that -- there are those that stay in some mountain at the source of the waters, and there are those that go as far as the sea.

302 But -- what the people say is that the snakes that -- do so much damage to the mountains and destroy the houses, can not go where they wanted -- they intended to go. 311 But those that don't, they are given permission by God; they go wherever they want to go. 314 But those that lose out before God do not arrive. So people tell it to this very day.

319 But -- we do not know if it is true. 323 But so people tell it. 324 That -- that snake -- at -- began with the female snake, and broke his horn. 331 But we didn't see it. If we had seen them begin to play, we would have laughed at them.

5. Man and Serpent

1 + 'a"iaŋ 'o'tron"te?e -- , '?o'hro"ner 'a'?kah"na + 'e?e -- , ta'ma're"ra + '?e?e -- . 'e"txan + 7 + ,'?a"iaŋ 'in'te?e"di 'ia + ,"txe 'ke'in"te?e + . 'ui"nik + ,"uar '?a'xa"na + .'ta 'mu?u"ti?i 'e"ha?a + 12 + ,'ie?e"ha?a "mei 'gra + 'por'ke?e -- . 'ta'ma?a'?kax"ha?a "?kin + 15 + ."mei 'gra'e"ha?a +

16 + ,'kon'da?a'?ko"toi + ,'ta'ma?a'u"ti?i 'e"ha?a + ,'u'ui"ra + ,'?ka"tar + ,'e"txan + 'ta "ma -- .'u"hor 'iŋ"gohr "pe 'nia + 23 + ."uar '?a'ua"ian '?e"txan + 24 + ,'?i'ha?a"xir + , 'ko"txa '?u'na?a"ti?ix + ,'ke?e'?e"txan + ,'?a "ian 'e'tu"min + . 'u'?ke"txa?a 'xa"na + 29 + ,'en"ton 'ses + ,'i"xin + '?e?e -- "txe?e -- . "txe + ,'?e"txa 'ni"ra + ,'?ka"nu?u 'iah"?ke?e 'nu'tu"min 'ko"ne?er + .'po"re 'su"?txa?ar "ua 'ra'ua"ian 'ta"ra +

37 + ,'?i"xin + ,'?ko"toi + ,'ta"ma 'u "ti?i 'e"ha?a + ,'?i"xin + 'ua?a"uan "to?o 're?e -- ,'?e"tun + 'u'ui"ra "ka?a -- . 'u'ui"ra 'ke?e '?a'ua"ien + 45 + ,'ta"ri + ,'u'?txa"mi + ,'u 'ma"txit + 'u'?txa"ki 'u"ne 'he?e -- ,'?e"txan 'ta"mar + ,'ie?e"txan + ,'kon'de'u"txe 'sen"tir + ,'?txah"ka 'u"neh + ,'lo"?koi + .'?ka"xi 'ta "ha?a +

55 + '?i?i -- , 'ma?a'ta"ka '?ix"na + , "kon 'da'txek"ta 'in"te?e + ,'no"xi '?i"?kar + .'ta"ma?a '?e"ha?a + 60 + ,'ie?e'ui"nik + ,'lo "ke '?u"txe + "ua?ar 'in"te?e -- ,'no"xi?i "te?e 'ta'ma'u"ti?i 'e"ha?a + ,'?i"xin + .'go"ru?u "?pa '?txu"uan 'ta"mar +

66 + '?ie?e -- ,'?e'no"xi?i "?kar + '?ka "xi 'ta'me?e -- ,'?e"ha?a + 'tu"no?or '?e?e -- '?e"sia?an "te?e 'ta'ma?a'?u?u -- , 'io"ri?i "ii 're"ha?a + ,"?ka?a"pa 'u'?ka"si + .'u'ia"ri 'ta "ha?a + 75 + "pe 'ru -- ,'?e'ui"nik 'ia"ha?a +

5. Man and Serpent

1 + aian otro vn-tee -- , ohron-er a-?kah-
na + e -- , ta-ma-r-er-ra + e -- . e-txan + 7
+ , aian vn-tee diia + , txe kee vn-tee + .
uinik + , ua-r a-xan-a + . ta-ma u&-tii e-haa +
12 + , i e-haa meigra + por kee -- . ta-ma ?kax
-haa-?kin + 15 + . meigra e-haa +

16 + , konda a-?kot-vi + , ta-ma u&-tii e-
haa + , u&-ir-a + , ?kat-ar + , e-txan + ta-ma
-- . u&-hor vn-go-h-r penia + 23 + . ua-r a-
uai-an e-txan + 24 + , i haax-ir + , ko-txa u&
-naat-a-ix + , kee e-txan + , aian e-tumin + .
u&-?ketx-e a-xan-a + 29 + , entonses + , vx-in
+ e -- txe -- . txe + , e-txan ir-a + , ?kan-i
u&-ah?k-u-en u-tumin koneer + . por eso ?txa-ar
ua-r a-uai-an tar-a +

37 + , vx-in + , ?kot-vi + , ta-ma u&-tii
e-haa + , vx-in + ua-au-an ta-hor e -- , e-tun +
u&-ir-a ka -- u&-ir-a kee a-uai-en + 45 + ,
tar-i + , u&-?txam-i + , u&-matxit + u&-?txak-i
u&-neh e -- , e-txan ta-ma-r + , i e-txan + ,
konde u&-txe sentir + , ?txah-ka u&-neh + , lo?k
-vi + . ?kax-i ta-haa +

55 + i -- , ma ta-ka ix-na + , konda txek-
ta vn-tee + , noxii i?k-ar + . ta-ma e-haa + 60
+ , i e-uinik + , lo kee u&-txe + ua-ar vn-tee
-- , noxii tee ta-ma u&-tii e-haa + , vx-in +
gor-i u&-?pa ?txu-uan ta-ma-r +

66 + i e -- , e-noxii i-?kar + ?kax-i ta-
ma e -- , e-haa + tunoor e -- e-sian tee ta-ma
u& -- , e-orii-ir e-haa + , ?kaap-a u&-?kas-i +
. u&-ar-i ta-haa + 75 + peru -- , e-uinik ia-
haa +

5. Man and Serpent

,'ko"txa '?u'si?ik"pa + '?e?e -- 'nuk"ta?a "te?e
'xe?e -- ,"ua?ar 'ta'mu?u"ti?i 'e"ha?a + ,'i"xin
+ .'?txu"uan 'ta"mar + 83 + .'lu"mui 'e'i"?kar
+ ."ma 'tu"?ka?a 'txe?e"na 'ta"kar +

85 + ,'i"kon 'da'u'koh"ko + '?i"xin -- ,
'?ix"na + ,'sis'?pah"na '?e'i"?kar + ,'en"ton
'ses + ,'?i"xin + ,'?u'ui"ra + "hai '?u'iu"?pi
'?u'lo?ok"se '?e?e -- .'?e'tu"min + 94 + ,'?ko
"toi + 'u'ka"txi?in 'te?e -- "la 'so'ta"ma '?e?e
-- ,'?u"ne 'he"txan 'ia"ha?a + ,'u'ke'reh"?pa
'lo"?koi + ,"kai + '?u?u -- ,'?u'io?o"?pi + .'?i
'ma?a"txa?a 'io?o?p"?tsa "tu?ut +

106 + ,'?en"ton 'ses + 'ta"ri + 'ta'ma?a
-- ,'ta'mo?o"tot + '?u'?txa"mi '?in"te?e '?u"ia
'txa + 111 + ."kai 'u'io"?pi 'ta"mar + 112 +
'?i"kon 'da -- ,'?u'io"?pi + 'pus"?ka 'ta"ri
'?e?e -- .'?e'tu"min 'lo'ke?e'?pu"?tur 'ta'mu?u
"neh '?e"txan + 116 + "pe 'ro + ,'?e'tu"min
'ia"ha?a + 'ma"ha?ax '?e?e -- ,"?paŋ 'ko'txe?e
'tu"min + '?e?e -- 'lo'ke?e -- ,'?a"ian + ."to?o
're"rum 'ta"ra + 124 + ,'?e'tu"min 'ia"ha?a +
."txe 'ke"?paŋ 'ko'txe'?e'?pa?ak"?pir '?uh
"?tsu?u?p +

126 + ,'?i'ha?a"xir + ."txe 'tu?u"ial 'ma
+ ,'ko"txa "tua?an 'sa"ti '?e'tu"mi 'ni"ra +
129 + '?in'na?a"ta "ne?eŋ 'ke?e -- ."?paŋ 'ko
'txe?e'ka'tu"min + 131 + ,'por'ke'?u'ui"ra
'?in"so 'lo + '?e?e -- ,'?pa?ak"?pir '?uh
"?tsu?u?p + .'?pu"?tur 'ta"mar +

135 + ,'?i'kon'dix"to + ,'u'?ke"txi?i "xin
'ta'mu?u'o"tot + ,'?ko"toi + '?u?u -- ,'?u'?pu
"?ti + .'ta"ma '?iŋ"gohr "?puhr + 141 + ,"txe
'ke?e'tu"min 'ia"ha?a + "mei 'gra + ,'?tsak"ta
'ux"gohr "?puhr + ,'?u'?pu"?ti 'ta"ka + .'?i
'ma?a"txi '?ka?a"pa + 146 + 'por'ke?e -- "txe
'ke?e -- .'txa?a"te?e '?e'ba"li 'ha + ,"?txu?ur

5. Man and Serpent

, ko-txa u&-siik-pa + e -- nuk-taa tee xee -- , ua-ar ta-ma u&-tii e-haa + , vx-in + . ?txu-uan ta-ma-r + 83 + , lum-vi e-i?kar + . ma tu?ka a-txe-e-na ta-ka-r +

85 + , i konda u&-kohk-o + vx-in -- , ix-na + , sis-?pa-h-n-a e-i?kar + , entonses + , vx -in + , u&-ir-a + hai u&-u?p-i u&-lo?k-se e -- . e-tumin + 94 + , ?kot-vi + u&-katx-i vn-tee -- laso ta-ma e -- , u&-neh e-txan ia-haa + , u&-ker-eh-?pa lo?k-vi + . ta-tak-in + 100 + i konda -- , u&-ker-eh-?pa lo?k-vi + , kai + u& -- , u&-io?p-i + . i ma atxi a-io?p-?tsa ta-u&-hut+

106 + , entonses + tar-i + ta-ma -- , ta-ma u&-otot + u&-?txam-i vn-tee u&-atxa + 111 + . kai u&-io?p-i ta-ma-r + 112 + i konda -- u&-io?p-i + pus-?ka tar-i e -- . e-tumin lo kee ?pu?t-ur ta-ma u&-neh e-txan + 116 + pero + , e-tumin ia-haa + ma haax e -- , ?pan ko-txa e-tumin + e -- lo kee -- , aian + . ta-hor e-rum tar-a + 124 + , e-tumin ia-haa + . txe kee ?pan ko-txe e-?pa?k-?pi-r uh?ts-u-u?p +

126 + , i haax-ir + . txe ta-u&-alma + , ko-txa tuaa vn&-sat-i e-tumin ir-a + 129 + vn& -naat-a na-en kee -- . ?pan ko-txe ka&-tumin + 131 + , por kee u&-ir-a vn-solo + e -- , ?pa?k-?pi-r uh?ts-u-u?p + . ?pu?t-ur ta-ma-r +

135 + , i konda-ix-to + , u&-?ketx-e vx-in ta-ma u&-otot + , ?kot-vi + u& -- , u&-?pu?t-i + . ta-ma vn-go-h-r ?pu-h-r + 141 + , txe kee e-tumin ia-haa + meigra + , ?tsak-ta ux-go-h-r ?pu-h-r + , u&-?pu?t-i ta-ka + . i ma atxi ?kaap -a + 146 + por kee -- txe kee -- . txaa-tee e-baliha + ?txu-ur

5. Man and Serpent

'ta'mu?u"pun 'tu'ta'mu?u"ne 'he"txan + .'por'ke "txe 'ke'?u"pun 'tu?u"neh '?a'xa"hro + ,'?i'ta 'ma'txa?a"xehr "ti?i + ."?txu?ur 'e'tu"min 'ta "mar +

153 + "txe 'ke?e -- ,'?pu?t"?ka '?ux"gohr "?puhr + ,'ta'ka'in"te?e 'ba"li 'ha + .'?i'ket "pa 'e'in"te?e + 157 + ,'?en"ton 'ses + ,'u'ma "ni 'o'trox"gohr 'u"?puhr + ."ka 'iu'?pu"?ti 'ta "mar + 160 + ,'kon'dix"to '?ka?a"pa 'u'?pu"?ti 'e'tu"min 'ia"ha?a + ,'ta'ma'?e"?puhr + ,'?i"xin '?u'?txa"mi + '?u?u -- ,'?u're'sen"sa 'rio + 'u?u -- ,'?u'?pu"?tu?ut 'e"?kahk 'ta"mar + ,'u '?tsu"?pa?a 'iuh"?tsu?u?p 'ta"mar + ,"kai 'u'?pu "?tsa + .'?e'?pu"hro?p 'ia"ha?a +

170 + ,'ta'ma"?o 'txo"di 'ia + 'ke?e'ua "ra?a -- ,'u'?pu"?tsu?ut + ,'?e'?pu"hro?p 'ia "ha?a + .'u'pa"si '?u'ui"ra + 175 + ,'?i'kon 'dix"to '?u'pa"si + ,'?in'so'lox"to 'tu"min + ,'?pu"?tur 'ta"mar + 'ko"txe?e -- ,'?e'tu"min + '?a"ian 'lo'ke?e -- .'?a'sah"ta +

182 + '?i?i -- ,'?en"ton 'ses + ."txe + 'ber"da 'ke?e -- ,'?e'tu"mi 'ni"ra + 'ia -- "ma "nik + "ka 'ii?i -- '?in"txe '?i?i -- ,'?e'?i"de 'ia'ta"kar + 'ma?a"txa?a "ni 'tua?a -- ,'?iŋ'gui "ra + .'?a'sut"pa 'tu"min + ,"pe 'ro'ko"ne?er + '?in'na?a"ta 'ke'ko"ne?er 'si -- .'?a'ia'nix"to '?e'tu"min + ,'?e'ui"nik 'ia"ha?a + "txe 'ke?e -- ,'ket"pa + '?e?e -- ,"ri 'ko + .'?po"ro '?u 'tu"min + 204 + ."pe 'ro'ta"ma '?u'tu"min '?e "txan +

205 + ,'?i'po"re 'so + ,'?e"hen 'te + '?u 'na?a"to?p 'ke?e -- '?e?e -- ,'e"txan + .'?a"ian 'u'tu"min + 211 + "por 'ke?e -- ."txe 'ke'?e "txan + "kon 'do?o -- ,'?a'lo"?koi 'ta'man"te?e 'ui"tsir + .'?a?a"xin + ,'?a'nuh"?pi + .'ta'ka?a -- ,'?u'uix"ka?ar + "tia?a -- '?ka"ni '?a?a --

5. Man and Serpent

ta-ma u&-puntu ta-ma u&-neh e-txan + por kee txe
kee u&-puntu u&-neh a-xahr-o + , i ta-ma txaa-xe
-h-r tii + . ?txu-ur e-tumin ta-ma-r +

153 + txe kee -- , ?pu?t-?ka ux-go-h-r u&-
?pu-h-r + . kai u&-?pu?t-i ta-ma-r + 160 + ,
konda-ix-to ?kaap-a u&-?pu?t-i e-tumin ia-haa +
, ta-ma e-?pu-h-r + , vx-in u&-?txam-i + u& -- ,
u&-resensario + u& -- , u&-?pu?t-i u&-hut e-
?kahk ta-ma-r + , u&-?tsu?p-a e-uh?ts-u-u?p ta-
ma-r + , kai u&-?pu?ts-a + . e-?pu-h-r-o?p ia-
haa +

170 + , ta-ma otxo diia + kee ua-r a -- ,
u&-?pu?ts-a u&-hut + , e-?pu-h-r-o?p ia-haa + .
u&-pas-i u&-ir-a + 175 + , i konda-ix-to u&-
pas-i + , vn-solo-x-to tumin + , ?pu?t-ur ta-ma-
r + ko-txa e -- , e-tumin + aian lo kee -- . a-
sa-h-t-a +

182 + i -- , entonses + . txe + berda kee
-- , e-tumin ir-a + ia -- ma nik + ka i -- vn&-
txe i -- , e-ideia ta-ka-r + ma atxi ani tuaa --
, vn&-ir-a + . a-sut-pa tumin + , pero koneer +
vn-naat-a kee koneer si -- . aian-ix-to e-tumin
+ , e-uinik ia-haa + txe kee -- , ket-pa + e --
, riko + . por-o u&-tumin + 204 + . pero ta-ma
u&-tumin e-txan +

205 + , i por eso + , e-hente + u&-naat-a-
o?p kee -- e -- , e-txan + . aian u&-tumin +
211 + por kee -- . txe kee e-txan + konda o --
, a-lo?k-vi ta-ma vn-tee uitsir + . a-vx-in + ,
a-nuh?p-i + . ta-ka -- , u&-ixka-ar + t-iaa --
?kan-i a --

5. Man and Serpent

.'?a'nuh"?pi + 222 + ,'?i"txe 'ke'tu"no?or + ,'u'tu"min + ,'?u'?ke"txe '?a'lo"?koi + .'?a?a "xin '?a'nuh"?pi 'ta"kar + 226 + ,'po"re 'so 'txe?e"no?p 'ke'?e"txan + '?e?e -- ."mei 'gra'?u 'tu"min +

229 + ."pe 'ro + ,"no?on + 'ko"txa 'ma?a "txi 'ka?a -- ,'ka'tah'ui + 'ma?a"txi 'ka'na?a "ta 'hai -- .'ber"da '?a"ia 'nu'tu"min + 235 + "pe 'ro'?e"hen 'te"?pa 'nu'?kah"tio?p 'ke?e"txan -- '?e?e -- ."mei 'gra'?u'tu"min +

5. Man and Serpent

. a-nuh?p-i + 222 + , i txe kee tunoor + , u&-tumin + , u&-?ketx-e a-lo?k-vi + . a-vx-in a-nuh?p-i ta-ka-r + 226 + , por eso txe-e-na-o?p kee e-txan + e -- . meigra u&-tumin +

229 + . pero + , na-on + kotxa ma atxi ka& -- , ka&-tahu-i + ma atxi ka&-naat-a hai -- . berda aian u&-tumin + 235 + pero e-hente ?pan u&-?kah-ti-o?p kee e-txan -- e -- . meigra u&-tumin +

5. Man and Serpent

1 There is another story -- that is told. About this Snake. 7 One day they say a man was walking along the river bank. 12 And there was a lot of water because it was the rainy season. 15 There was a lot of water.

16 When he came to the bank of the river he saw the snake, stretched across a big rock. 23 The snake was sleeping. 24 And he, since he knew that the snake had money that he was carrying ... 29 he went and said, "This snake is going to give me its money today. That is why he is lying, sleeping here."

37 He went to the edge of the water, and went to stand on top of the rock. He saw that it was sleeping. 45 He came and brought his machete, and chopped off the tail of the snake with it. And the snake, when it felt its tail chopped off, went and fell into the water.

55 And -- it wasn't long before a great wind came from the water. 60 And the man, what he did -- a big tree was standing there at the edge of the water; he went and wrapped himself around it and hung on to it.

66 And -- the great wind blew into the water all the many trees that were on the banks of the stream. It broke them all off and dropped them into the water. 75 But -- that man, since he had found the tallest tree, standing by the edge of the water, and had gone to hang on to it, -- the wind passed over him and did him no harm.

85 And when he had waited for a long time -- the wind calmed. Then he went to see whether he could get out the money. 94 He came and tied a rope to the tail of that snake, and he

hauled and it came out on dry land. 100 And when -- he hauled it out, he began to hit it, and it did not break for him.

106 Then he went to his house and got one of his hatchets. 111 He began to hit with it. 112 And when he hit, there poured out the money that the tail of the snake was full of. 116 But that money was not like the money that is on earth here. 124 That money, they say, was like molded incense.

126 And he said to himself, "How am I going to spend this money? I didn't know it wasn't like our money." 131 Because he saw it was only molded incense that it was full of.

135 And then when he carried it to his house, he went and filled a jug with it. 141 They say that there was so much money it filled three jugs, and that was still not the end of it. 146 Because they say that there were two bags hanging from the end of the snake's tail. Because they say the end of its tail was split, and from each part hung the money.

153 They say that three jugs were filled by one bag, and one remained. 157 Then he bought another three jugs and filled them with it. 160 Then when he had finished filling the jugs with the money, he went and got out his censer, and filled it with coals. He put the incense in it and began censing those jugs.

170 For eight days he went on censing those jugs. Then he opened them to look. 175 And when he opened them, only money like the money that is spent filled them.

182 And -- then he said, "It is true that

5. Man and Serpent

— this money -- if I hadn't had that idea about it, I wouldn't have looked to see if it had turned to money. But now, I know that today, yes -- it is now money." That man, they say he became rich; his money increased. 204 But it was money from the snake.

205 And therefore people think that the snake has money. 211 Because -- they say that the snake, when it comes out of the mountain, goes to mate with its wife where it wants to mate. 222 And they say that it carries all its money along, when it goes out to mate. 226 That is why they say that the snake had a lot of money.

229 But we, since we haven't found it, we don't know if it is true that it has money. 235 But the people tell it so, that the snake has much money.

GROUP I

NOTES

1. Sesimite

1.1 As an auxiliary, ?kan 'want' takes no personal affix. Here, person is marked for the entire construction by the prefix on txe. The same root ?kan also has more ordinary uses: 'u '?ka"ni 'tua?a'in"xin 'He wants me to go', 'I must go'.

1.1* From ?kan-i vn&-txe by V, C.

1.1-2 A variant of this formula begins all the tales recorded by Sr. González. As the fifth of a series (see the list of sources in the appendix) this is 'another' story.

1.2 The root used here, ohron, designates 'speaking' as distinct from 'saying' something to someone (aar-e), 'calling' (pehk), or 'crying out' (ar-o?p) to someone, and so on. No more specific term for tale or legend was found, though some informants called such tales as this Cuentos del Camino Real.

1.2* From otro vn-tee by V, C.

1.8 El Morral is an aldea just across the river from Chiquimula, West of Pelillo Negro. Houses inhabited by the Chorti are well dispersed, but tend to cluster in family groups. The limits of a given aldea are of no functional importance, and are frequently only vaguely known.

1.10* From ta-ma e-penia by A.

1.13* From i e-kohn by B.

1.14 There are two alternants of this root, ar and aar. One of them, probably the shorter, is apparently a back formation: a-aar-o?p-na automatically reduces to 'a?a'ro?p"na by the 3 rule, and there are clear cases of analogical perfective forms with short vowels corresponding to long-vowel imperfectives: u&-ir-a 'u'ui"ra 'he sees it', a-ir-on 'e?e"ron 'it looks, appears' (by R), 'e"ron 'it looked'. Here, an analogical perfective is the regular form: 'a'ro?p"na 'called, addressed'. The suffix o?p has nothing to do with the plural suffix; it is found only in the na constructions of this root. The na suffix is most comfortably interpreted as a passive marker. The introduction and Fought 1967 provide a syntactic analysis of its function.

1.15 There is a rather large stream by this lake 15 km. NE of Pelillo, but the text probably refers to the stream named Quebrada Arriba on government maps, which runs parallel to and N of the Xukinlih.

1.19 The Xukinlih, officially Chuquinlí, begins in an apparently precipitous ravine about 7 km. SW of Pelillo, and just E of El Morral.

1.24 Most other informants say 'mei"ra or "mei 'ra. This apparently native form is nevertheless anomalous in having penult stress.

1.26 One of several irregularities in the distribution of txe 'say, do' is this e suffix, found in na constructions only.

1.27 The intensive suffix -ir contributes to the difference in meaning between uinik 'man' alone and uiŋk-ir 'master'; the syncopation is regular.

1.35 The alternation of h and vowel length in ?pah?k (cf. 1.116) and a few other roots is almost automatic: most cases show vowel length before a consonant cluster or (especially) in a closed syllable, and h is regular in open syllables (cf. 'a'pah"no 'he digs' and 'a'pa?aŋ"gua 'it is dug').

1.35* From -se-on by R, B.

1.36* From ta-ma e-lugar by C or A, C.

1.44 Compare 'u"su 'iu"iok 'his heel': sui designates the angle at the base of an object, whether a leg or a cliff.

1.45 A ?txen may be a cave, or just an overhang or concavity. There are several roots designating objects in their appropriate positions of rest, among them ua 'stand (upright)' and tur 'sit (horizontally)'. Here, the cave 'sits', and in 1.49 the two women 'stand'. People may also 'sit' (= 'dwell'). Note that the Sesimite in 1.40 'lies' (?txa).

1.49 The tak suffix is a collective used more frequently in connection with people than with animals or objects. Compare 'max"tak 'children, kids' (max 'monkey').

1.53 The meaning of hut is elusive, but roughly 'the visible surface of an object', usually flat or convex. A semantic extension from its designation of 'eye', 'face', is not too implausible. Because of the morphophonemics of u&-hut, with the frequent loss of h, a competing form "u?ut also occurs in environments where a u prefix is excluded.

1.54 It is clear from the context that an imperfective sense is to be given to this construction, but there is no phonological difference between this group and the corresponding perfective: rule C eliminates the prefix.

1.57 Only the initial negative ma is clear in this form; its other constituents are apparently a root ir and either a or er suffixes. Since ir-a is a negative imperative element, it is not clear how to interpret the semantics of 'mee"ra.

1.63 Spanish vaca, Chorti 'ua"kax. The phonological adaptation suggests that this is an old loan.

1.63-7 The use of the h 'potential' infix here is typical. The situation is hypothetical (hai 'if') and the imperfective forms of otx 'enter' and au 'stand on' state a timeless circumstance in which a cow would be swallowed up. The root ?pu?k 'swallow' is used for foods not requiring chewing -- liquids or pastes, soups, and so on. The use of it here, reversing the ordinary relationship between the mud-like and animate participants, is a nice touch, and since

1. Sesimite

other choices are possible (mak-?tsa 'submerge') it must be considered deliberate.

1.69 The affirmative particle ?pan, like Latin sic, is closer to 'thus' or 'so' than to our 'yes'.

1.71* From a-otx-vi by A, V.

1.73* From a-lo?k-vi-o?p by V, C, R; V, A (lo?k-oo-o?p), 3, R would also work.

1.74 In forms like "kaa "txuo?p 'horns' (cf. "maa "lo?p 'evil ones') the Spanish and Chorti stress patterns cooccur. Note that in these, successive heavy-stressed syllables, geminate nuclei occur without laryngealization. This is virtually the only environment where Gonzalez does not laryngealize geminate vowels.

1.78 The adaptation of Spanish f to Chorti hu is a regular pattern, whether before a labialized vowel or not.

1.78* From txe-o?p by C or A, C.

1.79* From mak-uu e-anam by C, C (losing the uu in two steps), R, B.

1.84* From a-?pu-h-?k-a-o?p by C or A, C; from e-anam by R, B.

1.85* From u&-ir-a-o?p by &, C or A, C.

1.96 In the majority of its extended usage tii 'lip' refers to the edge of something, but it may also be read here as the mouth (rather than the sides) of the cave.

1.102 The ?ke?txuh, translated Sesimite by the informants, is a prominent part of the oral tradition. It is probably to be compared to the tzitzimime, a stellar diety of the Aztecs.

1.106 The form is probably to be further analyzed as ar-v?k, with the root ar 'man's son' followed by a suffix rather obscurely related to ?ka 'middle'. Compare, for instance, a-uai-an 'he sleeps', 'a-uai-?ka 'he dreams', and uai-v?k 'dream'. Note, however, that ar is a substantive root, not active like uai 'lay flat'. It is likely that ?p is a translative alternant; though this and a form i?p are instrumental forms, the semantic relationship to the translative, with its component of handling is not too devious.

1.107 The form tuaa serves as an independent possessive or, as here, in a roughly prepositional relation, when a substantive phrase is nested in a larger construction by it. The independent use (as a third person form) is shown, for instance, in "ha?ax 'e"?tsi?i "tua?a 'that's his dog'; compare 'ha?ax'e"?tsi?i 'ta'ni"?pa 'that's my dog', 'the dog of myself'.

1.113 There is a well-developed system of extended uses of body-part terms for spatial relationships of parts of objects of many kinds. Here, for instance, the 'neck' term nuu?k is used. Compare 'u"nu?u?k 'ni"?ka?p 'my wrist', where ?ka?p designates the arm and hand, and 'u "?ka?p 'e"te?e 'the tree-branch'.

1.122* From ma atxi u&- by A.

1.138 Typically, direct quotation is introduced by txe and a falling intonation, as here.

1.145 The ik suffix is cognate with plurals in certain other Mayan languages. It appears, as here, in a few Chorti attributes and as the plural of the imperative.

1.150* From u&-ho?ts-i by H, &.

1.160* From kee u&- by C, R.

1.165 The i?p suffix here is the 'instrumental' mentioned in 1.106 above. A '?txa"ri?p is a 'lying-place'.

1.168* There are a few instances, like 1.169, of gu- for syllable-initial u- with no &. This example should be grouped with them; it is

1. Sesimite

not a regular outcome of &. The same alternation is found below, in 1.178.

1.169* The assimilation of n to g is unrelated to & here, as is the occurrence of gu for u.

1.171* From konda a-vx-in by V, 3 or C.

1.172 The causative suffix occurs with the vh 'factitive' when the root is the i/ class, as mor 'gather' is.

1.172* From se-o?p by R.

1.175* From xan-a-o?p by C.

1.180* Only the weight rule applies to txe e-siits.

1.182* The loss of the first-person prefix here is unusual. Rules V, C and optional (but rare) reduction of geminates are required.

1.211 More closely, 'Going away was not to be his.'

1.215* From txutxuu-et-to by C, B or A, B and reduction of the geminate consonants.

1.216* From tuaa a-?kaap-a by C, C, A.

1.220* For ta-hor by H, A.

1.221* From vn-vx-i-to vn&-ak-ta-et i-vx-in by (from left) V, V, a regular permutation of the first person suffix before vowels, C, V, A, C, &, and V.

1.223* From ir-a i-sut-pa by A, from ua-ta -et by A (cf. 1.228).

1.227* From -a a&-hut by C, H, &, B.

1.230* From eso-ix-to by R.

1.231 The meaning of ?kah is clearest in ?kah-ar "?ka?ar 'remembering'. Cf. 'u'?kah"ti 'he tells'.

1.245* From ta u&-hut by &, H, C, or by &, H, A, 3. Note that the outcome of the form in 1.227 is not possible because of the position of & here.

1. Sesimite

1.247* From pero e-nuk by C.

1.254 The 'attributive' prefix and the 'instrumental'/'translative' suffix.

1.265 The toes are the 'head' of the leg; a parallel form is used for 'finger'.

1.265* Like other roots with initial h, hor 'head' is difficult to interpret grammatically because of its complex morphophonemics. Either another pair of competing forms, in this case hor and oor, must be postulated, or what seem to be the indicated affixes must be supplied in each environment. Here the likeliest, u&, is chosen, with the loss options of rules H and & being chosen, and A applying. But a basic e-hor would also be grammatically acceptable, and morphophonemically easier: H, A.

1.267 The segmentation given for 'u'?pa?a "xi is tentative; the form is not well understood. A close translation would be 'its self goes forward'.

1.269 The root ekm 'descend' is irregular: the segmentation given here is intended to fit it as closely as possible to the regular pattern, but the suffix is not vi.

1.270* From ta-ma u&-hut by C, &, H, or by A, &, H, and 3.

1.305 Compounds (as distinct from phrases) are recognized by the single heavy stress, as on '?ka'xi?p"ha?a.

1.315-322 Tales are often ended with some variant of this formula, but it is less frequent than the opening formula.

2. Serpent

2.6 The usual meaning of txan is 'snake'. These mythical serpents are also called txih txan (Yucatec chic chan); the first root designates large animals, usually horses. The cognates of txih in some Mayan languages designate deer, but Chorti 'deer' is masaa, a Nahua loan.

2.11* The alternants lum and num 'pass' are free variants.

2.14* The pause-filler 'e?e appears here without a perceptible pause, as in 2.18. In neither case is there a syntactic relation between e and the following element. See also 2.72.

2.15 The hesitation here is due to the e following ta-ma-r. The r suffix is found in proforms rather than before substantives, as in the typical use of ta-ka-r 'with it' in 2.92.

2.18* From ?txih-i by H.

2.20* There is a free variant ?kopot.

2.22 The root ?kaap emphasizes the completeness of an act. In many contexts, a translation as 'finished' or 'finished off' is most appropriate.

2.23 The choice of ?kutx here is strikingly appropriate: it means 'to carry on one's back'.

2.32* From ?kutx-i e-otot by C, R, B.

2.34* From e-otot by R, B.

2.50* From serka e-oriia by C, R.

2.54* From e-otot by R.

2.55-61 This point is elaborated below, in 2.75-112 and 2.154-186, and in texts 3-5.

2.62 Spanish infinitives, like conocer here, are freely adapted by means of this construction with txe.

2.72* The laryngealization and lengthening of the a- here is very rare in open syllables not followed by hesitation. This case parallels

2.14, and probably has to do with the very deliberate tempo of the speech in this text. Other examples are 2.81, 2.82, where the drawling effect of the hesitations may be responsible.

2.73* From mak-uu-ir by C, B.

2.74 None of the informants spoke of feathers, and they seemed surprised when I raised the question.

2.91* The alternant ixka for ixik is morphologically conditioned, but syncope is quite common in such cases. Compare 'ui"nik, 'uiŋ"kir.

2.75* Only the W rule applies.

2.92* From tuaa a- by C.

2.95 Note the parallelism of the alternants ?tsa, v?ts and ?ka, v?k.

2.96* From i e-txan by B.

2.104* From lo?k-vi-o?p by V, C, R, and from ta e-uitsir by A.

2.109* From tiaa a-lo?k-vi-o?p by 3, V, C, R.

2.110* From u&-txe-o?p by &, C.

2.120* Again, the suffixes undergo V, C, R. This is the commonest pattern for the vi suffix, repeated in 2.122 and elsewhere.

2.145* From e-otot by Ra, Rb.

2.159* From tu?ka e-otot by C, R, B.

2.186* From aldea-o?p by C, Ra, Rb.

2.193 Literally, 'until eight days had accumulated'.

2.198-200 A closer translation would be 'by nobody coming was he seen where he was lying because he was feared'.

2.207 Note the use of ?pu?t 'fill', here with a 'cursive' and in 2.213 with ?ka. It is the interior of the bags that is filled with money, and the available space along the banks

2. Serpent

that fills with people.

2.222 The informant compared the effect to being barely missed by a large fast bus. The form is built on <u>i?kar</u> 'wind' and <u>hut</u> 'visible surface'.

2.239* From <u>-to</u> <u>u&-i?kar</u> by A or R.

2.260–267 It is clear from the description in 'Stuckhorn' (Text 4) that the horns are, as one would expect, on the serpent's head, so that there is a deposit of money at both ends.

3. Landslide

3.3 'Town', *txinam*, is a Nahuatl loan.
3.4 Nueva Ocotepeque, Honduras, is about 24 km. SE of Esquipulas.
3.16 The root is *ir* 'see' with a *na* suffix and a substantive suffix. *Ir-na* alone means 'it was seen'.

3.28 A closer translation is 'not long gone'.
3.28* From *ma-to a-ix-na* by Bc, C.
3.36 The form *ilama* 'old woman', also compounded with *tuu* 'mother' as *'tui?i"la "ma* 'wife' is apparently a Lenca loan.
3.40 The form *txe aii*, *"txa?a 'ii* is much used by other informants where Gonzalez uses *txe*, in reporting speech.
3.41 The form is a plural imperative, with *ik* a morphologically conditioned alternant of the plural suffix.
3.43 The root is *kor* 'catch' with *pa* 're-flexive'. Compare *kor-p-es-na-i?p* *'kor'pes "ni?i?p*, a protective (rain) 'cape' or 'shel-ter'.

3.55 The *"ra* element is a variant of *ir-a*, the near demonstrative, whose root is doubtless *ir* 'see'.
3.64 Another example of the use of a Span-ish infinitive, *avisar*, with *txe* 'do'.
3.69 Spanish *loco* has a 'cursive' *r* and *an* thematic. The *h* is a 'factitive'. Compare the similar formation in 3.74 with *tarde* 'evening'.

3.81 Literally, the rain 'did not pass'.
3.87 The root is *sak* 'white', with 'facti-tive' and 'reflexive' suffixes. There is a var-iant *sok* in this construction only.
3.97 The root is *ki?p* (as in 3.105); in closed syllables, there is alternation between basic laryngealized stops and a lengthened lar-

3. Landslide

yngealized syllabic followed by a plain stop.

3.120 A plan is a raised open area.

3.153-179 The text in this passage illustrates the use of the plural suffix in Chorti. It has an elastic domain and is sparingly used. The hente 'townspeople' in this passage have singular active forms, for example.

3.158* From ta-ma u&- by A, as in 3.161.

3.179* From a-ua-ta-r by A. See 3.229.

3.180-187 Here, the events of the preceding section are summarized, but with plural concord for hente.

3.188-200 Here, uiŋk-ir plainly designates all those homeowners who went back for a second load and were buried. There is no plural marker in this passage, however.

3.188* From i u&- by B.

3.207-214 The townspeople have a plural active form here, but in 3.215-229 the same events are recounted with singular concord. Note that 3.230 is again a plural form.

3.235* From ket-pa-ix by A.

3.304-5 Here, only the active form has a plural suffix. The substantive might have had one instead, or both might have been marked for plurality.

3.309* From e-anam by R, B.

3.328* From vn-tee-ix by W.

3.333* From tur-u ani by A.

3.334* An anomalous form.

3.350-359 Again the active forms are plural but the substantives are not.

4. Stuckhorn

4.2 The root is ?kah, 'have in mind', or the like. Compare "?ka?ar 'remembering'.

4.18-20 The perfective aspect relates only to the appearance of the river. When that event had taken place, there had not been one for a long time.

4.32 More closely, 'there was a deep hollow from it'.

4.32* From u&-ham by & and H.

4.64 Literally, 'we went to see'.

4.71 'And the people were utterly terrified.'

4.80 Or, 'It became known that -- ' There are few examples of this ua suffix, but see 21.58 and 21.67.

4.93 It is not clear here, because there is no plural suffix, whether the serpent has one horn or more, but I assume it has two, like the others. Wisdom (1940:393) was told they have four.

4.112 Conacaste is a village on the northern slope of the valley, about 8 km. NW of Jocotán. The text probably refers to a ridge opposite it on the southern side whose slopes rise at almost a 45° angle for some 500 meters above the river, which bends around it, turning from NW to N and then W.

4.143 Most of Conacaste lies about 1 km. NE of the river, and perhaps 400 meters above it, but there is a smaller group of dwellings only a few hundred meters from the water.

4.153 The river turns S for about 1 km., then makes a sharp bend at the foot of a steep slope, and turns W for some 2 kms. to join the

Río Grande which flows NNE past Chiquimula. The sharp bend is the Rincón de Santa Bárbara.

4.207* From -r-u u&-?pa-o?p by W, and in the second syllable, by &, W, A. The alternation of me?k before vowels and meek before consonants is paralleled by many other roots with final laryngealized consonants.

4.229 I have not seen the place, but I suspect Stuckhorn is a very narrow ravine on the southern slope, about 1 km. NW of the confluence of the two rivers.

4.278 Wisdom's discussion of Chicchans (1940:292-7) suggests that the 'serpents' of the sky and the underworld belong in the same category, but it seems from texts 19 and 20 below that they are not associated with these water-serpents.

4.278* Consonantal assimilation is regressive, like that of vowels.

4.282* The o in nohp is real; it appears to be a lapse. Compare 4.293.

5. Man and Serpent

5.14 Literally, 'falling rain days'.

5.65 The root is gor 'wrap', used in the go-h-r 'container' classifier.

5.73 The root ?kas 'break off', 'snap', is one of several distinct forms for breaking objects of various kinds. Compare io?p 'break by a blow', and hit 'burst'.

5.125 Copal resin incense is sold in several forms. What is meant here is the discs, about 1 1/2" by 3/8", sold in stacks about 10" or 12" long, wrapped in corn husks. Each disc is molded around a flammable pith center. It is explained in 24.42-44 that discs of incense are payment, that is, money, for the gods.

5.151 The basic meaning of tii appears to be 'lip'; here the classifier derived from xer 'divide, cut', contributes the sense that the tail is split.

5.154 A ?puhr is illustrated in Wisdom (1940:fig. 7 o); it holds about three gallons. These jugs are used for carrying water.

5.164 Chorti censers are small, shallow pottery vessels with three arms rising from the lip and joined at the top, where a cord is tied, as shown in Wisdom (1940:fig. 7 j-m). Coals rest in the bottom and discs of incense are placed on them.

5.204 'But with the snake's money.'

II: Fables

6. Toad and Hawk

1 + '?a"ian 'in"te?e + ,'oh'ro"ner + ,'a '?kah"na + 'e?e — ,'?e"sa 'po + 'ta'ke?e — .'?e"muan + 8 + "txe 'ke?e — ,'tan'te?e"di 'ia + ,'?e"muan + .'u'?pih"nu + 12 + ,'i"xin + 'tia?a'tu"ru?u + ,'?e'ka'ta"ta?a + 'e?e — .'tu?ut"?kin + 17 + ,'u'tah"uu?u "?pa + 'ta"ka '?e?e — . 'e"sa 'po +

20 + ,'u'ia?a"re .'e"sa 'po + ,'ke?e"ne?en + '?ka"ni 'in"xin + ,'in'xa"na + ,'ti"txan + 'tia?a'tu"ru?u — 'e?e — .'?e"dios + 29 + ,'?e"muan + 'ie?e"sa 'po"txe 'ke?e + 'kom'pa "grio?p 'ta'ke?e — 'e?e — .'?e"sa 'po + 34 + ,'ha?ax"to 'e"sa 'po + "txe + 36 + .'u'ia?a"re 'u'kom"pa 'gre + 37 + .'?ka"ni 'in"xin 'ta'ka "ret +

38 + ,'n"ton 'ses + ,'?e"muan + '?e?e — ."txe + 42 + "ne?et 'mix'u'iu"?pik + .'txi"ket + 44 + "pe 'ro?o — ,'?e"sa 'po + "kai + 'u "txe + ,'bi'hi"iar + 'u"bol 'sa + .'u'kom"pa 'gre + ,'o"txoi + ."?txa?an 'ta"mar + 53 + "?i "kon 'da?a — ,'?u'?pih"nu + ,'?e"muan '?ii"xin + ,'?e"sa 'po + ,"iix "?txa?ar + 'ta"ma '?e?e — ."bol 'sa +

60 + ,"?i "kon 'dax"to + '?ko"toi — ,'?ko "toi '?e"muan + ,'tia?a'tu"ru '?e'di"os + ,'ie?e "sa 'po'ua?ak"txe 'ta"ka + .'lo"?koi 'ta"ma '?e "bol 'sa + 66 + '?i?i '?u'peh"ka 'u'kom"pa 'gre'?e?e — .'e"muan + .'i'ia?a"re + .'tu"?ko 'ra'io?o"pet 'ta"ra 'kom"pa 'gre +

70 + ,'?en"ton 'ses + "txe?e — .'?e"sa 'po + 73 + ,"ne?en + ."mas '?pah"xan 'io?o "pe?en 'ke"ne?et +

75 + 'e?e — ,'ha?ax"to + ,'e"muan 'txe + 78 + ,"pe 'ro'kom"pa 'gre + .'ko"txa 'ta"rie?et +

6. Toad and Hawk

80 + ."pe 'ro?o'ta"rie?en + ,"mas '?pah "xan + .'io?o"pe?eŋ 'ke"ne?et +

83 + ,'ha?ax"to + "kon 'da?a -- ,'sut"pa 'ta"ri + '?e?e -- ,"muan + 87 + ,'i'ha?a"xir 'ket"pa + 'ma?a'txix"tu?u 'iu"?pi "tua?a -- .'ua 'tar"ia?a + 90 + ,'?e"muan + ,'ko"txa '?a"ian 'u"ui?itx + 'ua?ak"txe 'ta"ka?a -- .'?txu"uan 'ta"ri + 94 + .'io?o"pa '?ka"xi 'ta"rum +

95 + ,'i'ha?a"xir + "ko 'txa'ma?a'txix "tu?u 'na?a"ta 'ko"txa 'tua?a -- ,'e?ek"mai + ,'?a'sut"pa '?u'ui"ra '?u?ut'e"rum + ,"txe 'tu?u "ial 'ma"pe 'ru'ki"sas + .'e"rer 'in"xin 'u"?pan +

101 + ,'?en"ton 'ses + ,'?u'iak"ta 'u"?pa 'ta"ri + .'?txu"uan 'ta"ri + ."tu?ut 'e"?kin + ,'i"kon 'da'io?o"pa '?ka"xi + ,'ta'mu?ut'e"rum + ,'in'iah"rer + .'he?ek"pa 'u"na?a?k + "tia?a 'io?o -- ."?u'io"?pu?u "?pa + .'io?o"pa '?ka"xi + 111 + ,'?in'iah"rer + '?e?e -- .'he?ek"txa 'u"na?ak +

114 + '?i?i -- ,"?i 'po"re 'so + ,'?e"sa 'po + ,'ka'ui"ra 'ko"ne?er + .'noh"ta?a 'u "na?a?k + 119 + ."?i?i -- .'?i"?an 'txu"?o?o 'ru'keh"re?p + 121 + ."por 'ke"txe 'ke"ha?ax 'e"tia?a 'u'io"?pu?u "?pa 'tia?a'io?o"pa '?ka"xi + 122 + "por 'ke?e -- 'ma?a'txix"to 'ta'res"na '?u"me 'nu?u -- .'?u'kom"pa 'gre"ia?a + 125 + ."?ak 'ta"na +

126 + 'i'po"re 'su"txe?e -- ,'?e"hen 'te 'ko"ne?er + "?e?e -- ,'?e"sa 'po + ,"?txi?i 'u "na?ak + ."por 'ke"ha?ax 'e"tia?a 'u'io"?pu?u "pa + 131 + ,"pe 'ro"ne?en + 'ma?ha?ax 'ia 'ua?a"re 'nin'gui"ra 'kon'da'io?o"pa -- .'?ka"xi 'ta'mu?ut'e"rum + ,'ke'si"ia 'ua?a"ren 'iŋ'gui "ra + .'in'la?a"?ta?a "ni 'ta"ma 'ni'?pi"tor + ."ta?a 'ma?a"txu?u 'io"?pu?u "?pa +

6. Toad and Hawk

1 There is a story that is told about the toad and the hawk. 8 They say that one day the hawk decided 12 to go where our Father is, in the sky. 17 He encountered the toad.

20 He said to the toad, "I'm going to go walking up above, to where God is." 29 The hawk and the toad, they say, were good friends with ... uh ... the toad. 34 Then the toad said, 36 he said to his friend, 37 "I want to go with you."

38 Then the hawk said, "You, 42 you aren't able to go!" 44 But the toad began to watch his friend's bag. He went in and lay down inside it. 53 And when the hawk decided to go, the toad was already lying in the bag.

60 And when he arrived ... the hawk arrived ... where God is, the toad immediately came out of the bag, 66 and spoke to his friend. The hawk said, "When did you come here, friend?"

70 Then the toad said, 73 "I came before you."

75 And then the hawk said, 78 "But friend, how did you get here?"

80 "But I was here, I came before you."

83 Then, when the hawk came back here, 87 he (the toad) remained; it was no longer possible for him to return. 90 The hawk, since he had his wings, immediately floated down here. 94 He came falling to earth.

95 And he, (the toad), since he didn't know how to come down, was looking back at the ground. He said to himself, "But maybe I can go

the same way."

101 Then he let himself go, floating in the sky, and when he came falling down to earth, all at once his belly spread out, where his body struck. He fell. 111 All at once his belly spread out.

114 And that is why the toad, we see today has a big belly. 119 And ... the top of his shoulders is wide. 121 Because, they say, that is where he struck himself, where he fell, 122 because he was not brought by his friend; he was left 125 behind.

126 And therefore the people say today that the ... the toad's belly grew large, because that is where he struck himself. 131 But I was not standing there looking when he came falling onto the earth, for if I had been looking, I would have caught him in my hat, so that he would not have struck himself.

7. Toad

1 + ,'?a"ian '?o'tron"te?e + ,'?e'?oh'ro "ner + .'ta'mar'ta"ka '?e"sa 'po + 5 + ,'?e"sa 'po'txe'ke'?a"ian — ,'in"te?e "di 'ia + ,'ta 'man"te?e 'noh"?kin + '?e?e -- ,"uar + ,'a'txe?e "nan 'te?e'nuh"?pia?ar + ,'?i'?a"ian 'e'lah "?pa?ar + ,'ta'mi?i'o"tot + 'ii"uar 'a'?kai"ue?e — ,'e"hen 'te'lo'ke?e'tu"ro?p 'ta'mi?i'o"tot +

15 + ,'?i'ha?ax"to '?e"sa 'po + ,'u'tah "uu?u "?pa + ,'ta'kan"te?e + ,'ui"nik + 19 + "kon -- ,"kon 'da'tah'ui"na + ,'u?p"na "tua?a + ,'ke"txi?i + ."uar 'a'?kai"iui + 'ta"ma?a -- .'?i'io"tot 'xe?e'tia?a"ian '?e'noh"?kin +

26 + '?e?e -- .'txe"tua?a + 28 + ,'tio "sa 'po + .'tia?a"uar 'i'io?o"pa 'ko?o"ra +

30 + ,'ha?a"xir "txe + ."iah 'ua'rin'io?o "pan 'xa"na +

32 + .'?en"ton 'ses'?a'ro?p"na + '?i?i -- '?a'na?a"ta 'ka"ne?et "txi?i -- 'ua'ra'?kai "iui?i — 'sa'koh"pa — ,'ta'noh"?kin 'sah"mi +

38 + .'?i'ha?a"xir "txe + .'i'kox"to 'ne?e 'na"?tsi +

40 + ,'in"ton 'ses + ,"txe?e 'ui"nik + ,'?en"ton 'ses + .'ka"nuah 'txi?i'?ka"iue?et +

44 + ,'?e"sa 'po"txe?e + .'?i'kox"to 'ka "nue?en +

46 + ,'?en"ton 'ses + .'txe"tua?a + 48 + 'ma?a"txi '?ka?a"ni?i -- '?a"txe?en "te?e -- 'to "na 'da -- ,'?ka"nu?um "?pi + .'?ka"nu?um "?pi 'ko?o"ra 'ko"txa "?i '?kai"iui +

53 + .'?en"ton 'ses'ha?a"xir "txe + ,"pe 'ro"ne?en + 'ma?a"txi 'u'iu"?pie?en 'iŋ'?kai"iui

7. Toad

— .'ta'ta'ki"nar +

57 + .'?en"ton 'ses'txe?e'ui"nik + .'i'ko "txix "ti?i '?kai"iui +

59 + ,"ne?en 'iŋ'?kai"iui + .'ta'me?e"ha?a + "?i?i -- ,'po"re 'so"ti?i 'ne?e -- '?ka"nu?u 'iu"?pi -- ,'ko"txa?aŋ '?kai"iui + 'u'?ka"ni 'tua?a -- 'u?u -- .'u'sah"ka 'e"ha?a 'u'iah "?ke?en +

68 + '?en"ton 'ses + '?e'ui"nik 'ia"ha?a "txe 'ke?e -- ,'?u'?txa"mi 'ko?o'ra"ha?a + 'u?u — '?txa"?pue?e -- ."sa 'po'ta"mar + 74 + ,'i "kon 'da'ix"to + '?o"txoi 'iue?e -- ,'?o"txoi "?txa?an '?e"sa 'po + ."kai '?kai"iui + 78 + ."txe + ."?tun "?tum + ."?tun "?tum + 81 + .'ha?ax"to '?u'to"na 'da +

82 + ,'?en"ton 'ses + ."txe "tua?a 'u"me 'ne'ui"nik + "pe 'ro"ne?et 'tio"sa 'po'me?e -- .'xe?e"ia?ax 'ma"ha?ax + 'ma"ha?ax -- ."ne?et 'ki"sas 'ua'ri'?kai"iui 'sa'koh"pa 'sah"mi 'u?um "?pi + "por 'ke?e -- ,'xe?e"ua 'ra'?kai"iui 'sah "mi + .'ga"lan 'u'iu?p"na?ar 'u'to"na 'da + 91 + ,"ne?et + .'ma?a'txe?e"re 'a'lo"?koi 'i'?kai 'iui +

93 + ,'?en"ton 'ses'e"sa 'po + ,'su'?pah "ra + 'u'iu"?pi "kuan 'do?o -- '?a'ro?o?p"na 'ke?e -- .'ma?a"txi '?o?o?p"na '?kai"iui + 98 + ,'por"ke '?u'to"na 'da + 'ma"ha?ax -- .'ga"lan '?u'iu?p"na?ar + 101 + ,'?en"ton 'ses'ha?a"xir + ,'u'me'ne'su?u"?par + ,'?es"tu?u '?tsuh"ri '?u 'na?a"?ku?ut + '?u'iu"?pi "kuan 'do'a'ro?p"na 'ke?e — .'ma?a"txu?u 'iu"?pie?et 'i'?kai"iui + .'su'?pah"ra + .'?es"to '?u'nu"kres 'u'na?a "?ku?ut +

108 + ,'i'po"re 'so + ,'ko"ne?er 'e"sa 'po

7. Toad

+ ,'?ko'?pi"rik 'u'na?a"?ku?ut 'ka'ui"ra + ,"kon 'da'?u'ui"ro?on + "?ehs 'to'?u'mu?uts"ru 'u'na?a "?ku?ut -- ,'?u'ui"ro?on + 114 + ,'i"kon 'do '?u'ia'ruh"se 'u'na?a"?ku?ut + .'u'?tsuh"ri 'ta "kix 'u'na?a"?ku?ut 'u'ui"ro?on + 116 + ,"por 'ke?e"txe 'ke?e'?u"me 'ne'su"?par + "por 'ke?e 'a'ro?p"na 'ke?e -- 'ma?a"txu?u 'iu"?pa?a?k -- .'ma?a"txo?o?p "na?a '?kai"iui +

120 + 'i?i -- ,'ta"ma 'res'to'ko"ne?er + ,'e"sa 'po + ."?pan '?a'?kai"iui "kon 'de "?txa?ar 'ta"ma '?e"ha?a + 124 + '?a"ian -- 'ia?a'la"gu 'na + "tia?a -- ,'?a?a"gua 'ne"ha?a + .'i"ia?a 'u'si?i?k"?po?o?p '?a'?txa?a"no?p 'ta"mar + "?i?i -- ,'?i'tu"no?or + ,'?e'?ak"?par + ,'?a"?txa?an + '?a'?kai"iuo?p 'ta'me?e -- ,"ha?a + 'u"txo?p '?e?e -- .'?e"?tun "?tum + 'por'ke?e -- ."?pan 'a'?kai"io?o?p +

139 + "pe 'ro?o -- "tu?ut 'ha?a"xir "txe 'ke?e -- .'ga"lan '?a'?kai"iui + 142 + ,"pe 'ro'ti"ko?oit "no?on + 'ma"ha?ax -- ."?kai 'lo 'ke?e'u"txe + 145 + "pe 'ro?o -- ,"no?on + 'ma 'ka'na?a"ta 'ka'ua?a"re 'ke'ma?a"txa?a 'lo"?koi 'a?k -- ,'a'?kai"iui + ."por 'ke?e'ma?a"txi '?ka "ni 'ka'su"?par 'e"mas 'ko'txe?e'su'?pahr"na 'ta 'mar'e'in"iahr +

7. Toad

1 There is another story about the same toad. 5 The toad, ... they say that one day there was a fiesta. A wedding was being held, and there was a band in the house. And the people who were there in the house were singing.

15 And afterward, the toad met a man. When he was met, he heard, "Who was singing in the house where the fiesta was?"

26 He was asked, "Uncle Toad, where are you coming from?"

30 He said, "I'm just walking along here."

32 Then he was asked, "And do you know who was singing at the fiesta when day broke earlier today?"

38 And he said, "Well, I was."

40 Then the man said, "Then you are one who has learned to sing."

44 The toad said, "Well, I learned."

46 Then he was asked, "Wouldn't you like to do your song? I want to hear it. I want to hear a little how you sing."

53 Then he (the toad) said, "But I can't sing when it's dry."

57 Then the man said, "And how do you sing then?"

59 "I sing in the water, and therefore whoever wishes to hear how I sing must find water and give it to me."

7. Toad

68 Then, they say, that man brought a little water and put the toad in it. And when the toad had gone in and was lying in it he began to sing. 78 He said, "?tun ?tum. ?tun ?tum." 81 That is his song.

82 Then he was told by the man, "But you, Uncle Toad, you must not be the one I heard singing at daybreak today, because the one who was singing earlier, his song was good to hear. 91 You, you can't sing at all."

93 Then the toad was ashamed to hear it, when he was told he could not sing, 98 because his song is not pleasant to hear. 101 Then he was so ashamed to hear this that his eyes widened, when he was told he could not sing. He was so ashamed his eyes grew large.

108 That is why we see the toad now has big eyes. When he sees us he closes his eyes. 114 And when he opens his eyes they widen; he sees us, 116 because, they say, it is from shame, because he was told he could not sing.

120 And so to this day, the toads sing the same way, when they are lying in the water. 124 There is a pond where water remains, and they lie in it, and every evening they lie singing in the water. They say, "?tun ?tum," because that is how they sing.

139 But, to himself, they say, (the toad) sings pleasantly. 142 But to us it is not singing that he does. 145 But we don't like to say that he can't sing, because we don't want to shame him more, since he was ashamed about it the other time.

8. Raccoon

1 + ,'?a"ian 'o'tron"te?e '?o'hro"ner + 'ta'me'ma"?e?e -- ,'?e'ih"matx + ,"txe 'ke?e'e 'ih"matx + ."hen 'te'?a"ni 'u"?pan +

6 + ,"txe 'ke'ia"ian 'in'te?e"di 'ia + ,'?a"ian + 'e?e -- ,'txa?a"te?e 'ui'ni"ko?p + 'ke?e -- 'u'na?a"to '?pa"ni?in 'te?e'?u?u -- ,'u "ma?a "nio?p + 'ke?e -- ,"kuan 'do'?ka"ni 'a'lo "?koi 'a'kor"mo?o?p + ,'u'txu"kio?p 'ia?a"?katx + ,'u'txu"kio?p 'e'txum"pi?i 'tua?a'u'be"si?i "no?p + ,'?i'ha?a"xo?p + ,'?pah"xan + 'e?e -- 'u "txo?p 'e?e -- 'in"te?e -- ,'?o'hro"ner + 'en "ton 'ses'n -- 'u'ia?a"re '?u?u -- ,'uix'ka?a "ro?p + ,'?a?a"guan + ,'i'ha?a"xo?p + .'a'lu'mu "o '?pi"o '?pu'iok'u'uix'ka?a"ro?p +

28 + ,'?i'kon'da?a'lu'mu"io?p + ,'in"ton 'ses + 'ua?ak"txe 'ta"ka?a 'sut"po?p + 'ia"ha?a -- ,'ih"matx + ,'ia?a'xi"no?p 'tua?a'u'be"si?i "no?p + ,'u'txu"kio?p 'e'txum"pi?i + ,'u'txu"kio '?pia?a"?katx + ,'u'?ka"txo?p 'ua"tar + 'a?a -- ,'so'koh"pa + 'e?e -- ,'e"?txa?ar 'e'txum"pi?i 'ia?a"?katx 'u'me'ne"ro?p + ,'ien"ton 'ses + 'e?e -- ,'e'i"xik + ,'a"ka 'iu"txe 'ta"mal + .'u "txe 'tu"no?or 'lo'ke?e'?ka"nu?u '?ku"xo?p +

46 + "pe 'ro?o -- ,'?ko"toi 'in'te?e"di 'ia + ,'e'ui'ni"ko?p 'ia"ha?a + ,'ma?a'txix"to 'lo"?koi + 'e?e -- 'u"txo?p 'ia?a'lo'ke?e -- ,'u "txo?p 'kos'tum"brar + ,'u"txo?p + 'i'nie"ha?ax 'e'i"xik 'ma?a'txix"to?o -- 'u'koh"ko 'ba"lor 'tua?a -- 'a?atx'pa?a"guan 'tua?a'lu"mu 'iu?u -- ,'a'lu"mui 'e'ui'ni"ko?p 'ia"ha?a + ."io '?pu'io "ko?p + 58 + 'u'?pa?a'krio'?pix'to"ia?a 'por 'kiu'ui"ro?p 'ke?e -- .'ma"ha?ax "hen 'te +

60 + .'ma?a'txix"tu?u 'iak"to?o '?pa'lu "mui 'io"?pu?u '?pi'ko?p"ia?a + 61 + ,'ha?ax "te?e "po 'bre'ui'ni"ko?p 'ia"ha?a + ,'a'?poh "?pa?a "ruo?p + ,'ma?a'txix"tu?u 'na?a"to?p 'ko

8. Raccoon

'txe'ta?a'sut"po?p "hen 'te + 'i?i -- "as 'ta 'ke?e -- ,'ha?a"xo?p 'u'uah"?pio?p 'e"pe 'nia + .'i"xin 'mu'kua"no?p +

68 + 'i?i -- ,'?pa'nix"to + '?ko"toi 'ket "pa 'e?e -- ,'ih"matx + 'i'ko"ne?er 'txe?e"hen 'te'ke?e -- 'e?e -- .'e'ih"matx 'u'ta"rer "hen 'te + 75 + 'i?i -- ,'ko"ne?er + ,'ka'ui"ra 'e 'ih"matx + "?paŋ 'ko'txa'u"iok 'e?e -- ,"hen 'te 'u"?ka?p + ,'tu"no?or + .'ke?e"hen "tio?p 'a"ni +

8. Raccoon

1 There is another story about the Raccoon. It is said the Raccoon used to be like a person.

6 It is said that one day, there were two men who knew one of those -- charms that -- when they were going to go hunting, they caught chickens and turkeys belonging to their neighbors, and they first -- said a -- story, then told their wives to stand, and they passed under the legs of their wives.

28 And when they passed through, then they suddenly turned into raccoons, and went to their neighbors', catching turkeys and chickens, bringing them back, and when daylight came, there lay the turkeys and chickens, by their doing. And then the women began to make *tamales*; they made everything they wanted to eat.

46 But there came a day when those men did not go out and do what they were accustomed to do, for the women no longer had the courage to stand so that the men could pass under their legs. 58 They were frightened then, because they saw that they were not people.

60 They would not let them pass beneath their skirts any more. 61 Then those poor men began to cry out: they did not know how to turn back into people, and until -- they took to the mountains and hid.

68 And thus, they remained raccoons, and nowadays people say that the raccoon is of the race of man. 75 And nowadays we see that the raccoon has feet and hands like man, and everything -- that he used to be a man.

9. Coyote

1 + 'e?e -- ,'?u'kon"ta 'ha'?e'ko"io 'te +
3 + ,"txe 'ke'?e'ko"io 'te'?a"ni + .'max"tak
'?a"ni + 5 + 'e?e -- ,'a"ia 'nin'te?e'ui"nik +
,'a"ian 'txa?a"koht 'u'max"tak + 'e'ui"nik 'ia
"ha?a + ,'kon'do"ua 'ra'tu"rua 'ne"nar + 'u'sa
"kre?e -- ,'u'iu'ne"no?p 'a?a"xin + ,'ma'ku?u
"txor + .'tua?a'u'koh"ko?p 'e"nar +

14 + ,'i"txe 'ke?e'ia"ro '?pe'max"tak 'ia
"ha?a + 'a'?ka -- 'in -- 'i'niahr"to 'a'?ko
"tuo?p 'ta?a -- ,'ta'u'iok"txor + ,'u'?ku"xo?p +
.'e"nar 'tsih"tsi + 21 + 'i?i -- ,'i'niahr"to
'a?a'xi"no?p + ,'ha?a"xo?p 'a'?ko'to"io?p 'ta'ka
+ ,'u'uah"pio?p 'e"nar + .'u'?ku"xio?p +

26 + ,'en"ton 'ses + '?ko"toi 'in'te?e"di
'ia + ,'ia"ro?p 'e'max"tak 'ia"ha?a + 'e?e -- .
'sut"po?p 'ko"io 'te + 31 + ,'ma?a'txix"to
'?ko"toi 'ta'e'u'io'to"to?p "ia?a + ,'ha?ax"to
'e'ui"nik + 'e?e -- ,'?ko"toi 'ta'u'io"tot + .'u
'ia?a"re?e 'uix"ka?ar + 37 + 'e?e -- ,'max"tak
+ .'tia?a'i'xi"no?p + 40 + 'e?ei -- .'e'i"xik
"txe + 'ha?a'xe"ra "xe?e -- .'i'xi"no?p 'ta"txor
+ .'me?e"ra?a 'io?o"po?p +

45 + ,'en"ton 'ses'e'ui"nik "txe + 'a?a --
.'sa"ber 'ma?a'txa?a"ian 'tu"?ka 'u'num"sio?p
'u?u'num"se 'u"?po?p 'e'max"tak 'i"ra + .'?ka
"nin 'xin'gui"ra + 49 + ,"?e 'ui"nik 'i"xin 'u
'ui"ra + ,'u'iu'ne"no?p + 'kuan'do -- ,'?ko"toi
'u'ui"ra 'ma'mah"txi?i + 'u?u -- ,'tah"ui 'ma
'ku?u"txor + ,'n"ton 'ses + ,'u'?pih"nu + 'e?e
-- ."txe 'tu?u"ial 'ma + 59 + 'a'sa"ber 'hai
-- 'e'max"tak 'i"ra?a 'sa"ber 'ma?a"txi?i --
'e?e -- .'sut'po"?pix 'ko"io 'te +

63 + "kai 'u?u -- 'tsor'ma"ian 'tu"no?or
'e?e -- ,'u"iok 'e"txor + ,'u'tso"ri?i "xin + ,
'tu"no?or 'u"ti?i 'e"txor + 'u'tah"ui 'e?e --
'u"iok 'e'max"tak 'ke?e -- .'o'txo"io?p 'ma"kuir

9. Coyote

'iŋ'gohr"pe 'nia + 71 + ,'i?ix"to 'ia"ha?a +
'e?e -- ,'max"tak + ,'u'sa"ti 'u"?po?p + ,'sut
"po?p 'ko"io 'te + ,'por'ke?e'u'?ku"xo?p 'e'tsih
'tsi"nar + ,'i'ta'rix"to 'ko"ne?er 'a'?kah"na
'ke?e'tsih'tsi"nar 'u'txe"mal 'ka'?ku"xi 'tsih
"tsi + .'por'ke'ka'sut"pa 'ko"io 'te +

79 + 'por'ke?e -- ,'max"tak 'ia"ha?a + ,
'?pa'nix"to '?ko"toi + ,'ket"po?p 'ko'io"tio?p +
'por'ke?e -- .'u'?ku"xio?p "mei 'gra'e'tsih'tsi
"nar + 85 + 'i?i -- ,'po"re 'so + ,'ko"ne?er +
,"no?on 'ka'?pa?a"kre 'tua?a'ka'?ku"xi 'e"nar
'tsih"tsi + .'?pah'?ka"tix 'ka'sut"pa 'ko"io 'te
+

9. Coyote

1 The story of the Coyote. 3 It is said that the coyote used to be a child. 5 There was a man with two children, and that man, when the corn was being harvested, sent his children into the cornfield to watch over the ears of corn.

14 And it is said that those little children, every time they came to the cornfield, ate ears of corn raw. 21 And ... every time they went, as soon as they arrived, they grabbed the corn and ate it.

26 Then, there came a day when those little children had ... turned into coyotes. 31 They didn't come back then to their house, and then the man ... came home and said to his wife, "The ... children -- where have they gone?" 40 And the woman said, "Since ... they went to the cornfield, they haven't come back."

45 Then the man said, "... I wonder if there isn't something that has happened to these children. I'm going to go see." 49 The man went to see his children. When ... he arrived, he saw no one, and ... found no one in the cornfield. Then, he thought ... he said to himself, 59 "I wonder if ... these children may have ... turned into coyotes?"

63 He began ... searching for a trail all ... over the cornfield, he went tracking them, all around the edge of the field; he found the footprints of the children that ... entered a big rock. 71 And right there, the ... children had turned themselves into coyotes, because they had eaten raw corn. And to this day it is believed that raw corn does harm if we eat it raw, because we turn into coyotes.

9. Coyote

79 Because those children, so it came to them, to remain coyotes, because they ate much raw corn. 85 And ... that is why today we are afraid of eating raw corn, because we risk becoming coyotes.

10. Armadillo

1 + 'a"ian 'o'tron"te?e -- ,'o'hro"ner + . 'a'?kah"na + "txe 'ke?e -- ,'ta"rix 'e"tiem 'po + .'a"ian 'in"te?e 'ui"nik + 7 + 'i?i -- "txe 'ke?e'e'ui"nik 'ia"ha?a + ,'uar'a'pat"na + .'io "?pe 'e'ha"ha?ar + 'i?i -- 'ha?a"xir + 'ma?a"txi — ,"u 'txe"ka 'so + ."uar 'a'?ka"xi 'e'ha"ha?ar + 16 + ,'u'ui"ra 'ke?e'uar'e?eih"?pi + ,'e'dio "so?p + 'lo'ke?e"uar -- ,'u'ta're"so?p 'e'ha "ha?ar + .'pe'ro'ha?a"xir 'ma?a"txu 'txe"ka 'so + 21 + ,"kai 'a'ro?p"na + 'u'me'nu?u — .'u 'pia?a"ro?p + ,'ak"tan 'e'pat"na?ar + 'por"ke?e — 'ua"ra 'ui"ra 'ke?e -- .'uar'e?eih"?pi "u?ut 'e"?kin + 28 + "?i '?pah"?kat -- 'u'ua "?tsio?on -- .'e'dio"so?p +

31 + .'i'ha?a"xir "txe + .'ko"txa?aŋ 'xiŋ 'uak"ta 'ni -- 'ni'ta"re 'a'ke?e -- 'me'e"ra?an 'lo?k"se 'ni'ta"re 'a + 'es"to?o -- ,"man 'lo?ok "se + ,'en"ton 'ses + .'e"rer 'i?iŋ"ri + 39 + 'txe"ke?e -- .'ua'ra"?kih 'na"ua?ar + 41 + , 'ta"ku?u 'ta"re 'a + .'por'ke?e'ma?a"txi '?ka"na 'lo'?koi"tu?ut + 'i'ha?ax"tue?e -- ,'u'pia?a "ro?p + ,'ua"ra 'ro?p"na + ,'ke'ak"taŋ + 'por "ke?e -- "uar 'e?eh"?pu?ut 'e"?kin + 49 + 'i 'ha?a"xir 'txe"hai -- ,'hai'?ka"nu 'ua'?tsi'?e "no?p + 51 + ,'i'tu"?ku 'u"txe + .'ko'txa"ma 'tu'?ka'ua"tar 'hai'?ka"nu 'ua'?tsie"no?p +

53 + ,"kon 'de"ha?ax + ,'u'txe'sen"tir + ,'ah"ka + ,'e'sen"te 'io + .'tia?a"ua?ar + 58 + 'i"txe 'ke?e -- 'kon"de?e -- ,'i"xin + ,'?ir "na + ,'u"me 'nu'pia?a"ro?p + ,"ia?a "?txa?ar + ,'pa"kar + 'to?o"ru?u -- .'u'ia'sa"don + 67 + 'i?i -- ,'i"kai + ,'?ir"na 'u'?pa"ke 'ru"pat + 'ma"ha?ax 'in"te?e 'ta'ka'e?e -- ,'?ke"uer + . "?txa?ar 'u'sein"iir 'ta"mar + 73 + 'i?i -- . "txe 'ke'ket"pa + 'e?e -- '?pa"nix 'ko"txa?a -- — 'e?e -- .'e"tun + .'u"pat 'tia?a'a'hah"?tsa 'u"me 'ne'dio"so?p + .'kon"da?a 'i"xin 'ir"na + .'u"me 'nu'pia?a"ro?p +

10. Armadillo

81 + ,'i'ha?ax"to + ,'a'?kah"na 'ko"ne?er
+ 'ke'?e'ui"nik 'ia"ha?a 'xe?e -- ,'hah"?tsa 'u
"me 'ne'dio"so?p + ,'tia?a"ua 'ra'pat"na + ,'a
"txe?e "na 'men"tar + ,'u"me 'ne"hen 'te'ko
"ne?er + .'ke"ha?ax 'e'men"ta 'do'i"?patx + 90
+ ,"por 'ke?ei"?patx + "?txa?ar 'e?e -- .'e"se
'nia'tu?u'?pa"ker 'u"pat + ."por 'ke?e"txe 'ke
"ha?ax 'e'tia?a'hah"?tsa + .'u"me 'ne'dio"so?p +
95 + ,'ket"pa + ,"pu 'ru"?pak + .'u"pat +

98 + ,"i 'ko"ne?er + ,'e?ei"?patx + 'e?e
-- 'ka'ui"ra '?a'xa"na + ,'ko"tor + ,'e'no"xi?i
"?pak + .'ta'ma'u'?pa"ke 'ru"pat + ,'pe'ro"txe
'ke?e'u"meŋ '?ke"uer + .'ket"pa 'ko'txe?e'ia
"ha?a + 'ma"ha?ax -- ,'po"re 'so + .'e'i'?patx
'ko"ne?er + ,'ma?a"txi 'u'?pa?a"kre 'e'ha"ha?ar
+ 'mo"tor + ,"uar 'a'?ka"xi 'e'ha"ha?ar + 'mo
"tor + ,'ak"?par + ,"pe 'ro'ha?a"xir + 'io?p --
.'ie"?pe 'e'ha"ha?ar + ,'a'xa"na + 'u'pah"ni 'e
"rum + 120 + ,'u'?kah"na?ar + ,'u'hu?u"ru
'u?ut'e"rum + ,'ta'mu?u"ni?i + .'tua?a'u'tah"ui
+ ,'e'lu'?kum + ,'ma'ku'e"rum 'u'?ku"xi + 'o?o
-- ,'a'al"gu 'nu"?pi?i + 'tu"?ki?k 'tu"?ki?k 'lo
'ke?e -- .'u'tah"ui 'ma"ku?u "rum + .'u'?ku"xe?e
'ko"kotx 'u"?pi?i + 'por"ke?e -- "ha?ax -- .'u
'sah"ka 'ma'kue?e"rum 'u'?ku"xi +

134 + ,'i'po"re 'so + "txe 'ke'kon"da '?a
'ro?p"na + 'u"me 'nu'pia?a"ro?p 'tua?a -- .'u
'iak"ta '?a"ne?e 'pat"na?ar + ,'ha?a"xir + 'u
'ia?a"re 'u?u -- .'u'pia?a"ro?p + .'hai'ma?a
"txi?im 'pat"na + .'ma?a'txiŋ"gue?e + 143 +
'e?e -- ,'ha"ha?ar + ,'u'ue?e"se?en + 'u?u -- ,
'u'txek"tes 'tu"?kaŋ '?ku"xi + ."pe 'ru'?ka"ni
'tua?am'pat"na + 149 + ,'i'po"re 'so + ,'ko
"ne?er + ,'ha?a"xir + ,'ma?a"txu '?pa?a"kre 'e
'ha"ha?ar + .'a'lo"?koi 'a'xa"na +

154 + ,'kon'da"ua 'ra'?ka"xi 'e'ha"ha?ar +
.'me"ho 'rix"tu?ut + 'por'kiu'na?a"ta 'ke?e --

10. Armadillo

.'a"ian 'tu'?ka'u'tah"uiu '?ku"xi + 'por'ke?e --
"txe 'ke?e -- ,'a"tsa?ai + .'kuan'du'ui"ra '?ka
"xi 'e'ha"ha?ar + 162 + ,'txe"ke 'u"ni?i + .
"ha?ax 'u'ia'sa"don + ."xe?e 'a'pat"na?a "ni 'ta
"mar 'a'pah"no + 168 + ,'ta"mar + ,'u'hu?u"ru
'u?ut'e"rum + .'u'sah"ka 'tu'?ku?u'?ku"xi 'ma"ku
'?e"rum + 171 + ,'kon'dix"to + 'i"xin + ,'ir
"na 'tia?a"?txa?ar + .'a'ro?p"na 'u'me'nu'pia?a
"ro?p + 175 + 'ber'dix"to 'ke?e -- ,'ua'ra"ni
'ka'ua?a"re?et 'ke?e'ak"tan + 'e'pat"na?ar + ,
'ma?a"txi 'u?u"pien + ,'i?i"ran 'tu"?ka?a 'num
"se 'a"?pa + ,'ber"da 'ke?e'hah"?tse?et + ,'i
"ran 'ko'txe"?txa?ar 'e'siaŋ'?ke"uer 'ta?a'pat'i
"ra + .'i'ket"pa "pu 'ru"?pak 'a"pat +

183 + .'i'ha?a"xir 'txe + 'pe're?e -- 'i
'txa"?pix "ta?an 'oŋ"ke?e -- 'e'ma?a"lir 'lo
'ke?e -- .'u'txe?e'dio"so?p 'i"ra 'ta'ka"ren + ,
'ko"ne?er + 'u'iah"?ke?e "no?p 'in"te?e 'ni?i --
'ni?i -- 'ni'kor"pes 'ni"?pir + ."tie 'ni"tiem
'po + '?ka"ni?i -- ,'u'?ku"xen 'e"?tsi?i + ,'i
'?ka"nu?u 'xi"xie?en + "pe 'ro?o -- 'ma?a"txia
'xi'nu?u -- ,'u'xi"xi 'ni"?puhk 'ko"txa?a 'ta
"?kix 'u'uah"pie?en + ,"por 'ke?e"ra + "ha?ax
'ni?i -- ,'ni'kor'pi"?pir "ia?a + ."tie 'ne"tiem
'po + .lo'ke?e'u'iah"?ke?en 'e'dio'si"ra +

204 + ,'ko"ne?er + ,'ket'pa"?pak 'ni"pat +
,'in'koht"?tsi?i + ,'a'io?o"pa 'u'uah"pie?en 'ta
'ni"pat + ,'ma'ko'txe?e"rer "ta?a 'u'txam"se?en
+ "por 'ke?e -- 'ma?a"txi?i -- 'o?o"txoi 'u?ut'u
"ieh 'ta'ma'ni?i -- .'ni"pat + "por 'ke?e -- ,
'ket"pa '?im"pim + .'?i'?a'?ke"?ko + 216 +
"ne?en 'ma"ha?ax -- 'ma"lir 'lo'ke?e -- .'u"txe
'e'dio"so?p 'i"ra 'ta'ka're"nia?a 'san + 'ni'kor
"pes 'ni"?pir 'xe?e -- 'u'iah"?ke?en 'i"ra 'ta
"ma?a -- .'ni"pat +

222 + "i 'po"re 'so + ,'e'i'?patx 'ko
"ne?er + 'in"tran 'to'a?a -- .'a'txa'mes"na '?u

10. Armadillo

"me 'ne"?tsi?i + 226 + 'por"ke?e -- ,'ta'me?e "?pak 'tu?u"pat + 'a?ahp"na 'u"me 'ne"?tsi?i + . 'i'ma?a"txa?a 'ku'kur"na + 'por'ke?e -- ,'a'?ke "?ko 'u"pat + "ma 'ko'txe?e"rer 'tua?a -- .'a 'uer"na 'u"me 'ne"?tsi?i + "por 'ke?e -- "txe 'ke?e -- ,'u'kor"pes 'ni"?pir + .'u'na?a"tah '?ku"na + 'u"me 'ne?e -- .'dio"so?p +

240 + "pe 'ro -- ,'lo'ke?e'ha?a"xir 'u'?ku "xi + ,'in"so 'lo + ,'e'lu"?kum 'ma'ku'?e"rum + ,'a'xa"na 'u'pah"ni + .'tu"no?or 'in'te?er"ti '?e'ak"?par + 'a'xa"na 'u -- 'pah"ni -- .'e'lu "?kum 'u'?ku"xi + 249 + ,"pe 'ro'kon"da 'tah 'ui"na + .'u"me 'ne"?tsi?i + .'ah'nes"na + 252 + ,'i'ko'txa'ha?a"xir + ,'ma?a"txa '?ah"ni + , 'ua?ak"txe 'ta'ka'a"?ko?oi + .'a'ku'kur"na 'u"me 'ne"?tsi?i + 256 + ,'in"ton 'ses + ,'lo'ke?e'u "txe '?e"?tsi?i + ,'a'suh"ta + ,'a'?txa?p"na 'ha "uar + 'en"ton 'ses'a'ka"ia?a -- .'a'xih"xa 'u?ut'u"na?a?k + 262 + "por 'ke?e -- ,"u?ut 'u "na?a?k + ,'ma"ha?ax "?pak + .'iŋ"?kun + 266 + ,'i'a?a"si?ik 'pa"na 'u"me 'ne"?tsi?i + .'a'xih "xa + 'i -- 'ko"txa?a 'a'?ko?oi + ,'mix"to 'ko "?pu?u 'txe"ia?a + "u 'iak"tu?u "?pa + ,'a'ua '?kar"na 'u'me'ne"?tsi?i + ,'a'?txa?p"na 'ha"uar + .'a'xih"xa 'u"me 'ne"?tsi?i + 275 + .'a'?kuh "xa +

276 + 'i"hai -- ,'ta'ku?u'uiŋ"kir 'e "?tsi?i + ,"lo 'ke?e'a'txe?e"na + ,'a"?keh 'txa?a"xin + .'a'?kuh"xa 'ta"mo?o "tot + .'u"me 'nu'e?e -- .'?e'?ah'ium"?tsi?i + 283 + ,'?pa 'nix"to ,'a'?ka?a"?pa + .'e'men"ta 'do'i"?patx 'ko"ne?er + 286 + '?kux"?pir + 'hur"?pir + , 'txa'mes"?pir 'ta'kie"?tsi?i + ,'?pa"na?a '?ka?a "?pa + ,'ko"ne?er 'i"ra + 291 + "pe 'ro"txe 'ke?e -- ."hen 'te'a"ni + .'e'i'?patx 'ia"ha?a + 294 + "?ah 'pat"na?ar + 'i?i -- ,'ko"ne?er + , 'u'?kah"na?ar 'a'xa"na + ,'u'hu?u"ru 'e"rum + , 'ta"mu?u 'si'e'hi"nah + 'tua?a -- .'u'tah"ui 'tu

10. Armadillo

'?ku'?ku"xi +

302 + "pe 'ro -- ,"no?on + ,"ma?a "txi 'ko?o"sre 'ka'?ku"xi + "por 'ke?e'ka'na?a"ta 'ke?e -- ."hen 'te'a"ni +

10. Armadillo

1 There is another story that is told. It
is said that a long time ago, there was a man.
7 And it is said that that man was working in
the rain, paying no attention to the rain that
was falling. 16 He saw that the Gods who were
bringing rain were causing lightning, but he
paid no attention. 21 His companions began
calling to him, "Leave off working, because --
you can see there is lightning in the sky. 28
And we're afraid the Gods will strike us."

31 And he said, "How can I leave my job
until — I've finished it? Then I can rest."
39 It is said he was getting angry with his
job, because he couldn't finish it, and then his
companions were calling for him to leave it, be-
cause there was lightning in the sky. 49 And
he said, "If -- if they're going to strike me,
what of it?" 51 What difference does it make
if they're going to strike me?"

53 At that moment, he heard the crash of
thunder where he stood. 58 And it is said that
when his companions saw him lying there, he was
face down on his hoe. 67 And they could see
that his backbone was not marked by just one
lash. 73 It is said that it became like stone
where his back was lashed by the Gods, when his
companions came to look.

81 And so, it is told today that the man
who was struck by the Gods where he was working
is called by people nowadays by the name of Ar-
madillo. 90 Because on the armadillo's back-
bone is the sign, because it is said he was
struck by the Gods. 95 His back became pure
bone.

98 And nowadays we see the armadillo walk-
ing bent over, with a big bone on his back, but

it is said that because of the lash it became that way, not -- therefore, the armadillo nowadays is not afraid of the rain; even if the rain is falling, even if it is night, he still walks in the rain, digging in the ground. 120 His mind is on ploughing up the ground with his muzzle, so as to find earthworms in the ground to eat, or some grubs, or anything he can find in the ground: he eats potato bugs, because he looks in the ground for what he eats.

134 And that is why when he was told by his companions to leave the work, he said to his companions, "If I don't work I don't eat. 143 The rain feeds me -- it causes what I eat to appear, but it means I must work." 149 And that is why today he is not afraid of the rain; he goes out walking.

154 When the rain is falling, it seems better to him, because he knows that he will find something to eat, because, it is said, he laughs when he sees the rain falling. 162 It is said that his snout is his hoe, which he uses to work with. 165 And nowadays it has turned into his snout, and he digs with it. 168 With it, he ploughs the ground, looking for something to eat in the earth. 171 Then, when they had gone to where he lay, his companions said to him, 175 "Isn't it true that we were telling you to leave work, and you didn't listen to me! See what has happened to you! You were struck, weren't you? See how the many lashes lie on your back, and how your back has turned to pure bone!"

184 And he said, "But -- I'm grateful for the misfortune that -- the Gods have given me. Today they have given me my -- shelter. Before, the dogs would bite me and rip me, but they

aren't going to rip my clothes when they grab me because this is my protection now, what the Gods have given me here."

204 "Now my back has turned to bone. If a dog comes and grabs me by the back, he can not kill me, because his teeth do not go into my back. Because it has become thick and tough. 216 To me it is not bad, what the Gods have done with me here; they have given me my protection here on my back."

222 And that is why it is difficult today for dogs to kill the armadillo, 226 because the bone on his back, dogs grab it, and he is not knocked down, because his back is tough, and it cannot be pierced by the dog because -- it is said, that is his protection, which he knows was given him by the Gods.

240 But what he eats is just worms in the ground. He goes and digs all night every night — he goes and digs worms to eat. 249 But when he is found by a dog, he is chased, 252 and since he can't run, he tires at once, and is knocked down by the dog. 256 Then, what the dog does is turn him over, lying on his back, and then he begins to rip open his belly. 262 Because his belly is not bone. It is soft. 266 And it is sought by the dog, and is ripped open. Since he is tired, there is nothing he can do about it; he is caught by the dog, laid down on his back, and ripped open by the dog. 275 He is eaten.

276 And if the dog's master is with him, what is done is he is carried off to be eaten at home by the owner of the dog. 283 That is the way it ends up for the one called armadillo nowadays. 291 But it is said he used to be a per-

10. Armadillo

son. 294 A worker. And now his concern is ploughing the earth around the roots of stalks, finding things to eat.

302 But we don't like to eat him, because we know he used to be a person.

11. Turkeys

1 + ,'?a"ian + ,'?o'tron"te?e + ,'?o'hro
"ner + .'?u'?kah"ti '?e"hen 'te + 5 + "txe
'ke?e -- ,'?e'?ah"tso?o + ,'ta"ka '?u"tu?u '?e
'txum"pi?i + "txe 'ke?e'kuan"do?o -- ,'nuh
"?pio?o?p + .'?a'tsa?a"io?p + ,"kon 'da'?u'iu
"?pio?p + 'tu'ru'?pa"na '?e?e -- ,'?e"mu 'si'ka
'ta'mi?i'o"tot + ,"kai 'txe?e"na '?e'lah"?pa?ar
+ ,'ha?a"xo?p + '?a'tsa?a"io?p + ,'ua?a"uaŋ "kai
'?ak"to?o?p + 'ta'me?e -- '?e"mu 'si'ka'lo'keu?u
-- ,'tu"ru 'ta'me?e'o"tot + .'por'ke?e'?a'tsa?a
"io?p +

22 + '?i? -- "txe 'ke?e -- ,"kon 'da'ix"to
+ ,'?ak'?pa"re + ,"uar '?a?ak"to?p + '?i?i --
'ha?ax"to '?e?e -- ,'?e'?ah"tso?o + ,'ka"rai +
"por 'ke?e -- "uar -- '?ah'?ku"na '?e?e -- .'?e
"txi 'txa'?u'iu"?txi + 35 + .'?i'ha?a"xir 'ka
"rai + 36 + ,"?i '?u"me 'ne'ka"rer + 'ko'txa?a
-- ,'sat"pa 'ka"rai + ,"txe 'ke?e'ua?a"uan + .
'lo'ko"hran +

41 + '?i?i -- ."kai + .'?a"ru + 44 + .
"txe + ."lok "lok "lok + 46 + ,'?en"ton 'ses +
,"txe '?e"hen 'te + '?ia"go 'ra'?e?e -- ,'?e'?ah
'nuh'?pia?a"ro '?pi"ra + "me 'ru'?ka"ni 'u?u --
.'?u'iah"?ku '?u"?po?o?p +

52 + ,'?i'ha?a"xir + "uar 'ua'ra?a"ru 'ta
'mu?u -- ,'ta'mu?ut'?io?o"tot + ,"ua 'ra?ak"ta +
"pe 'ro?o -- ."uar '?a?a"ru + 58 + ,'?i"ra 'hi
"rah + ."txe + ."lok "lok "lok + 61 + 'por
'ke?e -- .'ka"rai + '?i?i -- ,'ha?ax"to + '?e?e
-- ,'?e'?ix'ka?ar"?pir + 'ko'txa'?u'ui"ra 'ke?e
-- "ua 'ra?a"ru '?u?u -- ,'?u'no"xi?ip + ,'?en
"ton 'ses + ."kai '?a"ru '?u"?pan + 72 + ."txe
+ ."txo?ok "txo?ok "txo?ok +

74 + ,'?in"ton 'ses + "txe?e -- '?e"hen
'te'lo'ke?e'tu"ruo?p 'ta'me?e -- ,'?e'nuh
"?pia?ar + 'ia"go 'ra'?e?e -- ,'?e'?ah'nuh

11. Turkeys

'?pia?a"ro '?pi"ra + "me 'ro?o -- '?ka'nix"to '?u?u -- .'?u'iah"?ku?u "?po?o?p "ia?a + 83 + "txe 'ke'ha?ax"to '?e'?ah"tso?o + 'ko'txa?a -- , '?kih"ni?ix + '?u'ui"ra '?e?e -- ,"hen 'te'lo 'ke?e'tu"ru + '?i?i -- '?i?i -- "ua 'ru'ui"ra 'u?u -- ,'pia?a"ro?p + 'lo'ke?e -- ,'tu"ru + , 'ha?a"xir + ,'?i'nia"hrer + .'txa'koh"pa '?u"hor + 97 + "me 'ru?u -- ,"?txi?i?tx 'ket"pa '?u "hor + .'u"me 'ne'?kih"na?ar +

100 + ,"kon 'da'?u'ui"ra + ,'u'pia?a"ro?p + ,'?ko"toi + ,'?i'ha?a"xir + ."kai + .'txe + ."lok "lok "lok + 107 + ,'?en"ton 'ses + . "txe?e "mohr + .'lo'ke?e'tu"ro?o?p + ."me 'ru "ne?et 'ta"kix 'ui'ni"ket + 111 + .'ua?a"re?et "ua 'ria?a"ru + 112 + ,'si'?a'lo"?koi + ."ka?a 'ru?u"?pan + 114 + ,'?en"ton 'ses + ,'?e"mohr + ,'lo'ke?e'tu"ro?o?p + ,"kai + .'?u"txo?p + '?e?e -- ."lok "lok + "kai '?u'ta"krio?p '?a"ni '?e?e -- .'?e'?ah'nuh"?pia?ar 'ia"ha?a +

123 + ,"kon 'da'?ix"to + 'u'iu"?pi 'ke?e -- ,"uar '?a'ta'kar"na '?a?a"ru + .'?en"ton 'ses "txe 'ha?a"xir + ,"no?ox + ,"ua 'rua"to?ox + ,'ta"ma 'ni'noh"?kin + "ma 'ha?ax'por'ke?e -- . 'tu'?ku?u'pa"ter + ."no?ox '?u'pa"ter 'ni'uix "ka?ar + 133 + '?ka"ni?i -- .'?i'ui"re?eŋ'gua 'ra?an"ta 'ta"kar + 135 + 'por"re 'so"ua 'ra 'ua"to?ox 'u"?pan "pe 'ro -- ,'?ka"ni?i 'ui"ra + ,'ko"ne?er + .'?iŋ'gueh"ta '?i'ba"lor +

139 + '?en"ton 'ses"txe 'ke?e -- ,'?u'iak "ta '?u"?pa '?i"xin + ,'tu?u"ho 'ru'pia?a"ro?p + 142 + ."txe + .'hu?u"rik + .'hu?u"rik + 145 + .'hu?u"rik + 146 + .'u'?pah'?ku"se '?e"mohr +

147 + "pe 'ro + .'?e"mohr "txe + .'txe?e "no?p + "pe 'ro?o -- ,"no?on + '?a'ia"non 'tu "?ka 'ka'koh"ko 'ma?a"txi 'ka?a -- ,'ka'ueh"ta '?u'ba"lor + '?e?e -- .'?e'?ah'nuh"?pia?a 'ri"ra

11. Turkeys

+ 156 + "txe 'ke?e -- ,'him"po?o?p + ,'ta'?u "hor '?e'?ah'nuh"?pia?ar + ."kai + '?u'iah "?ko?o?p +

161 + ,'?i"kon 'da'ix"to + 'sa'koh"pa + , "txe 'ke?e'?in'ta"kix + ,'?tih"?tem '?tih"?tem + ,'?u"hor '?iah'nuh"?pia?ar 'ia"ha?a + ,"kon 'de 'sa'koh"pa + '?i?i -- ,'?a'ro?o?p"na + 'u"me 'nu?u -- .'u'uix"ka?ar + 171 + ,"ne?et + , 'ua?a"uan "kai 'a"rue?et + '?e'ma?a"txi -- 'lo "?ko?om "bien 'ta'ke?e -- ,'?e'nuh"?pia?a 'ri"ra + "por 'ke?e -- ,'?ka?a"?pah '?ku"ne?et + , '?txuh"?kun '?a'ui"ra + ,'u'tah"no?or "ia?ax + , 'in'ta"kix + ,'?tih"?tem '?tih"?te 'mu"me 'ne "ro?p + ,"por 'ke?e'ha?a"xo?p '?a'ia"no?p + ,'?i "ne?et '?a'?pah"ner + .'tu"?ka '?i"xi 'na"txe +

185 + ,'?i'?a'tsa?a"io?p + ."por 'ke?e "ne?en '?ũ?ũm"?pi + 186 + ,"kuan 'do'?u'iak 'te?e"to?p + .'txe?e"no?p + ,'ber'dix"to 'ke'?in 'ta"ka '?o"hron + .'ka'lo?ok"se '?i"xik "tu?ut + 191 + '?i?i -- ,'?i'ha?a"xo?p '?a'tsa?a"io?p + ."por 'ke?e'?ka?a"?pa '?u'iah'?ke?e"to?p +

194 + ,?i'ha?ax"to + .'?e'?ah"tso?o "txe + "pe 'ro?o -- .'ta'ma"ret '?u'iah'?ke?e"to?p + , 'ko"ne?er + '?iŋ'gua?a"re?et 'ke?e -- 'ma?a"txi "tua?a -- ,'ka'tu"ruan + '?im"?puts 'ka?a -- , 'ka"txe 'bi"bir + ,'si"no 'ka'?a'?kah"pa?a '?kah "pa + ,'ka"txe 'pe"liar + ,"por 'ke?e'ta'ma"ret + ,'?ka?a"?pa '?u'iah"?ke?en + .'?e'ui'ni"ko '?pi"ra + 208 + ."txe 'ke?e + ,"kuan 'do'?a?a "uan + '?a?a -- ,'tis'ki"ni + ,"to?o 're'ti"nah + "txe 'ke?e -- "ha?ax 'e'?ah"?kuts 'u"txe + "kuan 'do?o -- .'nuh"?pi + 217 + "por 'ke?e "txe 'ke?e -- "?pan 'u"txe '?e?e -- ,'?e'?pah "xan 'txum"pi?i 'xe?e'nuh"?pi?i + ,'?i'?pan"to 'u"txe?e 'txum"pi?i "?ehs 'to'ko"ne?er + '?a?a "uan 'a'tis'ki"ni +

11. Turkeys

222 + '?i"kuan 'do?o -- 'u'iah"?ku '?u "?po?o?p + ,'?in'ta"rer + ,'?e?em"pa "to?or 'u 'pia?a"ro?p + .'u'iah"?ku?u "?po?p + 227 + "por 'ke?e"txe 'ke?e -- "?pan '?u"txe '?e?e -- '?e?e -- .'?e'?pah"xan 'txum"pi?i + 231 + '?i 'po"re 'su"?pan '?u?u -- ,'?u'ia"ro '?pes'to'ko "ne?er + 'ma?a -- 'ma?a"txi '?a?a -- ,'?a'?tsoh "ii '?u'?pah'ne"ro?p + 'si"no 'ke?e -- ,'?in'ta "rer + ,'?u'?pu"?ti 'u"?po?p + ,"to?o 'ru'pia?a "ro?p + .'?u'iah"?kuo?p +

11. Turkeys

1 There is another story the people tell. 5 They say that the tom turkey, with the hen turkey, they say when -- they married, were happy. When they heard the setting up of the musicians in the house, the beginning of the playing, they were happy. They stood and began dancing to the music from the house, because they were happy.

22 And -- they say that -- when night came they were dancing, and -- then the -- the tom turkey got drunk, because he was being given chicha to drink. 35 And he got drunk. 36 And because of the drunkenness, since -- he became drunk, they say that he stood up and went crazy.

41 And -- he began to shout, 44 saying, "lok, lok, lok". 46 Then the people said, "And now the -- these spouses here seem to want to fight each other."

52 And he was standing on the floor of the house, dancing, but he was shouting 58 over and over, saying "lok, lok, lok". 62 Because -- he was drunk. And -- then the -- the wife, as she saw that -- her husband was shouting, then she began to shout too. 72 She said, "txo?ok, txo?ok, txo?ok".

74 Then the people who were there at the wedding said, "Now, these spouses are just going to fight each other now." 83 They say that then the tom turkey, since he was already angry, saw the people who were there and -- was eyeing his friends, who were there. All at once his head turned red. 97 His head just turned blood-red from anger.

100 When he saw his friends come out he began to say "lok, lok, lok". 107 Then the

others who were there said, "You are a real man.
111 You are standing there shouting -- 112
Well, we can shout too." 114 Then the others
who were there began to say "lok, lok". They
began to shout, the -- those guests.

123 When he heard that -- they were shout-
ing at him, then he said, "You, you came to my
fiesta, not for any other reason or interest,
you are interested in my wife. 133 You want to
see me dancing with her. 135 That is why you
came too. But -- if you want to see, now I will
test your courage."

139 Then they say that he threw himself on
top of his friends. 142 He said, "hu?urik, hu-
?urik, 145 hu?urik". 146 He frightened the
others.

147 But the others said -- they said, "But
we are many; what are we waiting for, not test-
ing the courage of this ... groom." 156 They
say that they piled on top of the groom's head
and began to beat him.

161 And then when day broke, they say that
the head of that groom was just pecked all over,
when day broke. And he was told by his wife,
171 "You were standing there shouting, and we
didn't come out well with this wedding, because
they beat you up. Look at your head, all pecked
up by them, because they are many. And you by
yourself, what were you doing?

185 "And they are happy, because I heard
187 when they left you, they said, 'He was just
talk -- let's take his woman from him.' 191
And they were pleased because they beat you all
up."

11. Turkeys

194 And then the tom turkey said, "But they beat me because of you. Now I tell you that -- we are not going to live well together, rather now and then we will fight, for because of you, they just beat me up, those men."

208 They say that when he is standing, strutting around the house lot, they say that that is the dance he did when he was married. 217 Because, they say, so did the first turkey who married, and so too do turkeys to this day; they go strutting around.

222 And when they fight, they all fall on top of their companions, and beat each other up. 227 Because they say that so did the -- the first turkey. 231 And therefore so its children to this day don't ... fight alone, but all at once pile on top of their companions and beat them up.

12. Buzzard

1 + ,'?ka"ni 'in"txe 'kon"tar + 'in"te?e -- ,'?o'hro"ner + ,'lo'ke?e'?u'?kah"ti '?a"ni + '?e?e -- .'?o"nia?aŋ "hen 'te + 7 + ,'?a"ian 'in"te?e + ,'?o'hro"ner + .'?a'?kah"na + 'ke?e -- ,'?a"ian 'in"te?e "di 'ia + .'tah'ui"na 'in 'te?e'ui"nik + 13 + ,'?ie?e'ui"nik 'ia"ha?a + "txe 'ke?e -- '?e?e -- ,'sak"sak "u?ut 'u"pix + 17 + '?i?i -- .'?a'ro?p"na + 19 + '?e?e -- , "ne?et + 'tu"?ka?a -- .'pat"na?ar '?a'na?a"ta + 23 + '?e?e -- "ua 'riŋ'gui"ra '?u?ut'a"pix "ia?ax 'ke?e -- 'in'ta"kix 'nn -- ."tan "tan +

27 + ."?a?a 'ha?a"xir "txe + 28 + , "ne?en + ,'ni'pat"na?ar + '?e?e -- "ha?ax '?e?e -- '?e?e -- '?e?e -- .'txe"iah 'o"tot + 35 + . "tia?a '?im'pehk"na + ,'tua?a'?a?an"txi '?iŋ"goh 'ro"tot + .'?in"xin + 38 + ,"por 'ke?e"ha?ax 'ni'pat"na?ar "ne?en + '?i'ta"mar 'in -- '?in 'num"se 'ni?i -- .'ni"?pa + 42 + .'ta"mar 'in 'ta"hui -- .'tu"?kaŋ '?ku"xi +

44 + ,'?en"ton 'ses + ."txe "tua?a + 46 + .'ko"txa?aŋ "kai 'ka"nue?et +

47 + .'ha?a"xir "txe + ,"ne?en + "kai 'ka "nue?en 'por'ke?e -- 'ni?i -- ,'pia?a"ro?p + , '?in"so 'lo + .'?al'ban"ii 'lo?p + 54 + ,'?i 'po"re 'so"ne?e 'nu"?pan + .'ka"nue?en + 'ii?i -- '?in"te?e "to 'ni'uer"maa "no?o?p + '?e?e -- ,"ha?ax '?u'pat'na?a"ro '?pu"?pan + ,"por 'ke?e "no?on + "ko 'txa?a -- "ha?a 'xe"ra 'ka?a -- 'ka?a -- ,'ka'pia?a"ro?p 'xe?e'?pah'xa"no?p + , '?al'ban'ii"lo?p + '?i'tu"no?o "ron "no?on "?pan 'ka'lo"?koi '?a?a -- .'?al'ban'ii"lon +

68 + '?en"ton 'ses + .'txe"tua?a + '?ie?e -- '?ie?e -- '?e?e -- '?e"kal + ."tia?a 'ta"hui '?a'ma"nil +

75 + 'ha?a"xir "txe?e -- 'ne?e -- ,'?e"kal

12. Buzzard

+ ."ne?en 'i"ra 'lo"?koi 'in"txe +

79 + '?e?e -- ,'en"ton 'ses + '?e?e -- , "txe "tua?a + 'ke?e -- "no?on '?ka'na?a"ni 'ka 'ui"ra + 'ko"txa?a '?a?a -- '?a"txe?e -- .'?e "kal 'lo'ke?e'?a'po'nio?o"tot 'ta"mar +

88 + '?i'ha?a"xir "txe 'hai'?ka"ni?iŋ 'gui "ra '?i?i -- .'?iŋ'guir"sio?ox + 90 + ,"txe 'ke?e'?i"xin + ,'?i"xin 'pa"kuan 'ta'man"te?e '?u'?ka?p"te?e + ,'?u'iak"ta 'ta"ri 'ta"rum + '?e?e -- '?e?e -- ."blaŋ 'ko'ko'txe?e"kal + 'ko 'txe?e'pu?u?k"?pir -- ."tan +

98 + ,'?en"ton 'ses + "txe "tua?a '?u"me 'ne?e -- '?e'ui'ni"ko?p 'lo'ke?e -- ,"uar '?o?o "hron 'ta"kar + 102 + ,"pe 'ro'si"ne?et + , 'ma?a"txi "ha?ax + ,'tu"?ka?a "xix "ua 'ra'?kam "pes + .'?a'ua?a"re 'ke'?al'ban'ii"len + 106 + ,"pe 'ro'si'?a"ta?a 'ta"ka?ah "txi?i + ."blaŋ 'ko + '?i'ta"mar 'ki"sas '?a?a -- .'?a'ua?a"re 'ke'?al'ban'ii"len +

110 + '?en"ton 'ses + ,'ha?a"xir + "txe -- 'ke?e'ma?a'txix"to '?o'hro"nian 'si"no 'ke?e -- '?e?e -- ,'lo'ke'ha?a"xi 'ru"txe + ,"kon 'de'?a 'ro?p"na + .'?u"txe 'u"nu?u?k + '?e?e -- ."hos "hos + ."hos "hos + "por 'ke?e"txe 'ke?e -- '?kih"na "kuan 'do?o -- '?a'ro?p"na 'ke'ta'mu?u "ta?a "uar 'u'ma"hres '?e?e -- .'?e"hen 'te'ke?e 'ha?a"xir '?al'ba"niil + ,'?in'ta'kix"to + , '?o?o'sre"ma + .'pa"kar 'ta'mu?u"?ka?p '?e"te?e +

126 + ."txe "tua?a '?u"me 'ne'ui'ni"ko?p + 127 + "hai '?i'?kih"na '?o?oi"?pi 'lo'ke"uar 'ka'ua?a"re?et + "pe 'ro"no?on "uar 'ka'ua?a "re?et + 'lo'ke'?e?e"ra?atx +

130 + 'ha?a"xir "txe 'ke?e -- ,'sut"pa 'u

12. Buzzard

'ui"ra '?e'ui'ni"ko?p 'ia"ha?a + "pe 'ro'?es
'to?o -- ."iax '?tuh"na '?u"hor + .'?u"me 'ne
'?kih"na?ar + 'ie?e -- '?e?e -- '?e'ui"nik 'ia
"ha?a 'xe?e"uar "txe 'ke?e'?al'ba"niil + "ha?ax
,'?a?a'ro?p"na 'ko"ne?er '?e?e -- .'?e'men"ta
'do'?u"sih + "txe 'ke?e -- ,'?e'?u"sih + '?e?e
-- '?u"ta?a '?tsu?u"?pa 'ke'ha?a"xir '?al'ban
"iil + ,'?i'ke?e'?e"rer ,'?a'lo"?koi '?u"txe 'o
"tot + '?i'ke'?a'lo"?koi '?u?u -- ,'?u'?po"ni'?o
"tot + '?e?e -- 'ta'ke?e -- '?e?e -- .'tua?a'?u
"txe 'sak"sak +

152 + '?i?i -- 'po"re 'so?o -- ,'ko"ne?er
+ ,'?e'?u"sih 'ka'ui"ra + ."blaŋ 'ku?ut'u"pix +
157 + '?i'tia?a'a"ta?an + "blaŋ 'ko + 159 +
"por 'ke?e -- "txe 'ke?e -- .'ha?a"xir '?al'ba
"niil +

162 + 'ha?a"xir "txe 'ke?e -- "kon 'da?a
-- '?ix"to + ,'?u'tah"uu?u "?pa 'ta'ke?e'ui'ni
"ko?p 'ia"ha?a + '?a"ian '?in"te?e 'txi"nam
'?a?a -- '?e?e -- ,'txe"ker + ,'tia?a'?u'tah
"uu?u "?po?p + .'?u'ia?a"ra?ai 'ie?e'ui'ni"ko?p
+ 'ke?e -- ,'?e"sia 'no'to"to?p 'lo'ke?e'?u'ui
"ra 'ia"ha?a + ,'ga'la"nik 'sak"sak + 174 + .
"pe 'ro'?in"so 'lo'ni'tra"ba 'ho + 175 + .'?in
"so 'lo"ne?en 'ko?o"ien 'ta"mar + 176 + .
"ne?en 'ka'uin"txi + 177 + ,'ga"lan + .'?u'uir
"na?ar + ,'?io?o'to"to?p 'ia"ha?a + "pe 'ro'?in
"so 'lo"ne?en "ka?a -- "ka 'ii?i -- .'im'?po"ni
+

183 + '?en"ton 'ses "txe?e 'ui'ni"ko?p
"pues -- 'hai -- ,'ie?e"ra?atx 'ke"ne?et + ,'?al
'ba'nii"let + "ti?in "di 'ia'ka?a"xi 'ka'txah
"niet 'tua?a -- 'tua?a -- '?a"txe -- .'?a"txe
'ko?o"tot + 191 + "por 'ke"no?on + 'ma?a"txi
'?a?a -- '?u'iu"?pio?on 'tua?a'ka"txe?e -- .'?in
"gohr 'ko?o"tot 'xe?e'sak"sak + 195 + '?i
"ti?in "di 'ia + 'ka?a"xi 'ka?a -- ,'ka'?txah

12. Buzzard

"nie?et + 'tua?a -- .'?a"txe '?iŋ"gohr 'ko?o"tot + 'xe?e -- .'xe?e'sak"sak +

202 + "txe 'ke?e -- .'?a'ro?p"na + ,'?u"me 'ne'ui'ni"ko?p 'ia"ha?a + 205 + ,"ne?et + '?o?o"tot 'tia?a'?i'ua"ien + 'ki"sas + .'ga"lan '?u'uir"na?ar +

109 + ,"?aa + "txe 'ha?a"xir + ,"?aa "ne?en + ,'ni'?o"tot + '?e?e -- .'ga"lan 'tia?a 'iŋ'gua"ian + 215 + ,'ma?a"txo?o "txoi 'e'si "sar + "nien -- ,"nien 'e'?i"?kar + 'ma?a"txo?o "txoi 'ta"mar "por 'ke?e -- ,'?kah"na?ar 'us'tam "?pir 'ni'me"ner + '?i?i -- .'ga"lan 'sak"sak 'tia?a'iŋ'gua"ian +

222 + ,'?en"ton 'ses"txe?e 'moh"ro?p + , "pues "no?on + .'ma?a"txu?u 'iu"?pio?on + 225 + "no?on 'ka"txa?a 'uan"tar '?e?e -- '?e?e -- , '?e'si"sar + "por 'ke?e'?o?o"txoi '?e?ei"?kar 'tia?a -- 'tia?a'ka'ua"ian + 230 + '?i?i -- '?i'po"re 'so + "no?oŋ + ,'ka"uar 'ke?en"te?e "di 'ia + '?ka"ni 'ka'?txa"nie?et 'tua?a -- '?a?a -- '?a"txe?e -- .'?a"txe 'ko?o"tot + 238 + "pe 'ro?o -- "no?on 'ma?a"txi 'ka'na?a"ta '?a?a -- ,'?a'ko"mi 'da'lo'kia'?ku"xi + ,'?a'sa "ber + .'tu"?ka?a 'tu"?ka?a '?ku"xi "ne?et +

243 + ,'ha?a"xir "txe + "ne?en 'ni?i -- , 'ni'ko"mi 'da'lo'ke'in'?ku"xi + .'?in"so 'lo "ue?er + 247 + ,"ne?en + 'ma?a"txi?iŋ '?ku "xi?i -- ,'tu"?ki?i?k "xix + "ne?en 'ta'ma"ue?er 'ta'ka'tu"re?en +

251 + '?i?i -- ."txe "tua?a + 253 + .'?i "tia?a 'tah"ui + '?e?e -- 'tua?a'?a'?ku"xi 'ke?e -- .'ko"txa?a 'ko"txa?a '?a'ta"hui +

257 + .'ha?a"xir "txe + 258 + ,"ne?en + 'ni?i -- ,'?e"ue?er 'lo'ke'?iŋ'?ku"xi + .'ma

12. Buzzard

"ha?ax '?in'te?e"ra + 262 + ,'?iŋ'?ku"xi '?e 'ua"kax + ,'?iŋ'?ku"xi '?e"txih + ,'?iŋ'?ku"xi '?e"?tsi?i + '?i?i -- ,'?a"?katx + ,'txum"pi?i + '?i?i "hai -- '?i"hai -- .'?iŋ"koht + ,"hen 'te 'tia?a "?txa?ar 'txa"men + .'?iŋ'?ku"xi '?u"?pan + 273 + ,"por 'ke"ne?en + ,'ni'ko"mi 'da + , 'xe?eiŋ'?ku"xi + ."ha?ax '?e'ga"lan '?o?oh"?tsun + 277 + "por 'ke'xe?e -- ,'?oh"?tsun + ."ha?ax '?iŋ'?ku"xi "ne?en +

280 + ,'?en"ton 'ses + ,"txe?e 'ui'ni"ko?p + "pe 'rok -- .'tu"?ka?a "ta?a 'tix'?e"ma 'soh "tsun +

284 + .'ha?a"xir "txe + ."kon 'da'?iŋ"koht 'ua"kax + .'?o?o'iŋ"koht "txih + ,'?txa?ar 'txa "men + 'ta'ma'?e?e -- ,"tres "di 'ia"?txa?ar 'txa"men + '?a"ka?ai '?o?o'?pok"na + '?i?i -- '?i?i -- '?a'txek"ta '?u'iuhts"ner + ,'?u'iuh "?tsi "ne?en + .'?in"xiŋ 'gui"ra + 296 + .'?i 'ta"mar 'ta'ka'tu"re?en + 297 + "ha?ax '?e"ra 'ni'ko"mi 'da"ne?en + 298 + '?i'hai -- ,"no?ox + '?ka"ni?i -- '?i'mah"nen "tua?an 'txi -- '?in "txe?e -- ,'io?o"tot + '?e?e -- ."pues + '?e"rer '?i?i -- '?i'txam"se 'iŋ"kohk '?i?i -- 'ua"kax + '?o?o -- ,'tu"?ka?a "ien 'ti?i"?pa + "pe 'ri?i -- '?i?i -- 'i'?txa"?pu 'tu?u"tahn '?e"?kin + '?e?e -- .'tua?a'?o?oh'?tsun"lan + ."tua?aŋ '?ku "xi + 317 + ,"por 'ke"ne?en + 'ma?a"txi?iŋ '?ku"xi '?in"te?e -- .'ko"mi 'da'xe'ma?a"txoh "?tsun +

320 + ,'?i'po"re 'so'ko"ne?er + ,'?iu"sih + ,'?u'koh"ko 'a'tuh"ran 'e"?tsi?i + ,'?e'ua"kax '?e"txih + '?e'?a"?katx + 'tu"no?or 'lo'ke?e -- '?a?a -- ,'?a'txa"mai + ,'?ia?a'tu"hran + .'ta "mar '?a"ue?e + 330 + "por 'ke"txe 'ke?e -- . "ha?ax '?e'?oh"?tsun '?u'na?a"ta + 332 + , 'ha?a"xir + "mix 'u'?ku"xi '?in"te?e -- '?in "te?e "ko 'sa'xe?e -- 'ma?a"txi 'to'?a?a -- .'?a

12. Buzzard

'puk"ta 'u"tui?ir + 337 + ,"por 'ke'ha?a"xir +
."txe 'ke'xe?e'?o?oh"?tsun '?u'?ka"ni +

339 + ,'ha?ax"to 'e"ra + ,'?u'kon"ta 'ha +
.'?iu"sih +

12. Buzzard

1 I'm going to tell a story that the old people used to tell. 7 There is a story that is told, that -- one day a man came along. 13 And that man -- they say, his knees were white. 17 And he was spoken to: 19 "You there, what work do you do? 23 I see that your knees there are all dusty."

27 And he said, 28 "Me, my work is that of -- house building. 35 Wherever I am called to put up a house, I go. 38 Because that is my work. And that is how I make my living. 42 That is how I get what I eat."

44 Then they said to him, 46 "How did you learn how?"

47 He said, "I learned how because my friends were all masons. 54 And so I learned also. And -- then one of my brothers -- it is his work too, because we, since -- it is they, our friends, who were the first masons. And all of us, we have also become masons."

68 Then they said to him, "And the lime, that you got on your mason's apron?"

75 He said, "The lime, I can make it."

79 And then, they said to him that -- "We would like to see how you make the lime that you spread on the house."

88 And he said, "If you want to see, I will show you." 90 They say that he went and roosted on a branch, and let fall to the ground something that was white, like lime, like watery mud.

98 Then the men who were speaking to him

said, 102 "But you -- that's not something you use -- you say 'I am a mason,' 106 but it's just that your droppings are white, and maybe that is why you say 'I am a mason.'

110 Then he, they say, -- could not speak. Instead, what he did when they said that to him, -- he said, in his throat, "Hos, hos. Hos, hos." Because they say that he was angry when he was told that with his droppings he was deceiving people, (saying) that he was a mason. And just then he was going "Hos, hos," perched on the branch of a tree.

126 He was told by the men 127 "If you get angry when you hear what we tell you -- well we are just telling you what is true."

130 He said that -- he looked again at those men. But -- his head turned bluish from anger. And -- the men who say they are masons, they say today, that the buzzard, they say, the buzzard, whose droppings pile up, is a mason, and that he can make houses, and that he spreads the houses with that which he makes white.

152 And therefore today we see that the buzzard's knees are white. 157 And where he leaves his droppings, it is white. 159 Because they say that -- he is a mason.

162 He said that -- when he met those men, there was a town -- there where they met. The men there said that -- the many houses they saw there were beautifully white.

174 "But it is just my work. 175 Am I even tired from it? 176 Have I collapsed? 177 Those houses look beautiful. But I alone plastered them."

12. Buzzard

183 Then the men said, "Well if it is true that you are a mason, how many days would it take for you to make us a house? 191 Because we are not able to make a house that is white. 195 And how many days would it take for you to make a house that is white?"

202 They say that those men said to him, 205 "You, your house where you sleep must be very pretty to look at.

209 He said, "Ah, my house, it is beautiful where I sleep. 215 The cold does not come in, nor does the wind come in, because it has been fixed up especially, by me. And it is very white where I sleep."

222 Then the others said, "Well, we can't do that. 225 We endure the cold, because the wind comes in where we sleep. 230 And so we want you to make us a house some day. 238 But we do not know what you eat at your meals. We wonder what you eat."

243 And he said, "Me, the meals that I eat are all meat. 247 I don't eat just anything. I live on meat."

251 And they said to him, "And where do you get what you eat? Where do you find it?"

257 He said, 258 "Me, my -- the meat I eat is not all the same. 262 I eat cow, I eat horse, I eat dog, and chicken, turkey -- and if -- and if there is a person lying dead, I eat him too. 273 Because I -- my meals that I eat smell wonderful. 277 Because what smells, that is what I eat."

280 Then the men said, "But -- what smells

the most?"

284 He said, "When a cow or a horse has lain dead for three days, it begins to rot. And -- and -- its smell appears, and I smell it and go to see. 296 And that is what I live on. 297 That is my meal. 298 And if you want to hire me to make your house, well, you must kill a cow for me, or -- whatever you have. But -- lay it in the sun, and -- so it will smell, so I will eat it. 317 Because I do not eat a meal that does not smell."

320 And so today the buzzard waits for the dog, the cow, the horse, the chicken; everything that dies, to become valuable, to become good for him to eat. 330 Because they say that he knows the smell. 332 He does not eat anything that does not have value, 337 because he -- they say that it is the smell he likes.

339 And that is the story of the buzzard.

13. Ants

1 + ,'?ka"nin "txe 'kon"tar + '?u 'io'hro "ner 'e?e -- ,'?e'?o'hro"ner + .'ta'me?e '?ti "sim + 5 + "txe 'ke?e -- "kon 'da?a -- 'ma?a "ta?a "ni 'tu"?ka?a -- '?e?e -- ,'?e"nar + ,'?a 'pah"?ka + '?e?e -- ,'ma?a'txi"to + '?a"ia?a -- '?a'txe?e"na 'ko'no"ser '?e?e -- ,'?e"nar + '?e?e -- "txe 'ke?e -- ,'tan"te?e "di 'ia + '?e?e -- .'?e'?ti"sim + '?u?u -- ,'?u'txek"tes + "por 'ke'txe?e"no?p 'ke?e"ia 'he?e -- '?e?e -- , '?a"ian '?in"te?e "dios + ,'?a?a'ro?p"na "san 'ma"nuel + '?e?e -- ."mon 'te'de"o 'ro + 28 + "txe 'ke?e"ia 'he?e -- '?e?e -- ,'?e"dios 'ia "ha?a + "?iatx -- ."?ia 'txek"te?e "nar '?pah "xan + 33 + '?i?i -- ,'?ie"hen 'te + ,'ma?a "txu?u 'na?a"to?p + 'ma?a"txu?u 'txok -- 'ma?a "txu?u -- '?u'na?a"to?o -- '?u'na?a"to?p 'ko"txa 'tua?a -- .'tu"?ka 'e"nar +

41 + ,'?en"ton 'ses'?e'?ti"sim + "txe 'ke?e -- ,"ko 'nda'sa'koh"pa + '?e?e -- 'tu"ru '?u?u -- '?u"muhr 'ta'ma?a -- .'u"su 'io?o"tot + 48 + '?i?ix"no?p 'kai'?u?u -- ,'?u'pik"to?o?p + ,'?u"muhr 'e'?ti"sim + ."txe 'ke'?u'tah"uio?p 'in"gohr "ier 'u'?ti"sim "?txa?ar 'ta"mar + , ,'?i?i -- ,"kon 'da'?ix"to + 'na?a"?ki 'ie're "nar 'ia"ha?a + ,"kai 'u'ke"tio?p + ."?ehs 'to 'ke"?pan 'u'?po'roh"sio?p + "txe 'ke'?pa'nix"to '?ko"toi 'txek"ta '?e?e -- .'?e"nar + ."pe 'ro '?e"nar "txe 'ke'ma'ku?u"rum 'ta"ri + 62 + "ha?a 'xe'?ti"sim '?u?u -- .'?u'txek"tes "to?or 'e"rum +

64 + ,'?i'po"re 'so'ko"ne?e 're"hen 'te + '?e?e -- ,'tia?a'?u'ui"ro?p 'tu"ru '?u"muh 're '?ti"sim + ,'?a"tsa?ai '?u'ui"ro?p + "por 'ke "txe 'ke?e -- '?e?e -- '?e?e -- .'?u"mu 'hre'?ti "sim 'ga"lan 'a'na"ri + 72 + "por 'ke'txe?e "no?p 'ke"ha?a 'xe'?ti"sim 'u?u -- .'?u'txek"tes 'e"nar +

13. Ants

1 I am going to tell his story -- the story of the ant. 5 They say that back when -- there was no corn to plant, and corn was not known, they say that one day the ants discovered it. Because they say that there was a God called San Manuel -- Monte de Oro. 28 They say that that God first discovered corn. 33 And people did not know -- how -- about corn.

41 Then the ants, they say, when day broke -- their anthill was right next to the house. 48 And (the people) went to stir up the anthill. They say that they found a little ant lying in it, and they took him and planted him. 54 And when that corn grew up, they kept it until it had multiplied. They say that that is how corn appeared. But they say that corn was within the earth. 62 And it was the ant that made it appear above the earth.

64 And that is why people today, where they see an anthill, they are happy to see it, because they say that the anthill is great for growing corn. 72 Because they say that it was the ants that brought forth corn.

GROUP II

NOTES

6. Toad and Hawk

6.4-5 An earlier version of this tale was the first I collected, in the summer of 1964. In it, Gonzalez interpolated at this point, 'u '?kah"te?e 'nuk"ta 'ui'ni"ko?p 'The old men tell it'.

6.7-8 The earlier version has the information from 6.29-33 here.

6.34-43 In place of this dialogue, the earlier version has the toad asking at this point, 'tu"?ka "di 'ii?i"xin 'tia?a 'tu"ru 'e "dios 'What day are you going to where God is?', and the hawk, mistakenly identified as the toad, answering, 'in"xin 'eh"?kar 'I'm going tomorrow'. The toad replies, 'in"xin 'ta'ka"ret 'I'm going with you'.

6.42 The ik 'injunctive' suffix with a negative. See Fought 1967:235-6.

6.48 Spanish vigilar 'watch over'. A bolsa is an agave-fiber bag, of open or tight weave, with a shoulder strap, as is commonly used all over Central America. A number are shown in the photograph in Wisdom 1940 facing 386.

6.51-2 This is missing from the earlier version, though the ix 'already' of 6.57 depends on it.

6.59 In the earlier version, this passage is added here: 'ie?e -- .'e"muan 'u'uah"pi 'e "bol 'sa'u'?ke"txi?i "xin 'And -- the hawk grabbed the bag and carried it away'.

6.69 The root ioop means 'arrive here' (i.e. where the speaker and addressee are), and ?kot means 'arrive there' (i.e. anywhere else). Thus, in 6.61-2 the narrator uses ?kot but the participants here use ioop for the same event.

6.71-72 Here the earlier version has 'e

6. Toad and Hawk

'kom"pa 'gre"?pir "txe 'the compadre said'.

6.74 Literally, 'I arrived here more first than you'.

6.75-82 This repetition is missing from the earlier version. Instead, it has 'i?i -- 'e 'kom"pa 'gre"?pir 'e"muan 'ma?a"txu?u 'na?a"ta 'i"ha?ax 'u?k -- .'u'?ke"txe 'u'kom"pa 'gre'i "xin 'And -- compadre hawk didn't know, and he -- carried his compadre along'.

6.89 Earlier 'e?ek"mai 'to come down'.

6.90 Earlier, 'e'kom"pa 'gre"?pir 'the compadre'.

6.91 In the earlier version, this replaces 6.94.

6.95-100 Omitted from the earlier version.

6.96 The earlier version interpolates just before this, 'a"si 'ke?e'?u'ui"ra 'u'kom"pa 'gre 'as he saw his compadre do'.

6.106 Earlier, 'ta"rum 'to the earth'.

6.108 Earlier, 'he?ek"txa 'u"na?a?k 'his middle spread out'. There are few examples of this tx suffix in the corpus, but its final vowel varies and it is, as here, roughly reflexive. Perhaps it is derivationally related to txe 'do'.

6.109-113 Omitted from the earlier version.

6.118-120 In the earlier version, 'noh "ta?a -- "?o 'ru'keh"re?p 'the top of his shoulders (or back) is big'.

6.121-130 The earlier version has instead only "por 'ke"txe 'ke?e'u'io"?pu?u "?pa 'tia?a '?ka"xi 'Because they say he broke where he fell'.

6. Toad and Hawk

6.131-136 Earlier, only _"pe_ _'ro"ne?en_ _'ma?a"txiŋ_ _'gui"ra_ 'But I didn't see it'. The kind of joke at the end of 6 is more normal.

7. Toad

7.26-31 Since Jocotán center lies in a valley, persons going downward on a trail are presumably going there, while those climbing up may be going to one of several settlements. Thus, the downward-bound participant in an encounter asks 'Where are you going?' as a greeting. The toad's response here is equally formulaic.

7.39 In Pelillo, '?pa'nix"to 'thus' is used more often; in Tunucó and Matasano, 'i'kox "to as here. These are not substitutable for 'ko"txa 'so, how, as', as in 7.58.

7.58* From -ix-to i-?kai-ui by A. The last syllable begins with a high front rounded vowel gliding to unrounded.

7.87 The expired, perfective portion of 'today' is sahmi; the imperfective part is koneer, hence, 'today' or 'nowadays'. The text here refers to the small hours of the morning of that day -- the usual use of sahmi.

7.91 Literally, 'it doesn't come out well, your singing'.

7.94 The root is su?p 'crumple'.

7.103 Literally, 'his eyes skinned'.

7.107 The root is nuk with 'cursive' and 'causative' suffixes. Compare nuk-ir tee 'a big tree', and nuk-taa hente 'big (old) people'.

7.110 This form is used only for large round objects. The ik is apparently a relic of the Mayan ik plural.

7.112 More exactly, 'he keeps blinking his eyes'. The root is muu?ts : 'u'mu?u"?tsi 'he closes his eyes (once)'.

7.119* From ma atxi a-u?p-na by B, C.

7.142* From ti-ka&-hut by H, &, B.

8. Raccoon

8.14 The root is *kor* 'keep'. Compare *u&-kor-vr-tee-ir e-nar* 'corn-crib', or 'wooden corn keeper'.

8.30 The root is *sut* 'turn'; the 'reflexive' suffix makes this an exact parallel of English 'turn into'.

8.60* From *-ix-to u&-ak-ta u&-?pa* by A, &; B, &.

9. Coyote

9.9 The ears of corn are *nar*.

9.10 The root *sak* 'send' is used for people; things are sent with *he?p* : *'iŋ'gue?p"ta* 'I send it (of a letter)'.

9.11 A man's child is *unen*; a woman's is *ar*.

9.74-75 Note the equivalence of the periphrastic reflexive with *?pa* 'self', 'body', and *-pa* 'reflexive'.

10. Armadillo

10.7-15 The Chorti do not work during thunderstorms, they say; they sit quietly indoors, not talking much or doing anything to attract attention to themselves until the storm passes.

10.16* From a-hih?p-i by H, B.

10.28 More closely, 'It is feared that...'

10.38 A regular alternant, from vn-hir-i.

10.40 The root is ?kin 'heat', 'sun', 'sky', with the h 'potential' infix.

10.72 Spanish seña. Compare 10.92.

10.102 Compare kot-vr here, 'crouching', with pak-vr '(lying) face down' above in 10.64.

10.117 Both io?p and ie?p are variants meaning 'under'.

10.142* From vn&-uee by &. Compare 10. 145.

10.145 More closely, 'the rain causes me to eat...'

10.175 Spanish verdad.

10.214 'Thick' in the sense of viscous is pim.

10.218 The san is an emphatic particle. It only appears in direct address, either actual or fictional, as here.

10.294 A typical use of the agentive prefix ah, for slightly intensive effect.

10.297 The root is ?kah 'have in mind'.

11. Turkeys

11.40 A Spanish loan, loco, is thematized here, with 'factitive' h, 'cursive' r, and thematic an.

11.96 The root is txak 'red'. Compare sak-oh-pa 'it got white' or 'light'; the variant sok-oh-pa is paralleled by a txok-oh-pa.

11.108 The root mor 'gather' here is used with an h infix as a substantive, 'others'.

11.121 Here ta-ka with a 'cursive' r and thematic e is an active form: to 'with', i.e. 'accompany' or 'assist' someone. Compare 11. 125.

11.174 From lo?k-vi-on bien by V, C, and assimilation of n.

11.177* From ?kaap-a ah?k-u-na-et by C; A.

11.202 Spanish vivir.

11.204 Spanish pelear.

11.225 The root is em 'descend', with a 'reflexive' suffix.

12. Buzzard

12.1 There are many parallels between this and texts 7 and 11. Since González did not remember this story at first, and then asked for time to think about it before recording it, I suspect it is somewhat scrambled, and that the comeuppance portion, 12.68-151, should follow the boasting of 12.162-319 and precede the explanation, 12.320-339.

12.39-41 More closely, 'by it I get along'.

12.96-97 More exactly, like *tan* 'dust' made into watery mud.

12.133 This is the active form of a compound color term, *iax* *?tun-en* 'black-and-blue', described as the color of a ripe bruise, or of rotten meat. The term for 'real' *iax* is *iaxax*; its range includes blue and green.

12.147 The root is *?pon* 'stain'.

12.170* From *u&-aar-e* *aii* *e-* by A; A.

13. Ants

13.4 The ?tis-vm (Spanish zompopos) are army ants.

13.25 San Manuel Monte de Oro or Sombrerón is a duente (Spanish duende) who hides from the thunder in the center of the earth. He receives the offering for rain on April 25 (formerly on March 25), consisting of chicks buried alive. He caught the blood of Christ at the crucifixion.

13.71 In almost every other occurrence, nar 'ear of corn' is a substantive. It is 'activated' here by simply affixing thematic and personal elements to it.

13.73 More directly, 'they caused corn to appear'.

III: Mores

14. *Indians and Ladinos*

15. *The Parent's Curse*

16. *The Henpecked Husband*

17. *The Henpecked Salesman*

18. *The Traveling Man*

14. Indians and Ladinos

1 + ,'?a"ia 'no'tron"te?e '?o'hro"ner + ,'u'?kah"ti 'e"hen 'te + ,'ta"rix + .'?e"tiem 'po + 5 + 'ke?e -- ,'ta'man"te?e "di 'ia + '?e?e -- ,'?e"dios + ,'?u'mo'roh"se + '?e?e -- ,'tu"no?or + ,'?e"hen 'te + ,'?u'mo'roh"se + .'u 'tu'ru"?pa 'ta'?u'ieh"?tser + 15 + .'?u'?kah "tio '?pa"ni + 'ke?e -- ,'tu"no?or "hen 'te + '?e?e -- .'?a"ian '?u"?txu?ur + '?e?e -- ,'?a'se "gun 'ko"txa + '?e?e -- ,'?e"ra 'sa'?e"hen 'te + .'txe?e"no?p 'ke'?a"ian 'u"?txu?ur + 25 + ,'u '?kah"tio '?pa"ni + 'ke?e -- .'ta'man"te?e "di 'ia + ,'?u"?txu?ur + '?e?e -- ,'?e"hen 'te + '?e?e -- ,'?e"ra 'sa -- ,'?in"di 'he'na + "txe 'ke?e -- '?in -- .'tan"te?e "di 'ia + ,'txe?e"na 'man"dar + '?u?u -- "me 'ne"dios + '?u'la"pi '?e?e -- .'?e'sa"pa 'to + '?i"kuan 'do?o -- ,'huh"ra + ,'ta'?u"iok + ,'txe?e"na 'man"dar + .'xa"na 'ta"kar + 47 + ."txe "tua?a + ,'ko "ne?er 'xa"ne?en + .'?ka"niŋ 'gui"ra "ha 'ii'xa "na 'ta"kar + 50 + '?i?i -- ,'?i'ha?ax"to + '?e?e -- ,'?e'?txu?ur"?pir 'ia"ha?a + ,"txe 'ke?e'ma?a"txi + ,'xa"na 'ta"kar + ,"nien 'tak "pa?a 'xa"na + ,'tsok"?tsa '?u"iok + .'ku'kre"ma '?ka"xi +

59 + .'?en"ton 'ses'?a'ro?o?p"na + ,'tu "?ko?t 'ma?a"txi '?u'iu"?pie?et '?i'xa"na + 'ta 'ka'?e?e -- ,'e'xa"na?p 'lo'ke?er'iŋ'guah"?ke?et + 63 + '?i?i -- .'ha?a"xir "txe + ,"ne?en + .'ma?a"txi?iŋ '?ka"ni + 67 + ,"ne?en + ,'me'ho "rix 'ta"niu?ut + .?in'xa"na 'pus'pus"nio?ok + 70 + ,'?en"ton 'ses + ,'sut"pa '?e"dios + ,'huh "ra + '?e?e -- '?e"?puhk 'ta -- .'ta"mar + 76 + .'?ah'?ku"na 'in"te?e '?u"sa 'ku + 77 + '?i "txe 'ke?e -- ,'?e'?txu?ur"?pir 'ia"ha?a + ,'nie 'nix"na + ,'la"par '?u'me"ner + .'u'uo?o"?tsi 'u 'txo"ki + "por 'ke?e -- "txe 'ke?e -- ."huer 'te '?e'ka"lor 'ta"mar + 85 + '?iu?u -- .'?u'ia?a "re '?e"dios + ,'?e"?puhk 'xia?a'uah"?ke?en + ,"ne?en 'ma?a"txi?iŋ '?ka"ni + 'por'ke?e -- .'u

14. Indians and Ladinos

'txa"pie?en 'e'ka"lor 'ta"mar + 91 + ,'?en"ton 'ses + ,'?e"dios + ."txe "pues + ,'hai'ma?a "txa?a '?ka"ni + .'pe'ro'?a"ian "ti?i 'nu'?ka"ni + 96 + ,'?i'ha?ax"to + ,'?u"?txu?ur '?e?e -- '?e?e -- ,'?e"?ah 'txi'na"mo?p + .'?ah'?ku"na '?u'la"pi +

101 + ,'?i"txe 'ke?e + ,'?ah'?ku"na 'ta'ka '?u'la"pi + ,'?a"tsa?ai + ."?ahs 'to'?a'to"?poi 'ti"txan + 105 + 'por'ke?e -- .'?ah'?ku"nu?u 'la"pi + 107 + .'?i'?puhk'se'na"bien +

108 + ,'?en"ton 'ses + .'txe?e"dios + ,'?i'kox"to + .'?e?en"te?e "ra + '?ul -- .'?u '?txa"mi 'lo'ke?e"ua 'riŋ'guah"?ku + 115 + ,'?en"ton 'ses + 'txe"ia 'he?e -- '?u"?txu?ur '?e?e -- '?e"ia 'he?e -- ,"hen 'te + .'?ah'?ko 'pat"hen 'te + 121 + 'ko'txa?a -- "?pan 'tua?a -- ,'?a'ket"pa + ,'?i"ne?en + ,"?pan "tua?aŋ 'ket"pa + ,'tu"no?or 'e"tiem 'po + .'?in'xa"na 'pus'pus"nio?ok + 128 + ,'?in'xa"na + .'ko 'txe'?ka"ni?in 'xa"na + 130 + ,"pe 'ro + 'ma?a "txi '?in"txe?e -- .'pen"sar + "por 'ke?e -- ,'ma"ha?ax + ,'?puhk'se'?pi"ren + 'ko'txe?e -- .'?e?en"te?e "ia?ax + 138 + ,"pe 'ro + ,'?in 'te?e"ra + ,'tua?a'ka'tur"uan + 141 + '?i"kuan 'do?o -- ,"ne?et + ,'?a'?kah"puo?on + ,'tua?a'?a '?txa"mio?on + ,'?a'tu'ru"?po?on 'ta'?a'ueh"tser "tie?e 'ne"tiem 'po + .'?in'te?e"ra 'tua?a'ka'tu "ruan 'ta'ka"ro?p + 147 + .'ia"ha?a 'tia?a'tu "re?et + 148 + '?i"tia?a -- ,'ka?a"xin 'ka'tu "ruan 'ta'ka"ret + ,'ko'txe?en'te?e"ra + ,'?puhk 'se"?pir + ,'?i'?pa"ne 'nu"?pan + ,'?u'?ka"ni 'tua?a'?puhk"se?en +

154 + ."pe 'ro"?ehs 'to"kuan 'do + '?e?e -- ,'?a'?ko"toi '?e"di 'ia + 'tua?a'ka?a -- ,'ka 'tu"ruan + ,'ko"mon 'ta'ka"ret + ,'ta'me?e"di 'ia'ia"ha?a + ,"ma 'mah"txi?ix + '?e?e -- ,"mas '?a"tsa?ai + .'ta'ka'?u"?puhk + .'si"no 'ke?e

14. Indians and Ladinos

'?in'te?e"ra 'tua?a'ka"tsa?ai +

166 + '?i?i -- ,'ta"mar "ne?en + ,"ne?en 'me'ho"rix + ,'tu"re?en + ,'ko'txe?e"ra + '?e?e -- ,'pus'pus"nio?ok + .'?i"ma 'tu"?ka 'ni"?puhk + 174 + ,"pe 'ro + ."ne?en + ."uar '?iŋ"koh 'ko + 'ke?e -- ."kuan 'do + ,'?in"xin '?ko"toi + '?e?e -- ."to?oit 'tia?a'tu"re?et + ."ne?e 'nu "?pan + .'?in"tsa?ai + ,'ko'txe'?in"te?e '?i"ra + .'?a"tsa?ai 'ta'ku?u"?puhk +

186 + ,'?i'po"re 'so'txe'?e"hen 'te + 'ko "ne?er 'ke?e -- ,'po"re 'so'?a"ian + '?e?e -- ,'?al"dee "io?p + ,'?a"ian "mei 'gra'?e"hen 'te 'ta'me?e -- ,'?e'lu'ga"ro?p + "tia?a -- '?e?e -- '?u"txo?p 'su"frir + 'ta'ka'?e?e -- "mei 'gra '?e?e -- ,'?e'pus'pu"sir + '?e?e -- ,'ui?i"nar + '?i?i -- .'?e'txuk"pa?ar 'ta'me?e'tu"min + 203 + 'por'ke?e -- 'txe?e"no?p 'ke?e -- 'ke?e -- ,"ha?ax + ,'ka"?txu?ur + ,'u"txe 'per"der + .'ma?a"txi '?u'?txa"mi 'lo'ke?e'?ah'?ku"na '?u "me 'ne"dios + 210 + ,'ha?ax"nik '?u'?txa"mi + 'lo'ke?e -- ,'?ah'?ku"na '?u"me 'ne"dios + ,"ma?a 'ni"ha?ax "?pan + .'tu"ro?oŋ 'ko'txe?e "ra +

215 + "pe 'ro?o -- ,'?a'ia"non + ,"ti?i 'ne'ka'ua?a"re + ,'u"?pan + 'ko'txe?e -- ,'?o 'hro"ner '?a'?kah"na + '?i?i -- ,'?i'?es'to'ko "ne?er + ,"mei 'gra'?e"hen 'te + '?e?e -- ,'ko 'txe?e"hen 'te'te?e'txi"nam + ,'ie"hen 'te'ta '?ko"pot + 227 + ,'?a"ian + ,'ti?i"non '?e 'ko?o"hron + .'ka'ua?a"re + ,'ke'hai'ta"ra + '?e?e -- ,'?a"ian 'ka'txuk"pa?ar + ,'ta'ma'?e'tu "min + ,'?a"ian + ,'?e'txuk"pa?ar + ,'ta'me?e 'ui?i"nar + ,'?a"ian '?e'txuk"pa?ar + .'ta'me?e 'pus'pu"sir +

239 + ,"pe 'ro + 'ko'txe?e -- '?a'?kah"na 'io'hro"ner 'ke?e -- .'?a'?ko"toi 'in'te?e"di

14. Indians and Ladinos

'ia + ."kuan 'do + ,"no?on + '?e?e -- ,'tu"ro?on + ,'tu?u"?ka '?pe"dios + '?e?e -- ,'ta"sie 'lo + ,'?en"ton 'ses + ,'ia"ha?a + ,'ma?a"txi + ,'u "txo?on + ,'ne'se'si"tar '?e"?puhk + ,'lo'ke?e 'ka'la"pi 'ta"ra + ,'ma?a"txi '?u"txo?on 'ne'se 'si"tar 'e'tu"min 'lo'ke?e'ka'?kam"pes 'ta"ra + ,'?i'ma?a"txi 'u"txo?on 'ne'se'si"tar + '?e?e -- .'lo'ke?e'ka'?ku"xi 'ta"ra + 260 + ,'si"no + ,'ke?e'ia"ha?a + ,'tua?a'ka'tu"ruan + ,'tu?u "?ka?p 'e"dios + ,'ka"tsa?ai 'tu"no?o 're"tiem 'po + ,'por'ke?e"?pan + .'?u'ia?a"rio?on +

267 + '?i?i -- ,'po"re 'so + ,'?a"ian + ."mei "gron + ,"tie?e 'ne'?a"ian + ,'ka'?ku'?pes "iah + 'ta'me?e -- ,'?o'hro"ne 'ri"ra + 'ke?e -- ,'ta"ra + "mei 'gra'?ex -- .'txuk"pa?ar +

279 + ,"pe 'ro + 'ma?a"txi 'ka?a -- ,'ma?a "txi 'ka'na?a"ta 'hai'ber"da + ,"ha?ax 'ka "?txu?ur + ,'?u'txe'per"der + ,'si"no + ,'?e "dios '?u'?ka"ni 'tua?a"?pan 'ka'tur"uan + '?e?e -- ,'ma"ha?ax + '?e?e -- 'ma"ha?ax '?e?e -- ,'ka "?txu?ur + ,'si"no + .'?e"dios + ,"?pan + ,'?u '?ka"ni + ,'tua?a"?pan + .'ka'lum"se 'ka"?pa +

297 + '?i?i -- ,"pe 'ro"no?on + '?e?e -- ,'?a"ian + 'ti?i"non 'e'ko?o"hron 'ko'txe?e -- '?o"hron '?e?e -- '?e?e -- '?e'ui"nik 'ia"ha?a 'xe?e -- .'xe?e'?a'?kah"na + ,'?i'?pa"non 'ko "ne?er 'u"?pan + .'?a"ian 'tie?e"non '?e"?pan 'ko?o"hron + 'ke?e -- '?a?a -- ,'?ko"toi 'in "te?e "di 'ia + ,'tua?a'ma?a"txi 'tua?a'ka"txe 'pen"sar + 'ta'ma?a -- .'lo'ke?e'?a"ian 'ta"ra 'ta"rum + 313 + ,'si"no + ,'ia"ha?a 'tua?a'ka "tsa?ai + ,'ta"ma + .'?u"?ka?p '?e'ka'uiŋ'ki"rar "dios +

317 + ,'?i'ko'txa'ma?a"txi 'ka'ui"ra "no?on + .'po"re 'so'ma?a"txi 'ka'?ku?p"se 'hai 'ber"da + ,'ha?ax"nik 'ka'ui"ra + .'ka"?ku?up"se

14. Indians and Ladinos

'?a"ni + 321 + "pe 'ro + ,'ma?a"txi '?ko"to?oŋ 'ka'ui"ra +

323 + "pe 'ro'ko"ne?er + ,"no?on + ,'xe?e '?ah'?ko'pa"ton + ,'?a"ian "mei 'gra + 'ti?i 'ne?e -- "uar 'u?u -- ,'kan"se '?u"?pa + '?u?u -- ,'u'?kam"pes + '?u'la"pi '?e?e -- ,'?e'sa"pa 'to + 334 + ,"pe 'ro + .'ma?a"txi 'ka'ku'kre "ma 'ta"kar + 336 + ,'?i'ta"ma 're"ra + 'ma?a "txi 'ka?a -- ,'na?a"ta + ,'hai'ber"da + ,'ka "?txu?ur + '?e?e -- 'ua'kar"pa 'ta'ke?e -- .'sa "pa 'to'kon'da?ah'?ku"na 'u'la"pi + 344 + ,"pe 'ro'?e"hen 'te + ,"?pan '?u'?kah"ti + .'?ehs'to 'ko"ne?er +

14. Indians and Ladinos

1 There is another story the people told in the old days. 5 That ... one day, God collected together all people; he collected them and set them down beside him. 15 They used to say that -- all peoples had their king. The ... for each of the races of people, they say there was a king. 25 They used to say that ... one day the king of the people -- of the Indian race they say, that that day he was ordered by God to put on shoes. And when -- they were on his feet he was ordered to walk with them. 47 He was told, "Now walk! I want to see if you can walk with them." 50 And then the -- that king, they say, did not walk with them, not even a short walk. His feet tangled, he stumbled and fell.

59 Then he was told, "Why can't you walk with ... the sandals I gave you?" 63 And -- he said, "I don't want them. 67 It is better for me that I walk in my bare feet." 70 Then, God continued, and the man put on clothes; 76 he was given a jacket. 77 And they say that -- that king scarcely put it on. He took it off and threw it away, because -- they say that -- it was very hot. 85 And ... he said to God, "The clothes which you gave me I do not want, because their heat roasts me. 91 Then God said, "Well, if you don't want them, there are those who do." 96 And then the king of -- of the townspeople was given them to put on.

101 And they say that when he was given them to put on he was so happy he jumped up into the air. 105 Because -- he was given them to put on, 107 and he was well clothed.

108 Then God said, "What about this one, who takes what I give him?" 115 Then the king said, he of the people -- the people of the bush -- 121 "Just as he remains (dressed), so I re-

main for all time walking barefoot. 126 I walk as I wish to walk. 130 But I do not -- think, because .... I am not dressed like that one. 138 But we will sit down in the same place. 141 And when you love us and receive us, you will seat us beside you some day. We will sit together in the same place, 147 there where you are. 148 And there we will sit down with you, that one dressed just exactly as he wants to be dressed.

154 "But when -- that day comes, when we sit down together with you ... on that day neither will be more pleased with his clothes; rather we will be equally pleased.

166 "And ... as for me, I am better off as I am, barefoot and without clothes. 174 But I am waiting, for when I come to you, there where you are, I will be as happy as this one is, with his clothes."

186 And that is why people say today that -- that is why there are villages; there are many people in places where they are suffering from great nakedness, hunger and the lack of money. 203 Because they say that -- that -- our king threw away, did not accept what he was given by God. 210 If he had taken what he was given by God, we would not be as we are.

215 But -- there are those of us who say it is as the story tells, and -- and to this day many people are like the people of the town, and the people of the bush. 227 There are those of us who tell it. We say here there is our lack of money; there is suffering from hunger; there is suffering from nakedness.

239 But as the story is told -- a day will

come when we -- will be in the hand of God, in heaven. Then He will not let us want for the clothes we wear; He will not let us want for the money which we spend here; and he will not let us want for the -- what we eat here. 260 Rather, there where we sit down, in the hand of God, we will be happy for all time, because so he tells us.

267 And -- therefore there are many of us who believe in this story, that -- here there is great hardship.

279 But we do not know if it is true, that our king caused the loss; rather, God wanted us so to live ... not the ... not the ... our king, but God. So he wanted us to spend our lives.

297 And -- but we -- there are those of us who tell the story as that man told it. And so today we are like him, there are those of us who tell the story that -- a day will come when we will not think about what there is on earth. 313 Rather, we will be happy there in the hand of our Lord God.

317 And since we have not seen it, therefore we do not believe it is true. If we had seen it we would have believed it, 321 but we did not go to see it.

323 But today we who are bush people -- there are many who are teaching themselves, who are used to wearing -- shoes. 334 But we do not stumble in them. 336 And because of this, we do not know if it is true that our king fell because of the -- shoes, when he was given them to put on. 344 But so the people tell it to this day.

15. Parent's Curse

1 + ,'?a"ian '?o'tron"te?e '?o'hro"ner + ,
'?a'?kah"na + .'ta"ri 'xe"tiem 'po + 4 +
'txe?e"no?p 'ke?e -- ,'?a"ian 'in'te?e"di 'ia +
'?e?e -- ,'?e"dios + '?u?u -- ,'?u'peh"ka + ,
'?in"te?e + ,'ui"nik + .'?i'iin"te?e '?i"xik +
'?i'e?e'ui"nik 'ia"ha?a "txe 'ke?e -- '?e?e -- .
"mei 'gra'u"ha?a?p + 16 + 'txe?e"no?p 'ha?a
"xo?p 'ke?e -- '?e?e -- "mei 'gra?a -- '?u?u --
,"ha?a?p + ,?i"?pan + .'?e?ei"xik + 23 + '?u
'?kah"tio?p 'ke?e -- '?e?e -- ,'?e?ei"xik 'ia
"ha?a + .'?a'sa"ki?i 'xu"hor + 27 + .'?i"?pa
'ne'ui"nik +

28 + '?i?i -- ,'ha?ax"to + '?e?e -- ,"dios
+ ,'?u"txe 'man"dar + '?e?e -- ,'ta'res"na +
'?in"te?e -- ,"ta 'bla + .'se"mi 'ta + 38 +
'?i?i -- ,'?i'?txa?a?p"na 'ta'man"te?e + '?e?e ,
"tra 'po + ,"blaŋ 'ko + ,'?i"?pan + ,'hah"ia + .
'ta'?u"hor + 45 + .'txe?e"no?p + 'ke?e -- ,
"kuan 'do + '?e?e -- ,'tu"ri?ix + '?e?e -- ,'?e
'se"mi 'ta + '?txa?a"rix 'ta'ma'?e?e -- ,"man
'ta + ,'xe?e"blaŋ 'ko + '?i'ha'ia"rix + '?e?e --
,'?e"tra 'po"blaŋ 'ko'ta'?u"hor + 'pehk"na 'ta
"ri + 59 + '?e?e -- .'?e'ui"nik + .'ie?ei"xik
+

62 + '?i?i -- .'?a'ro?o?p"na '?u"me 'ne
"dios + ,'ko"ne?er + '?e?e -- '?e'se"mi 'ta +
'lo'ke?e -- ,'?in"txe 'man"dar + ,'ta'res"na + .
'?in'?ka"ni + ."tua?a + ,'?a"txe '?in"te?e + ,
'?o'hro"ner 'ta'?u"hor + .'?ka"niŋ 'gui"ra 'ko
"txa '?a'lo"?koi +

75 + ,'?en"ton 'ses + '?e?e -- ,'?e"bie
'ho + ,'?ie?ei"la 'ma + ."txe + 80 + .'?u'ia?a
"re '?e"dios + 81 + '?e?e -- .'ni'uiŋ'ki"ret +
.'tu"?ka '?o'hro"ner 'a'?ka"ni "tua?a + 'in"txe
'tu?u"hor '?e?e -- .'?e'se"mi 'ta'?i"ra +

86 + ."txe '?e"dios + 87 + '?e?e --

15. Parent's Curse

"ne?en '?in'na?a"ta 'ke?e -- ,"ne?et + 'xe?e --
,"ua 'ri'?tox"ma + ,"ti?in "di 'ia + ,'?u'?ka"ni
"tua?a + ,'?a'?pa?a"xe + ,'?a'si?i"?tso?p + ,'?u
'?ka"ni 'tua?a'?a'?pa?a"xe + .'?a'gua"ro?p + 97
+ '?i?i -- ,'ha?ax"to + ,'?ka"ni '?iŋ'gua?a
"re?et + ,'tua?a'?a"txe 'in"te?e '?o'hro"ner + ,
'tu?u"hor + .'?e'se"mi 'ta'?i"ra +

103 + ,'?in"ton 'ses + '?e?e -- '?e?ei"la
'ma + '?u?u -- ,'?o"hron '?pah"xan + .'?u'ia?a
"re '?e"pan + 109 + ,'?txah"?pe?eix 'ta?a"?pa
+ 'lo'ke?e -- .'?a"txi?ix 'ta'ka"ren + 112 + ,
"ti?i 'ne"tiem 'po + "ti?i -- ."ti?i 'ne"tiem
'po + 114 + ,'?e"hen 'te + ,'ta"ma + ,'?e'ka
"lien 'te'?kih"na?a + ,'?u'mu'kie?e"to?p + .'?u
'?ku'xie?e"to?p +

119 + ,'?i"txe + 'ke?e -- ,"kuan 'do'?i
"xin + '?e?e -- ,'hah"txa + '?e?e -- ,'?e"man
'ta'tu?u"hor + '?e?e -- ,'?e'se"mi 'ta'ia"ha?a +
,'?ir"na + ,'ke'?u'mu"si?ik '?e?ei"la 'ma + ,
'?i'niah"rer + ,'?u'?kan'?txo"hres + ,'tu"no?or
+ '?e?e -- ,'?e'se"mi 'ta + .'?i'lu"mui + '?ehs
'to'?ka"xi + 'ta"ma '?e?e -- ,'?e"tra 'po + .
'xe?e"?txa?ar 'ie"?par + 139 + ,'?u'?kan'?txo
"hres + '?e?e -- .'?e'se"mi 'ta + 142 + "txe
'ke?e -- ,'?u'txe'par"tir + ,'lu"mui + 'ta'ma'tu
"no?or '?e'se"mi 'ta + ,'?i'lu"mui + ,'?ka"xi
+ "?ehs 'to'ta'ma'?e"man 'ta'xe?e -- .'xe?e
"?txa?ar 'ta"mar +

150 + '?i?i -- ,'?i'sut"pa + ,'pehk"na +
'?e?e -- .'?e"bie 'ho'ta"ri + '?a'ro?o?p"na +
156 + ,'ko"ne?er + ,"ne?et + ,'?o'hro"nen +
'?e?e -- ,'?e"mis 'mo'hro"ner 'xe?e'?u"txe +
'?e?e -- ,'?a'uix"ka?a 'ri"ra + .'?i"ha?ax 'iŋ
'?ka"ni 'tua?a'?a"txe '?u"?pan +

163 + '?i?i -- ,'?o"hron + ,'?e"bie 'ho +
'ko'txe?e -- '?o"hron '?u?u -- .'?u'uix"ka?ar +

15. Parent's Curse

169 + ,"pe 'ro + ,"kuan 'do'?i"xin + 'hah"txa 'e?e -- ,"tra 'po + 'ta?a -- '?u"hor 'e?e -- , 'se"mi 'ta'tia?a"?txa?ar + ,'?ir"na + 'ke + ,'?e "bie 'ho + 'ma?a"txi '?u?u -- ,'?ko"toi 'u'mu "si?ik + ,'ko'txa'?e?ei"la 'ma + ,'la'mi"ta 'ta "ka 'e'se"mi 'ta'?ko"toi + ,'?kan'?txo"hra 'u "men + '?u'mu"si?ik 'tia?a -- '?u?u -- '?u'iuh "ta "to?o 're?e -- .'?e'se"mi 'ta +

187 + ,'?i'po"re 'so + .'txe?e"hen 'te'ko "ne?er + 'ke?e -- ,'?a"ian '?e"hen 'te + "tie?e 'ne?e -- ,'?u'?pa?a"xe '?u'iu'ne"no?p + "tie?e 'ne?e -- .'?u'?pa?a"xe '?u'si?i"tso?p + 195 + "kuan 'do?o -- "kuan 'do?o -- ,'tu"?ka?a 'txe?e "na 'ta'ka"ro?p + ."kuan 'do + '?u'iu"?pio?p 'ke?e -- ,"ua'ra'?kai"no?p + '?u"me 'nu'iu'ne "no?p + '?o?o -- "ua 'ra'?kai"no?p 'u"me 'nu 'si?i"?tso?p + ,'?i'hai"ma + "kuan 'do?o -- , 'ma?a"txi + '?a?a -- ,'?a'?ku'?pes"no?o?p + '?u "me 'nu?u -- ,'?u'si?i"?tso?p + .'?i'ha?a"xo?p '?a'?pa?a'xua"no?p +

212 + 'po"re 'so'txe?e"hen 'te'ke?e -- '?e?e -- '?e"bie 'ho'?ie?ei"la 'ma'xe?e -- , 'txe?e"na 'man"dar '?pa?a"xuan 'u'me'ne"dios + , 'ket"pa '?ehs'to'ko"ne?er 'ta'ke?e'pa"ka?p 'e'ko "noh + 'por'ke?e'?a"ian "ti?i 'ne?e -- ,'ko "ne?er + ,'u'ius"re '?a'?pa?a"xuan + '?u'?pa?a "xe '?u?u -- .'?u'ia"ro?p + 222 + ,'?i'po"re 'so'?e"hen 'te'ko"ne?er + ,'?a"ian "ti?i 'ne'?u '?pa?a"kre + '?e"?pa?ax "kuan 'do'?u'iu"?pi 'ke?e -- ,'?a"?pa?ax '?a"ian + .'?a'?pa?ak"ta '?u'iu"?pi +

227 + '?i?i -- 'txe?e"no?p 'ke?e -- '?u "?pa?ax '?e?e -- ,'?e'tu?u"?pir + ,"mei 'gra + , '?i'ke?e'ma?a"txi + .'?e?eix"na '?a'?ka"xi + 234 + "por 'ke?e -- ,'ta'ma'rix"to 'ke?e'?o'hro "ner 'ia"ha?a + '?e?e -- '?u'iu"?pio?o?p + '?a '?kah"na + 'ke?e -- '?e?ei"la 'ma + 'kon'da'?u

15. Parent's Curse

'?pa?a"xe '?e'se"mi 'ta + ,'?e'u'?kan'?txo"hres + .'tu"no?or '?e'se"mi 'ta + 243 + '?i?i -- , 'txe?e"no?p 'ko"ne?er 'ke'?u"?pa?ax + '?e?e -- ,'tu?u"?pir + '?e?e -- ,"mei 'gra + ,'?i'ke?e 'ua?ak"txe 'ta"ka + .'?a'?ka"xi 'ta'ma"ron +

251 + '?e?e -- ,'ko"ne?er + ,'?a"ian '?e "hen 'te + '?e?e -- ,'txe?e"no?p + "kon 'da'?ka 'ni'u'?pa?a"xe '?u?u -- ,'si?i"?tso?p + ,'o?o + ,'?u'ia"ro?p + 'txe?e"no?p 'ke?e -- ,'?txah "?pe?eix 'ta?a"?pa 'lo'ke?e"ua 'ra"txe 'ta'ka "ren + ,'ma?a"txi 'a'?ku?p"se?en 'lo'ke?eiŋ 'gua?a"re?et + '?i?i -- ,'ma?a"txi + '?a?a -- , 'ta're"sen + ,'ta'ma'tu?u"?pir + "pe 'ro + "tie?e 'ne"tiem 'po + ,"?pan 'tua?a'?u"txe?et + .'?a'si?i"?tso?o?p + 272 + ,"?pan 'tua?a'?u "txe?et + '?a?a -- .'?a'ua'ro?p +

275 + ,'?en"ton 'ses + '?e?e -- ,'xe?e "ua 'ra'?pa?ax"na 'ia"ha?a + .'?a'?pa?ak"ta '?u'iu "?pi + 279 + 'por 'ke?e -- ,'?u'iu"?pio?p 'ke "?pa 'na'?kah"na + 'ke?e -- "?pan 'u?u -- '?u "txe '?e?e -- ."tiem 'po'ia"ha?a + 287 + ,"pe 'ro"ne?en + 'me?e'ra"to '?in'ma"ni '?e?e -- ,'?e 'se"mi 'ta + ,'?im'?pa?a"xe + 'tua?aŋ'gui"ra 'hai -- ,'ber"da + .'?iŋ'?kan'?txo"hres + 294 + ,"?pe 'ro'?e"hen 'te + ,"?pan 'u'?kah"tio?p + .'?ehs'to'ko"ne?er +

15. Parent's Curse

1 There is another story that was told in
time past. 4 They say that one day -- God --
called to a man and a woman. And that man, they
say, was very old. 16 They say that -- ... he
was many years old, and so was the woman. 23
They tell that -- that woman's head was already
white, 27 and so was the man's.

28 And then God ordered them to bring near
a large, flat loaf of bread. 38 And -- it was
laid on a white cloth, and so another was
stretched over it. 45 They say that when the
loaf of bread was already lying on the cloth,
which was white, and the white cloth was
stretched over it, they were called there, 59
the -- man and the woman.

62 And God said to them: "Today the loaf
of bread which I ordered brought near, -- I want
you to speak over it. I want to see how it (the
loaf) comes out."

75 Then the old man and the old woman
said, 80 they spoke to God: 81 "You are my
master. What do you want me to say over this
loaf?"

86 God said, 87 "I know that you who are
raising children -- a day will come that you
will curse your grandchildren; you will come to
curse your children. 97 And then, I will tell
you what words to say over this loaf."

103 Then the old woman spoke first. She
said to the bread, 109 "Thanks to you for what
you have done for me. Some day ... some day
114 people will put you in hot water, they will
cover you and will eat you up."

119 And they say that when she went to

raise the cloth from the top of that loaf, it was seen that the breath of the old woman had suddenly turned the whole loaf yellow. It had passed through to fall on the cloth that was lying underneath. 139 It turned the loaf yellow. 142 They say that it split and passed through the whole loaf, and passed through to fall on the cloth that -- that it was lying on.

150 And ... the old man was again called near. He was told, 156 "Today you must say the same words which your wife here said; I wish that you say the same thing."

163 And the old man spoke as the old woman had spoken. 169 But when he went to raise the cloth from the loaf, where it lay, it was seen that the old man's breath did not go as far as the old woman's; it reached half of the loaf, which was turned yellow by his breath where he blew on the loaf.

187 And that is why people today say that -- there are people, some, who curse their children, some who curse their grandchildren, 195 when -- when -- what is done with them -- when they hear that -- they are being quarreled with by their children, or -- are being quarreled with by their grandchildren. And if not, when they are not obeyed by their grandchildren. And they curse them.

212 And therefore people say that -- the old man and the old woman who -- were ordered to curse by God, are to this day among human beings because there are those today who want to curse, who curse their children. 222 And that is why people today -- there are those who fear a curse when they hear that -- there is a curse. They are frightened to hear it.

15. Parent's Curse

227 And they say that -- the mother's curses are many, and that they are fulfilled in a short time. 234 Because -- because of that story the -- they heard told, that -- the old woman when she cursed the loaf, she turned the whole loaf yellow. 243 And they say today that the curses of the mother are powerful, and that they are quickly fulfilled for us.

251 And -- today there are people -- they say, when they want to curse their grandchildren or their children, they say, "Thanks to you for what you do for me -- you don't obey what I say to you and you don't treat me like a mother. But some time your grandchildren 272 and your children will do the same to you."

275 Then the -- one who is cursed is frightened to hear it, 279 because they hear that as it is told, that so those people did it at that time. 287 But I have not yet bought a loaf and cursed it, to see if I would truly turn it yellow. 294 But so people tell it to this day.

16. Henpecked Husband

1 + '?a"ia 'no'tron"te?e -- ,'?o'hro"ner +
'?a?a -- ,'?kah"na + 5 + "txe 'ke?e -- ,'?a
"ian + .'in'te?e'ui"nik + 'ke?e -- ,"huer 'te +
.'?a?ah"?tsa 'u"me 'nu'ui"la 'ma + 11 + ,"txe
'ke?e'ui"nik 'ia"ha?a + ,'?e'i"xik + ,'a'lo"?koi
'a'xa"na + ,'?a?a"xin 'ta'txi"nam + '?i?i -- .
'?i'ma?a"txi '?a'io?o"pa 'tu?u'io"tot + 17 + ,
'?e'i"xik 'ia"ha?a + '?in -- ,'te?e"to 'do"miŋ
'go + '?a?a -- ,'?e?ek"mai 'ta'txi"nam + ,'pa
"kax + '?i?i -- .'?a'ket"po?oi "?txi + .'ma"ku?u
'txi"nam +

26 + ,'?i'ha?a"xir + ,'tu"ru "ua 'ra'kohk
"san + '?e?e -- ,'ma"ku?u + '?i?i -- ,'?i'e'i
"xik 'ia"ha?a + ,"kon 'da?a'?ko"toi + ,"?o 'tro
"di 'ia + "?i?i -- ,'?a'?ko"toi 'ta"ka + ,'a'tru
"uan + 'u'?ka"ie '?u?u -- ,'u'no"xi?ip + 39 +
'?i"kon 'de?e -- .'u'ta"hui + '?e'u'no"xi?ip
'ke?e -- ,"ma 'tu"?ka 'e"pa?a '?u'me"ner + 'o?o
-- ,"ma 'tu"?ka 'e"sa?a 'txe?e"?pir 'u'me"ner +
,'u'uah"pi 'ta'?ke"uer + .'u'ua"?tsi +

47 + '?e?e -- ,'?i'ha?ax"to '?e'ui"nik 'ia
"ha?a + ,"kuan 'do"uar '?a?ah"?tsa 'u"me 'nu'ui
"la 'ma + ,'ha?a"xir + ,'?in'ta"kix + .'?a'ma
"xia?a '?a?a"ru + 53 + "por 'ke?e -- '?a?ah
"?tsa 'u'me'nu'ui"la 'ma + 55 + ,'?i'ha?a"xir
+ 'ko'txa?a -- ,'?u'na?a"ta 'ke'?ah"?tsa 'u"me
'nu'ui"la 'ma + '?i'po"re 'so'kuan"do?o -- ,'?e
'i"xik 'a'lo"?ko 'ia'xa"na + ,'?a?a"xin 'ta'txi
"nam + ,'?i'ha?a"xir + ,"?txuhk "?txuhk 'u'me
"ner + .'tu"?ko 'ra'tua?a'?ko"toi + 64 + '?i?i
-- ,'?a?a"uan + '?a?a -- ,'ti'kru"ma + ,'u"txe?e
"pa?a + .'u'mu"xi '?e"sa?a + ,"tua?a '?u'iu"?txi
'?e'i"xik 'a'?ko"toi + "por 'ke?e -- 'a'?pa?ak
-- ,"ta + ."por 'ke?e'?u'na?a"ta 'ke'?ah"?tsa 'u
"me 'ne'i"xik +

75 + '?i'po"re 'so + 'e?e -- ,"kon 'da'lo
"?koi + '?u?u -- .'?u'ui"la 'ma'?a'xa"na +

16. Henpecked Husband

.'ha?a"xir + ,'ti'txan"to '?e"?kin + ,'?a?a"ua
'na'ti'kru"ma + '?u'sah"ka 'tu"?ka '?u'iah"?ku
'?e?e -- .'?e'i"xik 'a'?ko"toi + 85 + '?e?e --
,'ko"txa?a 'ta"kix + ,'?u'ui"ra + ,'a'txek"ta
'ua"tar + ,'ha?a"xir + ,'?in"tix 'a'ti'kru"ma +
,'u'uah"pi 'u"rutx + ,'u'po"ku?ut + "tua?a '?u
'iah"?ku 'e"ha?a '?e?e -- ,'?e?ei"xik + ."kon
'da'?o?o"txoi 'ma"ku?u + 96 + '?i?i -- ,'?u
'tu'ru"?pa + '?u?u -- ,'?e"?txe?eu + "tua?a -- .
'?a"ue?e '?e?ei"xik + 102 + ,'?in'te?e"to +
'?a?a"xin 'u?u -- ,'?u'uix"ka?ar + ,'ma"ku?u
'txi"nam + ,"?pan + .'?u"txe 'kon'da'?ko"toi '?e
'i"xik + 108 + "por 'ke'?u'na?a"ta 'ke?e -- .
'?ah"?tsa +

110 + ,'?i'en"ton 'ses + ,'?e'i"xik 'ia
"ha?a + ,'?a"ian "di 'ia'a'?ko"toi + '?e?e -- 'u
'?ke"txe '?e?e -- '?in"te?e -- ,'ui"nik 'a'?ko
"toi + 'xe?e -- ,'?e'ui"nik 'xe?e'?a'xa"na 'ta
"kar 'ma"ku?u 'txi"nam + ,'?a"ian "di 'ia + "txe
'ke?e -- ,'u'?ke"txe '?a?a"xin + ,'ta'mo?o"tot +
.'?a"ue?e 'ta"kar + 124 + '?en"ton 'ses + ,'?e
'ui"nik 'ia"ha?a + 'ko'txa?a'ta"kix 'a'txek"ta
'?e?e -- ,'?u'uix"ka?ar 'ua"tar + ,'tu?u'ni?i
"?pi?ir + '?iu'ui"ra 'ke?e -- 'ta"ka '?u?u -- ,
'?u'ui"nik "ua 'ra'?ko"toi + ,'?i'ha?a"xir + ,
'?in"tix 'a'ti'kru"ma + ,'?u'?txa"mi '?e"ha?a +
'u'iah"?ku '?e?e -- '?e'i"xik 'xe?e -- ."ua 'ra
'?ko"toi 'ia"ha?a +

138 + "pe 'ro?o -- "txe 'ke?e -- .'?a"ia
'nin"te?e "di 'ia + ,'?a"ian '?in"mohr 'ui'ni
"ko?p + '?e?e -- 'be"sii 'no'?pi"ro?p "tua?a --
'?e?e -- 'ui"nik -- .'?e'ui"nik 'ia"ha?a + 147
+ '?e?e -- ."txe?e "no?p + "ne?et + ,'?pa"ni 'xe
'ma"ha?ax 'ui'ni"ket + 151 + ,'tsah"tsa + "ua
'ru"txe?et '?e'i"xik + "lo 'ke?e -- ,'tu"re?et
'ta"kar + "por 'ke?e -- ,'ha?a"xir + ,'?a?a"xin
'ma"ku?u 'txi"nam + ,'?a"?txa?an + ,'?o?oi"?txi
+ ,"ii "kon 'da'io?o"pa + ,'?u'ta"res + ,'?u'ui

16. Henpecked Husband

"nik + ,'ta"mo?o "tot + ,'?i"ne?et + '?e?e -- , '?pa"nix 'ko'txa'in"te?e '?i"xik 'tu"re?et '?u 'me"ner + ,"ne?et 'ma"ha?ax 'ui'ni"ket + .'si"no 'ke'?i'xik"?pir 'tu"re?et 'ma"ku?u + 169 + "por 'ke?e -- ,'tia?a"ta?a 'ui"ra 'ui"nik + '?e?e -- ,"ha?ax 'a'ket"pa?a 'kohk"san + ,"ha?ax '?u'txe?e"pa?a + "ha?ax -- ,'?o?oi"?txu + , "ha?ax 'u"txe 'tu"no?or + '?e?e -- '?pa"ni 'xe?e -- ,"ma "ha?ax 'ui'ni"ket +

180 + ,'?en"ton 'ses + ,'?e'ui"nik "txe + ."pe 'ro'tu"?ka "tua?an "txe + 'si -- ."hai 'ma?a"txi '?in"txe + ,"lo 'ke'?u'ia?a"re?en + , 'u'?ka?a'pe"sen + .'ta'?ke"uer "kon 'da?a'io?o "pa + "por 'ke?e -- ,"kuan 'do'?u'ta'hu"ie?en + "ma 'tu"?ka '?iŋ'guah"?ku?u -- ,'?u'?ku"xo?p + , "kon 'da?a'io?o"po?op + '?e?e -- .'?u'ua "?tsie?eŋ "ko 'txe"ha?ax 'u'?ka"ni + 195 + , '?i'ta"mar "ne?en + ,'?im'?pa?ak"ta + 197 + , '?i'po"re 'so + .'?in"txe 'lo'ke?e'ha?a"xir '?u 'ia?a"re?en +

199 + "pe 'ro?o -- ,"txe + .'?e'ui'ni"ko?p + "pe 'ro?o -- ,'koh"kon + "no?on '?ka"ni 'ka?a -- "no?oŋ '?ka"ni 'ka?a -- .'ka'ui"ra 'ko"txa 'ka"txe + 207 + ,'?in"ton 'ses + "txe 'ke?e -- ,'?e'ui'ni"ko?p 'ia"ha?a + ,"kai + ,'xa"no?o?p + '?u?u -- 'tu"no?or '?e?e -- ,'?e"hue 'bes + "por 'ke?e'txe?e"no?p 'ke?e -- ,"di 'ia"hue 'bes + "ha?ax '?e?e -- 'hol"txan "di 'ia + 'ke?e -- . "no?on 'ma?a"txi 'ka'na?a"ta 'tu"?ka '?e'hol "txan + 221 + "pe 'ro?o -- "pe 'ro"txe 'ke?e -- '?ed -- '?e?e -- ,'?e"di 'ia"hue 'bes + 'ha?ax'?e?e -- .'?e'hol"txan "di 'ia +

228 + '?i?i -- ,'?en"ton 'ses + '?e?e -- , 'ui'ni"ko?p 'ia"ha?a + "txe 'ke?e -- 'u'?ke "txo?p 'in -- ,"tahtx "rutx + ,'u'ua"?puo?p + 'io"?pa?a -- 'in"te?e -- .'su"?pin + 239 + '?ie?e -- ,'?u'xi'ni"txi 're'su"?pin + '?e?e --

16. Henpecked Husband

"tia?a -- '?a?a -- ,'?a'txir"he?ei + ,'?en"ton 'ses + .'?a'?ka"xi 'ta'ma'?e"rutx 'xe?e"ua?a 'ru 'me'ne"ro?p + ,'iu'koh"ko?p 'tsak"ta "?o 'txo"di 'ia + '?i"xin + ,'u'ta're"so?p + .'?e"rutx 'xe?e "ua?ar '?u'me'ne"ro?p 'io'?pe?e'su"?pin +

251 + ,'?i"kon 'da'?ko"toi '?u'ui"ro?p + "txe 'ke?e -- '?a"ian '?im"?pihk "ha?a "ua?ar 'ta'ma?a -- '?e?e -- '?e"rutx + 256 + 'txe?e "no?p 'ke?e -- 'tak -- ,'ta"ka 're"ra + .'?a"ian "tua?a '?e're"me 'dio +

260 + ,'?en"ton 'ses + 'ta"ma?a -- ,"?o 'tron"te?e "hue 'bes + ,'?i'xi"no?p + ,"kai '?u 'sah"ko?p + '?e?e -- .'?e'si"nam + .'ma"kue?e "tun + 267 + '?i'?u'ta"huio?p + 268 + ,'?i 'ha?ax"to + '?e?e -- ,'u"pu?uk '?e'si"nam + "txe 'ke?e "kai '?u?u -- ,'?u"txo?o?p 'man"dar + '?e?e -- ,'?txihr"na "tu?ut 'e'se"met + '?e?e -- ,'?u'?pi?ik"to?o?p + '?u'ia?a"pro?o?p 'ta"ka '?u?u -- .'?u'ia"?pitx '?e'si"nam + 279 + '?e?e -- '?e?e -- '?u?u -- '?u'xi'ni"txir '?e?e -- .'su"?pin +

284 + '?i?i -- ,'?en"ton 'ses + ,"kai '?u 'ia?a"pro?o?p + '?i?i -- ,'u"txo?o?p 'man"dar + .'txa'mes"na '?iŋ"koh '?ta"?katx + 290 + ,'?i "xin 'u'peh"ko?p '?e'ui"nik 'ia"ha?a + '?e?e -- .'?u'iah"?kuo?o?p + '?e?e -- '?u'ma'hre"so?p 'ke?e -- '?e?e -- ,"no?on + ,"uar 'ka"txe?en "te?e 'ka'noh"?kin + '?i?i -- '?i'ka'ua?a"re?e -- "txe?e "na?aŋ 'koh'?ta"?katx 'ta'ke?e'?ar"ros + '?i'ka'?ka"na?a "ni "tua?a -- ,'?i?i"xi 'ni'ua "ra?a + "por 'ke?e -- ."guar 'ka'noh'?ki"ni +

305 + ,'?en"ton 'ses + '?e'ui"nik "txe + "pe 'ro?o -- 'ma?a"txi 'tu"ru 'ni?i -- ,'ma?a "txi 'tu"ru 'ni'uix"ka?ar + ,'?i"ha 'iu'ta'hu "ien 'ma?a"txi 'tu"re?en + .'?a?a"xu?u '?ka?a'pe "sen 'ta'?ke"uer +

16. Henpecked Husband

311 + .'?i'ha?a"xo?p 'txe?e"no?p + "hai -- ,'ka'ui"ra 'io?o"pa + .'ua"to?on 'ka'uak"te?et + 315 + ,'?i'ka'ua?a"re 'ke"no?on 'ka'?ke"txe?e '?pi"xe?et + "tua?a -- 'ma?a"txi?i -- .'?u'iah "?ke?et +

319 + '?in"ton 'ses + ,'?e'ui"nik 'ia"ha?a + ,"uar 'ta"ka 'a'?pa?ak"ta + .'?i"xin + 323 + '?i?i -- ,"kon 'da?a'?ko"toi + "txe 'ke?e -- 'txe?e"ni?ix + '?a're"glar '?e?e -- '?u'xi?i -- '?e?e -- '?e?e -- 'si"nam + '?ie?e'?u'ia"?pitx + '?u?u -- .'xi'ni"txi 're'su"?pin + 335 + ,'?ar 're"glaa "duix "ua?ar + '?e?e -- 'ta'ka'ko?o"ra '?u"kaal "duir -- ,'?a"?katx + '?ah'?ku"na '?u?u -- .'?u'iu"?txi +

341 + ."txe "tua?a + ,"ne?et + '?pa"nix '?e'?ah'mua"ket + '?e?e -- ,'dial"tii 'ru'tu "re?et + ,'?i'po"re 'so + '?e?e -- "uar 'ka?a "txe 'man"dar '?i'ta'res"na "tua?a -- '?ka"ni '?ka'ua?ah"?ke?et '?im"?pihk '?u?u -- "kaal "di 'ra"?ka 'txi"ra?a -- ,'?a'ku"mi + ,'tal"bes + '?i?i -- .'?iu?us"ta '?a"ni +

354 + ,'ha?a"xir + ,'?u'uah"pi 'ta"ka + . '?u'ku"mi + 357 + '?i"txe?e -- "pe 'ro?o -- 'tu"?ka?a "ian 'ta'me?e -- "kal 'du"ra "me 'ro?o -- "me 'ro?o -- '?a"ian 'in"te?e -- .'u'iuhts "nar +

364 + '?i?i -- "txet -- "txe?e -- .'?e'i "xik + "san "ha?ax '?e?e -- '?e?e -- .'?o"re 'ga 'no'ka"iin 'ia"ri 'ta"mar + 'ii?i -- 'i?i -- , '?i'nia"ri '?im"?pihk "txi 'le + '?a'sa"ber 'hai -- ,'?a'na?a"ta?a '?ku'xe?e "txi 'le + '?i?i -- .'?i'nia"ri 'ta"mar +

367 + ,'?en"ton 'ses + ,'txe?e'ui"nik + '?e?e -- '?e"txi 'le -- .'a"ka 'iiŋ'?ku"xi +

16. Henpecked Husband

372 + '?e?e -- .'txe"tua?a + "hai -- ,'a '?kan"to "mas + .'?i'nia"ri "to?o 'trom"?pihk +

377 + '?i"txe 'ke?e"ua?ar '?e?e -- '?e?ex -- ,'?e"txi 'le'ia"ha?a + ,'ia'?par"?pir 'ta"ka 'u?u -- "pu?uk '?e'si"nam + '?i'ta"ka '?e?e -- . 'u'xi'ni"txi 're'su"?pin + 384 + 'iah"ra 'ta 'mu?u -- .'u"kal 'du'tia?a"ua 'ru'ku"mi +

386 + ,'?i"kon 'da'?ix"to + ,'?ko"toi + , "?o 'tron"te?e 'do"miŋ 'go + ,'?ek"mai 'u'ui"la 'ma'ta'txi"nam + ,'?i'ha?a"xir + 'ma?a'txix"to '?u?u -- 'u'?pih"nu "tua?a '?u?u -- ,"txe?e "pa?a + ."nie 'nu'?pih"nu 'tua?a'?u"txe?e "sa?a + 395 + ,'ha?a"xir + 'uix"to '?u?u -- "txe 'sen"tir 'u?u -- 'ta'mu?u"kuer 'pu'ke?e -- .'?a '?ku'xur"na +

400 + '?i"txe 'tu?u"ial 'ma'ke?e -- ,'ko "txa 'ket"pe?en + ,"pe 'ro'si"ne?en "ma 'na?a "ta?aŋ '?kih"na + ,"ne?en '?im'?pa?a"kre '?a "ne?e 'i"xi 'ke"ra + ,"pe 're?e"ra + "ua 'rim '?pih"nu 'ke"hai -- ,'ke"hai + ,'sut"pa 'io?o"pa + 'ko"txe?e -- ,"ua 'ru"txe?en + .'ko"ne?er 'ma?a"txa?a 'kor"pa + 411 + ,'ko"ne?er "lo 'ke '?in"xin 'txc?e'ta"kar + ."ne?e 'nin"xin 'txam "se 'ta'?ke"uer +

413 + '?i"txe 'ke?e'i"xik 'ia"ha?a + ,'ko "txa?a 'ha?a"xir 'ma?a"txi 'u'na?a"ta + '?e?e -- 'tu"?ka "ua 'ra'txe?e"na 'ta"ka?a -- ,'?u'no "xi?ip + ,'ha?a"xir + ,'?ek"mai 'ta'txi"nam + , 'ket"pa 'ka'iu"?txi + '?i?i -- ,'?i'sa'koh"pa + '?e?e -- ,"di 'ia"lu 'nes + ,'?ko"toi 'ta'?u'io "tot + 'u'?ke"txe '?e?e -- '?e'ui"nik '?ko"toi 'xe?e -- .'?u'na?a"ta?a 'xa"na 'ta"kar +

429 + '?i + ,'?o"txoi 'ta"ka 'ma"ku?u + '?u'ui"ra 'ke?e -- '?e?e -- ,'?u'no"xi?ip 'xe?e 'tu"ru 'ma"ku?u + 'ma?a"txi '?u?u -- '?u?u --

16. Henpecked Husband

"txe "ka 'so"tua?a -- .'?a?ah'?ku"no?o?p 'ia "ha?a + .'?i"tua?a '?a'ue?e'se?e"no?p +

439 + ,'?en"ton 'ses + .'?u'ia?a"re '?e'ui "nik + ,'?i"ne?et + 'tu"?ka?a 'koh"ko 'ke?e -- '?e?e -- '?pa"ni 'xe?e -- 'ma?a"txa?a 'txe"ka 'so"tua?a -- .'?a'uah"?ko?o 'nim'?pihk"ha?a +

447 + ,'?en"ton 'ses + ."txe?e 'ui"nik + . "pues + ,'ko"ne?er + '?e?e -- .'txe?e"?pi 'rim "?pihk '?a"sa?a 'ua'?pu "?pir 'ni'me"ner + 453 + .'ta"rix "di 'ia + '?e?e -- ."ua 'ra'txa"ma?a 'tsah"ier 'ta'ma"ren + ,'?a'?ke"txa?a 'ui"nik '?a'io?o"pa 'ta'ma'nio?o"tot + ,'?i"ne?en 'tu "no?or 'in"txa?a 'uan"tar + '?i"lo 'ke?e -- '?a?a -- ,"kai + ,'?a'ua"?tsie?en + ,'ko"ne?er + .'?i'toh"ma +

464 + ,"txe 'ke'?e'ui"nik 'ia"ha?a + '?a 'ro?o?p"na 'ta"ka 'ke?e -- ,'ke?e"ma 'tu"?ka '?e "sa?a '?u'me"ner + ,'?u'?ka"ni 'u"sin 'txo'lo "?koi 'tu?u"na?ak + ,'?u'uah"pi '?e'?i"xik 'ia "ha?a 'ta'?ke"uer + ,'?ie?e'i"xik + .'?in'ta"kix '?a?a"ru + 471 + '?i'ha?ax"to '?e'ui"nik + '?e?e -- 'xe?e -- ,'?keh"txa '?ko"to 'ia"ha?a + '?pa?ak"ta '?u'ui"ra 'ke?e -- ,'?e'ui"nik + '?e?e -- ,"ua 'ra'?kih"na + ,'?i'ha?a"xir + . '?pa?ak"ta +

481 + ."pe 'ro'ha?a"xir "txe + 'ke?e -- , "ne?en '?a"ian 'ni'ba"lor + '?ie?e -- ,'?e'ui"ni 'ki"ra 'ke"fuer 'ta?a"?tsa'?u"me 'nu'ui"la 'ma + ,'?i"ne?en + .'tu"?kaŋ 'koh"ko + 488 + ,"txe 'ke'?u'iak"ta '?u"?pa '?i"xin + ,'tu?u"ho 're'ui "nik 'xe?e"ua 'ra'?u'ua"?tsi '?u'uix"ka?ar + '?ka"na?a "nu?u 'lo?k"se 'i"xik + 'tu?u"?ka?p '?e?e -- ,'ui"nik + ,'?i'ha?a"xir + ,"uar 'ta"ka '?a'?ko"toi + ,'hahp"na + ,'hu"hra 'ta"rum + , "ua 'ra'?ka"xi + ,'hahp"na '?a'pa"ta 'da + , '?koh"?ta 'u"nu?u?k + .'?i'txa'mes"na +

16. Henpecked Husband

501 + '?i?i -- '?ie?e -- ,'?e?ei"xik 'ia "ha?a + ,'?u"men 'ta"ka '?e'?ke"uer "tia?a "uar '?a?ah"?tsa + ,'txa"mai + ,"por 'ke?e 'kuŋ"ga 'na + .'ta'xar"na 'ta"rum + 508 + .'?i'txa"mai +

509 + ,'?i'?pa'nix"to + ,"txe 'ke?e + ,'?e 'ui"nik 'ia"ha?a + ,'?ko"toi + '?e?e -- ,'u'txam "se '?u'ui"la 'ma + ,"pe 'ro'ta'ke?e -- ,'?u'xi 'ni"txir '?e'su"?pin + ,'?i'ta"ka '?u"pu?uk '?e 'si"nam + .'pu?uk"?pir 'ta'ke?e"txi 'le +

519 + ,'?i'po"re 'so + "txe?e "hen 'te 'ke?e -- ,'?e'si"nam + '?e?e -- '?us -- '?u?u -- '?u'xi'ni"txir '?e?e -- ,'su"?pin + "txe 'ke?e — 're"me 'dio"tua?a -- ,'u"txe '?a'?kih"nan "te?e + 530 + '?i'po"re 'so'txe?e"no?p 'ke?e 'ui"nik 'xe?e'ma?a"txi '?ua?a -- ,'?a?a"?tso 'ta "ku?u 'ui"la 'ma + "mu?u 'na?a"ta '?u?u -- '?u 'ua"?tsi '?u'ui"la 'ma "txe 'ke?e -- '?e?e -- , '?u'xi'ni"txir '?e'su"?pin + '?i?i -- ,'?u"pu?uk '?e'si"nam + ,'pu?uk"?pir 'ta'ke?e"txi 'le + '?e?e -- '?u'iu"?txi 'ta'ke?e -- ,'?u"kal "dui 'ri'ia"?katx + ."txe 'ke?e're"me 'dio"tua?a '?a 'ka"no '?a?a"?tso '?e'ui"nik +

544 + "pe 'ro"ne?en 'ma?at -- ,"pe 'ro "ne?en 'ma?a"txi?iŋ 'gui"ra + "kai + ,'te'?ker "na '?e'ui"nik + .'?u"me 'nu"iet 'ui'ni"kir + '?i"ni? 'iŋ"ha?a 'xe?e'i"xik 'ma?a"txi?iŋ 'gui "ra?a -- ."kai '?koh"?ta '?u"nu?u?k + 551 + '?i'po"re 'so'ma?a"txi?i -- .'?iŋ'?ku?up"se 'hai 'ber"da +

553 + ,'?i"ne?en + 'ma?a"txi?i -- '?ũ?ũn "?txi '?u?u -- ,'xi'ni"txi 're'su"?pin + '?i 'ma?a'txi?in'xa"na?a 'sah"ka '?e'si?i -- "nam + "tua?a '?ũ?ũn -- '?ũ?ũn"?txi '?u"pu?uk 'ta'ke?e — ,'?e"txi 'le + "por 'ke'ma?a"txi '?ka"ni?in — .'?in'te?e"kruir 'ni"uet 'ui'ni"kir +

16. Henpecked Husband

1 There is another story that is told. 5 They say that there was a man who was beaten hard by his wife. 11 They say that that man's wife would go out and walk to town, and would not go back home. 17 That woman, every Sunday, went down to town, arrived and stayed to drink, in town.

26 And he, he stayed indoors, keeping house, and -- and that woman, when she came back the next day -- when she came back she would always scold her -- her husband. 39 And when she found her husband had made no tortillas, or had made no *chilate*, she would grab a rope and whip him.

47 And then that man, when he was beaten by his wife, he would cry out. 53 Because he was beaten by his wife. 55 And he, since he knew he would be beaten by his wife, therefore when the woman went out to walk to town, he watched and watched for her, (to see) what time she would return. 64 And he would get up and get busy making tortillas, making *chilate*, for his wife to drink when she came, because he was afraid. Because he knew that he would be beaten by the woman.

75 And therefore when she came, his -- his wife, walking, when the sun was high in the sky, he would get up and get busy looking for something to give to the woman who was coming. 85 And -- as soon as he saw her coming into view, he quickly busied himself, taking her gourd bowl and washing it, so as to give water to the woman when she came inside. 96 And -- he put down her -- bowl, so that the woman could eat. 102 Every time his wife went into town, so he would do when the woman came back. 108 Because he knew that he would be beaten.

16. Henpecked Husband

110 And then that woman came one day and brought a man along, the man with whom she walked into town. One day they say that she brought him along home to eat with them. 124 Then that man, since he had watched for his wife to come up the path, saw that she was coming with the man. And he at once got busy, took the water, and gave it to the woman who was coming there.

138 But they say that one day there were other men -- the neighbors of the man -- that man. 147 They said, "You, you are not a real man. 151 You let that woman you live with dominate you, because she goes walking into town, and you stay and grind, and when she comes back, she brings her man home. And you -- you live just like a woman because of her. You are not a man, but like a woman you're always indoors. 169 Because when you see a man who stays keeping house, making tortillas, grinding, and doing everything, -- then you are not a man."

180 Then the man said, "But what can I do since -- if I don't do what she tells me, she finishes me off with a whip when she comes. Because when she finds me, if I don't give them anything to eat when they come, she beats me as she pleases. 195 And that is what I am afraid of. 197 And therefore I do what she tells me."

199 But -- the men said, "But wait; we will -- we will -- see what can be done." 207 Then they say that those men began to go walking every -- Thursday, because they say that Thursday was Hol Txan day. We do not know what *hol txan* is. 221 But -- but they say that -- Thursday, that was Hol Txan day.

228 And -- then those men, they say, brought a gourd bowl, put it down under an aca-

cia tree. 239 And the -- acacia ants, where -- it dripped, then it fell in the gourd that was placed there by them. They waited for eight days to pass and went to get the bowl that was placed at the acacia by them.

251 And when they came and saw, they say that there was a little water standing in the bowl. 256 They say that -- with this, there would be a remedy.

260 Then, on the next Thursday, they went and began to look for a scorpion, under a stone. 267 They found some, 268 and then the -- the stingers of the scorpions -- they say, they began -- to order that they be toasted on the griddle, and -- they ground them up, and mixed them with the -- the urine of the scorpions. 279 Uh -- the -- the *acacia ants*.

284 And -- then they began mixing them, and -- they ordered a chicken killed. 290 They went to ask that man. And -- they gave it to him. They deceived him, (saying), "We are having a celebration. And -- we say -- a chicken with rice has been prepared. And we wanted you to come visiting. Because we are celebrating."

305 Then the man said, "But -- she isn't home, my -- my wife isn't home. And if she finds that I'm not home, she's going to finish me off with a whip."

311 And they said, "If we see her coming, we will leave you, 315 and we will tell her that we are bringing you, so that she will not beat you."

319 Then that man, who was afraid, went along. 323 And when he arrived, they say that

the an -- uh -- the scorpions were already prepared, and the urine of the acacia ant. It was already prepared in a little chicken broth, which was given to him to drink.

341 They said to him, "You seem a little sick, and very weak, and that is why we had you brought here, because we wanted to give you a little of this chicken broth to drink. Maybe it will fix you up."

354 He took it and drank it. And he said, "But -- what is in this broth? It -- it really has a -- an odor."

364 And the woman said -- said to him, "Oh that's just the oregano I put into it, and I put in a little chile. I wonder if -- you know that chile has a bite, and I put some in."

367 Then the man said, "Chile -- I can eat that."

372 Then she said to him, "Would you like some more? I'll put in a little more."

377 And they say that that chile was mixed with scorpion stings and -- acacia ants. 384 It was dropped into the broth that he was drinking.

386 And then when the next Sunday came, his wife went down to town. And he didn't feel like making tortillas, nor did he feel like making *chilate*. 395 And he soon began to have a prickly feeling in his body.

400 And he said to himself, "But what's happening to me? Am I the man who couldn't get angry? I used to be afraid of that woman, but

now I think if -- if she comes back again and -- the way she has been treating me, today it won't be safe. 411 Today, what I'm going to do with her, I'm going to kill her with the whip."

413 They say that that woman, since she didn't know what was being done with her husband she went down to town, stayed there drinking, and when daylight came, on Monday, she came back to her house, bringing with her the man who would go walking with her.

429 And she came in with him, and saw that her husband, who was sitting inside, paid no attention to her. They were not given water, nor anything to eat.

439 Then she said to the husband, "You, what are you doing this way, not paying any attention, not giving us a little water?"

447 Then the man said, "Well, there's a little *chilate* made today that I put out. 453 In the old days you used to take your pleasure with me. Now you bring your man and come into my house, and I put up with everything. But what you started, whipping me, today, you pay for."

464 They say that that man, of whom it was said that he had not prepared *chilate*, he took off his belt from his waist, and hit that woman with the whip. And the woman began to cry out. 471 And then the man, who -- the one she went out with -- was frightened to see the husband -- the man getting angry, and he was afraid.

481 But he said that, "I am brave, and this man was beaten hard by his wife, and I -- what am I waiting for?" 488 They say that he

threw himself on top of the man who was beating his wife. He wanted to get the woman out of the man's hands. And when he came out, he was grabbed and thrown to the ground. And as he fell he was hit by a kick. His neck was wrung, and he was killed.

501 And that woman, from the whipping she was given, she died, because she was so trampled on the ground, 508 and she died.

509 And so, they say, that man came to kill his wife, but with acacia ants and scorpion stings put into chile.

519 And that is why people say that scorpions and uh -- acacia ants, they say, the remedy makes a person angry. 530 And that is why they say that a man who doesn't fight with his wife, who doesn't know how to punish his woman, they say that acacia ants and scorpion stings, put into chile, and drunk with chicken broth, they say it's a remedy for teaching a man to fight.

544 But I didn't -- but I didn't see when the man began being kicked by his fellow-man, nor did I see the woman begin to have her neck wrung. 551 And that is why I don't know if it is true.

553 And I don't drink uh -- acacia ants, and I don't go looking for scorpions to drink their stings with chile. because I don't want to trample on my fellow-men.

17. Henpecked Salesman

1 + '?a"ia 'no'tron"te?e -- ,'?o'hro"ner +
,'?a'?kah"na + .'ta"ri 'xe"tiem 'po + 5 + ,
"txe 'ke?e'?a"ian 'in"te?e 'ui"nik + '?e?e -- ,
'?e'ui"nik 'ia"ha?a + '?a?ah -- ,'?ah'xot"man +
'ta'ma?a -- ,'tu"?ki?ik 'tu"?ki?ik + ,'?u'xot'ma
"ni + ,'?a?a"xin + .'?u'txo"ni '?in"naht + 15
+ '?i?i -- ,'sa"tar + "?es 'to?o -- ,"?o 'txo"di
'ia + .'ma?a"txi '?a'?ko"toi 'ta'?u'io"tot +

20 + '?i?i -- '?ie?e -- ,'?e'i"xik + ,'xe
'?u'uix"ka?ar + "txe 'ke?e -- ,'ma?a"txi + '?u
'?pa?a"kre '?u?u -- .'no"xi?ip + 28 + '?e?e --
,'ha?ax"to '?e'ui"nik + ,'?ko"toi 'in"te?e "di
'ia + '?a'ro?o?p"na '?u"me 'nu?u -- .'?u'be"sii
"no?p + ."txe "tua?a + ,"ne?et + ,'ua?a"ret "ua
'ri'xa"na + '?a?a -- ,'?a'si?ik"?pa '?a'tu"min +
'?ii?i -- ,'?a'uix"ka?ar + .'ma?a"txa?a 'na?a"ta
'tu"?ka "ua 'ru"txe 'ta'ka"ret + 41 + ,'ha?a
"xir + 'ma?a"txi "ua 'ru?u -- ,'u'?pa?a"kre?et +
"por 'ke?e -- ,'ha?a"xir + "kon 'da?a -- ,"ne?et
+ ,'?i'lo"?koi 'i'xa"na + ,'?i'ha?a"xir + ,'?u
'io"se '?in"te?e 'ui"nik + .'?a'ua"ian 'ta"kar +

52 + ,'?i'ha?a"xir + 'ma?a"txi 'u'?ku?u?p
"se "hai -- 'ber"da 'lo'ke?e -- "ua 'ru?u -- .
"txe '?u'uix"ka?ar + 56 + ."txe + "pe 'ro'ko
"txa?a -- ,'ma?a"txi "ua 'riŋ'gui"ra "ne?en +
"ma 'ko'txe?e"rer "tua?a -- '?iŋ -- '?iŋ'gua?a
"re 'ke?e -- ,'ber"da + "por 'ke'ma?a"txi 'riŋ
'gui"ra + 64 + "?es 'to'ke"ha?ax + ,'ne?e"natx
'?iŋ'gui"ra + 'ta'mu?u"na?k "niu?ut + ,'?en"ton
'ses + .'?iŋ'?ku?u?p"se + 69 + '?i?i -- ,'ha?a
"xir + 'ma?a"txi '?u?u -- ,'?ku?u?p"se + ,'ma?a
"txu?u 'ta'res"ka 'so + .'lo'ke'?a'ro?o?p"na '?u
"me 'nu'be"si 'no + 75 + "pe 'ro?o -- ,'?in
'te?e"to + '?a'lo"?koi '?a?a -- ,'?a'xa"na + ,
"naht '?a'txon"ma + ,"ie?ei "xik + ,'ko'txa?a
"tix + ,'?u'ui"ra + '?a?a -- '?a'lo"?koi '?u?u
-- ,'no"xi?ip + ,'?a'xa"na + ,'?u'uah"pi '?u
"?puhr '?a?a"xin + .'ta"kar "tu?ut "ha?a + 89

17. Henpecked Salesman

+ '?ie?e -- ,'ui"nik + 'xe?e -- ,'?a'?ko"toi + , '?a'ua"ian 'ma"ku?u + "ia?a '?u?u -- ,'ta"hui '?u"?po?o?p + "tu?ut "ha?a +

97 + ,'?u'ia?a"re '?e'ui"nik + ,'ke?e'ni 'no?xi?ip + ,'?i"xin 'txon"ma + '?i?i -- '?i 'ma?a"txi '?a'io?o"pa + '?e?e -- ."di "io?p '?i "ra + 104 + ,'?en"ton 'ses + ,'?e'ui"nik '?a "tsa?ai + "por 'ke?e -- ,"ha?ax '?a'ket"pa + '?e?e -- .'ta'ke?e'?i"xik +

110 + ,'?i'?ko"toi '?e"di 'ia + ,'?a 'ro?o?p"na '?o'tro"niahr + .'?e'ui"nik 'ia"ha?a '?u"me 'nu'be"sii "no?p + 113 + .'?a'ro?o?p"na + 'ma?a"txa?a '?ku?u?p"se 'lo'ke?e -- ,'ka'ua?a "re?et + ,"pe 'ro + ,'?a'uix"ka?ar + ,'ma?a "txi?ix + .'?u'?pa'?kahr"se?et + 120 + "por 'ke?e -- ,'ha?a"xir + 'ma"ha?ax 'ke?e -- 'uar"to '?u?u -- ,'u'ta're"set 'ta"ma '?u'no"xi?ip + 'ha?a"xir + '?a"ian '?o'tron"te?ei 'xe?e -- '?e?e -- 'tu"ru -- '?e?e -- .'ta"kar +

131 + ,'ha?ax"to '?e'ui"nik 'ia"ha?a + "txe 'pues + 'ma?a"txin 'na?a"ta "hai -- ,'ber "da + ,"ha?ax 'ni'kin'na?a"ta + 'ke?e -- ,'ber "da + .'?iŋ'?ku?u?p"se '?a"ni +

139 + '?i"txe 'tua?a'?u"me 'ne?e -- .'?u 'be"sii "no?p + ,"tua?an 'na?a"ta + 'ke?e -- "uar -- ,'ka'ua?a"re?et + ,'?i"ma "ha?ax 'ta'ma 'men"ti 'ra"uar 'ka'ua?a"re?et + ,"ma "ha?ax 'in 'ta"ka "uar -- 'ka'ma'hre"set + '?e?e -- .'txe?e "no?p "kuen 'ta + ,'?a'ui"ra + ."?es 'to'ke"ma '?a'ta"huio?p + 151 + '?i?i -- ,'ma"na + '?ab -- ,'tu"?ka "ko 'sa'?ka"na?a 'ma"ni + ,'ma"na + '?i?i -- '?a"txe "ma 'nia'ke?e -- .'?ka"ni?i "xi 'txon"ma + 159 + ,'?i?i"xin '?a'tur "?pa + , '?in"naht + .'?i'sut"pa 'ua"te?et + 162 + ,'?i "?txa?an + '?e?e -- ,'tu?u"pat '?o"tot + 165 + ,'?i"ia + .'ia?ak'?pa"re + 167 + ,"tua?a '?u

17. Henpecked Salesman

'ui"ra "hai + '?e?e -- .'?in'ta"ka "uar 'ka'ma 'hre"set +

170 + '?ie?e'ui"nik 'ia"ha?a + ,"kai + , '?u'ma"ni + ,'tu"?ka 'xe'?ka"na?a "xin 'u'txo"ni + ,'?i"xin + ,'?u'ma"ki '?u'tu'ru"?pa 'ta"maŋ "go 'hro"tot + ."tia?an "naht + 177 + .'?u 'ia?a"re 'u'uix"ka?ar 'lo"?koi + 178 + ,"ne?en '?in"xi 'ne"ra + 'ma?a"txi "tua?a -- '?in'sut "pa?a -- '?e?e -- 'se"ma 'na"ra + 'si"no 'ke?e -- "?ehs 'to'ta'ma?a -- ."kin 'se"di 'ia'?a'koh "kue?en + 186 + "por 'ke?e -- ,'?in"naht + , '?ka"ni?in "xin 'xa"na + .'?i'ma?a"txi "tua?a 'nio?o"pa + 190 + ,'?en"ton 'ses + "txe '?e?e -- '?u'ia?a"re '?u?u -- ,'uix"ka?ar + ,'?txa "?pun 'ni"pa?a + ."tua?aŋ '?ke"txe '?ã?ã"xin + 196 + "por 'ke?e -- '?e?ex"na "ren 'ĩ?ĩn"xin + 198 + ,'?i'ha?ax"to + ,'?e'i"xik + "kai '?u?u -- ,'?txa"?pu '?e"pa?a + ,'?u'?pa"si + ,'?u'iah "?ku '?e'ui"nik + .'?u'?ke"txe?e 'lo"?koi +

205 + ,'?i'ha?a"xir + ,'ket"pa + ,'?i"kon 'da'?ix"to + ,'?ak'?pa"re + ,'ma"xa?an '?u?ut'?e "rum + ,'?ko"toi '?e'ui"nik + .'xe?e'?u'na?a "ta?a '?ko"toi + 212 + ,'?ko"toi + ,"kai + '?e?e -- ,"uio?o?p + '?i?i -- ,'?ie?e'ui"nik + 'xe?e -- '?u?u -- "txe 'ke?e -- ,'?i"xin 'xa"na + 'u'koh"ko 'ta"ka + ,'iam"pa "?u?ut '?e"rum + ,'?o"txoi "?txa?an + ,'ma"kui?i 're'?ko"pat + '?e?e -- .'tu?u"?pot '?o"tot + 228 + .'?ka "nu?u 'ui"ra + .'tu"?ka '?a"ian + 230 + ,'?i 'ha?a"xir + ."ia "?txa?ar "kon 'da'?ko"toi 'e'ui "nik + '?in"ton 'ses + "txe 'pues + .'ber"dah "txi?i "ua 'ra?a'no?or"na '?i"ne?en 'ma?a"txi?iŋ '?ku?up"se + 235 + "pe 'ro?o -- '?e"ra 'si?i -- .'?iŋ'gui'rix"to "ia?a +

238 + '?i?i -- ,"ia "?txa?ar 'tu'?po?o"tot + ,'?u'iu"?pi + ,"pe 'ga'a'tse?e"ne '?e'i"xik 'ta'ke?e'ui"nik + '?e?e -- .'?u'lo?ok"su?u

17. Henpecked Salesman

"nu?uk '?a"tse?e "nio?p + 244 + '?i?i -- ."kai "uio?o?p + 245 + ,'ha?a"xir + ,'?in'ta"ka 'tu "ru?u 'iu"?pi + .'tu"?po?o "tot + 248 + ,'?i '?u'koh"ko + ,'?ak'?pa"re + ,'u'tah'pe"so?p '?e "?kahk + ,'?i'ha?a"xir + ."ia 'tu"ru + ,'ma'ku?u '?ko"pot + ,"ua 'ru'?koh"ko + .'tu"?ko 'ra"tua?a 'ua'ie"no?p +

256 + "kon 'da?a -- ,'?u'koh"ko + ,'?txaŋ '?ka"?po?o?p + ,'?i'?i"xin + ,'tu"ruan + ,'ta 'mu?u"su 'ie"puer 'ta + ,'?i"ia 'tu"ru + "kon 'da -- '?e?e -- ,'?atx"pa '?e'ui"nik + '?e?e -- ,'lo"?koi + .'pa"tir + 269 + '?i'ha?a -- '?ie?e'ui"nik 'xe?e -- ,'tu'ru"ua 'ra'kohk"san + ,'tu?u"su 'ie"puer 'ta + '?e?e -- ,'lo"ke '?u "txe + ,'ha?a"xir + ,'?u'?txu"?pa '?in"te?e + , "?txa?an 'ta"mu?ut '?e"puer 'ta'paa"tir + ,'u 'ka"txi + 279 + ,'?i'ha?ax"to '?e'ui"nik 'xe?e'?ka"na?a "na?a 'lo"?koi 'paa"tir + .'ma?a "txa?a 'pas"?ke?e "puer 'ta"tu?ut + 281 + "?i?i -- .'?u'ia?a"re?e 'i"xik + 283 + ,'tu "?ka "ga 'na'?e"puer 'ta"ra + ,'ma?a"txa?a 'pas "?ka +

285 + '?e?e -- ,'?e'i"xik "txe + .'?a'sa "ber 'tu"?ka '?u'koh"ko + .'?eh'?kar"to 'ka'ui "ra + 289 + '?e?e -- '?e?e -- ,"txe "tua?a '?u "me 'ne'i"xik + "hai -- ,'?ka"na?a "txe '?a'man "da 'do + ,'?e"rer + .'?ia?a"uan 'ta"mu?ut '?e "puer 'ta + 296 + .'?eh'?kar"to 'ka'ui"ra 'tu "?ku?u 'koh"ko 'e"puer 'ta + 297 + ,'?i"txe 'ke?e'ui"nik 'ia"ha?a + "kai '?u?u -- '?u"txe '?u?u -- ,"ha?a + .'ta"mu?ut '?e"puer 'ta +

302 + ,'?ie?e'ui"nik + "ia 'tu"ru "ti?iŋk — "ti?iŋ 'si'?pa"ner + '?u?u -- ,'?u'ui"ra + , '?i"kon 'da'?ix"to + ,'?u'ui"ra + 'ke?e"ua 'ru "txe '?u?u -- "ha?a '?e'ui"nik + 'ta"mu?ut '?e "puer 'ta + ,'?u'uah"pi + ,'?u'te'hro"mar + ,'?e 'ui"nik 'ia"ha?a + ,'ua?ak"txe 'ta"ka + '?u?u --

17. Henpecked Salesman

,'?u'xu"ri 'ta'man"te?e 'na"ba 'ha + ,'?ke"txe 'ru'me"ner + '?e?e -- ,'hu?uk"?pir + 321 + '?i?i -- 'tas"?pir 'ta"ka 'u"txe '?e?e -- .'?e '?u'te'hro"mar '?e'ui"nik 'ia"ha?a + 324 + , '?i'ia?a"tix + ,'ua'kas"pa '?e'ui"nik + ,'?ka"xi 'ta'mu?u"su 'ie"puer 'ta + 'me"nix -- .'?o"hron +

329 + ,'?i'ha?ax"to + ,'?e?ei"xik + ,'?atx "pa '?u'ui"ra + ."txe + .'tu'?kix"tu?u 'koh "kue?e 'ui"ni 'ki"ra + '?pa"ni 'xe?e -- ,'ku'kre "ma + 336 + '?i?i -- "kon 'da?a -- ,'?atx"pa '?u'ui"ra + ,"ka 'iu'peh"ka + '?e?e -- 'tu'?kix "ta?a 'koh"ko "me 'ro?o -- .'ku'kre"me?et 343 + '?ie?e -- ,'ui"nik + ,'ma?a"txi?ix '?o"hron + "por 'ke?e -- .'txa"mi?ix + 348 + "kai + '?u?u -- ,'?u'sah"pi + ,'?u"ho 're'ui"nik + '?u?u -- , 'po"hro 'in"te 'ru"kuer 'po + "hai -- ."ma 'tu "?ka '?u'koh"ko + 356 + '?i?i -- "ma 'tu"?ka?a -- .'?u'koh"ko + 359 + '?i?i -- ,'ha?a"xir + , "uar '?u'ia"txi + ,"ua 'ru'peh"ka + '?i'ma?a "txi?i -- .'?o?o"hro 'ne'ui"nik + 365 + ,'?en "ton 'ses"txe + '?a -- ,'?a'sa"ber 'ma?a"txi?i -- .'txa"mai '?e'ui"ni 'ki"ra + 369 + ,'?ia"go 'ra + "ma "ha?ax 'ni?i -- ,'ni'no"xi?ip + 'tu "?ka?a '?kam'pan"txe 'ta"kar "hai -- ,'txa"mai + ,"tu?ut 'o"tot 'ta"ra + .'?a?a"xa?a 'ta'hui"na + 376 + '?u"me 'ne?e -- .'ui"nik + ."?iah "iu 'mo "tot +

379 + '?i?i -- ,'?atx"pa + ,"kai + ,'?u 'sah"?pes + ,'?e"?kahk + .'?u'?txuh"?ku 'tu "?ku?u 'koh"ko + '?i?i -- "kon 'da?a -- ,'?u'ui "ra + ,'ke'?e'ui"nik + ,"ha?ax + '?u?u -- ,"te 'hro"mar + .'xu"hra + 393 + ,'?en"ton 'ses"txe + ,'?i"txa?a'na'nu?u'me"ner + 'txa'mes"ne '?e'ui "ni 'ki"ra '?ia"go 'ra'ke?e -- ,'ma?a"txi 'tu"ru 'ni'no"xi?ip + .'tu"?ka?a '?kam"pan "txe 'ta"kar + 398 + '?i"txe 'ke?e -- ,'ta'kiak"?par + 'ua?a"uaŋ "kai -- ,'ti'kru"ma 'ta"kar + ,'u'ka

17. Henpecked Salesman

"txi '?u"nu?u?k + ,'?e'ui"nik 'ia"ha?a + ,'ta 'man"te?e + ,"la 'so + '?u?u -- ,'ke'reh"?pa 'lo "?koi + .'?i"xin + 409 + "por 'ke?e"txe 'ke?e -- ,'?a"ia 'nin"te?e '?u'uam"kohn + ,'?a'ket"pa + '?i?i -- '?i'ia"ha?a 'ta'mu?u -- ,'ta'me?e "kohn + "ua?ar 'in"te?e "pe 'nia'ke?e -- "mei 'gra?a -- ,'?u"ial "tir + 418 + '?i"txe 'ke?e -- ,'?u'ke'reh"?pa '?i"xin + ,'ta'kiak"?par + , 'ta'me?e"la 'so + ,'?i"xin + '?u?u -- ,'?u'?txa "?pu "to?o 're"pe 'nia + '?i?i -- ,'?u'uah"pi + ,'?u'io"hres + .'?i"xin 'ta"mu?ut '?e"pe 'nia +

429 + ,'?i"kon 'da'?ix"to + ,'sa'koh"pa + ,'?ta"?pai 'e"?kin + '?e'ui"nik 'ia"ha?a 'ma?a "txi '?a?a -- ,'?a'?ko"toi 'tu?u'io"tot + ."ua 'ra'kohk"na '?u"me 'nu'uix"ka?ar + 435 + ,'?i ?ta"?pai 'e"?kin 'ma?a"txi '?ko"toi + ,'?en"ton 'ses + ,'?e?e'i"xik + ,'ta"ri + '?u?u -- ,'?u 'sah"ka + ko"txe?e '?u'na?a"ta "tia?a -- '?a?a -- ,'?a?a"xin '?a'ua"ian + .'ta"ri '?u'sah"ka + 445 + ,'io?o"pa + ,'ta'mio?o"tot 'ia"ha?a + . '?u'ia?a"re '?ei"xik + 'ma?a -- 'ma?a"txi 'ka?a -- 'io?o"pa 'ni?i -- ,'no"xi?ip 'ta"ra + ,'ta "rie 'niŋ'gui"ra + 'ke?e"ma?a "txa?at -- ,'?a '?ko"toi + '?i'ko'txa'na?a"ta 'ke?e -- ,'ta'ka "ret 'ua"ta 'ra'ua"ian 'ta"ra + 457 + .'po"re 'so'ra'ua"te?en '?u?um"?pi +

458 + ,'?en"ton 'ses'txe?ei"xik + .'ma?a "txi '?i"ra '?a'io?o"pa 'ta"ra +

460 + "pe 'ro?o -- ,'ma?a"txi '?a'?ko"toi 'tu?u'io"tot + ,'?i"ne?eŋ "gua 'riŋ'koh"ko + . 'ma?a"txa?a'?ko"toi + 464 + ,'ma"tia?a '?ah "?kiŋ 'ko'txe?e"ra + '?e?e -- '?a?a -- ,'?a'io?o "pa '?a'ua"ian 'ta'ka"ret 'ta"ra + "pe 'ro?o -- ,'?a?an'?txak"na 'ta"ka + .'ua"rix 'a'?ko"toi 'tu?u'io"tot +

471 + .'?en"ton 'ses"txe?ei "xik + "pe

17. Henpecked Salesman

'ro?o -- 'ma?at -- .'ma?a"txi "ua 'ra'io?o"pa +

475 + '?i?i -- ,'?en"ton 'ses + '?e'i"xik + ,'lo'ke'?u"txe + ,'?i"xin + '?e?e -- ,'?u 'txa?a'bi"sar + '?e?e -- '?e -- ,'?au'si"liar + ,'?atx"pa + "kai 'u?u -- ,'txa?a'si"tar + ,'?e "hen 'te'lo"?koi 'ta"kar + '?e?e -- ."kai '?u 'sah"ko?p + 494 + ,'txe?e"no?p 'ke'tal"bes '?a "ian + '?e?e -- ,'tu"?ku?u 'num"su?u "?pa + 497 + ,"kai '?u'sah"ko?o?p + '?i?i -- '?i'ko"txu?u 'na?a"to?p 'ke?e -- ,'?e'ui"nik 'ia"ha?a + '?e?e -- ,'se'pa"ra 'di'io"tot "tia?a '?ko"toi 'a'ua "ian + .'?i"xin '?u'sah"ko?o?p + ,'?ko"to?o?p 'ta'mio?o"tot 'ia"ha?a + ,"kai + ,'?u'tso"rio?p + '?e?e -- '?e"ras 'tro"tia?a -- ,'?a'?ko"toi 'e 'ui"nik + ,'?i"txe 'ke?e'?u'ta'hu"io?o?p + '?e?e -- ,'?e"se 'nia"tia?a + '?e?e -- .'lo"?ko 'ie'ui "nik 'ia"ha?a +

515 + '?i?i -- '?e'i"xik 'lo'ke?e"kai -- , 'na?a"uan 'ti'kru"ma 'ta'kiak"?par + 'u'ui"ra 'ke'?ko"toi 'e?e -- ,'?e"hen 'te'tu?u'io"tot "ua 'ra'kohk"na '?e'ui"nik + ,'?i'ha?a"xir + '?e?e -- .'?pa?ak"ti?ix + 523 + ,'?u'ui"ra + 524 + '?i?i -- ,"kai + '?txuhk"na '?e?e -- '?e?e -- , "ras 'tro"tia?a '?a?a"xin + ,"txe 'ke'?ko"toi + 'ta'ma?a -- ,'ta'man"te?e "?u?ut "?txen + 'ham "biahr 'tia?a -- ,'?u'io"hres '?i"xin + '?i?i -- '?ia'?a"ian "tia?a -- ,"?u?ut "kohn + '?a"ian 'tia?a -- ,"?u?ut 'ui"tsir + '?a"ian 'ta?a -- 'ta'mo?o -- ,'ta"mo?o 're"tun + ,"ia "ka 'iu 'kreh"?pa 'lu"mui +

543 + ,'?en"ton 'ses + ,'?ir"na + 'ke?e -- ,'?e'ui"nik + '?e?e -- .'txa'mes"?pir + 549 + '?i?i -- ,'nien'tak"pa 'xa"no?p + ,'?ko'to"io?p + 'ta'ma?a -- 'ta'man"te?e -- ,'?u?ut"tun + ,'u 'ta"huio?o?p + ,'u'tsu"tser 'u"ho 're'ui"nik + 'tia?a -- ,'?u'pa"hri + ,'lu"mui 'ta"mu?ut 'e "tun + 560 + ,'?en"ton 'ses + '?e?e -- "txe?e

17. Henpecked Salesman

— '?e"hen 'te"pues -- ,'?e'ui"nik '?i"ra + , '?ka"ni?i 'ui"ra + ,'ma?a"txi?ix 'tu"ru + "por 'ke?e — '?a"ia 'nu'tsu"tse 'ru?u -- '?u"hor "tia?a — .'ke'reh"na 'lu"mui +

571 + ,'?en"ton 'ses + ,'?u"txe 'se"gir + "kai '?u?u — '?i'xi"no?p 'ta'me?e'?e"se 'nia 'tia?a — 'ke'reh"na '?e?e -- ,'ui"nik 'ia"ha?a '?i"xin + '?i?i -- ,'?i'xi"no?p + '?i?i -- ,'?i '?ko"tuo?o?p + ,"to?or '?e"pe 'nia"tia?a '?o 'hres"na '?e'ui"nik 'ia"ha?a + '?e?e -- '?u?u -- .'?u'ui"ro?o?p 'ke?e"ia?a '?o'hres"na '?i"xin + 585 + ,'?ek"mai '?i'xi"no?p + ,'tu'ua'me"kohn + ,'?ko"toi + ,'?u'ui"ro?o?p + ,"ia "?txa?ar 'e'ui "nik + 'ta'ma?a — '?u?u -- ."su 'ie"pe 'nia + 593 + ,"ia "?txa?ar + .'txa"men +

595 + ,'?i"kai + '?u'ui"ro?p 'ket -- ,'tu "?ka '?u'koh"ko + "pe 'ro?o -- "txe 'ke?e -- , "ma 'txe"ker + ,"por 'ke?e'ui"nik + ,'?in'iah "rer + '?e?e -- ,'pux"?ka '?u"hor 'tia?a'?ko"toi '?ka"xi "to?o 're'tu"no?p + .'ta'miu?u"su 'ie"pe 'nia + ,"por 'ke?e"mei 'gra'?u'ial"tir + .'?e"pe 'nia + 608 + '?i?i -- ,'ma?a"txi + ,'txek"ta + ,'ko'txa + ,'txa"mai + '?e?e -- ,'?e'ui"nik 'ia "ha?a + "pe 'ro?o — '?e'i"xik 'txe?e"na '?u"kar 'go'ke?e — 'ke?e -- ,'ta"mar + ,'txa'mes"na '?e 'ui"nik + "por 'ke?e -- ,'ta'mu?u'io"tot 'tah'ui "na + '?e?e — '?e"ras 'tro'tia?a -- ,'?u'ke'reh "?pa '?i"xin + ,'?i'ta"ma '?u'tsu"tse 'ru"hor '?e'ui"nik + ,"dial 'ma + '?e?e -- 'tu"ra?a"xin 'ta'mu?ut'?e"tun 'tia?a -- 'kreh"?pa?a 'lu"mui + 630 + ,'?i'ta"mar + ,'?ko"toi + 'txek"ta 'ke?e — ,'ke?e"ha?ax + .'?u'txam"se +

635 + ,'?pa'nix"to + ,'?ko"toi + '?ka?a"pa '?e'ui"nik 'xe?e — '?a?a -- ,'?ko"toi 'a"ni + '?a'ua"ian 'ta'ka?a -- '?u?u -- ,'uix"ka?ar + . '?u"iet 'ui'ni"kir + 644 + "pe 'ro?o -- '?pa 'nix"to 'ta'me?e -- ,'ko'txe?e'ia"ha?a + ,'?ko

17. Henpecked Salesman

"toi + ,'?ka?a"pa + '?e?e -- ,'?u'iak"ta '?u'tsu "tse 'ru"hor 'ta"mu?ut '?e"tun + 'ko'txe?e -- . '?a'ke'reh"?pna 'e"?tsi?i + 653 + ,"pe 'ro "ne?en 'ma?a"txi?iŋ 'gui"ra + '?i'ma?a"txi?in -- .'ta"kre 'u'kreh"?pa +

17. Henpecked Salesman

1 There is another story that was told a long time ago. 5 They say there was a man, and that man was a re-seller. He went around re-selling everything, selling far away. 15 And he was gone as long as a week, not coming home.

20 And the woman who was his wife, they say that she was not afraid of her husband. 28 Then a day came when the man was spoken to by his neighbors. They said to him, "You are going around looking for money, and your wife, you don't know what she's doing to you. 41 She isn't afraid of you, because she, when you go out traveling, she brings in a man and sleeps with him."

52 And he didn't know if that was really what his wife was doing. 56 He said, "But since — I don't see it, there's no way I can say that it's true, because I don't see it. 64 When I see that with my eyes, then I will believe it." 69 And he didn't believe it. He paid no attention to what he was told by his neighbors. 75 But each time he went out walking, selling far away, the woman, as soon as she saw the husband go out, went and took her water jar and walked with it to the spring. 89 And the man who came and slept with her, there they would meet, at the spring.

97 She said to the man, that, "My husband has gone selling, and won't be back for the next few days." 104 Then the man was happy, because he stayed with the woman.

110 And a day came when he was spoken to again, that man, by his neighbors. 113 He was told, "You don't believe what we tell you, but your wife does not obey you. 120 Because she doesn't -- isn't -- treating you like a husband.

17. Henpecked Salesman

There is another -- living with her."

131 Then that man said, "I don't know if it's true. If I knew it was true I would believe it."

139 And he was told by his neighbors that "I know that what we are telling you -- and that we're not just lying to you." They said, "Watch them until you don't find them. 151 And buy whatever you want to buy, buy and pretend you're going to go selling. 159 Go put it down somewhere far away, and come back again. 162 And lie behind the house. 165 And there wait until night. 167 So as to see if we are just deceiving you."

170 And that man began to buy things which he would go selling. He put them away inside a house where they were far away. 177 He told his wife he was going. 178 "I'm going now. I won't be back this week. Instead, look for me in two weeks. 186 Because I'm going far away, walking, and I won't be back." 190 Then he said, he told his wife, "Make my tortillas, so I can carry them along. 196 Because I'll be gone a long time." 198 Then the woman began making tortillas, wrapped them up and gave them to the man; he carried them away.

205 And she stayed. And then when night fell and it was dark on the ground, the man came who was accustomed to coming. 212 He came and they began to eat. And the man who said that he had gone waited for it to be dark on the ground, and came to lie in the brush behind the house. 228 He wanted to see what was up. 230 And he was lying there when the man arrived. Then he said, "It's true, what I was told. And I didn't believe it. 235 But this, yes, now I believe

it."

238 And lying there, behind the house, he heard the woman keep laughing with the man; they threw their heads back with laughter. 244 And they began to eat. 245 He just stayed, listening, behind the house. 248 And he watched it become dark; they put out the fire, and he stayed there in the brush, waiting for the time when they were asleep.

256 When -- he waited until they fell silent, and went to sit at the doorstep, and there he waited until the man got up and came outside. 269 And the man who was there waiting at the doorstep, what he did, he hung a vine on the outside of the door, tied it. 279 And then the man who wanted to go outside, he couldn't open the door in front of him. 281 And he said to the woman, 283 "What's got into this door? It won't open."

285 The woman said, "I wonder what happened? Tomorrow we will see." 289 And -- and he was told by the woman, "If -- you want to do your business, you can, standing against the door. 296 Tomorrow we will see what's got into the door." 297 And they say that that man began to make water against the door.

302 And the man, waiting there in the dark saw, and when he saw that the man was making water against the door, he grabbed his penis, that man's, and suddenly cut it off with a pocket knife carried by him. Uh -- well sharpened. 321 And with one slice he did it -- that man's penis. 324 And immediately the man fell down at the doorstep, not making a sound.

329 Then the woman got up to see. She

17. Henpecked Salesman

said, "What's the matter with this man? He seems to have fallen down." 336 And when she got up to see, she began calling to him, "What's the matter with you? Have you fallen down?" 343 And the man did not speak, because he was already dead. 348 She began to stroke the head of the man, and felt all over his body, to see what was the matter. 356 And she found nothing. 359 And she was lifting him and calling to him, and the man did not speak. 365 Then she said, I wonder if this man is dead? 369 And now he is not my -- my husband. What am I going to do with him if he's dead? On the floor of my house here he's going to be found. 376 By my husband, the master of the house."

379 And she got up and began to light a fire, looking for what was the matter. And when she saw the man's penis was cut off, 393 then she said, "And by whom was this done? Was this man killed? And now my husband isn't here, what am I going to do with him?" 398 And they say that during the night she got busy with him, tied a rope around the neck of that man, and dragged him out, away. 409 Because they say that there was a ravine, and there at the ravine was a rock that was very high. 418 And they say that she dragged him in the night, by the rope, going to lay him on top of that rock. And she took him and dropped him from that rock.

429 And then when it got light, the sun came up, and that man didn't come to his house, where he was awaited by his wife. 435 And the sun came up and he didn't come. Then the wife came looking for him, since she knew where he was going to sleep, she came looking for him. 445 She came into that house and told the woman "Isn't — didn't -- my husband -- come here? I've come looking for him, because he didn't

come home, and since I know that he was coming to sleep here with you. 457 That's why I'm coming to ask."

458 Then the woman said, "He isn't coming here."

460 "But he isn't coming home, and I am looking for him. He hasn't come home. 464 There's never been a day like this. He's coming here to sleep with you, but as soon as it gets light, he comes home to his house."

471 Then the woman said, "But he isn't -- he doesn't come here."

475 And then the woman, what she did was to go notify the *auxiliar* in the village. 487 And the *auxiliar* got up and got people together, and they began to look. 494 They said that perhaps something has -- something has happened to him. 497 They began looking. And since they knew that that man -- uh -- there was a different house where he went to sleep, they went looking for him, and came to that house. They began to follow the track where the man had gone, and they say that they found the traces where that man had gone.

515 And that woman began to get up and get busy during the night; she saw that the people were coming to her house looking for the man, and she became frightened. 523 They looked, 524 and the track where he had gone began to be noticed; they say that he went into a deep gorge, and it was easy to see where he had been dropped. And it went where there were streams, where there were peaks, over rocks, there he had been dragged along.

17. Henpecked Salesman

543 Then it was seen that the man had been killed. 549 Nor had they gone far when they came to a rock and found hair from the man's head where he had been scraped over the rock. 560 Then the people said, "Well, this man, you will see, is already dead, because here are hairs from his head where he was dragged along."

571 Then they continued, and began -- they went along the trail where that man had been dragged. And they went along, and came to the top of the rock from where that man had been dropped, and they saw that there he had been dropped. 585 They went down into the ravine and came to see where the man was lying at the foot of the cliff. 593 There he was lying dead.

595 And they began to look to see what was the matter, but they say that it was not apparent, because the man's head was completely shattered when he fell from the top of the rock to the foot of the cliff, because the cliff was very high. 608 And it was not clear how he died, that man. But it was said to be the fault of the woman that -- because of her the man was killed, because at her house the trail was found, where she dragged him along, and many hairs from the man's head were on the rocks where he was dragged by. 630 And through that, it became apparent that she had killed him.

635 Thus came the end of the man who used to come to sleep with the wife of his fellow man. 644 But -- so by -- as -- he came to his end, leaving his hair on the rocks like a dog being dragged. 653 But I didn't see it. And I didn't help drag him.

18. Traveling Man

1 + ,'?a"ian 'o'tron"te?e 'ui"nik + ,'?a '?kah"na + 3 + "txe 'ke?e -- ,'?e'ui"nik 'ia "ha?a + '?e?e -- ,'ma?a"txi '?a'tu"ruan 'tu?u'io "tot + ,'?in'ta"ka + '?a'xa"na '?u?u -- ,'?u"txe 'ga"nar + ,"tia?an "naht + ,'ma?a"txi '?a'tu "ruan + .'tu?u'io"tot + 13 + '?i?i -- ,'ha?ax "to + ,'?u'uix"ka?ar + ,'a'ket"pa + ,'txo"kem + ,'?u'me"ner +

19 + '?i?i -- ,'?i"txe 'ke'?a"ian + 'in "te?e -- ,'ui"nik + '?e?e -- 'a'ket"pa?a -- , "ser 'ka + .'ta'ke?e'o"tot 'tia?a'tu"ro?o?p + 27 + ,'?ie?e'ui"nik 'ia"ha?a + "kon 'da?a -- , '?u'ui"ra 'ke'?a'lo"?koi + '?a'xa"na '?u?u -- , '?u'be"si 'no + ,'ha?a"xir + ,'?o?o"txoi + '?a?a -- 'ua"ian 'ta'ka?a -- .'?e'i"xik +

37 + '?i?i -- 'ie?e -- ,'?e'ui"nik + 'xe?e -- ,'?a'lo"?ko 'ia'xa"na + '?e?e -- ,'ha?a"xir + .'ma?a"txi 'a'?kih"na + ,'?a?a'ro?o?p"na + 'ke?e -- ,'?a'uix"ka?ar + 'ma?a"txi "ua 'ru?u -- '?u?u -- ,'?u'?pa'?ka"hre?et + "pe 'ro'ha?a"xir 'ma?a "txi?i -- .'?a'?kih"na '?u'iu"?pi + 53 + . 'ha?a"xir 'ma?a"txi '?a'tu"ruan + 54 + "por 'ke?e -- "txe 'ke?e -- 'ma?a"txi 'a?a -- '?a'?pa '?kahr"na '?u"me 'nu?u -- ,'uix"ka?ar + '?i?i -- '?i?i -- "ma "ha?ax '?in"te?e 'ui"nik + '?e?e -- '?e?e -- .'?a'?kih"na +

65 + ,"txe 'ke?e'ui"nik 'ia"ha?a + ,"kon 'da'tu"ru 'tu?u'io"tot + ,'?a'txe?e"na 'man"dar + '?a'?txa?a?p"san 'u"me 'nu?u -- .'?u'uix"ka?ar + 70 + ,'?i'?a"ian "di 'ia + "kuan 'do?o -- 'ma?a"txi '?a?a -- '?u"txa?a 'pu"rar '?e?e -- , '?e"pa?a + ,"txe 'ke'?a'?pak'?pu"na '?u"?ka?a?p + ,"tu?ut 'se"met + .'?u"me 'nu'uix"ka?ar + 78 + "por 'ke?e'ma?a"txi '?a?a -- .'?a'lo"?koi '?a '?txa?ap"san + 80 + 'ma?a"txa?a "na?a '?pa '?kahr"na '?u"me 'nu?u -- .'uix"ka?ar +

18. Traveling Man

82 + '?i?i -- ,'?i"txe 'ke'?e'ui"nik 'ia "ha?a 'xe?e'?o?o"txoi + ,'?a'ua"ian 'ta'ke?e'i "xik + "kon 'do?o -- ,"ha?ax 'a'?ko"toi + ,'?en "ton 'ses + '?e?e -- '?e?e -- 'ui"ni 'kia"ha?a 'xe?e'no'xi?i"?pir 'tua?a -- ,'?e'i"xik + "txe 'ke?e -- ,'?a'txe?e"na 'man"dar + ,'?a?a"?txa?an + ,"tu?ut '?o"tot + '?a?ah"ia '?e?e -- ,'si "?ti?it 'ta"mu?ut '?e"rum + '?o?o -- .'?a "?txa?an 'ta"mar + 100 + '?ie?e -- ,'ui"nik 'ia"ha?a 'xe?e"ua 'ra'?ko"toi + ,"ha?ax + '?a?a -- .'?a'ua"ian 'ta'ke?e'i"xik +

105 + ,'?in"ton 'ses + ,'?a"ian 'in"te?e "di 'ia + '?a'ro?o?p"na?a -- '?u"me 'ne?e?e -- . '?in"te?e '?u'be"si 'no + 110 + ,'?a'ro?o?p"na + ,"ne?et + ,'tu'?ka?a"non 'a'ui'ni"kir + ,'ke?e 'tsah"tsa + ,"ua 'ru"txe?et + '?e?e -- ,'?e?ei "xik 'tu"re?e 'ta"kar + 117 + ,"nien 'ni?i '?kih"na + ,'?a'ui"ra + .'lo'ke?e"ua 'ru"txe + 120 + ,'tu"re?et '?a'ui"ra + ,'?u'io"se?en "te?e 'ui"nik + ,'?a'ua"ian 'ta"kar + ,'?i"ne?et + ."tia?a '?i'ua"ian +

125 + ,'ha?a"xir "txe + "kon 'do?o -- ,'?a '?ko"toi + '?e?e -- ,'?e?en"te?e ,'ui"nik '?a'ua "ian + ,"ne?en + '?e?e -- ,'tu?ut"rum + '?u?u -- ,'?u'uai'ne'se"no?p + '?i"ia '?u'ua"io?p '?e?e -- ,'si"?ti?t + ."tua?a '?in"?txa?an 'ta"mar + 138 + .'?i'ha?a"xo?p '?a'ua'ie"no?p + .'ko"mon +

140 + ,'?en"ton 'ses + ,"txe 'tua?a + .'?u "me 'nu'be"si 'no + "pe 'ro"hai -- ,'?i'?pa?ak "ta + '?i"ma 'tu"?ka?a 'ba"lor 'tua?a -- 'tua?a -- '?a?a -- '?a'?ka"ie 'ta"ma?a -- ,'?a'uix "ka?ar + ."txen '?in"te?e "pre 'ba + 'ke?e -- , 'ki"ki?i 'xa"ne?en + ,"tal "di 'ia + '?i?i -- '?a"txe?e "ma 'nia'ke?e -- ,'?i?i'xi"ni 'xa"na + ,"tua?a 'ha?a'xi"ro?p 'a'ket"po?p + .'?a'ket "po?p '?u'?pah'ne'ro?p + 159 + ,'?i"ne?et + ,

18. Traveling Man

'?a'koh"ko + ,'?a?ak'?pa"re + ,'?io?o"txoi + , 'tsus'ta"ka + .'kon'da?a'koh"ko '?a'ua'ia"no?p + 165 + ,'?io?o"txoi + ,'?i'tu"ruan + '?e?e -- , 'io"?pe?e 'txak"te?e + ,'tia?a'?a'ua'ia"no?p + '?o?oi"?pi 'hai -- .'?a?a"ru '?u"nio?o?p + 172 + ,"pe 'ra?a'koh"ko '?a'ua'ie"no?p + .'tua?a 'ma?a"txi '?u'ui"ro?p 'io?o"txoi + 174 + ,'?i 'ma?a"txi '?a'uir"so?oit + ,'tua?a'ma?a"txi '?u 'ui're?e"to?p + ,'tua?a'?u'na?a"ta + '?e?ei"xik 'ke?e -- .'ma?a"txi 'tu"re?et + 179 + '?i"kon 'da?a -- ,"ia 'tu"re?et 'io"?pe?e 'txak"te?e + ,'?a'koh"ko?o?p + ,'?ia?atx"pa 'tsus'ta"ka + , 'a'po"hro '?u'te'hro"mar + ,'?e'ui"nik + 185 + ,'?a'tsa"ki '?a'xu"ri + ,'?i'lo"?koi 'ua?ak"txe 'ta"ka 'ta"kar + .'?i?i"xin +

188 + ,'?ie?e'ui"nik 'ia"ha?a "txe'ke?e "?pan '?u"txe + ,'lo"?koi + '?i"xin 'xa"na '?u 'ia?a"re '?e?e -- ,'?e'i"xik + ,'ke"ne?en '?ka "ni?in "xin + ,'?in'xa"na + .'?i'ma?a"txi '?in 'io?o"pa + 195 + '?e?e -- ,'?a'ui"ra 'tu"?ka "di 'ia + .'a'koh"kue?en + 198 + ,"ne?en + . '?e?ex'na"ren 'in"xin +

200 + "txe 'ke?e -- ,'?e?ei"xik 'ia"ha?a '?a"tsa?ai + ,'kct"pa '?u'?pah"ner + '?i?i -- , 'lu"mui 'tu"ruan + '?e?e -- '?e'ui"nik 'ta"kar + .'?i'nia"hrer + 208 + "por 'ke?e -- '?u'ia?a "re 'ke?e -- '?e?e -- ,'ni'no"xi?ip + ,'xe?e'tu "re?en 'ta"kar + ,'ha?a"xir '?i"xin + .'?i'ma?a "txi 'tua?a'io?o"pa + 215 + '?e?e -- '?e"rer 'i?i -- .'?i'lu"mui '?i'tu"ruan 'ta'ka"ren "ne?et + 218 + ,'?ie?e'ui"nik 'ia"ha?a + .'lu "mui 'tu"ruan 'ta"ka '?e'i"xik +

220 + '?i"txe 'ke?e -- ,'?e'ui"nik 'ia "ha?a + '?e?e -- .'?u"txe 'ko'txe?e'?a'ro?p"na '?u"me 'nu'be"si 'no + ,'?u'koh"ko '?ak'?pa"re + "kai + ,'?u"txa?ar 'ri"mar + ,'tu?u"pat '?o"tot + ,'ma"kui?i 're'?ko"pat + .'u'koh"ko '?ak'?pa

18. Traveling Man

"re + 230 + ,"kon 'da'?ix"to + '?u'koh"ko 'ke?e -- ,'sah"mi?ix '?ak'?pa"re + ,'?o"txoi 'tsus'ta"ka + '?u?u -- ,'?u'pa"si '?e"puer 'ta 'tsus'ta"ka + '?u?u -- .'?u'pa"si '?e"puer 'ta 'tsus'ta"ka '?o"txoi 'ma"ku?u + 238 + '?i?i -- '?u'iu"?pi 'ke?e -- ,'?a?a"ru '?u"nio?p + .'?e '?ah'uai'ni"ho?p + ,'?i"xin + ,'tu"ruan + '?e?e -- ,'io"?pe?e '?txak"te?e + '?u'iu"?pi "hai -- "hai -- .'?a?a"ru '?u"nio?o?p + 249 + '?i?i -- ,'ha?a"xir + ,"lis 'to'?ke"txer + '?in"te?e -- ,'na"ba 'ha'?u'me"ner + ,"kai '?atx"pa + ,'io "?pe?e '?txak"te?e 'tsus'ta"ka + '?u?u -- ,'?u 'po"hro + ,'?u'te'hro"mar '?e'ui"nik + '?e?e -- ,'?u'uah"pi 'ta"ka + ,'u'tsa"ki '?u'xu"ri + , '?i'lo"?koi 'ta"kar + '?ie?e -- ,'?e?ei"xik + 'ko"txa?a -- ,"ua 'ra'ua'ia"no?p + .'nia?a"txi '?u"txo?p 'sen"tir + 'tu"?ko 'ra?a -- .'xu"hra '?e'ui"nik +

270 + ,'?i"kon 'dix"to + ,'?pix"?ka '?e'?i "xik + '?u"txe 'sen"tir 'ke?e -- 'ke?e -- ,'ku "xur "?u?ut 'e?e -- ,'e"pohp "tia?a '?a'ua'ie "no?p + '?e?e -- ."txe + ,"ne?et + 'tu'?kix"to "ua 'ra"txe -- '?e?e -- '?pa"ni 'xe"to?o 're "ha?a '?txa?a -- ,"to?or "ha?a '?txa?a"rum 'ka 'ua"ian 'a'me"ner + '?e?e -- 'tu"?kot 'ma?a"txi 'lo"?kue?et 'paa"tir 'ke?e -- ."tu?ut 'txak"te?e "ua 'ra"txe '?a"ha?a + ,'?ie?e 'ui"nik + 'ma?a "txi '?a?a -- ,'?o?o"hron +

289 + .'ha?a"xir "pe 'ga'u'peh"ka + '?e?e -- ,"ua 'ru'ia?a"re 'ki"ki?i 'paa"tir + '?ka?a "pi?i 'xa?a -- '?a?a -- ,'?a'?tsa'iu?ut '?e"pohp + ,"to?or "ha?a '?txa?a"run 'a'me"ner + 296 + '?atx"pe?en 'lo'?kem"pat + .'lo"?kem 'pa"tir +

298 + '?ie?e'ui"nik 'ia"ha?a "txe 'ke?e 'ma?a"txi '?a?a -- ,'?a'?pix"?ka + ,"pe 'ga'?u 'nih"?kes + .'ma?a"txi '?a'lo"?koi + 302 + , '?en"ton 'ses + '?atx"pa '?u?u -- ,'tsah"?pe 'se

18. Traveling Man

"?kahk + ,'?u'ui"ra + 'ke?e -- ,'?e'ui"nik + ,
'txa"men + 309 + '?i"to?o 're?e -- ,"?txi?i?tx
"?txa?ar 'ha?a"xir + .'?a'ua"ian + 312 + ,'?i
'ma?a'txix"tu?u 'na?a"ta 'ko'txa'tua?a'?u'txe
"ia?a + ,'?en"ton 'ses"txe 'ia"go 'ra + '?e?e --
'tu'?kix"to '?n?n -- ,'?u'nu?um"su?u "?pe?e 'ui
"ni 'ki"ra + 'ke?e -- 'ke?e -- "ma "ha?ax -- .
"ma 'tu"?ka 'u'koh"ko 'tu?u"kuer 'pu + ,'?i"kai
'?u'po"hro '?u'ui"ra + '?e?e -- .'?u'teh'ro"mar
'?e'ui"nik + "ma 'tu"?ka?a +

325 + ,'?i'ma?a'txix"tu?u 'na?a"ta "tia?a
'ta?a"xin 'ta"kar "ia?a + ,'?atx"pa + "ka 'iu?u
-- ,'tsah"pes 'e"?kahk + '?i?i -- ,'?u'uah"pi +
'?e?e -- ,'?in"te?e "txu 'sa + ,"kai + '?u'io"ri
'e"?txen 'ta'mu?u -- ,'ta'mu?u"ti?i '?e"?kahk +
"tia?a -- ,'?u'xu"ni '?e"?kahk + "ka 'iu?u -- ,
'?u"txe '?e"?txen + ,'?in"te 'ro"no 'txe + ,'tu
"ru '?a'pah"no + '?u'koh"ko 'ke?e -- ,'tsak"ta
'?e"?txen + '?i"xin "ka 'iu?u -- '?u?u -- ,'io
"hres '?e'ui"nik + ,'?o"hri 'ta'txak"te?e +
'?e?e -- .'?u'ia"ri 'ta"?txen + 350 + '?i?i --
,'ua?ak"txe 'ua?ak"txe + "ka 'iu?u -- ,'?u'?pu
"?ti '?e"rum 'ta"mar + ,'sa'koh"pa "mas 'sa'koh
"pa + "ka 'i?u?u -- ,'?u'?to"ri '?e"?kahk "to?o
'ru'mu"hrer '?e'ui"nik 'ia"ha?a + '?i"txe 'ke?e
"ka 'iu?u -- '?u'pu"si '?e"tan 'ta'me?e -- '?e?e
-- ,'?e"?txi?i?tx + '?ie?e -- ,'?e"pohp 'ia"ha?a
+ ."kai '?u'po"ki "bien 'ta'ke?e'?kih"na?a +

364 + ,'?i'kon'da'han'?txak"na + ,"kai
'pohr"na '?e'ui"nik 'ia"ha?a + ,'ma?a"txi 'ta
'hui"na + 'ko"ra 'ko"ra "pe 'hur -- '?a'pohr"na
'?u"me 'nu?u -- ,'?u'uix"ka?ar + .'ma?a"txa?a
'ta'hui"na + '?e?e -- .'?ko"toi '?a'ro?o?p"na
'?e'i"xik + 'ma'ka"ha?ax 'ta'ka'sa'koh"pa '?e?e
-- ,'?e'ui"nik 'ta'ka"ret + .'ma?a"txa?a '?ko
"toi 'tu?u'io"tot +

376 + .'ha?a"xir "txe 'ke'ma?a"txi + '?i?i

18. Traveling Man

-- ,'ha?a"xir '?u'na?a"ta 'ke?e'?u'mu"ki?ix + .
'tu?u'tu"ri?ip '?e"?kahk + 380 + "pe 'ro'?e'ui
"nik 'xe?e -- '?ko"toi '?u'xu'ri'?e?e -- ,'?e'ui
"nik + "txe 'ke?e -- ,'?u'xu"ri 'ta"ka + ,'?i
"xin + 'ta'man"te?e "kohn + "kai '?u?u -- ,'?u
'ua"ti '?u"na?a?k + '?e?e -- '?e'ui"nik 'ia"ha?a
'xe?e -- ,'?u'xu"ri + ,'kai'?u'?pu"?tia "?tsam
'ta"mar + .'?u'ta'kih"se +

394 + '?i?i -- ,'ta'ma"kin 'se"di 'ia +
'sut"pa 'io?o"pa + '?u'ia?a"re '?u?u -- .'?e'i
"xik + ,'?in'ta"res '?im"?pihk "ue?er 'ia"ra + ,
"tua?a '?a'?ku"xi + ,'ta"ma 'do"miŋ 'go'lo"?koi
'hur"ma 'ni'pa"tron + '?e?e -- ,'?u?u"ri '?iŋ
"koht 'ma"sa?a + '?i?i -- ,'?u'iah"?ke?e 'nim
"?pihk 'iŋ'?ke"txe 'ta"ri 'tua?a'?a'ueh"ta + .
'ko"txa 'tu'ru?u"tse?ei 're'ma"sa?a + 407 + ,
"txe 'ke?e'?u'ma"hres + '?e'?u'uix"ka?ar 'ke?e
-- .'?u'ue?e"rir 'ma"sa?a + .'?ah'?ku"na 'ta'mon
"ta 'nia + '?i?i -- '?i'ha?a"xir "ua 'ru'na?a"ta
'ke?e -- ,"ha?ax + ,'?e'ui"nik 'xe?e'?a'ua"ia
'na"ni 'ta'ke?ei"xik + ,"ha?ax '?u'xu"ri + 416
+ "ua 'ru'?ke"txa?a 'ro?o"pa '?u'iah"?ku '?u?u
-- .'uix"ka?a 'ru'?ku"xi +

418 + '?i?i -- 'kon'dix"to 'tu"ru '?a"ue?e
-- '?e?e -- ,'?e'i"xik + "ka 'iu'iu"?pi + '?ie?e
-- .'?e'ui"nik 'xia?a'io?o"pa?a 'ua'ian'ta'ka
"ret + ."tia?a '?a"non '?i"xin + 426 + "me 'ru
'ma?a"txa?a 'txek"tu?ut + 427 + .'?i"ne?en
"gua 'rin"txe "kuen 'ta'?e"ra?aŋ 'gui"ra 'ke
'ma?a"txa?a 'txek"tu?ut +

428 + '?ie?ei"xik "txe 'ke?e -- '?e?e --
'?i"xin -- 'xa"na '?i?i -- .'ma?a'io?o"pa +

433 + .'?i'ha?a"xir "txe + "pe 'ro'ko
"txa?a -- ,'io?o"pe?e 'xam"?par 'tu?u"ho 're'ui
"nik 'i"ra + "mu?u 'na?a"ta?a -- .'?a'lo"?koi 'a
'xa"na + .'?ie"ra 'ke'lo"?koi 'xa"na + 439 + .

18. Traveling Man

'?i'ha?a"xir 'tu"ru + 440 + '?i?i -- ,'?u'ia?a "re?ei "xik + .'tu"?kaŋ "?ku "mah 'tu?u'tu'?o "to 'ri"ra + 443 + '?pa"ni 'xe?e -- ."huer 'tia'?ku"me?e 'iu?ut'io?o"tot +

445 + '?e?e -- '?e?e -- .'i"xik "txe + . 'ki"sas '?u'ia"?puix "?tsi?i 'iŋ'?ku"mah 'ta 'mu?u"su 'ie"puer 'ta + 449 + ,'?i'ha?a"xir + .'?i"rah 'i"rah 'u'iu"?pi 'ke?e'tu"?ka '?aŋ'?ku "mah 'ta'mu?u"su 'ie"puer 'ta + 451 + ,'?i"kon 'da'?ix"to + ,'?ka?a"pa "ue?e '?e'i"xik + .'?u 'ia?a"re '?e'i"xik + 'ber"dix 'to'ke?e -- 'ko "txa?a 'ta"hui '?u?u -- '?u"tse?eir '?e?e -- '?e "ue?er 'to'ke?e -- ."ua 'ra'?ku"xi +

459 + '?e'i"xik "txe 'ke?e -- ,'ga"lan + . '?in"tsah + .'ga"lan 'u"tse?eir + 463 + .'ma '?a"ni "tia?aŋ '?ku"xi 'e'ma"sa?a '?in'tu"?ka "di 'ia"ua 'riŋ'gueh"ta +

464 + ,'?en"ton 'ses"txe?e 'ui"nik -- 'ber 'dix"to + ,'?in'tu"?ka "di 'ia + ,'?a'ueh"ta '?u "tse?eir + ,'?e'ui"nik 'xe?e'?i'ua"ia 'na"ni 'ta "kar + '?e?e -- .'?e"ia?ax '?ka?a'?pes"?pir 'ta?a'?ku"xi '?u'ue?e"rir + 470 + ,'?i'ko "ne?er + ,'na?a"tan + ,'ke"ha?a 'xe'ui"nik 'lo "ke '?i'ua"ia 'na"ni 'ta"kar + ."ha?ax "ua 'ra '?ku"xi '?u'ue?e"rir +

474 + ,'?en"ton 'ses + ,'?e'i"xik + ,"txe 'ke'?i'nia"hrer + ,'su'?pa"hra '?u'iu?pi + ,"kon 'da?a'ro?p"na + '?i?i -- .'?a'ro?o?p"na + 481 + '?e?e -- ."txe 'tua?a'?u"me 'ne'ui"nik +

483 + '?ie?e -- ,'?u"kuer 'pu + .'tia?a'?i "xe?e 'ta"kar + ,'ha?a"xir "txe + ."ne?en 'ma?a "txi 'riŋ'gui"ra + 488 + ."ma 'tu"?ka?a 'riŋ 'gui"ra "ne?en + 489 + ,"pe 'ro'ma?a'txix"to + '?e?e -- 'u"me 'nu'na?a"ta 'tu"?ka 'tua?ah -- , '?u'?kah"ti + "por 'ke?e'?pa?ak"ta '?i'nia"hrer

18. Traveling Man

"kuan 'da?a'ro?p"na 'ke"ha?ax '?e?e -- ,'?e'ui
"nik 'xe?e'?a'ua"ian 'ta"kar + ."ha?ax "ua 'ru
'?ku"xi '?u'ue?e"rir +

496 + ,'?pa'nix"to + ,'?ko"toi + ,'?ka?a
"pa '?e'ui"nik + ,'xe?e'?o?o"txo 'ra"na 'ua"ian
+ ,'ta'ke?e'i"xik + ,'?ie?e'i"xik + 'txe?e"na?a
-- ,'txe?e"na '?u'?ku"xi + ,'?u'ue?e"rir + ,'?e
'ui"nik 'xe?e'?a'ua"ian 'a"ni 'ta"kar + "por
'ke?e -- ,'ha?a"xir + 'ma?a"txa?a "ni '?u'?pa
'?kahr"se '?u?u -- .'?u'no"xi?ip + "pe 'ro?o --
"ne?en 'ma?a"txi?i -- ,'?ko"tue?en + ,'?in'ta
"kre 'pah"no 'ti?iŋk'si'?pa"ner + .'ma?a"txi?iŋ
'gui"ra 'tu"?ka "ka 'iu"txo?p + 515 + ,'?i'po
"re 'so + 'ma?a"txi?iŋ '?ku?u?p"se "hai -- .
'ber"da +

18. Traveling Man

1 There is another man they tell of. 3 They say that that man did not stay in his house -- he just went walking to earn money, far away. He did not stay in his house. 13 And then, his wife remained, left alone by him.

19 And they say that there was a man who stayed near the house where they lived. 27 And that man, when he saw that his neighbor had gone out walking, he came in and slept with the woman.

37 And the man who went out walking, he did not get angry when he was told, "Your wife is not afraid of you. But he did not get angry hearing it. 53 He did not stay. 54 Because they say that he was not feared by his wife. And -- and he was not a man who got angry.

65 They say that that man, when he stayed home, was given orders to make tortillas, was ordered to make tortillas by his wife. 70 And one day, when he did not make tortillas, they say that his hand was pressed down on the griddle by his wife. 78 Because he did not go out, and he made tortillas. 80 He was not respected by his wife.

82 And they say that that man, who came in to sleep with the woman, when he came then, the man who was married to the woman, they say that he was ordered to lie on the floor of the house, and rushes were laid on the ground, and he would lie on them. 100 And that man who came slept with the woman.

105 Then one day he was told by one of his neighbors, 110 he was told, "You, what kind of man are you, that your wife is putting you down? 117 And you don't even get mad. You see what

she does, you stay there looking when she brings in a man to sleep with her. And you, where do you sleep?"

125 He said, "When he comes, the man who sleeps, I uh — on the ground -- they make me sleep — and they lay out rushes for me to lie on. 138 And they sleep together."

140 Then he was told by the neighbor, "But if you are afraid, and do not have the courage to quarrel with your wife, try this: say 'I'm going walking' on a certain day, and pretend to go walking, so they will stay together. 159 And you, wait for night, and come in silently, when you have waited for them to go to sleep, 165 and come in, and stay under the bed where they are sleeping, and listen for their snoring. 172 But wait for them to sleep, so they won't see you come in. 174 And you won't show yourself, so they won't see you. So your wife will think that you weren't there. 179 And when you are there, under the bed, wait for them, get up silently, find his — find the penis of the man. 185 You whack it off, and go away immediately with it."

188 And that man, they say that so he did. He went out to go walking, saying to his wife that, "I'm going to go walking, and I won't be back. You'll see what day to expect me. 198 I'm going away for a long time."

200 They say that that woman was happy. She was left alone. And the man came over to live with her once and for all. 208 Because she said that, "My husband, who lives with me, he has gone and is not coming back. You can come and live with me." 218 And that man came to live with the woman.

18. Traveling Man

220 And they say that the husband did as he had been told by his neighbor. He waited until night. He began to come near behind the house, in the brush. He waited for dark. 230 Then he waited until the middle of the night, came in silently, opening the door silently. He opened the door silently, and came inside. 238 And he heard that they were snoring, the sleepers, and he went to stay under the bed, and listen for their snoring. 249 And he carried, ready, a pocket knife. He got up under the bed, silently found the man's penis, and seizing it, whacked it off, and went out with it. And the woman, since she was sleeping, did not hear at what time the man had been cut.

270 And then when the woman woke up, she felt that the mat where they were sleeping was wet. She said, "You, what are you doing? Here we are sleeping on water because of you. Why didn't you go outside, instead of making water on the bed?" And the man did not speak.

289 She went on talking to to him, saying, "Go outside, you've already wet the bed. We're lying on water because of you. Get up and go outside."

298 And they say that that man was not alive. He went on twitching, and didn't go outside. 302 Then she got up and lit a light, to see that the man was dead. She lit a light and saw that the man was dead. 309 And she had been lying, sleeping, on blood. 312 And then she didn't know what she was to do. Then she said, "Now, uh — what's wrong with this man? There — nothing -- nothing was wrong with his body. And she began to look, and saw that the man had no penis.

18. Traveling Man

325 And she didn't know where to go with him then. She got up and began to light a fire, and took a digging stick, and began to dig a hole beside the fire, where the fire was laid. She began to make a hole. All night she was digging, waiting for the hole to be finished. Then she tipped him down from the bed, and dropped him down into the hole. 350 And very rapidly she began to fill it with dirt. And at the break of dawn she began to build a fire on the grave of that man. And they say that she began sprinkling ashes on the blood, and she began to wash the mat well with hot water.

364 And when dawn had come, that man began to be sought. And he was not found. He was being sought everywhere by his wife, and she did not find him. She came and said to the woman, "The man didn't spend the night with you, did he? He hasn't come home."

376 She said, "No," and she knew that he was already buried under the house. 380 But the man who came to cut the man, they say that he went to a stream and began to bathe the penis of that man whom he had cut, and to pack it with salt; he dried it.

394 And in two weeks he came back and said to his wife, "I've brought you a little meat here, for you to eat. On Sunday my boss went hunting and shot a deer, and he gave me a little. I'm bringing it for you to eat, since it has the flavor of venison." 407 They say that he deceived his wife, that -- it was deer meat given to him in the mountain. And he knew that it was the man who had been sleeping with his wife, whom he had cut. 416 He had brought it back to give to his wife to eat.

18. Traveling Man

418 And then as the woman ate, she began to hear, "And the man who comes to sleep with you, what's become of him? 426 He really does not seem to be anywhere in sight, and I'm just realizing that I can't see him anywhere around."

428 And the woman said that, "He went away and hasn't come back."

433 And he said, "But how did walking come into that man's head? He didn't plan to go out walking, and here he's gone out walking!" 439 And he sat down. 440 And he said to the woman, "What stinks in this house? 443 There's some kind of strong stench in this house."

445 The woman said, "Maybe it's dog urine stinking on the doorstep." 449 She every little while heard, "What's that stinking at the doorstep?" 451 And when the woman had finished eating, he said to the woman, "Really, how do you find the flavor of the meat you've been eating?"

459 The woman said, "It tastes good, it has a good flavor. 463 I had never eaten venison until trying it today."

464 Then the man said, "Really, today you are trying the taste of the man you were sleeping with. You've just finished eating his flesh. 470 And today, know that the man you were sleeping with, that is his flesh you were eating."

474 Then, they say, the woman all at once was shamed to hear it, when she was told what she was told by the man.

483 "And his body, where did you go with

it?" He said, "I don't see it. 488 I don't see anything." 489 But there was nothing more -- she knew to -- she said, because she was frightened all at once, when she was told that that was the man she was sleeping with whose flesh she had been eating.

496 So it came about that the man finished off the one who had been coming to sleep with his wife, and the woman was said -- was said to have eaten the flesh of the man who used to sleep with her, because she did not respect her husband. But I didn't go there to help did in the darkness, and I didn't see what they began doing. 515 And that is why I don't know if it's true.

GROUP III

NOTES

14. Indians and Ladinos

14.49* From hai i-xan-a by W.

14.62 A variant of uar common in rapid speech appears here as the -r in 'lo"ke?er. Compare 14.114.

14.68 Perhaps 'it seems better to me that I walk barefooted'.

14.87* From xee a&-ah?k by C, R, B.

15. Parent's Curse

15.15 This is the only use of ha?a?p 'years', 'age' in Chorti. In counting or naming years, Spanish año is used.

15.93 The root ?paax 'curse' is typical of Chorti roots in having active formations, with thematic suffixes e (in groups 93, 95, 192, 194, 220, 240, 256, 290) uan (211, 215, 219) as well as a na form (276) and uses as a bare root with a substantive sense (225, 229, 244).

16. Henpecked Husband

16.91 A rutx is a roughly hemispherical bowl made from half a gourd; a ?txeen, mentioned in 16.99, is a low pottery bowl.

16.238 The su?pin 'bull acacia' is a small tree with numerous large, paired, hollow thorns, each with a small hole near the point. The trees are inhabited by colonies of slender red ants that live in the thorns, and swarm over anyone brushing against them, giving unforgettably painful bites. This uniquely hostile combination is cordially hated by the Chorti, who must clear it by hand from fallow milpas.

17. Henpecked Salesman

17.9 A reseller buys goods produced by others and carries them to the villages or to other town markets for resale. Most Chorti sell goods they produce themselves.

17.135-138 Here is a typical use of nik in a counterfactual conditional expression. Note also the presence of the past progressive ani, which might call for translation as 'I would have believed it'.

17.243 Literally, 'they stuck their necks out laughing'.

17.303-304 The form is 'iŋk'si"?pan 'dark' apparently with an 'attributive' prefix. Gonzalez says it has replaced an older form 'iŋ'ku "?pen. Other forms with the Maya root for 'black' are 'ik'tsu"ren 'grey' and 'ik'na"?pen 'black'.

17.313 Compare tehrom 'boy'.

17.484 The auxiliar is the town mayor's deputy for an aldea or settlement.

18. Traveling Man

18.97 The si?ti?it are the pithy hearts of the tule rushes, left over after the hard outer layers are peeled away for use in making mats (pohp).

18.150 Spanish prueba.

18.342-343 More closely, 'watching for the hole to be sufficient'.

IV: Disease and Curing

19. Belief in Diviners

1 + .'e'?ku'?pe"siah 'ta'ma'iah'?ki"no?p +

2 + ,'iah'?ki"no?p + ,"kon 'da?a"ian 'txi
'a'mo"kran + ,'en"ton 'ses + .'a'?txah"ma "ti?in
'u'na?a"ta 'a'?ki"ni + 6 + ,'hai'ak"?par + ,'a
'?ka"xi 'in"te?e 'ah"muak 'ta'mi?i'o"tot + ,'ta
'ka're"ra 'iak"?par + .'a?a"xin 'a'?txah"ma + .
'tua?a'u'?ki"ni 'u'ui"ra 'tu'?ku?u"men 'txu"kur
'e'?ah"muak 'ia"ha?a + 11 + ,"kon 'da'?ko"toi
'tia?a"?txa?ar 'e'ah"muak + ,'u'?pah"iu 'u"mut +
.'tu?u"nu?u '?ku"?ka?p + 14 + ,"o?o + ."u?ut
'u"txu?u + .'hai"?txa?ar 'u"mut +

17 + ,'en"ton 'ses + .'u'?kah"ti 'e"?kuhts
'u'?ko"ii + 19 + .'a"ka?ai 'u'?ki"ni + 20 +
.'u'sah"ka 'hai'?poh"?pir "muak + .'o?o'ier'ah
'?ka"xer "muak "?pan 'ta"ka + 22 + ,'hai'ma
"ha?ax 'atx"?pir + .'u"meŋ 'o'tron"te?e +

24 + ,"kon 'da"uar 'o?o"hron 'ta'ka'u"ta?a
'u"iok + ."txe 'ko'txe?e"ra + 26 + ,"sa 'bio
'sa'hu"rin + .'sa'be"dor + ,"tia?a 'txoh'?pes
'?pi"ret 'u"me 'ne"dios 'ta'ma'ni'?txi"?txer + ,
'ta"ma 'u'?ka"?pa 'e'ka'uiŋ'ki"rar "dios + .'i
'ta"ma 'u'?ka"?pa 'e"rei 'na'ma"ri 'a'san"ti 'si
'ma + ."rei 'na'san'ta'lu"si 'a + .'e"rei 'na
'san'ta'te"re 'sa + ."rei 'na'de'gua'da"lu 'pe +
."rei 'na'de'kus"to 'dio + ."rei 'na'de'pas"to
'ra + "rei 'na'de're"hu 'hio + ,'ta'ma'u'?ka"?pa
'e"?an 'hel'saŋ'ga"briel + ,'e'saŋ'mi"gel 'ar
"kaŋ 'hel + ,'e"?aŋ 'hel"san 'to'to"mas 'be"ro
'ni'ko + ,'e"?aŋ 'hel'saŋ'kus"to 'dio + .'e"?aŋ
'hel"san 'ra'fa"el + 42 + .'i'ta"ma 'u'?ka"?pa
'e'a"pos 'tol'saŋ"huaŋ 'bau"tis 'ta + .'e'saŋ
"mar 'kos'e'baŋ"he 'lio + 'e'san'fe"li 'pe + .'a
"pos 'tol'de"kris 'to + 46 + .'ta'ma'u'?ka"?pa
'e'pa"tron 'san"tia 'go'de'ga"li 'sia'des"pa
'nia + ."due 'nio'de'ba"ta 'ia + .'kon'ben'se
"dor 'de'iŋ"hu 'ria + ."due 'nio'de'sa'hu"rin +
,'tia?a'a'uak"ta 'txoh'?pes"?pir + ,'na'ual"?pir

19. Belief in Diviners

+ .'ta'ma'ni'?txi"?txer + 53 + ,'e'pa"?ka?p 'e 'ko"noh + ,"to?or 'e"rum + ,'tia?a"uar 'ka'?ka '?pah"se 'i'?ka"?pa?a + ,"no?ox 'i'xa"uan 'ko "ne?er + ,'a'po'de"ra 'do'a'bo"ga 'do + ,'de'fen "sor + ,"sa 'bio'sa'be"dor + ,'ko'ne?e'rix"to 'a 'uah"?ko?on 'ka'na?a"ta "xe '?e?e"ra?atx + 61 + ,'txek"tes 'ko"ne?er 'ti"ko?oit + .'e'kas"ti 'go'a"so 'te + .'tia?a"?txa?ar 'a?a"si 'tu?u"hor 'e'kria"tu 'ra'e'me"nor + .'tia?a"uar 'a'txe?e "na?a 'me'na"sar 'u"iaŋ 'hel'ku?u'na'ua"lir +

65 + ,"sa 'bio'sa'be"dor + ,'ah'?ku"non 'ka'na?a'ta"nik + ,'in'ta'ka"ka '?atx"pa + .'e 'hus"ti 'sia'i"ra + 69 + .'tal"bes 'in'ta"ka 'ta"ri + 70 + .'tal"bes 'ah'?te?en"sah 'i'?ka "ro?p + 71 + ,'tal"bes 'i?ka"ro?p + .'to?or 'e'ui'tsi"ro?p + 73 + .'hol"txan 'i'?ka'ro?p "tik + 74 + .'o'hol"txan 'to'ka"ro?p "to?or 'e'ui"tsir + 75 + .'tal"bes 'ah'iohk"sah 'to 'ka"ro?p + 76 + .'tal"bes "prin 'si"po?p "to?or 'e'ui"tsir +

77 + ,'i'pu"rui "ka + 78 + ,'ie?e"ra "katx "pa 'ta"ra + ,'u"ti?i "?kahk 'hus"ti 'sia "tik + ,"o?or "?txuh '?pe'no?p"tik + 81 + , 'tal"bes "ha?ax 'e"san 'ta"bie 'ha + ."uar 'a '?te?en"san + 83 + ,'tal"bes 'u'ti'ka'ui "ru?ut + .'e"san 'ta"bie 'ha + 85 + ,'o?o'u 'ti'ka'ui"ru?ut + .'e"san 'an"to 'nio + 87 + ,'tal"bes "ha?ax "uar 'a'?tsoh"ii + ,'ta"ka 'u 'le'?ko"nir "u?ut + ,'u'he?e'ra"iir "u?ut + 90 + ,'o'u'tuh"ki?i?p 'ta"no?o?p + ."uar 'a'?te?en "san + 92 + .'tia?a'ka"nik 'ta"ri 'e'hus"ti 'sia'i"ra +

93 + ."sa 'bio'sa'be"dor + .'i"ra 'a'ma 'hre"son + 95 + ,"tia?a 'u'iak"te?et 'i'ka'iu "mar "dios 'ti'ka"?txi"?txer + ."ma "ha?ax 'tua?a'i'ma'hres"ian + .'si"no 'tua?a'i'tsor'ma "ian + ,'i"tua?a 'i'txek'su"ian + .'ta"ma 'e?e

19. Belief in Diviners

"ra?atx +

100 + .'o?o"me?e "so?p 'ka"uar 'a'?te?en "san + 101 + ,'tal"bes + .'u'tuh'ki?i?p"so?o?p + 103 + ,'tal"bes + .'ha?ax'e'noh'kon"ben 'to "rial + .'e"noh 'kon"ben 'to'ma"ior + 106 + , 'tal"bes 'u'nu"?ti?ix 'u"?pa + ,'ta'ka'u'hol'txa "nir + .'e'nues'tra"ma 'dre'san"ti 'si'ma + 109 + ,'es'tu'me'ka"to?o?p "tik + .'tue?e'ka"tu?u "mun 'do + 111 + ."om 'bres'es'tu"me 'kas + . "re 'ies'tu"me 'kas + 113 + ."om 'bres'ka'pi "tan + ."rei 'ka'pi"tan + 115 + .'tal"bes "ha?ax 'uar'a'?tsoh"io?o?p + 116 + ,'o?o'ti "txan "ka 'ta"ri + 117 + .'tal"bes 'u'ua'ra "rir 'u?ut 'e'saŋ'gre"go 'rio + 118 + .'tal "bes 'ia'nih"ki 'ta"ri 'e'hus"ti 'sia'i'kas"ti 'go + ,'atx"pa 'ta"ri 'ta'ma'e?ein'iax'a'la"gu 'na + .'e?ein"sak 'a'la"gu 'na + 121 + ,'ta "mar 'e?ein"iax "saŋ 'gi + "ia 'gua + .'e?ein "sak "saŋ 'gi"ia 'gua + 124 + ,'u'nu"?ti 'u "?pa + 'ta'ka'e'?in"iax 'a'la"u 'na'ui 'ho + .'e '?in"sak 'a'la"gu 'na"ui 'ho + 127 + ,'ta'ka'e "om 'bres'ba'ta"ion + ."rei 'ba'ta"ion + ,'e"aŋ 'hel'se"re 'no + ."rei 'se"re 'no +

131 + ,'ta"mar 'e?ein"iax "rue 'de + . 'e?ein"sak "rue 'de + 133 + ,"om 'bres'ku'le "brin + ."rei 'ku'le"brin + 135 + ,"om 'bres 'ti'bo"ron + ."rei 'ti'bo"ron + 137 + ,'ta"mar 'e'in"iax "pi 'la + .'e'?in"sak "pi 'la'de"a 'gua + ,'ko'txa'ia?a"si 'doŋ"huan 'de'se"re 'no + .'e'do'nia"hua 'na'de'se"re 'na + 141 + ,'u 'mak'txa"nir "u?ut + .'u'hol'txa"nir "u?ut + 143 + ,'ta"kar 'doŋ"huan 'de're'mo"li 'no + . 'e'do'nia"hua 'na'de're'mo"li 'na + 145 + , "ha?ax 'uar'a'iohk"san 'ha'ra"rio?p + ,'ta'ka'u 'hol'txa"nir "u?ut + ,'u'ti'ka"uir "u?ut + .'e san'gre"go 'rio'de"a 'gua +

149 + ,'ah'su"tut 'i'?ka"ro?p + ,'ah'na

19. Belief in Diviners

"ual 'i'?ka"ro?p + .'ah'moi'moi'te?e"ian 'i'?ka
"ro?p + ,"om 'bres're'mo"li 'no + ,"rei 're'mo
"li 'no + ,'a?atx"pa 'ua"tar + .'ta'ma"kua 'tre
'rer"ti?i 'u'iees'ki"nir 'e"mun 'do + 156 + ,
'u'noh'ko"mo 'nu?u"?pa + .'ta"ka 'e'noh'a'la"gu
'na'ie"?par 'e"mun 'do +

158 + ,"ti?in 'ka"nik 'es"ta 'do + .'e"mun
'do'ta"ri 'ta"mar + 160 + .'tal"bes 'ta'ma're
"ra 'e'pri"mer 'es"ta 'do + 'o?o -- .'ta'me'e
"dos 'es"ta 'do'e"mun 'do'ta"ri + 'o?o -- .'ta
"ri "ka 'ta'ma'e'ki"nien 'to'es"ta 'do'del"mun
'do + 165 + ,'tal"bes 'ia'nih"ki 'ta"ri 'e'hus
"ti 'sia'e'kas"ti 'go + ,'hu'sti"sia 'iŋ"hier
'na"lo?p + ,'iŋ'hier"nal 'i'?ka'ro?p"tik + ,'atx
"pa 'ta"ri 'ta'ma'e'ki"nien 'to'es"ta 'do'del'iŋ
"hier 'no +

169 + ,'a?a"si 'ua"tar + ,'ta'ma'e'noh'a
'la"gu 'na'ie"?par 'e"mun 'do + ,'ta"ma 'e?ein
"iax 'a'la"gu 'na + .'e'?in"sak 'a'la"gu 'na +
173 + ,'ko'txa'ia?a"si 'tu"no?or 'ah'?te?en'sa
"ho?p + ,"om 'bres're'mo"li 'no + ."rei 're'mo
"li 'no + 176 + ,'ah'pe"teht 'i'?ka"ro?p + .
'ah'moi'moi'te?e"ian 'i'?ka"ro?p + 178 + .'ah
'mai"hut 'i'?ka"ro?p + 179 + .'ah'lam"?pat 'i
'?ka"ro?p + 180 + .'ah'sis'?pa"?ta?a 'i'?ka
"ro?p + 181 + .'ah'he?e"rai 'i'?ka"ro?p + 182
+ ,'ha?ax"to 'e"ra 'a?a"sio?p 'ua"tar 'ta'ma'e
'ki"nien 'to'es"ta 'do'del'iŋ"hier 'no + ,'a'tek
'pa"ni 'ua"tar 'ta'ma + .'u'io'ri"iir 'e"mun 'do
+ 185 + ,'ha?ax"to + ,'a'iohk"san 'ha'ra"rio?p
+ ."to?or 'e'?pa"?ka?p 'e'ko"noh +

188 + .'ta'me?e"muak 'a?a"xo?p + 189 + ,
'hai'?txi?itx'na?a"?kir + ,'o'?txi?itx"ni?ir + .
'u'sah"ko?o?p 'ti"txan + 192 + ,"por 'ke?e
'txe?e"no?p 'ke"kon 'da'a"?txa?an 'e"rue 'de
'tu?ut'e"?kin + ,'txe?e"no?p + ,'ke"ha?ax 'e'saŋ
'gre"go 'rio"dia 'gua + .'uar'a?a"ti + 196 + ,

19. Belief in Diviners

'i'ke"ha?ax 'e"di 'ia + .'xe'?ka"ni 'a'?ka"xi 'e 'ha"ha?ar + 198 + .'po"re 'so'a"?txa?an "tu?ut 'e"?kin + 199 + ."ha?ax 'e'?ir'se"iah 'ta'ma '?e'ha"ha?ar 'ta'ma'e'?kax'ha?a"?kin +

200 + ,'txe?e"no?p + ,'ke"ha?ax 'e"mar + . "uar 'a'?ta'?pes"na 'ti"txan + 203 + ,'ie?e "rue 'de'ia"ha?a + .'txe?e"no?p 'ke"?paŋ 'ko'txa 'e"pi 'la + ."pe 'ro"mei 'gra + .'ko'txan"te?e 'a'la"gu 'na + 207 + ,"txe 'ke?e"ha?ax 'e"?o 'ra'ia"ha?a + ,'?pu"?tur "uar 'a?a"si 'tu"no?or 'a'ni'ma"lo?p + .'tu"no?or 'na"ual 'ah'ma'?pam "?pan + 210 + ,'txe?e"no?p 'ke"ha?ax 'a'iohk 'sa"no?p + .'tu"no?or 'na"ual + 212 + ,"txe 'ke?e'u'su"ti 'e'?kux'ho"rir + .'pu"rer 'si"sar + ,'?ke'?ke"ua?a + 215 + ,"txe 'ke'u'le'?ko "nir 'e'saŋ'gre"go 'rio + .'a'?te?en"san + 217 + ,"por 'ke'txe?e"no?p 'ke?e'u'ua'ra"rir 'a'ua 'ra"ri + .'ta'ma'tu"no?or "o?or 'e"rum + 219 + ,"ha?ax 'a'?te?en"san + .'ta'ma'tu"no?or 'e'lu 'ga"ro?p +

19. Belief in Diviners

1 Belief in diviners.

2 The diviners, when there is someone who becomes ill, then someone who knows how to divine is brought. 6 If it is night, and someone in the house falls ill, that same night someone goes to get him, so that he will divine and see in whose grasp that sick person is. 11 When he comes to where the diseased person is lying, he feels his pulse in his wrist 14 or on his breast, to see if his pulse is there.

17 Then he asks for tobacco, chews it, and 19 begins to divine. 20 He inquires if it is an ordinary disease, or a little disease which befalls anyone just like that, 22 if it wasn't raised by someone else.

24 When he is speaking with the calf of his leg he says this: 26 Wise Diviner, knowing one, where you are cherished by God in my blood, in the name of our master God, and in the name of the holiest Queen Mary, Queen Santa Lucia, Queen Santa Theresa, Queen of Guadalupe, Queen of Custodio, Queen of Pastora, Queen of Refugio, in the name of the angel San Gabriel, of the archangel San Miguel, the angel Santo Tomas Veronico, the angel San Custodio, the angel San Rafael, 42 and in the name of the apostle Saint John the Baptist, the evangelist Saint Mark, San Felipe, apostle of Christ; 46 in the name of the patron Santiago of Galicia in Spain, patron of battle, avenger of injury, patron of diviners, where you remain, cherished spirit in my blood: 53 the human beings on the earth, where we are proclaiming your name, you stand up today, mighty advocate, defender, wise and knowing, now, today give us knowledge of what is certain, 61 reveal to us today the punishment and bondage where it plays over the head of this

19. Belief in Diviners

little creature, where his angel and spirit are being threatened.

65 Wise and knowing one, give us knowledge whether this punishment was raised up. 69 Perhaps it just came. 70 Perhaps it was sickening winds, 71 perhaps it was winds over the peaks, 73 it may have been Hol Txan winds, or 74 Hol Txan clouds over the peaks. 75 Perhaps it was hovering clouds, 76 perhaps Old Angels over the peaks.

77 Are you burning? 78 Did this rise up here, perhaps a fireside judgement, on hearthstones, perhaps. 81 Perhaps it is the Holy Old Woman making you sick. 83 Perhaps it is the warmth of the Holy Old Woman, 85 or the warmth of San Antonio. 87 Perhaps he is beating us with his heat, his fitful glowing. 90 Or the lime-dump is causing sickness. 92 Where could this judgement have come from?

93 Wise knowing one, do not deceive us. 95 When our master God placed you in our blood, it was not so that you should deceive, but rather so that you should trace and so that you should reveal what is certain.

100 Or are [consecrated] tables causing the sickness? 101 Perhaps it is the hole where the _chilate_ is poured? 103 Perhaps it is the Great Royal Temple, the Great Major Temple. 106 Perhaps our Holy Mother has joined up with the Hol Txan. 109 Estumekas of our Mother World, 111 Estumekas men, Estumekas king, 113 Captain men, Captain king, 115 perhaps they are beating, 116 or coming up above. 117 Perhaps it is the Beam of San Gregorio. 118 Perhaps this punishment judgement was dislodged there and came here, rising up in the blue lake, the

white lake; 121 in the blue water channel, the white water channel. 124 It joined with the blue Lake Güija, the white Lake Güija; 127 with the batallion men, the batallion king, Serpent angel, Serpent king.

131 In the blue ring, the white ring, 133 serpent men, serpent king, 135 shark men, shark king. 137 In the blue basin, the white basin of water, as Don Juan of the Serpent, Doña Juana of the Serpent, 141 their rainbow surface, their Hol Txan surface. 143 With him Don Juan of the Whirlwind, Doña Juana of the Whirlwind. 145 He is shedding his beams with the Hol Txan surface, the warm surface, of San Gregorio of Water.

149 The turning winds, the spirit winds, the sweeping-up winds, whirlwind men, whirlwind king, he comes rising up from each of the four corners of the world, 156 he joins his body with the big lake underneath the world.

158 From which level of the world did it come? 160 Perhaps it was from the first level, or from the second level -- or did it come from the five-hundredth level of the world? 165 Perhaps there the punishment judgement was dislodged and came, hellish punishments, hellish winds may have risen and come from the five-hundredth level of hell.

169 It came playing from the big lake underneath the earth, from the blue lake, the white lake, 173 since all disease-causers play there, whirlwind men, whirlwind king, 176 distaff winds, sweeping-up winds, 178 illusion winds, 179 <u>lam?pat</u> winds, 180 freezing winds, 181 coal-glowing winds. 182 They were playing, coming from the five-hundredth level of

19. Belief in Diviners

hell, towering up at the edge of the world. 185 Now they shed their beams over mankind.

188 They go to the sick person. 189 If he has body-bleeding or nose-bleeding they look above, 192 because they say that when the ring lies around the sun, they say that that is San Gregorio of Water who is bathing, 196 and that that's the day when it's about to rain. 198 That is why it lies in the sky. 199 It is the sign of rain in the rainy season.

200 They say that that is the sea, raised up above. 203 And that ring, they say it is like a basin, but large, like a lake. 207 They say that at that time, it is full of all the animals playing, all the evil spirits. 210 They say they are hovering, all the spirits. 212 They say that headache, chills and fever, hardening, come back, 215 they say the searing of San Gregorio causes disease. 217 Because they say that his beams play about over all the earth. 219 They cause disease everyplace.

20. Curing

1 + ,"kon 'da"uar 'a'ni"ruo?p 'e"?ah 'ni 'ro"mo?p + ,'u'?ka'?pah"sio?p + ,'tu'?ka"?pa?a 'tu'?ka"?pa?a + .'tu"no?or 'lo'ke?e'u'tah"ui 'ta 'ma'u'?ki"no?p +

5 + .'txe?e"no?p 'ko'txe?e"ra + 6 + .'ah 'ti'txa"ner 'hu'sti"xiox + ,'tia?a"uar 'i'xa"si 'ua"to?ox 'ta'ma'e?ein"iax "rue 'de + ,'e'in'sak "rue 'de + .'tue?e'saŋ'gre"go 'rio "dia 'gua + , 'ta'ka'u'mak'txa"nir "iu?ut + .'u'mak'txa"nir 'i 'ue"roh + ,'u'ti'ka"uir "iu?ut + .'u'ti'ka"uir 'i'ue"roh + ,'u'le'?ko"nir "iu?ut + .'u'le'?ko "nir 'i'xam"?par +

16 + ,'tia?a'i'noh'ko'mo"ni 'i"?pa + ,'i 'xa"si 'ua"to?ox 'ta'ma'e'?in"iax "pi 'la + .'e '?in"sak "pi 'la + 19 + ,"ia 'a?a"si 'e"ni 'nio'san'gre"go 'rio'ta"ka 'u'?tsa?p'ta"ru?ut + .'u'?tsa?p"tar 'u'ie"roh + ,'u'ua'ra"rir "u?ut 'u'ua'ra"rir 'u'xam"?par + ,'u'ti'ka"uir "u?ut + .'u'ti'ka"uir 'u'ie"roh +

24 + ,'tia?a'i'xa"si 'ua"to?ox 'ta'ka'u 'mak"he?eir 'i'xam"?par + .'u'mak"he?eir 'i'uah "ner + ,'u'lam'?pa"tir 'i"?ka?p + .'u'lam'?pa "tir "io?ok + ,'u'sis'pa'ne"nir 'i"?ka?p + .'u 'sis'pa'ne"nir "io?ok + ,'u'mai'hu"tir "iu?ut + .'u'mai'hu"tir 'i'ue"roh +

32 + ,'ta'ka'u'?ke'?ko"ue?eir 'i'xam"?par + .'u'?ke'?ko"ue?eir 'i'uah"ner + ,'u'sa'ma"mir "iu?ut + .'u'sa'ma"mir 'i'ue"roh + 36 + ,'ta 'ka'u"ti?ip "txan '?pa'ke"rir 'i'xam"?par + .'u 'ti?ip"txan '?pa'ke"rir 'i'uah"ner + 38 + . '?ah'ti?ip'txam"?pak 'o?oi"sen 'te + .'ah'io?p 'te?e"?pak 'o?oi"sen 'te + .'ah'su'tut"hut 'o?oi "sen 'te + .'ah'?txuhr"he?ei 'o?oi"sen 'te + . 'ah'ue?k'ue?k"he?eir 'o?oi"sen 'te +

43 + ,'ua"to?ox 'ta'ka'u'tsur'tsa?a"rir 'i

20. Curing

'uah"ner + .'u'tsur'tsa?a"rir 'i'xam"?par + ,'u
'txan"len '?pa'ke"rir 'i'xam"?par + ,'u'txan"len
'?pa'ke"rir 'i'uah"ner + 47 + ,'ta'ka'u'sus
"te?eir '?pa"kir 'i'xam"?par + .'u'sus"te?eir
'?pa"kir 'i'uah"ner + 49 + ,'ta'ka'u'sak'po'io
"mir 'i'ta"rer + .'u'sak'po'io"mir 'i'ta"ri?p +
51 + ,'ta'ka'u'si?p'na?a"?kir 'i'ta"rer + .'u
'si?p'na?a"?kir 'i'ta"ri?p + 53 + ,'ta'ka'u
'leh"tsir 'i'xam"?par + 'u'leh"tsir 'i'uah"ner +
55 + ,'ta'ka'u'kex'ka?a"rer 'i'xam"?par + .'u
'kex'ka?a"rer 'i'uah"ner + 57 + ,'ta'ka'u
'io?ots"ner 'i'ta"rer + .'u'io?ots"ner 'i'ta
"ri?p + ,'u'so?o"rer 'i'ta"rer + .'u'so?o"rer 'i
'ta"ri?p + 61 + ,'ta'ka'u'he?e"ra?ai 'im"?pak
'i'ta"rer + .'u'he?e"ra?ai 'im"?pak 'i'ta"ri?p +
63 + ,'ta'ka'u'?txuhr'he?eir"sihm 'i'ta"rer + .
'u'?txuhr'he?eir"sihm 'i'ta"ri?p + ,'u'sis'pa
"tir 'i"?ka?p + .'u'sis'pa"tir "io?ok + 67 + ,
'ta'ka'u'?tsu?u'iam"?pak 'i'xam"?par + .'u
'?tsu?u'iam"?pak 'i'uah"ner +

69 + ,'tia?a"uar 'i'xa"si 'ua"to?ox + .
"uar 'ix'uahr'me?ein'ha'ra"ri + 71 + ,"uar 'ix
'uahr'me?ein'hol'txa"ni + ,'u'hol'txa"nir "iu?ut
+ .'u'hol'txa"nir 'i'ue"roh + ,'u'ti?ip'txa"nir
"iu?ut + .'u'ti?ip'txa"nir 'i'ue"roh + 76 + ,
'ta'ka'u'ta'kim'?pa'ke"rir 'i'ta"rer + .'u'ta
'kim'?pa'ke"rir 'i'ta"ri?p + 78 + ,'ta'ka'u
'ni?ik'txam"?pak 'i'xam"?par + .'u'ni?ik'txam
"?pak 'i'uah"ner +

80 + ,'tia?a"uar 'i'iu'puk'te?e"res 'u"iaŋ
'hel'e'krea"tu 'ra'e'me"nor + ,'uar'i'la'?tah
"res 'u"me?ein + ,'u'na'ua"lir + 83 + ,'ko'txa
"no?ox 'xe'?ah'ma'hres'ia"hox + ,'ah'ma'hres"iah
'i'ta"rer + .'ah'ma'hres"iah 'i'ta"ri?p + 86 +
.'ah'mah'res"iah 'o?oi"sen "tiox + 87 + .'ah
'ma'hres"iah 'na'ua"lox + 88 + .'tia?a"uar 'i
'xan'tah"res + .'u"me?ein 'e'krea"tu 'ra'e'me
"nor +

20. Curing

90 + .'iix"to "uar + ,'i'tih'ti"hres 'u "me?ein + .'i'tih'ti"hres 'u'na'ua"lir 'tia?a "uar 'i'la?a"tru + 93 + ,'i"?pit 'txa'pa"hres 'u'na'ua"lir + 95 + ."ia 'ua"rix 'na'?pa"hre 'tu?u"hor + .'uar'ix'?pa'hra"mi 'tu?u"hor 'u "me?ein + 97 + ,'ix'?pa'hra"mi "to?or 'u'na'ua "lir + ,'ko'txa"no?ox 'xe?e"uar 'ix'?pa'hra"mi + .'tu?u"hor 'iah"muak 'i"ra +

100 + ,"uar 'i'lo'?txoh"res 'u'na'ua"lir + .'i'le'?peh"res 'u"me?ein + 102 + ,"uar 'i'leu 'leu"res 'u"me?ein + ."uar 'i'leu'leu"res 'u'?pa "ker + 104 + ,'tia?a"uar 'i'lah"?kes 'u'to "?kor "u?ut + ,'u'to"?kor 'u'ie"roh + ."uar 'i 'ta'xa"hru 'u"me?ein + 107 + .'i'ta'xa"hru 'u 'kux"tar +

108 + ,'tia?a"uar 'i'?pi?i"ru 'e'krea"tu 'ra'e'me"nor + ."uar 'i'ke'xeh"res 'u"ial 'ma + 110 + ,'ta'ka'u'ti'ka"uir "iu?ut + .'u'ti'ka "uir 'i'xam"?par + ,'u'?pu'ri"txir "iu?ut + 'u '?pu'ri"txir 'i'ue"roh + 114 + ,'ta'ka'u'kiŋ "ka?ar 'i'xam"?par + .'u'kiŋ"ka?ar 'i'uah"ner + 116 + ,'ko'txa"ia '?pu'?tu"rox 'ix'ma'ra'?tak "na 'tu?u"hor + .'tia?a"?txa?ar 'kas'ti"ga 'do'a 'so"ta 'do'i'me"ner +

118 + ,"uar 'i'ton'to?o"res 'u"hor 'tia?a '?pu'?tu"rox 'ix'ka'sak"na + .'tu?u'ieh"?tser 'e 'krea"tu 'ra'e'me"nor + 120 + ,'tsah"tix "u?ut + .'tsah"tix 'u'ie"roh 'i"men + 122 + ."mix "ha?ax 'tua?a'e'kux"tar + ."mix "ha?ax 'tua?a'e 'kor"pa?ar + .'i'me"ner +

125 + ,'san"no?ox 'ix"to + .'u'?txu?u"rox 'e'txa"mer + .'u'?txu?u"rox "muak + ,'u'?txu?u "rox 'tu"no?or 'na"ual + .'ah'ma'?pam"?pan + 130 + ,'no?ox'ix"to + ,'ix'iohk"san + ,'ix '?te?en"san + ,'ix'ha'ra"ri + ."to?or 'e'pa "?ka?p 'e'ko"noh + ."to?or 'e"rum + 136 + ,

20. Curing

'ko'txa"no?ox 'i'si?ik"?pa + .'e'?txan'txe?e"di 'ia + .'e'?txan'txe?e"?o 'ra + ,'tua?a'ix"na '?pah"re + ,'ix'hol'txa"ni + ."to?or 'e'pa"?ka?p 'e'ko"noh + 142 + ,'ko'txa"no?ox + .'u'ta"rer 'ah'xuhtx'i'xam"?par + .'u'ta"rer 'ah"xuhtx 'i 'uah"ner +

145 + ,'pe'ro'ko"ne?er + ,'ha?a'xe"ra 'e "?o 'ra + ,'ha?a'xe"ra 'e"di 'ia + ,'ta'ma'u'?ka "?pa?a 'tu"no?or 'e'dio"so?p + .'tia?a"uar 'ka '?ka'?pah"se + ,'tu?u"hor 'iah"muak 'i"ra + 151 + ,'ko"ne?er 'e"ra + .'e'kor'pe"siah 'e'po"der 'tu?u"hor 'e'krea"tu 'ra'e'me"nor + .'tua?a'i "lo?o 'u"iaŋ 'hel + 154 + .'i"lo?o 'u'na'ua "lir + .'tia?a"?txa?ar 'kas'ti"ga 'do + .'a'me 'na"sa 'do'i'me"ner +

157 + ,'pe'ro'ko"ne?er + ,'in"txo?ox 'en 'tre"gar + .'tu?u"?ka?p 'e'aŋ'he'les'pi'ri'to "san 'to + .'i'tu"no?or 'e"?aŋ 'he"lo?p + 161 + ,'ha?a'xix"to + .'tua?a'u'iah'ne"sox 'i'xah"ni + 163 + .'u'ia"rio?ox 'tu?u"?txu?ur 'mon"ta 'nia + 164 + ,'ha?a'xix"to + .'tua?a'u'?ka "txo?ox 'a"pun 'te"ra 'ia + .'a"pun 'te'sen"te 'io +

20. Curing

1 When the curers are curing, they proclaim, name by name, everything found in the divining.

5 They speak like this: 6 You judgements from above, where you are coming to play in the blue ring, the white ring, of San Gregorio of Water, with the rainbow of your appearance, the rainbow of your expression, the warmth of your appearance, the warmth of your expression, the heat of your appearance, the heat of your walking.

16 Where you pile yourselves up, coming into the blue basin, the white basin, 19 the child San Gregorio is playing there, with the reflection of his appearance, the reflection of his expression, the beams of his appearance, the beams of his walking, the warmth of his appearance, the warmth of his expression.

24 Where you have come to play, with the water-dam of your walking, the water-dam of your running, the lam?pat of your hands, the lam?pat of your feet, the numbness of your hands, the numbness of your feet, the hallucination of your appearance, the hallucination of your expression.

32 With the hardening of your walking, the hardening of your running, the lassitude of your expression; 36 with the jaundice of your walking, the jaundice of your running, 38 the jaundice-ghost, the bone-breaker ghost, the dizziness ghost, the water-drip ghost, the water-slosh ghost.

43 You come with the trembling of your running, the trembling of your walking, the vein-distension of your running; 47 with the

impaling of your walking, the impaling of your running, 49 with the thick mucus of your presence, the thick mucus of your coming, 51 with the bloating of your presence, the bloating of your coming, 53 with the nausea of your walking, the nausea of your running, 55 with the panting of your walking, the panting of your running, 57 with the itching of your presence, the itching of your coming, the tickling of your presence, the tickling of your coming, 61 with the body-burning of your presence, the body-burning of your coming, 63 with the mucus-dripping of your presence, the mucus-dripping of your coming, the coldness of your hands, the coldness of your feet, 67 with the body-draining of your walking, the body-draining of your running.

69 Where you are playing, you come and are playing your ghost beams, 71 you are playing your ghost Hol Txan, the Hol Txan of your appearance, the Hol Txan of your expression, the jaundice of your appearance, the jaundice of your expression, 76 with the dessication of your presence, the dessication of your coming, 78 with the bone-bending of your walking, the bone-bending of your running.

80 Where you are tossing end over end the angel of this little creature, you are playing cat and mouse with his ghost, his spirit; 83 you who are deceivers, deceiver your coming, deceiver your arrival, 86 deceiver ghosts, 87 deceiver spirits, 88 where you are guiding the ghost of this little creature.

90 And now you are diminishing his ghost, you are diminishing his spirit, when you toy with it. 93 You carry his ghost on a litter, you carry his spirit on a litter, 95 there you

are already metamorphosing over his head. 97 You are becoming beasts of prey over his ghost's head, you are becoming beasts of prey over his spirit, like you who become beasts of prey over the head of this sick person.

100 You are clutching at his spirit, you are clawing at his ghost, 102 you are softening his ghost, you are softening his bones 104 when you waste away the healthiness of his appearance, the healthiness of his expression. You are trampling on his ghost, 107 you are trampling on his vitality.

108 When you tug at this little creature, you are making his soul pant 110 with the warmth of your appearance, the warmth of your walking, the sweat of your appearance, the sweat of your expression, 114 with the roaring of your walking, the roaring of your running. 116 As you are all crowding together, gnashing together over his head where he lies whipped and punished by you.

118 You make him unconscious where you crowd together, snorting beside this little creature. 120 His appearance is made sorrowful, his expression is made sorrowful by you. 122 He has no vitality, no protection because of you.

125 Truly, you are the kings of death, the kings of disease, the kings of all evil spirits. 130 You are now hovering, sickening, casting your beams over mankind, over the earth, 136 since you seek the Silent Day, the Silent Hour so as to transform yourselves, to Hol Txan over mankind, 142 since your walking is like a thief's presence, your running is like a thief's presence.

20. Curing

145 But today, this is the hour, this is the day; in the name of all the gods which we are proclaiming over the head of this sick person here, 151 this day let there be protective power over the head of this little creature, so you will release his angel, 154 release his spirit where it lies threatened and punished by you.

157 But today I deliver you spirits of disease into the hands of the angel Holy Spirit, and all the angels. 161 So, they chase you running, 163 throw you to the King Mountain. 164 So, Lightning Aimer, Thunder Aimer carry you away.

21. Funeral Ceremony

1 + ,'?ka"nin 'txe'kon"trar + ,'kon"tar + .'?o'tron"te?e '?o'hro"ner +

4 + 'ta'ma?a — ,'ni'lu"gar 'tia?a'tu "re?en + ,'kon'da?a'txa"mai '?e"hen 'te + 'tia?a 'tu"re?en + 'kon -- ,'da'?u'ui"ro?o?p + ,'ua"rix + .'u'ua"?ki '?u"?pa + '?e'?ah"muak 'xe?e -- , "?txa?ar 'ua'ra'txa"mai + ,'u'tu'ru"?po?o?p + , 'u'xa"na?p + ,'u'?txa"?po?o?p 'u'ma"txit + , 'ta?a'u'ieh"?tser + ,'u'tu'ru"?po?p 'u"rutx + , 'u'mu"rur + '?i?i -- ,'?u"?kuhts + ,'?u'?txa "?po?p + ,'iŋ'gohr"pi 'pa + ,'ta?u'ieh"?tser + . '?u'?pi"tor +

26 + "txe 'ke?e -- ,'?e"pi 'pa + .'tua?a 'txam"bri 'ta"mar + ,'ie?e'?u'mu"rur + .'tua?a '?u'iu"?txi '?e"ha?a 'ta"mar + ,'iu?u"rutx + , "txe 'ke'tua?a'u'iu"?txe?e "ha?a 'ta"mar + 33 + ,'iu'?txa"?po?o?p 'in"tahtx "?txe?eu 'ta?a 'u 'ieh"?tser + ."txe 'ke?e"tua?a '?a"ue?e 'ta"mar + 35 + ,'e'ha?a"xo?p + ,'txe?e"no?p 'ke"?pan + '?e?e -- "siem 'pre'ko'txe?e -- .'tu"ro?on '?pi "xir +

40 + "?pan 'u?u -- ."txo?p + .'?u?txa "?po?o?p '?u'xa"na?p + .'?u"txo?o?p 'ko'txe'tu "ru '?a"ni '?pi"xir + 'tu"no?or 'lo'ke'?u'?kam "pes + '?i?i — ,'?u"txo?p '?an"dar + ,'?a '?txa?a?p"na '?e"pa?a + .'u'tu'ru"?po?p 'ta?a'u 'ieh"?tser + 49 + '?u"txo?o?p 'man"dar '?a?a — .'txah"?pa 'e"ku?um + ,'?a'?txa?a?p"na 'ta'mu "na?a?k 'e"pa?a + '?a'?txa?a?p"na 'ta'mu?u'ieh "?tser + 'txe"ka?e -- ,"tua?a '?u'?ku"xi + ,'ta 'ma'?e"?pi?ir 'tua?a'?a?a"xin + 'xe?e'txa"mai 'ia"ha?a + "?i?i -- '?i"kon 'da?a -- ,"uar '?a 'pa?aŋ"gua '?e"?txen + ,'?a?a"xin + '?e?e -- , '?e"pa?a + '?e?e -- ,'?ia?a"?katx + ,'tia?a"uar + 'a?a -- .'?a'pa?aŋ"gua 'e"?txen + 68 + , 'tua?a'u'?ku"xi 'e"hen 'te + .'xe?e"uar 'a'pah "no?o?p +

21. Funeral Ceremony

70 + 'i'kon'da'tu"ri?ix -- ,'?e"?txen + ,
'ua"to?o?p + ,'xe?e"ua 'ra'?pah"no?o?p + .'ua
"to?p 'ta'mo?o"tot + ,'u'?ti"sio?p 'e'txa"pahr +
"tua?a 'u'?pi"tio?p 'e?e -- .'?e'de"hun 'to'?a?a
"xin 'ta"mar + 78 + ,'ie?ei'xik"tak + .'?a?a
'xi"no?p + .'?u'?ke"txo?o?p + .'?ux"gohr "?puhr
"ha?a + "tua?a -- '?u'tu"kio?p "to?o 're?e -- ,
'?u'mu"hrer + .'?e'de"hun 'to'xe?e"ua 'ra'muh"ka
+ ."por 'ke'txe?e"no?p 'ke?e + ,'?e"ha?a + ,
"ha?ax + "tua?a — ,'?a'ket"pa '?u?ut"ha?a +
"tua?a '?u'iu"?txi 'xe?e -- ."uar '?a'muh"ka 'ia
"ha?a + 93 + ,'?i'po"re 'so + ,'?u"txo?p 'kos
'tum"brar + '?u'?ke"txo?p '?e"ha?a -- ,"mei 'gra
+ .'?u'tu"kio?p "to?o 'ru'mu"hrer 'kon'de"ua 'ra
'muh"ka +

98 + '?i"kon 'da -- ,'tsak"ti?ix + .'?e"?o
'txo"di 'ia + ,'muk"?pir + ,'?u'koh"ko?p + ,'ta
"ka '?e'ta"mal + '?u?u -- ."txo?p 'man"dar + ,
'?a?a"xin + ,'?a'?txah"ma + "to?or '?u'muh"rer +
.'?a"me 'dio"di 'ia + 110 + ,'?a?a'txe?e"na
're"sar + ,'ta'?u"hor + .'tia?a"?txa?ar + 113
+ '?i"kon 'da -- ,'?a?ak'?pa"re + ,'?a'tur'?pa
"na '?e'ta"mal + .'ta"mu?ut '?e"me 'sa + 117 +
,'?a'ua?a?p"na '?e"sa?a + ,'?i'tu"no?or 'lo'ke?e
'?u'?ku"xi '?a"ni + .'tu"no?or '?u'tu'ru"?po?p +
,'por'ke?e"uar 'u'koh"ko?p + .'por'ke?e'tsak
"ti?ix '?e"?o 'txo"di 'ia + 'por'ke'txe?e"no?p
'ke?e -- ,'ta'ka'tsak"ta "?o 'txo"di 'ia + '?en
"ton 'ses'?e'xe?e -- ,'txa"mai + ,'?a'sut"pa '?a
'?pix"?ka + .'pe'ro'ma?a'txi?ix"to 'tua?a'?u'ui
"ro?o?p 'u?ut"ia?a +

128 + "pe 'ro"txe?e -- ,"txe?e 'no?p'ke?e
'ta'ma"?o 'txo"di 'ia + ,'?a'sut"pa '?a'?pix"?ka
+ "to?or 'u'mu"hrer 'tia?a'?i"xim 'mu?k -- ,'muh
"?ka + '?i'txe?e"no?p 'ke?e -- ,'ke?e'ta'me?e"di
'ia'ia"ha?a + .'?a?ai"?tsa + ."kon 'da?a'?pix
"?ka + .'por'ke'txe?e"no?p 'ke?e"uar '?a'ua"ian
+ 138 + '?i'po"re 'so + '?u'tu'ru"?po?o?p +

21. Funeral Ceremony

'?e?e -- '?e'ta"mal + .'kon'da'?tsak"ta 'e"?o 'txo"di 'ia + 143 + '?u?u -- ,'tu'ru"?po?p '?e 'kan"de 'la + '?i'kon'da'?tsak"ta '?e'seis"mes + ,'txa"men + .'?a'sut"pa '?u'koh"kuo?p + 148 + ,'ko'txe'?e"di 'ia'tia?a'txa"mai + "?pan '?a'sut "pa '?u'koh'kuo?p + ,'?u'tu'ru"?po?p '?e'ta"mal + '?u'ua"?po?p '?e"txi 'txa + '?i?i -- '?u'tu'ru "?po?p '?e?e -- .'?e'kan"de 'la +

155 + .'?i"kon 'da'?tsak"ta '?e"?a 'nio + ,'txa"men + ,'?a'sut"pa '?u'koh"kuo?p + .'?u'tu 'ru"?po?p '?e'ta"mal + '?u'tu'ru"?po?p 'tu"no?or 'lo'ke?e -- .'?ka"ni '?u'tu'ru"?po?p + 'por'ke?e 'txe?e"no?p 'ke?e -- "ha?ax '?e?e -- "?a 'nio 'tia?a -- ,'txa"mai + '?e?e -- ,'?e'de"hun 'to + ,"txe 'ke'?a'?ko"toi '?u'ua'rah"se '?u'io"tot + ,'?i'po"re 'so + 'ha?a"xo?p '?u'koh"ko?o?p + . 'ta'me?e"di 'ia'ia"ha?a + 171 + ,'kon'da'?tsak "ta '?e"?a 'nio + 'xe?e"uar + ,'?u'koh"ko?o?p '?e'de"hun 'to + ,'?i'ta'me?e"?a 'nio + ,'?u'ua "?po?o?p '?e"txi 'txa + ,'?u'peh"ko?p + ,"tie?e 'ne'?a"ian 'u'gi"tar 'ra + ,"tie?e 'ne'?a"ian 'u 'kor"dion + ,'u'peh"ko?p 'tua?a'?a'lah"?pa + . 'tu"no?or '?e"no 'txe +

181 + '?ie?e -- '?e'ui"nik 'xe?e -- ,"ua 'ru'txe're"sar + 'tu?u"hor 're?e -- ,'ta"mal + , "txe 'ke'?u'pa"ter '?e'de"hun 'to + ,'?e'ui"nik 'ia"ha?a + ,'?a?atx"pa + ,'?a?ak"ta + ,'?u'?pah "ner + .'?a?a"uan '?a?ak"ta + 192 + ,"txe 'ke?e"uar + '?e?e -- ,'?u'iah"?ku"tes + '?e?e -- ,'de"hun 'to'xe?e"ua 'ru'koh"ko?p + ."txe 'ke?e "ha?ax 'ua'ru'ua"?pua?ak "ta + 198 + ,'?i'po "re 'so + .'ha?a"xir '?a?a"uan '?a?k"ta 'u'?pah "ner + .'?u'lah"?pa '?u"?ka?p +

201 + '?i?i -- ,"ma 'mah"txi?i + '?a'?kah "na 'tua?a'?a?ak"ta + "kuan 'do -- ."kuan 'do"ua 'ra?ak"ta + ,'?e'ui"nik 'xe?e"ua 'ru'txe're"sar "to?o 're'kan"dee "lo?p + "ma 'mah"txi?i '?a

21. Funeral Ceremony

'?kah"na 'tua?a'?a?ak"ta 'ta"ma '?e?e -- .'?e"mu 'si'ko'xe?e'tu"ru + 209 + "por 'ke?e -- ,'?u '?pah"ner 'ta"ka 'tua?ak"ta + "por 'ke"txe 'ke "ha?a 'xe?e -- ,'?e'de"hun 'to'xe?e"ua 'ra'kohk "na + ."ha?ax "ua 'ru'ua"?pua?ak "ta + 214 + , '?i'po"re 'su + .'?a?a"uan '?a?ak"ta '?u'?pah "ner +

216 + .'tan"te?e "tiem 'po + ,'kon'da "ne?en 'max'ta'ken"to + '?a"ian 'in"te?e 'ni?i — ,"pri 'mo + .'?iŋ'gui"ra 'txa"mai + 221 + , '?i'kon'da'?tsak"ta '?e"?a 'nio + ,'mah"na '?e '?in"te?e '?u"?puhk + ,'?txa?a?p"na + .'ta"mu?ut '?e"me 'sa'tia?a'tur'?pa"na '?e'ta"mal + 225 + ."txe 'ke?e'tua?a'?u'la"pi + 226 + '?i'?a"ian 'in"te?e 'ni"ma 'ma?a'?u'?ka"?pa?a "mar 'kos + , 'ha?ax"to + ,"kai + ,'u'txe're"sar 'tu?u"hor 'e 'ta"mal + ,'?i?iŋ'gui"ra + ,"kai + ,'ua?a"uan + .'?ak"ta '?u'?pah"ner + 234 + ,'por'ke?e"txe 'ke?e"ua 'ru'ua"?pu + .'?u?u'so"bri 'no'?a?ak"ta + '?i?i -- '?ie?e'ui"nik -- '?e"si?its 'ia"ha?a 'xe?e -- ,'txa"mai + ,'me?e"ra?an '?e?ex"na + '?u?u -- .'?a'nuh"?pi 'ta'ka'?u'ui"la 'ma + 243 + .'ie?e'?eh"?txok 'ia"ha?a + '?a'ro?o?p"na '?u "me 'nu'?pi"xam + 'tur"uan 'ta'mu?u"ti?i '?e?e — '?e'?txak"te?e 'tia?a — 'tu"ru '?e?e -- ,'?e 'ta"mal + 'ta'mu?u -- .'u'io'ri"iir '?e"me 'sa + 251 + ,'?a'ro?p"na '?u'?txa"mi '?in"te?e '?u "?kahn + .'tu"ruan 'ta"mar + .'?e?eh"?txok 'ia "ha?a +

254 + '?a'ro?p"na 'ke?e -- ,"ne?et + , 'ma?a"txi 'tua?a'ia?atx"pa '?a"txe 'man"da 'do + 'ma?a -- ,'me?e"rer 'ia?atx"pa 'iu?u"?txu + , 'por'ke'?a"bie 'ho + ,"uar '?a'?tsak"ta '?u"ia 'nio + ,'ko'txe'txa"mai + ."ha?ax 'uar'ka'koh"ko + ,"ne?et + ,'tu"ren + ,'?i"ria?atx "pa + 'por 'ke?e -- ,'?a"bie 'ho + .'?a'io?o"pa 'ko"ne?er +

269 + .'por'ke?e"txe?e "no?p + 'ke?e --

21. Funeral Ceremony

'?e?e -- .'?e'ui"nik 'xe?e'txa"mai + '?i?i -- , '?u'iak"ta '?u'ui"la 'ma + ,'kon'dix"to '?a '?tsak"ta '?e"?a 'nio + '?o?o -- '?e"?a 'nio '?o?o -- ,'?e'seis"mes 'txa"men + "txe 'ke'?ak — ,'kon'da?a'?ko"toi + "tu?u 'io"tot + ,'ha?a "xir + ,"siem 'pre + .'?kan"to '?u'?ku"xi 'u "ti?i '?u'ui"la 'ma + 285 + ,'?i'po"re 'so + , '?e?eh"?txok 'ia"ha?a + '?a?a -- ,'tu'ru'?pa"na + 'ta'ma'?u?u -- ,'io'rii"iir '?e"me 'sa + ."por 'ke'txe?e"no?p 'ke'tua?a'ta?a'?kuh"xa 'u"ti?i '?u"me 'nu"bie 'ho +

292 + ,'po"re 'so + ,"?pan 'txe?e"no?p + "pe 'ro"no?on 'ma?a"txi 'ka'ui"ra '?k -- ,'?a '?ko"toi + ,'?e'ui"nik + ,'?u'?tsuh"tsu?u "ti?i '?u'ui"la 'ma + 'por'ke?e -- ,"no?on 'ka'ua?a"re 'ke"ti?i 'ne'txa"men + 'ma?a"txi?ix -- ,"?ka?ar + .'e"?tsuhts "ti?i 'u'me"ner +

21. Funeral Ceremony

1 I'm going to tell another story.

4 In the place where I live, when people die, where I live, when they see that he is already expiring, the sick person who is lying dying, they lay out his sandals, they lay down his machete beside him, they lay out his gourd cup, his gourd bottle, and his tobacco, they lay down a pipe beside him, and his hat.

26 They say that the pipe is for him to smoke with, and the bottle is for him to drink water with, and the cup is for him to drink water with. 33 And they lay down a bowl beside him; they say that it is for him to eat with. 35 They say that it is just as if he were alive.

40 Thus they do it, they lay down his sandals, and act as if he were alive; everything he uses, and -- order that tortillas be placed beside him. 49 They order that eggs be cooked and laid in the middle of the tortillas, and laid beside him. They say that it is for him to eat on the road he is to walk, the one who is dead there, and when -- they are digging the grave, the tortillas and the chicken go to where they are digging the grave 68 for the people to eat who are digging the grave.

70 And when the grave is ready, those who are digging come to the house and lash together a litter, so as to carry the dead man along on their shoulders. 78 And the women go along carrying three jugs of water to pour over the mound of the dead man who is to be buried, because they say that the water is to become a spring for him to drink whom they are burying there. 93 And because of that they customarily carry a lot of water to pour over the mound

where he is being buried.

98 And when a week has gone by since he was buried, they wait with tamales -- they send them to be placed on the mound at mid-day. 110 Prayers are said over his head where he is lying. 113 And when it becomes dark, the tamales are placed on the table, 117 chilate is poured out, and everything which he used to eat. They put out everything, because they are waiting, because a week has gone by, because they say that with the passage of a week, then the one who died comes back to life, but no longer so they can see him there.

128 But they say that in a week he comes back to life, on top of the mound where he had gone to be buried. And they say that on that day, he is hungry, when he comes to life, because they say that he was sleeping. 138 And that is why they put out tamales when the week has passed. 143 They put out candles and when six months have passed, they await him again. 148 Like the day he died, so they await him again. They put out tamales, they pour chicha, and they put out candles.

155 And when a year has gone by they again await the dead one; they put out tamales, they put out everything they want to put out, because they say that -- that -- year when he died -- the dead man they say comes to visit his house, and for that reason they await him on that day. 171 When a year has passed, those who are awaiting the dead man, and in a year, they pour chicha, they call for one who has a guitar, for one who has an accordion, they call them to play all night long.

181 And the man who is saying the prayers

over the tamales, they say that he is the defender of the dead man; that man rises, and dances by himself, he stands and dances. 192 They say that he is making the dead man dance, whom they are awaiting. They say that he is inviting him to dance. 198 And for that reason he stands and dances by himself, clapping his hands.

201 And nobody is intended to dance when — when the man who is saying the prayers over the candles is dancing, nobody is intended to dance for -- the musicians who are there. 209 Because he is to dance alone, because they say that the dead man is awaited; he is being invited to dance. 214 And because of that he stands up and dances by himself.

216 A long time ago, when I was a kid, there was a cousin of mine I saw die. 221 And when a year had gone by one of his outfits was bought, and laid on the table where the tamales were placed. 225 They say it was for him to wear. 226 And there was one of my uncles whose name was Marcos who then began to pray over the tamales and I saw that he stood up and danced by himself, 234 because they say that he was inviting his nephew to dance, and the man -- the boy who died, he had not long before married his wife. 243 And that girl was told by her father-in-law to sit on the edge of the bed where the tamales were placed at the -- side of the table. 251 She was told to get one of her benches and sit on it, that girl. 254 She was told, "You are not to get up, to work, you don't have to get up to grind corn, because your husband has been dead for a year now. We are awaiting him. You, sit down! You can't get up, because your husband is coming today."

269 Because they say that the man who died

21. Funeral Ceremony

leaves his wife, until a year has passed, a year or six months dead, they say that -- when he comes to his house, he always wants to kiss his wife. 285 And that is why that girl was seated at the edge of the table, because they say that it was so she could be kissed by her husband.

292 That is why they say that, but we did not see -- the man come and kiss his wife, because we say that anyone who is dead does not remember kissing.

22. Tsikin

1 + ,'?a"ian + ,'?o'tron"te?e 'kos"tum
'bre + .'tia?a'tu"re?en + 4 + 'ta'me?e -- ,
'pri"me 'ro'di'no"biem 'bre + .'txe?e"no?p 'ke?e
"mei 'gra'noh"?kin + 7 + ,'tua?a'tu"no?or + .
'?e'txa'me"no?p + 9 + ,'ke?e"ha?ax '?e"di 'ia
+ ,"tia?a + ,'?e?ek"mai + ,'tu"no?or + .'?e'txa
'me"no?p + 14 + ,"pe 'ro + ,'?e"di 'ia + ,'ia
"ha?a + ."mei 'gra + ,'noh"?kin + ."tu?ut 'e"hen
'te + 'ta'ni?i'lu"gar +

21 + .'?a'noh"?ki"nio?o?p + 22 + ,'u'tu
'ru"?po?p '?e'ta"mal 'ta"me 'sa + ,'u'tu'ru
"?po?p 'e"xe?p + .'u'tu'ru"?po?p 'e'?pah'?pur
"sa?a + 25 + .'u'tu'ru"?po?p 'e"txa?ap "?txum
+ 26 + .'u'tu'ru"?po?p 'e'na"ran 'ha + .'u'tu
'ru"?po?p 'e'ke"ne?e + 28 + ,'u'tu'ru"?po?p 'e
'uis"kil + .'u'tu'ru"?po?p + ,'?e'si"?ka?p + 31
+ ,'?u'?txa"?po?o?p '?e"?kuhts + .'ta"me 'sa + ,
"tua?a + ,'u'txam"bri 'e'de"hun 'to + '?u?u -- ,
"txo?p 'man"dar + ,'?a'tu'ru'?pa"na + ,'?e'?ar
'ros"?pir + ,'a"?katx + ,'u'ua"?puo?o?p + ,'in
"te?e + ,'mu'ruh"rutx + ,"txi 'txa + .'ta"me 'sa
+ 45 + ,'?u'ma"nio?p '?e"pan + ,'u'tu'ru"?po?p
+ ,'kon"da + .'a'tar'de"ran + ,'u'tso"rio?p 'e
"?kahn 'tu"no?or 'u"ti?i 'o"tot + ,"txe 'ke?e
"tua?a + .'a'tu'rua"no?p + .'e'de"hun 'to'xe?e
"uar 'a'kohk"no?p +

53 + ,'?a"ian 'a"ni 'in"te?e + ,'ui"nik +
.'u'?ka"?pa?a 'do"lo 'res'fe"li 'pe + 56 + ,
'kon'de"uar 'a'tsik"ni + ,'u'?txa"mi 'u"?kahn +
,'a'tu"ruan 'ta"kar + .'tu?u"ti?i "puer 'ta +
60 + ,'?u"txe 'man"dar 'a'tso"hra 'e"?kahn + ,
'tu"no?or 'u'ti?i'o"tot + 'a?a -- ,'ha?a"xir + ,
'a'tu"ruan + .'ta"puer 'ta + 66 + ,'?u'peh"ka
+ ,'tu'?ka"?pa?a 'tu'?ka"?pa?a + 'tu"no?or 'lo
'ke?e -- ,'txa"men + ,'u'ier"maa "no?o?p + ,'u
"prii "mo?o?p + ,'u'so"brii "no?o?p + ,"?o?o '?u
'ia"mii "go?o?p + ,'u'ta'ta?a"bie "ho?p + ,'tu
"no?or 'u'pa"rien "tio?p + .'u'peh"ka 'tu'?ka

22. Tsikin

"?pa?a 'tu'?ka"?pa?a + .'?o?o"txoi 'ma"ku?u +
90 + ,'?i"ti?i 'ne"ua 'ru'peh"ka + ,'?o?o"txoi
+ ,'tu'?ka"?pa?a + ,'?a?a"xin + ,'?u'iah"?ku 'u
"?kahn + ,'iu'?ke"txe '?u"?ka?p + "txe 'ke?e --
"uar '?u?u -- .'?u"txe 'sa'lu"dar 'ta"kar +
.'xe?e"uar '?o?o"txo?p 'ia"ha?a +

100 + "por 'ke?e'txe?e"no?p 'ke?e -- 'ta
'me?e -- ,'?e"di 'ia'ia"ha?a + 'tu"no?or '?e?e
-- ,'?e'de"hun "to?p 'xe?e'txa'me"no?p + ,'ta"ri
'xe"tiem 'po'?e?ek"mo?p + 'tua?a -- .'?e?ek"mo?p
+ "tua?a '?u'ua'rah"se '?u?u -- .'fa"mii "lio?p
'tia?a'?u'iak"to?p + 110 + ,'?i'po"re 'so + .
'a'kohk"no?p 'ta'me?e"di 'ia'ia"ha?a + 112 + .
'txe?e"no?p 'ke?e"mei 'gra'noh"?kin + .'tu?u
"to?p +

114 + ,'tu"no?or 'u"ti?i 'o"tot + ,'?a
'?pu?t"?ka '?a?a"xin + 'ta"ka '?e?e -- .'tu
"no?or 'u'tu'ru"?po?p + 118 + ,'por"ke?e '?u
'xi"?txio?p + .'?e"man 'ta'ta'mu?ut'?e"rum +
'?e?e -- ,'pohtx"?pir + ,'?i'tu?u"hor + ,'?u'ua
"?po?o?p + '?e?e -- ,"sa?a + ,'?e'?txa?ap"?txum
+ ,'ke"ne?e + ,'tu"no?or 'lo'ke?e'?ka"ni '?u'tu
'ru"?po?o?p + '?u'tu'ru"?po?p -- .'in'te?e"ra +
131 + 'por'ke?e -- ."txe 'ke?e"mei 'gra + .
'xe?e"uar '?a'?ko"toi '?a'gua"ro?p 'ia"ha?a +

134 + 'ie?e -- ,'lo'ke?e'?a'tu'ru'?pa"na
'ia"ha?a + ,"kon 'da'ix"to '?a'?ka?a"pa '?a
'txe?e"na -- '?e?e -- 're"sar 'tu?u"ho 're?e --
.'e'ta"mal + 140 + '?en"ton 'ses'a'puh"ka 'ta
'ka'?e"hen 'te'lo'ke?e -- ,'?a'?ko"tuo?p + .'?u
'ui"ro '?pe'noh"?kin + ,"ha?ax '?ah'?ku"no?p 'e
'ke"ne?e + ,'si"?ka?p + ,'?e'?a"?katx + ,'ta"mal
+ .'tu"no?or 'lo'ke?e'?a'tu'ru'?pa"na + '?e?e --
.'?ah'?ku"no?p + 150 + "por 'ke?e"txe 'ke?e --
'?e'?ah"rer '?u"me?ein '?u'?ku"xi '?e?e -- .'?e
'de"hun 'to'xe?e"ra?a '?ko"tuo?p + .'xe?e"ua 'ra
'kohk"no?p + 154 + "pe 'ro?o -- '?e?e -- '?e?e

22. Tsikin

— ,'?e"me 'ro'ta"mal 'xe?e'tu"ru + .'ma?a"txi 'u'?ku"xo?p + ,'?i'po"re 'so + ,'ha?a"xo?p + ,'u 'tu'ru"?po?p + ,'tu"?ki?ik 'tu"?ki?ik + ,'tua?a '?u'?ku"xi + .'lo'ke?e"uar 'u'koh"ko?o?p +

165 + ,'xe?e'?a'?txah"ma + ,'u"txe 're"sar + .'tu"no?or 'iak"?par + 168 + ,'?a'xa"na + . "uar '?a'xa"na 'u'txe're"sar "?ehs 'to'?a'sa'koh "pa "?o 'tro"di 'ia + 170 + ,'?i"mei 'gra"hen 'te'?a'xa"na 'ta"kar + "por 'ke?e -- ,'ha?a"xir + ,'tia?a'?ko"toi + ,'?i?i'?e'ta"mal 'xe?e'a'tru '?pa"na + "ha?ax '?u?u -- .'pu"ki 'ta'ke?e"hen 'te + 177 + ,'?i'po"re 'sue"hen 'te + ,'?a '?txu"uan '?a'xa"na + .'tu?u"pat "tia?a '?a'xa "nu?u 'txe're"sar +

180 + ,"kon 'da'?ix"to + '?a?a -- ,'?a'sa 'koh"pa + ,'?ia?a'?ka?a"pa '?u"txe 're"sar + , '?en"ton 'ses + 'tia?a'?a"ian '?e?e -- ,"txi 'txa + ,'a"ka?ai + ,'?u'iu"?txio?p 'e"txi 'txa + '?a"ian 'tia?a -- '?a"ian '?e?e -- '?e"mu 'si'ka 'ta'ke?e -- ,'bio"lin + ,'ta'ke?e'gi"tar 'ra + 'ta'ke?e -- .'?e'a'kor"dioŋ + 196 + .'?a?ak "to?o?p + 197 + ,"uar '?a'ka'ra"io?p + .'?a?a "xin '?e"tar 'de + 199 + "por 'ke"txe 'ke?e -- ,'a'tsa?a"io?p + 'por'ke?e -- ,"uar + '?e?e -- . '?a'noh'?ki"nio?p + 205 + ,"uar '?u'koh"ko + . '?u'de"hun "to?o?p + 'tu"no?or 'lo'ke?e -- ,'txa "men + ,'u'ta"to?o?p + ,'u'ier"maa "no?o?p + 'tu "no?or 'lo'ke?e -- .'?u'pa"rien "tio?p + ."uar 'u'koh"ko?p + 214 + ,'?i'po"re 'so + ,'?u'ma "nio?p + "mei 'gra'?e?e -- .'?e'kan"de 'la + '?u?u -- ,'?tsah'pe"so?p +

220 + '?a"ian "tie?e 'ne?e -- ,"mei 'gra + .'?e'kan"de 'la + 223 + ,"por 'ke?e"txe 'ke?e '?in'te?en"te?e + "tua?a '?u?u -- '?ak -- "ka 'da — 'de"hun 'to'xe?e -- ,"ua 'ru'koh"ko?p + . '?in'te?en"te?e '?e'kan"de 'la"tuo?o?p + 230 + ,'ie'kan"de 'la'ia"ha?a + ,"txe 'ke?e"ha?ax 'u

22. Tsikin

'?kah"ko?p + ,'tua?a'?ko"tuo?p + .'tu?ut 'e"dios 'ta"kar + 234 + ,'po"re 'so'ha?a"xo?p + ,"?pan '?a'?ku"?pe 'sia"no?p + 'ke?e -- 'ke?e -- ,'?e 'kan"de 'la + ,"ha?ax + ,"tua?a '?u"txo?p + , '?en'tre"gar + ,'a'?ko'to"io?p + .'ta'ke?e"dios + 256 + '?e?e -- '?u"?tsah 'pe"so?p 'tua?a '?a?a -- ."ka 'aa'de"hun 'to'lo'ke'?e?e'ru'koh "ko?o?p + 259 + ,'?i'ta'me?e'txi"nam + '?e?e -- ,'ta'ma'?i"gle 'sia + ,'?a'?toht"na '?e'kam "pa 'na + ,"?ehs 'to'?a'?ko"toi + .'?a'las"dies + 'ta'ma'?e?e -- ."di 'ia"tia?a 'sa'koh"pa 'e 'tsi"kin + 267 + ,"por 'ke?e"txe 'ke?e + "ha?a -- ,'?e'kam"pa 'na'ia"ha?a + '?e"?u '?tam -- , '?u'?ta"?pes 'ni"?pir + '?e?e -- ,'de"hun "to?o?p 'ia"ha?a + 'lo'ke?e -- ,"uar '?a'xa"na + '?u?u -- ,'fa"mii "lio?p + ,'?u'pa"rien "tio?p + ,'?i'ha?ax"to + ,'?a'?ta"?pes"no?p 'ta'ke?e'kam "pa 'na + ,'?i'po"re 'so + ,'?e'kam"pa 'na'ta'ma '?i"gle 'sia + ,'ta'?e'txi"nam + ,"ua 'ra'?toht "na + ."?ehs 'ta'?ko"toi 'a'las"dies + 288 + 'por'ke?e -- "txe 'ke?e -- ,"ha?ax + ."ua 'ra '?ta'?pes"no?p 'ta'ke?e'kam"pa 'na'ia"ha?a +

292 + ,'?a"ian 'in"te?e '?al"de 'ia + .'?u '?ka"?pa?a "mi 'na + 294 + ,'i'al"de 'ia'ia "ha?a + ,"kon 'da'sa'koh"pa 'e'tsi"kin + 'tu "no?o 're"hen 'te'xe?e -- ,'tsik"nio?p + ,'?i "kon 'da'sa'koh"pa + '?u?u -- ,'?ke'txo?p"to + '?e?e -- ,'ta"mal + ,'?e'?txa'?pu'?pir "pa?a + 'u'tu'ru"?po?p "to?o 're?e -- ,'?e"kam 'po"san 'to + ,'tia?a'muk"?pi 're'de'hun"to?p + '?a?a -- 'tu"no?or "tie?e 'ne?e -- ,'?a"ia 'nu'de"hun 'to 'muk"?pir + 'u'?ke"txe?e -- .'?e'?txa'?pu'?pir "pa?a + .'?u'tu'ru"?pa + 313 + 'i?i -- ."ia?a '?u'pu"kio?p +

315 + ,"?a '?pu?t"?ka '?e"hen 'te + "to?o 're?e -- .'?e"kam 'po"san 'to'kon'da'so'koh"pa 'e'tsi"kin + 318 + '?i"txe 'ke?e -- ,"mas 'ta "rix 'tiem 'po + '?e?e -- '?e'kan"de 'la'tia?a

22. Tsikin

— ,'u'pu"to?p + "txe 'ke?e -- ,'kon'da?a'so'koh
"pa + ,'u'?ke"txo?p + ,'?e?ek"mai + ,'ta'me?e
'txi"nam + '?u"txo?p '?en'tre"gar + 'ta"ka '?e?e
— '?e"pa 'gre'tua?a -- .'?u'?ta?a?p"se + 332
+ .'?in"so 'lo"?pan '?a"ni 'u"txo?p + 333 +
"por 'ke?e -- 'txe?e"no?p '?a"ni 'ke?e -- ,'?e
'tsi"kin + ,'ma"ha?ax 'kual"ker 'noh"?kin + 'si
"no 'ke?e -- '?e?e -- ,"ha?ax + ,'u'noh'?ki"nar
+ "tie?e 'ne?e -- .'txa'me"no?p + 343 + .'por
'ke?e'tu"no?or '?e?ek"mo?p +

344 + ,'?i'po"re 'so + .'ta"ri 'xe"tiem
'po + "kuan 'do?o -- ,"tia?a 'tua?ak'?pa"re?e
'tsi"kin + .'a'?ka"xi 'e'txir"ha?a + 349 +
'txe?e"no '?pa"ni 'e"hen 'te'ke?e -- ,"ha?ax + .
"ua 're?em'se"no?p 'ta'ke?e'txir"ha?a + 352 +
"pe 'ro?o -- ,'ko"ne?er + 'ma?a"txi 'a'?ka"xi
'?e?e -- ,'?e'txir"ha?a 'ta'me?e'tsi"kin + ,
"pues + ,'ka'ua?a"re 'ke'ki"sas + 'ma?a'txix
"to?o -- ,'ua"tar 'e'de"hun "to?o?p "ia?a + 'po
"re 'so'ma?a"txi?ix -- .'?a'?ka"xi 'e'txir"ha?a
+ 362 + 'por'ke?e + 'ta"ri 'xe"tiem 'po'txe?e
"no?p 'ke?e -- ,"ha?ax + ,'?e?ek"mo?o?p + ,'ta
'ke?e'txir"ha?a "kon 'da?a'?ka"xi 'e'txir"ha?a
'de"tar 'de + ,"pe 'ro'ko"ne?er + ,"kon 'da?a
'?ko"toi + ,'?e'tsi"kin + ."ma 'tu"?ka '?e'txir
"ha?a + 371 + "pues + ,'po"re 'so'ka'ua?a"re
'ke'ki"sas + ,'ma?a'txix"to '?a?ak'ta"na '?e?ek
"mo?o?p "ia?a + 'por'ke?e -- .'ma?a"txi '?u'ta
're"so '?pe'txir"ha?a +

376 + ,'?i'?po"re 'so + ,'ma?a"txi '?a'lo
"?koi '?e'?peh"uar + "por 'ke?e -- ,"ma 'tu"?ka
'?e'txir"ha?a + .'u'ta"res 'e'de"hun "to?o?p +
381 + ."por 'ke?e'?u'?kah"tio '?pa"ni + 'ke?e
— '?e'de"hun "to?o?p 'xe?e -- ,'?a'txa"mo?o?p +
"txe 'ke?e -- ,"?pan + 'ko'txe?e -- .'?u'sol"da
'do'?e'go"bier "no?p + 'ke?e -- ."ia 'ma"kar + .
'?u'me"ner + 392 + '?i?i -- '?i"kuan 'do?o --
,'?a'?ko"toi '?e"?a 'nio + ,'?en"ton 'ses + ,

22. Tsikin

'?a?ak'ta"na + .'ua"to?o?p + '?e?e -- ,'?u'ua 'rah"sio?p + '?u?u -- ,'fa"mi "lio?p + ,'lo'ke?e '?u'iak"to?o?p + 'por'ke?e -- ,'me?e"rer '?a'lo "?kuo?p + ,'kual"kier "tiem 'po + ,'por'ke?e 'ha?a"xo?p + 'tu"ro?p 'ta'mu?u -- ,"?ka '?pe "dios + .'?i"ma 'ko'txe?e"rer 'ta?a'lo"?kuo?p +

410 + ."?pa 'na"ni 'u'?kah"tio?p + 'ke?e -- ,"kon'da?a'txa"mai + ,'?e"hen 'te + ,'?a?a "xin + ,'tu?ut'e"dios + ,'?i'ia"ha?a + '?e?e -- "ma 'ko'txe?e"rer 'tua?a -- ,'?a'lo"?koi + ,'por 'ke?e'ha?a"xir + ,'?e"txer + .'ko'txan"te?e '?ah '?kam"pa?ar + 423 + ,"?pa 'na"ni '?u'?kah "tio?p + .'ta"ri 'xe"tiem 'po + 425 + '?i?i -- ,'?i'?pan"to + .'u'?kah"tio?p '?ehs'to'ko "ne?er +

22. Tsikin

1 There is another custom where I live. 4 On the first of November, they say it is a great festival 7 for all the dead. 9 That is the day that all the dead come down, 14 but that day is a great festival for the people in my village.

21 They celebrate. 22 They put out tamales on the table, they put out *xepes*, they put out sour *atol*, 25 they put out sweet squash, 26 they put out oranges, they put out bananas, 28 they put out *güicoy* squash, they put out sugar-cane, 31 they put out tobacco on the table, so the dead man will smoke it, and they order that chicken with rice be put out, and a gourd bowl of chicha be set on the table. 45 They buy bread, and put it out when evening comes; they line up benches all around the house. They say that is for them to sit on as they are waiting for the dead man.

53 There was a man whose name was Dolores Felipe. 56 When he was celebrating the Day of the Dead, he took his bench, and sat down on it in his doorway. 60 He ordered the benches to be placed in line all around the house -- he sat down at the door. 66 He called by name all the dead: his brothers, his cousins, his nephews, or his friends, his grandfathers, all his relatives he called by name to come inside. 78 He did not see them. 80 But since he knew -- what the names were of the men who were dead, he called them by name to come inside. 90 And to each one he called by name to enter, he went and gave a bench, and raised his hand: they say -- he was giving a greeting with it to those who were coming in there.

100 Because they say that on that day everyone -- the dead men who are dead, long ago

would come down -- they would come down to visit their families where they had left them. 110 And that is why they are awaited on that day. 112 They say that it is a great festival for them.

114 All around the house they fill it with everything they put out. 118 Because they spread a cloth on the ground, washed, and on top of it they set atol, sweet squash, bananas, everything they want to put out, they put out together. 131 Because they say that many are coming to visit there.

134 And -- what is put out there when the prayers have been finished over the -- tamales, 140 then they offer them to the people who come to see the celebration; they are given bananas, sugar cane, chickens, tamales, everything that is put out they are given. 150 Because they say that only the spirit eats -- the dead man who comes there who is awaited. 154 But -- the -- real tamale which is there they do not eat, and that is why they put everything out to eat, those who are waiting.

165 The one who was brought says prayers all night; 168 he walks saying prayers until it gets light the next day. 170 And many people walk with him, because where he comes, the tamales which are put out he offers to the people. 177 And that is why people follow along behind where he walks saying prayers.

180 Then, when it grows light, the prayers are finished, and then when there is chicha they begin to drink the chicha, and when there is music, with a violin -- a guitar, with an -- accordion. 196 They dance. 197 They get drunk as the evening passes, 199 because they

say that they are happy because they are celebrating. 205 They are awaiting the dead men, all who are dead; their fathers, their brothers, all who are their relatives, they are awaiting. 214 And that is why they buy many candles, and light them.

220 There are some who have many candles, 223 because they say that for each one of the dead whom they are awaiting there is a candle for him. 230 And that candle, they say that it is his light for him to come before God with. 234 That is why they believe that -- the candle is for them to give up when they come to God.

244 They say to him that, "We were awaited." And that is why they buy many candles, each for each. 256 They light them for each dead man who is being awaited. 259 And in the town, in -- the church the bell is tolled until it comes to be ten o'clock of the day when the Day of the Dead comes. 267 Because they say that -- that bell is the elevator of the dead who are going to their families, their relatives. And then, they are raised up by the bell. That is why the bell in the church in the town is tolled from when it grows light; it is tolled until ten o'clock comes. 288 Because they say that they are raised up with that bell.

292 There is a village called La Mina. 294 And that village, when the Day of the Dead dawns, all the people celebrate it. And when it grows light, they carry tamales, flat tortillas, they carry them up to the cemetery where the dead are buried -- everyone who has a dead man buried there, they carry the flat tortillas and put them out. 313 And there they offer them.

315 People fill the cemetery when the Day

of the Dead dawns. 318 And they say that a longer time ago, the candles where -- they burned them, they say that when it grew light, they carried them down into town and gave them to the priest to keep. 332 Only thus did they do it. 333 Because they said that the Day of the Dead was not just any festival, but that -- it was the festival of those who were dead. 343 Because all of them came down.

344 And that is why long ago when where it gets dark on the Day of the Dead and a drizzle falls, 349 the people say that -- "They are bringing down the drizzle." 352 But nowadays, if the drizzle doesn't fall on the Day of the Dead, well, we say that maybe the dead didn't come down there, and so the drizzle didn't fall. 362 Because long ago they say that they came down with the drizzle when the drizzle fell in the evening, but today, when the Day of the Dead comes without drizzle, 371 well, we say that maybe they were not allowed to come down there, because they did not bring the drizzle.

376 And that is why there is no second harvest, because there is no drizzle the dead bring. 381 Because they used to tell that the dead who died, they say that just like -- the soldiers of the government, shut up there by it, 392 and when a year has gone, then they are allowed to come -- they visit their families which they left, because they can't get out just any time, because they dwell in the hand of God, and there is no way for them to get out.

410 So they used to tell it that when people die, they go before God, and there, there is no way for them to get out, because one is held there like a servant. 423 So they used to tell it long ago. 425 And so they tell it to this day.

23. Devil

1 + ,'?a"ian 'o'tron"te?e '?o'hro"ner + , 'a'?kah"na + .'ta"ri 'xe"tiem 'po + 4 + '?e?e -- ,'ia"ha?a + 'ta'me?e -- '?al'pri"me 'ro + , 'de'no"biem 'bre + ,'a'txe?e"na 'kon -- ,'stum "brar + .'a'txe?e"na '?e'tsi"kin + 12 + ,'?i 'tu"no?or '?e"hen 'te + .'?a'tsik"nio?p +

14 + '?i"txe 'ke?e'?a"ian 'in'te?e -- . "tiem 'po + '?e?e -- "uar + ,'a'tsik"ni 'tu "no?or 'e"hen 'te + '?i?i -- ,"kon 'da'sa'koh"pa + ,"uar '?a'txe?e"na '?e'?o?oi"?txer + 'tu"no?or '?e?e -- ,'?e'?al"de 'ia + .'tu"no?or '?e'lu'ga "ro?p + 25 + '?i?i -- ,'?i"txe + ,'?a'?kah"na + ,"?es 'to'ko"ne?er + 'ke?e'?a"ian + '?in"te?e 'ui"nik + ,'ha?a"xir + ,'ma?a"txi '?ko"toi + 'xa "na 'ta'me?e -- .'?e'tsi'ki"no?p 'tia?a"uar 'a 'txe?e"na +

35 + "pe 'ro?o -- ,"txe 'ke?en"naht + , '?ka"ni '?a?an'?txak"na + ,'kon'da'?ko"toi + . 'pehk"na '?u"me 'nin"te?e 'ui"nik + 40 + ,'?a 'ro?o?p"na + ,'?i"ne?et -- '?e?e -- 'tu"?ka?a -- "ga 'na'ma?a"txi?i -- '?ka"ni?i -- '?i'lo"?koi 'i'xa"na 'ko?o"ra?a -- .'?i'txuhk"san 'te?e'noh '?ki"no?p +

48 + ,'?i'ha?a"xir "txe + ,"ne?en 'ma?a "txi '?ũ?ũ"sre '?in'lo"?koi + "por 'ke?e -- ,'?e 'noh"?kin + '?e?e -- ,'?a"iam "be 'ses'ma?a"txi 'ka'lo"?koi + "bien 'ta'ke?e -- ,'?e'xam"?par 'te?e'noh"?kin + 'por'ke?e -- '?e?e -- 'tal"bes + ,'?im'?pus"ta?a "ni '?txa?a"ron + '?e?e -- , 'ma"kui?ir 'ko?o"tot + ,'?i'ka'lo"?koi 'ka'xa "na + '?i?i -- '?i'ma?a"txi 'ka'na?a"ta + 'tu '?ka 'ka"ni 'tah"ui 'na -- .'ka'tah"ui + 67 + '?i?i -- 'ta"mar "ne?en + 'ma?a"txi?in 'lo"?koi 'in'xa"na 'ta'me?e'noh'?ki"no?p + "por 'ke?e -- '?a"ian "mei 'ra + ,'?tsoh"iir 'a'txe?e"na + '?e?e -- ,'ta'me?e'noh'?ki"no?p 'ko'txe?e"ra + , "por 'ke?e'?e"hen 'te + 'ma?a"txi '?o?oi"?txio?p

23. Devil

'tsus'ta"ka +

77 + 'ha?ax"to '?e'ui"nik 'xe?e -- ,"uar '?a'?ko"toi + '?u'lo?ok"se '?e?e -- ,'?e'ui"nik 'ta'mu?u'io"tot + ."txe + "pe 'ro?o -- ,"ma "ha?ax 'tu"no?o 're"di 'ia + ."?pan '?a'nu"mui + 85 + ,'?e"ra + ,'?iŋ"ko?o 'xa'na"kon + ,'?a?a '?txah"ma?ar 'ta"rie?en + '?i?iŋ'?ka"ni 'tua?a -- .'?i"xi?i 'xa"na 'ko?o"ra 'ta'ka"ren +

90 + .'?e'ui"nik "txe + "pe 'ro"ne?en 'ma?a"txi?i -- ,'?in"xin + '?i?i -- '?in"txe?e 'ta'gra'de"ser 'ke?e -- 'ma?a"txe?e -- ,'?a "txe?e "huer 'sa'tua?a'in"xin 'ta'ka"ret + "por 'ke"ne?en 'ma?a"txi '?ka"nin 'lo"?koi 'por'ke?e -- '?e?e -- .'?im"?puts '?txa?a"ren 'ta'nio?o "tot +

100 + ."pe 'ro'?e'ui"nik "txe + "pe 'ro?o -- ,'hai'ma?a"txi + ,'?i?i"xin 'ta'ka"ren + , '?en"ton 'ses + 'ko'txe?e -- "ua 'ra'?pa?a"kre 'ke?e -- ,'?a"ian '?a"uet 'ui'ni"kir + ,'?a '?ka?a"pa 'txa'mes"?pir + ,'?i'hai"ua 'ra'?pa?a "kre + "pues + ."ne?et 'pri"me 'ro + ,'?i?i"xin + ,'?i'?ka?a"pa 'txa'mes"?pir + .'por'ke'ma?a "txi '?ka"ni?i "xi 'ta'ka"ren +

115 + ,'?en"ton 'ses + ,'?e'ui"nik + , '?pa?ak"ta '?u"ial 'ma'?u'iu"?pi + ."kon 'da 'ro?o?p"na 'ko'txe'ia"ha?a + 119 + ,'?en"ton 'ses + ,'?u'ia?a"re + '?u?u -- ,'?u'uix"ka?ar + .'ki"sas '?in"xin 'ta'ke?e'ui"nik 'i"ra + "por 'ke?e -- ,"ua 'ru'ia?a"re?en + .'?ka"ni '?in"xin 'ta"kar + 127 + "por 'ke?e -- ."txe?e 'ui"nik + ,"hai 'ii?i"xin 'ta'ka"ren + ,'?in"txe?et 'kui "dar + 'tua?a -- "ma 'tu"?ka?a 'num"sa?a "?pa + ,'?i"ra '?a"txe 'pen"sar + ,'ta'ka"ren '?i?i"xin + ,'?i'ta'ka"ren + ."ma 'tu"?ka "tua?a '?a'num "sa?a "?pa + 137 + ,"ne?en '?in"txe?et 'kui "dar 'ha'ia"ian 'txi'?ka"ni + ,'?u'iah"?ke?et +

23. Devil

,"pe 'ro"ne?en + ,'õ?õn'se'ni"?pa + .'ta'ma"ret +

142 + ,'?en"ton 'ses + '?e?e -- ,'?e'ui "nik + '?e?e -- ,'?u'uah"pi + '?u?u -- ,'ma"txit 'lo"?koi 'ta"kar + '?i?i -- ,'?ko'to"io?p + , 'tia?a"uar + '?a'txe?e"na '?e?e -- ,'?o?oi"?txer + ,'tu"ru '?e'noh"?kin + 'tu"ru '?e?e -- ,'lah "?pa?ar + ,'ta'mi?i'?o"tot + ."ua 'ra?ak"ta '?e "hen 'te + 159 + "?i?i -- '?a'ro?op"na '?u"me 'ne'ui"nik 'xe?e -- .'?ko"toi 'lo'?kes"na + 162 + ."txe "tua?a -- ,'ket"pe?en 'ta"ra + ."ne?en '?ka"ni?in "xin 'ma"ku?u + 165 + ,'ha?a"xir 'ket"pa 'tu"ruan + ,'tu?u"pat 'o"tot 'ma"kui?i 're'?ko"pot + ."tia?a 'ma?a"txi '?e?er"na + 168 + "?i?i -- "?i 'ha?a -- "?i?i -- ,'?i'ha?a"xir + ,"uar + ,'?u'ui"ra + '?e?e -- 'tu"?ka "ua 'ru "txe '?e'ui"nik 'xe?e -- '?ko"toi 'lo'?kes"na + 177 + '?i?i -- ,'ha?a"xir 'tu"ru '?u'ui"ra + , 'tu?u"pot 'o"tot + ,'?e'ui"nik 'ia"ha?a + ,'?ko "toi + ,'tu"ua 'me"hen 'te + ."ma 'mah"txi?i 'u 'peh"ka + '?i"nien 'ha?a"xir 'ma?a"txi 'pehk"na 'u"me 'ne"hen 'te +

185 + ,"pe 'ro'ha?a"xir + "txe 'ke?e -- , '?ko"toi 'ta"ka + '?e?e -- ,'ta'mi?i'o"tot + , '?o"txoi 'ma"ku?u + '?e?e -- 'tu"ua 'me"hen 'te 'tia?a -- ."uar '?a?ak"ta + 194 + "pe 'ro?o -- ,"ma 'mah"txi '?u"mem 'pehk"na + '?i"nien 'ha?a "xir 'ma?a"txi 'u'peh"ka '?e?e -- .'?e'?ah'?ku "to?p 'lo'ke?e"ua 'ra?ak"to?p + 198 + ,'ha?a "xir "txe 'ke'tu"ru '?u'ui"ra + '?e?ei -- '?i "kon 'da?a -- ,'lo"?koi + '?u'?ke"txe?en 'te?e -- ,'mu'ruh"ruhtx + ."txi 'txa'lo"?koi + 205 + '?u'iah"?ku '?e?e -- '?e?e -- '?e'ui"nik 'xe'tu "ru '?a?a -- '?a'kohk"san 'to'?po'?o"tot + 209 + '?e?e -- ."txe + ,"ne?en + 'txe?e'ne"nix '?a?a -- ,'?a'ten"der + '?ah'?ku'ne"nix 'ni?i -- ,'ni "tra 'go'?ũ?ũn"?txi + '?i?i -- '?iŋ'?ka"ni 'tua?a -- .'ko?oi"?txi 'ko"mon +

23. Devil

219 + '?e'ui"nik "txe "pe 'ro"ne?en 'ma?a "txa?a "ni '?ka"nũ?ũn "?txi 'por'ke?e -- ,'?im '?pa?a"kre + ,'?e'ka"rer + 'por'ke?e -- "ne?eŋ + "kuan 'do?o -- ,'?iŋ'ka"rai + ,'ma?a"txi?iŋ '?ko "toi 'ta'ni'?o"tot + 'si"no 'ke?e -- '?iŋ'ku'kre "ma "tu?ut "?pi?ir + .'?i"ia?aŋ 'gua"ian + 230 + '?i?i -- ,'?pah"?kat + 'al"gun -- ,"bo 'lo'?a 'lu"mui "tu?ut "?pi?ir + ,'u'iah"?ke?en + '?i?i — ,'ta"ma 're"ra + .'im'?pa?ak"ta '?ũ?ũn"?txi +

238 + ."pe 'ro'ha?a"xir 'txe + '?i'ma "ka?an 'gua?a"re?et 'ke?e -- ,"ne?en + '?ko'tu "re?e -- '?ko"tue?en + ,'?in'lo?ok"se?et 'to?o "tot + '?i?i -- ,'?in"txe?et 'kui"dar + 246 + '?i?i -- "ma 'tu"?ko?ot '?i'?pa?ak"ta + 'por 'ke?e -- .'ta'ka"reŋ 'gua"ri 'xa"na + 250 + , '?en"ton 'ses + ,'?e'ui"nik 'ia"ha?a + 'u'iu "?txi '?e?e -- .'?e"txi 'txa'lo'ke?e'?ko"toi 'ah '?ku"na +

254 + '?i?i -- '?en -- ,'?en"ton 'ses + '?e?e -- .'?e'ui"nik "txe + ,"hai '?ka"na?a 'ui "ra + 'ko"txa?a -- 'ko"txa '?in'lo?ok"se '?e?e — ,'?e"txi 'txa"ne?en + ,'?iŋ"ko?o + .'tu"re?en "to?or 'ti"nah + 265 + ,'?e'ui"nik 'ia"ha?a + '?atx"pa '?i"xin + 'tu"ruan '?e?e -- "mas -- . "ser 'ka'?e'io?o"tot + 270 + ,"txe 'ke?e'?ko "toi 'tu"ruan + ."to?or 'in"te?e "?txen + .'tu?u "pot 'o"tot + 273 + '?ie?e — ,'?u'ui"ra + '?e?e -- '?e"siaŋ "hen 'te + "ua 'ra?ak"to?p + '?e?e — 'ko'txe?e -- "to?or 'ti"nah + '?i'ma "ku?u + "uar '?a?ak"ta '?e"hen 'te + 283 + "por 'ke?e"mei 'gra"hen 'te + ,'?i'ha?a"xir "txe 'ke'tu"ru '?u'ui"ra + '?i?i -- "kon 'da?a -- '?e 'ui"nik 'ia"ha?a -- ,'?ko"toi + '?o"txoi '?o 'tron"iahr + 'ma"ku?u + '?i?i -- ,'?i'ua?ak"txe 'ta"ka + 'sut"pa 'lo"?koi 'ta"ka?a -- "?o 'tron "te?e -- .'mu'ruh"rutx "txi 'txa + 296 + '?u 'iah"?ku '?u?u -- '?e?e -- 'ui"nik 'xe?e -- "ua 'ru?u — .'?ke"txa?a 'xa"na + 301 + '?en"ton

23. Devil

'ses + "txe?e 'ui"nik + 'ko'txa"ua 'ra'lo?ok
"se?e -- "tra 'go"ne?en 'ma?a"txi?i -- 'ma?a"txi
'?ũ?ũm"?pi -- '?e?e -- '?o'hro"net + '?im --
'ma?a"txi '?ũ?ũm"?pi?i 'pehk"net "kon 'da?ah'?ku
"net '?e?e -- .'?e"tra 'go + 312 + '?en"ton
'ses'txe?e -- .'?e'ui"nik + '?e?e -- "hai '?ka
"na?a 'ui"ra + .'?iŋ"ko?o 'ta'ka"ren 'ma"ku?u +

317 + '?en"ton 'ses + '?e'ui"nik + 'ia
"ha?a '?i"xin + '?e?e -- 'tu?u"pat + '?i?i -- ,
'?i"kon 'da'?o"txoi 'ma"ku?u + ,'?o"txo?o?p
'txa?a'ter"tio?o?p + 'ma?a"txi 'pehk"no?p + '?i
'ha?a"xir + "por 'ke?e'tx -- '?a'ro?p"na + '?i
"ra 'txa?a'peh"ka + 330 + '?i'ha?a"xir + '?o
"txoi 'ma"ku?u + ,"ua 'ra?ak"ta '?e"hen 'te + .
"pe 'ro"ma 'mah"txi 'u"men 'a'pehk"no?p + 334
+ ,'?i'ha?a"xir '?ko"toi + '?e?e -- 'ua?a"uan
'tu?u -- ,'tu?u"pat 'e"?peht + ."tia?a "uar 'e
"txi 'txa + 339 + ,"kai '?u'lu"pi + '?u'iah
"?ku '?u?u -- .'kom'pa"nie 'ro'xe?e"ua 'ru'?ke
"txa?a 'xa"na +

342 + '?i?i -- '?en"ton 'ses + "txe '?e'ui
"nik + 'tu?u"ial 'ma + '?e?e -- 'tu'?kix"ta?a
'tse?e"ran "ton 'ses + ,'?e'ui"ni 'ki"ra + 'ki
"sas 'ma"ha?ax -- '?e?e -- .'kual"ker "hen 'te +
352 + ,'?a'sa"ber 'ma"txi + ."ha?a 'xe"dia 'blo
+ 354 + '?i?i -- '?i"txe 'ke?e -- ,'?e'ui"nik
'ia"ha?a + ,'ua?ak"txe 'ta"ka + '?u?u -- '?u
'na?a"tah 'tu?u -- ,'?u'na?a"ta + ,'tu?u"ial 'ma
+ .'?u'ia?a"re '?e'ui"nik + ,'?en"ton 'ses + ,
"ne?et + ,'ma"ha?ax + .'?a"mii "guet 'ta'ka"ren
+

366 + ."txe?e 'ui"nik + '?e?e -- ,'ma?a
"nik "ha?ax 'a"mii "guen + .'ma?a"txa?a"ni 'ta
"rien 'ta'ka"ret +

370 + "pe 'ro?o -- '?i'kux"to '?a'ua?a
"re?en 'ke?e -- '?e"ha?ax 'ah"txi?i '?e"dia 'blo
+ ."ua 'rin'xa"na 'ta"kar + 374 + .'?i'ko"txa

23. Devil

+ "ia 'ke?e'ko"ne?er '?a'na?a"ta 'ke?e -- "ne?en + ,'?e"dia 'bo"len + "pues + 'ko"ne?er + '?iŋ '?ka"ni 'tua?a'ko?oi"?txi 'ko?o"ra + 381 + '?i 'po"re 'soŋ'gua?a"ret 'ke"hai 'ma?a"txi + '?a '?ku?u?p"se 'lo'ke?e -- "ne?en '?iŋ'gua?a"re?et + "ne?et '?i?i"xi 'txa'mes"na + 385 + "pe 'ro 'ha'ia'?ku?u?p"se?en 'lo'ke"ne?en '?iŋ'gua?a "re?et + '?e?e -- 'ma?a'tx -- ,"ma 'tu"?ka 'tua?a'num"se 'a"?pa + 'si"no 'ke?e -- '?a'ui"ra 'lo'ke?e -- '?e?e -- ."tua?a 'lu"mui 'ta'me?e 'noh"?kin 'i"ra +

393 + '?en"ton 'ses + '?e'ui"nik + "txe 'ke?e -- ,"mas '?pa?ak"ta + 'i'tu"no?or 'lo'ke?e '?a'ro?op"na + 'tu"no?or '?u'?ku?up"se + '?e?e -- 'tua?a'ma?a"txi + '?a?a -- ,'?a'txa'mes"na + ,'?i'ha?a"xir + "kai + 'luh"pa '?e"txi 'txa + . '?ah'?ku"na '?u'iu"?txi + '?i?i -- "kon 'da'?ix "to + ,"kai 'ka"rai '?e"hen 'te + '?u'ia?a"re '?e?e -- '?e?e -- .'?e'ui"nik + ."txe + ,'ko "ne?er + '?e?e -- ,'lo"?ken 'tu"ren + ,'nah"ti 'ru"pa 'tio?o"tot 'tia?a'txe"ker + ."tua?a 'ui "ra 'tu"?ka?a 'nu"mui + 419 + '?e?e -- "ke?e -- .'?e'ui'ni"ko '?pi"ra + '?e?e -- '?ko"ti?ix '?e"?o 'ra'tua?a -- .'?a?a"sio?p + 425 + '?i?i -- ,'?i'hai'?ka"na?a 'ui"ra + '?e?e -- ,'tu"ren + ,'nah"tir 'u"pa 'tio?o"tot 'ia"ha?a + '?i 'tia?a -- '?e?e -- 'tia?a'ma?a"txi '?u?u -- .'?u 'ui're?e"to?p +

434 + ,'?en"ton 'ses + '?e'ui"nik 'xe'lo "?koi -- ,'?ko"toi 'lo'?kes"na 'tu?u'io"tot + , '?i'xin'tu"ruan + ,"ua 'ra'?pa?ak"ta + 'pe'ro "txe 'ke?e -- ,'?a'lu"mui '?e"hen 'te'tu?u'ieh "?tser + .'ma?a"txi '?a'pehk"na + 442 + '?e?e -- '?a"ian "ti?i 'ne?e -- '?e?e -- ,'?e'ui'ni "ko?p + ,'?e?ei'xik"tak + "ia?a '?ko"toi '?a?a -- ,'?a'tu'rua"no?p + '?e?e -- ,'tu?u'ieh"?tser + ,'?u'ui"ra?a '?ko"to 'ie?ei'xik"tak + ,'a'tu "ruan 'tu?u'ieh"?tser + .'?e'ui'ni"ko?o?p + 454

23. Devil

+ ,"pe 'ro'ha?a"xir + .'ma?a"txi '?a'pehk"na + .
'ma?a"txi '?e?er"na +

457 + '?i?i -- ,"kon 'da'?ix"to + ,'?ko
"toi + '?e?e -- ,'?e"?o 'ra + ,'?en"ton 'ses + ,
'?e"dia 'blo + ,"txe 'ke?e'?o"txoi + .'ma"ku?u +
466 + ,"kai + '?u?u -- '?u"sihts "ha?a '?e"hen
'te'ta'me?e -- 'ta'mu?u'ia?a"rua?a -- ,'u'ia?a
"ra 'ru"ti?i + '?i?i -- ,'ii?i"xin + ,'ta'me?e
"?peht 'tia?a"ua 're"txi 'txa + '?u?u -- .'?u'ia
"ri 'u"ia?a 'ru"ti?i 'ta'me?e"txi 'txa + 476 +
,'?i'ua?ak"txe 'ta"ka + ,"kai 'lo'ko"hra 'ne"hen
'te + 'ua?a"uaŋ 'kai -- 'ti'kru"mo?o?p "kai -- .
'?a"ruo?p +

481 + ,'?en"ton 'ses'lo"?koi + '?u'ia?a
"re?e -- .'?e'ui"nik + .'xe?e"ua 'ru'?ke"txa?a
'xa"na + 'ber'dix"to 'ko'txe?eŋ'gua?a"ret 'ke?e
— 'ke?e -- ,'ua"rix 'a'?ko"to 'ie"?o 'ra + .
"tua?a '?e'ui'ni"ko '?pi"ra '?a?a"sio?p + '?i
'tua?a -- ,'ta?a'ui"ra + ,"ne?et + ,"ne?en + ,
'?ka"ni?in "xin + 'ta?a -- .'tu?u'ha"mo?p + ,
"txe 'ke?e'?e"dia 'blo + ,'?ko"toi + ,'tu?u'ieh
"?tser '?e'ui'ni"ko?p 'ia"ha?a + 'ie?e -- ,'ie?e
'ui"nik 'xe?e"uar + '?u'uah"pu?u "?po?p 'ta'ke?e
— "kor 'bo"ua 'ru?u -- ,'?u?u -- 'la?a"?tio?p +
'?e?e — '?e?e -- ,'?e'ma"txit + ,"txe 'ke?e'?ko
"toi 'ta"ka + 'tu?u'ieh"?tser '?e'ui'ni"ko?p 'ia
"ha?a 'xe?e"ua 'ru?u -- ,"ua 'ru'iah"?ku?u
"?po?p + '?i'kon'da?a -- ,'?ko"toi + ,'?u'lo?ok
"se '?in"te?e 'txak'txak'pa"iuh + 'ta"ma?a '?u?u
-- ,'?u"bol "sir + '?u?u -- .'ka"mi 'sa + 518
+ ,'?u'uah"pi + .'?u'ua"ii 'tu?u'na"?ku?ut
'?e?en"te?e + 520 + ,'?en"ton 'ses + ,"kon 'de
'?ah'?ku"na + '?i?i -- ,'?in'iah"rer + .'lo"?kes
"na '?u"hor + '?i?i -- '?i"kon 'da?a -- ,'ku'kre
"ma '?e'ui"nik + ,'?ka"xi 'ta"rum + ,"kon 'de
'txa'mes"na + '?i'ha?a"xir + '?e?e -- ,'ua?ak
"txe 'ta"ka + '?u'lo?ok"se '?in"te?e -- "ba 'so
'ta'mu?u -- ,'?u"bol 'sa + '?u?u -- '?u'?txa"mi

23. Devil

'?e?e -- ,'?e"?txi?i?tx 'tia?a"ua 'ra'lo"?koi + .'u'iu"?txi + '?i?i -- ,'?en"ton 'ses + '?u'?txa "mi '?in -- '?u?u -- ,'?in'te?e"ba 'so + '?u'iah "?ku '?e?e -- .'ui"nik 'xe?e"ua 'ru'?ke"txa?a 'xa"na + 547 + ."txe + '?e?e -- "ia 'ke?e -- , "uar 'ko?oi"?txi + ,'pues + '?e?en'te?e"ra?a -- '?e?e -- ,"bi 'no + '?i?i -- ,'?i'hai'?ka"na?a 'ueh"ta 'ko'txa'tu"ru?u "txe?eir + '?e'?iŋ'?ka "ni 'tua?a -- .'ko?oi"?txi 'ko"mon +

559 + ,'txe'ke?e'ui"nik + ,'uix"ta?a '?pa?ak"ta "ia?a + "por 'kiu'ui"ra 'ke?e -- , "ha?ax 'u'?txi"?txer + ,'?e'ui"nik 'xe?e'txa'mes "na + ,'?i"ha?ax "ua 'ra?a"xi 'nu'ta"res + .'?i "txe 'ke?e"bi 'no + 566 + ,'?en"ton 'ses + , 'ha?a"xir + '?e?e -- ,'uix"ta?a '?pa?ak'ta"ia?a + "pe 'ro?o -- ,'?u'iu"?txi + 572 + '?i"kuan 'do?o -- 'u'iu"?txi '?e?e -- ,'?e"?txi?i?tx + "txe 'ke?e -- ,'?iŋ'ga"lan 'in"tsah 'u'na?a"ta + '?e?e -- 'ke?e -- .'ga"lan 'in"txi?i + 580 + , '?en"ton 'ses + ."txe "tua?a '?u"me 'ne"dia 'blo + 'ber'dix"to 'ko'txe?eŋ'gua?a"re?et 'ke?e -- '?e"ia 'he?e -- '?e?en"te?e -- "kla 'se?e -- , "tra 'go"ra + .'ga"la 'na"?tsi?i '?u'iu?tx"na?ar +

588 + .'?e'ui"nik "txe 'pues + .'ga"lan 'ber"da +

590 + '?en"ton 'ses"txe 'ke?e -- "ia 'ke?e -- '?e?e -- ,'ko"ne?er + ,'?u'?txi'e"tix 'ta'ka "ren + ,'?i'ko"ne?er + .'?i"ra?a '?kah"tu?u '?ka "?pa?a '?e"dios + "por 'ke?e -- ,"ne?en + ,'?e "dios + .'ni'ue'ne"mi 'go + 601 + '?i"ra?a '?ka"tu?u '?ka"?pa?a + ,'si"no 'ke'kuan'do'?ka "ni 'o?oh"ron + .'ni'?ka"?pa '?a'?kah"ti + 604 + '?i?i -- '?i"hai -- '?ka"na?a -- '?a'ueh"ta '?e?e -- 'ko'txe?e -- '?e?e -- "ua 'ru"txe?e -- 'ui"nik 'ia"ha?a '?u?u -- ,'?u'txam"se '?u"iet 'ui'ni"kir + 613 + ."ne?en '?iŋ'guah"?ke?et

23. Devil

'?a'ba"lor + 614 + '?i'ko"ne?er 'ke?e -- ,'?u '?txio?o"nix 'ko"mon + '?e?e -- ,'ko"ne?er + . 'ni'ua"mii "guet +

619 + ,'?en"ton 'ses + .'?e'ui"nik "txe + .'tu?u"ial 'ma + 622 + "pe 'ro?o -- "ia 'ke?e -- ,'ha?a"xir "ua 'ru"txe?eŋ 'kui"dar + "pues -- '?ka"ni '?i?i -- '?in -- '?in"txe '?o?o -- ,'be 'de"ser 'lo'ke?e'?u'ia?a"re?en +

630 + ,'?ien"ton 'ses + ."txe "tua?a '?u "me 'ne"dia 'blo + ,"ia 'ke'?a'ui"ri?ix + ,'tu "no?or 'lo'ke?e'nu"mui + '?e?e -- .'?i"txe "tua?a + "hai + '?ka"ni '?ak"ta '?u"?pan 'ta 'me?e -- ,'?e'lah"?pa?ar 'lo'ke?e"ua 'ru"txo?p 'ia"ha?a + '?e?e -- .'?iŋ"ko?o + 641 + '?i?i -- ,'?e'ui"nik + "txe 'ke?e -- ,'?ko"toi 'ta"ka + '?e?e -- 'ua?a"uaŋ 'kai -- .'?ak"ta + 647 + "pe 'ro + ,'ma 'mah"txi?i '?u"men + ,'?a'pehk"na + 650 + .'?i'ha?a"xir "txe + 'tu?u"ial 'ma 'ke?e -- ,'tu"?ko?t '?a"non + 'ma?a"txi '?u?u -- ,'peh"ke?e 'ne"hen "tio '?pi"ra + '?o?o -- ,"ua 'ra'?kih"na '?u'ui're"no '?pa'sa"ber 'ko'txa?a "non + ."pe 'ro'ma?a"txu?u '?peh"ke?e "no?p + 658 + .'?i'ta'ni'ueh"?tser '?a'lu"muo?p + 659 + '?i?i -- ,'?i'?u'pa"txio?o '?u"pat "niok 'tia?a"ua 'ra?ak"to?p + .'?i'ma?a"txiu?u 'peh 'ke?e"no?p +

662 + .'?en"ton 'ses'txe -- ."txe "tua?a '?u"me 'ne"dia 'blo + ,"pe 'ro"ne?et + .'ma?a "txi "ua 'ri'xa"na 'ko'txe?e'kual"ker "hen 'te 'ko'txe?e'tu"ro '?pi"ra + 666 + ,"ne?et + "ua 'ri'xan -- ,'?i'xa"na 'ta'ka"ren + .'na'ual"?pir + 670 + ,'?i'po"re 'so'ma?a"txu?u 'ui"re?et '?e"hen 'te + ,"por 'ke?e"ne?en + 'ma?a"txu?u 'ui"re?en 'tia?a -- ,'?in'xa"na + ,"ne?en + '?in 'tu"ruan 'tu?u'ieh'?tse"ro?p + '?ĭ?ĭ -- ,'?in 'txi"kro?o?p + '?i'ma?a"txi '?u?u -- ,'?u'ui're "no?p + ,"por 'ke?e"ne?en + .'na'ual"?pir 'in'xa

23. Devil

"na + 673 + ,'?i"kuan 'do"ne?en + '?ka"ni +
'?in -- '?i?i -- '?in"txe '?u?u -- ,'?u'iah
"?ku?u "?po?o?p + ,"ha?ax 'ni'pa"iu 'hi"ra?aŋ
'?kam"pes + ,"ha?ax '?õ?õm"?pu?u 'na'?ku?u'to?p
"tor + 'xe?e -- ."tua?ah '?ku"na + 683 + "por
'ke?e -- ,"hai 'ma?a"txi '?õ?õm"?pi '?u'na'?ku?u
"to?p + ,"ma 'ko'txe?e"rer 'tua?ah'?ku"no?p + ,
"por 'ke'?u'ui"ro?o?p + '?e?e -- ,'?e'ma"txit
'tia?a"ua 'ra'?tsah"na 'tu?u'ho"ro?p + .'?u'ui
"ro?p 'tia?a'ua"tar + ,'?i'ha?a"xo?p '?u'la?a
"?tio?p + 691 + "pe 'ro?o -- "kuan 'do?o --
"ne?en '?in'?ka"ni "tua?a -- ,'?a?ah'?ku"no?o?p
+ ,"ha?ax 'ni'pa"iu 'hi"ra + ,'?in'?kam"pes + .
"tua?a '?õ?õm"?pi '?u'na'?ku?u"to?p 'ta"mar +
698 + ,'?i'en"ton 'ses + ,'?a?ah'?ku"no?p + .
'?a?ah'?ku"no?p +

701 + '?i?i -- ,'?i'ha?ax"to '?e'ui"nik
'ia"ha?a + ."txe 'pues + ,'?e"no?on 'ma?a"txa?a
"ni 'ka'na?a"ta + ,'?a"ian + ,'?in'te?e"di 'ia'u
"?pan + ,"ne?en + '?e?e -- "kai '?in -- '?ã?ãh
"pi 'ni"?pa 'ta'kan"te?e -- ,'ni"uet 'ui'ni"kir
+ "pe 'ro?o -- ,'ma?a"txin 'tah"uiŋ 'guah"?ku +

714 + ,'?en"ton 'ses"txe?e "dia 'blo + "pe
'ro?o -- 'ma?a"ni 'ha?a -- "ma "ha?ax "ia 'ua?a
"ren 'ta'ka"rox + '?e?e -- .'ta'me?e"?o 'ra'ia
"ha?a + 721 + '?i'po"re 'so?o -- '?e?e -- ."ma
'tu"?ka '?a"txe + 724 + "pe 'ro?o -- ,"kuan
'do"ne?en + ,"ia?a 'ua?a"ren + ,"ne?en + '?e?e
-- ,'?õ?õm"?pi 'u'na"?ku?ut + '?e?e -- ."tie?e
'ne"tua?ah '?ku"na + 732 + ,'?i"hai '?ka"na?a
'ui"ra + ,'?a"ia 'nin'te?e"di 'ia + ,'?in"xin +
'?ĩ?ĩ -- ,'?in"txe 'ta'ka"ret + '?i'ke?e"kuan
'do?o -- '?e?e -- ,'?ka"ni + ,'?a'txam"se '?a
"uet 'ui'ni"kir + .'?a'peh"ke?en + '?in"xin 'ta
'ka"ret "tua?a -- ,"ne?en + .'?õ?õm"?pi 'u'na
"?ku?ut 'xe'?ka"na?a 'txam"se + 746 + '?i"txe
'ke?e -- ,"kuan 'duix"to + '?e?e -- ,'?u'ui"ra +
,'txa'mes"na '?e'ui"nik 'ia"ha?a + ,"to?o 're'ti

23. Devil

"nah + '?i?i -- ,'?i'u'ui"ra + 'ke?e'tu"no?or
'?e?e -- ,'?e?ei'xik"tak + ,"kai + ,'?a?a"ruo?p
'ta'me?e'ui"nik 'xe?e'txa'mes"na + '?ie?e -- '?e
'ui'ni"ko?p 'ia"ha?a + .'?ka?a"pa '?pa?ak"to?p +

761 + ,'?en"ton 'ses + ."txe?e "dia 'blo +
'ber'dix"to 'ke?e -- 'ga"la 'na"?tsi "kuan 'do?o
-- ,"ne?en + ,'?o?on"txoi '?u?un"?txi 'tu?u'ha
"mo?p + .'ga"la 'na"?tsi '?a'nu"mu 'ie'noh"?kin
+ 768 + ,"ne?en '?in"tsa?ai + ."kuan 'du?uŋ
'gui"ra 'u"txo?p 'ko'txe?e"ra + ,"por 'ke?e'ha?a
"xo?p + .'?a?a"ruo?p + 'ta'mu?u'pia?a"ro?p 'ke?e
-- .'?a'txa"mai + 774 + ,'?i"ne?en + .'?in
"tsa?ai + .'?iŋ'gui"ra + ,'?i'po"re 'so"ne?en +
'?e?e -- "kuan 'do?o -- ,'txe?e"no?p 'ke?e'?ka
"ni 'ka'ua"?pu?un 'te?e'ka"tra 'go + ,'tua?a
'ko?oi"?txi 'te?e'noh"?kin + ."ne?en 'in"tsa?ai
+ .'?ũ?ũm"?pi + 784 + "por 'ke?e'?in'na?a"ta
'ke?e -- .'?ka"nu?un "?txi 'ta'ka"ro?p + '?i?i
-- '?i"ne?et + "hai -- ,"ti?in "di 'ia + '?ka"ni
'?a?a -- ,'?a"txe?en "tia?a 'noh"?kin + .'a'peh
'ka'ni"ken + 793 + '?e?e -- '?i?i -- '?i"hai
-- ,'?kan"to 'a"txe 'se"gir + '?a?a -- ,'?i'xa
"na 'ta'ka"ren + '?e?e -- ,'?e"ra + ,'iŋ"ko?o +
.'ta'ma?a"?o 'tron"te?e 'o"tot + 'ia"ha?a '?a
"ia 'ne?e -- ,'noh"?kin + .'ia?a"ia 'ne'lah
"?pa?ar "ua 'ra'txe?e"na + 796 + 'por"ke?e --
,'ta"ra + 'ma?a"txi?ix 'tu"ro?o -- ,'ta"ma?a --
,'?ah"?kut + 803 + "por 'ke?e -- ,'?ka?a
"?pi?ix '?pa?ak"to?p + .'?in"so 'lo'?a"rua?ar
'tu"ru?u "txo?p + 806 + '?e?e -- '?a"sies
'ke?e -- 'ta"ra?a -- 'ma?a"txi?ix 'iŋ'?kah"ier
-- ,'tu"ro?on + "por 'ke?e -- .'?ka?a"pi?i 'xe
'noh"?kin + 813 + "pe 'ro?o -- ,'?a"ian +
'io?o'to"to?p 'tia?a -- .'uar"to '?a'noh'?ki
"nio?p +

817 + ,'?i"txe 'ke?e'?keh"txa '?i"xin + ,
'ta"mo?o 'troŋ"go 'hro"tot + '?i'?ko"toi 'ia
"ha?a + '?e?e -- ,'?pu"?tur '?e"hen 'te + ."ua

23. Devil

'ra?ak"to?p + 823 + '?i?i -- '?ie?e -- ,"sia 'ni'xik"tak + ,'?pu"?tur + ,'ta'me?e'ko"si 'na "uar + '?e?e -- ,'u"txu?u 'man"daa "do?p + ,'?i 'ia?a"ian "tie?e 'ne"ua 'ra?ak"to?p + .'?ia?a "ian "tie?e 'ne"ua 'ra'ka'ra"io?p +

832 + "txe?e -- .'?e"dia 'blo + 'ma?a"txi 'ka?a"no?os "ru?ut 'in"te?e -- '?e?e -- '?e?e -- '?en'txok'ta"ko?p 'ia"ha?a 'lo'ke?e -- ,'tu"ro?p 'ta'me?e'ko"si 'na'ia"ha?a + 839 + ,"txe?e 'ui "nik + ."pues + "bieŋ 'ke?e'?ũ?ũ"sre '?a"ni "pe 'ro?o -- ,'ko"txe "tua?a '?in"txe + "por 'ke?e -- .'tuam"hen 'te +

845 + ."txe?e "dia 'blo + '?a?a -- 'si'ta 'ka"ren + ,'?i"ra?a "txe 'pen"sar + "ne?en 'ta 'ka"ren 'tu"no?or 'lo'ke?e -- ,'?a'?ka"ni + ,'tu "no?or '?iŋ'guah"?ke?et + '?i"hai -- '?ka"ni 'a?a -- '?a"txe?e -- ,'pro"bar + ,'?iŋ'koh"to?p + '?ka"ni?in "xin + .'?in'lo?ok"sio?p +

859 + ,'?en"ton 'ses + ."txe?e 'ui"nik 'pues + ,"hai 'ne?et'ix"to '?ka'na?a"txe?e 'fa "bor + .'?e"rer '?i?i"xin + 862 + '?i?i -- , 'ha?a"xir + .'tu"ru '?u'ui"ra + 864 + '?a 'ro?o?p"na 'ke?e -- ,'ki"ki?i 'tu"ren 'ia"ha?a + '?e?e -- ,'ma"ku?u '?e'sihk"?txa?an + .'?i"ia?ax '?a'?ko"toi '?u'tah"ui"iet + 869 + '?i?i -- , '?i'ha?a"xir + ."txe 'ke?e'tu"ru '?u'ui"ra +

872 + '?ie?e -- ,'?e"dia 'blo + ,'?ko"toi 'ta"ka + '?e?e -- ,'?u'uah"pi + ,'?in"te?e '?ih "?txok + '?u?u -- ,'?u'ia"ri + '?u'ia?a"ra 'ru "ti?i 'ta'mu?u -- 'ta'mu?u -- .'u"na '?ku'txi "kin '?eh"?txok + 883 + ,'?ie?eh"?txok 'ia "ha?a + ,'ua?ak"txe 'ta"ka + '?e?e -- 'ket"pa?a -- ,"lo 'ko + '?i'ua?a"uaŋ "kai -- '?e?e -- ,'su 'tre"ma "to?or 'ti"nah + .'ko"ra 'ko"ra?a '?txuhk"san + 892 + '?i?i -- ,"uar + ,'?a'pehk "na '?o?o"txoi '?u"me 'nu'pia?a"ro?p 'ma"ku?u +

23. Devil

,'?a?a'ro?p"na '?o"txen 'ma"ku?u + 'ua'ra'ui"ra
'ke?e -- ,'?in"so 'lo'ui'ni"ko?p '?pu"?tur + .
"to?or 'ti"nah + 899 + ."pe 'ro'ha?a"xir 'ma?a
"txi '?o?o"?pian + 900 + 'ko"ra 'ko"ra "uar
'?a?a -- ,'a'su'tre"ma "to?or 'ti"nah + ,"ua 'ru
'?ku"xo?or 'u"?ka?p + '?i?i -- '?a'?txuhk"san
"hai -- "ma 'mah"txi?i -- ."ua?ar +

907 + ,'?en"ton 'ses + '?e?e -- ,'?e"dia
'blo + '?i"xin '?u'ia?a"re?e 'ui"nik 'xe?e'tu"ru
'?a?a'kohk -- .'?a'kohk"san 'ma'ku?u'sihk
"?txa?an + 912 + ."txe + '?e?e -- ,'ko"ne?er +
'?e?e -- 'xe?e -- '?iŋ'?ka"ni 'tua?a -- ,'?a'lo
"?koi 'u'tah"uiet 'ta"ra + ,"ua?a "rix "to?or
'ti"nah "ua 'ra'?txuhk"san + '?i?i -- .'?ir"se
"no?oit + 922 + ,'?i"kuan 'do'?u'ui"re?et + .
'?a"txa?a 'pa'iuh"tu?ut + 924 + .'?i'ua?ak"txe
'ta"ka?a "xa 'io?o"pu?u 'tah"uie?et +

925 + ,'?en"ton 'ses + ,'?e'ui"nik 'ia
"ha?a + '?e?e -- ,'lo"?koi 'ua?a"uan + '?e?e --
"tia?a -- ,'txe"ker + '?i?i -- ,'?ir"na '?u"me
'ne?eh"?txok + '?i'ha?a"xir + .'?u"txe 'u'pa'iuh
"tu?ut + 936 + ,'?ie?eh"?txok 'ia"ha?a '?a
"tsa?ai + ,'?u'ui"ra + ,"kuan 'do'txe?e"ne?e 'pa
'iuh"tu?ut + ,'?i"xin + .'?u'ta"hui '?e'ui"nik +
941 + '?i'?ko"toi 'ta"ka + .'?u'mo"ru?u 'me
"?ke?e 'ui"nik + .'?a'?txu"uan 'tu?u"nu?u?k +
944 + ,'?ien"ton 'ses + '?e?e -- ,'?e'ui"nik
'ia"ha?a + "txe 'ke?e -- ,'u'?ke"txe '?eh"?txok
'?i"xin + ,'ma"ku?u '?ko"pot + ,'?i"ia 'sa"tar
'ta"kar + .'?i"xin '?e"tar 'de +

952 + '?i?i -- ,'?ien"ton 'ses + ,'?i"kon
'daix"to + 'sut"pa '?ko"toi '?e?e -- ,'?eh"?txok
'ma"ku?u + '?a'ro?o?p"na '?u"me 'nu?u -- .'?u
"tu?u + 'ke?e -- ,'tu'?kix"to + "gaa "net "ne?et
'?ih"?txok 'ke?e -- ,"ma "tia?a "txe 'ko'txe?e
"ia?ax + '?ie?e -- '?ie?e"ia?ax 'ke?e -- ,"ua
'ra?a"su '?pa'ra"?pa + '?pa"ni 'xe?e -- ,'?a"ian

23. Devil

'tu"?ka?a "txe 'na?a"ta "ne?en + "por 'ke?e -- . '?ix"na 'sat"po?oit + 970 + ,'?i"ua 'ra'ui"ra 'ke?e'?pu"?tur + '?e?e -- ,"sian 'ui'ni"ko?p "to?or 'ti"nah + '?i"ne?et -- 'nie"nix 'ko?o"ra '?i?i -- ,'?i'su'?pah"ra + ,'ua?a"ret "ua 'ri'su 'tre"ma "to?or 'ti"nah + 'ua?a"ret "ua 'ri?i -- ,'ua?a"ret "ua 'ri'sta"ri + ,"ua 'ra"?kux 'ua'ra "?ka?p "tu?ut '?e"hen 'te + '?ie?e -- .'?e'ui'ni "ko?p 'tu"?ka 'mu?u'ui"ra 'ni"ko?p + 'ke?e -- , 'tu"?ka?a 'nuŋ"ga 'na'a"txe 'ko'txe?e"ia?ax + . 'ke"ma "tia?a "txe +

985 + "pe 'ro?o -- .'ha?a"xir "txe + "pe 'ro?o -- 'ma?a'txix"to 'ka'na?a"ta "pues 'ke?e — '?e?e -- ,'?e"dia 'blo + ,"ha?ax '?u'iah "?ko?oŋ 'ka'ba"lor + ,'tu"?ka 'tua?a'ka"txe + '?i'ka"txe 'lo'ke?e'?ka"ni 'ka"txe?e -- ."no?on + 995 + ,"ne?en '?in'na?a"ta 'ke"ha?ax + '?e?e — '?txu"uan 'ta'ni?i -- ,'ta'ni'sen"ti 'do + '?i'ua?a'ua"neŋ "kai -- .'su'tre"men "to?or 'ti "nah +

1001 + ,'?en"ton 'ses'txe?e"dia 'blo'?u 'ia?a"re?e 'ui"nik + "ber 'dix"to 'ke?e -- 'ke?e — .'?e'uix"tu?u '?kah"ti 'ni'?ka"?pa?a '?u'?pa "nia?a + 1005 + '?i?i -- ,"ne?eŋ + ,"kuan 'do '?a'?kah"na 'ni'?ka"?pa?a + ,'?in"tsa?ai + "?ehs 'ton -- "?ehs 'to'?a?aŋ"kta + 1011 + "por 'ke?e'?in"tsa?ai 'ke?e -- ."tie?e 'nu'?kah"ti 'ni'?ka"?pa?a +

1013 + '?i?i -- ,'?pa'nix"to + "txe 'ke?e — ,'?e'ui"nik 'ia"ha?a + '?ko"toi '?e?e -- , '?ah'?ku"na '?e"txi 'txa'?u'iu"?txi + ,'?i'lo '?kes"na '?u'uih"?txok + '?e?e -- .'?ah'?ku"na 'ta'?ko"pot + 1022 + 'tu"no?or 'txe?e"na 'ta "ka '?u"me 'ne"dia 'blo + 1023 + "por 'ke?e 'ha?a"xir '?u?u -- .'?u'?ku?up"se '?e"dia 'blo + 1025 + ,'?in"ton 'ses + .'?a'ro?p"na '?o'tron "iahr + .'?iŋ'guah'?ke?e"tix '?e"txi 'txa'?o?oi

23. Devil

"?txi + 1028 + ,'?o?oi"?txi?ix '?e"bi 'no'ta
'ka"ren + '?ie?e"ra '?a?a -- .'?a"txi?ix 'pro
"bar 'in'te?e'?a'uih"?txok + 1031 + .'?i'tu
"?ka "mas 'a'?ka"ni + 1032 + '?e?e -- 'hai --
,'?a"ian 'tu"?ka?a '?ka"ni + .'?a're"nen + .'?i
"ne?en '?iŋ'guah"?ke?et +

1037 + .'?en"ton 'ses'txe?e'ui"nik "pues +
"ia 'ke?e -- 'ko"ne?er + '?in -- ,'?in"txi?ix
'kom'pro'me"ter + "tua?a '?iŋ -- ,'?ku?up"se?et
+ 'hai -- '?a"txe 'tan'te"ier 'ke?e -- "ne?et --
'?a'uah"?ke?en 'tu"no?or 'lo'ke?eiŋ'?kah"ti + .
"pues + "ne?en 'iŋ'?ka"ni '?a'ne?e -- 'tua?a'uah
"?ke?en '?e?e -- .'?im"?pihk 'ni'tu"min + 1052
+ ,'?en"ton 'ses + .'txe?e"dia 'blo"pues + .'hai
"ha?ax '?a'?ka"ni '?iŋ'guah"?ke?et 'u"?pan +
1056 + ,'?e'ui"nik 'ia"ha?a + "txe 'ke?e --
"kon 'de?e -- ,'?u'?kah"ti '?e'tu"min + ,'?ie?e
"dia 'blo + ,'ua?ak"txe 'ta"ka + ,'?u'io"se '?u
"?ka?p 'ta'mu?u"bol 'sa + 'u'lo?ok"se 'in"te?e
-- ,'pa"ke 'ta'tu"min + .'?u'iah"?ku '?e'ui"nik
+ .'?u'ia?a"re + ,'ta'ke?e"ra + 'ta"kar 'ta"ka
"tua?a -- .'?a'?po"ro "to?oit +

1070 + ,'?e'ui"nik 'ia"ha?a + "txe 'ke?e
-- ,'?ko"toi 'tu?u'io"tot + "kai '?u"txe 'kon
"tar 'ta'ku?u'uix"ka?ar 'ke?e -- ,'?e'ui"nik + ,
'xe?e'io?o"pa '?u'lo?ok"se?en + ,'?ak"?par + .
'ma?a"txi "ha?ax 'kual"ker "hen 'te + 1078 +
"por 'ke?e -- ,"ne?en '?iŋ'gui"ra + ,'tu"?ka?a
'tu"?ka?a "ka 'iu"txe + ,'ta'me?e'noh"?kin +
'?e?e -- 'ma?a"txi 'ka?a -- 'lu"mu 'ie?e -- ,'?e
'?au'si"liar 'u'txe?e"na?a 'si"tar 'ta"ra +

1086 + ."txe?ei "xik "pues + ,'lu"mui +
'?e?e -- ,'han'?txak"na 'ta"ka + ,'lu"mui +
'?e?e -- "txe 'ke?e -- 'txe?e"na '?in"te?e -- .
"muer 'to'ta'me?e'noh"?kin +

1095 + ."txe?e 'ui"nik + 'sin -- ."ne?en

23. Devil

'?iŋ'gui"ra + ."ia 'tu"re?en 'kuan'do'txe?e"na + 1099 + "pe 'ro?o -- '?e?e -- '?e'ui"nik 'xe?e -- ,'?u'io?o"pu?u 'lo?ok"se?en + 'ma?a"txi "ha?ax 'kual"ker 'ui"nik 'si"no 'ke?e -- ."dia 'blo'?ah"txi?i + 1105 + '?i?i -- ,"ne?en + , '?u'iah"?ke?en '?e"txi 'txa'?ũ?ũn"?txi + ,'?i'?u 'iah"?ke?en + '?e?e -- ,'?e"bi 'no + '?i?i -- . '?i'?u'lo?ok"se '?in'te'?ih"?txok 'u'iah"?ke?en 'ta'?ko"pot + 1113 + '?i?i -- .'?u"txe 'man "dar 'ka'iak"te?en 'ta'ke?e'i'xik"tak 'ma"ku?u +

1115 + ,'?en"ton 'ses + .'txe?e'i"xik + , "pe 'ro"hai "?pan + ,"hai '?a"txi?ix 'lo'ke?e "ua 'ra'ua?a"re?en "ia?ax + ,'?en"ton 'ses "ne?en + .'ma?a"txi?iŋ 'ket"pa 'ta'ka"ret + 1121 + ,"por 'ke?e"ne?en + ,'ni'dio"sir + "ha?ax '?ka"ni -- .'?iŋ'?ku?up"se 'tu"no?o 're "tiem 'po + 1125 + ,'?i"hai "ne?et + ,'sut 'pe?e"tix 'ta'ke?e"dia 'blo + .'?i'ket"pa?a '?pah"ner +

1128 + ,'?en"ton 'ses"txe?e 'ui"nik + "pues + "ko 'txa"ne?et '?a'na?a"ta "hai -- '?ka "ni?i -- ,'?i?i"xin + ,?e"re 'ri?i"xin + "pe 'ro?o -- ,"ne?en + '?e?e -- ,'ta'mi?i'xik"tak + 'ma?a"txi?i -- 'u"txe?en -- ,'ne'se'si"tar + "por 'ke?e -- ,'?i'xik"tak + '?e?e -- ,'lo'ke '?in'?ka"ni "ne?en + .'?a"ian + 1146 + "ne?en '?a'ro?p -- ,'?u'ia?a"re?en + ,'ni'pa"tron + 'xe?e"ua 'rin"xan 'ta"kar 'ke?e -- ,'ko"ne?er "ne?en + 'ma?a"txi 'tua?a -- '?iŋ'?kah"ti '?u '?ka"?pa?a '?e"dios + "por 'ke?e -- "ha?ax 'u '?ka"ni "tua?a -- .'?iŋ'?ka'?pah"se 'tu"no?o 're "di 'ia +

1156 + ,'?en"ton 'ses + ."txe?e "ia 'he?e -- '?e"po 'bre'i"xik "pues "ne?en '?in"xin + 1159 + ,'?in'tah"ui 'ni"tu?u + .'?in'tah"ui 'ni 'ta"ta?a + 1161 + .'?i'ket"pe?e "ne?et +

23. Devil

1162 + '?i?i -- ,'po"re 'so + ,'ko"ne?er '?e"hen 'te + 'ta'ni?i -- ,'lu"gar + ,'?u'?kah "tio?p + ,"?es 'to'ko"ne?er + .'?i'ia'?ku'?pe 'sia"no?p 'ta"mar + 1170 + 'txe?e"no?p 'ke?e -- 'ke?e -- ,'?e"txi 'txa + ,'?e"bi 'no'?e"ua 'ro + ,"ma "ha?ax "tua?a '?e"dios + .'si"no 'ke?e"tua?a '?e"dia 'blo + 1176 + "por 'ke?e -- 'ta'ma'rix"to 'ke?e -- '?a'?kah"na 'ke?e -- '?e?e -- ,'?e'ui"nik 'ia"ha?a + 'xe?e -- '?u'ui "rak -- ,'tu"?ka "ka 'iu"txe '?e"dia 'blo + , 'ha?a"xir '?u'ui"ra + ,'u'tuh"?pa '?e"txi 'txa + '?i?i -- .'?i'?u'?pih"txi + 1188 + ,'?i'po"re 'so + 'txe?e"no?p 'ke?e -- '?e?e -- ,'?e"txi 'txa + ,'?pihtx"?pir + '?u"me 'ne?e -- '?e"dia 'blo + '?i'po"re 'so + ,"fuer 'te'?a'txe?e"na + ,'?al"gun '?tsoh"iir + "?o?o -- '?a?a -- '?o?o '?u'txam"su?u "?po?o?p "ti?i 'ne?e -- ,'?o?oi "?txio?p + "por 'ke?e -- 'ta'rix"to 'ke?e -- , '?e"txi 'txa + ,'ma"ha?ax + ,'?ak'ta"?pi 'ru"me 'ne"dios + 'si"no 'ke?e -- '?e?e -- "tua?a '?e?e -- .'?e"dia 'blo + '?i"?pan '?a?a -- .'?a'?ku "?pe 'sia"no?p "?es 'to'ko"ne?er + 1213 + "?pa 'nu'?kah"tio?p + ,"por 'ke?e'ha?a"xo?p + '?e?e -- "?ka?ar '?u'me'ne"ro?p 'lo'ke?e -- '?e?e -- . '?o'hro"ner 'lo'ke?e'?a'txe?e"na 'kon"tar 'ta"ri 'xe"tiem 'po +

1219 + '?i?i -- 'txe?e"no?p 'ke?e -- ,'ke 'tu"no?or + '?e?e -- '?e'?i'xik"tak 'xe?e -- '?u 'iu"sre '?a'xa"no?p 'ma'ku?u'?ko"pot 'ta'ka?a -- ,'?al"gun 'ui"nik + 'txe?e"no?p 'ke?e -- "ma "ha?ax "por 'ke?e -- ,'?u'?kah"na?ar + 'si"no 'ke?e'?u"me 'ne"dia 'blo + ,'?a'txe?e"na + '?a?a -- '?a'?txu"uan 'ta'mu?u -- ,'?u'sen"ti 'do'?in 'te?e"hen 'te + '?i?i -- '?i'?ka"ni '?u?u -- , 'tu'ru"?pa + 'txa?a"te?e '?u?u -- ,'?u'uix"ka?ar 'in"te?e 'ui"nik + ,'?ie?e'i'xik"tak + '?a"nu?u 'tru"?pa 'txa?a"te?e '?u?u -- .'no"xi?ip + 1242 + 'in"te?e '?ka"nu?u -- ,'tu'ru"?pa 'tu?u'io"tot + '?i'in"te?e -- '?i'?ka"ni 'u'tru"?pa?a -- .'ta

23. Devil

'?ko"pot 'ta"ka 'nah"tir + 1247 + "pe 'ro"txe 'ke?e -- .'?u"me 'ne"dia 'blo + 1249 + "por 'ke?e -- ."?pan '?a'?kah"na +

1251 + "por 'ke?e"txe 'ke?e -- ,'?e'ui"nik 'ia"ha?a + 'xe?e'?ah'?ku"na '?u?u -- ,'?u'tu"min + ,'u"me 'ne"dia 'blo + ,'?i'ha?a"xir + ,"ma?a 'ta"ka '?ix"na + .'?po"ro '?u'tu"min + '?e?e -- ,"kai + '?e?e -- '?u'xot'ma"ni + ,'?e'tu"?ki?ik 'tu"?ki?ik + ,'u'txo"ni + ,'?i"kai 'u'?to"xi 'a "?katx + ,"kai 'u'?to"xi '?e'txi"tam + ,"ka 'iu '?to"xi 'e'ua"kax + '?i"ka 'iu'?to"xi '?e?e -- . 'tu"?ki?ik 'tu"?ki?ik + 1270 + '?i?i -- '?i?i -- 'ma?a"txi + '?a?a -- ,'?a'txa"mai "tu?ut + 'si"no 'ke?e -- .'?a'?po"ro + 1277 + "por 'ke?e"txe 'ke'?u"men '?e?e -- ,"dia 'blo + .'?ah '?ku"?pir 'tu"no?or 'lo'ke?e'u'?ka"ni + 1280 + '?i'po"re 'so'e"hen 'te'ko"ne?er + "?es 'to?o -- ,'ko"ne?e 'ri"ra + ,'?a"ian "tie?e 'na'?ku'?pe "sian 'ta"mar + '?e?e -- '?a"ian "tie?e 'ne 'txe?e"no?p 'ke?e -- '?e?e -- ,'?u"me 'ne"dia 'blo'?a?ah'?ku"no?p + .'tu"?ka?a "ian "tuo?o?p + 1289 + '?i?i -- "txe 'ke?e -- '?a"ian "ti?i 'ne?e -- .'?u'?kah"tio?p 'ta"kar "tua?a '?a?ah '?ku"no '?pe'tu"min +

1293 + "pe 'ro?o -- "ne?en + 'ma?a"txi '?in'na?a"ta "hai -- .'ber"da + 1297 + '?e?e -- '?a"ia 'ne?e -- ,'?e'ui'ni"ko?p + "ti?i 'ne?e -- ,'?u'iu"srio "?pu?ut + ,'?al"gun '?ih'?txok "tak + ,'?a'xa"no?p 'ta"kar + ,'?i'ha?a"xo?p + '?e?e -- ,'?u'?kah"tio?p '?u'?ka"?pa?a '?e"dia 'blo + ."tua?a '?ah'?ku"no?p + "por 'ke?e -- '?u 'na?a"to?p 'ke?e -- 'ber"di?ix 'lo'ke?e -- .'?a '?kah"na + 1312 + '?i'po"re 'so?o -- ,'?a"ian + ,'?u"mei 'gra'?u'?ku"?pes 'ia"no?p 'ta"mar + 'ke?e -- "ti?i 'ne?e -- ,'?ka"ni '?u'ui"ra '?e 'tu"min + "ti?i 'ne'?ka"nu?u 'ui"ra '?e?e -- '?a "ian 'tu"?ka?a "ia 'nu?u -- "tua?a '?u?u -- ,'?u 'num"su?u "?pa 'ta"kar + 1322 + ,'pues -- ,

23. Devil

'ha?a"xo?p + 'txe?e"no?p 'ke?e -- .'?e"dia 'blo
'?u'iah"?ku 'tu"no?or + 1326 + ,'txe?e"no?p
'ke?e"dia 'blo'u'iah"?kue?e 'tu"min + 'u'iah
"?kue?e -- ,'ua"kax + ,'u'iah"?ku 'tu"no?or +
,'?e"nar + ,'?e"?pu?ur + .'tu"no?o 'ru'iah"?ku +

1333 + "?i '?a"ian "ti?i 'ne?e -- '?e?e --
,'?u'?ka'?pah"se + ,'tua?a"?tix + ,'?a'lo"?koi
'u"nar + ,'tua?a"tix 'u'iah"?kue?e 'tu"min +
'tua?a"tix '?a'?po"ro?o -- ,'tu"?ka "ko 'sa
"tu?ut + '?e?e -- .'?u'?kah"ti '?u'?ka"?pa '?e
"dia 'blo + 1343 + "pe 'ro'?a"ian "ti?i 'ne?e
-- ,'?u'?kah"ti 'u'?ka"?pa '?e"dia 'blo + .'?i
'lo"mis 'mo"ma 'tu"?ka 'u'tu"min + 1346 + '?i
'po"re 'so + "ne?en 'ma?a"txi?i -- 'iŋ'?ku?p"se
"hai -- ,'ber"da + "por 'ke?e -- ,"ne?e 'ni"ra +
'?e?e -- 'ma?a"txi '?ka"ni?i -- ,'?in"txe 'ni'pa
"tron 'ta'me?e"dia 'blo + ,'?i'po"re 'so + ."ma
'tu"?ka?a 'ni'tu"min +

1357 + ,'?i'ko'txa"ma "ha?ax "ia?a 'ua?a
"ren + '?iŋ'gui"ra "kuan 'do?o -- ,'?ah'?ku"na
'?e'tu"mi 'ne'ui"nik 'ia"ha?a + '?i?i -- ,'?i
'ma?a"txiŋ 'gui"ra + 'ko"txa "kai -- 'ua?a"uan
'su'tre"ma '?e?eh"?txok "to?or 'ti"nah + '?i
'ma?a"txin 'gui"ra 'ko'txa'ua?a"uaŋ "ka 'iu?u --
,'?u'?kux"ro?or 'u"?ka?a?p + '?e?e -- 'sta"ri
"tu?ut '?e?e -- 'ui'ni"ko?p + '?i'po"re 'so'ma?a
"txi?i -- '?iŋ'?ku?u?p"se "ne?en "hai -- .'ber
"da + 1373 + ."por 'ke'ma"ha?ax "ia 'tu"re?e
'niŋ'gui"ro?o?p +

23. Devil

1 There is another story they told long ago. 4 On the first of November, it was customary to celebrate the Day of the Dead. 12 And all the people celebrated the Day of the Dead.

14 And they say that at one time, all the people were celebrating the Day of the Dead, and when it grew light, they were doing the drinking in all of the villages, in all the places. 25 And they say, it is told to this day, that there was one man, and he did not come to celebrate the Day of the Dead where it was being celebrated.

35 But they say that before it got light, he was spoken to by a man. 40 He was asked, "And you, why don't you want to go out and have a good time at the fiestas?"

48 And he said, "I don't want to go to the fiesta because -- sometimes we don't come out well on the journey to the fiesta, because -- sometimes we are being good, lying down inside our houses, and we go out -- and we don't know what we are going to be met with -- what we will meet. 67 And so I don't go out to the fiestas, because there are many fights, in fiestas like that, because people don't drink quietly."

77 Then the man who was there to get the man out of his house said, "But -- it isn't every day it happens thus. 85 Now let's go for a walk. I'm to bring you to it, and I want to -- come walk a little with me."

90 The man said, "But I'm not going, and -- I will thank you not -- to force me to go with you, because I don't want to go out, because -- I'm being good and lying down in my house."

23. Devil

100 But the man said, "But if you don't come with me, then since -- you are afraid that there are your fellow men who were killed off, and if you are afraid, then you are going to be killed off first, because you wouldn't go with me."

115 Then the man was frightened in his heart to hear it, when he was spoken to like that. 119 Then he said to his wife, "Maybe I'll go with this man here, because he is telling me I'll go with him." 127 Because the man said, "If you go with me I will take care of you, so nothing will happen to you; don't think about it. You're going with me, and with me nothing will happen to you. 137 I will take care of you if there is someone who goes for you, but I will go in with you."

142 Then the man grabbed his billhook and went out with him, and they came to where the drinking was being done, where the fiesta was, and the music was, in a house; the people were dancing. 159 And he was spoken to by the man who had come to get him out. 162 He said to him, "Stay here. I'm going inside." 165 He stayed there behind the house in the brush where he was not seen. 168 And -- he was watching what the man did who had come to get him out. 177 And he stayed watching behind the house, that man, he went among the people and did not speak to anyone, nor was he spoken to by the people.

185 But he, they say that he came to the house, and went inside among the people where -- they were dancing. 194 But he was not spoken to by them, nor did he speak to the dancers who were dancing. 198 They say that he stayed watching, and when he came out, he carried a

gourd bowl of rum out. 205 He gave it to the man who was waiting and watching behind the house. 209 He said, "I waited to give myself a drink to drink, and I want us to drink together.

219 The man said, "But I didn't want to drink, because I'm afraid of being drunk, because when I get drunk I don't come back to my house, but instead I fall down on the road and there I sleep. 230 And there is a danger that some drunk will pass along the road and hit me, and because of that I'm afraid to drink."

238 But he said, "And didn't I tell you that I came -- came to get you out of your house and I would take care of you? 246 And there is nothing for you to fear, because I am walking with you." 250 Then that man drank the rum which he was given.

254 And then the man said, "If you want to see how I get the rum out, go sit on the yard." 265 That man got up and went to sit nearer to the house. 270 They say that he went and sat on a hollow behind the house. 273 And he saw the many people dancing, since he was on the yard, and inside, the people were dancing. 283 Because there were many people, and they say that he sat there watching, and when that man went and entered again, inside, he immediately came back out with another gourd bowl of rum. 296 He gave it to the man whom -- he had brought. 301 Then the man said, "How are you getting the drinks? I didn't hear what you said and -- I didn't hear what was said to you when you were given the drinks." 312 Then the man said, "If you want to see, go with me inside."

317 Then that man went behind him, and when he entered inside, the two of them entered,

and were not spoken to, and he, because -- he was told "Don't speak." 330 And he went inside and the people were dancing, but they were not spoken to by them. 334 And they went to stand behind the bowl where the rum was. 339 He began to dip it out and give it to his friend whom he had brought along.

342 And then the man said to himself, "What is this? Now, this man, maybe he isn't just anybody. 352 I wonder if he isn't the Devil?" 354 And they say that that man suddenly -- he knew in -- he knew in his heart; the man said, "You then, aren't you my friend?"

366 The man said, "If I weren't your friend, I wouldn't have come with you."

370 "But how can you tell me that 'this one is the Devil I am walking with'? 374 And since you know now that I am the Devil, well, now I want us to have a little drink. 381 And that is why I tell you that if you do not obey what I tell you, you are going to be killed. 385 But if you obey what I tell you, then no -- nothing will happen to you; instead, you will see what is going to happen at this fiesta.

393 Then, they say that the man was more frightened, and everything he was told he obeyed, so as not to be killed, and he began to dip out the rum, and he was given some to drink, and when next the people began to get drunk, the man spoke. He said, "Now go out and sit down far behind the house where it can be seen, so you can see what happens. 419 That -- these people, the time has already come for them to play. 425 And if you want to see, go sit far behind the house, where they will not see you."

23. Devil

434 Then the man who went out, went out behind the house, and sat down; he was afraid, but they say that people came beside him and he was not spoken to. 442 And there were some of the men and the women who came out there to sit — beside him, and he saw the women come out to sit beside the men, 454 but he was not spoken to; he was not seen.

457 And when the time came, then the Devil they say went inside. 466 He began to spit on the people -- with his -- saliva, and he went to the bowl where the rum was, and he dropped a little of his saliva in the rum. 476 And immediately the people began to go crazy, stood up, and began to fight and to shout.

481 Then he came out and said to the man whom he had brought along, "Isn't it true as I told you, that the time has come for these men to play, and for you to see, I am going to go among them." They say that the Devil came beside those men and the men who were -- grabbing machetes and catching billhooks; they say that he came beside the men who were striking at each other, and when he came he took out a red handkerchief from the pocket of his shirt. 518 He took it and laid it over the eyes of one of them. 520 Then, when he was struck, his head was taken off at once, and when the man fell writhing to the ground, when he was killed, he suddenly took a glass out of his pocket, took the blood where it was coming out, and drank it, and then took a glass and gave it to the man he had brought along. 547 He said, "Since we are drinking, here is some wine — and if you will try its flavor, I want us to drink together."

559 They say that the man was very frightened at that, because he saw that it was the

blood of the man who had been killed, and he was coming to bring it, and saying it was wine. 566 Then he was very frightened, but he drank. 572 And when he drank the blood, they say that he thought it tasted good, that it was very sweet. 580 Then he was told by the Devil, "Isn't it true as I told you that -- this is some drink here? Very tasty drinking!"

588 The man said, "Well, it's truly fine!"

590 Then he said that, "Since today you drank with me, today you are no longer to say the name of God, because God is my enemy. 601 Don't speak his name: when you want to speak, call my name. 604 And if -- you want to try -- as -- he did -- that man who killed his fellow man, 613 I'll give you the courage. 614 And today we have drunk together. Today you are my friend."

619 Then the man said to himself, 622 "But since he is taking care of me, I will -- obey what he says to me."

630 And then he was told by the Devil, "Since you have already seen everything that happened," he said, "if you want to dance also to the music they are making there, go." 641 And the man said that he would go, and stood up and danced. 647 But he was not spoken to by any of them. 650 And he said to himself, "How come don't these people speak to me? Or -- are they angry to see me? I wonder what the matter is? But they don't speak to me. 658 And they pass beside me. 659 And they tramp on my insteps where they are dancing, and they do not speak to me."

662 Then he was told by the Devil, "But

you are not going around like just any one of the people who live here. 666 You are going with me, as a spirit. 670 And that is why they do not see you, the people, because they do not see me where I walk; I sit beside them, I tickle them, and they do not see me, because I walk as a spirit. 673 And when I want them to strike at each other, I use my handkerchief here. I cover their eyes with it, those who are to fight, 683 because if I don't cover their eyes they can not fight, because they see the bill-hook where it swings over their heads, they see where it is coming. And they parry it. 691 But -- when -- I want them to fight, I use my handkerchief here; I cover their eyes with it. 698 And then they strike and strike at each other.

701 And then that man said, "Well, we did not know. There was a day like that: I set myself against one of my fellow men, but I didn't manage to strike him."

714 Then the Devil said, "But didn't he -- I wasn't with you there at that time. 721 And that is why you did nothing. 724 But when I am there, I -- cover the eyes of the one who is struck. 732 And if you want to see, there will be a day, when I will go do it with you, and when you want to kill your fellow man you will call me, and I will go with you to -- I will cover the eyes of the one you want to kill. 746 And they say that -- when he saw that man killed on the yard, and he saw that all the women began to cry over the man who was killed, those men became completely terrified.

761 Then the Devil said, "Isn't it true that it is good when -- I enter to drink among them? What a fine fiesta! 768 It makes me

happy when I see them doing that, because they are shouting to their friends that he is dying. 774 And I am happy to see it. And that is why I -- when -- they say 'Let's have a drink, to drink to the fiesta!' I am happy to hear that, 784 because I know that I will drink with them, and you, if one day you want -- to give a fiesta invite me! 793 And if you want to continue going with me, let's go now to another house; there there is a fiesta and there is music being played. 796 Because here, there is nothing in this fiesta -- they are not going on dancing, 803 because they are all so frightened. They are only crying. 806 So there is no interest in our staying here, because the fiesta is finished. 813 But there are houses where they are still celebrating."

817 And they say that he was taken along to another house and they came to that one; it was full of people dancing. 823 And many women filled the kitchen, where they were busy, and there were some dancing, and there were some getting drunk.

832 The Devil said, "Don't you want to get into one of those girls who are -- in the kitchen there?" The man said, "Well, sure I would like to, but -- how am I going to do it, because they're in the midst of the people."

845 The Devil said, "Ah, if you're with me, don't think about it. With me, everything you want, I will give to you. And if you want to try one of them, I'll go get them out."

859 Then the man said, "Well, if you want to do me the favor, you can go." 862 And he stayed to see. 864 He was told to "Stay there. Go and wait over there in the brush, lying down,

and there she will come to find you." 869 And he, they say, waited to see.

872 And the Devil came to grab one of the girls, and dropped some saliva from his mouth into the side of the ear of the girl. 883 And that girl suddenly got up and went out, walking around and around the lot, looking all around. 892 And she was being called in by her friends inside, calling to her, "Come inside! You see that there are just men filling up the lot!" 899 But she did not hear. 900 She kept on turning around and around the lot, chewing her fingers, and looking to see if there was anybody standing there.

907 Then the Devil went to speak to the man who was lying watching in the brush; 912 he said, "Now the one I want to come out to find you here is standing in the yard looking around. Show yourself! 922 And when she sees you, wave your handkerchief to her, 924 and she will immediately come to find you."

925 Then that man stood up where he was visible and was seen by the girl, and he waved his handkerchief to her. 936 And that girl was happy to see him; when the handkerchief was waved to her, she went to find the man. 941 And she came to him and gathered the man into an embrace and hung around his neck. 944 And then that man, they say that he carried the girl off into the brush and stayed away with her all evening.

952 And then, when the girl came back inside, she was asked by her mother, "What came over you, girl, that -- you never did such a thing, and there you were making a spectacle of yourself, just like a -- I think you did some-

thing, because -- you were gone a long time. 970 And you saw that there were many men on the lot, and you -- weren't even ashamed, standing and turning around and around on the lot and -- flouncing around there biting at your fingers in front of people. And the men, how could they help but see you -- what got into you to act that way, that you never did before?"

985 But she said, "But -- we didn't think that -- well, the Devil, he gives us the courage to do what we do. And we do what we want to do. 995 I think that he was in my mind and made me get up and circle around on the lot."

1001 Then the Devil said to the man, "Isn't it true that -- just as soon as you said my name it was like that? 1005 And I, when my name is spoken, I am happy, to the point of dancing, 1011 because I am happy that someone has said my name."

1013 And so they say that that man came to be given rum to drink, and his girl was brought out and given in the brush. 1022 All was done by the Devil. 1023 Because he obeyed the Devil. 1025 Then he was told another time, "I'll give you rum to drink. 1028 Drink wine with me and try a girl. 1031 And whatever else you want. 1032 If there is anything you want, tell me, and I will give it to you."

1037 Then the man said, "Well, since -- now I have already promised to obey you, if you will give me anything -- you give me everything I ask for, well, I wanted -- you to give me -- a little money." 1052 Then the Devil said, "Well if that is what you want me to give you, all right." 1056 That man, they say, when he asked for the money, and the Devil immediately put his hand in his bag, he took out a packet of money, and gave it to the man. He said, "With this, there is enough for you to make it increase."

1070 And that man, they say that he went to his house, and began to tell his wife that, "The man who came to take me out last night was not just anybody. 1078 Because I saw every little thing that he did in the fiesta, and -- didn't the *auxiliar* pass by to arrest me here?"

1086 The woman said, "Well, he passed as it grew light, he passed by, and said that there had been a death at the fiesta."

1095 The man said, "Yes -- I saw it. I was there when it happened. 1098 But the man who came to take me out, he is not just any man, but rather -- the Devil is who it is. 1105 And I, he gave me rum to drink and he gave me wine, and he brought out a girl and gave her to me in the brush. 1113 And he ordered me to dance with the women inside."

1115 Then the woman said, "But if that is so, if you did what you are telling me here, then I am not staying with you. 1121 Because I, my God wants me to obey him all the time. 1125 And if you returned to the Devil, you remain by yourself."

1128 Then that man said, "Well, since I know that you are going to go, you may go, but I -- I have no lack of women, because women, when I want them, there they are. 1146 I am sp -- he tells me, my boss, whom I walk with, that today I do not have to -- call the name of God, because he wants to be named every day."

1156 Then the poor woman said, "Well, I'm

going. 1159 I'll find my mother, and I'll find my father. 1161 And you stay."

1162 And that is why nowadays people in my -- place, they tell until today and they believe in it, 1170 they say that rum, wine, brandy are not of God, but of the Devil. 1176 Because of this, it is thought that that man who saw -- what the Devil did, he saw the rum spat in, and he touched it. 1188 And because of that they say that rum has been touched by the Devil, and that is how it becomes strong enough to cause some fights, or -- for them to kill each other, those who drink it, because rum is not left by God, but is from the Devil, and so they believe until today. 1213 So they tell it, because they -- it is remembered by them that -- story which was told long ago.

1219 And they say that today, the women that want to go into the brush with -- some man, they say that it is not because of their desire, but because of the Devil doing it -- that he gets into the mind of a person that he wants to keep two wives for one man, and the women want to keep two husbands. 1242 One wants to stay in his house, and one you want to keep in the brush far away. 1247 But they say that is because of the Devil. 1249 Because so they tell it.

1251 Because they say that that man who was given his money by the Devil, it was not long before he increased his money. He began to resell everything; he bought and began to raise chickens, and began to raise pigs, and began to raise cattle, and began to raise everything. 1270 And it did not -- die on him, but increased. 1277 Because they say that it was from the Devil everything that he wanted was given. 1280

23. Devil

And for that reason people today until this very day, there are some who believe in it. And there are some who say that they are given what they have by the Devil. 1289 And they say that there are some who ask him to give them money.

1293 But I do not know if it is true. 1297 There are some men who want some girls to go with them, and they call the name of the Devil to give them, because they think it is true what is told. 1312 And that is why there are many who believe in him, that -- some want to see money, and some want to see what there is -- happening to him, 1322 well, they say that the Devil gives everything. 1326 They say that the Devil gives money, gives cattle, gives everything: corn, beans, everything he gives.

1333 And there are some who call him by name, just so their corn will come up, just so he will give them money, just so that their affairs will prosper, they call the name of the Devil. 1343 But there are some who call the name of the Devil and still have no money. 1346 And that is why I do not believe it is true, because I don't want to take the Devil as my boss, and so I have no money.

1357 And since I was not standing there to see when that man was given the money, and -- I didn't see it as the girl began to circle around the lot, and I didn't see how she began to bite at her fingers, and flounce around before the men, for that reason I don't believe it is true. 1373 Because I wasn't there to see them.

24. Exorcising Disease

1 + "kon 'da'e"muak 'atx"?pir + ,'u'men'e
'?ah'na'?pa"ren 'ui'ni"ko?p + ,'o?o'i"xik + ,'en
"ton 'ses + ,'e'?ah"?kin 'a'tsor'ma"ian 'ko"ra
'ko"ra 'ta'ma'u"?kin + ,"ehs 'to"ma 'u'tah"ui +
.'tia?a'pehk"na 'u'uiŋ"kir 'e"muak 'ia"ha?a +
8 + ,'tu"?ka?a 'tu"?ka?a 'u'?ka"?po?o?p + ,'u
'?ki"ni 'u'ui"ra 'tia?a'pehk"?pir 'e"muak 'ia
"ha?a + "hai 'ta'ka'e"rue 'de + 'e"saŋ 'gre"go
'rio + "o?o 'ta'ka'e'sa'nan"to 'nio'del"mun 'do
+ "o?o 'ta'ka'e'sa'nan"to 'nio"ser 'bi"sian 'te
+ "o?o 'ta'ka'e"san 'ta'ma'da"le 'na'del"mun 'do
+ "o?o 'ta'ka'e'san'ma"nuel "mon 'te'de"o 'ro +
"o?o 'hai"iŋ "hier 'no'pehk"na 'e"muak 'ia"ha?a
+

17 + ."por 'ke?e'txe?e"no?p 'ke'?a"ian 'o
'tron"te?e 'lu"gar 'eh"mar + .'ie"?pe?e "rum 'i
"ra + 19 + ,'ie?e'txi"nam 'ia"ha?a + ."ia '?pu
"?tur 'e"sia?an "maa "lo?p + 21 + "ia "?txa?ar
'e"rei 'ma"lom 'bre + 22 + ,"txe 'ke?e"kon 'da
'ta'ka'e"maa "lo?p 'ia"ha?a + ,'a'pehk"na 'u'uiŋ
"kir 'e"muak + ,'ha?ax"to 'xe?e"ma 'tu"?ka?a + .
'u'?ku?u?p"se + ,"nien 'ni"roh + ."nieŋ '?kah'pe
"siah +

28 + ,'en"ton 'ses'a'si?ik'?pa"na 'e'nuk
"ta?a '?ah'ni'ro"mo?p + ,'xe?e'u'na?a"to?p + .'u
'?ka"?pa?a 'e'uiŋ'kir'?pir 'tua?a'e"muak 'ia
"ha?a + 31 + ,'e'?ah'ni"rom 'ia"ha?a + ,'u'?ki
"ni 'u'ui"ra + ,'ko'txa'u'?ka"ni 'tua?a'a'lo
"?koi 'e"muak 'ia"ha?a + ."hai 'toi"?pir 'ta'ka
'e'dio"so?p + 35 + ,'en"ton 'ses + ,'u'ia?a"re
'a'mah"na 'iuh"?tsu?u?p + ,'e'?pi"?kit 'kan"de
'la + .'txa?a"te?e 'nuk"ta?a 'kan"de 'la +

39 + ,"kon 'da'tu"ri?ix 'e'kan"de 'la + ,
'iuh"?tsu?up + .'u'?ki"ni 'u'ui"ra 'hai"te?e
"bam 'ba'iuh"?tsu?u?p 'u'?ka"ni 'tua?a'u'pu"to?p
+ 42 + ,"por 'ke"txe 'ke?e'iuh"?tsu?u?p 'ia
"ha?a + ,'tua?a'ni"?pir 'tua?a'e'dio"so?p 'ti

24. Exorcising Disease

"txan + .'ie?e"?aŋ 'he"lo?p 'tua?a'u'iah'ne"so?p
'a?ah"ni 'u'uiŋ"kir 'e"muak + 45 + ,'e'noh
"ta?a 'kan"de 'la + ,'txe?e"no?p 'ke?e"ha?ax 'ko
'txa'in"te?e "?kahk + .'tua?a'u'uir"se?e 'u
"?po?o?p "tu?ut 'u'tur"tar 'e"dios 'ti"txan + .
'ke?e"uar 'u'?txa'?puh"res 'u"?po?o?p "tu?ut +
49 + ,'e'kan"dee "lo?p 'ia"ha?a + ,'in"te?e
'txe?e"no?p 'ke'tua?a'e"dios + .'in"te?e 'tua?a
'u'?ke'?ko'ni"?pir 'u"me?ein 'iah"muak + 52 +
,'iah'?kah'pes"iah + .'u'num"se 'e'kan"de 'la'ia
"ha?a 'tu?u"hor 'iah"muak 'tia?a"?txa?ar + 54
+ .'en"ton 'ses'a"ka?ai 'a'?kah'pe"sian +

* * * * *

55 + ."txe 'ta'ma'u'?kah'pe"siah + 56 +
,'ka'dio'si"ret + ,"no?on 'e'?pa"?ka?p 'e'ko'no
"hon "to?or 'e"rum + .'a"ian "mei 'gra'ka'txuk
"pa?ar 'ta'ma"ret + 59 + ,'ko"ne?er + ,'ka
'?kah"pes 'a'?ka"?pa?a + .'ta'ma"siŋ 'ko'pa'gre
"nues 'tro'i"dies "a 'bes'ma"ri 'ia + ,'ko'txa
"ne?et 'e"ra + 'a'uak"ta '?tsih'?pa"?pir + .'ke
'?pa"ne?e "ra 'tua?a'ka'?kah'pes"ian "to?oit +
65 + ,'en"ton 'ses + ,'u"txe 're"sar "siŋ 'ko
"be 'ses'e"pa 'gre"nues 'tro + .'i"dies "be 'ses
"a 'bes'ma"ri 'ia + 67 + ,'i"tuam 'e"re 'so'ia
"ha?a + ,"uar 'u'?ka'?pah"se 'tu"no?or 'e'dio
"so?p + .'e'?aŋ'he"lo?p +

70 + ."txe 'ta"ma '?u"re 'so +

71 + ."e 'ia"nues 'tro'di"bi 'no'e"ter 'no
+

+ ."e 'ia"nues 'tro'se"nior "he 'su
"kris 'to +

+ ."e 'ia"nues 'tro"pa 'dre'es"pi 'ri
'to"san 'to +

+ ."e 'ia'san'mi"gel 'ar"kaŋ 'hel +

+ ."e "iaŋ 'hel'es"pi 'ri'to"san 'to +

24. Exorcising Disease

72 + ,'ko"ne?er 'ka'?ka'?pah"se 'a'?ka "?pa?a + .'ta'kan"te?e 'pa'gre"nues 'tro'i'txa?a "te?e "?a 'bes'ma"ri 'ia +

[One Our Father and two Hail Marys are said in Spanish.]

74 + ,"ta '?i'?ka"?pa?a 'ah'ti'txa"ner 'dio"sox + ,'ko"ne?er 'ka'uah"nes 'tu"no?or 'na "ual 'ah'na'?pa"ren + ,'tia?a'?pu'?tu"ro?p "uar 'a?a"sio?p 'tu?u"hor 'e'kre'a"tu 'ra'e'me"nor + ,"tia?a "?txa?ar 'kas'ti"ga 'do'u"iaŋ 'hel'a'so "ta 'do'u'na'ua"lir + "tia?a '?pu'?tu"ro?p "uar 'u'?pa'hram're"so?p + .'u"me?ein 'e'krea"tu 'ra 'e'me"nor +

80 + ,"ne?et 'a'na?a"ta 'tia?a'tu"ru 'e 'pa"?ka?p 'xe?e'mal'o"bris 'ta + ,'e'ko'ra"son "ne 'gro + ,'e'ko'ra"son 'iŋ'hier"ne 'ro + , 'tia?a'tu"ru 'a'hol'txa"ni 'ta'ma'e'?txan "txe?e "di 'ia + ,'e'?txan"txe?e "?o 'ra + ,"tia?a 'tu "ru "uar 'u'toh'ti?i"ies + .'u'ia"mi 'go'iŋ'hier "nal + 87 + ,'ko'txa'ha?a"xir 'u'ia"mi 'go + . "ha?ax 'e"rei 'ma"lom 'bre + .'e"rei 'lu'si"fer + .'e'dom"fuan 'del"mun 'do + .'e"don 'ia"hua 'na'del"mun 'do + .'e"rei 'sam'ma"nuel "mon 'te 'de"o 'ro + .'e"rei 'sa'nan"to 'nio'del"mun 'do + .'e"rei 'san'rei"mun 'do + .'e"do 'nia'rei"mun 'do + .'e"rei 'na'san'ta'ma'da"le 'na'del"mun 'do + .'e'doŋ"huan 'dem"bu 'te + .'e"do 'nia"hua 'na'dem"bu 'te +

99 + ,'ko"txa 'ia?a"sio?p 'ta'ma'e'ki"nien 'to'es"ta 'do'del'iŋ"hier 'no + .'ie"?par 'e"mun 'do + 'ia?a"si 'ua"to?p 'ta'ma'u'ui"?ka"rir "u?ut 'ia?a'la"gu 'na + 102 + ,'u'noh'ko'mo"ni 'u"?po?p 'ta'ka'e"?om 'bres'ba'ta"ion + ."rei 'ba'ta"ion + ,"om 'bre'se"re 'no + ."rei 'se"re 'no + ,'e"?om 'bres'ku'le"brin + ."rei 'na'ku'le "bri 'na + ,"om 'bre'se'si"mi 'te + ."rei 'se'si

24. Exorcising Disease

"mi 'te +

110 + ,"pe 'ro'ko"ne?er + ,'ta'ma'i'?ka "?pa?a + ,'ka'dio'si"rox + .'ka'uah"nes 'a?ah"ni 'e'na"ual 'ah'na'?pa're"no?p 'i"ra + ,'a?ah "nio?p + .'ko"txa 'na'ual'?pi"ro?p 'tua?a'e"maa "lo?p 'ie"?par 'e"mun 'do + 116 + ,"pe 'ro "no?ox 'i'puk"se 'a?ah"nio?p + ,'a"pun 'te"ra 'ia + .'a"pun 'te'sen"te 'io + 119 + ,'txe"nik 'kon'hu"rar 'txi"ko?p + ,'tia?a'atx"pa 'ta"rio?p + .'ie"?par 'e"mun 'do +

122 + ,'ko"ne?er 'i'uah"?ku 'u're"tii "ro?p 'in'me'dia'ta"men 'te + .'tia?a"?txa?ar 'a '?ko'?to"rio?p "to?or 'e'krea"tu 'ra'e'me"nor + 124 + ,'ko'txa"ha?ax 'e'tan"lum 'mu"si?ik + .'e 'xe"ror 'mu"si?ik + ,'e'hol"txan 'mu"si?ik + .'e 'mak"txan 'mu"si?ik + ,'e'?pa"hram 'mu"si?ik + . 'e'?ah'na'?pa"ren 'mu"si?ik + .'tia?a"uar 'u'iuh "ta + ,'e'ko'ra"son "ne 'gro + .'e'mal'o"bris 'ta + 133 + ."pe 'ro"no?ox 'i'xa"uan 'a'bo"ga 'do'tu?u"hor 'e'krea"tu 'ra'e'me"nor +

* * * * *

134 + .'en"ton 'ses'a?atx"pa 'tia?a'ko"tor 'u"txe 're"sar + 135 + .'a'lo"?koi 'pa'kax"pat 'pa'kax"pat 'ta'ka'e're'sen"sa 'rio + 136 + , 'i'ta'u"re 'so'u"txe 'men"tar 'u'?ka"?pa?a 'e '?ah'po'so"ner + ,'u'?pu"?tsa?a 'tu"no?or 'u"pat 'io?o"tot + ."ehs 'to'a'lo"?koi 'ta'ma'u'nie "?pi?ir +

24. Exorcising Disease

1 When the disease is raised by a were-animal, man or woman, then the diviner traces it out with his gift of divination until he finds out from where the master of that disease was summoned. 8 Name by name he divines to see from where that disease was summoned, whether from the wheel San Gregorio, or from San Antonio of the Earth or from San Antonio the Servant, or from Santa Magdalena of the Earth, or from San Manuel Monte de Oro, or whether that disease was summoned from Hell.

17 Because they say that there is another place below, under this earth. 19 And that town there is filled with many evil ones. 21 There lies the Evil King. 22 They say that when one of those evil ones is called as master of the illness, then he who does not believe neither cures nor prays.

28 Then a great curer is sought who knows the names of the masters of those diseases. 31 That curer divines to see how it will be necessary for that disease to leave, if it must be paid for to the gods. 35 Then he says that incense is to be bought, small candles, and two large candles.

39 When the candles are ready, and the incense, he divines to see if the discs of incense are to be burned. 42 Because they say that that incense is payment to the gods above, and the angels, for putting the master of the disease to flight. 45 The large candles they say are like a light, to show them the dwelling-place of God above, that they are to abase themselves before him. 49 Those candles, one, they say, is for God, and one is for strengthening the spirit of the sick person. 52 The prayer-sayer passes that candle over the head of the

sick person where he lies. 54 Then he begins to pray.

* * * * *

55 He says in his prayer, 56 "You are our God. We, the human beings on the earth, great is our need of you. 59 Now we pray your name in five Our Fathers and ten Hail Marys, since you have left it written that so you are to be prayed to." 65 Then he says the Our Father five times and the Hail Mary ten times. 67 And in the midst of that prayer he names all the gods and angels.

70 He says in his prayer,

71 "Oh Our Divine Eternal One,
"Oh Our Lord Jesus Christ,
"Oh Our Father Holy Spirit,
"Oh Saint Michael Archangel,
"Oh Angel Holy Spirit,

72 Today we name your name in one Our Father and two Hail Marys.

[One Our Father and two Hail Marys are said in Spanish.]

74 In your names, gods above, today we chase all were-animal spirits where they crowd together playing over the head of this little creature, where his angel lies punished, his spirit whipped, where they crowd together preying like beasts on the spirit of this little creature.

80 You know where the human who works evil dwells, the black heart, the infernal heart, where he stays, Hol Txaning in the silent day,

the silent hour, where he stays imploring his infernal friend. 87 Since he is your friend, he is the Evil King, the King Lucifer, Don Juan of the World, Doña Juana of the World, the King San Manuel Monte de Oro, the King San Antonio of the World, the King San Reimundo, Doña Reimundo, Queen Santa Magdalena of the World, Don Juan Dembute, Doña Juana Dembute.

99 Since they are playing on the five-hundredth level of Hell under the earth, and they are coming to play in the wind of the lake, 102 they are joining themselves with the fighting men, fighting king, serpent men, serpent king, viper men, viper queen, Sesimite men, Sesimite king.

110 But today, in your names, our gods, we put to flight these were-animal spirits, they run away, since they are spirits of the evil ones under the world. 116 But you put them to flight, Lightning Aimer, Thunder Aimer. 119 Conjure them where they rose to come here, under the earth.

122 Today give them their leave immediately where they lie dominating this little creature. 124 Since it is the dust-breath, the blight-breath, the Hol Txan-breath, the rainbow-breath, the tiger-breath, the were-animal-breath where they are blowing, the black heart, the evil-doer. 133 But you stand as an advocate over the head of this little creature."

* * * * *

134 Then he gets up, where he was crouched to pray. 135 He goes out backward with the censer. 136 And in his prayer he calls the witch by name, and censes all the outside of the house, until he goes out to the walk.

GROUP IV

NOTES

19. Belief in Diviners

19.1 Divining and curing are the diagnostic and therapeutic phases of the Chorti response to disease. These may be performed by the same person, but the gift of divination is not given to all curers: some must collaborate with a diviner who does not cure.

19.16 A mut is also a 'bird'.

19.20-23 The distinction is between 'ordinary' diseases, brief, with no supernatural cause, and diseases raised by someone and with supernatural vectors.

19.24 Divination is done by asking yes or no questions: when the sensitive object, almost always the calf muscle, sometimes a forearm muscle, gives a twitch, the answer is affirmative. The diviner names the causes one after another, until a yes answer is obtained.

19.26 The ultimate source of sahurin, by way of Spanish zahori 'geomancer' is Arabic.

19.28 'Cherished' is an approximation of 'txoh'?pes"?pir: 'in'txoh"?pes 'ni"la 'pis 'I'm taking good care of my pencil'. Usually 'ak'ta "?pir 'left' is used for gifts of God.

19.60 This is a weaker way of making a request than the use of an imperative, as in 19.66. The two parts of these two expressions are not interchangeable: *'a'uah"?ko?on 'ka 'na?a'ta"nik is not acceptable.

19.70 The root is ?tehn: 'u'?teh"nu 'he causes disease in someone', said of a spirit. The alternation of postvocalic h in open syllables and vowel length in closed syllables has been noted before: compare '?te?em"?pir 'sickened'.

19.73 Regrettably, no informants could explain the meaning or significance of hol txan.

19. Belief in Diviners

González supplied a folk etymology 'like a rainbow' (mak txan). The term is associated with Thursday, and there is a hol txan ceremony, not very well known, performed in secret by a man and a woman next to a pit containing candles. They expose their genitals, fill in the pit, and thereby put a spell on some specified person.

19.75 The root is iohk 'pass over, hover': 'u'ioh"ko 'it passes over something'.

19.76 The principo?p are angels who were blinded by the kumix angel (the Archangel Michael) when he destroyed their tower to heaven. They now bring drizzles rather than real rains (compare the drizzles brought by the returning dead in text 22) and unlike other angels, they live in mountains.

19.77 This is asked of the patient.

19.80 The ?txuh?p 'tripod' term designates the three stones of the hearth (here), and the tripods placed at either end of a Chorti house (in the traditional pattern, not illustrated in Wisdom 1940) so that the ridge-pole can be laid between them. These ?txuh?p then become the framework for the rest of the roof structure.

19.81 The santa bieha is the hearth-?txuh?p spirit.

19.83 The heat here is radiant, as from a hot stone, or a truck standing in the sun.

19.87 The root is ?tsohi 'whip, punish, beat'; there are no u forms.

19.88 The root is le?k 'sear' -- a more intense radiant heat than that of 19.83; 'u'le"?ke, 'a'le"?kon 'it sears'.

19.89 This expression describes the glowing of coals.

19.90 Near the house, usually behind it, spent lime from food preparation is dumped each day. The plants in this area soon die. González thinks that this effect causes some anxiety

19. Belief in Diviners

that the spirit of the earth will be burned by the lime and retaliate by causing a disease.

19.92 The ka 'interrogative' particle occurs in second position, here after tiaa.

19.98 A few roots, like txek 'appear' take a su causative alternate.

19.109 González could not explain the significance of estumekas.

19.104-105 These phrases refer to the area of ground near the houses, where the New Year ceremony is held, and the Planted Cross stands. See texts 32 and 33.

19.121 The sangi are small canals dug for the irrigation of rushes.

19.125 This is Lake Guija in El Salvador.

19.131 This wheel or ring is thought to be a pool in the sky. See texts 27 and 28.

19.158 The levels of the world are described in texts 25 and 26.

19.179 Another form for which González supplied only a folk-etymology is lam?pat, which he connects with freezing (?pat 'hail'). This is the Chorti cognate of the Yucatec day-name lamat, Tzeltal lambat (See Thompson 1960:77), the etymology of which is not clear.

19.186 As both 'beam of light' and 'cane', harar embodies a metaphor only slightly different from ours.

19.189 'Body-bleeding', ?txi?itx naa?k, is dysentery.

19.212-214 These diseases are headache, fever with chills, probably malaria (burning-freezing), and 'hardening', a disease characterized by thickening and hardening of the skin.

20. Curing

20.4 González is assuming that the divination and curing are done by the same person.

20.5 González considers the language of this text to be very difficult, due primarily to the obsolescent technical vocabulary, whose associations he is none too sure of.

20.10 The first of a series of structurally interesting invocations begins here. Syntactic parallelism, with its repeating rhythms and mnemonic advantages, is played off against a slowly progressing, interlocked series of images, roughly of this form: the A of your W, the B of your X; the C of your W, the D of your X; the A of your Y, the B of your Z ... J. Eric S. Thompson called attention to strikingly similar structures in the books of Chilam Balam (1960: 61-3). Note also that these chains of images are associated with a deity and his attributes — in 20.10-68 all seem to be tied to the rain god and thus to the beliefs about weather.

20.11 A person's _eroh_ is the cast of his features, whereby one can not only identify him, but also tell if he is well, happy, or whatever; it is his face, and the expression on it.

20.15 The use of _xan-?p-vr_ _'xam"?par_ instead of _eroh_ here is probably a lapse: the elements appropriate for possessed and possessor environments in the syntactic framework are quite freely combinable; doubtless a skilled _ah-nir-om_ can improvise indefinitely in this pattern.

20.16 The unusual number and complexity of compound forms in this text may well be an index of its age and formality. Here _noh_ 'great' and _komon_ 'joined together' (Spanish _común_) form an active stem with thematic _i_.

20.23 Note that the semantic ranges of the elements in the parallel constructions are usually of inclusion or overlapping, rather than of antithesis or opposition. One might go farther and say that as hut '(overall) appearance' is to eroh '(facial) expression', so walking is to running.

20.24 A mak-haa-ir is an enclosed volume of water, and thus, as a disease, the inability to urinate.

20.34 This disease lasts a long time; the patient is pale, wastes away, has a slight fever in the morning, and swelling.

20.36 Although ?pak is 'bone', this is a special sense; its general sense is 'core'. Here, it means 'body-jaundice', apparently hepatitis.

20.38 'Body-puffing' is a closer translation of 'u'ti?ip"txan '?pa'ke"rir. An 'o?oi"sen 'te (from ah-ausente) is the spirit of a person who did not die of a disease, but was murdered or died accidentally.

20.46 The characteristic of this disorder is swollen veins in the hands and arms.

20.48 A sus-tee 'sharp stick' is a digging stick.

20.49 Literally, 'white mucus'. The form tar-er 'coming' is a cursive; tar-i?p is an instrumental.

20.51 The roots are si?p 'inflate' and naa?k 'torso'.

20.63 It is worth emphasizing that compounding on this scale is a possibility one would not suspect even after considerable study of colloquial Chorti. The root ?txuhr 'drip from something' is probably onomatopoetic: compare 'a'?txuhr"?txa 'it is dripping', and "?txah "?txah 'drip, drip'.

20. Curing

20.70 This form is compounded of three roots: uahr 'blow (as wind)', meein (or mahin) 'ghost', and harar 'cane' or 'beam', the stem thematized by an i suffix. The form in 20.71 parallels it.

20.76 'Body-dryness' is a closer translation: a-tak-i 'it dries', tak-in 'dry'.

20.80 Note the presence in this compound and above in 20.39 of the tee 'stiff' element.

20.82 The root la?t 'catch, support from beneath' has 'factitive', 'cursive', and 'causative' suffixes here. Compare 20.91.

20.88 The roots are xan 'walk' and tar 'bring, come'.

20.91 'His spirit is contracted or diminished', in a gasp or shudder. It is not clear what relationship exists between this and '?pah 'ku"tir 'fright', caused by a spirit seizing one when he is frightened, and characterized by high fever, scaly skin, and loss of hair.

20.92 Again, the root is la?t 'catch' in a preconsonantal alternant. The 'cursive' suffix, as before, is iterative with this root.

20.93 The txapahr is the litter the dead are carried on; u&-?pit-i 'he carries it (on his shoulder)'.

20.95 An evil person whose spirit takes the form of an animal -- a were-animal -- is an ah-ha?p-ar-en. The form here is thematized by the e and an -h- infix in the suffix: compare ?pa?k-a-h-r-na 'feared'.

20.96 The translation of ?pahram as tigre 'jaguar' is usual, but the Chorti do not know much about them. A tour of the Guatemala City zoo with a group of informants revealed that any predatory feline is a ?pahram.

20.100 The root is lo?tx 'clutch'; compare

20. Curing

u&-lo?tx-i 'he clutches it (once)', u&-lo?tx-ro 'he keeps clutching it', a cursive, and u&-lo?tx -vh-r-es 'he makes him keep clutching it', with added 'factitive' and 'causative' suffixes, like the parallel form in 20.101, with le?p 'claw at'.

20.102 This attributive stem is of the common reduplicated type: in-leu-leu 'soft, pliable', here with 'cursive' and 'causative'.

20.104 The root is la?k 'wear out', 'waste away': a-la-h-?k-a 'it wears out, is used up', here a 'causative'; in the text it refers to emaciation.

20.106 The root is tax; compare the 'cursive', u&-txa-ru 'he scuffs, wipes his feet on it'.

20.108 The root is probably ?pih 'tug, stretch', thus 'u"?pi?i 'he hauls at it' by H, and the imperative "?pi?in 'pull!'.

20.109 The root kex 'pant' occurs with this 'factitive-cursive-causative' combination as well as the rare -ka suffix (compare 20.116 and 20.55-56). A closer translation of u&-kex-vh-r-es is 'it makes him pant'.

20.112 Gonzalez says 'a'?pur"txi 'he's sweating'; others, including the father of one of his best friends, say 'a'?pul"txi. The conditions and distribution of the sound change *l > r are not yet clear.

20.114 The patient hears this roaring noise inside his head; it is compared to the roaring of a river at high water: a-kin-ka ni&-hor 'my head is roaring'.

20.116 Both mar-a?t-ak-na and har-a?t-ak-na are common for 'gnashing' or 'grinding together'; the segmentation is tentative: compare a-kas-ak-na 'he is snorting'.

20.118 This form is a 'cursive-causative'

with Spanish tonto as the root.

20.125 The san particle indicates anger or vehemence of the speaker; it is used only in direct address.

20.130-135 The shadow of the spirits is cast upon the sick person and penetrates him, causing the disease and delirium. Gonzalez compares it to a flock of swallows flying in circles over a person, their shadows flickering over him.

20.137 The ?txan-txee diia is the 'silent day', that is, the night.

20.153 The root is probably loh. Compare ?pih (20.108); 'u"lo?o 'he loosens it', and the imperative "lo?on.

20.165-166 The angels who aim thunder and lightning at the evil spirits are the same ones who chop the clouds into rain. They are doubtless the Maya Chacs in superficially Catholic clothing. The missiles they are believed to fire are ancient Maya stone chisels, found fairly often, and believed to have curative powers.

21. Funeral Ceremony

21.26-39 The ceremony described in this text differs in many details from that reported in Wisdom 1940:302-306. Unfortunately, it is seldom possible to determine just where Wisdom made which observations. The pretense that the deceased is about to make a journey is more elaborate in this text than in Wisdom's report.

21.77 The dead are carried to the cemetery wrapped in a rush mat, tied around them, on a litter, followed by the women carrying water in jugs.

21.105-109 Compare Wisdom 1940:304: "No food is offered within or above the grave", and see 21.135-137 for the explanation of the offering.

21.192-198 This aspect of the ceremony is described in more detail below, in 21.226-250.

21.292 Although this is not a tale but a narrative prepared at my request, González supplies a variant of the usual ending formula for tales.

22. Tsikin

22.56 Note the syncope of the vowel of <u>tsikin</u> before a heavy stressed syllable (the thematic). The etymology of the form is troublesome: it is not laryngealized, so I suspect a reborrowing from Spanish, or perhaps a hypercorrect form, but this is only speculation.

22.305 Wisdom (1940:302) wrote that "all the family's dead are buried somewhere on its own land..." but this text seems to speak of an aldea cemetery, at least for La Mina.

23. Devil

23.21* From _ah-u?tx-er_ by H, B.

23.26 Although _naht_ means 'distant', the idiom means simply 'some time before'.

23.76 The formation of _tsus-ta-ka_ is not entirely clear, but it seems likely that _ta-ka_ 'with' is the one constituent of a compound.

23.86 This is an 'injunctive' construction but _in-koo_ is irregular in any case; it is used exclusively in constructions like this one. The injunctive suffix is _-k_.

23.148 A billhook has a metal head with a curved 'bill' mounted in a wooden handle one or two feet long; it is the chief utility and agricultural implement, but most Indians who can afford one prefer a commercially made _machete corvo_ as a weapon, and most carry one. See below, 23.500-510.

23.212 This form, like that in 23.214, has the _na_ suffix, contracted before a personal pronoun.

23.347 There is an affirmative particle _atsi_ in this form; it is rare, and its usage not clearly understood.

23.377 The alternant _diabol_ of _diablo_ here is not called for by any phonotactic pattern. Although the form is hard to explain, it is probably more frequent than one would at first assume, and so a likely candidate for morphophonemic adaptation of this kind.

23.380 The root 'drink' is _u?tx_; the alternation is regular. See 23.594 for a perfective showing the root without prefixes.

23.834 A pun: the 'cursives' of the roots

23. Devil

us 'fix, want' (as a cursive) and os 'insert' are the same in the second person singular.

23.902 Nail biting or finger-chewing is regarded as a sign of acute sexual arousal in women. See below, 23.970–984 for the mother's reactions.

23.1010 The root is ak or akt 'dance' (only thematic forms are attested); the permutation of radical vowel and first person singular prefix is regular.

23.1114 The form is kai ak-ta-en (or akt-a-en), not first person plural.

24. Exorcising Disease

24.2 Diseases are also caused by ah-pos-on-er 'harmers', who do not transform themselves into animals, but work magic.

24.17-21 These matters are taken up in texts 25 and 26.

24.61 These prayers are in Spanish, so I have not included them here. They are said between 24.73 and 24.74, but see the note on 24.71.

24.71 The first diety is invoked, then the ah-nir-om continues through 24.72-73, says the indicated prayers in Spanish, goes on to the end of 24.133, and then returns, invokes the second deity in group 24.71, and repeats through 24.133 and so on for five cycles in all. The eia in 24.71 is an exclamatory particle.

24.97 This attribute is probably derived from Spanish embustear 'tell lies', but may also be from embutir 'drink'.

24.105 The sereno here has nothing to do with watchmen or dew, but rather refers to man-made water channels (usually for tule irrigation) which are said to be like the txih txan serpents.

V: The Universe

25. What the World Used to be Like

1 + ,'?e"hen 'te'?u'?kah"tio?p + ,'?a"ni
'ta"ri 'xe"tiem 'po + ."ke?e + ,'?e"mun 'do + ,
'ta"ri 'xe"tiem 'po + .'?i"ra 'hi"rah '?a'sat"pa
+ 7 + ,"txe 'ke?e + ,'?a'?ta"?pai + ,'?e"mar +
,"to?or '?e"rum + ,'?i'?a'?pu?t"?ka 'tu"no?or
"?o?or 'e"rum + .'ta'ke?e"ha?a + 13 + ,'?ie?e
"rum + ,'?a'ket"pa + .'?a"nam + "?es 'to'ke'?a
'?ka?a"pa + '?a?p -- ,'?a'ket"pa + ."ha?a 'tu
"no?or "?o?o 're"rum + ,'?ie?e"hen 'te + ,'?a
'?ka?a"pa + .'?a'txa"mo?p + .'?u"me 'ne"ha?a +
24 + 'por"ke?e -- ,'?a'?ka?a"pa '?a'?txu"uan +
,'?e"hen 'te'lo"ke?e '?a"ian "to?o 're"rum + .
'?a'?ka?a"pa?a '?txu'ua"no?p 'ko'txe?e"suhk
'to?o're"ha?a +

28 + '?i?i -- ,'nien"mut + ,"ma 'tu"?ka?a
'ket"pa + ,"nien "?txahtx + ,"nien 'ma"sa?a + ,
"nie 'nu"sih + ,"nien "muan + ."ma 'tu"?ka?a + ,
'?a'ket"pa + 'por"ke?e -- ,'?i'niah"rer + '?a
'sat"pa 'tu"no?or 'lo'ke?e -- .'?a"ian "to?o 're
"rum + "por 'ke"txe 'ke?e -- ,'ta"ri 'xe"tiem
'po + ."ma?a 'ni'tu"?ka?a '?e'ui"tsir + "to?or
-- "ta 'me?e -- .'?e"mun 'do + 47 + "por 'ke?e
"txe 'ke?e -- ,'?i'niah"rer 'a"ni + ,'?in'ta"ka
+ ,'xi?i"?txir + ,'?e"mun 'do"to?o 're"ha?a + .
"ma 'tu"?ka?a '?e'ui"tsir + .'ko"txe?e 'ko
"ne?er +

54 + "pe 'ro?o -- "kuan 'do -- '?e'di"os
'?u'ui"ra 'ke?e -- 'ke?e -- ,'?a'sat"pa '?e'?pa
"?ka?p + ,'ta'me?e"mun 'do + ,'?en"ton 'ses + ,
'?in'te?e"di 'ia + "kuan 'do -- '?pu?t"?ka 'e?e
-- ,'?e"ha?a "to?o 're"rum + .'ket"pa "pu 'ro'?a
"nam + 'tu"no?or '?e?e -- .'?e"mun 'do + 68 +
"?i 'kon -- ,'?i"kon 'do"kai + ,'ta"ki + ,'?i
"xin + '?ie?e"ha?a 'ia"ha?a + 'tia?a"kai '?u'mo
'roh"se 'u"?pa '?i"xin + ."kai '?u'txa"hri + .
'?e"rum + 76 + ,'?en"ton 'ses + ,'kon"da + ,
'txek"ta 'tu"no?or + ,"kohn + ,'ui"tsir + '?i?i
-- ."tun + 83 + .'tu"no?or 'lo'ke'?a"ian +

25. What the World Used to be Like

84 + "?ka?a 'txek"ta '?i"xin + ,'por'ke "txe 'ke"ha?a 'xe"ha?a + ,'tia?a"kai 'ta'ki?i "xin + '?i'tia?a"kai 'u?u -- ,'?u'mo'roh"su?u "?pa + ."kai '?u'txa"hri '?e"rum + 90 + '?i?i· -- ,'txek"ta 'tu"no?or + '?e?e -- ,"sian "tun 'lo'ke'?a"ian + .'txek"ta '?i"xin +

95 + "pe 'ro?o -- .'ta"ri 'xe"tiem 'po"txe 'ke'ma?a"ni 'tu"?ka?a + 97 + 'ke?e -- ,'?i'nia "hre 'ra"ni + '?e?e -- ,"?txa?ar "?u?ut '?e"rum 'tu"no?or + '?e?e -- .'?e'lu'ga"ro?p + 103 + , 'ko"ne?er + ,'ka'ui"ra + ,"mei 'gra'ui"tsir + '?e?e -- '?e"ian '?e?e -- ,"sian 'koh"no?p + "por 'ke?e -- '?pa'nix"to 'ke?e -- ,'ta'me?e"di 'ia'ia"ha?a + 'ke?e -- "ha?a 'xe?e -- ,'?e"ha?a + ,"kon 'da"kai '?u'mo'roh"se 'u"?pa + .'?ka?a "pa '?u'txa"hri '?u?ut'?e"rum + 117 + '?i?i -- ,'?ka?a"pa 'ket"pa '?e"siaŋ 'ui'tsi"ro?p '?i"xin + ,'ta'me?e'lu"gar +

120 + 'por"ke?e -- .'?u'?kah"ti '?a"ni '?e "hen 'te'ta"ri 'xe"tiem 'po + ,'ke?e'?e"mar + , '?i"rah '?i"rah + ,'?a'?ta"?pai + ,'?u'ioh"mar + '?i?i -- .'?a?atx"pa '?a?a"uan + 'ko"txe?e -- , '?e'to"kar + 130 + ,'?i'kon'da?atx"pa '?a?a "uan + ,'?en"ton 'ses + ,'u'iak"tu?u '?pa'ua"tar + .'u'?po?o"?txi 'tu"no?or "?o?o 're"rum + 134 + "?pa 'na"ni '?u'?kah"tio?p 'ke?e -- ,"por 'ke?e'ta"ri 'xe"tiem 'po + '?u'?kah"tio?p 'ke?e -- ,'?e"mar + '?e?en -- ,'re'de"dor + ,'io?o "ri?i 'lia'?a"mun 'do + ."?txa?ar 'ta"mar + ,'?i 'po"re 'so + ,'ua?ak"txe 'ta"ka + ,'?u'?po"?txi '?o?o're"rum + ,"kuan 'do'?ka"ni '?a'?ta"?pai + 'ta"ma?a -- ."o?o 're"rum + 148 + ."?pan '?a "ni '?u'?kah"tio?p + .'ta"ri 'xe"tiem 'po +

150 + '?iu?u'?kah"tio '?pa"niu?u -- ,'?a "ni '?u'?pan + ,"txe 'ke?e'?e"mar + ."ma "ha?ax '?in'te?e"ra + 154 + ,"txe 'ke'?a"ian '?in 'te?e"mar + ,"txak "txak + ,'ia?a"ian '?in'te?e

25. What the World Used to be Like

"mar + ,"sak "sak + ,'?ia?a"ian 'in"te?e "mar + ,'?in'ta?ak"ta?ak + .'ko'txe'?e"bre 'ia + 161 + ,'?i"txe 'ke'?a"ian '?in'te?e"mar + ,"pu 'ru "?txi?i?tx + .'?in'ta"kix 'txa'ko"?pen + 164 + ,"pe 'ro"no?on + .'ma?a"txi 'kai'?ko"to?on 'ka 'ui"ra + 166 + ,"txe 'ke'?a"ian '?in"te?e "mar + .'ke?e"mei 'ra + 168 + '?i"?pan 'ko -- ,'ko "txa '?e"le 'txe + '?in'ta"kix "sak "sak + '?u '?kah"tio?p 'ke?e "ia -- "ia?a -- 'pe"ga 'do "u?ut '?e"?kin + .'ta'ke?e"mar +

175 + .'?i"ia 'tu"ru '?e'dio"so?p + 176 + ,'?i"txe 'ke'?e"mar 'ia"ha?a + 'ke?e -- ,'?in 'te?en"te?e '?ah"?kin + 'tak'?e'iak -- ,'?ak "?par + .'?e?eh"?pi + 182 + ,"por 'ke?e"txe 'ke?e + ,"ia 'tu"ru + '?e?e -- .'?e'dio"so?p + 186 + "pe 'ro'ma?a"txi 'ka'na?a"ta 'hai -- . '?pam'ber"da 'lo'ke'?u'?kah"tio?p + 188 + '?i 'txe?e'no?p"ke?e -- ,'ta'me?e"mar + ,'?a"ian + , "mei 'ra'?a'ni"mal + .'?pu"?tur 'ta"mar +

193 + ,'?i'po"re 'so + '?a"ian '?in'te?e 'txi"nam + '?u'?ka"?pa?a + "bar 'rio + '?e?e -- ,'ua'te"ma 'la + 'ke?e -- '?a?ak -- ,"ia + '?a?k -- ,"?txa?ar '?e"mar + '?i?i -- .'?u'?kah"tio '?pa"ni 'ta"ri 'xe"tiem 'po + 'ke?e -- ,'?i"ra 'hi"rah + ,'?ka"ni '?a'lo"?koi 'ia?a'ni'ma"lo?p 'ia"ha?a + 'ta'ma'?e?e -- ,"bar 'ko + ,'?ka"na?a '?ka"xo?p 'ta'me?e'txi"nam + 212 + ,"pe 'ro 'ma?a"txi '?a?ak'ta"no?p '?u"me 'ne'sol"daa "do?p + ,'?o?oh"ro?p + .'?a'sut"pa '?a?a"xo?p + 215 + ,"pe 'ro"no?on + .'ma?an"iahr '?ko"to?on 'ka'ui"ra +

217 + "pe 'ro -- ."?pan '?u'?kah"tio?p + 219 + '?u'?kah"tio?p 'ke?e -- ,'?a"ni + 'txe?e "no?p 'ke?e -- 'tu?u"pat '?e"mar + ,'?a"ia 'ne "hen 'te + ."kua 'tro'?u'na?a"?ku?ut + 227 + "txe 'ke?e + ,'?a"ian 'in"mohr "hen 'te + ,'?a "ian 'u'na?a"?ku?ut 'ta'mu?u"pat '?u"hor + ,

25. What the World Used to be Like

'?ia?a"ian + .'de"lan 'te + 232 + 'txe?e"no?p 'ke?e -- 'de"kua 'tro"?o 'ho + 234 + '?i'ha?ax "to '?e"hen 'te'ia"ha?a 'xe'?a?a?k -- .'?a'?ku 'xua"no?p + 236 + .'u'?ku"xo?p 'e"hen 'te + 237 + ,"pe 'ro'txe?e"no?p '?a"ni + 'ke?e -- . 'tu?u'pat"mar '?a"ian + 240 + '?i?i -- ,'?i "txe 'ke?e'?a"ian + '?e"hen 'te'ke?e -- ."ma 'tu "?ka '?u"hor + 244 + '?ia?a"ian '?e?e -- ,'?e "hen 'te + 'ke?e -- ."pa 'txu'?u"hor + .'tu "no?or 'u'?kah"tio '?pa"ni + 249 + ,'ke?e'tu?u "pat "mar + "mix "ha?ax "hen 'te'ko'txe?e -- . '?a"ian 'tia?a'tu"ro?on +

252 + .'?i'po"re 'su?u'?kah"tio '?pa"ni + 'ke"hai -- '?a?ak'ta"na?a 'lo"?kuo?p + ,'?u"men + ,'?e'go"bier 'no + .'?u'sa"tio '?pe"hen 'te + "pe 'ro?o -- 'txe?e"no?p 'ke?e -- 'ma?a"txa?ah '?ku"no?p 'lu"gar + "no 'ke?e -- ,'?e"hen 'te'lo 'ke?e'?a"ian 'tu?u"pat '?e"mar + .'?ka"ni '?a'lo "?kuo?p + '?i?i'?a?a -- .'?a'?pa?ak"to '?pa"ni +

266 + ,'?u'?kah"tio '?pa"ni + ,'ke?e'?a "ian 'in"te?e 'lu"gar + .'?u'?ka"?pa?a '?es"ta 'dos + .'?u"ni 'do + 270 + "txe 'ke?e -- ,'?e "hen 'te + ,'ta'me?e'lu"gar 'ia"ha?a + ,'?e"hen 'te'?a"ian 'u'tsu"tser + '?iu?u -- ,"?iu?ut '?u '?ka?a"?po?p + .'?ko'?pi"rik + 277 + '?i"txe 'ke?e'ha?ax"to 'xe?e -- '?u'?ku"xo '?pa'ne?e"hen 'te + "por 'ke"txe 'ke?e -- .'?a?a"?txi?i '?u 'tsu'tse"ro?p + 281 + ,'?i'po"re 'so + ,'ta"ri 'xe"tiem 'po + '?e?e -- '?a'?pa'?kahr"na '?a"ni + .'?e"hen 'te'xe'a'?ko"to?o?p 'ta'me?e'nah"tir 'lu"gar + ,'xe?e'ma?a"txi '?a'txe?e"no?p 'ko'no "ser + ,'?a'?pa'?kahr"no?p '?a"ni + ,'?a'mu"kuan + ,'e'max"tak 'tu?u"to?p + 'tu?u -- '?e?e -- , 'tu"no?or '?e'i'xik"tak 'a'mu'kua"no?p + "kon 'do?o -- ,'?u'ui"ro?p + .'?a'mu'kua"no?p + ,'?ka "?pe?eik + ,'?e'ua?a"uan + 'in"te?e -- ,'in"te?e "ger 'ra + .'ta'man"te?e 'lu"gar +

25. What the World Used to be Like

301 + ,'?u'?kah"tio '?pa"ni + ,'ke?e"hen 'te'ia"ha?a 'tia?a"ua 're"ger 'ra + "kuan 'do "?a?a -- '?a'ia"hra + '?e?e -- ,"bom 'ba'tu?u'ho "ro?p + ,"txe 'ke?e'ma'ku?u'?e"mar 'u'tsi'ru?u "?po?o?p + "ia?a 'kor"po?o?p + .'?i'po"re 'so 'ma?a"txi '?a'txa'mes"no?p + 310 + "pe 'ro?o "txe 'ke?e -- ,'?ko"toi 'in'te?e"di 'ia + ,'ia "hra '?e'be"ne 'no'ta'me?e"mar + ,'?en"ton 'ses + .'?ka?a"pa 'txa"mo?o?p + 315 + "pe 'ro"txe 'ke?e -- ,'hur"?pir 'a'txe?e"no?p + ,'ma?a"txi '?a'txa'mes"no?p + 'por'ke?e -- 'ma'ku?u'?e"mar 'u'tsi"ru?u "?po?o?p + "?es 'to'ke?e -- 'ia"hra '?e'be"ne 'no'ta'me?en -- ,'?e"mar + ,'?en"ton 'ses + .'?ka?a"pa 'txa"mo?p + 325 + "?pan '?u '?kah"tio?p '?a"ni +

25. What the World Used to be Like

1 People used to tell long ago that the world, long ago, would be destroyed again and again. 7 They say that the sea rose over the earth and filled all the earth with water. 13 And the earth became mud, until it finished -- it turned to water all over the earth, and the people were completely killed off by the water. 24 Because -- they ended up floating, the people who were on the earth, ended up floating like rubbish on the water.

28 And no birds remained, nor foxes, nor deer, nor buzzards, nor hawks; nothing remained, because all at once, everything was destroyed on the earth, because they say that long ago, there were no mountains on the -- world. 47 Because they say that the world was once just stretched over the water; there were no mountains like today.

54 But when God saw that the humans in the world were destroyed, then one day, when it was filled with water all over the earth, and it had become pure mud, all over the -- world. 68 And when it began to dry, it went, and that water, where it began to gather, went away, and began to wash away the earth. 76 Then was when everything appeared: streams, mountains, and stones. 83 Everything there is.

84 It all became visible, because they say that that water, where it dried away, and where it began to gather together, washed away the earth. 90 And everything appeared, and the many rocks there are became visible.

95 But long ago they say that there was nothing. 97 That all at once, all the places lay about on the surface of the earth. 103 Today we see great mountains, and -- there are

many streams, because so, on that day, it was -- the water, when it began to gather itself, completely washed away the surface of the earth 117 and the many mountains became visible in the country.

120 Because the people used to tell long ago that the sea, from time to time, rose up, in its waves, and rose up standing like the clouds. 130 And when it rose up standing, then it let itself come down, and covered everything on the earth. 134 So they used to tell it, because long ago, they tell that the sea lay all around the edges of the world, and that is why it immediately covered over the world when it was rising in -- the world. 148 So they used to tell it long ago.

150 And they used to tell too that the sea was not all one. 154 They say there was one sea that was red, and one sea was white, and there was one sea that was sticky like tar. 161 And they say there was one sea that was pure blood, perfectly red. 164 But we did not get there to see. 166 They say there was one sea which was very large, 168 and just like milk, perfectly white; they say that they were stuck together, the sky and the sea.

175 And there lived the gods. 176 And they say that that sea every day as every night, there was lightning. 182 Because they say that there lived the gods. 186 But we do not know if it is really true, what they tell. 188 And they say that in the sea there were many animals, filling it.

193 And that is why there was a town whose name is Barrios -- Guatemala -- where -- the sea lies -- they tell that long ago that from time

25. What the World Used to be Like

to time those animals tried to come out in -- ships, wanting to fall on the town. 212 But they were not allowed by the soldiers; they shot and they turned and went. 215 But we didn't get there to see.

217 But so they tell it. 219 They tell that -- they used to say that beyond the sea there are people who have horns. 225 There are people with four eyes. 227 They say that there are other people whose eyes are behind their heads, and some in front. 232 They say they have four eyes. 234 And then those people who -- they eat. 236 They eat people. 237 But they said that beyond the sea they are. 240 And they say there are people who -- they have no heads. 244 And there are -- people -- whose heads are flat. They used to tell all this. 249 That beyond the sea there are no people like -- where we live.

252 And that is why they told that -- if they were allowed to go out, by the government, they would destroy the people, but -- they say that -- they were not given permission. No -- the people who are beyond the sea wanted to go out and -- they were feared.

266 They told that there was a place named the United States. 270 They say that the people in that place, the people had hair, and -- their arms were big around. 277 And they say that when -- they used to eat people, because they say that their hair grew. 281 And that is why long ago, they were frightening, people who came from distant places who were not known, they were feared, and they hid the children from them and -- all the women they hid when they saw them. Once they made a -- a war in a place.

25. What the World Used to be Like

301 They used to tell that those people where there was a war, when bombs were dropped on their heads, they say that they went into the sea, and there they were protected, and for that reason they were not killed. 310 But they say that there came a day when poison was dropped in the sea; then they all died. 315 But they say that when shots were fired they were not killed, because they went into the sea; not until the poison was dropped in -- the sea did they all die. 325 So they used to tell it.

26. Earth, Sky and Water

1 + ,'?ka"ni?in 'txe'kon"tar + '?e?e -- , '?in"te?e '?o'hro"ner + ,'lo'ke?e'?ũ?ũm"?pi '?a "ni '?a'?kah"na + .'ta"rix '?e"tiem 'po + 6 + ,'u'?kah"tio?p '?a"ni + .'?e'?o"nia?aŋ "hen 'te + 'ke?e -- '?e?e -- ,'?e"mun 'do'lo'ke?e'tu "ro?on 'ta"mar + .'txe?e"no?p '?a"ni + 'ke?e + , 'ie"?par + '?e?e -- ,'?e"mun 'do + ,'lo'ke?e'tu "ro?on "tar + ,"mas + .'?eh"mar + ,"txe 'ke?e + .'?in"so 'lo"ha?a +

21 + '?i"txe 'ke?e + ,'ie"?par + '?e?e -- ,"ha?a + ,'lo'ke?e"uar '?a"ian "?o 'tron"te?e + '?e?e -- .'lu"gar + 28 + 'ko'txe?e -- .'ta"ra + 30 + ,'?i"txe 'ke?e'?e'lu"gar 'ia"ha?a + , "ia '?pu"?tur + 'tu"no?or '?e"ia 'he?e -- '?e "hen 'te'xe?e -- '?a?a'ro?p"na?a -- ."ma 'lo +

36 + '?i?i -- 'txe?e"no?p -- 'txe?e"no?p -- ,'ke'?e'lu"gar 'ia"ha?a + ,'?u'tu"ri?i?p + . "maa "lo?p + 42 + '?e?e -- ,'po,'ke?e'txe?e "no?p + ,'ke'?e'lu"gar 'ia"ha?a + ."?paŋ 'ko 'txan"te?e 'txi"nam + 'ke?e -- "mei 'gra -- , "mei 'gra"hen 'te'?pu'?tu"ro?p 'ta"mar + "pe 'ro?o -- ,'ha?a"xo?p 'txe?e"no?p + 'ke?e -- . "maa "lo?p + 53 + '?e?e -- 'ha?a"xo?p '?u?u -- ,'ha?a"xo?p + '?u'txa"?puio?p 'ke?e -- '?e"ma 'lo'?i?i -- '?in"te?eix 'n -- .'?in"te?eix "hen 'te +

60 + ,"txe 'ke?e + ,"kon 'da + ,'ta"ra '?a'nam"?tsa '?e"?kin + ,'?i'?a?ak'?pa"re?eŋ '?e?ek'sih"?pa + .'txe?e"no?p + ,'ke?e'ta'me?e 'lu"gar 'ia"ha?a + "uar '?a'lu"mui '?e?e -- '?e?e -- .'?e'ka'ta"ta?a + 69 + "ia "uar '?a?an'?txak"na + .'?a?an'?txek"na "sian + 71 + .'?i'ta"ra '?iŋk'si"?pan + 72 + ,'?i"txe 'ke "kon 'de'?a'lu"mui + '?e?e -- ,"?kin + ,'ta'me?e 'lu"gar 'ia"ha?a + 'tu?u"hor '?e'ui'ni"ko?p 'ia "ha?a + 'ke?e -- 'ke?e -- ,"mas + "fuer 'te'?u?u -- .'ka'lo"ri "ru?ut +

26. Earth, Sky and Water

82 + '?i"txe 'ke?e -- ,'?e"hen "tio?p 'ia "ha?a + ,"mix 'u'na?a"ta + ,'tu"?ka 'u"txo?p 'u "men + '?u'ka'lo"ri "ru?ur -- ."?u?ut '?e"?kin + 88 + '?e?e -- ,'ha?a"xo?p + '?u?u -- '?u'na?a "to?p 'ke?e -- ,'?a"ian + ,'?o'tron"te?e '?u?ut "?kin '?eh"mar 'tia?a'tua?a'lu"mui + '?e?e -- "ia 'he?e -- .'?e"?kin + 97 + "por 'ke?e -- . "?pan 'u'?kah"tio?p + 'ke?e -- .'?a"ian "?o 'tron"te?e 'lu"gar + '?i'ke'?eh"mar '?a?a -- 'ie "?pa 're?e -- ,'?e"rum 'lo'ke?e'tu"ro?on + ,'ta "mar + ,"ia?a '?a'nu"mui + ,'e"?kin + "kon 'da 'ta"ra '?e?eiŋk -- .'?e?eik'sih"?pa +

109 + ,"pues + .'ka'na?a"ta 'ke?e -- .'?a "ian "?o 'tron"te?e 'u?ut"?kin '?eh"mar + 112 + ,'?i"txe 'ke'?e'lu"gar 'ia"ha?a + '?e?e -- , '?in'te?e"ra + 'ta"ka + ,'xe?e + 'txe?e"no?p '?e?e -- .'?e'lu"gar '?in"fier 'no + 119 + "por 'ke"txe 'ke?e -- '?e?e -- ,'?e'lu"gar + . 'xe'?a?a'ro?p"na '?in"fier 'no + ,'ke"ia '?a?a "xi 'tu"no?or "ti?in 'u"txe '?e'ma'?pam'?pa"nir + ,'tu"no?or + '?e?e -- .'ha?a"xo?p 'txe?e"no?p + 127 + ,'tu"no?or "ti?in '?u'na?a"ta?a '?pa?a "xuan + "ti?i 'ne?e -- ,'?a'txam"san + ,"ti?i 'ne?e -- '?u?u -- '?u?u -- 'txe?e -- ."bur 'la '?u"pia?ar + "ti?i 'ne'?u'na?a"ta '?u"txe?e -- , '?a'men"ti 'ra + '?i?i -- ,'tu"no?or + ,'ma'?pam '?pa"nir + ,"txe 'ke'?in"so 'lo + ,"ia '?a?a"xin + .'?a'?pu?ut"?ka 'ta"ma '?e'lu"gar 'ia"ha?a + 145 + ,'txe?e"no?p 'ke"ha?ax '?e'lu"ga 'rin "fier 'no'tia?"ua?ar 'in"te?e "?kahk + ,"ua 'ra '?tsah"?pa + '?i'ke?e -- .'ma?a"txi '?a'tah"pa + 149 + "txe 'ke?e -- ,"ia?a '?ko"toi + .'tu "no?or "ti?i 'ne'?a'txa"mo?o?p +

152 + "pe 'ro?o -- ,"ma "ha?ax 'in'te?e"ra + '?u?u -- '?ku'?pe'sia"ho?p 'ta'me?e -- '?e"ia 'he?e -- '?e?e -- .'lu"gar '?in"fier 'no + 159 + "por 'ke?e -- 'txe?en -- '?a?a -- ,'?a"ian + "ti?i 'ne?e -- 'txe?e"no?p 'ke?e -- ,'ke?e"ti?i

26. Earth, Sky and Water

'ne'?a'txa"mai + '?i?i -- ,'i'ta"ma "?a 'nio + '?a?a -- ,'?a'?ko"toi '?e"?aŋ 'he"lo?p + .'?a'lo '?kes"na + ."to?or 'e"?kahk 'ia"ha?a + 172 + , "ia?a "ian + "ti?i 'ne'txe?e"no?p 'ke?e -- 'ke?e -- ,"ha?ax 'in"te?e 'tur"tar + 'tia?a "ma '?eh "?kar 'tua?a -- '?a?a -- ,'?a'lo"?koi + .'ia "ha?a "tie?e 'ne'?a'txa"mai + ."tie?e 'ne"mei 'gra'?u'ma'?pam'?pa"nir + ,'por'ke"txe 'ke + '?e "ia 'he?e -- '?a"ian 'in'te?e -- .'?a"ian "?o 'tron"te?e 'lu"gar + ,"tia?a + ,'?a'?ko"toi "ti?i 'ne'?a'?ka?a"pa 'txa'mes"?pir + "ti?i 'ne?e -- '?a?a -- ,'txa"mai 'ta"ha?a + ,"ti?i 'ne'?o?ots'po?o"hri + ,'tu?u"?ka?p "te?e + "ti?i 'ne'o?ots'po?o"hri 'tu?ut -- 'tu?ut"?txen + . "txe 'ke'?a"par 'te'?e'lu"gar 'tia?a'tu"ruo?p + 195 + "por 'ke?e -- .'txe?e"no?p 'ke"ma "ha?ax 'u'?poh"?pir 'txa"mer 'u'tah"ui + 'i'ke'?a"par 'te'?e?e -- .'?e'lu"gar 'tia?a'tu"ro?o?p + 199 + '?e?e -- "txe 'ke?e -- '?e?e -- ,"txe 'ke?e'e 'lu"gar 'ia"ha?a + '?e?e -- "ia 'tur -- ,"ia 'tu "ru 'tu"no?or + '?e?e -- .'?e"hen 'te'xe?e'?ah 'ma'?pam"?pan +

208 + '?e?e -- ."txe + 'ke?e -- ,'?a"ian 'in'te?e'u'?ku'?pe'sia"ho?p + 212 + ,"txe 'ke "kon 'da + ,'?a'txa"mai + '?e?e -- ,'?e'ui"nik + ,'xe?e'?a'txam"san + '?o"hai -- ,'?txa"kuan + . '?i"kon 'da'?ko"toi 'ia"ha?a + .'?e?er'se"na + '?e?e -- ,'?u"hor '?e'ui"nik 'xe?e'?u'txam"se + ,'?o?o + '?i'hai -- ,'?txa?a"kuan + ."txe 'ke?e '?e?er'se"na 'e"?txi?itx + 'lo'ke?e -- ,'u'lo?ok "se + .'?e?er'se"na "kon 'da?a'?ko"toi +

230 + '?i?i -- .'?i'txe?e"no?p + 'ke?e "ti?i 'ne -- '?u'na?a"ta '?u?u -- '?u'po"si '?u?u -- ,'?u"pia?ar + ,'tua?a'txa"mai + "txe 'ke?e"tie?e 'ne -- ,'?e'?a'txa"mai + '?e?e -- '?u"me 'ne?e -- ,'lo'ke?e'?u"txe 'u'pa"te 'ru "pia?ar + .'xe?e"txe 'tua?a"bru 'ho + 243 + , "txe 'ke"kon 'da'?a'txa"mai + "ia + '?e?e -- .

26. Earth, Sky and Water

'?e'ui"nik 'ia"ha?a + ,'xe?e -- 'txa"mai + "kon
'da?a -- 'pos"na 'u"me 'ne?e -- ,'?e'ui"nik
"to?or 'e"rum 'ta"ra + "txe 'ke?e + ,"ia?a '?a?a
"xin '?a"?txa?an + ,'tu?u"ham + '?e?e -- .'?e
"maa "lo?p 'ia"ha?a + 257 + .'?i"kon 'da?a'?ko
"toi + ,'ta'ke?e"di 'ia'?a'txa"mai + ,'xe?e'?a
'pos"uan + ,'?en"ton 'ses + .'?a'?ko"toi 'ia
"ha?a + 262 + ,'?u'lo?ok"se + 'xe?e -- '?e?e
-- .'xe?e'?u'txam"se + 266 + ."?pan 'tu"ru '?u
'?ku'?pes'ia"ho?p +

267 + '?i"txe 'ke"ti?i 'ne?e -- ,'?u'na?a
"ta '?a'po"suan + '?o?o -- 'ko'txe?e'ka'ua?a"re
'ke?e -- ,"bru 'ho + "txe 'ke"kon 'de'?a'txa"mai
+ '?e?e -- ,'?a'kah"txa?a 'txu?u?p"na + ,"to?or
'e"?kahk + '?i?i -- "tun -- 'ta'ma?a -- ,"ia
'tua?a"?txu?ur + ,'tu"no?or '?e"tiem 'po + ,'?i
'ke"ma '?eh"?kar + 'tua?a + .'?u'to"ii 'tu"no?or
'lo'ke?e'?u"txe + 284 + .'txe?e"no?p 'ke?e
"ia?a "?txu?ur + .'?pu?uts "?pu?uts 'u'na"?ku?ut
+ 286 + 'u?u -- .'u"me 'ne"?kahk 'tia?a
"?txu?ur + 288 + ,"txe 'ke"tie?e 'ne'?u'na?a
"ta '?u"txe 'men"ti 'ra + ,"ia "?txu?ur "to?o
're"?kahk 'ia"ha?a + '?e?e -- '?e?e -- ,'?ko
"ro?tx '?ko"ro?tx + ."?o?or 'u'ia?ak + .'u"me
'ne"?kahk + 295 + "?pan 'tu"ru '?u?u -- .'?ku
'?pe'sia"ho?p +

297 + ,'por"ke?e + .'txe?e"no?p + 'ke?e --
,"mei 'gra + ."mar + .'ie"?pa 're"mun 'do + 303
+ '?a"ian '?e?e -- .'?e"mar "blaŋ 'ko + '?i?i --
.'?a"ian '?in"te?e "mar 'txak"txak + 307 + ,
'txe?e"no?p 'ke?e'?a"ian '?in"te?e "mar + '?e?e
-- ,"ber 'de + ,'?a"sul + 311 + '?i?i -- '?i
'txe?e"no?p 'ke?e -- ,'?a"ia 'nin"te?e "mar + .
'ko'txe?e"le 'txe + 'ke?e -- 'txe?e"no?p 'ke?e
-- ,"no?on + .'to?or "mar '?txu?u"ron +

319 + .'?i'po"re 'so'txe?e"no '?pa"ni +
'ke?e -- 'ke"hai -- '?e?e -- .'?e"mun 'do'lo

26. Earth, Sky and Water

'ke?e'tu"ro?on 'ta"mar + ,'?ka"ni + '?a?a -- ,'?a'nih'kes"na + ,'ua?ak"txe 'ta'ka + '?e?e -- ,'?a?a"xin 'ma'ku?u"ha?a + .'i"no?on 'ka'?ka?a "pa + 331 + "por 'ke?e -- 'txe?e"no?p 'ke?e -- .'?in"so 'lo'ha?a'ie"?pa 're"rum + 334 + '?i 'tu?u"hor 'e?e -- 'e"ha?a + .'?txu?u"ron "no?on +

337 + ,"por 'ke?e"txe 'ke?e + ,'tia?a'ke "ter + 'ke"ter '?u?u -- ,'?u'io"rii "iir + ,'?e 'mun"do + 'lo'ke?e -- ,'tu"ro?on "tar + '?i'ta 'me?e -- ,'?u'io"rii "iir + ."txe 'ke'?in"so 'lo "ha?a + '?e?e -- 'xe'txe?e"no?p 'ke?e -- ."mar "bre 'ia + 350 + "por 'ke?e -- ,'txe?e"no?p 'ke?e"mar "bre 'ia'por'ke?e"txe 'ke?e"ia + '?e?e -- ,"ia 'nu"?tur + ,'?u'io"rii "iir '?e"mun 'do + .'ta"ku?ut '?e"?kin + 356 + 'i'ke?e -- ,'ia "ha?a + ,"mix 'mah"txi '?a'?ko"toi + 'nien -- , "bar 'ko + ,'nien '?a"bion + .'me?e"ra '?ko"toi +

363 + 'por'ke"txe 'ke?e -- 'ta'me?e -- , '?u'io'rii"ii 're"mun 'do + ,'tu?u'io'rii"ii 're "mar + ."ia 'tu"ru '?e"?aŋ 'he"lo?p + 368 + '?i"txe 'ke?e -- 'txe?e"no?p 'ke?e -- "hai -- , 'ia"ha?a '?a'?ko"toi '?in"te?e + '?e?e -- '?in "te?e -- '?e?e -- ,'?ah'?o?o'ru"mir "hen 'te + , 'ke'ua?ak"txe 'ta"ka + ,'?e?eh"?pi 'e"?aŋ 'he "lo?p + ,'?i?i'?u'io'hre"so?p '?o?o"hri + ."hai '?in"te?e '?a"bion '?ka"ni '?a'?ko"toi + "por 'ke + ."txe 'ke"ia 'pe"ga 'do + ,'?e?e -- "sie 'lo + '?e?e -- .'xe?e'ka'ua?a"re "?u?ut 'e"?kin + 386 + 'ta'ka?a -- '?e?e -- .'?e"mun 'do + 389 + "por 'ke'txe?e"no?p 'ke?e"ia 'he?e -- '?e?e -- ,'?e"mun 'do'ie?e"?u?ut 'e"?kin + ,'tu "ru + 'ko'txe?e -- '?e?e -- 'ko'txe?e -- '?e?e -- ,'?u"pat 'e"xux + .'tu?u'?tsah"kir 'tu?u '?tsah"kir 'tu"rua?a "xin +

399 + '?pa?a -- .'txe?e"no?p 'ke"?pan 'e

26. Earth, Sky and Water

"mun 'do + 'ke?e -- '?e?e -- 'ke?e -- ,"?u?ut 'e
"?kin + ,'ti"txan + 'lo'ke?e'ka'ui"ra 'ta"ra + .
"txe 'ke?e'mon"ta 'nia + 408 + ."ber 'de +
409 + '?i?i -- ,'?i"mas + ,'ti"txan + "tui?i
'xe?e -- .'txe?e"no?p 'ha?a"xo?p 'ke'tu?u"pat
'?e"sie 'lo'ti"txan + 'ke?e -- '?a?a -- ,"iaa +
,"ia '?e'lu"gar + 418 + .'?a"ian 'in"te?e 'lu
"gar + .'?in"te?e 'txi"nam + 'ko'txe?e -- .'ko
"txia?atx 'ka'ui"ra 'ta"ra + ,"txe 'ke"ia + ,'tu
"ru + '?e?e -- ,'tu"no?or + "ti?i 'ne?e -- '?a?a
-- ,"tie?e 'ne'a'txa"mai + ,'ta"ra + ,'ke"ia
'?a?a"xin 'a'tu"ruan + 'ta'ma'?e?e -- .'?e'lu
"gar 'ia"ha?a + 433 + '?i?i -- ,'?i"mas 'ti
"txan + '?a"ian "?o 'tron"te?e -- '?e?e -- ,'lu
"gar + .'ke"ia 'tu"ru '?e'dio"so?p +

439 + ,'po"re 'so + .'ta"rix 'e"tiem 'po +
"kuan 'do?o -- '?e?e -- '?a"ian "ti?i 'ne?e -- ,
'?a'?kah'pes"ian + ,'?a"ni + ,"tu?ut '?e"dios +
."txe + ,"tia?a 'ua?a"ret + ,"tia?a + ,'tu"re?et
'ta'ma + .'?u"pat '?e"sie 'lo + 452 + 'por
"ke?e -- '?u'?pin"nu 'ke?e -- 'ke'?e?e -- ,
"?u?ut '?e"?kin 'lo'ke?e'ka'ui"ra 'ti"txan + ,
'ke"ma "ha?ax '?u'tur"ta 're"dios + 'si"no 'ke?e
-- ,'?u'tur"ta 're"dios '?a'ket"pa + ."mas 'ti
"txan + 460 + ,'?i'po"re 'so + "?pan 'na?at --
.'?u'na?a"to?o?p 'ke?e -- ,'?eh"mar + '?e?e -- ,
'?a"ian + '?e?e -- ,'?a"ian "?o 'tron"te?e +
'?e?e -- ,'lu"gar + .'?eh"mar + 471 + .'ni'?a
"ian '?in"te?e "mar +

472 + '?i"txe 'ke?e -- "tia?a -- 'nu?t --
"tia?a -- ,'nu"?tur + ."?u?ut '?e"?kin + 'ta'ka
'?e?e -- ,'?e"mun 'do'lo'ke'tu"ro?on 'ta"mar +
'i'ta"ma?a -- 'ta'ka -- 'tu"no?or 'lo'ke?e'?u?u
-- ,"txo?p 'men"tar + 'ke?e -- 'ke?e -- ,'nu
"?tur + '?e?e -- ,"mun 'do + ,'u'?kah"tio?p '?a
"ni + 'ke?e -- '?e"ia 'he?e -- '?e'ka -- ,'?e'ka
'ta"ta?a "dios + ,'ha?a"xir + ,'tu"ru + ,"des
'de'ta'mu"pat 'e"sie 'lo'ti"txan + ,'?i"ha?ax
'txu"kur 'u'me"ner + ,'tu"no?or '?e'lu'ga"ro?p +

26. Earth, Sky and Water

'e?e -- ,"mar + '?i"txe 'ke?e -- '?e"mun 'do'lo 'ke?e'tu"ro?on 'ta'ri"ra + 'ha?a -- 'txe?e"no?p 'ke?e -- '?e?e -- ,'ta"ma + '?e?e -- '?u?u -- , '?u"tah 'nu"iok + '?e?e -- .'de'te"ni 'du?u'me "ner + 'i?i -- .'po"re 'so'txe?e"no?p 'ke'hai "ha?ax + ,'?ka"ni '?u'nih"?kes + ,'ke'ua?ak"txe 'ta"ka + ,'?e?ein"txa 'e"mun 'do'ta'ka"ron + .'i 'ka'sat"pa +

518 + 'por'ke'txe?e"no?p 'ke?e -- ,'ke'?e "mun 'do + .'in'ta"ka "?txu?ur + .'ta'ka"ron + 'ko'txe?e -- '?a?a -- '?a'?txu"uan '?e?e -- ,'?e '?txa"?pi?i "to?o 're"ha?a "kon 'de"uar 'ka'txa "pi + '?i?i -- 'n -- .'ta"ka '?a'?txu"uan '?o?o 'ioh"?ki "to?o 're"ha?a + "txe 'ke?e -- ,"txe 'ke"?pa 'ne"mun 'don'ta"ka "?txu?ur + ,'?o?o 'ioh"?ki 'ta'ka"ron + '?i?i -- ,'?i'de'te"ni 'do 'u"me 'ne'ka'ta"ta?a "dios + .'ta'mu?u"iok + 535 + ,'i'ke"hai "ha?ax '?u'nih"?kes 'ta'ka"ron + ,'?en"ton 'ses'ua?ak"txe 'ta"ka + '?e?e -- , '?e"mun 'do'?i"ra + '?a?a -- 'ke?e -- ,'ua?ak "txe 'ta"ka '?e"mun 'do'?i"ra + ,'?u"txe 'kon'su "mir 'ta'ka"ron + ,'?i'?a'?ta"?pai 'e"ha?a "to?o 're"rum + ,'tua?a'ket"pa + ,'?in"so 'lo + ."mar "o?o 're'ru"mi 'ri"ran +

547 + 'txe?e"no?p 'ke?e -- '?e?e -- .'?e "mar "bre 'ia + 'xe'?u"txo?p 'men"tar 'tia?a -- '?tsa"kar "u?ut '?e"?kin 'ta'ka'?e?e -- ,"mun 'do + .'txe'ke'ga"lan 'a'?tsa?a'pru"ma + 554 + ,'po"re 'so'txe?e"no?p + 'ke"?paŋ 'ko'txa'?e?e -- '?e?e -- "ti?in "txe 'ke?e -- ,"mar "bre 'ia + ,'?i"ti?in 'txe?e"no?p 'ke?e'?e"mar + .'kris 'ta"li 'na + 561 + "por 'ke?e -- ,'txe?e"no?p 'ke'ga"lan + .'?a'?tsa?a'pru"mu?ut +

564 + '?i?i -- ,'?u'?kah"tio '?pa"ni + 'ke?e -- 'ke'?e?e -- ,'?e?ei"?kar + ,'?e'ta"ki 'ni"?kar + ,'xe?e'a'uahr"san + ."to?or 'e"rum 'ta"ra + 572 + '?i'ke?e -- ,'ma"ha?ax + ,"mei

26. Earth, Sky and Water

'gra + '?e?e -- '?u"ial "tir 'lo'ke?e -- '?a?am — '?a?a — .'?ta"?pai 'ta"mar + 580 + , 'txe?e"no?p 'ke?e"mas 'ti"txan + ,'?a"ian 'o 'tron"te?e '?i"?kar 'xe?e'?a'uahr"san + 'ke?e -- ,"ha?ax + '?u?u -- ,'ma?a"txi '?u'iak"ta + , '?e?ei"?kar 'xe?e'?a'uahr"san 'ta"ra "to?o 're "rum + .'ma?a"txi '?u'iak"ta '?a'nu"mui 'ti"txan + 588 + ,"por 'ke'txe?e"no?p 'ke'?e?ei"?kar 'xe'?a'uahr"san 'ta"ra + '?e?e -- '?e?e -- 'ma?a — '?e?e — ."ma '?pam"?pan + 594 + '?e?e -- , 'txe?e"no?p 'ha?a"xo?p 'ke?e + 'ma"ha?ax '?n?n — .'sa"gra 'do + 598 + ,"por 'ke?ei"?kar 'ta "ra + ,'?u'ua"hri + ,'tu"?ki?ik 'tu"?ki?ik + , 'lo'ke'?a"ian "to?or 'e"rum + '?e?e -- '?e?e — '?u?u — ,'?u"tui?ir '?al"gu 'na"ko 'sa'lo'ke'?a "ian "to?o 're"rum + ,'?i'tu"no?or + ,'?e'ma '?pam'?pa"nir + ,'lo'ke?e'?a"ian "to?or 'e"rum + '?i?i -- 'ha -- .'?e'?a'ua"hro 'ta"mar + 612 + ,"pe 'ro"txe 'ke?e + '?e?ei"?kar 'xe?e -- , "?txa?ar "mas 'ti"txan + 'ma?a"txi?ix '?u?u -- 'ma?a"txi?ix '?u?u -- ,'ma?a"txi '?u'iak"ta '?a 'nu"mui + ,'?e?ei"?kar 'xe'?a'uahr"san 'ta"ra + .'tua?a'ma?a"txi '?a'nu"mui + .'?e'ma'?pam'?pa "nir 'ti"txan + 621 + 'i"txe 'ke?e -- ,"mas 'ti"txan + .'?a"ian "o 'tron"te?e '?i"?kar + . "?txa?ar + 625 + 'ke?e -- 'ke?e -- ,'?e?ei "?kar 'ia"ha?a + ,'txe?e"no?p 'i"?kar 'sa"gra 'do + "por 'ke?e -- "mix 'tu"?ka '?u?u -- ,'ma '?pam'?pa"nir + '?ue?e -- .'?a"ian 'ta"mar +

634 + ."pues + ."?pan 'tu'ru"?pu?u '?ku '?pes'ia"ho?p + 636 + ,"por 'ke?e"txe 'ke?e + ,'?e?ei"?kar 'xe?e"?txa?ar 'ta"mu?ut '?e"?kin + '?i?i -- 'txe?e"no?p 'ha?a"xo?p + 'ke?e -- , '?e?ei"?kar + '?e?e -- ,'sa"gra 'do + 'ke?e -- ."ma 'tu"?ka '?e'ma'?pam'?pa"nir 'ta"mar + 646 + "por 'ke"txe 'ke?e -- ,"ha?ax + '?e?e -- '?e?e -- '?e?ei"?kar 'xe?e"?txa?ar 'ta -- ,'ti"txan + ,"txe 'ke"ha?ax 'la"?tar + '?e?e -- ,"?u?ut 'e "?kin + .'?u'me"ner +

26. Earth, Sky and Water

656 + '?i?i -- .'?i'txe?e"no?p + ,"ke?e + '?e?ei"?kar 'xe?e -- ,"?txa?ar 'ti"txan + 'tia?a -- '?e?e -- ,'pe"ga 'do + 'tia?a -- .'xe?e'pe"ga 'do'ta"ku?ut 'e"?kin + 666 + ,'?i'ke"ha?ax + '?u"txe '?a?a -- ,'u"txe '?a'kor"tar + '?u?u -- .'?u'?kah"ke "?u?ut 'e"?kin + 671 + "por 'ke 'txe?e"no?p 'ke?e -- 'ke?e -- ,'ma"nik '?e?ei "?kar 'ia"ha?a + ,'ke'?a'?tsah"?pa '?a"ni '?e "mun 'do'?i"ra + 'u"me 'ne -- ,'u'?kah"kir "?u?ut '?e"?kin + ,'lo'ke'?a'lu"mui 'ti"txan + "por 'ke?e -- ,"txe 'ke?e"?kin + ,'xe'ka'ui"ra 'ti"txan + ."?kahk + 682 + ,'i"hai "ma 'tu"?ka '?e?ei"?kar 'ia"ha?a + "tua?a '?u?u -- "tua?a '?u?u -- ,'?u"txa?a 'kor"tar + .'?en"ton 'ses'?a '?tsah"?pa 'e"mun 'do + 687 + ."?pa 'na"ni '?u '?kah"tio?p +

688 + ,'po"re 'so'txe?e"no?p 'ke'?e?ei "?kar + ,'lo'ke?e"?txa?ar '?a'uahr"san 'ta"ra + '?i'ke?e -- "ma 'tu"?kan "te?e "tiem 'po'tua?a -- ,"ma 'tu"?ka?a + ,'por'ke"txe 'ke + ,'?e?ei "?kar + ,'xe'a'uahr"san 'ta"ra + ."mei 'gra'u '?kam'pi?i"?pir + 697 + ,'?i'ke'?ak'ta"?pir 'u "me 'ne"dios 'tua?a"ha?ax + ,'?e?e -- '?u'ua"hri "ko?oit + '?i?i -- '?i"tua?a -- ,'?u'sis'?puh "res "?o?o 're"rum + .'tua?a'ma?a"txi '?a'?tsah "?pa + '?i"tua?a 'ma?a"txi '?a?a -- ,'?a'txa"mai '?e'pa"?ka?p '?e'ko"noh + '?u"me 'ne?e -- '?e?e -- .'?u'?kah"kir "?u?ut 'e"?kin + 709 + ,'po "re 'so'txe?e"no?p + ,'ke'?e'ta"kin 'i"?kar 'xe?e"?txa?ar '?a'uahr"san 'ta"ra + 'ma'tu"?ka?a "tiem 'po'xe?e -- .'?a'lo"?koi + 713 + ,"por 'ke"txe 'ke'?e'ta"kin '?i"?kar + ,'?a"par 'te'ke "?txa?ar 'tu"no?o 're"tiem 'po + ,'ia?a"par 'te '?e?ei"?kar + .'xe?e'ua"tar 'ta'ke?e'ha"ha?ar +

717 + ,'?e?ei"?kar 'xe?e'ua"tar 'ta'ke?e 'ha"ha?ar + '?u'?kam'pi?i"?pir "ha?ax '?e?e -- , '?u'ta"re 'se'ha"ha?ar + ."na?a 'xe'?u'?ta?a?p "se?e "?aŋ 'he"lo?p "tu?ut '?e"?kin + 721 + ,

26. Earth, Sky and Water

"pe 'ro'?e'ta"kin 'i"?kar 'xe"?txa?ar + ,'tu "no?o 're"tiem 'po + ,"txe ke"tua?a 'ta"ka + '?e?e — '?u'uah — ,'u'uah"rio?on + ,'tua?a 'ma?a"txi 'ka'?tsah"?pa + ,'?u"men + .'?u'?kah "kir "?u?ut 'e"?kin + 730 + ."?pa 'na"ni '?u '?kah"tio?p +

731 + .'txe?e"no?p 'ke'ta"ri 'xe"tiem 'po + ,'a'?kah"pa?a '?kah"pa '?a"ni + '?a?a — ,'?a 'sat"pa '?e"mun 'do + .'ta'ke?e'pa"?ka?p '?e'ko "noh + 736 + ,"por 'ke?e'txe?e"no?p 'ke'?a"ian '?in"te?e "?aŋ 'hel + '?e?e — 'ha?a"xo?p 'txe 'ke?e'?e?e — "?aŋ 'hel'ke?e — 'ma?a"txi '?u '?ku?u?p"se 'u?u — .'?u'ta"ta?a + ,'ke"ha?ax 'e 'ka'ta"ta?a + .'e'ka'ta"ta?a "dios + "txe 'ke?e "ia 'he?e — ,'?e"?aŋ 'hel'ia"ha?a + '?e?e — , '?a'?kah"pa?a '?kah"pa + '?e?e — ,'?u'iu"sre + '?u'nih"kes '?e?e — '?e?e — "por 'ke'txe?e "no?p 'ke?e'?a"ian — '?n?n — ,"ti?in 'u'?kah "tio?p 'ke'?a"ian + .'u'koi'ki"nar '?e"mun 'do + '?e?e — '?o?o — .'u'uo"iir +

759 + "txe 'ke?e + ,'e"?aŋ 'hel'ia"ha?a + '?a?a — ,"kon 'da'?ah'?ku"na "ga 'na + '?u?u — ,'?u'iuh"?ku + ,'?u'uo"ii 're"mun 'do + ,'?ien "ton 'ses + '?e?e — '?e?e — ,'txe?e"no?p 'ke '?e"mun 'do + ,'ua?ak"txe 'ta"ka + '?a?a — , '?a?a"xin 'ma'kue?e — '?e?e — ."na?a + '?ia "hu?u "txa '?e?e — .'tu"no?or 'e"mun 'do'ta 'ke?e'pa"?ka?p 'e'ko"noh + 777 + 'txe?e"no?p 'ke?e — .'ta"ri 'xe"tiem 'po + .'?a'?kah"pa?a '?kah"pa + .'?a'sat"pe?e "mun 'do +

781 + "pe 'ro?o — "txe 'ke?e — '?a"ian + 'in"te?e — ."tiem 'po + "kon 'da?a — '?e?e — '?e'ka — ,'?e'ka'ta"ta?a "dios + ,'?ko?oi"ran + ,'i"ra 'hi"rah + ,'u"txe 'hor"mar + ,"?o?o 're "mun 'do + .'ta'ke?e'pa"?ka?p '?e'ko"noh + 795 + '?i?i — 'en"ton 'ses'kon'da?a — '?u'ui"ra '?e"dios 'ke?e — '?e?e — '?u'sa"ti?i — '?a

26. Earth, Sky and Water

'?kah"pa?a '?kah"pa + ,'u'sa"tio?p '?e'pa"?ka?p
'?e'ko"noh + ."txe "tuo?o?p + 'ke?e -- ,'ke
"no?ox + ,'ma?a"txi?i 'uak"ta + ,'?e'pa"?ka?p
'?e'ko"noh + .'lo'ke"ne?en 'in'?to"xi + 808 +
'?i'ke?e -- ,"ne?en + ,'?in"txe 'hor"mar + '?e?e
-- "?o?or 'e?e -- ,'?e"rum + ,"tua?a 'tu'ra"no?p
"tar + ,'?i"no?ox + ,'?i"ra 'hi"rah + '?i?i -- .
'?i'hu?u"txes + ,'ko"ne?er '?us'ta"nik + 'ko
'txe?e -- "?paŋ 'ko'txe?e -- 'ta'ua"rox 'tua?a
-- '?i?i -- '?i?i -- ,'sa"ti + '?i"?pan 'ta'ua
"rox 'tua?a -- '?e?e -- .'iu?us"tes +

829 + ,"txe 'ke?e + ,'?e"?aŋ 'he"lo?p 'ia
"ha?a + ,'ua?a'ua"no?p + 'ke?e -- ,"mix "ti?in +
'?u"na?a -- .'ta'tu"?ku?u "txo?o?p + ,'ke'?a?a
"xin ,'?u'tsu"io?o?p + ,'?e"rum + ,'?u'pu
"sio?o?p "to?or 'e"ha?a + ,'i"txe 'ke?e"rum 'ia
"ha?a + ,'?a'?ka"xi '?a'?ka"xi + ,'?a'hu?u"txa +
'?a?a -- .'?a?a"xin 'ma'ku?u"ha?a + "nie?e -- .
"nie 'na'txek"ta 'tia?a'?a?a"xin + 846 + '?i?i
-- .'?a'?kai"no?o?p + .'?u"me 'ne'ka'ta"ta?a
"dios + ."txe "tuo?o?p + 'kox"to "tua?a + ,'?i
'sa"ti + ,'ta'ua"rox + ,'?i"tua?a '?i"txe '?o
'tro"niahr + '?e?e -- .'ma?a"txu 'iu"?pio?ox +
856 + .'?en"ton 'ses + ,"txe 'ke'ta"ri + ,"?o
'tron"te?e "?aŋ 'hel + ,'u'?ka"pa?a + ."san 'rai
"mun 'do +

861 + ,'?e"?aŋ 'hel'san'rei"mun 'do'?i"xin
+ '?u'uah"pi '?e'hi?i -- '?e?e -- '?e?e -- '?e?e
-- ,'?im'?pihk"rum + .'?u'pu"si "to?o 're"ha?a +
868 + ,'?i"txe 'ke'?ka"xi 'ta"ka + '?e?e -- '?e
"rum 'ia"ha?a "to?o 're?e -- ,'?e"ha?a + ,'pu
'kuh"?ki?i "xin 'tu"no?or "?o?o 're"ha?a + ,'leh
"mai '?u"ho 're"ha?a '?u'me"ner + '?i?i -- '?i
'ii?i -- ,'?txu"uan 'i"xin + ,'i'ua?ak"txe 'ta
"ka + "kai '?ke"?ko 'ta"ri 'ko'txe?e -- ,'a'?ke
"?ko + '?e?e -- .'?txa"?pi?i "to?o 're"ha?a +
882 + "txe 'ke?e -- .'?txu"ua 'ni"xin + ,"to?o
're"ha?a + ,'tu"no?or "?ehs 'to'ke?e"ma + ,'?u

26. Earth, Sky and Water

'?po"?txi 'tu"no?or + ."?o?o 're"mar + .'sut"pa "?o 'tro"niahr + '?e?e -- '?e?e -- ,'?e"mun 'do + '?i?i -- .'?tox"pa '?e"hen 'te'ta"mar + 'txe?e "no?p 'ke"des 'de -- ,'ta'me?e"di 'ia'ia"ha?a + ,'ma?a"txi?ix 'sut"pa + ,'sat"pa "mas 'e"mun 'do + .'ta'ke?e'pa"?ka?p '?e'ko"noh + 899 + ,'?i 'po"re 'so'txe?e"no?p 'ke?e + .'ke'ko"ne?er '?a "ian "mei 'gra'?e"hen 'te + ."por 'ke'?e"mun 'do 'ma?a"txi '?a'sat"pa 'ko"ne?er +

902 + ."txe 'ke?e + 'ie?e -- ,'?e'?ah'sat "pa?ar "hen "tio?p 'ia"ha?a + ,"ti?i 'ne"kai 'sah"to?o?p + '?e?e -- .'?ka?a"pa 'sut"po?o?p "txai + 908 + ,'txe?e"no?p 'ke?e"txai + '?e?e -- ,'?e"txai 'txek"ta + "por 'ke?e -- '?e?e -- , '?i"ra 'hi"rah '?a"ni '?a'sat"pa '?e"hen 'te + , '?i'?e?e"hen 'te'ia"ha?a + 'lo'ke?e -- '?a?a -- '?a'hu?u -- '?a?a -- ,'sat"pa + '?e?e -- ,"mun 'do'ta'ka"ro?p + .'?a'?puh"ko?p '?u"me 'ne"ha?a + '?i?i -- .'?a'sut"po?o?p "txai + 925 + ,"?pa 'na"ni 'u'?kah"tio?p '?e"hen 'te + .'ta"ri 'xe "tiem 'po + ,'ke'?e"txai + ."hen 'te +

929 + ,"ma "ha?ax '?in'te?e"ra + '?u?u -- ,'?u"txo?p 'kon"tar + '?a"ni 'e?e -- ,"hen 'te 'ta"ri 'xe"tiem 'po + 'ko'txe?e"re 'tu"ru '?e?e -- ,"?u?ut '?e"?kin + 'ie?e -- '?e?e -- .'?e"rum + 939 + ,'?a"ian "ti?i 'nu'?kah"tio '?pa"ni + 'ke?e -- ,'ke'?a"ian + '?e?e -- 'ke?e -- ,'?u 'ies"kii "nir + '?e?e -- '?e"mun 'do'xe?e -- , "txe 'ke'?a"ian + 'e?e -- 'u"uoi -- '?u?u -- .'u 'oi'ii"ro?p + 952 + 'i"txe 'ke'ta'ma'?e?e -- '?e?e -- ,'?e?e'?oi"io?p 'ia"ha?a + ,"ua?ar '?e "?an 'he"lo?p + '?e?e -- .'txu"kur 'u'me'ne"ro?p + 958 + 'txe?e"no?p 'ke?e -- 'kuk -- 'ke?e -- ,"kon 'de"ha?ax + ,'?u'iuh"kuo?p + ,'?u'uoi"ii 're"mun 'do + ,'?en"ton 'ses + '?e?e -- ,'?a'nih "ki + '?e?e -- .'tu"no?or '?e"rum + ."por 'ke?e '?a'?ku'?pes'ia"no?p '?a"ni 'ta"rix 'e"tiem 'po + 'ke?e -- 'ko'txa?a -- '?e?e -- ,'?i"ra 'hi"rah

26. Earth, Sky and Water

+ '?a'nu"mu 'ia"ni '?e?e -- .'?e'iuk"?par + '?a
'?ku'?pes'ia"no?p 'ke?e -- ,'ke?e"?aŋ 'he"lo?p
'ia"ha?a + ."ha?ax '?u'iuh"kuo?p + ,'?u?u + ,'?u
'uoi"iir + '?e"mun 'do + .'?i'ke?e'?ka"ni 'u'sa
"tio?p +

983 + ,"pe 'ro'ma?a"txi '?ah'?ku"no?o?p
'lu"gar + ,'?u"me 'ne'ka'ta"ta?a "dios 'ti"txan
+ 'tua?a -- 'tua?a -- .'?u'sa"tio?p + 988 +
"pe 'ro'ha?a"xo?p "txe 'ke?e -- .'?a'?ko?oi'ra
"no?p + ,'tia?a'ua?a"ro?p 'ta"kar + ,'txu"kur
'u'me'ne"ro?p + 992 + ,'?i'ha?a"xo?p '?a"ni +
.'?u'sa"tio?p + 994 + ,"pe 'ro'ma?a"txi '?a?ah
'?ku"no?p 'lu"gar 'u"me 'ne'ka'ta"ta?a "dios + .
'?u'iah"tu?ut + .'?e'pa"?ka?p '?e'ko"noh + .
'tua?a'sat"pa +

1001 + ,'?a"ia 'na"ni '?in"te?e "ie 'ran
"sia 'no + .'?a"kai 'u'?kah"ti + '?e?e -- '?in
"tia?atx '?u?u -- .'?u"txe 'kon"tar + ,'ha?a"xi
'ru'?kah"ti '?a"ni + 'ke?e -- .'?u'iu"?pan '?a
'?kah"na + .'ta"ri 'xe"tiem 'po + 1010 + ,'ke
'?e"mun 'do + .'?i"ran 'lo'ke?e'tu"ro?on 'ta"mar
+ 'ke?e -- ,'in'ta"ka "?txa?ar + ,'?u'iah"?ku?u
"buel 'ta + "txe 'ke?e -- ."kon 'da + '?e?e -- ,
'?e?ek'sih"?pa 'ta"ra + "txe 'ke?e -- '?e?e -- ,
"?u?ut '?e"?kin + 'ti"txan '?a?a -- .'?a'nu"mui
'eh"mar + 1024 + ,'?i?i + ,'?e"mun 'du"ra + .
'?a'?ta"?pai 'ti"txan + 1027 + 'i"kon 'du'?e?e
-- ,"mun 'du'ta"ra + '?a?a -- ,'?a'nu"mui '?eh
"mar + ,'?ien"ton 'ses + .'ka'ui"ra '?e"?kin 'ti
"txan + 1033 + .'?i"kon 'da + ,'?e?e -- "?u?ut
'?e"?kin + '?eh -- 'ti"txan "uar '?a'lu"mui '?eh
-- ,'?eh"mar + '?i"no?on -- '?i"no?on -- '?e?e
-- '?i"no?on "txe 'ke?e -- .'tu"ro?on 'ti"txan +

1044 + '?e?e -- .'?a"kai 'a"ni '?a?a'ro?p
"na + "pe 'ro'kox"to 'ma?a"txi 'ka"txe 'sen"tir
'tu"?ko?o 'ra -- .'tu"?ko 'ra'ka'?txu"uan 'xir
"koht + 1048 + .'ha?a"xir 'txe'?a"ni + ,'ko

26. Earth, Sky and Water

'txa'ka?a"xi 'ka'txe'sen"tir + ,'ke"no?on '?ah
'ma'?pam'?pa"non + .'?i'ma?a"txi 'ka'na?a"ta +
1052 + '?i?i -- ,'ko"txa '?u'po"der 'e"dios 'ta
'ka"ron + .'i'po"re 'so'ma?a"txi 'ka'txe'sen"tir
'tu"?ko 'ra'ka'?txu"uan 'xir"koht + "?pa 'na"ni
'?a?a -- .'tu"ruan '?o?o'hro"no '?pa"ni +

1057 + ,"ti?in + ,'txe?e"no '?pa"ni + .'ke
"ha?ax '?e"mun 'do'?a'su'tre"ma 'ta'ka"ron +
1060 + '?i?i -- "ma "ha?ax '?in'te?e"ra 'u?u --
.'?u"txo?p 'kon"ta 'ra"ni + 1063 + '?e?e -- ,
'?a"kai 'a"ni 'u'?kah"tio?p + 'ke?e -- ,'?e"?kin
+ ,'xe'?a'lu"mui 'ti"txan + "?paŋ 'ko'txa'?e?e
-- ,'?e"tren + ,'ka'ui"ra 'ko"ne?er + 'ta'ka?a
-- .'ta'ka'?u"?kahk + 1073 + '?u'?kah"tio?p
'ke?e -- 'ke?e -- "?txa?ar '?e?e -- '?e"li 'nia
-- '?e?e -- ."tia?a '?a'xa"na 'ta"mar +

1079 + '?e?e -- ,'?a"ka 'ia"ni 'u'?kah
"tio?p + 'ke?e -- 'ke?e -- ,'lo'ke?e'?a"ian + ,
'ko"ne?er + ,"to?or "mun 'do + 'ka'ui"ra '?e?e
-- ,'?e"?kahk 'lo'ke?e'a"ian 'ta'me?e'txi'na
"mo?p + .'i'ka"ian 'iŋ'guah"tio?p + ,"ke?e + ,
"ha?ax '?e"dios + '?u?u -- '?u'iah"?ku '?u?u --
'?u"ia 'hu?u -- ,'?u'sen"ti 'do'?e"hen 'te +
"to?o 're?e -- ."to?o 're"rum 'ta"ra + 'ko"txa
'tua?a -- ,'u"txo?p + ,"por 'ke?e"tia?a 'tu"ru
'?e"dios + ."?pan + ,'?i?i'po"re 'so + 'txe?e
"no?p 'ke?e -- '?e?e -- '?e'lu"se 'ra'lo'ke?e --
,'ka'ui"ra 'ta'mu?ut 'e"?kin + "txe 'ke?e --
'?e?e -- 'txe?e"no?p 'ke?e -- ."lus '?e"lek 'tri
'ka + 1110 + "por 'ke?e -- .'txi"nam +

1112 + "pe 'ro?o -- 'ma?a"txi 'ka'na?a"ta
'hai -- .'ko'txe?e"ra + 1115 + ,"pe 'ro'ha?a
"xo?p + ."?pan 'u'?kah"tio?p +

26. Earth, Sky and Water

1 I am going to tell a story which I heard told long ago. 6 The old people used to tell that the world where we live, they said that under the -- world which we live on, farther down, they say that there is just water.

21 And they say that under the -- water, what there is is another -- place. 28 Like here. 30 And they say that that place there is filled with all the people -- called evil.

36 And they say -- they say that that place is the home of the evil ones. 42 Because they say that that place is just like a town, that is large and filled with many people, but they say that they are evil. 53 They -- they say that -- the evil are -- different people.

60 They say that when the sun sets here, and the night grows dark, they say that in that place, the -- Our Father is passing. 69 There it is growing light, and things are becoming visible. 71 And here it is dark. 72 And they say that when the sun passes through that place, over the heads of those men, that it -- is stronger -- its heat.

82 And they say that those people don't know what to do because of the heat of -- the sun. 88 They think that -- there is another sun below where it passes, the sun. 97 Because so they tell it, that -- there is another place, and that it is below -- under the earth where we live, and there passes the sun when it is -- dark here.

109 Well, we think that there is another sky below. 112 And they say that that place is one with the place called -- Hell. 119 Because they say that the place which is called Hell,

that there go all those who have committed sins, all -- who have committed them. 127 All who know how to curse, who have killed, who have chopped, -- who -- have made sport of their fellows, who have thought lies and all sins, they say they alone go to fill up that place. 145 They say that that is the place, Hell, where there is a fire lit, and that it doesn't -- go out. 149 They say that there go all who die.

152 But their beliefs about the place, Hell, are not all the same. 159 Because they say -- there are those who say that some who die, in a year the angels come to take them out of that fire. 172 And there are some who say that it is a resting-place from which there is never an exit, for those who die who have sinned greatly, because they say that the -- there is a -- there is another place, where those who were killed come, and those who died in water, those who fell from tree-branches, those who fell into caves, they say the place where they stay is separate. 195 Because they say that they did not meet an ordinary death, and that the place where they stay is separate. 199 They say that -- they say that that place is where all the people who were sinners stay.

208 They say that -- there is a belief of theirs. 212 They say that when the man dies who kills or if he has chopped, when he comes there he is shown the head of the man whom he killed, or if he chopped they say that he is shown the blood which he drew; he is shown it when he arrives.

230 And they say that -- there are some -- who know how -- who hurt their friends so they die; they say that there are those who -- die by -- what their friends do, who are witches, 243

26. Earth, Sky and Water

they say that when they die, those men who die, when hurt by men on earth here, they say that there they go to rest, among the evil ones there. 257 And when they arrive, on the day they die, who hurt, then they come. 262 Those whom they killed are taken out. 266 So they still believe.

267 And they say that those who know how to hurt or -- are like what we call -- witches, they say that when they die, they are tied over the fire, and -- there they hang, for all time, and that there is never a payment for all they have done. 284 They say that there they hang, with smoke in their eyes. 286 From the fire where they are hanging. 288 They say that those who know how to tell lies, there they hang over the fire, and their tongues are roasted by the fire. 295 So they still believe.

297 Because they say that a great sea is under the world. 303 There is the white sea, and there is a red sea. 307 They say that there is a sea like milk, that -- they say that we float on a sea.

319 And that is why they used to say that the -- if -- the world which we live in would be made to flex suddenly, and go into the water, and we would be finished. 331 Because they say that there is just water under the earth. 334 And over the water we are floating.

337 Because they say that where the edge of the world remains, which we live on, and at the edge, they say, there is just water -- which is called -- the sea of tar. 350 Because they say that it is the sea of tar because they say that there -- there they join, the edge of the world and sky. 356 And there nobody goes, nei-

ther ships nor planes can go there.

363 Because they say that at the edge of the world at the edge of the sea, there live the angels. 368 And they say that if any of -- one of -- the earth-dwelling people comes there, that he is immediately struck with lightning by the angels, and they bring it down if a plane is coming, because they say that there is sealed heaven, which we call the sky, 386 and the earth. 389 Because they say that the world an- the sky are like -- like -- the back of a wasp, coming together at a joint.

399 So -- they say that the world is thus, that -- that -- the sky, above, which we see here, they say it is mountains. 408 Green. 409 And farther up, to -- they say that beyond the heavens above, that there is a place. 418 There is a place, a town like -- just like we see here; they say that there live all who die here and that there they go to live in that place. 433 And farther up there is another place, that there live the gods.

439 That is why long ago when there were those who prayed to God, they said, "Where you are standing, where you live beyond the heavens" because they believed that the sky which we see above is not the dwelling-place of God, but that the dwelling-place of God is farther up. 460 And that is why they thought thus, that below there is another place, below. 471 And there is a sea.

472 And they say that where -- where the sky is joined to the world which we live in, and where everything is we know; that -- that -- the world joins together. They used to tell that Our Father God, he lives way beyond the sky a-

bove, and it is caught by him; all the places, the sea, and they say that -- the world where we live, here, they say that -- it is held by the sole of his foot, and that is why they say that if it flexes, that the world will immediately be flattened with us, and we will be destroyed.

518 Because they say that the world is just floating with us, like foam floats on the water when we are cooking, and we are just floating, rippling on the water; they say that so too the world is just floating, rippling with us, and held by Our Father God with his foot. 535 And that if he makes it flex with us, then immediately this world -- that immediately this world will be consumed with us, and the water will rise over the earth, until it becomes sea all over this earth we see.

547 They say that the -- sea of tar which we know where the sky is put together with the world, they say it glistens beautifully. 554 That is why they say it is just like a -- some say that it is the sea of tar and some say it is the crystal sea. 561 Because they say that its surface glistens beautifully.

564 And they used to tell of the -- wind, the dry wind which blows over the earth here. 572 And -- it doesn't rise to a very high altitude. 580 They say that farther above there is another wind which blows, that it does not let the wind which blows here over the earth, it does not let it pass above. 588 Because they say that the wind which blows here is -- bad. 594 They say that it is not -- sacred. 598 Because the wind here blows everything over the earth -- the -- the -- whatever thing is on the earth, and everything bad that there is on the earth is blown by it. 612 But they say that

the wind which lies farther up is not -- is not -- does not let the evil pass above. 621 And they say that farther up, there is another wind lying, that that -- that wind is called the sacred wind, because there is no evil in it.

634 Well, so their beliefs continue. 636 Because they say that the wind which lies in the sky is called the sacred wind, and there is no evil in it. 646 Because they say that it, the wind that lies above, they say that the sky is supported by it.

656 And they say that the wind which lies above, where -- it is stuck -- which is stuck to the sky, 666 that it cuts off the fire of the sky. 671 Because they say that -- that if it weren't for that wind, that this world would be burned up by the fires of the sky, which pass above. Because they say that the sun, which we see above, is fire. 682 And if there were not that wind to -- to -- cut it off, then the world would burn up. 687 So they used to tell it.

688 That is why the wind which blows down here, and which -- there is no time that -- it does not, because they say that the wind which blows here is a great shelter, 697 and that it was left by God to blow in front of us, and to cool the earth, so that it does not catch fire, and so that -- mankind does not die from the fires of the sky. 709 That is why they say that the dry wind which lies blowing here, at no time does it go away. 713 Because they say that the dry wind lies separate all the time, separate from the wind which comes with the rain.

717 The wind which comes with the rain, it is the protection of the one which -- brings the

rain, which is raised up by the angels into the sky. 721 But the dry wind which lies all the time, they say it is so it blows on us, so we are not burned by the fires of the sky. 730 So they used to tell it.

731 They say that long ago, it was known that the world was destroyed, with mankind. 736 Because they say that there was an angel, and they say that the angel did not obey his father, who is Our Father; they say that that angel, he wanted to cause a quake -- because they say that there -- there are some who tell that there were the braces of the world, or its corner-posts.

759 They say that that angel, when he decided to shake the corner-posts of the world, then they say that the world immediately went into the -- water, and all the world with the human beings was engulfed. 777 They say that long ago, it is known that the world was destroyed.

781 But they say that one time, when Our Father God was tired, here and there he formed the world, with mankind. 795 Then when God saw that -- he destroyed it, and destroyed mankind, (God) said to them, "You do not leave the human beings, whom I have raised. 808 And that -- I formed on the earth, where they are living. And you, you flooded them everywhere. Now fix them up, since you had the power to -- destroy them, so you have the power to fix them up."

829 They say that those angels got up, and that they hardly knew what they were doing; they went and got earth, and poured it on the water, and they say that that earth fell and fell, and dissolved, and went into the water, and nothing appeared where it was going. 846 And they were

berated by Our Father God; he said to them, "What is this? You have the power to destroy, but to make again, this you cannot do!" Then they say that there came another angel, whose name was San Raimundo.

861 The Angel San Reimundo went, and took a little earth, and dropped it on the water. 868 And they say that as that earth fell on the water, it swirled all over the water, and the water was covered over by it, and it immediately began to harden like foam on the water. 882 They say that it went on floating on the water, until it thickened all the water of the sea; the world came back again and the people increased upon it; they say that from that day, the world has no longer been destroyed again, with mankind. 899 And that is why they say that today there are many people, because the world has not been destroyed now.

902 They say that that destroyer of people, some of those he destroyed turned completely into fish. 908 They say that fish -- fish appeared because people were destroyed everywhere, and those people who were destroyed -- and the world with them, were covered by the water, and became fish. 925 So people used to tell long ago, that the fish were people.

929 There was not just one thing the people used to tell long ago, about how it was in the -- sky and -- the earth. 939 There were some who used to tell that the -- corners of the world -- had corner-posts. 952 And they say that at those corner-posts were angels standing, holding them. 958 They say that when they shook the corner-posts of the world, then it quaked all over the earth because they believed it long ago, that so it used to happen from time

to time, the shaking; they believed that those angels shook the corner-posts of the world, and that they were going to destroy it.

983 But they were not given permission by Our Father God above to -- destroy it. 988 But they say that they were tired, standing there, holding on to them. 992 And they wanted to destroy it. 994 But they were not given permission by Our Father God to destroy it. 996 Because they say that Our Father God loves us, the human beings, and will not destroy us.

1001 There was another little old man who began to tell that -- he just had one story -- he would tell that he had heard tell long ago, 1010 that the world here that we live on, that it lies, and curves around; they say that when it is dark here, they say that the sun above, passes underneath. 1024 And in that world it rises. 1027 And when the world here -- it passes below, then we see the sun above. 1033 And when the sun -- above is passing below, and we -- and we -- and we they say live above.

1044 He began to be asked, "How come we don't feel it when we are turned over?" 1048 He used to say, "How are we going to feel that we are sinning? We don't know! 1052 And such is the power of God over us. And that is why we don't know when we are turned upside down." So he used to tell them.

1057 Some used to say that the world is turning with us. 1060 There was not just one thing they used to tell. 1063 They used to tell that the sun which passes above is like a -- train, which we see now, with -- a light. 1073 They say that the line lies there where it goes.

26. Earth, Sky and Water

1079 They used to tell that -- what there is today in the world we see -- the lights there are in the towns, that it was God who -- gave to -- the -- people on this earth the knowledge to make them, because where God lives, so it is, and that is why they say that the lights we see in the sky, they say that they are electric lights. 1110 Because it is a town.

1112 But we don't know if -- that is how it is. 1115 But they, so they told it.

27. Rainy Season

1 + .'e'?ir'se"iah 'ta'ma'e'?kax'ha?a"?kin
+

2 + ,'ti"ko?oit "no?on + .'a"ian 'in"te?e
'ir'se"iah 'ta"ma 'e"?kin 'ie?e"lu 'na + .'ie?e
"rue 'de'xe?e'a"?txa?an 'tu?ut'e"?kin + 5 + ,
'ta'me?e'lu"gar 'tia?a'tu"re?en + .'a"ian 'txa?a
"te?e 'ui"tsir "ua?ar + 7 + .'in"te?e 'u'?ka
"?pa?a 'bol"kan + .'in"te?e 'u'?ka"?pa?a 'nia
"rar + 9 + .'e'ui"tsir 'ia"ha?a "mei 'gra +
10 + ,"ha?ax 'e"ra 'a?a'ro?p"na 'ta'txuk"ti?i +

11 + ,'e"?kin 'xe?e'a'nu"mui 'ti"txan + .
'?pa"nix 'ka'na?a"ta 'ke?e'tu?u"pat 'e'ui'tsi
"ro?p 'ia"ha?a 'a'txek"ta 'ua"tar + 13 + .'ka
'ui"ra 'a'lo"?koi 'ta"mo?or 'e'ui"tsir + 14 +
,'ta'me?e"ne 'ro + ,'he"bre 'ro + ,"mar 'so + .
'ka'ui"ra 'a'txek"ta 'ua"tar 'tu?u'?pi'sa"rir 'e
'ui"tsir 'bol"kan + 19 + .'?i'?a'nam"?tsa
'tu?u'?pi'sa"rir "o?or 'e'ui"tsir 'mo'riuh
"?tsu?u?p +

20 + .'i'ta'mia?a"bril 'ua"rix 'a"ka?ai 'u
'ui"si 'u"?pi?ir + .'ko"nix 'ka'ui"ra 'in"te?eix
"la 'do'a'to"?poi + 22 + ,'en"ton 'ses + .
'ma?a"txi?ix 'a'nam"?tsa 'tu?u'?pi'sa"rir "o?or
'e'ui"tsir 'mo'riuh"?tsu?u?p + 24 + .'tu?u
'?tehr'ta'rix"to 'a'nu"mui "ia?a + 25 + ,'in
'te?er"ti?i 'e'me"so?p 'ia"ha?a + ,'ia?a"bril
"ma 'io + ."uar 'u'ui"si 'u"?pi?ir +

28 + ,'ko"nix 'ka'ui"ra + .'ke'?ka"nix 'a
'?ko"toi 'tu?u'?pi'sa"rer 'e'ui"tsir 'nia"rar +
30 + .'ka'ua?a"re 'ke'?ka"nix 'o?o"txoi 'e'?kax
'ha?a"?kin + 31 + ,"pe 'ro'kon'da'in'nah"to +
,'tua?a'a'?ko"toi 'tu?u'?pi'sa"rer 'e'ui"tsir
'nia"rar + .'e?ex'na"to 'e'be"ra 'no +

34 + ,"por 'ke?e'ta'me?e"hu 'nio + ,'e"hu
'lio'a"gos 'to'sep"tiem 'bre + ,'ke?e"ha?ax 'e

27. Rainy Season

'me"so?p 'ia"ha?a + ,'ka'ui"ra 'ke?e'u'lo "?ki?i?p 'e"?kin + ."ia?a 'txek"ta + ,'tu?u'?pi 'sa"rir "o?or 'e'ui"tsir 'ia"ha?a + .'nia"rar + 43 + ."ia 'ka'ui"ra?a 'to"?poi + 44 + ,'kon "da 'a'nam"?tsa + .'ka'ui"ra?a 'nam"?tsa "to?or 'e'ui"tsir 'xin'xi"ra?a + 46 + ,'kon'da"?kix 'a'lo"?koi + ,'e'?kax'ha?a"?kin + .'a"ka?ai 'a 'sut"pa 'tu?u'?poh'pi"rer 'u'?pi?ir +

49 + ,'a"ian 'o'tron"te?e 'ir'se"iah + . 'ta'ma'e"lu 'na + 51 + ,'ta'me?e'?kax'ha?a "?kin + ,"kon 'da'ma?a"txi "uar 'a'?ka"xi 'e 'ha"ha?ar 'ie?e'hi'na"ho?p "uar 'a'ta"ki + .'u "me 'ne'be"ra 'no + 54 + ,"pe 'ro'e"lu 'na'u 'uir"sio?on 'e'?ir'se"iah "kon 'da'?ka"nix 'a'nu "mui + .'o?o"kon 'da'a'sut"pa 'ua"tar + 56 + , "kon 'da'e"lu 'na'a'?txu"uan 'xir"koht + ,'i'?pa "nix 'o?o'ioh"?ki 'ka'ui"ra + ,'en"ton 'ses'ka 'ua?a"re + .'u'ta"res 'e'ha"ha?ar 'e"lu 'na +

60 + ,'ia"iam "be 'ses'a'?ka"xi 'e"di "io?p 'ia"ha?a + ,'i"kon 'da"ma 'tu"?ka 'e'?ir 'se"iah 'u'ta"res + ."kon 'da'a'sut"pa 'ka'tur "?pa "kuen 'ta + .'kon'da'a'?petx"?ka + 64 + , "por 'ke?e"kon 'da'a'?petx"?ka + ,'a'?ka"xi "to?or 'e'ui"tsir + .'a'xir'koh"tran + 67 + , 'i'ta"ma 'u'?teh"rir 'a'?txu"uan + .'?pa"nix 'ko 'txe?e'to"kar + 69 + ,'txi"?kih 'txi"?kih + , 'ta'ka'e'txak"txak + .'ko"txia?ax 'e'txu"ruhp 'in'ta"ka '?txi?i"?txu?ut + 72 + ,'ie?e"lu 'na 'ia"ha?a + ,"kon 'da'a'xir'koh"tran + .'?pa"nix 'ko'txe?e'o?o'ioh"?ki +

75 + ,'en"ton 'ses'ka'ua?a"re + .'ke?e'?ka "ni 'u'txe?e"sian 'ha"ha?ar + 77 + ,'i'kon'da 'ix"to 'a?a"uan 'e"sian 'ha"ha?ar + .'nie"nix '?e?ei"ri + 79 + ,"kon 'da'a?an'?txak"na + ,'a 'txa'koh"pa "u?ut 'e"?kin + .'tu?u'ta'ri"?pir 'e "?kin + 82 + ,"kon 'da"uar 'a'tih"?pi 'e"?kin "to?or 'e'ui"tsir + ,'tia?a"uar 'ua"tar 'u'ua'ra

27. Rainy Season

"rir + .'in'iah"rer 'a'?txi?itx"ran "u?ut 'e
"?kin + 85 + ,"kon 'da'a'txek"ta 'u'?teh"rir
"to?or 'e'ui"tsir 'i'?pan"to "ia?a "o 'tro"di
'ia + ,"kon 'da'ix"to 'a'ke'tru"ma 'e'ha"ha?ar +
,'nu"men "di 'ia + .'ma?a"txi 'a'?ka"xi +

89 + ,'en"ton 'ses'u'su"ti + .'e"sia?an
'ta"kin 'i"?kar + .'ah"?kin 'ah"?kin + 92 + ,
'ia"?txa?an 'e"sia?an 'txak"txak 'to"kar + .'ta
"mu?ut 'e"?kin + 94 + .'u'ua"iu?u "?pa?a "xin
"to?or 'e'ui'tsi"ro?p + 95 + .'u'txu?u"?pa 'ko
'txe?e"txih + 96 + 'i'ta'ma'rix"to 'txe?e"hen
'te + .'txih'to"kar + 98 + ,'txe?e"no?p 'ke?e
'e'to"kar 'ia"ha?a + .'a'hua?a"?kin + 100 + ,
'ma?a"txi 'u'iak"ta 'a'?ke"?ko 'e'to"kar "to?or
'e'ui"tsir + ,'xe?e'to"kar 'xe?e'u'ta"res 'e'ha
"ha?ar + ,"por 'ke"txe 'ke?e'txak"txak 'to'ka
"ro?p 'ia"ha?a + .'ah'ua?a"?kin + 104 + ,'i
"ha?ax + .'ma?a"txi 'u'iak"ta 'a'?ka"xi 'e'ha
"ha?ar +

106 + ,'ie?e"sia?a 'ni"?kar + 'a"?txa?an
"kon 'da?a"xi 'e"tar 'de + ."ma "ha?ax 'ko?o"ra
'ta"ka + 109 + ,'ie?e'mak"txan + ,'xe'a
"?txa?an + ,'ko"ra 'ko"ra + .'a?atx"pa + ,"por
'ke"txe 'ke?e'mak"txan + .'ma?a"txi 'u'iak"ta 'a
'?ka"xi 'e'ha"ha?ar + 115 + ,"kon 'da'a'?txu
"uan 'e'to"kar + ,"to?or 'e'ui'tsi"ro?p + .'xe?e
"tua?a 'u'ta'ri"?pir 'e'ha"ha?ar + ,'ie?e'mak
"txan 'ia"ha?a + ,'u'xo"tu?ut + ."ia "?txa?an 'e
"sia?an 'ta"?kin 'i"?kar + 121 + ,'uar"xix 'ka
'ui"ra + ,'a'sat"pa 'e'to'ka"ro?p 'ia"ha?a 'xe?e
"tua?a 'u'iak"ta 'e'ha"ha?ar + .'a'?ka"xi +

124 + ,'e?en"te?e 'ir'se"iah + ,'xe?e'ka
'ui"ra + ,"kon 'da'e"?ar 'ko'xe?e'a"?txa?an
'tu?ut 'e"?kin + .'e"?ar 'ko'ia"ha?a 'a'xa"na +
128 + ,"kon 'da?a'nam"?tsa "to?or 'e'ui"tsir +
."tia?a 'a'nam"?tsa 'e"?kin + .'ka'ua?a"re 'ke?e
'u'?ka"ni 'e'be"ra 'no + 131 + ,"pe 'ro"kon

27. Rainy Season

'da'e"?ar 'ko'ia"ha?a + ,'a?an'?txak"na "to?or 'e'ui"tsir "tia?a 'to"?poi 'e"?kin + ,'en"ton 'ses + .'ka'ua?a"re 'ke?e'u'?ka"ni 'e'ha"ha?ar + 135 + ,'ie?e"?ar 'ko'ia"ha?a + .'?pa"nix 'ko 'txe?e'?a'?txi"ri?i +

137 + ."?o 'tron"te?e 'ir'se"iah 'xe?e'ka 'ui"ra + 138 + ,'a"iam "be 'ses + ,'a'?ka"xi 'e'to"kar + .'ta'me?e'xu"kur + 141 + 'u'?puhk "se 'tu"no?or 'e'lu"gar + 142 + ."ua?ar 'in "te?e "pe 'nia + ,'u'?ka"?pa?a 'pe"li 'io + 144 + .'a'?puhk'se"na 'u"me 'ne'to"kar + 145 + .'u 'xi"?txi 'u"?pa 'ta"ma 'tu"no?or 'u"uam 'e'koh "no?p + 146 + .'?pa"nix 'ke?e"uar 'u'ieh"?tsu 'tua?a'?ka"xi 'e'ha"ha?ar + .'ka"tsa?ai 'ka'ui "ra +

148 + ,'i"kon 'da'ko?oi"?pi 'a'?kai"iui 'e 'ua"ko?o + .'ka'ua?a"re + ,'a?a"ru 'e'ua"ko?o + .'ha"ha?ar 'u'?ka"ni + 152 + ,"por 'ke?e'ua "ko?o 'ia"ha?a + .'ha"ha?ar "uar 'u'peh"ka + 154 + ,"por 'ke"txe 'ke?e'ua"ko?o + .'pa"gri 'no + ,"o?o + .'ah"pehk 'ha"ha?ar + 158 + , 'ie?e'mu"to?p + ,'ko"ra 'ko"ra + 'a'?tso?o?k "no?o?p + ,"tuam "kohn + ,"ti?ik "ti?ik + .'tu?u '?ka?p"tio?o?p + 164 + ,"pe 'ro"kon 'da'ka'ui "ra + ,'a"?txa?an 'e"?pu?ts 'ma"iui + ,'ta"ma 'e 'lu"gar + .'ka'na?a"ta 'ke?e'?ka"ni 'u"txe 'e'be "ra 'no + 168 + ,'ie?e'to"kar + ,'ta"ma "u?ut 'e"?kin + .'a?ah"ni "mei 'ra +

171 + ,'e"?o 'ra'xe?e"uar 'a'?ka"xi 'e'ha "ha?ar + ,"hai 'de"di 'ia + .'?i'e?e"ron 'e"?kin + ,'?i'?a?a"?tso 'ta'ta'ki"nar + ,'tia?a'ma?a "txi "uar 'a'?ka"xi 'e'ha"ha?ar + 176 + ,"?i 'e?eh"?pi 'tia?a'e?e"ron 'e"?kin + .'ka'ua?a"re 'ke'?ka"ni 'a?a"xin 'e'ha"ha?ar + .'i'?ka"nu?u "txe?e 'be"ra 'no + 179 + ,'ie?e'mak"txan + . "tia?a 'ma"tia?a + ,'a?atx"pa + .'ta'me?e'lu'ga "ro?p + 183 + '?i'?a"?txa?an + ,'e"sia?an 'su

27. Rainy Season

"tut 'ia"?kar + ,'ie?e"sia?an 'txak"txak 'to"kar + ,'ko"ra 'ko"ra?ah "ni + .'ta"mo?or 'e'ui'tsi "ro?p +

27. Rainy Season

1 The signs of the rainy season.

2 For us, there is a sign from the sun and the moon and the wheel which hangs in the sky. 5 In the place where I live there stand two peaks. 7 One is named Volcano and one is named Niarar. 9 That mountain is large. 10 It is the one called Ta Txuktii.

11 The sun which passes above, we know that it comes into view from behind those mountains. 13 We see it come out over the mountain. 14 In January, February, and March, we see it appear in the direction of the mountain Volcano. 19 And it sets in the direction of the mountain Moriuh?tsu?p.

20 And in April it is already beginning to change its path. Soon we see it is already rising to one side. 22 Then it no longer sets in the direction of the peak of Moriuh?tsu?p. 24 It is already passing along the side of it. All during the months of April and May it is changing its path.

28 Next we see that it is going to come into line with the peak of Niarar. 30 We say the rainy season is about to set in. 31 But so long as it remains distant from lining up with the peak of Niarar, the drought continues.

34 Because in June, July, August, and September, those rainy-season months, all those months, the sunrise appears there, in the direction of that peak, Niarar. 43 There we see it come up. 44 When it sets, we see it set over the mountain of Xinxiraa. 46 When the rainy season is going away, it begins to turn back to its usual path.

27. Rainy Season

49 There is another sign, from the moon. 51 In the rainy season, when the rain is not falling and the shoots are drying up because of the drought. 54 But the moon shows us the sign when it is about to pass, or when it is coming back. 56 When the moon floats turned over, and we see it seem to ripple, then we say, "The moon is bringing the rain."

60 And there are times when it falls that same day. And when the sign brings nothing, we keep count when the moon comes back, when it grows full. 64 Because when it grows full, it goes down over the mountain and turns downward. 67 And on its side it lies, like a cloud. 69 It is mixed with red, as if the waters of the sky were mixed with blood. 72 And when it has turned, it is just as if it ripples, the moon then.

75 Then we say that it is going to cause the heavy rains. 77 And then there are the heavy rains, which do not stop. 79 When it grows light, the sky reddens where the sun comes up. 82 When the sun comes out over the mountain, where its beams are falling, then the sky reddens completely. 85 When it appears to one side over the mountain, and it is already another day, then the rain holds back, and during the day it doesn't fall.

89 Then the strong, dry wind comes back, day after day. 92 The big red clouds lie there in the sky. 94 They stretch out over the mountains. 95 They take shapes like horses. 96 And because of that people say they are "horse clouds". 98 They say that those clouds are lords of the sky. 100 They do not let the clouds take shape over the peaks -- the clouds which bring the rain -- because it is said that

those red clouds are lords of the sky. 104 And they do not allow the rain to fall.

106 And the big winds come up as the afternoon goes, and not just a little. 109 And the rainbows which lie scattered around come out, because it is said that the rainbow does not let the rain fall. 115 When the clouds are floating over the mountains -- those which are the bringers of rain -- the rainbow bars them. There stay the strong, dry winds. 121 At once we see those clouds destroyed which were to bring the rain falling.

124 One sign we see when the arc which lies in the sky, that arc moves. When it sets behind the mountain where the sun sets, we say that there is going to be drought. 131 But when that arc comes up behind the mountain where the sun rises, then we say that there is going to be rain. 135 And that arc, it is as if it gleams.

137 There is another sign which we see. 138 There are times when the clouds fall onto the streams. 141 They cover every place. 142 There is a rock whose name is Pelillo. 144 It is covered by clouds. 145 They stretch along all the watercourses. 146 It is as if it were trying to rain, and we are glad to see it.

148 And when we hear the *waco* singing, we say, "The *waco* is calling. It is going to rain." 152 Because that *waco* is calling for rain. 154 Because it is said that the *waco* is a *padrino*, or a rain-maker. 158 And the birds, here and there, burst out, in the stream beds, everywhere, in the tree-branches. 164 But when we see the smoke-haze lying over the place, we know it is going to be a drought. 168 And

the clouds in the sky run fast.

171 At the time when the rain is falling, if it is during the day, and the sun shows, and shines where it is dry, and the rain is not falling, 176 and there is lightning where the sun shows, we say that the rain is going to go away, and there is going to be a drought. 179 And the rainbows here and there rise up in the villages. 183 And the big whirlwinds come, and the big red clouds run everywhere over the mountains.

28. Rainmaking

1 + '?ka"ni?in 'txe'kon"tar 'u?u -- 'ko
"txe '?u?u -- ,'a'?kah'pes"ian + ,'e'pa"gri 'no
+ ,'kon'da"uar + .'u'peh"ka '?e'ha"ha?ar + 7 +
,'?pah"xan + 'e?e -- 'u"txe 'man -- ,"dar + ,'a
'txe?e"na + 'in -- ,'in"te?e + ,'ra"ma 'da + .
'ko'txe'?u'ta"rer 'iŋ"gohr 'o"tot + 16 + 'n --
'nah"tir + ,'io?o"tot +

19 + ,'?i'kon'da'?o?os"ta + 'e?e -- ,'u
"txe 'man"dar + '?a?a -- ,'?a'ua?a?p"na + 'ux
"te?e -- ,"krus + ,'u'txe'man"dar + 'a?a -- ,'a
'txe?e"na?a 'dor"nar + ,'ta"ka 'e"?kom + '?ie?e
-- ,'?e'kan"de 'la + .'?pah"xan + 33 + 'e?e --
,'?u'tu'ru"?pa + ,'txa'txa?a"te?e '?e'ui'ni"ko?p
+ ,'a"ka 'da'?al"de 'ia + 'e?e -- "txe 'ke?e --
,'?e'ui'ni"ko?p 'ia"ha?a + .'sa'kum'?pi"ro?p
'tua?a'?e'pa"gri 'no + 41 + ,'ie?e'sa'kum'?pi
"ro?p 'ia"ha?a + ,'a'xa"na '?u'mo'roh"sio?p 'e
'tu"min + '?e?e -- ,'?e"nar + ,'ia?a"?katx + ,'e
'txum"pi?i + ,'?e'?uh"?tsu?u?p + .'ta'ma'tu
"no?or '?e'ial"dee "io?p +

49 + ,'?i'po"re 'so + ,'ta'ma'tu"no?or
'?ial"de 'ia + ,'u'tu'ru"?pa + '?e?e -- 'txa
'txa?a"te?e -- 'sa'kum'?pi"ro?p + .'tua?a"ha?ax
'?u'mo'roh"sio?p 'tu"no?or 'lo'ke'tua?a'?kam"pa
+ 56 + '?i"kon 'da?a -- '?a?a -- .'?e'sa'kum
"?pi"ro?p 'ia"ha?a 'a'?ko"tuo?p 'ta'ke?e'tu"min
+ 'tu"no?or 'lo'ke?e -- ,'u'mo'roh"si "io?p
'te?e -- '?al"de 'ia + ,'a'?ko"toi + '?a?a -- .
'?a?ak'ta"na 'tu?u'io"tot +

65 + ,'?en"ton 'ses + ,'?u'tu'ru"?pa '?e
"di 'ia + .'ke'tu"?ka "di 'ia'tua?a'noh'?ki
"nio?p + 67 + ,'i'e'sa'kum'?pi"ro?p 'ia"ha?a
+ ,'?a?a'xi"no?p + '?e?e -- ,'u'pa"?kio?p 'iuh
"?tsu?u?p + '?e?e -- 'tu"no?or 'lo'ke?e -- ,
"tua?a 'u'?kam'pe"so?p + .'u"txo?p 'a'dor"nar +

75 + ,'?i"kon 'da'ix"to + .'tu"ri?ix + ,

28. Rainmaking

'tu"no?or 'lo'ke?e'?ka"ni 'u'?kam'pe"so?p + 78 + '?en"ton 'ses'?a?a"xin 'a'pehk"na 'tia?a -- . 'ma"kar 'tu"ru 'tu?u'io"tot + 80 + "por 'ke?e -- .'?e'pa"gri 'no'ia"ha?a + ,'u'?kah"na?ar 'u 'tu'ru"?pa '?u"di 'ia + ."?es 'to'ta'ma"?o 'txo "di 'ia + 84 + '?u'ia?a"re 'e'sa'kum'?pi"ro?p 'ke?e -- 'e?e -- 'ke?e -- ."tal "di 'ia'ka'noh '?ki"ni + 88 + ,'i'ha?a"xir + 'u'ma"ki 'u "?pa?a "?txa?an 'tu?u'io"tot + ,'u'?pah"ner + , "por 'ke"txe 'ke"uar + .'u'koh"ko 'u"?pa +

93 + "por 'ke?e -- 'txe?e"no?p 'ke"ia 'he?e -- ,'?e'pa"gri 'no'ia"ha?a + "kon 'do -- 'tua?a'?o?o"hron 'ta'ke?e -- 'e?e -- ,"dios 'i'e 'an'he"lo?p + 'e'u'?ka"ni 'ke?e -- ,'ha?a"xir + 'e?e -- .'u'koh"ko 'u"?pa + 104 + 'e?e -- , '?a?a"ti + '?a?a -- ,'ah"?kin 'ah"?kin + .'?a?a "ti + 'tua?a -- "txe 'ke?e -- '?e?e -- 'ma?a"txi 'a?a -- 'a'puhk"tu?ut "kon 'de"uar '?o?o"hron 'ta'ke?e -- .'?e'dio"so?p + 115 + .'u'koh"ko 'u"?pa 'es"to 'ta'ma"o 'txo"di 'ia +

116 + 'tua?a -- '?e?e -- .'?a'?kah'pes"ian + "kon 'de?e -- 'u'?kah"ies 'u'ia'hu?u -- ,'?u '?kah'pes"iah + ."txe + 123 + ,'?e'sa'kum'?pi "rox + ,'ko"ne?er + '?e?e -- 'e"?o 'ra'tua?a -- 'ka'?kah'pes"ian 'tu?ut'?e?e -- ,'?e"?aŋ 'he "lo?p + ,'mo'roh'se"nik 'i"?pa 'ta"ra + '?i'?u 'mo'roh"se + .'ko?o"ra '?pi'?kit 'max"tak + 132 + ,'?e'?pi"?kit 'max"tak 'ia"ha?a + ,"txe 'ke "ha?ax + '?e"ia 'he?e -- .'?an'xe"ro?p + 136 + ,'a"ka?ai + .'?a'?kah'pe"sian + ,'u'uo"?pi 'u "hor 'ta'man"te?e + 'ia"ha?a -- ,"blaŋ 'ko"tra 'po + .'u'uo"?pi 'u"hor 'a'tu"ruan + 142 + 'ie?e -- ,'sa'kum'?pi"ro?p 'u"?pan + ,'u'?puhk "se 'u"?po?p + 'ta'man"te?e -- 'e"tra 'po -- , "blaŋ 'ko + ,'u'uo"?pi 'u"hor 'u"?po?o?p + 'e?e -- .'tu'no?o"ro?p + 151 + ,'tua?a'a'tur'ua "no?p + ,'tu?u'ieh"?tser + '?e"ia 'he?e -- .'?e 'pa"gri 'no +

28. Rainmaking

155 + ,'en"ton 'ses + ,'?e'pa"gri 'no + . 'a"ka?ai 'a'?kah'pe"sian + 158 + .'i"txe + 159 + '?e?e -- ,'ko"ne?er + .'?e"di 'ia + 'lo 'ke?e -- 'ua?a -- ,'ua?a"ron + ,'i'tu"ro?oŋ 'uar 'ka'pe'tru"ma + ,'?ka"ni + ,'ka'?kah'pes"ian + ."to?oit +

169 + ,'?pah"xan + 'u?u -- '?u'ia?a"rio?p 'e"dios 'xe?e -- 'ka'ua?a"re '?e?e -- "nues 'tro?o -- ."pa 'gre?e"ter 'no + 175 + ,"ha?ax + .'u'peh"ka '?pah"xan + 177 + .'i"txe + ,'ke "ne?et + '?e?e -- ,'xe'?i'?ko'to"ri + ,'ta'ma 'tu"no?or + '?e?e -- ,'?e'ian'xe"ro?p + ,'ta'ma 'tu"no?or 'lo'ke'?a"ian + 'ta'ma'tu"no?or 'lo 'ke?e -- '?e?e -- .'a"ian "to?or 'e"rum + 188 + ,"ne?et 'i'?ko'to"ri + 189 + ,"por 'ke"ne?et '?a"txu?ut 'e"?kin + ,'?a"txe?e "rum + ,'ia"txe 'tu"no?or + .'lo'ke'ka'ui"ra + 193 + ,'i'ko "ne?er + "no?on 'ka?a -- ,'ka'peh"ke?et + 'ke "tua?a -- .'?a'ue?e?p"ta + 198 + '?a?a -- ,'?a 'uan'xe"ro?p + ,'?u'ue"?txe + '?e?e -- 'u'ue "?txe '?u?u -- ,'ben'di'sio"no?p + ,'ti"ko?or 'ta"ra + ,'por'ke"no?on -- 'ta"ra 'tu"ro?on "uar 'ka -- 'e?e -- ,"uar 'ka'num"se 'ka"?pa "mei 'gra + ,'ta'ke?e'ui?i"na?ar + 'ta'ke?e -- ,'ta 'ki?ih"ti?ir + .'por'ke"ma 'tu"?ka 'ka'tah"ui + 213 + 'i?i -- ,"ne?et + ,'?tsin"?tsa 'ka"ual 'ma + ,'a'ui"ro?on + 'ke?e -- ,'tia?a'tu"ro?on 'ta"ra + "uar 'ka?a -- ,"uar 'ka'num"se 'ka"?pa + ,'ta'ka"mei 'gra'e'ui?i"nar + .'por'ke"ma 'tu "?ka 'ka'ta"hui 'ka'?ku"xi + 223 + '?i?i -- , '?i'ko"ne?er + "no?on 'ka'ko?o -- 'ka?a -- ,'?a "ian "mei 'gra'ka'txuk"pa?ar + 'ta'ma'?e?e -- . '?e'ben'di"sion 'ta?a"?pa + 'ke?e'?e?e -- .'?eh "tan + 232 + '?e?e -- ,"ha?a 'xe"ran + 'e?e -- 'e"?o 'ra'lo'ke'tu"ro?on 'tia?a"uar 'kap -- .'ka'pe"ti 'ka"?pa + 237 + ,'ko?o"hron 'ta'ka "ret + .'?eh"tan + .'a?a'uan'xe"ro?p + .'ta"rik + 'tua?a -- ,'?u'?tsa?a"io?p + ,"to?or 'e"rum + ,'tia?a'tu"ro?on "uar 'ka'kohk"san + 'ta'ka?a --

28. Rainmaking

'e?e -- 'tu"no?or "ti?i 'ne?e -- "?txa?ar 'ie 'ru?u -- ,'hi'na"ho?p + ,"ua 'ra'ta"ki + .'u"me 'ne"?kin + 252 + .'por'ke"ma 'tu"?ka 'e"ha?a 'ta"mar +

253 + ,'i'ko"ne?er + 'e?e -- ,'tia?a'tu "ro?on 'ta"ra + ,"ua 'ra'ui"ra + 'ke?e -- , 'tia?a"uar + ,'u'sa"ti 'u"?pa + '?e?e -- ,'?e'pa "?ka?a?p + ,'?u'tu'ru"?po?p + ,'tu'?ki?k"xix + 'lo'ke?e -- '?e?e -- ,'u"txo?on 'ne'se'si"tar + '?i'ie?e -- ,'?e'pa"?ka?p + ,'?e'?al"de?e "io?p + .'ha?a"xo?p + ,"uar 'u'sa"ti 'u'?po?p + . 'tua?a'u'tu'ru"?po?p 'tu"no?or 'lo'ke'tu"ru 'ka 'nie"ner '?i"ra + 273 + 'i?i -- ,'ta"mar 'e"ra + '?a?a -- ,'tua?a'ni"?pir + ,'?i'ke'ta"mar + 'tua?a -- .'tua?a'?i'sut"pa '?a'ui"ro?on + 280 + ,'?ep"tan + ,'?a'uan'xe"ro?p 'ta"rik + ,"ha?a 'xe"ra + ,'?e'?o 'ra'tia?a'tu"ro?on 'ta'ri"ran + 'ke?e -- "no?on + .'?a"ian "mei 'gra'ka'txuk "pa?ar + ,'ta'ma + '?e?e -- ,'?e"ha?a + "por 'ke?e -- "ua 'ra'ui"ra 'ke?e -- '?e'pa"?ka?p 'ua 'ra?a -- '?a'txa"mai 'tu"ru 'u"me 'ne?e -- ,'?e 'ui?i"nar + '?i?i -- "tia?a -- ,"ma 'hai"te?e + ,'ie"ro?p 'e'?pi"?kit + ,"uar '?a?a"ruo?p + ,'u "me 'ne'ui?i"nar + ."por 'ke"ma 'tu"?ka '?u'ta "hui 'u'?ku"xo?p +

302 + 'i'in -- "ton 'ses + ,'?a"ka?ai + , 'u'peh"ka 'tu"no?or + '?e"ia 'he?e -- .'?e"?an 'he"lo?p + 308 + ,'?pah"xan 'u'peh"ka + 'e?e -- ."txe + 311 + '?e?e -- "?aŋ 'hel'saŋ'gab -- .'gab"riel + "aŋ 'hel"san 'to -- ,"san 'to'to "mas + 'e"?aŋ 'hel + '?e?e -- .'?e"san 'to'to "mas 'be"ron 'i'ko + 319 + 'i?i -- "?aŋ 'hel -- .'saŋ'mi"gel 'ar"kaŋ 'hel + 322 + ,"txe 'ke?e'saŋ'mi"gel 'ar"kaŋ 'hel + "ha?ax '?e?e -- '?a?a -- ,'a'?ko'to"ri + 'i"ha?ax '?u?u -- '?u?u -- ,'u'peh"ka 'tu"no?or + '?e?e -- ,'?u"iet 'an 'xe"rir + .'tua?a'?a?atx"pa '?a'lo"?koi 'ta"kar + 332 + .'en"ton 'ses + ,'kon'da'?ka?a"pa 'u

28. Rainmaking

'peh"ka + 'tu"no?or '?e'?aŋ'he"lo?p 'ia"ha?a 'lo
'ke?e"tua?a — ,'u'?ka"txe 'a'lo"?koi 'ta"kar +
'?a?a — ,'pat"na + 338 + ,'n"ton 'ses + 'u
'peh"ka '?e?e — ,'?e"san 'lo"ren 'so + ."txe +
342 + .'san'lo"ren 'so + 343 + ,"bar 'ba'de"o
'ro + ."bar 'ba'de"pla 'ta +

345 + '?e'ie?e — ,'san'lo"ren 'so'ia"ha?a
+ ,"ha?ax + '?e?e — ."kon 'da'?u'iu"?pi + '?a
'toht"na '?e?e — ,'?e'tam"bor 'u'me'ne'?an'xe
"ro?p + .'?en"ton 'ses'ha?a"xir '?a?atx"pa 'ua
"tar '?u'ui"ra + 353 + '?e?e — .'po"re 'so'?e
'pa"gri 'no"txe + '?e?e — ,"san + .'lo"ren 'so
+ .'ma'ma?a'?pi"ret 'te?e'?an'xe"ro?p + ,'?atx
"pe?en + 'ko"ne?er "la?ar + '?e?e — ,'?i'ra"non
+ 363 + ,'tia?a'tu"ro?on + ,"uar 'ka'txa"mai +
,'?u"me 'ne'ui?i"nar + 366 + 'tia?a'tu"ro?on
"uar 'ka — ,"no?on 'uar'ka"txe 'su"frir + .
'?atx"pe?en + 369 + ,'?i'?ta?a?p"sen + '?a'so
"brii "no?p + ,'ti"txan + ,'tua?a'u'ue"?txo?p 'e
'ben'di"sion 'ti"ko?or + '?e?e — .'ko"ne?e 're
"ra + 375 + 'por'ke?e"ma 'ta'ua"ton 'tua?a'ka
'ui"ra + ,"tan 'to'ui?i"nar 'lo'ke?e'?a"ian +
377 + ,'i"no?on "ma 'ta'ua"ron + ,'tia?a'tu
"ro?on "uar 'ka'txa"mai + .'?ia?a"ro?p 'e'?pi
"?kit + 380 + ."ua 'ra'?ka?a"pa?a 'txa"mo?o?p
+ 381 + '?i?i — ,'?ep"tan + .'?i'rah"xi?ix +
384 + '?a?a — .'?e'ben'di"sion 'ti"ko?or +

386 + .'?e'pa"gri 'no'ia"ha?a + "uar 'a
'?kah'pe"sian 'tu"ru + .'?i"uar + ,'?u'tsu"ii +
'?e?e — ,'?iuh"?tsu?u?p 'lo'ke?e'pa?a?k"?pir
'ia"ha?a + '?e?e — ,'?u'tsu"ii 'tu?u'tah'nu
"?ka?p + .'u'?ke"txe 'tu?ut'?e"?kin + 395 +
'?iu?u — .'?u'uir"se + '?e?e — .'?e"?aŋ 'he
"lo?p + 399 + 'kon'da'?u?u — ,'?u'?ke"txe '?u
"?ka?p 'tu?ut"?kin + 'ta'ke?e — '?e?e — ,'?iuh
"?tsu?u?p 'tu?u"tahn 'u"?ka?p + ."txe + 405 +
."?an 'xe"rox + 406 + ,"no?ox + .'?i"ra '?ix
'koh'ka"?pi + 408 + ,'ta"ra 'tu"ru + .'?i

28. Rainmaking

'tua?a'ni"?pir + 410 + ."ha?a 'xe"ra + ,'sut 'pe?e"nik + ,'?i'ra"nik + ,'tia?a"no?on 'tu "ro?on + ."uar + ,'ka'ku"ni 'ka"?pa?a + .'ka'peh "ko?ox + 417 + ,'sut'pe?e"nik + .'?i'ra'ni"kon + 419 + ,'?i"ra '?i'ui"ro?on + ,'su'tur"hut + .'?i'ra"non + ,'pa'sar"hut + ,'?i'ui"?txi?ik + , '?i'ben'di"sion + .'ti"ko?or + ,'tia?a'tu"ru + , '?e'ni'sa'ku"no '?pi'ri"ran + 428 + .'?i'ha?a "xo?p + ,'?u'pa"ti?ix 'u"?po?o?p + .'xa"no?p + 431 + ,'?u'peh"ko?o "?pu?ut 'tu"no?or + '?e?e — ,'?e'pa"?ka?p + ,'tia?a'tu"ru + .'tua?a'?u 'iah"?ku + .'lo'ke?e'?a"ian 'tuo?o?p + 437 + , '?i'ta"ra 'tu"ru + '?e?e -- ,'ka'me"ner + 440 + ,'?i'ko"ne?er + ,'?i'ra"nik + .'?i'?txa"mi?ik + .'pa'sar"?ka?p +

444 + ,'?i'ko"ne?er + '?a?a -- ,'sut"pa + '?e?e -- ,'?u'?ke"txe?e 'ie"ro?p '?e'?pi"?kit "rutx 'ia"ha?a + ."tu?ut '?e"?kin + 450 + .'?u 'ia?a"re + 451 + '?an'xe"rox + ,'ta"ra + .'tu "ru + "ierr '?e -- ,'?e'kum"ha?a 'ka'me"ner 'ti?i"?pa + .'ke'ka'na?a"ta + ,'ke"no?ox + , 'ma?a"txi '?i'?kam"pes + 'ko'txe?e -- ."no?on + 461 + ,"pe 'ro'ka'na?a"ta + .'ke'?u"me?ein + , "ha?ax + .'xe?e'?i'?kam"pes "no?ox + 465 + . '?u'?ke"txe '?u'?ka?p 'tu?ut"?kin + 466 + , '?in"ton 'ses'?a"ka?ai + '?e?e — .'?o?o"hron + 469 + .'?i"txe + 470 + "?aŋ 'hel -- .'saŋ'ga "briel + 472 + ."san 'mi"gel '?ar"kaŋ 'hel + 473 + ,'ko"ne?er + ,'tia?a'tu"ro?on + ,"uar 'ka '?kah'pes"ian "tiu?ut + .'tek'pa'nie?e"nik 'ko "ne?er + 477 + .'i'ke"no?on + ."uar 'ka'kohk "san + 479 + ."?iŋ 'ko"?pi?ix 'e"di 'ia + , "uar 'ka'kohk"san 'tu"ro?on + ,'por'ke'?a"ian 'ka'txuk"pa?ar + .'ta'ma'?e'ben'di"sion + .'ti?i "?pa +

484 + ,'?en"ton 'ses'?a"ka?ai + '?e?e -- '?a"ka?ai '?u?u -- ,'?u'tso"ra?a "xin + .'?e'ui 'tsi"ro?p + 'tua?a'?e?e -- "txe 'ke'tua?a'?a?a

28. Rainmaking

— ,'?e'to"kar 'ia"ha?a + ,'?a'tek'pa"ni + .
'?e?e -- 'ta"nio?or '?e'ui'tsi"ro?p + 495 + ,
'a"ka?ai + ,'u'iah"?ku + ,'u'?ka"?pa '?e'ui'tsi
"ro?p + 498 + '?e?e -- "ti?i -- ,'tu"?ka 'tu
"?ka?a 'ui"tsir 'lo'ke?e'?u'na?a"ta 'u'?ka"?pa?a
+ .'u'iah"?ku?u '?ka"?pa?a + 502 + ,'ke"ia
"tua?a + ,'a'tek'pa"ni + '?e?e -- .'to"kar +
506 + ,'por"ke?e 'to"kar 'ia"ha?a + ,"txe 'ke?e
"ha?ax + '?e?e -- ."ha?ax + .'e"?puhr 'tua?a'?e
"?aŋ 'he"lo?p + 511 + ,'?en"ton 'ses + "txe?e
-- '?e'pa"gri 'no'ke?e -- 'ke"hai -- ,'a"ian
'tia?a'tu"ru + ,'in"te?e + 'e?e -- ,'?ah"ma
'?pam"?pan + ,'na'ua"lir + "uar '?u?u -- ,'?u'xo
"tiu?ut + ,"pe 'ro'ko"ne?er + ,'txe"nik + ,'koŋ
'hu"rar + '?a'?es -- .'?a'?es"pa 'da + 527 + ,
'txe"ni 'koŋ'hu"rar + '?a?a -- 'sen -- .'?a'sen
"teio + 531 + ,'?i"ri?i 'uak"ta + .'?a'?ko'to
"ri + 533 + ,'?i'ko"ne?er + ,'tia?a"ma 'hai
"te?e + ,'na'ua"lir + ,'?ah"ma '?pam"?pan + .
'txe"ni 'koŋ'hu"rar +

538 + ,'?u'peh"ka + ,'tu"no?or + '?e?e --
,'?e"?aŋ 'he"lo?p + .'tu'?ka"?pa?a 'tu'?ka"?pa?a
+ 543 + .'?i"txe + 544 + ."?aŋ 'hel + ."saŋ
'ga"briel + ,'txok"he?ein + .'txok"he?ein + 548
+ 'iax'muh"re?e -- ,'iax'mu"hres + ,'e'lu'ga
"ro?p + 551 + ,"?aŋ 'hel"san 'ta'to"mas + ,
'txok"he?ein + .'txok"he?ein + 554 + ,'iax'mu
'hre"sik 'tu"no?or + .'?e'lu'ga"ro?p + 556 + .
"san 'mi"gel 'ar"kaŋ 'hel + ,'?ah'?ko'to"ret + ,
'ta'ma'tu"no?or + '?e?e -- .'?an'xe"ro?p + 561
+ "txoi -- '?e?e -- ,'txok"he?ei "nik + ,'?i'iax
'mu'hre"sik 'tu"no?or + '?e"la -- .'?e'lu'ga
"ro?p + .'tia?a'tu"ro?on + 568 + ,"uar 'ka
'?tsin"?tsa + 'u"men 'e?e -- .'e'txuk"pa?ar +
571 + ,'ko"ne?er + ,'txek'te"sik + ,'tu"no?or +
,'?i'ia"rum + 'ia?a -- ,'iax'mu'hre"sik + .'tu
"no?or + .'?u'tra"ba 'ho + '?e'pa"?ka?p 'lo'ke?e
— ,'tu"ru + ,"uar + .'?a'?tsin"?tso?o?p + 583
+ 'tia?a -- ,'tia?a"uar + ,'u'mor"?pa + ,"?ier

28. Rainmaking

'?u'hi'na"ho?p + ,'iax'mu'hre"sik + 'txoi -- .
'txok'he?ei"nik 'ta"mar + 590 + .'tia?a
"?txa?ar 'a?a"si + ,'?e'xe"ror + .'ma"iui + .
'ta'ta'ki"nar + 594 + .'ko"ne?er + .'?ta?a?p
'se"nik + '?i'ia"rik .'tu?u'?txu?ur'mon"ta 'nia
+ 597 + .'por'ke"no?on 'ka'?ka"ni + .'ke?e + .
'?e'lu"gar + .'iax'mu"ren + 601 + ,'?i'ke?e"ia
+ ,'ka'tah"ui + ,'tu"no?or + ,'lo'ke"no?on + .
'ka'?ku"xi 'ta"ra + "to?or 'e"rum + 607 + ,
'hai'?a"ran + ,'tu"?ka 'pa"?ka?p + ,'tu"ru + ,
"uar + ,'?a'xe"ror 'mu'sii"?ki + 612 + .'ko
"ne?er + ,'ka'peh"ko?ox + ,'ke?e"no?ox + ,'tua?a
'?ix'?ko'to"ri + 'ta?a -- .'ta?a'?u"hor + 618
+ ,"?aŋ 'hel"san 'ta'to"mas + .'be"ro 'ni'ko +
620 + ."par 'ra'ma"dor + ,'ue?e"txrun 'ko"ne?er
+ .'?e?ein"iax "to 'ma + .'?e?ein"sak "to 'ma'de
"a 'gua + ,'ue?e"?txrun + ,'ko"ra 'ko"ra + ,
'tua?a"non 'ka'?txa"mi + ,'ta"ra + '?e?e -- .'?e
'ben'di"sion + 630 + .'?e'txoh'?pes"iah 'ti?i
"?pa +

631 + ,'?ah'tek"pan + .'to'ka"rox + 633
+ ,'?atx'pe?e"nik + .'?i'?ka'?kue?e"nik + 635
+ ,'ta"mar + ,'?e?ein"iax '?a'la"gu 'na + .
'?e?ein"sak '?a'la"gu 'na + ,'?ke'?kue?e"nik + .
"to?or + 640 + .'?e"iax 'mon"tan "io?p + .
"to?or 'e'ui'tsi"ro?p + 642 + ."por 'ke'ta"mar
'a?a"?tsi + 643 + ,"ha?ax '?u'ua?a"ri?i?p + ,
'?u"iok '?e"?an 'xe"ro?p + .'?i'ko"ne?er + .
'?atx'pe?e"nik + '?i'?ke'?kue?e -- .'?ke'?kue?e
"nik + ."to?or + 'e'ui'tsi"ro?p +

651 + ."?an 'xe"rox + ,'sut'pe?e"nik + .'i
'ra"nik + .'tu"no?or + 'e?e -- .'pes"te 'ho + ,
'tia?a'tu"ru 'ka'me"ner + ,'ta"mar + 659 + .'e
"noh 'kom"ben 'to + ,'ta"mar + .'e"iax 'kom"ben
'to'ma"ior + ,'tia?a'tu"ro?on + ."uar 'ka'pe"te
'ka"?pa + 664 + ,'a'?kah'?pe"sian "tiu?ut 'ko
"ne?er + ,'iax'ta'hre"sik + .'?e'lu'ga"ro?p + ,
'iax'ta'hre"sik + ,'?u"iok 'u'txo"ro?p + '?e?e

28. Rainmaking

— ,'?e'ni'sa'ku"no?p 'i"ra + ,'tia?a'tu"ruo?p +
,"ua 'ru'pa"tu?u "?po?p + ."tiu?ut +

674 + ,"por 'ke?e'pa"?ka?p + ,'tia?a"uar
'?e?ei'xim"ian + .'a'pa'tah"ian + 677 + "ma
'ta'ua"ro?p 'tua?a'?e?e -- .'?e'ne'se'si"da +
679 + ,"ma 'ta'ua"ro?p + ,'tua?a'tu"no?or +
'?e?e -- 'lo'ke?e -- .'ka'num"se 'ka"?pa + 684
+ .'?tsai'me?e"nik 'ko"ne?er + ,'pa"sar 'u?ut
"?kin + 686 + 'txok'ha?a'hen -- ,'txok'ha?a
'ie"nik 'ko"ne?er + .'pa"sar "u?ut "?kin + 689
+ ,'ah'tek"pan + .'to'ka"rox + ,'ah'tek"pan + .
'?i'?ka"rox + 693 + ,'ko"ne?er + ,'?ke'?kue?e
"nik + ,'ta'ma"?u?ut 'e"?kin + 696 + ,'?ah'tek
"pan + .'i'?ka"rox + 698 + ,'ko"ne?er + .
'?puhk'se"nik + ,'tu"no?or + ,"u?ut 'e"?kin + ,
'tia?a'?ka"ni + ,'a'pat"na + .'?e'?an'xe"ro?p +
705 + ."san 'lo"ren 'so + ,"bar 'ba'de"o 'ro +
."bar 'ba'de"pla 'ta + ,'ko"ne?er + .'xe?e'?a'so
"brii "no?p + 710 + '?i'ta'ka?a -- ,'ta'kar
"sah + ,'ke?e'ha?a'xi"ro?p + ,'pat'na"ko?p + .
'ko"ne?er + 715 + ,"no?on + ,'ma?a"txi 'a"?tsi
'?ka"ni + ,'ka'koh"ko + '?e?e -- ,'tua?a"to '?e
"mei 'gra"di 'ia + 720 + ,'por'ke?e'?a"ian +
.'ka'txuk"pa?ar + 722 + ,'?i'ko"ne?e 're"ra +
.'ka'?ka"ni + 724 + .'tua?a'?ix'txok'?pes"ian
'ti"ko?or +

725 + .'?a"ian '?e'txuk"pa?ar + "tua?a --
,'?e"ni 'nio'ha'uai"li 'ka + .'e"ni 'nia'ha'uai
"li 'ka + 729 + ,'?e'ha'uai"li 'ka + ,"txe 'ke
"ha?ax + 'e?e -- 'lo'ke?e -- .'e'hi"nah 'ie?e
"?pu?ur + 734 + ,'po"re 'so + ,'txe?e"no?p "ni
'nio'ha'uai"li 'ka + .'i"ni 'nia'ha'uai"li 'ka +
737 + ,"txe 'ke?e"ha?ax '?u'?ka"?pa?a '?e"nar +
.'ie?e"?pu?ur + 739 + .'i"txe + 'tia?a --
'tia?a -- ,'tu"ro?o?p + ,"uar '?a'txa"mo?o?p + .
'?u"me 'ne'ta'kih"ti?ir + 745 + ,'ko"ne?er + ,
'ue?e"?txi?ik + ,'?i'ben'di"sion + .'tu?u'ho
"ro?p + 749 + ,'?i'ke"ha?ax + ,'?e'?a'li"men

28. Rainmaking

'to'ta?a'tu"no?or + .'?e'pa"?ka?p 'e'ko"noh
"to?or 'e"rum +

752 + ,"kon 'da'ix"to + ,'?a'?ka?a"pa +
'?a?a -- ,'?a'?kah'pes"ian + '?e?e -- ,'tia?a'ko
'to"ro?p + 'tu?u'ieh"?tser 'e?e -- ,'e'u"bar 'ko
'de"sa?a + ,'?i'uh"?tsu?u?p + .'?i'tu"no?or 'lo
'ke?e'tu"ru?u 'me'ne"ro?p + 762 + ,'?en"ton
'ses'a'lo"?kuo?p + ,'?a?a'ua"no?p "to?or 'e'ti
"nah + 'ta'ka'tu"no?or 'e?e -- ,'?e"?an 'xe"ro?p
+ .'ie?e'sa'kum'?pi"ro?p + 767 + ,'?a'lo"?koi
+ .'?a?a'ua"no?p "to?or 'e'ti"nah + 769 + '?u
'?ke"txo?p 'in'te?en"te?e -- ,"pu 'niu'?uh
"?tsu?u?p + .'tu?u"ta 'hnu'?ka"?po?p + 772 + ,
'?a'lo"?ko?p 'ta"kar 'pa"tir + '?ie?e -- .'?e're
'sen"sa 'rio'ta'kiuh"?tsu?u?p + 775 + "uar '?u
'pu"tu?u + '?u?u -- ,'?u'iuh"mo?p + ,'?e're'sen
"sa 'rio + ,'?e'u'?ke"txo?p + 'e"?pu?uts 'ta?a
— .'ti"txan + 782 + ,'?iu'?ke"txe 'u'?ka
"?po?p 'ti"txan + ."tu?ut 'e"?kin + .'ta'kiuh
"?tsu?u?p + 785 + '?i?i -- ,'?a?atx"pa?a 'ua
"no?p + .'?i'sut"pa '?a'ko'tua"no?p + 788 + .
"ma "ha?ax '?in"iahr 'ta"ka 'u"txo?p + 789 +
'?e?e — ,'tu"no?or + '?e'ia'he?e -- ,'?e'sa'kum
'?pi"ro?p 'ia"ha?a + '?ie?e -- ,'?an'xe"ro?p +

795 + .'?e'pa"gri 'no"txe + 796 + ."pa
'gre"nues 'tro + .'kes"tas 'en'lo"sie 'los +
798 + '?ie?e"ia 'he?e -- '?e"?an 'xe?e -- ,'?e
"?an 'xe"ro?p + ,'ie?e'sa'kum'?pi"ro?p 'ia"ha?a
+ "ha?ax 'u'?ka?a'pe"so?p 'tu"no?or 'e?e -- "ia
'he?e -- .'e?e"pa 'gre"nues 'tro + 805 + "pe
'ro?o — "uar '?a?a -- ,'?o?o'hro"no?p + '?i"uar
'?a?a — .'?a'ko'tua"no?p + 810 + '?i"ua 'ru?u
— ,'?u'?pu?u"?tso?p 'ko"ra 'ko"ra + .'e
"?pu?u?ts 'ia"ha?a 'tua?a'?a?a"xi 'tua?a'u'ue
"?txu?u "?pa 'ko"ra 'ko"ra + 813 + ,'ie?e'pa
"gri 'no + '?e?e -- ."ua?ar + ."ua 'ru'?ke"txu?u
"?ka?p "tu?ut 'e"?kin 'ta'kiuh"?tsu?u?p + 817
+ '?e?e — ,'kon"da '?ix"to + .'?a'?ka?a"pa '?u

28. Rainmaking

"txe 'tu"no?or '?e'ia"ha?a + ,'?n"ton 'ses + , '?u'?ke"txe 'tu"no?or + '?e?e -- ,'?u'pia?a"ro?p 'lo'ke?e"uar 'u"txe 're"sar 'ta"kar + .'?o?o "txoi 'ma"ku?u +

825 + ,'kon"da '?ix"to + ,'?ka?a"pi?ix 'tu "no?or + '?u?p -- ,'?en"ton 'ses + '?ũ?ũm -- , '?a"ka?ai + ,'?u'txam"sio?p 'tu"no?or + '?e"ia 'he?e -- ,'?e'ia"?katx + ,'?e'txum"pi 'lo'ke?e 'tu"ru 'u'me'ne"ro?p + 'i?i'a"kai '?u?u -- .'?u 'tu"kio '?pe"sa?a 'ta'me?e"?txen 'xe?e'ior"?pir 'u'me'ne"ro?p + 837 + ,"kon 'da?a'?ka?a"pa + . '?u"txe 'man"dar + '?a?a -- '?a'?keh'txa?a'?e?e — ,'?e"sia 'na"?katx 'ia"ha?a + '?e?e'ta?a -- 'ta'mio?o"tot 'tia?a'tu"ru '?e"ia 'he?e -- '?e?ei'xik"tak 'xe"ua 'rut -- '?u?u -- .'?u "txo?p '?e'man"da 'do + 847 + .'?u"txe 'man "dar 'a'?pehr"na?a "xi 'tu"no?or + .'tua?a'?o?os 'ta"na '?e'ia"?katx 'ia"ha?a +

849 + ,'?i'ha?a"xir + ,'?u'ia?a"re + '?e?e — ,'sa'kum'?pi"ro?p 'ko"ne?er + '?a'ket"pa "tu?ut 'ta'ka"rox 'tu"no?or 'lo'?ke'u'?kan"to 'tua?a — '?a?a -- ,'?a'nu"mui + 856 + ,'?a 'ket"pa '?e'sa'kum'?pi"ro?p 'ia"ha?a + '?a"ka?ai 'u?u — '?ak -- .'?u'pu"to?o?p 'iuh"?tsu?u?p 'tu "no?or 'lo'ke?e'tu"ru + 860 + 'i?i -- ,'?a "ka?ai + .'?a'puk'ma'ia"no?p + .'?e?e -- '?e "sa?a 'lo'ke?e -- ,'tu"ru?u 'me'ne"ro?p + .'a "kai'u'pu"kio?p 'ta'ka'?e"hen 'te'lo'ke?e'a'?ko "toi + 'i?i -- '?ie?e -- 'ma?ak"sa?a 'lo'ke?e -- ,'?u'tu'ru"?po?p 'ia"ha?a + 'a"kai 'u?u -- '?e?e — ,'u'xu"?tio?p + ,'im"?pihk 'im"?pihk + '?e?e — '?u'iah"?ko?p '?e?e -- '?e?e -- .'?e'?pi"?kit 'max"tak + 879 + 'por'ke"txe 'ke?e -- ,'?e 'ma?ak"sa?a 'ia"ha?a + "ha?ax '?e?e -- ,'?u 'tua?a'ni"?pir + '?e"ia 'he?e -- '?e?e -- .'?e "san 'lo"ren 'so + 886 + '?a"ka?ai 'u?u -- 'u?u -- ,'?u'xu"?tio?p + ,'?u'iah"?ko?p 'tu "no?or 'e'?pi"?kit 'max"tak + .'lo'ke?e'a'?ko

28. Rainmaking

"toi +

891 + ,'?i'ha?a"xir + ,'?a?a"xin + .'?a?a "xin 'ma"ku?u + 894 + '?e?e -- ,'?u'?txuh "ku?u 'ia"?katx 'tia?a"uar 'o?os'ta"na + ,'?i'?a "ka?ai + .'?u'si?ik"?pa "ti?i 'ne?eim"?pahr + 898 + ,'?u"txe 'man"dar '?o?os'ta"na '?a"par 'te + .'tua?a'?u'?ku"xi 'ha?a"xir + 900 + "por 'ke?e -- "txe 'ke?e -- ,'ha?a"xir + ,'?i'ko'txa "ha?ax "ua 'ru'?kah"ti '?e'ha"ha?ar + '?iu'?ka "ni 'ke?e -- 'tua?a -- ,'?u'?ku"xi 'ha?a"xir + "ha?a 'xia?a"?katx 'xe?e'?a?a -- '?e?e -- .'?a 'noh"ran + 910 + ,'?i'po"re 'so + ,'?u'?kah "na?ar '?a?a"xin 'ma"ku?u 'tia?a'tu"ru '?e'?i 'xik"tak + ,'?a"ka?ai + '?e?e -- '?u?u -- '?u 'txui'u"ru?u 'ia"?ka"txo?p 'tia?a'tu"ru + . 'tua?a'u?u'ta"hui "ti?i 'ne?eim"?pahr +

917 + ,'?ie?e'sa'kum'?pi"ro?p 'ia"ha?a + , '?i"rah 'i"rah '?a'lo"?koi + ,'?a?a'ua"no?p "to?or 'e'ti"nah + .'?u'ui"ro?p "hai "uar '?a?atx"pa '?e'to"kar "to?or '?e'ui"tsir + 921 + .'?i"hai '?i"xin '?e"tar 'de + "mai 'tu"?ka?a -- ,'?a"ian + ,'?u'koh"ko?p '?a'?ko"toi "?o 'txo "di 'ia + .'?i"ma 'tu"?ka 'e'ha"ha?ar + ,'sut"pa + ,'?a"ka?ai '?u'mo'roh"sio?p '?o'tron"iahr + '?e?e -- .'xe?e'txe?e"no?p '?a'pre'ben"sion + , '?a'xa"na 'e'sa'kum'?pi"ro?p 'ta'ma'tu"no?or '?al"de 'ia + '?e?e -- ,'?u'mo'roh"sio?p + ,"?o 'tro"niahr + .'tu"no?or 'lo'ke'?ah'?ku'no"?pix 'a"ni + 935 + .'tua?a'?a'sut"pa '?u'tu'ru "?po?p '?o'tro"niahr + 936 + ."pe 'ro + '?ep -- .'?e'pa"gri 'no'xe'?a'?kah"na?a "ni '?o"ni?ix + '?e?e -- ,'?e'pa"gri 'no'ia"ha?a + "txe 'ke?e 'u'?ka"?pa?a '?a"ni 'ia"ha?a -- ,'?in"te?e + '?e?e -- ,'?u'?ka"?pa?a '?a"ni + '?e?e -- ,'ber 'na"be "lion + ,'iin"te?e + '?a?a'ro?p"na '?a"ni + 'ta'ma'bi"sien -- .'bi"sen 'te"lion +

951 + ."txe 'ke?e'pa"grii "no?p 'ia"ha?a

28. Rainmaking

'?a"ni + 952 + ,"uar 'tok"to + ,'?a"ka?ai + , '?a'?kah'pe'sia"no?p + 955 + "por 'ke"txe 'ke?e"ia 'he?e -- '?e?e -- '?e'ber'na"be?e -- , 'ia"ha?a + "txe 'ke'des'de?e -- ,'?e'kux"na + . '?u"me 'nu"tu?u + '?e?e -- 'pa"kar '?iŋ"koht 'pek"pek 'tu?u -- 'tu?u -- .'tu?u'?pa"ke 'ru"pat + 966 + 'i"txe 'ke?e"ia 'he?e -- ,'?e'par"te 'ra'xe?e"uar + '?e?e -- ,'?u'ui"ra 'e'?txur "?ka?a?p 'ia"ha?a + 'kon'da?a -- ,'?u'ui"ra + , 'e'?txur"?ka?a?p 'ia"ha?a + .'?ka"xi + 974 + , 'i'pa"kar 'e'pek"pek + ,'tu?u'?pa"ker 'u"pat + . '?u'ia?a"re 'e'tu?u"?pir + ,'?ak"tan + .'?i"ra '?a'lo?k"se + "por 'ke?e -- ,"ie 're"si '?tsi"ra + ,'ma?a"txa?a 'na?a"ta + .'tu"?ka 'u"?kam 'pi "?pir "ti?i 'ne"tiem 'po + 983 + ,'e"si?its 'i "ra + ,'?pa"nix + ."ha?ax + ,"tua?a + ,'?in"te?e '?ah'?kah'pe"siah + ,'ta'ma'tu"no?or + '?e?e -- ,'?u'pia?a"ro?p + ,"ti?i 'ne"tiem 'po + 992 + ,'i'ke"ha?ax + .'?u'?pi"?pir + ,'?u'io'hro"ner + .'?u"me 'ne'dio"so?p +

996 + '?i"txe 'ke?e -- "ia 'he?e -- ,'?e "si?its 'ia"ha?a 'kai"?txi?i + 999 + ,'?ko"toi 'in"te?e "di 'ia + '?e?e -- .'?u'ia?a"re 'u"tu?u + ."na 'na + "ier 'ni?i -- ,'ni'pek"pek 'ia"ra + .'?ka"ni 'a?a"ti + 1006 + ,'ta"res 'im"?pihk "ha?a + 'ta'man"te?e "rutx 'xe?e'ma"ha?ax 'ah '?ka -- .'ma"ha?ax 'a_'?kam"pa?ar + 1009 + , '?ka"nin '?txa"?pu 'ta"mar + ."por 'ke'?ka"na?a "ti "ier 'ni'pek"pek +

1001 + ,'i"txe 'ke?e'tu?u"?pir 'ia"ha?a '?i"xin + 'u'pe"te?en -- '?n -- ,'?im"?pihk "ha?a + ,'ta"ma '?e"rutx 'ia"ha?a + .'xe?e'ma "ha?ax 'iah'?kam"pa?ar + 1017 + "kon 'da?a -- ,'u'?txa"?pu 'e'pek"pek 'ia"ha?a 'ta"mar + , 'ua?ak"txe 'ta"ka + .'ki'rik"na "?u?ut 'e"?kin + 1021 + .'?u'ia?a"re 'u"tu?u + 1022 + ."na 'na + ,'?pa"nix 'e'?u?ut"?kin + ,'?a'ki'rik"na + 1025 + ,'?e'tu?u"?pir "txe + 1026 + 'e?e -- .

28. Rainmaking

'ha"ha?ar 'u'?ka"ni + 1028 + '?i'?an -- ,'?a 'na?a'ta"ka + ,'tu'?ka"tar + ,'ki'rik"na "?u?ut 'e"?kin 'ia"ha?a + 1032 + ,'?e'tu?u"?pir "txe + 1033 + '?pa"nix 'in'na?a"ta 'ke?e -- ."por 'ke?e'?a'?txa"?pu '?a'pek"pek 'ta"ma '?e"ha?a + 1035 + ,'ha?a"xir + ,'sut"pa + .'?u'?txuh "?ku?ut '?e"?kin + 1038 + '?i?i -- ,'?i "?txa?ar + '?e?e -- ,'?e'pek"pek 'ia"ha?a 'ta"ma '?e"ha?a + .'sut"pa 'ki'rik"na "?u?ut 'e"?kin +

1043 + ,'?i'lo"?koi '?e'tu?u"?pir + ,'?u 'ui"ra + ,"to?or 'ti"nah + '?u'ui"ra 'ke?e -- , 'ke'ko"ra 'ko"ri?ix + ,"ua?ar "?u?ut 'e"?kin 'a?a"xin + .'ta"mo?o 're'ui'tsi"ro?p + 1050 + ,'?in"ton 'ses + .'?u'ia?a"re 'u"tu?u + 1052 + ,'ko"ne?er + .'?ku?u?p"sen + 'ke?e -- .'?e'ni 'pek"pek "i 'ra + 1056 + ,'ke"kon 'da"ha?ax + ,'?in'?txa"?pu + ,'ta'ma'?e"ha?a + ,'i'ke?e 'ua?ak"txe 'ta"ka + 'tua?a'?ka"xi 'e'ha"ha?a -- .'e'ha"ha?ar + 1062 + .'?e'tu?u"?pir "txe + 1063 + ."?i 'ho + 1064 + .'?en"ton 'ses"ne?et + ,'?pa"nix + ,'?u'ta"rer "dios + .'?a'uir"na?ar + 1068 + ,"por 'ke"no?on + ,'ma?a"to '?in"iahr 'ka'ui"ra 'in"te?e + ,'ui"nik + .'ko'txe?e"ne?et + 1072 + ,"pe 'ro"ne?et + ,'?pa"nix + ,'?a"uet '?o'hro"ner + .'?e'?an'xe"ro?p + .'tua?a'?e'ka 'ta"ta?a "dios +

1077 + ,"txe 'ke'?ko"toi 'in"te?e "di 'ia + ,'ua?a"uan + '?e?e -- '?in"te?e 'be"ran -- . '?in"te?e 'be"ra 'no + 1082 + "por 'ke?e -- , "txe 'ke?e'ta"rix 'e"tiem 'po + ,'?e"hen 'te + , '?a'pa?a?k"mo?p 'a"ni + 'ta"ma 're"ra '?e?e -- '?e?e -- .'?e"mar 'so + 1089 + ,'?ie?e"di 'ia 'ia"ha?a + ,'?ka?a"pa '?e"mar 'so + ,'?o"txoi 'ia?a"bril + ."ma 'tu"?ka '?e'ha"ha?ar + 1093 + ,'?en"ton 'ses + ,'ta'ma'?a"bril + '?e?e -- . '?ko"toi '?e"siaŋ "hen 'te"tu?ut + 1097 + . "txe "tua?a + ,"ne?et + .'?a'txek"ta 'ko?oi"?pi + ,'ke"ne?et + "des 'de'ke?e -- 'kux"ne?et

28. Rainmaking

"to?or 'e"rum 'er -- ,'?i"ra + ,'?a"ian '?iŋ
"koht 'iah'pek"pek + '?e?e -- .'kux"na 'ta'ka
"ret + 1107 + ,'i"no?on + ,'ka'?ka"na?a "ni +
'tua?a -- .'?a'uir"sio?oŋ 'ko'txe?e"re + 1111
+ 'por'ke?e -- ,"no?on + ,'ta"rix "di 'ia + ,
"kai + .'pat"no?on + 1116 + ,'i"uar 'ka'kohk
"san 'tu"ro?on + ,'ta'ma'?e'ha"ha?ar + .'?i"ma
'tu"?ka?a + 1119 + ,"pe 'ro + ,'tal"bes + ,
"ne?et '?a"ni + .'?u'iu"?pie?et '?e"dios 'ko
"ne?er +

1123 + ,'?en"ton 'ha?a"xir "txe + "pe
'ro?o -- ."ma 'tu"?ka '?i'ta"res + .'tua?a'ka
'uir"se?e "?aŋ 'he"lo?p + 1127 + ,'?en"ton
'ses + .'?e'ui'ni"ko?p 'ia"ha?a "txe + ,"pues +
,"ma 'tu"?ka 'ka'ta"res + 1131 + "pe 'ro?o --
,'ma?a"txi '?ka"nik '?u'iu"?pio?on + .'?u'iu
"?piet + ,'?e"dios + ,"?pan 'ta"ka +

1136 + .'?en"ton 'ses + .'ha?a"xir "txe +
.'?e"rer 'in"txe + 1139 + 'pe'ro?o -- ,"ne?en
'iŋ'gua?a"rio?ox + 'ke?e -- ,'?e'dio"so?p + ,'u
'?ka"ni + ,'tua?a'ka'uir"se + '?e?e -- .'tu"?ka
'lo'ke?e'ka'?kam"pes 'ta"ra + 1147 + ,'ha?a
"xo?p + .'ma?a"txi 'u'?ku"xo?p + 1149 + .'pe
'ru'?ku"xo?p '?u"me?ein + 1150 + '?i?i -- ,
'txe'ke?e'?u'uah"pi + ,'?e'pek"pek 'ia"ha?a + ,
'?u'?txa"?pu 'ta'me?e"ha?a + '?i?i -- .'?u'peh
"ka + .'?e"?aŋ 'he"lo?p + 1157 + .'?i"txe +
1158 + .'ta"ta?a '?pi"ret + 1159 + ,'xe?e'tu
"re?et + ,'?i'?ko'to"ri + .'ti"ko?or + 1162 +
,'?ep"taŋ 'ko"ne?er + ,'?a'uan 'xe"ro?p + .'ti
"ko?or + 1165 + .'?u'peh"ka + .'?e"?aŋ 'he
"lo?p + 1167 + ."txe + 1168 + ."?aŋ 'hel'saŋ
'ga"briel + 1169 + ."?aŋ 'hel + .'san'to'to
"mas + 1171 + ."san 'mi"gel 'ar"kaŋ 'hel +
1172 + .'?i'tu'no?o"rox "ti?i 'ne"?an 'xe"ro?p
+ 1173 + .'tua?a'?e"nues 'tro'di"bi 'no'e"ter
'no + .'ke"ha?ax + ,'ka'iu"mar + ,"ha?ax + .'?a
'iu'ma"ri 'ti"ko?or + 1178 + ,'txok'he?e"nik +

28. Rainmaking

.'?tsai'ne?e"nik "to?o 're"rum + 1180 + ,'iax 'ta'hre"sik + .'e'lu'ga"ro?p 'i"ra + .'iax'ma 'hre"sik 'tu"no?or + .'?e'lu'ga"ro?p + 1184 + "por 'ke?e — .'?e'pa"?ka?p 'i"ra + ,'tia?a'tu "ro?o?p 'ta"niu?ut + ."uar '?a'?tsin"?tso?o?p + 1188 + ,'?a"ian + .'?u'txuk'pa?a"ro?p + 1190 + ,'?i'ko"ne?er + ,'ue"?txi?ik + .'?i'ben'di "sion + 1193 + .'tek'pa'nie?e"nik 'ko"ne?er + 1194 + .'por'ke?e'pa"?ka?p 'i"ra + .'?ka"ni '?u 'ui"ro?o?p + .'?i'rah"xi?ix 'i"ra + 1197 + . '?i'txoh'?pe"siah +

1198 + ,"txe 'ke"uar 'tok"to + ,'?o?o"hron 'tu"ru + ,"kuan 'do + .'ki'rik"na "?u?ut 'e"?kin + 1212 + .'?en"ton 'ses + 1203 + ."txe "iah 'e'ui'ni"ko?p 'ia"ha?a + .'?e?e"ra?atx 'ah"txi?i + 1205 + ,'?e'ui"nik 'i"ra + ,'?o?o?p"na + 'tua?a -- ,'?u'ta"res + .'?e'ha"ha?ar + 1210 + "por 'ke?e + ,'?u'?pi"?pir + ,'?u'io'hro"ner + . '?u"me 'ne'dio"so?p + 1214 + .'?u"me 'ne'an'xe "ro?p + 1215 + ,"txe 'ke'?e'ui"nik 'ia"ha?a + .'ma"ha?ax "mei 'gra + ,'u'io'hro"ner + 'tua?a '?a'tu"ruan '?a?a -- ,'?a'?kah'?pe"sian + ."pe 'ro'ha?a"xir '?u'?pi"?pi 'ra"ni + .'?u'io'hro "ner '?u"me 'ne'dio"so?p + 1222 + "txe 'ke?e -- 'ta'ma?a -- ,"txahr + ,"uar '?a'?ko"toi + '?a 'pehk"nu?ut '?u"me 'ne?e -- ,'?e'ui'ni"ko?p 'ia "ha?a + ,'?ie?e'ui'ni"ko?p 'ia"ha?a '?u'?ko'te 'so'?pix"to "ia?a + 'tu"no?or 'lo'ke?e -- '?e?e -- '?e?e -- .'?u'?ka"ni + '?e?e -- ,'?uh "?tsu?u?p + '?e?e -- ,"nar + .'tu"no?or + 1238 + ,'?a"?katx + ,'txum"pi?i + ,'?ko"toi + '?u?u — ,'?u'iah"?ko?o?p + '?i?i -- "ka 'iu?u -- ,'?u 'ia?a"re 'tur'?pa"na + ,'?e'sian"sa?a +

1247 + ,"ton 'ses + ,'?u'ia?a"re '?e'sa 'kum'?pi"ro?p + 'ke?e -- .'na?a'ta"nik + .'ke'lo 'ke?e"ua 'tar'tur'?pa"na + 1252 + ,'ma"ha?ax + 'por'ke?e -- ,'ua"tar '?e"?an 'xe"ro?p + '?u?u — '?u?u -- '?u'?ke"txo?p 'tu"no?or 'lo'ke?e --

28. Rainmaking

,'tu"ru 'ka'me"ner + 1259 + ,"pe 'ro'?u"me?ein
+ ."ua 'ru'?ke"txo?p + 1261 + ,'?i'ha?a"xir +
,'ka'iŋ'?kah'?pe"sian 'ta'ka'?u?u -- 'ta'ka'?e?e
— .'?u'ian'xe"ro?p + 1265 + '?i?i -- "ha?ax
'ta"ka "siem 'pre'lo'ke?e'?e?e -- "ka 'iu?u --
'?kah'?pe"sian 'ta"mar "ha?ax 'ta"ka '?o?o -- .
'?o"hron 'ta"mar 'o'tro"niahr + 1270 + ,'txe
'ke"uar 'tok"to + '?o?o"hron 'tu"ru + "kon 'da
— .'ki'rik"na "?u?ut 'e"?kin + ,'?i'kai"xix
'?atx"pa '?e'to'ka"ro?p "to?or 'e'ui"tsir +
1275 + '?i?i -- '?e?e -- ,'to"kar 'ia"ha?a + ,
'ua?ak"txe 'ta"ka + .'u'?puhk"se "u?ut 'e"?kin +
1280 + "txe 'ke?e -- .'kai"xix '?ka"xi 'e'ha
"ha?ar + 1282 + ,'?i'po"re 'so + "txe '?e?e --
'?a"ni 'e"hen 'te'ke?e -- .'?e'pa"gri 'no'ia
"ha?a + ,'?u'?pi"?pir 'a"ni '?u'io'hro"ner + ,
'?u"me 'ne"dios + ,"por 'ke'ha?a"xir + ,"uar
'tok"to + .'?o?o"hron + ,'tu"ru + ,"ua 'ra'?kah
'?pe"sian + 'tu -- ,"tu?ut '?e'dio"so?p + ,
'ie?e'ha"ha?ar + ,'ua"rix '?a?a -- .'?a'?ka"xi
"to?o 're'ui'tsi"ro?p +

1298 + "pe 'ro + ,'e'pa"grii "no?p 'lo
'ke?e'kai"to '?iŋ'gui"ro?o?p "ne?en + ,"ma 'in
"iahr '?iŋ'gui"ra + 'a?a -- ,'xe?e"uar 'tok"to
'?o?o'hro"no?p + .'?i'ua"rix 'a'?ka"xi '?e'ha
"ha?ar + 1304 + "pe 'ro -- ,'ha?a"xo?p + .
'?o?o'hro"no?p "mei 'gra + 1307 + ,"mei 'gra
'?u'?kah'?pe'sia"ho?p + "tu?ut '?e?e -- ."tu?ut
'?e"dios + 1310 + ,"pe 'ro + ,'ma?a"txi + ,
'ma?a"txi 'ta"kix + '?o?o?p"na?a -- '?u?u -- ,
'?u'?kah'?pe'sia"ho?p + ,'?u"me 'ne"dios + "por
'ke?e'ma?a"txi 'a?a -- ,'?a'?ka"xi 'e'ha"ha?ar +
.'ko'txa'ta"kix "uar '?o?o'hro"no?p + 1320 +
"ne?en 'ma?a"txin 'na?a"ta "hai -- "ua 'ra'lo
"?koi 'in -- ,'?iŋ'?kah"ti 'e'ha"ha?ar + 1323
+ ,"pe 'ro'hai'ta"ra 'ma?a"txi '?a'?ka"xi + ,"pe
'ro"ne?en 'in'na?a"ta 'ke'?a?a"xin '?a'?ka"xi
'ta'ni'lu"gar + ."por 'ke'?a"ian 'ni'hi"nah
"?txa?ar +

28. Rainmaking

1326 + 'i"kon 'da?a -- '?u?u -- .'?e'pa "gri 'no + .'?u'ui"ra + .'ke'ua'ra'?ka"xi + , "mei 'gra'?e'ha"ha?ar + "?i 'ke?e -- 'ma?a "txi?ix '?u'iu"?pi '?a?a -- ,'pat"na 'e"hen 'te 'u"me 'ne'ha"ha?ar + ,'?en"ton 'ses + ,'?e'sa 'kum'?pi"ro?p 'ia"ha?a + ,'?a'?ko?oi'ra"no?p '?u 'me'ne'ha"ha?ar + ,'?a"ka?ai + ,'?a?a"xin 'u'peh "ko?p "u?ut '?e'pa"gri 'no + '?e?e -- .'txe?e "no?p + 1342 + .'ta"ta 'pa"gri 'no + ,"no?on + ,"uar 'ka'io?o"pa + ,'ka'peh"ko?oit 'ta"ra + "por 'ke?e -- ,'?e'dio"so?p '?i"ra + ,'ma?a "txi?ix + ,'u'iu"?pi 'ka'pat"na + .'?u'me'ne "ro?p + 1351 + "por 'ke?e -- "ua 'ra?a -- ,'?a '?tsai"mo?o?p + ."mei 'gra + 1355 + '?e?e -- , '?en"ton 'ses + '?e?e -- ,'pa"gri 'no + '?u'?kah "ti?i -- '?o?o -- '?e?e -- 'lo'ke?e -- ,"tua?a '?u'tu'ru"?po?o?p + 1364 + ,'?e'sa'kum'?pi "ro?p 'ia"ha?a + ,'?a'lo"?koi + ,'?u'mo'roh "sio?p + 'ta"ma?a -- ,'?e'ial'de"io?p + .'tu "no?or 'lo'ke?e'tua?a'u'?kam'pe"so?p + 1370 + '?e?e -- ,'sut"pa '?a"ka?ai + ,'?a'?kah'pe"sian '?e"ia 'he?e -- .'?e'pa"gri 'no'?o'tro"niahr + 1374 + '?u'peh"ka '?e?e -- "?aŋ 'he"lo?p 'ia "ha?a 'tu -- 'tu"no?or 'lo'ke?e -- '?e?e -- . '?ah'pat'na?a"ro?p +

1379 + .'?u'ia?a"re + 1380 + ,"?an 'xe "rox + ,'ko"ne?er + ,'ka'uah"?ko?ox + .'?i'des "kan 'so + .'?i'hi"ria?ar + 1385 + "por 'ke?e -- ,'?e'pa'?ka"?po '?pi"ra + ,'me?e"rer + , 'tua?a'?a'pat"no?o?p + ,'?i'ko"ne?er + ,'ka'uah "?ko?ox + ,'?i'hi"ria?ar + 'kohk -- ,'koh'kia?a '?pe?e"nik + 1394 + ,'koh'ka?a'?pe"nik 'ko "ne?er + .'?an'xe"rox + 1396 + .'san'lo"ren 'so + .'koh'ka?a'?peŋ 'ko"ne?er + ,'?txah "?pe?eix + ,'ti?i"?pa + .'ke"no?ox + ,'?i'uah "?ko?o "nix + ,"mei 'gra + .'?e'ben'di"sion + 1404 + ,'?i'iax'mu'hre"si?ix + ,'?i'iax'ta'hre "si?ix + .'tu"no?or '?e'lu'ga"ro?p + .'tia?a'tu "ro?on + 1406 + ,'?i'ko"ne?er + .'koh'kia?a

28. Rainmaking

'?pe?e"nik +

1410 + '?e?e -- .'?u'ia?a"re 'tu"no?or + '?e?e -- ,'?e'to'ka"ro?p + ,'lo'ke?e"kai '?u'peh "ka + "kuan 'do?o -- '?e?e -- "ua 'ru'peh"ka 'tu "ru '?e?e -- ,'ha"ha?ar + ,'?i'tu"no?or 'lo'ke "ka 'iu'peh"ka + ,'tu"no?or '?u'iah"?ku + '?e?e -- .'?u'hi"ria?ar + 1423 + ,'?i'?u'ia?a"re + , 'ke'hi'rie?e"nik + .'koh'ka?a'?pe"nik + 1426 + ,'ha?ax"to '?e"ra + '?ũ?ũ -- ,"kai 'ũ?ũm"?pi "ne?en + ,'ko'txa'?a'?kah'?pe"sian + '?e?e -- . 'pa"grii "no?p + .'a"ni +

1433 + "pe 'ro?o -- ,'?a"ian 'in"te?e "mes + .'xe?e'ma?a"txi?ix + 'e?ei"ri '?e'ha"ha?ar + 'ii?i -- '?i?i -- ,'?a'lo"?koi "mei 'gra'ki "?pits + ,'ta'ma'?e'lu'ga"ro?p + ,'ta'me?e'ui 'tsi"ro?p + 1442 + "txe 'ke"ia 'he?e -- .'?a "ian 'in"te?e "?aŋ 'hel + ,'?u'?ka"?pa?a + ."?aŋ 'hel'ku'le"bri 'na + 1446 + ,'?i"txe 'ke"ha?ax + ,"kon 'do"ha?ax '?a'pat"na + ,'?a"ian "mei 'gra'?e'ha"ha?ar + '?i?i -- ,'?a'lo"?koi 'ko"ra 'ko"ra '?e'ki"?pits + ,'ta'ma'?e'ui'tsi"ro?p + 1452 + ,'?en"ton 'ses + ,'?e'pa"gri 'no + ,'?u 'tur"?pa + ,'tu"no?or + 'lo'ke?e -- '?e?e -- , '?u"txe 'a'kos'tum"brar + ,'?u'tu'ru"?po?p + 1460 + ,"txe 'ke'?u'tua?a'ni"?pir + '?e"ia 'he?e -- .'?e"?aŋ 'hel'ku'lu"bri 'na +

1463 + ,'?i?i + ,'?e"?aŋ 'hel'ku'le"bri 'na'ia"ha?a + '?a?a -- ,'?a'tu'ru'?pa"na + 'tu?u "?ka '?pe?e -- '?e?e -- ."san 'mi"gel '?ar"kaŋ 'hel + 1470 + ,"por 'ke?e"san 'mi"gel '?ar"kaŋ 'hel + "ha?ax 'e?e -- '?a'ko'to"ri 'ta'ma'tu "no?or '?e?e"?aŋ 'he"lo?p + 1473 + '?i'po"re 'so"ia 'he?e -- '?e?e -- ,'?e"?aŋ 'hel'ku'le"bri 'na'ia"ha?a + ,'?a'tru'?pa"na + 'tu?u"?ka?p '?e?e -- ,'?e"?aŋ 'hel + '?e?e -- .'?e"san 'mi "gel 'ar"kaŋ 'hel + 'ke?e -- 'ka'ua?a"re 'ke?e -- .'ke"ha?ax '?e'ku"mix "aŋ 'hel + 1483 + "ia

28. Rainmaking

'he?e -- .'?e"?aŋ 'hel'ku'le"bri 'na'ia"ha?a + '?u"men '?e?e -- '?e"?aŋ -- ,'?e'ku"mix "?aŋ 'hel'tua?ah'?ku"na '?u'hi"ria?ar + 'tua?a'ma?a "txi '?a?a -- '?a?a -- '?a'?ka?a"pa '?u?u -- . 'sa"ti 'tu"no?or '?e'lu'ga"ro?p + "por 'ke?e -- '?e?e -- ,'?e"?aŋ 'hel'ku'le"bri 'na + "txe 'ke?e -- 'ia"ha?a -- ,"ha?ax + ,'iu'mar"?pir + 'tua?a'?e?e -- .'tu"no?or '?e'txa"no?p 'lo'ke'?a "ian 'tu?ut -- 'ma'ku?u'ui"tsir +

1502 + ,'?i"kon 'da'?ix"to + '?a'tua?a"na '?e'?a?a -- '?e"ia 'he?e -- ,'?e"?aŋ 'hel'ku'le "bri 'na + ,'?a'koh'ka?a"?pi '?e'ha"ha?ar + . 'ta'ma'?e'lu'ga"ro?p +

28. Rainmaking

1 I'm going to tell how the padrino prays when he calls for rain. 7 First he orders that an arbor be built, the size of a house. 16 The house is at a distance.

19 When it is ready, he orders that three -- crosses be stood up, and he orders that they be decorated with *conte*, and -- candles first. 33 He has two men in each village; they say those men are older brothers of the padrino. 41 And those brothers go gathering money, corn, chickens, turkeys, and incense, in all the villages.

49 And that is why in all the villages there are two of the -- older brothers, so they can gather everything that is used. 56 And when -- those brothers arrive with the money, and all they have gathered in the villages, they go and leave it at his house.

65 Then the day comes which is the day for them to celebrate. 67 Those brothers go and mold the incense, and -- everything -- to be used, they decorate.

75 And when everything they are going to use is all ready, 78 then they go to call him where he is shut up in his house. 80 Because that padrino is careful to wait for his day, until in a week 84 he says to the brothers, "Such and such a day we will celebrate." 88 And he shuts himself up, lying in his house alone, because they say that he is waiting.

93 Because they say that that padrino when he speaks with God and the angels, he waits. 104 He bathes day after day, he bathes so -- they say that -- he will not be soiled when he speaks with the gods. 115 He waits for a week.

28. Rainmaking

116 For the prayer, when he begins his prayer, he says, 123 "You brothers, now is the time for us to pray to -- the angels: gather yourselves together here." And he gathers up a small child. 132 That small child, they say he is the Angel. 136 He begins praying, covering his head with a white cloth; he covers his head and sits down. 142 And the brothers too put on white cloths, cover their heads, all of them, to sit down beside that padrino.

155 Then the padrino begins praying. 158 And he says, 159 "Today is the day we are here, and we are sitting tailor-fashion; we are going to pray to you."

169 First he speaks to the God we call Our Eternal Father. 175 He calls to him first. 177 And he says, "You who rule over all the angels, over everything there is, over everything there is on the earth, 188 You rule, 189 because you made the heaven, you made the earth, and you made everything we see. 193 And today, we call to you so that you send 198 your -- angel spreads -- he spreads his blessing over us here, because we who are living here -- great hunger is happening to us, from drought, because we find nothing. 213 And you, you see us, our hearts are humble; here where we live, we experience great hunger, because we find nothing to eat. 223 And today we -- our need is great for your blessing -- give it. 232 This is the time when we sit down where we live. 237 We speak with you. Let your angels come to carve over the earth where we stay watching for you, with -- all whose -- corn seedlings lie drying from the heat. 252 Because there is no water for them.

253 And today, where we live, you see that

where they are depriving themselves, the people, they put out everything which they need, and the humans, the villages, they are depriving themselves to put out everything which is placed here. 273 And this is your -- payment, and with it, turn to look at us. 280 Send your angels here. This is the time when we who live here have great need for -- water, because -- you see that -- humans are dying here of -- hunger, and where -- it is nothing that little ones are crying from hunger, because they find nothing to eat."

302 Then he begins to call to all the angels. 308 First, he calls, saying, 311 "Angel San Gabriel, Angel Santo Tomas. Angel Santo Tomas Veronico. 319 Angel -- San Miguel Archangel." 322 They say that San Miguel Archangel is the ruler, and he calls to all his fellow angels to rise up and come out with him. 332 Then, when he has finished calling all the angels who are -- he is bringing along to work, 338 then, he calls San Lorenzo. He says, 342 "San Lorenzo! 343 Golden Beard, Silver Beard!"

345 And San Lorenzo, when he hears that -- the drum is beaten by the angels. Then they rise up and come to look. 353 That is why the padrino says, "San Lorenzo, you are the uncle of the angels. Rise now and come here; look at us. 363 Where we live we are dying from hunger. 366 Where we live we are -- we are suffering. Rise! 369 And raise up your nephews above, so they will spread the blessing over us today. 375 Because you can not stand to see us, so much hunger is there. 377 And we can not stand it that where we live we are dying. And the little ones. 380 They are dying out. 381 And -- send now 384 your -- blessing on us."

28. Rainmaking

386 That padrino continues praying, and he burns the incense which was molded, he sets it in his hand, and holds it up to the sky, and shows it to the angels. 399 When he holds it up to the sky with the incense in his hand, he says, 405 "You angels, 406 you watch; 408 here is your payment. 410 Turn here, see us where we are living; we humble ourselves, we call to you. 417 Turn, see us. 419 Do not look upon us with eyes turned away; look on us with open eyes, and spread your blessing over us, where my brothers here live. 428 And they followed along. 431 They called to all the people who were there to give what they had. 437 And here it is, by our doing. 440 And today, see us and take from us with open hand."

444 Then he turns back and holds the small gourd up to the sky. 450 He says, "Angels, here is a little *chilate* for you from us, though we know that you don't use it as we do. 461 But we know that its spirit is what you use." 465 He holds his arm up to the sky. 466 Then he begins to speak. 469 He says, 470 "Angel San Gabriel, 472 San Miguel Archangel, 473 today where we live, we pray to you. Tower up today. 477 And we will watch for you. 479 The time is ripe; we are sitting watching for you, because we have need of your blessing."

484 Then he begins to trace out the peaks, whose -- they say that those clouds build up over the peaks. 495 He begins to give the names of the peaks. 498 Each and every peak whose name he knows, he gives its name. 502 So that there the clouds will build up. 506 Because that cloud, they say that it is the jar of the angels. 511 Then the padrino says that "If there is somewhere an evil spirit at work, today, conjure your sword; 527 conjure your

thunderbolt. 531 Do not let them rule. 533 And today where there is no evil spirit, conjure."

538 He calls all the angels by name. 543 And he says, 544 "Angel San Gabriel, throw, throw down the water. 548 Make it green -- make the places green. 551 Angel Santo Tomas, throw, throw down the water, 554 make all the places green. 556 San Miguel Archangel, you are the ruler over all the angels. 561 Throw down the water, and make all the places green where we live. 568 We share the grief from our need. 571 Now reveal all the world and make it green. All the work of people that -- they sympathize with each other. 583 Where they are, they gather their little seedlings. Make them green, and throw down the water on them where the blight and delirium lie playing in the drought. 594 Rise now and pour out over the mountains, 597 because we want the places to be green. 601 So that there we will find everything we eat here on the earth. 607 If there is some human here blighting with his breath, 612 today we call to you to dominate him. 618 Angel Santo Tomas Veronico, Parramador, spread over us today the green source, the white source of water, spread all around, so that we may take it here, the blessing, 630 the compassion you have.

631 You towering clouds, rise up, take form in the green lake, the white lake; take form over 640 the green mountains, over the peaks. 642 Because truly, 643 it is the support of the angels' legs; and now rise up, take form over the peaks.

651 Angels, return, see us today, the _pestejo_ where we live by it. 659 The great altar,

the green great altar, where we live, we kneel 664 to pray before you today. Bring green to the places, bring green to the cornfields; my brothers here where they live have been working for you.

674 Because people, where they raise corn, working, 677 they cannot endure need, 679 they cannot endure all that -- happens to them. 684 Pity them today; open the sky. 686 Throw the water -- throw down the water now, with open sky. 689 You towering clouds, you towering winds, 693 today take form in the sky. 696 You towering winds, 698 today, clothe all the sky where the angels will work. 705 San Lorenzo, Golden Beard, Silver Beard, today your nephews 710 will assist you; let them work today. 715 We will just await that great day. 720 Because we have need. 722 And today we want you to have mercy on us.

725 We have need of the Boy Hauailika, the Girl Hauailika. 737 They say that that is the name of the corn and the beans. 739 And they say that where they live they are dying of drought. 745 Today spread your blessing over their heads. 749 And that is the food of all human beings on the earth."

752 Then when he finishes his praying, where they are bent over beside his bowl of *chilate* and the incense, and everything placed there by them, 762 then they go out and stand on the lot with all the angels and the brothers. 767 They go out to stand on the lot. 769 And they carry each a fist-full of incense in their palms, 772 both it and the censer with the incense 775 burning, and they fan the censer, and carry the smoke up, and hold their arms up to the sky with the incense. 785 And they

stand up and come back to crouch. 788 They do not do this just once, 789 all the -- brothers there, the angels.

795 The padrino says, 796 "Our Father, who art in heaven," 798 and the angels and the brothers there, they finish all the Our Fathers. 805 But they are speaking, and they are crouching. 810 And they are censing everywhere with the smoke which is spreading itself all around. 813 And the padrino is standing holding his arm up to the sky with the incense. 817 Then when they finish doing all that, then he brings all his friends who were praying with him and goes inside.

825 When all is finished, then he begins to kill all the chickens and the turkeys which were placed there by them, and to pour the *chilate* into the hole which was dug by them. 837 When he has finished, he orders many chickens brought into the house where the women are -- are working. 847 He orders that everything be fetched so that those chickens are fixed.

849 And he says to the brothers, "Now everything is left for you to -- go through." 856 Those brothers keep on burning all the incense that is left. 860 And they begin to stir the *chilate* that is set out by them; they begin to share it with the people who are coming and the *chilate* which they put there. They share it little by little, giving it to the little children. 879 Because they say that that *chilate* is the payment of San Lorenzo. 886 They begin to give it out to all the little children who came there.

891 And he goes inside, and looks at the chicken where it is being fixed, and begins to

look for one which is heavy. 898 He orders it fixed separately, for him to eat. 900 Because they say that he, since he was calling the rain, and he wants to eat, he gets the chicken which grew biggest. 910 And that is why he is concerned to go back inside to where the women are and begins to pick up the chickens, where they were placed, to find which is the heaviest.

917 And those brothers, they go out to stand here and there on the lot, looking to see if the clouds are rising over the peaks. 921 And if the afternoon goes and there are none, they watch for a week, and if there is no rain, they come back, and begin to gather another time, which they call precautionary, and the brothers walk through all the villages gathering another time everything which they had been given already, 935 so as to put it out again. 936 But the padrino who prayed before, that padrino, they say his name was -- one -- was named -- Bernabe Leon, and one was called by Vicen -- Vicente Leon.

951 They say those padrinos 952 were always praying. 955 Because they say that Bernabe, they say, from when he was born of his mother, he was followed by a toad. 966 And they say that the midwife when she saw -- the afterbirth, when she saw that afterbirth, she fell down. 974 And the toad came, bent over, behind him; his mother said, "Let it be -- don't put it out, because, this little boy, you don't know what use he may be someday. 983 This boy, he will surely be a prayer-sayer for all his friends some day." 992 And this was heard, her speech, by the gods.

996 And they say that that boy began growing. 999 And there came a day when he said to

his mother, "Mother, this toad of mine, he is going to bathe. Bring a little water in a bowl which has not been used. 1009 I am going to lay hir in it, because he wants to bathe, my little toad."

1011 And they say that the mother went and put a little water into that bowl which had not been used. 1017 When he laid the toad in it, immediately it thundered in the sky. 1021 He said to his mother, "Mother, it is thundering in the sky!" 1025 The mother said, 1026 "It is going to rain." 1028 "Do you know why it is thundering?" 1032 The mother said, "This I know -- because you laid your toad in the water." 1035 He looked again at the sky. 1038 And his toad was lying in the water; it thundered again in the sky.

1043 And the mother went out to look in the lot; she saw that it was everywhere over the peaks. 1050 Then he said to his mother, 1052 "Believe today that my toad, 1056 that when I put my toad here in the water, that immediately it is going to rain." 1062 The mother said, 1063 "Son, then your appearance is truly a gift of God. 1068 Because we have never seen a man like you. 1072 But you are truly in conversation with the angels of Our Father, God."

1077 They say that a day came when a drought set in. 1082 Because they say that long ago people used to plant in -- March. 1089 That day, when March ended, and April began, there was no rain. 1093 Then in April, many people came to him. 1097 They said to him, "You, we have heard that you, since you were born into this world, there has been a toad that was born with you. 1107 And we, we want you to show us what it is like. 1111 Because we started working long ago. 1116 And we have kept waiting for the rain, and there is none. 1119 But maybe you, maybe God heard you today."

1123 Then he said, "But you have brought nothing to show to the angels." 1127 Then those men said, "Well, we've brought nothing, 1131 but he can't hear us: God hears you, just like that."

1136 Then he said, "I can do it. 1139 But I tell you that the gods want us to show them what we use here. 1147 They do not eat. 1149 But they eat the spirits." 1150 And they say that he took that toad, and laid it in the water and called the angels. 1157 And he said, 1158 "Father, you who live and rule us, 1162 send now your angels to us." 1165 He called the angels. 1167 He said, 1168 "Angel San Gabriel, 1169 Angel Santo Tomas, 1171 San Miguel Archangel, 1172 and all you who are angels 1173 of Our Divine Eternal One, He that is our Master; he has mastery over us. 1178 Let the water fall, carve it for me over the earth, 1180 bring green to the places here, make all the places green. 1184 Because these humans, where they live before, are grieving. 1188 They are in need. 1190 And now spread your blessing. 1193 Tower up today, 1194 because these humans want to see right now 1197 your love."

1198 They say that just as he said that, it thundered in the sky. 1202 Then, 1203 those men said, "You are truly the one. 1205 This man was heard by Him, and he brought the rain. 1210 Because his speech was heard by the gods. 1214 By the angels." 1215 They say that that man did not speak much when he sat down to pray, but he was heard speaking by the gods. 1222 They say that twice he was asked by those men, and they came to him bringing everything that he wanted: incense, corn, everything. 1238 Chickens, turkeys, they came to give him, and he would say to put out lots of chilate.

1247 Then he said to the brothers, "You know that what is put out here, 1252 is not so the angels will come to carry off all that was put out by us, 1257 but its spirit they will carry off. 1261 And this I pray for to the angels." 1265 And always as he began to pray to them, as he began to speak with them another time, 1270 they say that just as he sat down to speak, it thundered in the sky and the clouds at once began to build up over the peaks. 1275 And those clouds immediately covered the sky. 1280 They say that the rain began to fall at once. 1282 And that is why -- they -- people used to say that that padrino's speech was heard by God, because just as soon as he sat down to pray to the gods, the rain began falling on the peaks.

1298 But of the padrinos whom I saw, not once did I see one who just spoke and the rain fell. 1301 But they spoke a lot. 1309 They prayed a lot to God. 1310 But they were not heard right away praying by God, because it did not start to rain as they were speaking. 1320 I don't know if I could manage to call for rain. 1323 But if it was not raining: but I know that it is going to rain in my place, because my seedlings are out.

1326 And when the padrino saw that it was raining a lot, and that the people could not work because of the rain, then the brothers grew tired of the rain and began to go to ask the padrino, saying, "Father padrino, we come here to ask of you this because we are not allowed to work by the gods, 1351 because they carve a lot." 1355 Then the padrino told them what to put out. 1364 The brothers went out to gather things in the villages, everything they used. 1370 He came back and the padrino began to pray again. 1374 He called all those working angels.

1379 He said, 1380 "You angels, now we give you your rest, your rest. 1385 Because these humans cannot work, and today we give you your rest. Wait. 1394 Wait today, you angels. 1396 San Lorenzo, wait today; thank you for giving us great blessings. 1404 You have already made it green, and brought green to all the places where we live. 1408 And today, wait."

1410 He said to all the clouds which he had called, when he was sitting calling the rain, and everything which he had called he gave a rest. 1423 He said, "Rest! Wait!" 1426 Then I heard how the padrinos used to pray.

1433 But there was one month when the rain did not stop, and there were many landslides in the places in the mountains. 1442 They say there was one angel whose name is Viper Angel. 1446 They say that he, when he works, there is much rain and there are landslides all over in the mountains. 1452 Then the padrino puts out everything they are used to putting out. 1460 They say that it is the payment to the Viper Angel.

1463 And that Viper Angel is placed in the hands of San Miguel Archangel, 1470 because San Miguel Archangel rules over all the angels.

28. Rainmaking

1473 And that is why the Viper Angel is put in the hands of the angel -- San Miguel Archangel, who we say is -- is the Young Angel. 1483 That Viper Angel is given his rest by the Young Angel so that he does not completely destroy the places, because the Viper Angel, they say that he is the master of all the snakes there are inside the peaks.

1502 And when the Viper Angel is paid, the rain stops in the places.

29. Astronomy

1 + ,'a"ian 'in"te?e 'lu"se 'ra'noh"ta?a +
.'ie?en"te?e 'txu"txu?u + .'a'ma"xia?an 'to?or'e
'ui"tsir "mo 'riuh"?tsu?u?p + 4 + ,'ma?a"txi
'ka'ui"ra 'de"di 'ia + ,"es 'to'ke?e'a'nam"?tsa
'e"?kin + ,'i"uix 'a'iam"pa "u?ut 'e"rum + .
"tui?ix 'e?ek'sih"?pa + 8 + ,'en"ton 'ses'a
'txek"ta 'a'tur"uan + ,"to?or 'e'ui"tsir + .'e
'lu"se 'ra'ia"ha?a + 11 + .'txa?a"ni 'e'?o
"nia?an "hen 'te + ,'ke?e'u'?ka"?pa?a 'san'ra
"mon + .'ah'?txuhk"sah "to?or 'e"rum + 14 + ,
'e'?o'nia?aŋ"hen "tio?p 'ia"ha?a + ,'iŋ'gui"ra?a
"ni + .'a'?kah'?pes'ia"no?p "tu?ut + 17 + ,
"kon 'da'a'ma"xia?an + ,'a'ko'tua"no?p 'tu?u"pat
'o"tot + .'ta"ka 'u'kan"dee "lo?p + 20 + ,'u
'?tsah'?pe"so?p "tu?ut + .'ko"txe?e 'u"txo?p
"tu?ut 'e"lu 'na +

22 + 'a"ian 'o'tron"te?e -- 'o'tron"te?e
'lu"se 'ra + ,'a'to"?poi 'kon'da"uar 'tok"to + .
'a'ma"xia?an + 26 + .'ko'txe?e'a'la"sie 'te +
27 + ,'e'lu"se 'ra'ia"ha?a + ,'tu"no?or 'iak
"?par "uar 'a'xa"na + ."tu?ut 'e"?kin + 30 + ,
"kon 'da'?ko"toi 'a'las"kua 'tro + ."tui?ix 'a
'sa'koh"pa + 32 + ,'e'lu"se 'ra'ia"ha?a + ,
"uix 'a'?ka"xi "to?or 'e'ui"tsir + .'tia?a'nam
"?tsa 'e"?kin + 35 + ,"kon 'da"txe 'a'?ko"toi
'a'la"siŋ 'ko + ,'e'lu"se 'ra'ia"ha?a + .'nam
"?tsi?ix 'tu?u"pat 'e'ui"tsir + 38 + ,'e'lu"se
'ra'ia"ha?a + ,'tu"ru?u '?ka"?pa?a 'u'me'ne"ro?p
+ .'ta"ma 'san'o'ro"man 'ah"?txuhk"sah "to?or 'e
"rum +

41 + ,"txe 'ke?e'tur'?pa'?pi"ro?p 'u'me'ne
"dios + .'ko'txe?e'ah'?txuhk'sa"ho?p "to?or 'e
'?pa"?ka?p 'e'ko"noh + 43 + ,'txe?e"no?p 'a
"ni 'ke?e'lu"see "ro?p 'ia"ha?a + ,'u'?kah"na?ar
'ak'ta'?pi"ro?p + ,'ah'?txuhk'sa"ho?p + ,"to?o
're'?pa"?ka?p 'e'ko"noh + .'tua?a'nie'nin"te?e
'mo"men 'to + ,'a'ket"pa 'txo"kem + .'e'?pa
"?ka?p 'e'ko"noh "to?or 'e"rum + 50 + ,'i'po

29. Astronomy

"re 'so + ,'tu?u"pat 'e?en"te?e + .'ua"tar 'o 'tron"te?e + 53 + ,'i'tu?u"pat 'e?en"te?e + . 'ua"tix 'o'tron"te?e + 55 + ."por 'ke?e"txe 'ke?e'u"ie '?tah'ne"ro?p 'e"?kin + ,"?i + .'e "tok '?pi"ro?p 'tua?a'e"?kin + .'ak'ta'?pi"ro?p 'u"me 'ne'ka'ta"ta?a "dios + 59 + ,'po"re 'so + ,'ha?a"xo?p 'a'?kah'?pe'sia"no?p 'a"ni + . "tu?ut 'e'lu"se 'ra'ia"ha?a +

62 + ,'a"iam "be 'ses + .'u'nu"?ti 'u"?pa 'ta'ka'e"lu 'na + 64 + .'i"txe?e "hen 'te + "kon 'da'e'lu"se 'ra'ia"ha?a 'u'nu"?ti 'u"?pa 'ta'ka'e"lu 'na + ."ha?ax 'in"te?e '?ir'se"iah + .'ke?e'?a"ian "ti?i 'ne'?ka"ni 'u'txam"se 'u"?pa 'ta"ma 'e'lu'ga"ro?p + 68 + ,'hai"ma + ."ger 'ra'?ka"ni 'a'txe?e"na 'ta'ma'e'txi'na"mo?p + 70 + .'?pa'nix"to 'a'?ku'?pe'sia"no?p + ,"por 'ke"ha?a 'xe"ra + ,'e'?o"nia?aŋ "hen 'te + , "?pan 'a'?ku'?pes'ia"no?p + ,"ke?e 'lu'se"ro?p 'ia"ha?a + ,'xe?e'a'xa"no?p + .'ah'?txuhk'sa "ho?p "to?or 'e'?pa"?ka?p 'e'ko"noh "to?or 'e "rum +

77 + ,"i?i + ,'i"xe?e 'ka'ui"ra + ,'ma?a "txi 'a'xa"no?p + ,'txe'ke?e"?kahk + ,"tua?a 'ma?a"txi 'e?ek'sih"?pa 'i'niah"rer + ."o?or 'e "rum + 83 + ,"por 'ke"txe 'ke?e + ,"hai 'e?ek 'sih"?pa + ,'in'iah"rer + ,'a'lo"?koi 'tu"?ki?k 'tu'?ki?k"xix 'a'ni"mal + ,'u'uiŋ"kir 'ui'tsi "ro?p + .'u'?ka?a"pes 'e'?pa"?ka?p "to?or 'e "rum + 89 + ,"txe 'ke?e'po"re 'so'ak'ta"?pir + ,'e'lu"se "ro?p 'ia"ha?a + .'ko'txa'in"te?e '?ir 'se"iah 'ta"ma "u?ut 'e"?kin +

92 + ,"kon 'da"?kix 'a?an'?txak"na + ,'ko 'txe?e'a'las"kua 'tro + .'a'lo"?koi 'o'tron"te?e + 95 + .'u'peh"ko?p 'ta"ma "ni 'nio'sam'pas "kual + 96 + ,'?e'?o"nia?aŋ 'hen"tio '?pa"ni + 'ko'txa?a'tix'a'lo"?koi + 'e'lu"se 'ra'ia"ha?a "to?or 'e'ui"tsir + ,'ta'ka'u'kan"de?e "lo?p + ,

29. Astronomy

'tu?u"pat 'u'io'to"to?p + .'a"ka?ai 'a'?kah'?pe
'sia"no?p "tu?ut + 102 + ,"ia 'ko'to"ro?p + .
"ehs 'to'a?an'?txak"na + ,'por'ke?e'lu"se 'ra'ia
"ha?a + .'tu?u'pat"xix 'ua"tar 'e"?kin + 106 +
.'a'?kah'?pe'sia"no?p 'tua?a'ma'tu"?ka?a 'u'nu
'me"ro?p "nie 'nu'max'ta"ko?p + 107 + ,'a'?kah
'?pe'sia"no?p 'ta'ma'tu"no?or 'e'pa"?ka?p + .
"to?or 'e"rum +

109 + ,'e'lu"se 'ra'xe?e'ka'ua?a"re 'mor
'mo"re?e?k + ,"por 'ke?e'nu"?tur 'a'xa"no?p + ,
'txe?e"hen 'te'ke?e"sie 'te'lu"see "ro?p 'ia
"ha?a + .'a'xa"no?p 'nu"?tur 'e'lu'se?e"ro?p 'ia
"ha?a + 113 + 'ah'uaŋ'?kin"to 'a'to"?poi +
114 + ,'kon'da"txe 'a?an'?txak"na 'e'lu"see
"ro?p 'ia"ha?a + .'nam"?tsi?ix +

116 + ,'i'lo'ke?e'ma?a"txi 'a'xa"no?o?p 'a
"iam "be 'ses'ka'ui"ra + .'o?o"hri 'ua"to?o?p
"tu?ut "?kin + 118 + ,'?pa"nix "u?ut "?kahk
'txe'ke'?in'ta"ka + ,'e?es"pa 'a'tur'ua"no?p + .
'ta"ma 'u?ut'e"?kin +

121 + ,'e'ki"lis 'a'?pa"?kahr"na 'u'me'ne
"hen 'te + .'kon'da?a"?txa?an 'ta"ma "u?ut 'e
"?kin + 123 + "por 'ke"txe 'ke?e -- ,'e'ki"lis
'ia"ha?a + 'hai'ah'?ku"na "tiem 'po + ,'u'me'ni
"dios + .'e'ki"lis 'ia"ha?a 'u'?ku"xi 'e"?kin +
.'o?o'?e"lu 'na + 129 + ,'i'po"re 'so + ,
'txe?e"no?p 'ke'kon'da'e"?kin 'o?o'e"lu 'na + ,
'a?ahp"na 'u'me'ne'ki"lis + ,'en"ton 'ses + .'e
"lu 'na'u'txom'pa"ti 'e'pa"?ka?a?p 'e'ko"noh
"to?or 'e"rum + .'tua?a'ma?a"txi 'a'?kuh"xo?p 'u
'me'ne'ki"lis + 135 + ."por 'ke"txe 'ke?e'hai
'a'nu"mui 'in"te?e "di 'ia + ,'o?o + ."dos "di
'ia + ,"ma 'tu"?ka 'e"?kin + .'e?ek'sih"?pa
"o?or 'e"rum + 140 + .'a?atx"pa 'tu"no?or 'a
'ni"mal 'lo'ke?e'?a"ian + ,'ta'me?e'ui'tsi"ro?p
+ ,'ta"ma 'e'ma"ro?p + .'i'tu"no?or 'e'na'ual
'?pi"ro?p 'lo'ke?e'txa'me"no?p 'ko"txia?atx

29. Astronomy

'ti?in'a'?ka?a"pa 'txa'mes"?pir + 144 + 'ie?e 'na"ual 'ia"ha?a + ,'a'?pix"?ko?o?p + ."?i '?u '?ku"xo?p 'e"hen 'te'xe?e'a'?pi'xi"ri "to?or 'e "rum +

29. Astronomy

1 There is one large star and one small one when it becomes dark over the peak Moriuh-?tsuu?p. 4 We do not see them by day, until the sun sets and it is already becoming dark on the ground. 8 Then that star appears in place over the peak. 11 The old people used to say that its name is San Ramon Watcher-over-the-Earth. 14 Those old people, I used to see them praying to it. 17 When it grew dark, they bent over behind their houses with their candles. 20 They prayed to it as they did to the moon.

22 There is another ... another star that rises when it has just become dark. 26 At about seven o'clock. 27 That star, every night it travels across the sky. 30 When it gets to be four o'clock, it is already about to get light. That star is already setting over the peaks where the sun sets. 35 When it gets to be five o'clock, that star has already set behind the peak. That star has been named by them as San Oromán Watcher-over-the-Earth.

41 It is said that it was set in place by God as a watcher over mankind. 43 They used to say that those stars had been left on purpose as watchers over mankind so that not even for a moment would man remain abandoned on the earth. 50 And so, behind the one comes another. 53 And behind that one, already comes another. 55 Because it is said that they are fellow runners with the sun, and mates of the sun, left by God Our Father. 59 So, they used to pray to that star.

62 There are times when it unites its body with the moon. 64 And people say, "When that star unites its body with the moon, that is a sign that someone is going to kill himself in the villages. 68 If not, a war is going to be

made in the towns." 70 So they believe, because this is what the old people believed, that those stars which travel are watchers over mankind on earth.

77 And those which we see not traveling are said to be fires, so that it does not become completely dark on the earth. 83 Because it is said that if it gets completely dark, all of the animals of the master of the peaks will come out, and finish off man on the earth. 89 It is said that that is why those stars were left, as a sign in the sky.

92 When it is just about to grow light, at about four o'clock, another comes out. 95 They call it Child San Pascual. 96 The old people, just as that star came out above the peak, used to begin, with their candles, behind their houses, to pray to it. 102 There they bent over until it became light, because that star there, just behind it came the sun. 106 They prayed for nothing to happen to them or their children. 107 They prayed for all men on the earth.

109 The stars we call Star-group, because they go together, people say that those seven stars travel joined together. 113 They rise just at daybreak. 114 When it becomes light, those stars have already set.

116 And those which do not move, at times we see them fall down from the sky. 118 Like coals, it is said that they move in the sky.

121 The Eclipse is feared by people when it lies in the sky. 123 Because it is said that ... that eclipse, if given time by God, that eclipse would eat the sun or the moon. 129

29. Astronomy

And so, they say that when the sun or the moon is grabbed by the eclipse, then the moon offers up mankind on the earth, so as not to be eaten by the eclipse. 135 Because it is said that if one day passes, or two days, there will be no sun; it will become dark on the earth. 140 All the animals there are will rise up in the peaks, in the seas, and all the spirits who are dead, just like those who are completely dead. 144 And those spirits will come to life and eat the people who are alive on the earth.

30. Other Signs of the Weather

1 + ,"kon 'da'ka'ua?a"re 'ka'?ka"nix 'a'nu "mui 'e"lu 'na + ,"ha?ax "kon 'da'u'?ka'ni"tix "tres "di 'ia 'o?o"dos "di 'ia + .'tua?a'a'nam "?tsa + 4 + ,"kon 'da'a?an'?txak"na + .'ka'ui "ra 'a'sa'koh"pa "to?or "tix 'e'ui"tsir + 6 + ,'en"ton 'ses + ,'e"di 'ia'xe?e"tia?a 'a'nu"mui + .'ma?a'txix"to 'ka'ui"ra + 9 + ."pe 'ro'a'nu "mui 'ta'ka'e"?kin + 10 + ."pe 'ro'ma?a"txi 'ka'ui"ra + 11 + ."por 'ke?e'u'nu"?tu?u "?pa 'ta"ka 'e"?kin + 12 + .'i'po"re 'so'ma?a"txi 'ka'ui"ra +

13 + ,'en"ton 'ses + ,'ta'ma"dos "di 'ia + .'xe?e'ma?a"txi 'ka'ui"ra + ,'ta"ma 're"ra + ,'e "dos "no 'txe'ia"ha?a + ,"kon 'da'a'ma"xa?an + . 'ka'ui"ra 'ke?e'txe'ke"rix "to?or 'e'ui"tsir + 20 + .'ha?ax"to 'ka'ua?a"re 'ke?e'sut"pi?ix 'e "lu 'na + 21 + ."por 'ke?e"uar 'a'nah"tran 'ta 'ka'e"?kin +

22 + ,'e"rue 'de'ia"ha?a + ,'a"?txa?an 'ta 'mu?ut'e"?kin + .'nien'ka'ui"ra 'tu"?ko 'ra'a 'txek"ta + 25 + ,'txak"txak + .'i"iax 'ta"ren + 27 + .'ka'ua?a"re 'ke"ha?ax 'u'ta'res"ni?i?p 'e'ha"ha?ar + 28 + ."?paŋ 'ko'txa'e'mak"txan 'xe?e'ka'ui"ra "to?or 'e"rum + 29 + ,"kon 'da 'ma?a"txi 'e?eix"na + ,'a'sat"pa + ,'a'?ka"xi 'e 'ha"ha?ar + .'a?a"xi 'e"tar 'de + 33 + ,'i"kon 'da'ta"kar 'es'to'a'nam"?tsa 'e"?kin + .'ka 'ua?a"re 'ke"ma 'tu"?ka 'e'ha"ha?ar +

30. Other Signs of the Weather

1 When we say that the moon is about to pass, that is when it is going to be almost three days, or two days until it sets. 4 When it gets light, we see it become light just over the peak. 6 Then, the day that it passes, we do not see it. 9 But it passes with the sun. 10. But we do not see it. 11 Because it joins itself with the sun. 12 And so we do not see it.

13 Then, for two days we do not see it, then, on that second night, when it gets dark, we see that it is visible over the peak. 20 Then we say that the moon has turned around. 21 Because it is getting farther from the sun.

22 That wheel hangs in the sky, and we don't see what time it becomes visible. Red and gray-green it is. 27 We say that it is the bringer of rain. 28 So too with the rainbow which we see over the earth. 29 When it does not go away, the rain ceases falling in the afternoon. 33 And when it is around until the sun sets, we say there will be no rain.

GROUP V

NOTES

25. What the World Used to be Like

25.6 In all its occurrences, irah irah definitely means 'again and again'. Moreover, it is clear from the first phrases that cyclical destruction of a world peopled as it is now is just what is meant. A few other contemporary myths continue this ancient trait (see J. Eric S. Thompson 1965).

25.150-174 These colored seas are obviously a vestige of the ancient Mayan color-direction symbolism. In 26.297-355 there are said to be four seas: milk white, blood red, blue-green and pitch black.

25.276 That is, 'big around'. In general, the Chorti, whose heavy work is mostly done with the legs and back, do not have prominently developed arms.

25.278 This belief in cannibalism in the United States is widespread among the Chorti. I heard it from several informants, who told of a train being loaded with people who were shipped off to be fattened and eaten 'during the war'. Shortly before González left Jocotán with me for New Haven, he was visited by an old uncle who, convinced González would never return, wished to say goodbye.

26.736-758 The oi is one of four forked tree-trunks set in the ground to support the roof and walls of a house. For similar episodes in other Mayan myths, see J. Eric S. Thompson 1965.

26. Earth, Sky and Water

26.108 This form follows the same pattern as the other compound color terms: "iax '?tu "nen 'It is black and blue', 'iax'?tuh"na 'It turned black and blue', "?kam '?pu"nen 'It is lemon yellow', 'a'?kam'?puh"na 'It is turning lemon yellow', and so on. Only the suffix vowel of "ik 'si"?pan is different.

26.175 The literal translation is 'no tomorrow'; it is sometimes contracted to 'meh "?kar.

27. Rainy Season

27.4 This wheel or ring is the Milky Way. Girard (1949:458-464) discusses some of the beliefs about it.

27.5-10 Volcán is a peak just N of a long high ridge extending SW of it. A village near the S end and a small stream there are named <u>El Chucte</u>; near the N end, about 14 km. just S of E from Pelillo Negro, is the village Nearar, which the Chorti consider two villages, <u>niarar</u> and <u>ti pakai</u>. The ridge is also known as <u>niarar</u>. The peaks on this ridge, all above 1500 m. and one at 1615 m. are the highest ground visible from Pelillo in that direction. In June, the sun rises directly over the village of <u>niarar</u>, and in January, slightly N of it, but S of Volcán.

27.19 This peak, whose name means 'Incense gathering', is just W of Pelillo, and slightly higher. It is just N of the ridge <u>Xinxiraa</u> (see 27.45).

27.28-30 Rafael Girard first reported that the Chorti make such observations (1962:57); since this has not been accepted by everyone, it should be noted that this text confirms it.

27.45 <u>Xinxiraa</u> is a ridge S of Pelillo Negro.

27.56 The crescent moon is tipped to one side, like a bowl or jug being emptied of water. See Girard (1962:134) for an illustration.

27.109-114 A <u>mak txan</u> 'rainbow' is like a <u>mak tee</u> 'corral', because it confines the rain.

27.180 Compare + ."tua?a 'ma"tua?a + ,"pe 'ro'ko"txa '?ka"nu?u "txe "tua?a + "His or not his, it's going to be used by him just the same!"

28. Rainmaking

28.14 A _ramada_ or arbor is constructed of saplings or canes arched over the cross, altar, or image to be venerated. Some have house-like roofs as well. Wisdom 1940 (facing 421) shows one; Girard 1966 (photo 24) shows a more elaborate one.

28.78-79 Compare the ritual confinement of the saint in 36.17-26.

28.132-135 Many curers also use a child as a medium. Note again that the medium is an _anxer_, while an angel is an _aŋhel_.

28.136-141 Girard (1966, photos 21, 33, 121, 122, etc.) shows a kerchief knotted around or over the head of the prayer-sayer.

28.200 Literally, 'sprinkles' or 'scatters'.

28.510 Rain is beaten or chopped from the clouds by the angels being invoked throughout this passage.

28.518-519 The angels who bring rain strike at evil spirits, firing thunderbolts at them.

28.591 'Blight' is meant literally here: a number of plant diseases causing withering and discoloration of leaves are known as _xer-or_; one, _tan xer-or_ 'dust blight' results in a yellow powdery coating over the leaves. _Xer-or_ is caused by the breath of an _ah-pos-on-er_ (see 28.607-611, and compare text 15).

29. Astronomy

29.7 San Ramón is Venus as the Evening Star. The less bright star which follows it I am unable to identify for the present.

29.109 This is the constellation Pleiades. See Girard (1949:453-455) for a discussion of its use in determining zenith passages of the sun.

29.121 This is Spanish _eclipsis_ adapted and metanalyzed to _kilis_ with an _e_ prefix.

29.133 Mankind is put up as security, or in escrow. The details of the transaction are obscure.

30. Other Signs of the Weather

30.1 Girard (1949:466) speaks of the _confusion_ of the moon; the Chorti term is simply 'passing'.

30.22 This is apparently the Milky Way. See Girard 1949:458-460.

VI: Religion

31. Esquipulas

I

1 + ,'e'?pah"xan 'noh"?kin + ,'ta'ma'e'u
'?kah'ies'ia"hir 'e"?a 'nio + .'ta"ma 're"ra 'el
"kua 'tro'de?e"ne 'ro + 4 + .'a"ka?ai 'a?a"xin
'e"hen 'te'ta'noh"?kin 'es'ki"pu 'la +

5 + ,"kon 'da"tui?ix 'ka?a"xi 'ta'noh"?kin
+ ,'ka'uix"ka?ar + ,'a"ka?ai 'u'lo?k"se 'e'mux
'mux"pa?a + .'xe?e'ka'ua?a"re 'sar"pat + .'tua?a
'ka'ku"txi 'a?a"xin 'ta'noh"?kin + 10 + .'ka
'?ka"txe "mei 'gra + ,'tua?a'?tsak"ta 'ka'?ku"xi
+ ,'es"to 'tia?a'ka'io?o"pa + 13 + ,"kon 'da
'a?ak'?pa"re + ,"tui?ix 'ka?a"xin 'u'ius"ta
'ia?a"?katx 'tua?a'ka'?ku"xi 'ta"?pi?ir + ,'u'go
"ri 'e'?pu?t"na?a?k + ,'u'mu"xi 'e"?txah + 17
+ ,"kon 'da'tu"ri?ix 'tu"no?or + ,'u'?pu"?ti 'ta
"man "te?e "txihr + .'ka'ku"txa?a "xin +

20 + ,"kon 'da'ka'?ko"toi 'ta'ma'e'txi"nam
'o"lo 'pa + ,'ka'ma"ni 'e'kan"de 'la + ,'ko?o
"txoi 'ta"kar + ."tu?ut 'e'ka"tu?u 'pas"to 'ra +
24 + .'ka'uir"se + 25 + ."por 'ke?e"txe 'ke
'?ix'ka?ar"?pir 'tua?a'e'mi'la"gro 'so + 26 +
,"ia 'ka'lo"?koi + ,'ka'?ko"toi 'ka'ua"ian + .
'ta"kohn 'saŋ"huaŋ + 29 + ,"ia 'ka'?ku"xi?i 'a
"?katx + .'lo'ke'ka'lo?k"se 'ti'ko?o"tot + 31
+ ,'u'?pa"ker 'ia"?katx 'ia"ha?a + ,'ma?a"txi
'ka'uak"ta + ,'ka'?pa"si 'ta"ma 'e"xe?ex + .
"tua?a 'ka'su"ti 'ua"tar 'ti'ko?o"tot + 35 + ,
'por'ke"txe 'ke?e"hai 'ka'uak"ta + ,'e"?pak 'ia
"ha?a + .'a'ket"pa 'u"me?ein 'ia?a"?katx 'ta'ma
'e'lu"gar 'ia"ha?a + 38 + .'i'ma?a"txi 'a'?tox
"pa 'ti"ko?oit +

39 + ,'a?an'?txak"na + ,'ka'lo"?koi 'tia?a
"uar 'ka?a"xi 'ta"?pi?ir + .'ua"rix 'ka'sah"ka
'ka"si?i + 42 + ,'ka'?kat"?pu "to?or 'ka"txihr
+ ,'tua?a'ka"txe?e "?kahk "tar + .'tia?a'ka'?ko
"toi 'ka'tur"uan 'es'ki"pu 'la + 45 + ,'ka'?ko
"toi 'ta"kohn 'san"tia 'go + .'tu"no?or 'e"hen

31. Esquipulas

'te'a?a"tio?p + 47 + ,"por 'ke"txe 'ke'me?e
"rer + ,'ko?o"txoi "tu?ut 'e'mi'la"gro 'so + .
'hai"ma "ha?ax 'a'tes'?pi"ron +

50 + ,"kon 'da'ka'?ko"toi + .'tu?u"ti?i
'txi"nam + .'ka"ka?ai 'ka'txe're"sar + 53 + ,
"uar 'ka'txe're"sar + .'es"to 'ko?o"txoi 'ma
"ku?u 'san"tua 'rio + 55 + ,'as'ta'?ka?a"?pa
'ka"txe 're"sar + ,'ka'lo"?koi + .'ka'sah"ka
"tia?a "tua?a 'ka'tu"ruan + 57 + .'a"ka?ai 'ka
'txa"pi 'ka"?pu?ur +

58 + ,"o 'tro"di 'ia + ,'ka?a"xi 'ka?a"uan
'tu"uam 'e"hen 'te + ,"tia?a 'tso'ro"ro?p + .
"tua?a 'ka'lu"mui 'tu?u"pat 'e'ka'ta"ta?a 'mi'la
"gro 'so + 62 + ,"por 'ke?e'ta'ma'e'txi"nam
'ia"ha?a + ,"ua?ar 'in'te?e"dios + .'u'?ka"?pa
'mi'la"gro 'so +

II

65 + ,"txe 'ke?e"dios 'ia"ha?a + .'tah'ui
"na 'ta'ma'in"te?e "u?ut "ia 'no + 67 + .
"ua?ar 'ga"lan 'a'?txi"ri?i 'u"?puhk + 68 + .
"txe 'ke'u'mo'roh"se 'u"?pa 'e"hen 'te'tua?a'u
'ui"ro?p + 69 + ,"pe 'ro'e"dios 'ia"ha?a + .
'ma?a"txi 'u'iak"ta 'u"?pa 'tua?a'a'?pihtx"nu?ut
+ 71 + ,"por 'ke"txe 'ke'a"ian "ti?i 'ne'?ka
"ni 'u'ta"res + .'u'ua"?pu 'ta'u'io"tot +

III

73 + ,"kon 'da'ix"to + ,"kai 'txe?e"na 'u
'io"tot "tu?ut 'e"ia 'no'ia"ha?a + ."txe 'ke
'ma?a"txi 'u'?ka"ni 'tua?a'ket"pa 'ia"ha?a + 76
+ ,'por'ke?e"ua?ar 'in"te?e 'no"xi?i 'a'la"gu
'na + .'ta"ma 'u'io'ri"iir 'e"ia 'no +

78 + ,"txe 'ke"kon 'da'a?an'?txak"na 'o
'tron"te?e "di 'ia + ,'a?a"xin 'e?er"na 'ta"ma

31. Esquipulas

'u'io"tot + .'tia?a'txe?e"na "tua?a 'ket"pa?a
"ni 'ta"mar + 81 + .'ma'mah"txi?i + ,'kon'da
'a?a"xin 'e?er"na + ."ia?a "ua?ar 'tu?u'io'ri
"iir 'ia?a'la"gu 'na + 84 + ,'in'iahr"to 'in
'iahr"to + .'a'?keh"txa 'a'ua?a?p"na 'ta'u'io
"tot + .'ma?a"txi 'a'ket"pa +

IV

87 + .'e'hen"tio?p 'ia"ha?a 'txe?e"no?p +
.'ko"txa "tua?a 'ka"txe 'u'io"tot 'e'ka'ta"ta?a
'ta"ra + 89 + ."por 'ke?e"mei 'gra'ia?a'la"gu
'na + 90 + ."ma 'ko'txe?e"rer + ,"por 'ke"hai
'ka'?tsohi"ro + .'tue?e"ra 'u'?txa"mio?on 'e
"sier '$_r$o'u'uin"kir 'ia?a'la"gu 'na +

V

93 + "pe 'ro"txe 'ke?e -- ,'in"te?e 'i'la
'ma + .'uai'?kih'res"na 'u"men 'u'uiŋ"kir 'ia?a
'la"gu 'na + 96 + .'a'ro?p"na 'ta"ma 'u'ua
"ia?k + ,"hai 'u'toi'ie?e"no?p 'ko'txe?eŋ'?ka"ni
"ne?en + .'e"rer 'u"txo?p 'io?o"tot +

VI

99 + ,'e'hen"tio?p 'ia"ha?a + ."kai 'u'mo
'roh"se 'u"?po?p + 101 + ,'u'tu'ru"?po?p 'ia?a
"katx + ,'iah"tso?o + ,'iuh"?tsu?u?p + ,'e'kan
"de 'la + .'e"pan + 106 + ,'u'mo'roh"se 'u"?pa
'e'i'xik"tak + ,"kai 'u"txo?p 'e"sa?a + ."ti?in
'ta'?pehr"ha?a + 109 + ,"kon 'da'tu"ri?ix 'tu
"no?or + .'u'?pu"?tio?p 'e"sa?a 'ta'ma'e"?puhr +
111 + ."kai 'u'?pa"sio?p 'e'txum"pi?i 'ta'ma'e
"txihr + 112 + ,'ia?a"?katx + ,'u'ku"txio?p 'i
"xin 'ta'u'io'ri"iir 'ia?a'la"gu 'na +

114 + ,'u"txo?p 'ko"tuan 'e'?i"la 'ma'xe?e
'uai"?ka + .'tua?a'?kah'?pe"sian "tu?ut 'e"sier
'po'ia"ha?a +

31. Esquipulas

VII

116 + ."kai '?kah'?pe"sian 'e'?i"la 'ma + 117 + .'u'ia?a"re 'e"sier 'po + ."rei 'na"san 'ta'ku'le"bri 'na + ."rei 'ku'le"bri 'na + 120 + ,'ah'?ko'to"ret + .'i'iu'ma"ret 'ta'mia?a'la "gu 'na'i"ra + 122 + ,"no?on + .'e'?pa"?ka?p 'e'ko'no"hon + .'u'nem'?pi"ron 'tua?a'e'?ah'ti 'txa"ner "dios + ,"uar 'ka'io?o"pa 'ka'toh"ti?i 'ie"set + ,'ta"ka 'u'ia"ra?k 'e"san 'ta'ma'ga"le 'na + .'xe?e'i'iu'mar"?pir 'ta'ma'ka'ua"ra?k + 128 + ,'i'ta"ka 'u"txu?u 'e'txoh'?pes"?pir "tio?o?p + .'u"meŋ 'ka'uiŋ'ki"rar "dios + 130 + ."ha?a 'xe"ra 'a'tua?a'ni"?pir + 131 + .'i "ra 'a'ui"ra 'su'tur"hut + 132 + .'?txa"ma 'pa 'sar"?ka?p + 133 + .'u"?piŋ 'ka'?kah'?pe"siah + 134 + ."no?oŋ 'ka'txuk"pa?ar + "tua?a -- . 'tua?a'uah"?ko?on 'lu"gar 'tia?a'ka?a"txi 'iŋ "gohr 'o"tot 'ta?a'ueh"?tser + 137 + ,"por 'ke?e"dios 'xe?e'txek"ta 'ti"ko?oit + .'?pa"nix '?ka"ni 'a'?ko'to"ri "to?or +

139 + ,"kon 'da'u'lo?k"se 'e'o'hro"ner 'ia "ha?a 'e'?i"la 'ma + .'ia?a'la"gu 'na'ki'rik"na 'ko'txa"u?ut 'e"?kin +

VIII

141 + ,"txe 'ke?e'?pa?a?k"ta 'e"txan 'ia "ha?a + .'kon'da'u'iu"?pi 'e'?ka"?pa?ah '?ko'to "rer + 143 + ,"kon 'da'?ka?a"pa '?kah'pes"ian 'e'?i"la 'ma + ,'i'?ka?a"pi?ix 'u'xu"rio?o?p 'u 'nu?u?k'iah"tso?o + ,'ia?a"?katx + ,'atx"pa 'e '?i"la 'ma + .'oh"ron + .'u'ia?a"re?e "hen 'te + 149 + ,"?en 'tre"o 'txo"di 'ia + .'i'?kah"ies 'e'tra"ba 'ho +

IX

151 + ,"kai 'u'?pi"sio?p + .'u'ua?a"ri?p 'io?o"tot + 153 + ,'u'?txa"?po?o?p 'u"saŋ"hir

31. Esquipulas

+ ,'tia?a"tua?a 'u'tso"rio?p 'e"tun + .'ua"tar 'ma'ku?u"rum + .'xe?e'u'hah"txi?i?p 'io?o"tot + 157 + ,"pe 'ro'ta'kiak"?par + ,'ia?a'la"gu 'na + ,'tia?a"uar 'o?o'ioh"?ki + .'a'?ka?a"pa 'u'uin "txu 'tu"no?or + 161 + ,"kon 'da?a'sa'koh"pa + .'ma'tu"?ka 'a"ian + 163 + .'a'?ka?a"pa 'e?ein "txa 'a?a"xi 'ta"ha?a + 164 + ,"kon 'da'a'sa 'koh"pa "o 'tro"di 'ia + ,'a?a"xin + 166 + ,'u 'ui"ro?p + .'ma'tu"?ka?a "ian + ."xe 'u"txo?p + 169 + .'i"?pan 'tu"no?or "di 'ia + 170 + . "kai 'oh'ro"no?p + 171 + .'txe?e"no?p + .'in 'ta"ka 'ka'sa"ti 'ka"?pa + 173 + ,'ma?a"txi 'lo"?koi + .'tu"?ka 'u"txe 'e'?i"la 'ma'i"ra +

X

175 + .'sut"pa 'uai"?ka 'e'?i"la 'ma + 176 + .'a'ro?p"na 'ta"ma 'u'ua"ia?k + ,'ke'u 'uin"kir 'ia?a'la"gu 'na + .'u'?ka"ni 'u"ma?an +

179 + ,"kon 'da'sut"pa 'uai"?ka 'e'?i"la 'ma + ,'u'mo'roh"se 'u"?pa 'tu"no?or 'e"hen 'te + .'xe?e"uar 'a'pat"no?o?p + 182 + .'u'ia?a "rio?p 'e'i"la 'ma + .'u'sah"ka 'ta"ma 'u"?kin + "tua?a 'u'na?a"to?p + ,'ko"txa 'u'?ka"ni 'u "ma?an + .'e"txan 'ia"ha?a + .'hai'?pi"xir 'o 'txa"men + 188 + ,'txek"ta 'ta'ma'e"?kin + . 'ke"?pi "xir 'a'?kan"na +

XI

190 + ,'i"kon 'da'txek"ta + ,'ke?e'?pi"xir "hen 'te'u'?ka"ni 'e"sier 'po + ,'en"ton 'ses + ,'e'hen"tio?p 'ia"ha?a + 'xe?e"uar 'a'pat"no?o?p + .'txe?e"no?p + ,'u'?ka"nia?atx "tua?a 'ko?o "txoi 'ka?a"uan + ,'in"te?en 'tio?o"natx + .'ma "kui?ir 'e"mes 'kla + .'?pi"xir '?pi"xir + 200 + ,"por 'ke"txe 'ke?e + ,'u'?kah"tio?p 'a"ni 'e 'o"nia?aŋ "hen 'te + ,'ke?e'o"tot 'ia"ha?a + , "kon 'da"kai 'hah"txa + .'u'ui?i"ro?p 'ta"ri 'ma

31. Esquipulas

'ku?u"rum + 205 + ,"txe 'ke?e + ,'txa'txa?a "te?e 'e'ui'ni"ko?p + ,'ua?a?p"no?o?p + .'ta"ma 'u'ies"ki?i "nir + 209 + ,"txe 'ke'?pi"xir '?pi"xir + ,'e'ui'ni"ko?p 'ia"ha?a + ,'o'se"na 'ua?a?p"no?o?p + ,'ma"kui?ir 'e"mes 'kla + 'tia?a'hah"txa 'u'uo?oi"ro?p +

XII

214 + ,"es 'to'ke?e + ,'u"txo?p 'ko'txe'ia "ha?a + ,'en"ton 'ses + .'atx"pa 'io?o"tot 'tu?u "to?p + 218 + ,'kon"da 'us"ta + ,"tui?ix + ,'u '?ka?a'pe"so?p + ,'ho?ots"pa 'in"te?e 'al'ban "iil + .'ta"ri 'ta"rum + 223 + ,'tu'ru"to 'u 'se?ein"iir 'u'me'ne"ro?p + .'es"to 'ko"ne?er + 225 + ,"txe 'ke?e'al'ban"iil 'ia"ha?a + .'ah '?es"pa 'nia'a"ni +

XIII

227 + ,"txe 'ke"ha?ax 'e"sier 'po'ia"ha?a + ,"kai '?txa"muan + 229 + ,'?pa'nix"to + , '?ko"toi 'txek"ta + .'e'txi"nam 'ia"ha?a + 232 + ,'po"re 'so'ko"ne?er + ,'txe?e"hen 'te'ke?e 'san"tua 'rio'ia"ha?a + ."to?or 'a'la"gu 'na "ua?ar + 235 + ,"txe 'ke'kon"da 'us"ta 'tok"to + ,'i"rah 'i"rah 'a'ki'rik"na + .'ko'txe"u?ut 'e "?kin + 238 + ,"es 'to'ke?e'kah"txa 'u"nu?u?k 'e"sier 'po'u"men 'e'mi'la"gro 'so + .'u'iak"ta 'e'ki'rik"na?ar + 240 + ,'ko"ne?er 'txe"ker 'e 'ia"lam 'bra'sa"nar + ,'ua"tar "to?or 'e'san"tua 'rio + .'a?a"xin 'ma'ku?u"rum + 243 + ,"por 'ke?e"txe 'ke?e"ha?ax 'e"txan 'ia"ha?a + .'ka "txar "?txa?ar +

XIV

245 + ,'txe?e"no?p 'a"ni + .'ke?e'ta"rix 'e"tiem 'po + ,'ta'ma'e'noh'?ki"no?p + ."mei 'gra"hen 'te"kai 'ket"pa + 249 + ,'ia"ha?a + ,

31. Esquipulas

'ui'ni"ko?p + ,'i'xik"tak + ,'max"tak + ,"por 'ke?e"txe 'ke?e + ,"kon 'da"uar 'a'nu"muo?p 'ta 'ka'ma"rin + ,'tia?a"?txu?ur 'e'mi'la"gro 'so + ,"tu?ut 'u'ku'ru"sir + ,'tia?a'a'lu"muo?p 'ko "tor 'ko"tor + ,'tu?u"pat 'e'mi'la"gro 'so + . "txe 'ke'?a"ian "ti?i 'ne'a?a?p"?tsa "u?ut 'e"ta 'bla'ta"kar + 260 + .'o?ots"pa 'a?a"xin 'ta 'me?e'a'la"gu 'na + 261 + ."ti?in 'a'sut"pa 'u 'nu?u?k 'tu?u"pat + 262 + ,'txe?e"no?p 'ke "ha?ax + ."tie?e 'ne'ma"ha?ax 'in'te?e"ra 'u '?pih'nu"siah + 264 + ,"txe 'ke'u"men 'e'mi'la "gro 'so + .'a'suh"ma 'u'nu?u"?ko?p + 266 + . 'a'txa"mo?o?p +

XV

267 + ,"kon 'da"uar 'a'nu"muo?p 'tu?u"pat 'e'mi'la"gro 'so + ,'tia?a"?txu?ur + .'tu"no?or 'u'iak"ta 'u'tu'mi"no?p "tu?ut + 270 + ."ti?in 'u'iak"ta 'in"te?e 'kan"de 'la'tu?u'ieh"?tser + 271 + ."txe 'ke?e"tua?ah '?ku"na 'mas'u'kux"tar 'u"me 'ne"dios 'ia"ha?a + 272 + ,"por 'ke"txe 'ke?e"dios 'ia"ha?a 'ta"uar + "tua?a 'u'lo?k"se 'tu"no?or 'ma'?pam'?pa"nir + .'lo'ke?e'a"ian 'ta "ma 'e'ui"nik +

XVI

275 + ,'po"re 'so + ,'ta'ma'e'noh"?kin 'ia "ha?a + .'a'?ko"toi "mei 'gra"hen 'te + 278 + ,'u"txo?o?p 'e'pe'ni"ten 'te + .'tua?a'a'kor'pes "no?o?p 'tu?u'ma'?pam'?pa'ni"ro?p + 280 + , 'tar'tok"to 'u"ti?i 'e'txi"nam + ,'a'ko'tua"no?p + ,'ko"tor 'ko"tor + ,"to?or 'u'pi"xo?p + .'es "to 'a'?ko"tuo?p 'tia?a"?txu?ur 'e'mi'la"gro 'so + 285 + ,"ti?i 'ne"uar 'a'?ko?oi "o?or 'u"pix + ."tia?a 'ra?a"xi 'ko"tor + .'ta"ka 'ia + 288 + ,"ti?i 'ne'?pu"?tur "ua 'ra'xa"no?p 'ta"ka 'ia + .'u'ua"ii 'u"saa "ko?o?p 'tu?ut'e"rum + 290 + ,"ti?in 'u'po?otx"hor + ."ti?in 'u"sa 'ba'na +

31. Esquipulas

,'tua?a'nu"mui 'ta"mar + .'xe?e"uar 'a?a"xi 'ko "tor "to?or 'u"pix +

294 + ,"ti?i 'ne"uar 'a?a?p"?tsa + .'u"sa 'ko + ,'u'ui'xa?a"xi + ,'u'xi"?txi 'de"lan 'te + ,"es 'to'ke?e'u'?ko'te"so?p + .'tia?a"?txu?ur 'e 'mi'la"gro 'so + 300 + ,"pe 'ro'a"ian "ti?in 'a'txa"mai + .'u"me 'ne'?ko?o"ier + 302 + . 'txe?e"no?p 'ke"ha?ax 'e"mei 'gra'u'ma'?pam'?pa "nir + 303 + .'po"re 'sua'txa"mai +

XVII

304 + ,'po"re 'so + ,"kuan 'do"uar 'a'lo "?koi + ,'tu?u'io'to"to?p + ,'u"txo?p 're"sar + .'tua?a'ma'tu"?ka 'u'num"se 'u"?po?o?p 'ta "?pi?ir + 309 + ,'a"ian 'e'ku"rus + ."ua?ar 'a?a"xin 'ta"?pi?ir + 311 + .'nah'tok"to 'u'ui "ro?p + ,'a"ka?ai 'u'?ka"sio?p 'u'ni"txir 'e'?ko 'pot + .'hai"ma 'u'?ka?p'tah"te?e + ,'u'ua"?tsi 'u"nu?u?k 'u'io"ko?p 'ta"mar + 315 + ,'u'?txa "?pu?u 'iak"to?p 'tu?ut'e"krus + .'tua?a'ma?a "txi 'a'?ko?o"io?p +

317 + ,"ti?i 'ne'ma?a"txi 'u'tah"ui 'tu "?ka "tar 'u'ua"?tsi 'u"nu?u?k 'u"iok + ,'u'uah "pi 'u'?pi"tor + .'u'ua"?tsi 'u"nu?u?k 'u"iok 'ta"mar + 320 + ,'hai"ma + ,'u'uah"pi 'iŋ'gohr "tun + ,'u'?pi"ti "to?or 'u'keh"re?p + .'tua?a 'u'?txa"?pu "tu?ut 'e"krus + 324 + .'i"?pan 'kon"da 'sut"pa 'tu?u'io'to"to?p +

XVIII

325 + ,'e'noh"?kin 'ia"ha?a + .'a"ka?ai 'ta'ma'e'pri"mer "di 'ia'e"ne 'ro + 327 + , "ti?in 'a?a"xi 'ta'me'el"kua 'tro + .'a'io?o"pa 'tu?u'io"tot 'el"o 'txo + 329 + ,"ti?in 'a?a "xi 'ta'me?el"?on 'se + .'a'io?o"pa 'ta'me'al "kin 'se'tu?u'io"tot +

31. Esquipulas

331 + ,'ka'lo"?koi 'ka?a"xin 'es'ki"pu 'la + .'ta'me?e"di 'ia"mar 'tes + 333 + ,'i"iah 'txe'iah"so?o?p + ,'e"di 'ia'tia?a'sa'ta"ron 'es 'ki"pu 'la + ,'ta're"ra 'e"di 'ia"hue 'bes + ,'u 'ia"rio?p 'e'i"xim 'ta"ha?a + .'tua?a'e"sa?a + , 'ta'me"di 'ia"bier 'nes + .'u'ui"truo?p "u?ut 'e 'i"xim + 340 + ,'i"o 'tro"di 'ia + ,'xe?e "ha?ax 'e"sa 'ba'do + .'sa'koh"pa 'ta'ka'a'ka?a "io?p 'u'?pi?ik"to?o?p + 343 + ,'i'kon'da?ak '?pa"re + .'a"ka?ai 'u'txa"pio?p +

345 + ,'ta'me?e"di 'ia"sa 'ba'do + ."mei 'gra'u'pat'na"ro?p + 347 + ,'por"ke?e 'i'xik "tak + ,"uar 'u"txo?p 'e"sa?a + ,'in"mohr + ,'a "ka?ai 'u'mu"xi 'u'?kuh"mar 'e'ta"mal + ,'in "mohr + ,"uar 'u'ius"ta 'e'txum"pi?i + .'ia "?katx + 354 + ,'ie?e'ui'ni"ko?p + ,'in"mohr + ,"uar 'u'si?ik"?pa 'e"si?i + ,'in"mohr + ,'a?a 'xi"no?p 'ta'xur"lau + .'tua?a'e"?pas 'ta"mal + 360 + ,'kon'dix"to 'tu"ri?ix 'tu"no?or + ,'?pu 'iur'?pi"rix 'tu"no?or 'e'txum"pi?i + .'a"ka?ai 'e'?i'xik"tak 'ta'ka'e"?pas 'ta"mal + 363 + , 'e'ta"mal + ,"kon 'da'a?an'?txak"na + .'ta"?kan +

366 + ,'ha?ax"to 'e'ui'ni"ko?p 'xe?e'tu "ruo?p + ,'in"te?en 'tio"?patx 'a'lo"?koi 'a?a "xin 'ta"?pi?ir + ,'ta'ke?e'ta"mal 'ie?e"sa?a + ,'tua?a'u'?ku"xi + .'xe?e"uar 'a'io?o"pa 'ta'noh "?kin + 371 + ,'i'ua?ak"txe 'ta"ka + ,'a'sut "pa 'ua"tar 'ta'mo?o"tot + .'tua?a'u'ia?a"re 'a 'lo"?kes "na 'e"krus + 374 + ,'e'i'xik"tak 'a "ka?ai 'u'?u"ri 'u'?puh"ko?p + .'xe?e'po?otx "?pir +

376 + ,'u'me"?kio?p 'e"krus 'a'lo"?koi 'tu?u'ni"?pi?ir + ,'tua?a'o?ohts"na "u?ut + ,'i 'tua?a'e'?pi'sir"hut + ,'e'ui"nik 'xe?e"uar 'a 'io?o"pa 'ta'noh"?kin + .'ie?e'ah're'sa"dor + 381 + ,'e'i"xik 'u'me"?ke 'e"krus + ,'ie?e'ui

31. Esquipulas

"nik 'u'iuh"mu 'e're'sen"sa 'rio'ta'kiuh"?tsu?p
'ko"ra 'ko"ra +

385 + ,'hai'ma?a"txa?a "xin 'a'ta'hui
"no?o?p 'ta"?pi?ir + ,'u'pu"to?p 'iŋ"gohr "kue
'te'tia?a'ham'biah"rix 'io?o"tot + ,'tua?a'na?a
'taŋ"gua 'u"me 'ne'tu"ro?p 'ta'mo?o"tot + .'ke
"uix 'a'?ko"tuo?p "io?o?p 'noh'?ki"no?p + 389
+ ,'ko"ra 'ko"ra + .'mo"ror 'e"hen 'te + 391 +
,"tu?ut "?pi?ir 'a'kohk'sa"no?p + ,'tua?a"xo?p
'ta'mo?o"tot + .'ta'ke?e'xe?e"ua 'ra'io?o"pa 'ta
'noh"?kin + 394 + ,"por 'ke'?ka"ni 'u'iu
"?txio?p 'e"sa?a + 396 + ,'i"tua?a 'a'ta'kar
'sa"no?p + .'u"txo?p 're"sar +

398 + ,'a'lo"?kuo?p 'tu?u'ni"?pi?ir 'ta
'ke?e'ku"rus 'xe?e"uar '?puhk'se"?pir 'u'me'ne
"ro?p + 'ma"kui?ir 'io?o"tot + ."tua?a 'u"txo?p
're"sar "tu?ut + 401 + ,"uar 'u'?pu"?tso?p
"u?ut 'ta'ka'iuh"?tsu?u?p + ."es 'to'ke'u'io
"sio?p 'ma"ku?u + 403 + ,"por 'ke'txe?e"no?p
'ke?e'u'na'ua"lir 'e'mi'la"gro 'so + ,'a'?ko"toi
'ta'ka"ro?p + ."kon 'da"uar 'a'io?o"pa 'tu?u'io
'to"to?p +

406 + ,"kon 'da"uar 'o?o"txo?p 'ma"ku?u +
,'e'i"xik 'xe?e'u'me"?ke 'e"krus + ,'ie?e'ui"nik
'xe?e"uar 'u'?pu"?tsa "u?ut + .'u'?ku"nir 'u'?ku
"nir 'a'xa"no?p 'ta"kar + 410 + ,"kon 'da'?ko
"to?o?p 'tu?u"ti?i 'e"puer 'ta + ,'o?o"txoi 'e'i
"xik 'ta'ke?e"krus + .'ie?e'ui"nik 'xe?e"uar 'u
'?pu"?tsa + 413 + ,'tu?u"pat + ,'o?o"txoi
'xe?e"uar 'u"txe 're"sar + .'ie?e — 'ah'ium'noh
"?kin + 417 + ,'tu?u"pat 'e're'sa"dor 'ie'ah
'ium'noh"?kin + ,'u'tok"txu?u "?po?o "txoi 'tu
"no?or 'e"sia?aŋ "hen 'te + ,'xe?e"uar 'a'ta'kar
'sa"no?p + .'u"txo?p 're"sar + 421 + ,"tie?e
'ne'ma?a"txi + .'a'ket"po?p "to?or 'ti"nah +
423 + .'a'kohk'sa"no?p "es 'to'a'?ka?a"pa 'e're
"sar + 424 + ,"por 'ke'ha?a"xo?p + ,'o?otx

31. Esquipulas

"xo?o?p + .'i'ah"?kux 'ta'ma"lo?p +

427 + ,"uar 'a'?ko"tuo?p + 'e'i"xik 'a'?ko
"toi 'ta"ka + ,'ta'mu?u"ti?i 'u'txak"te?eir 'e
"krus + .'u'ua"?pu 'e"krus 'tu?u'ua'ri"?pir +
431 + ,'i'u'iak"tu?u "?pa 'a'ko'tua"no?p 'tu
'no?o"ro?p + ,'ie?e'ui"nik 'xe?e"ua 'ru'?pu"?tsa
"u?ut 'e"krus + ."es 'to'a'?ka?a"pa 'e're"sar +
434 + ,"ia 'ko'to"ro?p + ."es 'to'ke"ma 'a
'?ka?a"pa 'e're"sar 'a?atx"po?o?p +

XIX

436 + ,'kon'da'ix"to + ,'a'?ka?a"pa 'e're
"sar + ,'a'mo'roh'se"na 'tu"no?or 'lo'ke?e"uar
'a'ti'kru"mo?o?p + ,'ta'ke?e'ah'txe"iah "sa?a +
'o?o'se"no?p + ,'iŋ'koh"tatx 'iŋ'koh"tatx +
'tua?a'suhk"na 'e'kan"de 'la'tu?u'ho"ro?p + .'tu
"no?or 'e'?pi"?kit 'max"tak + 444 + ,"por
'ke?e'txe?e"no?p + .'ke"ha?ax 'u'txoh'?pe"siah
'e'mi'la"gro 'so'xe?e"uar 'a'io?o"pa 'u'?kah
"tio?p + 446 + ,"ha?ax 'uar'u'pu"ko?o?p + .'ta
'ka"ti?i 'ne'ma?a"txi?i "xin 'ta'noh"?kin + 448
+ ,"kon 'da'?ka?a"?pa + ,'en"ton 'ses + ,'a'lo
'?kes"na 'e'ta"mal + .'e"sa?a + 452 + ,"kon
'da'u'koh"ko?p 'a'ma"xia?an + ,'a'ka?a"io?p + .
'ta"ka 'e'pu"rut 'uh"?tsu?u?p + 455 + ,'u'pu
"to?o?p 'e"kue 'te + ,'e"bom 'ba + ,'tu"no?or 'e
'al'de"io?p + 458 + ,'ta"ka 'e'pu"rut "kue 'te
+ ,"kon 'da'a?ak'?pa"re + ,'a'?ko"toi 'es'to'a
'las"do 'se'de'la"no 'txe + .'e?ei"rio?p +

XX

462 + ,"por 'ke'kon'da"uar 'u'pu"to?p 'iuh
"?tsu?p + ,"ha?ax 'e"?o 'ra + .'xe?e"uar 'a'?kah
'pe'sia"no?p + 465 + ,'u'?kah"tio?p + .'tu
"no?or 'lo'ke'u'?ka"nio?p + ,'u'kux'ta"ro?p + ,
'u'na"ro?p + ,'u'?pu?u"ro?p + ,'u'te?e"rar 'u'ka
"fio?p + .'u'?kah"tio?p "tua?a 'ma?a"txi 'a'ta

31. Esquipulas

"ki 'u"me 'ne"?kin +

475 + .'u'ia?a"rio?p 'e'mi'la"gro 'so + ,
'tia?a"uar 'ka'io?o"pa + ,'ka'ui"re?et + 'ah'?ku
"no?on 'lo'ke"no?on 'ka'?ka"ni + ,'tua?ah'?ka"re
'tu"?ka 'ka'?ku"xi + .'ti'ko?o"tot + 481 + .
'ma"nik "ha?ax 'sah'?pes"?pir + .'ti"ko?oit +
483 + .'ah'?ku"no?on 'u'to"?kor "ko?oit 'u'to
"?kor 'ka'ue"roh + 484 + ,'i"ra?a 'uak"ta + ,
'o?o"txoi 'e"muak + .'ti'ko?o"tot + 487 + ,'tu
"no?or 'na"ual 'ah'ma'?pam"?pan + ."ne?et 'i'?ko
'to"ri 'tu?u"hor + 489 + ,'ia"ra 'ta"ma 'e'mon
"ta "nio?p + .'tia?a"ma 'tu"?ka 'e'pa"?ka?p 'e
'ko"noh +

XXI

491 + ,'ha?ax'e"ra 'e'ak"?par 'ia"ha?a + ,
'ta"me 'iel"kin 'se'de?e"ne 'ro + ,"ti?i 'ne"uar
'a'noh'?ki"ni + ,'ta"ka 'u'ua?a"ri?p 'u'io"tot +
.'xe?e'a?a'ro?p"na 'li"mos 'na + 496 + ,"kon
'da'a'?ka"xi 'e"?kin "to?or 'e'ui"tsir + .'a
"ka?ai 'e'mux"sa?a + 498 + ,"uar 'a'muh"xa + .
'es'ta?ak'?pa"re + 500 + ,"kon 'da'?ko"toi 'a
'las"nue 'be'de'la"no 'txe + ,'a"ka?ai 'a'?pehr
"na 'e"sa?a + .'ta'ra"ma 'da + 503 + ,'en"ton
'ses + ,'a'las"do 'se'de'la"no 'txe + .'a'?ka?a
"pa 'e'?kah'pes"iah + 506 + ,'a"ka?ai 'a'puh
"ka 'e"sa?a + ,'ta"ka 'e"hen 'te + .'lo'ke?e'tu
"ro?p + 509 + ,'a'sa'koh"pa "o 'tro"di 'ia + .
'a"ka?ai 'a'ue?e'se?e"na 'tu"no?or 'e"hen 'te +
.'ah'?ku"no?p 'e'ta"mal + 512 + ,"kon 'da?a
'?ka?a"pa 'e'?kux'ta"mal + ,'a"ka?ai 'a'pu'kuh
"?ki 'e"hen 'te + .'a?a"xin 'tu?u'io'to"to?p +

31. Esquipulas

I

1 The first celebration in the beginning of the year is on the fourth of January. 4 The people begin to go to the Esquipulas celebration.

5 When it is time that we go to the celebration, our wives begin to get out the brittle tortillas, which we call 'crack-backs', so that we can carry them along to the celebration. 10 We carry many, so there will be enough for us to eat until we come home. 13 When night falls, so that we can go right on she has prepared a chicken for us to eat on the road, wrapped up some stuffed tortillas, and has ground parched corn-meal. 17 When everything is there, she fills up a net with it, which we carry along on our backs.

20 When we arrive in the town of Olopa, we buy candles and go in with them, in front of our Mother, the 'Pastora'. 24 We show them to her 25 because they say that she is the wife of the 'Milagroso'. 26 Then we leave, and go to San Juan Creek to sleep. 29 There we eat the chickens which we took from our houses. 31 The bones of those chickens we do not leave behind; we wrap them in corn husks so as to return them to our houses, 35 because they say that if we leave those bones, the spirit of the chickens remains in that place, 38 and ours do not thrive.

39 As it grows light, we go out to where we are going along the road. We are already looking for our firewood. 42 We lay it flat across the tops of our nets, so as to make a fire with it where we are going to stay in Esquipulas. 45 We arrive at Santiago Creek, and everyone bathes, 47 because they say that we can-

not come before the 'Milagroso' if we have not been bathed.

50 When we arrive at the edge of town we begin to pray. 53 We are praying until we enter his sanctuary. 55 When we have finished praying we go out and look for where we will stay. 57 We begin to boil our beans.

58 The next day we go stand among the people, where they are lined up, so that we may pass behind Our Father, the 'Milagroso'. 62 Because in that town there stands a God whose name is 'Milagroso'.

II

65 They say that that God was found in a flat clearing. 67 He was standing, with his clothing glittering beautifully. 68 They say the people gathered together so as to see him. 69 But that God did not allow himself to be touched. 71 Because, they say, some wanted to bring him, to stand him up in his house.

III

73 When his house began to be built, on that clearing, they say that he didn't want to remain there. 76 Because there was a big lake at the edge of the clearing.

78 They say that when it was light the next day people went to look in his house, which had been built so that he would remain in it. 81 There was nobody when they went to look; there he was standing at the edge of the lake. 84 Time after time he was carried and put in his house. He did not remain.

31. Esquipulas

IV

87 Those people said, "How are we to build the house of Our Father here? 89 Because the lake is large. 90 It can't be done, because if we bother the serpent who is master of the lake, he might get us."

V

93 But they say an old woman was caused to have a revelation by the master of the lake. 96 She was told, in her dream, "If I am paid as I desire, they may build the house."

VI

99 Those people began to gather together; 101 they put out chickens, turkeys, incense, candles, and bread. 106 They gathered together, the women, and began to make *chilate*, and some, to carry water. 109 When everything was there, they poured the *chilate* into the jugs, 111 they began to wrap the turkeys in nets. 112 The chickens they carried to the banks of the lake.

114 They had the old woman kneel, she who had dreamed, so she would pray to that serpent.

VII

116 The old woman began to pray. 117 She said to the serpent, "Holy Queen Snake, King Snake, 120 You who are ruler and master of this lake here; 122 we, the human beings, sons of the Highest God, we are coming to entreat and move you, with the poultry of Saint Magdalene who is mistress of our poultry, 128 and with the milk of the trees blessed by our Master,

31. Esquipulas

God. 130 This is your payment. 131 Do not turn your face away; 132 take it with open hands. 133 Hear our prayer. 134 We, our need is that you give us a place where we may raise a house by your side. 137 Because the God who appeared before us likewise will rule over you."

139 When the old woman came out with that speech, the lake thundered like the sky.

VIII

141 They say that that snake was frightened when he heard the name of the ruler. 143 When the old woman had finished praying, and when they had finished cutting the throats of the turkeys and chickens, the old woman rose and spoke. She said to the people, 149 "After eight days, begin the work."

IX

151 They began to measure out the supports of the house. 153 They laid out its trenches, where they were to line up the stones, and which went into the ground, as the 'risers' of the house. 157 But with the night, the lake kept lapping, and completely undermined everything. 161 When it became light, there was nothing. 163 It was entirely eroded and gone into the water. 164 When it became light the next day they went 166 to look, and nothing they had done was there. 169 And so, every day. 170 They began to speak of it. 171 They said, "We are just wasting ourselves. 173 It hasn't come out the way this old woman said."

X

175 The old woman dreamed again. 176 She

was told in her dream that the master of the lake wanted servants.

179 When the old woman had dreamed again, all the people who were working gathered together. 182 They told the old woman to seek by divining to find out how that snake wanted his servants, whether alive or dead. 188 It appeared from the divining that live ones were wanted.

XI

190 And when it became clear that the serpent wanted live people, then those people who were working said, "It is necessary that we go and stand, some of us here, in the mortar, alive." 200 Because they say that the people of olden days used to say that that house, when it began to go up, had its roots in the ground. 205 They say that two by two, men were stood up in its corners, alive they say. 209 Those men were inserted, standing up, in the mortar, where the cornerposts rose.

XII

214 When they had done that, then the house rose before them. 218 When it was ready for them to complete, a mason fell down to the ground. 223 His picture, put there by them, is there to this day. 225 They say that that man was a -- Spaniard.

XIII

227 They say that that serpent accepted. 229 And so that town appeared. 232 That is why people say nowadays that that church is standing over a lake. 235 They say that when

the place had just been completed, it thundered all the time, like the sky, 238 until the neck of the serpent was tied by the 'Milagroso', and he gave up thundering. 240 Today the wire is visible, hanging down coming down over the church and going into the earth. 243 Because they say that there is that serpent, lying, tied.

XIV

245 They used to say that a long time ago, at the celebration, many people remained each time 249 there, men, women and children. Because they say that when they were passing behind the 'Milagroso', they say there were those under whom the planks slid away. 260 They fell and went into the lake. 261 Others' necks turned themselves backwards. 262 They say that they were those whose thoughts were not pure. 264 They say that by the 'Milagroso' their necks were wrung. 266 They died.

XV

267 When they are passing behind the 'Milagroso', where he hangs, all leave their money in front of him. 270 Some leave a candle beside him. 271 They say that is so they will be given more life by that God. 272 Because they say that that God has the authority to take away every sin which exists in man.

XVI

275 Therefore to that celebration many people come 278 and do penance, so that they will be saved from their sins. 280 Upon arriving at the edge of town they crawl along on their kneecaps, where they are walking along,

kneeling, in the street. 288 Some of those filling the street walk along, laying out their jackets on the ground; 290 others, their head cloths, others their sheets, for them to pass over them, those who are going, kneeling, on their knees.

294 Some, when their jackets are free, quickly go and stretch them out ahead, until they bring them to where the 'Milagroso' hangs. 300 But there are some who die from fatigue. 302 They say that they are the ones who have much sin; 303 therefore they die.

XVII

304 Therefore, when they go out of their houses, they say prayers so that nothing will happen to them on the road. 309 There are crosses standing on the road, as they go along. 311 They see them from quite a distance. They begin to break off flowers from the bushes. If not, pine branches, with which they lash their ankles. 315 They leave them lying in front of the crosses, so that they will not get tired.

317 Those who do not find something with which to lash their ankles grab their hats, and lash their ankles with them. 320 If not, one grabs a rock, sets it on his shoulders, so as to lay it in front of the cross. 324 And likewise when they have turned back toward their houses.

XVIII

325 That celebration begins on the first day of January. 327 He who goes on the fourth, comes back to his house on the eighth. 329 He who goes on the eleventh comes back to his house on the fifteenth.

31. Esquipulas

331 We leave on our way to Esquipulas on Tuesday, 333 and the chilate makers, the day when we are away in Esquipulas, on Thursday, throw the corn in the water for chilate. On Friday they break up the corn grains. 340 And the next day, which is Saturday, they begin to grind it fine when it gets light. 343 And when night comes they begin to boil it.

345 On Saturday they have a lot of work. 347 Because the women are making the chilate; others are beginning to grind the dough for tamales, others are fixing turkeys and chickens. 354 And the men: some are looking for firewood; some are going banana-leaf cutting for tamale wrapping. 360 Then, when everything is there and all of the turkey is cut up into pieces, the women begin with the tamale wrapping. 363 The tamales, when it is daylight, are yellow.

366 Then the men who are there, one of them goes out along the road with the tamales and chilate, for those who are coming back from the celebration to eat. 371 And immediately he returns to the house, so as to order the cross taken out. 374 And the women begin to put on their clothes, which are washed.

376 They cradle the crosses and go out on the trail, so they may be bowed to, and for the sign of the cross by the men who are coming back from the celebration, and the prayer leader. 381 The woman cradles the cross and the man swings the censer with the incense, so the smoke of the incense spreads itself all around.

385 If nobody goes to meet them on the road, they fire a rocket, from the place where the houses are first visible, so that it is

31. Esquipulas

known by those who stayed at home that the celebration-goers are about to come back. 389 All around, people are clustered. 391 Along the road they are waiting, so as to go to the houses with those who are coming home from the celebration. 394 Because they want to eat tamales, and want to drink chilate, 396 and in order to assist those saying their prayers.

398 They go out on the path with the cross which was adorned by them inside the house, for them to pray before. 401 They cense it with incense until they bring it inside. 403 For they say that the spirit of the 'Milagroso' comes with them when they arrive at their houses.

406 When they are going inside, the woman who is cradling the cross and the man who is censing it walk very very slowly with it. 410 When they have arrived at the door, the woman enters with the cross, and then the man who is censing it. 413 Behind, enters the one who is saying the prayers, and the one in charge of the celebration. 417 Behind the prayer-sayer and the one in charge of the celebration, all the many people who are assisting in the praying jam themselves together entering. 421 Those who do not, remain on the house plot. 423 They wait until the praying finishes 424 because they are chilate drinkers and tamale eaters.

427 They arrive; the woman comes with -- to the edge of the altar of the cross; she stands the cross on its support. 431 And they let themselves fall to their knees, all of them. And also the man who is censing the cross, until the praying is finished. 434 There they kneel; they do not get up until the prayer is over.

31. Esquipulas

XIX

436 When the praying is finished, everyone who was working is gathered together with the chilate makers; they go in one by one for the candles to be rubbed against the heads of all the little children. 444 Because they say that it is the blessing of the 'Milagroso' that they are praying will come. 446 He is separating out those who did not go to the celebration. 448 When this is finished, then the tamales and chilate are taken out. 452 When they see it is becoming twilight, they begin with the burning of copal. 455 All the villages fire rockets and bombs. 458 With the firing of rockets when night falls it comes to be as late as twelve o'-clock at night before they rest.

XX

462 Because when they are burning incense, that is the time when they pray. 465 They ask for everything that they want: their health, their corn, their beans, their chickens, their cattle, those who have some, their coffee trees. They ask that they not be dried up by the heat.

475 They say to the 'Milagroso', "Where we are coming, we see you. Give us what we want, so that there is an abundance of what we eat in our houses. 481 Let there not be a scarcity for us. 483 Give us a healthy appearance, healthy expressions. 484 Do not let disease enter our houses. 487 All the evil spirits: you are dominant over them. 489 Throw them into the mountains, where there are no human beings."

31. Esquipulas

XXI

491 It is that evening, on the fifteenth of January, that some celebrate on their house lots, which is called 'Limosna'. 496 When the light falls on the peaks, the *chilate* grinding begins. 498 It is ground until night falls. 500 When it comes to be nine o'clock at night, they begin to go back and forth carrying *chilate* to the bower. 503 Then at twelve o'clock at night the praying ends. 506 They begin to distribute the *chilate* among the people who are there. 509 When it gets light the next day, all the people begin to be fed. They are given tamales. 512 When the tamale eating is finished, the people begin to disperse, going to their houses.

32. Preparations for the Limosna

1 + ,"kon 'da'a'?ko"toi 'e"di 'ia'e'noh
"?kin 'xe?e'a'ro?p"na 'li"mos 'na + ,'tu?u'txa
"?pi?ir + ,'u'mo'roh"se 'u"?pa 'e'ui'ni"ko?p + .
'a"ka?ai 'u"txo?p 'e'ra"ma 'da + 5 + ,'?pah
"xan 'a?a'xi"no?p + .'u'si?i?k"?po?o?p 'e"te?e
'ta'?ko"pot + 7 + ."ti?in 'u'ta"res 'u'uoi"iir
+ 8 + ."ti?in 'u'ta"res 'u"ti?i + 9 + .
"ti?in 'u'ta"res 'ki"rih + 10 + .'u'?ke"txo?p
'ua"tar +

11 + ,"kon 'dix"to 'a'io?o"po?o?p 'ta
'ke?e"te?e + .'a'ue?e'se"no?p + 13 + ,"kon 'da
'?ka?a"pa?a "uio?p + .'en"ton 'ses'a'ka?a"io?p
'u'io"rio?o?p 'e"?txen + ."tua?a 'u'ua"?puo?o?p
'e"?oi + 16 + ,"kon 'da?a'?ka?a"pa 'u'ua
"?puo?p 'u'uoi"iir + ,'u'?kat"?puo?p 'u"ti?i + .
'u'?txa"?puo?p 'u'ku"laa "tir + 19 + .'en"ton
'ses'u'ua"?puo?o?p 'e"txuhp + 20 + ,'ta'me?e
"txuhp + ,'u'?kat"?puo?p 'in'te?e"te?e 'tu?u"hor
+ ."tua?a 'u'?ka"tri?p 'e'kal"son "tio?p + .
"tua?a 'ua"tar 'u'?pah"ri?p 'e'ki"rih +

24 + ,"kon 'da'?ka?a"pa 'u'?pa"rio?p 'e'ki
"rih + .'u'xi"?txio?p 'u'io"por 'e'ke"ne?e 'tu?u
"hor + 26 + ,'u'na"?tio?p 'ta'ke?e"te?e + .
"tua?a 'ma?a"txi 'o?oh'res"na 'u"me 'ne'i"?kar +

28 + ,"pe 'ro'e'ra"ma 'da + .'u'?kah"na?ar
'tu"ru 'u"pues "tir + 30 + ,"ha?a 'xe"ra 'xe?e
'u'?kam"pes 'a"ni 'e'?o"nia?an 'ah"ium + .'ta"ma
'u'ua?a"ri?p 'io?o"tot 'ia"ha?a + 32 + ,"ha?a
'xe"ra 'e"krus 'xe?e'pa?a?k"?pir + .'u'me"ner +
34 + ,'e"krus 'ia"ha?a 'a"?txi?i + .'a'ket"pa
'no"xi?i "te?e + 36 + ,'i"tia?a "guar 'e"te?e
'ia"ha?a + .'in'te?e"to 'noh"?kin 'a'txe?e"na +
38 + ."ia '?a?ah"txa 'e'ra"ma 'da + 39 + ,
"por 'ke'u'?kah"na?ar + .'ket"?pir 'e"pues 'to
'ia"ha?a 'tua?a'ta"ka 'u'tu"ri?i?p 'e"sa?a + .
'te?e'li"mos 'na +

32. Preparations for the Limosna

42 + ,'po"re 'so + ,'a'txa"mai 'e'ta'ta?a
"?pir + ,'xe'?u'?kah"ies 'e'li"mos 'na + .'a'ket
"pa 'e'?u'nem"?pir + 46 + ,'i"ha?ax 'ta"ka 'e
"pues 'to'ia"ha?a + .'a'sut"pa 'u'?kam"pes + 48
+ ,'ia?a'txa"mai 'u'nem"?pir + ,'e'si?ts'?pi
"ro?p + .'ha?ax'ta"ka 'a'sut"pa 'u'?kam'pe"so?p
+ 51 + ,"por 'ke"txe 'ke?e"pues 'to'ia"ha?a +
."?pan 'ko'txan"te?e "me 'sa'xe?e'tua?a'ka'ue?e
'ni"?pir +

53 + ,"txe 'ke?e"ia '?ta'?pes"?pir 'u'pa
'lan"ga 'na + .'u'na'ua"lir 'e"rum + 55 + ,
"txe 'ke'kon'da"uar 'a'tu'ru'?pa"na 'tu"no?or +
,"sa?a + ,'a"?katx + ,'txum"pi?i + ,'uh"?tsu?u?p
+ .'txe?e"no?p 'ke"ko 'ma"ke?e + ,'to?or'e"me
'sa'ia"ha?a + ."uar 'u'tu'ru"?po?p 'tu"no?or +
63 + ,'i"ia?atx "pa 'u'na'ua"lir 'e"rum + .'u
'?txa"mi 'tu"no?or 'lo'ke?e"uar 'a'tru'?pa"na
"tu?ut +

65 + ,'kon'do?os"ta 'e'ra"ma 'da'ia"ha?a +
,'in"te?e "di 'ia'in'ta"ka + .'ma"kar "ua?ar +
68 + ,"o 'tro"di 'ia + ,"tia?a 'tua?ak'?pa"re
'e'noh"?kin + ,'?ka?a'pa"tix 'u"txo?p 'e"uia?ar
+ .'a'ka?a"io?p 'ta'ke?e'a'dor'na"sion + 72 +
,'u"txo?p 'a'dor"nar + ,'e"?a 'ro'ie?e"krus + .
'ie?e'txa?a"te?e 'kan"de 'la'nuk"ta?a + 75 + ,
'ha?ax"to + .'a'txe?e"na 'tu"no?or 'e"di 'ia +

77 + ,'i"kon 'da'ix"to + ,'a'?ka"xi 'e
"?kin "to?or 'e'ui"tsir + ,'a'kim"?pu "na 'e
"si?i 'ta"?kahk + .'tua?a'u'ia"ri 'u'ia?ak"rer +
81 + ,'u'?kah"na?ar 'u'sah"ko?p 'e"te?e + .'u
'io"?pio?p 'xe?e'tua?a'?kam'pes"na "u?ut 'u'?kah
"kir 'ta'kiuh"?tsu?up + 83 + ,'a"si?k '?pa"na
'e'mu"rak + ,'e'txa"kahr + ,'e'?txo"ror + ,'por
'ke?e "te?e 'ia"ha?a + .'ga"lan 'a'he?e"rai
"?u?ut + 88 + .'i'ma?a"txi 'a'tah"pu?ut 'ta
'ke?e'uh"?tsu?u?p +

32. Preparations for the Limosna

89 + ,"es 'to'ke'a'?ko"toi 'e"?o 'ra + ,'a
"ka?ai 'a'?pehr"na 'e"sa?a + ,'a'tsoh"pu?u "iok
'e'txum"pi?i + ,'ia?a"?katx + ,'a'?txa?p"na
'tia?a'tso"ror 'e'kan"de 'la'ia"ha?a + 'ie?e
"krus 'tu?u'iu"xin 'ie'bar"ko?o?p 'ia"ha?a + .'a
'ko"tuan 'iah'?kah'pe"siah + 95 + ,'?i'?ux
"te?e 'e'ui'ni"ko?p 'a'tur'ua"no?p 'ma"kui?ir 'e
'ra"ma 'da + ,'tua?a'a'ta'kar'sa"no?p + ,'a'lo
"?koi 'u'?txa"mio?p "u?ut 'e"?kahk + .'tia?a'tu
"ru '?tor"?pir +

99 + ,'i'kon'dix"to + ,'a'xuh"ru?u "nu?u
'?ke'txum"pi?i + ,"ha?ax 'u'xu"rio?p 'u"nu?u?k +
,'u'tso"pio?p 'u"iok + 'u"ui?itx + .'tua?a'ma?a
"txi 'a'ti'kru"ma 'e'txum"pio?p 'ia"ha?a + 105
+ ,'i'e'ah'?kah'pes"iah + ,"kon 'de"uar 'a'?txi
"?txen 'e'txum"pi?i + ,'e"?txi?tx 'ia"ha?a + ,'a
'?ka"xi 'ta'me?e"?txen + ,'ah'iah'?kah'pes"iah +
.'tu"ru "uar 'a'?kah'pes"ian 'ta'ka'u'na'ua"lir
'e"rum +

111 + ,'kon"da?a '?ka?a"pa 'e'xu'ru'nu?u?k
'txum"pi?i + ,'en"ton 'ses'a'lo"?kuo?p + .'ta
'mu?u'nie?e'?pi?i"ro?p 'ta'ka'e"sa?a "iu?ut 'e
"?kahk + 114 + ."ti?in 'u'?ke"txe "u?ut 'e
"?kahk + 115 + ."ti?in 'u'la"?ti 'e"sa?a +
116 + ."ti?in 'u'?ke"txe 'iuh"?tsu?p + 117 +
,'ta'rix"to + ,'ux"te?e 'e'ui'ni"ko?p 'ia"ha?a +
,'a'tur'ua"no?p 'ah'ta'kar"sah + .'tua?a'iah
'?kah'pes"iah 'xe?e'pehk"?pir +

121 + ,'kon'da?a'?ka?a'pa?a'ia"hra 'e"sa?a
+ ,'ta'me?e"?txen 'ia"ha?a + ,'ie?e'u'?txi"?txer
'e'txum"pi?i + .'u'?txe?e"nar 'iuh"?tsu?u?p + ,
"kon 'dix"to '?ka?a"pi?ix 'tu"no?or + ,'u'pak
"?puo?p 'in"gohr 'no"xi?i "tun 'ta"mar + ,'tua?a
'ma?a"txi 'u'lah"?txi 'e"?tsi?i + .'lo'ke?e'a
"ian 'ta'me?e"?txen +

129 + ,'e"?txen 'ia"ha?a + ."ia 'ma"kar

32. Preparations for the Limosna

"es 'to'a'?ko"toi "?a 'nio + ,'ko'txe?e"tua?a '?ka"xi 'e'noh"?kin 'o'tro"niahr + .'a'sut"pa 'u 'pa"sio?p + 133 + .'i"ma 'mah"txi 'e"rer 'u 'pih"txi 'e"pues 'to'ia"ha?a + 134 + ."por 'ke "txe 'ke'a'?te?en"san + 135 + ,'i'po"re 'so + ,'hai'ka'na?a"ta 'ke?e'u'tu"ri?p "sa?a + .'me'?e "rer 'ka'ioh"ko + 138 + ."por 'ke"txe 'ke'a '?te?en"san + 139 + .'u'su"ti 'e'?txi?i?tx 'na?a"?kir 'ie?e'sam"pa?ar +

140 + ,'e"di 'ia'tua?ak'?pa"re 'e'noh"?kin + .'a"ian "mei 'gra"ti?i 'ne"uar 'a'ta'kar'sa "no?p + 142 + ,'u"txo?p 'tu"no?or + .'lo'ke 'tua?a'a'?kam"pa 'ta'me?e'noh"?kin +

144 + ."ti?in 'uar'u'pa"?ki 'iuh"?tsu?u?p + .'ti?in'guar'a'xur'la"ui + ."ti?iŋ "guar 'u '?tso"tio?o?p 'e'ia"ual + 147 + ,'ie?e'i'xik "tak + ."uar 'a'ti'kru"mo?o?p 'ta'ka'e'txe'iah "sa?a + 149 + ,"mei 'gra'tra"ba 'ho"tuo?o?p 'ta'me?e"di 'ia'ia"ha?a +

150 + ,"kon 'da'?ko'tes"na 'e"lau + .'a "ka?ai 'a"?pa?an 'lau"io?p + 152 + ,"uar 'a '?pas'ta'ma"lio?p + ."es 'to'a'?ko"toi 'a'las "dos 'de'la'ma"nia 'na + 154 + ."ma 'tu"?ka 'uai"ner "tuo?o?p +

155 + ,'a"ian 'in"te?e 'i"la 'ma + ,'xe?e 'a?a'ro?p"na 'ka'pi"ta 'na + .'ke?e"ha?ax 'a'kan 'se"ian + .'ta'ma'tu"no?or 'lo'ke'a'txe?em"pa + 159 + ,"ha?ax 'u"txe 'man"dar 'ta'ma'tu"no?or 'e'?i'xik"tak + ."xe '?o?oi'?txu"muo?p + 161 + ,'ha?ax"tix "?ka?ar 'u'me"ner + .'tu"?ka?a 'tu "?ka?a "tua?a 'txe?em"pa + 163 + .'ke'tu"?ko 'ra'a'lo"?koi 'e"sa?a + 164 + ,'i"ha?ax 'u'pu "?ki 'e'txo'ko"la 'te + .'u'ia"ri 'ta'ma'e"sa?a + 166 + ,'ie?e'u'tsu"tser 'e'txum"pi?i + ,'u '?pa"si 'ta'me?e"lau + ,"tua?a 'u'txe'man"dar + ,'a'mah"ka 'ma'ku?u"rum + .'tia?a'tu"ru 'u'pues

32. Preparations for the Limosna

"tir 'e"?txi?itx + 171 + ,'ta'me?e"me 'sa 'tia?a'tru'?pa"na 'e"sa?a + .'i"tia?a 'xu"hra 'u "nu?u?k 'e'txum"pio?p + 173 + ,'ma?a"txi 'u 'iak"ta 'a'txok"pa + .'e"tsuts 'ia"ha?a + 175 + .'tu"no?or 'u'?pa"si + 176 + ,'i'po"re 'so + ,'u'?kah"na?ar 'a'pehk"na + ."tua?a 'ta"ka 'u'ui "ra 'tu"?ka?a 'tu"?ka?a 'tua?a'a'txe?em"pa +

179 + .'i"?pan 'e'ui'ni"ko?p + 180 + ,'a "ian 'in"te?e + ,'a'tu'ru'?pa"na 'u"men 'iah"ium 'noh"?kin + ."tua?a 'u'ui"ra 'tu"?ka?a 'tu"?ka?a 'tua?a'a'txe?em"pa + 183 + ."ti?in 'u'sa"kre 'a?a"xin 'ta'xur"lau + 184 + ."ti?in 'u'sa"kre 'a?a"xin 'ta"?tsot 'ia"gual + 185 + ."ti?in + ,'u"txe 'man"dar + .'u"txa?a 'dor"nar + 188 + ,"i "ti?in + .'u'iah"nes 'a?a"xin 'ta'ta'res"iah 'o'iok'ke"ne?e + 190 + ,"por 'ke'u'?kah"na?ar 'tu'ru'?pa"?pir + ,"tua?a 'u'ia?a"re 'a'txe?e"na 'tu"no?or 'lo'ke?e'u'?ka"ni + .'ta'me?e'noh"?kin 'ia"ha?a +

32. Preparations for the Limosna

1 When the day comes for the celebration which is called *limosna*, two days before it the men get together and begin to build the *ramada*. 5 First they go looking for the wood in the bush. 7 One brings its cornerposts, 8 another brings its side plates, 9 another brings stringers. 10 They come carrying them.

11 When they come with the wood they are fed. 13 When they have finished eating, then they dig the holes so as to stand the cornerposts. 16 When they have finished standing the cornerposts, they lay the side plates, and lay the end beams. 19 Then they place the tripod braces. 20 Over the tripod braces they lay a log on top as a rest for the rafters, so they come for lashing on the stringers.

24 When they have finished lashing the stringers, they lay out the leaves of banana plants on top. 26 They pinch them down with sticks so they are not made to fall by the wind.

28 But the *ramada*, it is placed in its location on purpose. 30 That is where it was used by the old owners of that house-plot. 32 That is the cross which was planted by them. 34 That cross grows, and becomes a big tree. 36 And where that tree stands, each celebration is held, 38 and there the *ramada* is put up, 39 because that place is saved on purpose so as to be the receptacle of the *chilate* in the *limosna*.

42 That is why, when the father dies, he who began the *limosna*, the son remains. 46 And he, with that place, returns to use it. 48 And when the son dies, the grandsons return to use it. 51 Because they say that that place is like a table which is for us to eat from.

32. Preparations for the Limosna

53 They say that there it was put up, the basin of the spirit of the earth. 55 They say that when everything is being set down, *chilate*, chickens, turkeys, incense, they say that it is as if on that table they had placed everything. 63 And the spirit of the earth rises and takes everything which was placed in front of him.

65 When that *ramada* is finished, it just stands shut up for one day. 68 The next day, when the night of it is the celebration, the meal (breakfast) having been finished, they begin the ornamentation. 72 They ornament the arches and the cross, and the two large candles. 75 And that is done all day long.

77 And then, when the sunlight falls on the peaks, firewood is piled high on the fire, so as to make the coals break off. 81 They look especially for wood and chop down those whose coals are used with incense. 83 *Spanish Plum*, *Palo Jiote*, and oak are sought because those woods glow well, 88 and are not extinguished by the incense.

89 When the time comes, the *chilate* begins to be carried in, the legs of the turkeys are tied together, and the chickens, and they are laid where those candles and the cross are lined up, beside those bowls, and the prayer-sayer kneels down. 95 And three men sit inside the *ramada* with him, so as to help, going out and getting coals where they sit piled up.

99 And when the turkeys' throats are cut, they cut their throats, they bind their feet and wings so that those turkeys do not jump around. 105 And the prayer-sayer, when the turkeys are bleeding, that blood falls into the hole, the prayer-sayer is seated praying to the

spirit of the earth.

111 When the turkey-throat-cutting is finished, then they go out on the nearby paths with the *chilate* and the coals. 114 One carries the coals. 115 One carries the *chilate*. 116 One carries the incense. 117 Thereupon those three men sit as helpers of the prayer-sayer who was invited.

121 When the *chilate* has all been poured down into that hole, and the blood of the turkeys, the incense is placed in the hole. And when everything is finished, they put a big stone on it, so that no dog digs up what there is in the hole.

129 That hole, it is covered there until a year is up. As the celebration comes again they come back and open it again. 133 Nobody can touch that place, 134 because they say that it causes sickness. 135 And that is why, if we know that it's a *chilate* container, we can't step over it. 138 Because they say that it causes sickness; 139 it gives dysentery or swelling.

140 The day before the night of the celebration there are many who are helping. 142 They make everything which is used in the celebration.

144 One molds the incense. One is banana-leaf-cutting. One is rolling ring-shaped stands 147 and the women are jumping around making *chilate*. 149 There is much work for them on that day.

150 When the banana leaves have been brought, they begin banana-leaf-roasting. 152

32. Preparations for the Limosna

They are tamale-wrapping until it comes to be two o'clock in the morning. 154 There is no sleep for them.

155 There is one woman who is called a captain, and she teaches how everything is done. 159 She gives orders to all the women who are grinders. 161 She is wholly concerned with each thing which is done. 163 What time the _chilate_ goes out (of the kitchen). 164 And she distributes the chocolate and drops it into the _chilate_. 166 And the turkey feathers, she wraps in banana-leaf, so as to send them to be enclosed in the ground where the place for the blood is, 171 on the table where the _chilate_ is placed and where the turkeys' necks are cut. 173 She does not allow those feathers to be thrown away. 175 She wraps everything. 176 And that is why she is especially invited, so as to help and see that each thing is done.

179 And so the men. 180 There is one, chosen by the giver of the celebration, so as to see that each thing is done. 183 He sends one to go banana-leaf-cutting. 184 He sends one to go ring-wrapping. 185 He orders one to make decoration, 188 and he chases one off to the bringing of banana-palm trunks. 190 Because he is chosen especially so as to say what must be done for that celebration.

33. Offering to the Earth Spirit

1 + ,'a"ian 'in"te?e 'noh"?kin + ,'a'txe?e "na + ,'ta"ma '?e'lu"gar + 'tia?a — .'tu"re?en + 6 + 'i?i — ,'ma"ha?ax + ,'ah"rer 'ta'ka + , 'ta"ma 'e'lu"gar + ,'tia?a"ne?en 'in'tu"re?en + 'e?e — .'tu"no?or + ,'e'?al"de?e "io?p + 'e?e — ,'u"txo?p + .'e'noh"?kin 'ia"ha?a +

17 + 'ta"ma — ,'el"kin 'se'de?e"ne 'ro + 'tia?a"uar 'a'io?o"pa 'e?e — ,'e"hen 'te + ,'ta 'noh"?kin 'is'ki"pu 'la + "ti?i 'ne — 'u'na?a "ta — 'u"txe 'li'mo"snar 'e?e — ,'u'ua?a"ri?p 'u'io"tot 'tia?a'tu"ru + 'a?a — ,'ta'ma're"ra 'e"ah 'e"tar 'de'ia"ha?a + ,'tia?a"uar 'a'io?o "pa 'ta'noh"?kin + ,'a"ka?ai 'a'muh"xa + ,'e "sa?a + 'a'?pu?t"?ka 'e?e — ,'e"sian 'i'xik"tak + ,'tua?a'u"txo?p 'e"sa?a + ,'e'ui'ni"ko?p + 'tua?a — 'e?e — ,'a'pat"no?p + 'ta"ma '?e?e — .'e'noh"?kin 'ia"ha?a + 40 + ,"kon 'da'u'koh "ko?p + ,'a'?ka"xi 'e"?kin + "to?or 'e'ui"tsir + ,'ko'txe?e'a'las"kua 'tro + ,"o '?a'la"sin 'ko + ,'a"ka?ai + ,'e'mux"sa?a + ,'uar'a'muh"xa 'es"to '?a'?ko"toi + ,'a'la"sie 'te + .'o'a'la"so 'txo +

50 + ,"kon 'da'ix"to 'tu"ri?ix + 'e?e — , 'e"sa?a + ,'?a?a"?pi?ix 'puh"?ka + ,'a"ka?ai 'a '?pehr"na + 'a?a"xin — ,'ta'ra"ma 'da + ,'tia?a "ua?ar + .'e'ra"ma 'da + 59 + 'a"ian "ti?i 'ne?e — ,'u'tu'ru"?pa + "es 'to?o — ,'siŋ"kuen 'ta"bar 'ko + ,"ti?in "trein 'ta + ,"ti?in "bein 'te"siŋ 'ko + ,"ti?iŋ 'kua"ren 'ta + ."pe 'ro "?pan 'u'tu'ru"?po?p + 67 + 'e?e — 'kon'da?a "ka?ai 'a'?pehr"na 'e?e — ,"sa?a 'ia"ha?a 'a 'ua?a?p"na + 'e?e — ,'ta"mu?ut 'e"krus + , 'tia?a"uar 'e'ra"ma 'da + ,'a'tsoh"ra 'a?a"xin + 74 + ,"kon 'da'?ka?a"pa + 'a?a — ,'a'ua?a?p"na + 'e?e — ,'e"nuk 'ta"bar 'ko + 'xe?e — .'e?e + ,'e"txi?i "txi?i "sa?a + 'e?e — ,'a'iah"ra 'e "pan + ,'tu?u"hor + ."ie?e — "ie?e — .'txo'ko "la 'te + .'xe'ka'ua?a"re 'ka"kau + 89 + ,

33. Offering to the Earth Spirit

'i?in"ton 'ses'ua"tar + ,'txa?a"te?e 'ia"ro?p
'?pi'?kit"rutx + ,'e"?pan 'ta"ka + 'ma"ha?ax 'ta
'ka?a -- ,"txa?a?p + ,'nien'ta'ka"pan + 95 +
'e?e -- ,'txa?a"te?e "rutx 'ia"ha?a + ,"txe 'ke
"ha?ax + 'e?e -- "tua?a 'e?e -- .'e"?aŋ 'he"lo?p
+ 101 + ,"por 'ke"txe 'ke?e"aŋ 'he"lo?p + ,
'ma?a"txi 'u'iu"?txio?p "mei 'gra + 'e?e -- .
"mei 'gra + 105 + 'i?i -- ,'a'ua?a?p"na + 'in
"te?e 'no"xi?i -- ,"bar 'ko + ,'xe?e'u'tah"ui +
,"mei 'gra'e"sa?a + 'ie?e -- ,'e"bar 'ko'ia
"ha?a + ."kon 'da + 114 + ,"kon 'da'ix"to + ,
'tu"ri?ix + .'tu"no?or + .'ta"me?e 'ra"ma 'da +

118 + '?ka?a"pi?ix 'ua?a?p"na 'e?e -- 'e?e
-- ,'e"sa?a + 'i?i -- ,'ka'txa"rix + ,'u"iok
'iah"tso?o + 'e?e -- ,'iu?u"tu?u 'e'txum"pi?i +
,'ia?a"?katx + ,'i'tu"ri?ix 'tu"no?or + ,'en"ton
'ses + ,'a"ka?ai + 'e?e -- "ti?i 'ne?e -- "ua
'ru?u -- ,'e"ti?i 'ne?e'pehk"?pir + 'tua?a'u
'?ka?a -- 'u'?ka -- 'u?u -- 'u'num"se 'ia"he?e
-- ,'e'li"mo 'sna'ia"ha?a + ,'a"ka?ai + 'e?e --
.'a'?kah'pes"ian + 142 + ,"uar 'a'?kah'pes"ian
+ ,"ehs 'to'?a'?ko"toi + 'a?a -- .'a'las"do 'se
'de'la"no 'txe + 146 + ."por 'ke'?e?eix"na + ,
'a'tur"uan + ,'a'?kah'pes"ian + "por 'ke?e -- ,
'i"iah '?kah'pes"iah 'ia"ha?a + ,'u'?kah"na?ar +
.'a'pehk"na + 153 + .'u"me 'ne'ah"ium 'noh
"?kin + 154 + "pe 'ro"ti?i 'ne -- ,'ha?a"xatx
+ ,'u'na?a"ta + 'ko"txa 'tua?a -- ,'a'?kah'pes
"ian + .'ma?a"txi 'u'peh"ka 'o'tron"te?e + 160
+ ."pe 'ro'ha'iah"ium 'noh"?kin + ,'ma?a"txi 'u
'na?a"ta + 'e?e -- ,'ko"txa 'tua?a'?kah'pes"ian
+ ,'u'peh"ka 'o'tron"te?e + ."ti?in 'u'na?a"ta +
166 + 'i?i -- ,'iah'?kah'pes"iah 'ia"ha?a + ,
'kon'da"uar + ,'a'?kah'pes"ian 'tu"ru + .'u'ia?a
"re + 'e?e -- 'xe'txe?e"no?o?p 'ke?e -- 'e?e --
,'u'na'ua"lir + 'e?e -- .'e"rum +

177 + 'e?e -- ."txe 'ko"txe?e "ra + 179
+ 'e?e -- .'nues'tra"ma 'dre'san"ti 'si'ma +

33. Offering to the Earth Spirit

181 + "tia?a -- ,'ak"ta '?pi"ret + ,'u"men + , 'e'ka'uin'ki"rar 'di"os + ,'xe?e'?pi"xir 'tu"ru 'tu?ut"?kin + 186 + ,'i"ne?et + ,'u'iak"te?et + 188 + ,'i"no?on + ,'tu"ro?on + 190 + "uar 'ka?a -- 'ka'lah"?tsue?et + 192 + "uar 'ka"txe 'tu"?ki?ik "xix + 193 + 'e?e -- ,'ta'ka"ret + 195 + 'ke?e -- ,"no?on 'a'ui"ro?on + .'ma'?pam "?pan + 198 + .'ma'?pam'?pa"non + .'tu'?ki?ik "xix 'a'ui"ra 'ka"txe + 200 + "pe 'ro'i"ra '?ka?a"pa?a 'pas -- ,'i"ra '?ka?a"pa 'a'pa"sen 'sia + 202 + ,'a'ui"ro?on + ,'txoh'?pe"son + , 'i"ra?a 'ui"ro?on 'su'tur"hut + 205 + 'tu'ru "?pan + 'a?a -- ,'a'txoh'?pes"iah 'ta'ma"ron + , 'i'ko"ne?er + ,"no?on + ,'e'pa"?ka?p 'e'ko'no "hon + ,'uar"to + ,'ka'?kah"?pue?et + ,'ta'ka'ka 'ua"ra?k + .'tia?a"uar + 'e?e -- .'ka'?to"xi + 217 + 'i"no?on 'ka'?ka"ni 'ke?e -- ,'ke"ne?et + ,'tua?a'txoh'?pe"son + ,'i"ra?a 'uak"ta + ,'a '?ka"xi 'e"muak + ,'ta'ma'ka'max"tak + ,'i'ta'ma "ron + ,'ta'ma'tu"no?or 'ka'ua"ra?k + .'lo'ke "no?on 'ka'tu'ru"?pa + 226 + ,'ta"ra 'ka'ta "res + 'e?e -- ,'ka'ua"ra?k + ,'ka"ha?ax 'a 'tua?a'ni"?pir + ,'i'ta"mar 'ka -- .'ka'toh"ti?i 'ie"set + 232 + ,'i'ra"non + ,'pa'sar"hut + , 'i'iah'?ku"non + ,'tu"?ka 'ka'?ku"xi + ,'pa'sar "?ka?p +

237 + ,'e'ui"nik 'ia"ha?a + ,'a'tur"uan + ,'a'?kah'pes"ian + 240 + ."mei 'gra + .'u'?kah 'pes"iah + 242 + ,'u'?kah"ti + ,'tua?a'ma?a "txi 'o?o"txoi 'e"muak + 244 + ,'u'?kah"ti 'tua?a'ma?a"txi 'a'txa"mai 'ia?a"?katx + 245 + ,'u'?kah"ti 'tua?a'ma?a"txi 'a'txa"mai 'e'max "tak + ,'tua?a'ma?a"txi 'a'?ka"xi 'in'te?e"muak + ,'ta'me?e'o"tot + 248 + ,'por"ke?e + ,"txe 'ke?e + ,'po"re 'so'a'tua?a"na + 'ta'ke?e -- , 'iuh"?tsu?p + ,'e'txum"pi?i + .'ia"?katx + 255 + ,"txe 'ke"ha?ax 'u'tua?a'ni"?pir + ,'tua?a 'ma?a"txi 'u'iak"ta 'o?o"txoi 'e"muak + 'a'?ka "xi 'ta'ma'e?e -- .'o"tot +

33. Offering to the Earth Spirit

259 + "kon 'da — ,'ix"to 'a'?ka?a"pa + , 'a'?kah'pes"ian + ,'en"ton 'ses + ,'a"ka?ai + , 'a'lo"?kuo?p 'tu?u"nie?e "?pi?i "ro?p + ,'ta "ku?ut 'e"?kahk + 'ie?e — .'re'sen"sa 'rio + 268 + ,"uar 'u'pu?u"?tso?o?p + ,'u?ut'e"?pi?ir 'a?a'xi"no?p + 'ta — 'u'?ke"txo?p 'in — ,'in "te?en 'te?e"rutx "sa?a + .'u'ia"rio?p 'ta'mu?u 'nie?e"?pi?ir + 274 + ,'iu'?ke"txo?p "ko?or "u?ut '?kahk + ,'ta'kiuh"?tsu?p + "tua?a — 'e?e — ,'u'ia"rio?p 'ta'me?e"?txen + ,'tia?a'u'io "rio?p + .'u'me'ne"ro?p + 281 + ."por 'ke?e + ,'e"?txen 'ia"ha?a + ,'a'ioh"ra + 'ko'txa?a"tix + ,'a'nam"?tse?e "?kin + 286 + ,'a"ka?ai 'a'xa "na 'a'ioh"ra 'e"?txen + .'ta'ma'u'nie?e'?pi "ro?p + 288 + 'e?e — ,'in"te?e 'a'ioh"ra + 'e?e — ,'tua?a'tuh"ka 'e"sa?a 'ta"mar + ,'in "te?e 'a'ioh"ra 'tua?a'a'tur'?pa"na "u?ut 'e "?kahk 'ta"mar + .'tia?a'ta?a'pu"rui 'iuh"?tsu?p +

294 + 'i"txe 'ke?e"ia 'he?e — 'ia"ro?p 'e?e — ,'e"?txen 'ia"ha?a + "xe?e — ,'a?a'tuh "ke?e "sa?a "tar 'i"tia?a 'tur'?pa"nu?ut 'e "?kahk 'ta'kiuh"?tsu?p + ."txe 'ke"ha?ax 'ko 'txan"te?e 'mak"te?e + 300 + ,'tua?a'ma?a"txi 'a'nu"mui + 'e?e — 'e?e — ,'u'uiŋ"kir 'e"muak + 'o?o — ,'tu'?ka?a"xix 'na'ua"lir + lo"ke?e — ,'?ka"ni 'o?o"txoi 'ta'me?e'o"tot + ,"pe 'ro "txe 'ke"ha?ax + 'e?e — 'e?e — 'e"sa?a 'ia "ha?a 'ie'uh"?tsu?p + ,"ha?ax + ,'ko'mo"ha?ax + .'u'tu'ru"?po?o?p 'ko'txan'te?e'mak"te?e + . 'tua?a"ma 'tu"?ka?a 'nu"mui 'ta"mar + 317 + 'i?i — ,'los"kua 'tro + 'u'ies"ki?i "nir 'e?e — ,'u"nie?e '?pi"ro?p 'ia"ha?a + ,'a'xa"na + , 'u'ia"rio?p 'e"sa?a 'ta"mar + 'ta — .'ie?e'uh "?tsu?p 'ta'ku?ut'e"?kahk + 325 + "txe 'ke?e — ,'ko'txan"te?e 'mak"te?e "uar 'u'ma"ki "u?ut 'u'io'to"to?p 'ta"mar + .'ta?a'ma?a"txi 'o?o "txe?e "muak + 328 + .'i"kon 'da +

33. Offering to the Earth Spirit

329 + ."pe 'ro + "ia 'he?e -- ,'xe?e"mas + 'e?e -- 'e"pues 'to'xe?e"mas "mei 'gra'u?u -- , 'u'?kam'pi?i"?pir + ."ha?ax 'e"tia?a "ua?ar 'e 'ra"ma 'da + 336 + 'por'ke?e -- ,"ia + ,"ua?ar 'in"te?e "krus + 'xe?e -- ,'pa?a?k"?pir 'u'?kah "na?ar + .'u'me'ne"ro?p + 342 + ,'i'ta'mu?u "sui 'e"krus 'ia"ha?a + ,"ia?a 'a'tuh"ka 'e"sa?a + "ia?a -- 'a?a -- ,'a'xuh"ra 'u"nu?u?k 'ia?a "?katx + ,'iah"tso?o + .'i'u"tu?u 'e'txum"pi?i + 349 + ,"ia + 'a?a -- ,'a'tuh"ka + ,'in"te?er "ti?i "bar 'ko + ,'e"sa?a + 'e?e -- ,'xe'txe?e "no?p 'sak"sa?a + 356 + ,"i?i + .'ie?e'txa?a "te?e '?pi'?kit"rutx + ,'xe?e'txe?e"no?p 'ke "tua?a 'e"?aŋ 'he"lo?p + ."ia?a 'u'tu"kio?p + 'ta"ma 'u"sui 'e -- .'e"krus 'ia"ha?a + 362 + ,'i"kon 'da'ix"to + ,'a'?ka?a"pa 'tu"no?or + , 'en"ton 'ses + ,'a"ka?ai + ,'u'pu"kio?p 'e"sa?a + ,'lo'ke?e"ua?ar 'u'me'ne"ro?p + 'e?e -- "xe?e -- 'e?e -- "sa?a + ,'txe"?pir 'ta'ke?e"txa?p + 'ie?e -- ,"pan 'tu?u"hor + .'a"ka?ai 'u'pu"kio?p 'ta'ke?e"hen 'te +

376 + ,"kon 'da'?ka?a"pa + 'e?e -- ,'puk 'ma"iah 'ia"ha?a + ,'ta'ka'e"sa?a + 'e?e -- ,'e "hen 'te + ,'a"ian "ti?in 'a?a"xin 'tu?u'io"tot + .'ia?a"ian "ti?i 'ne'a'ket"pa + 384 + ,'a 'tur"uan + 'por'ke?e -- ,'ma?a"txa?a 'ua'ie"no?p + "por 'ke?e -- 'e'ui"nik 'xe?e -- 'pehk"?pir "uar 'u'num"se -- 'o?o -- 'o?o -- "xe?e -- "ua 'ra'?kah'pes"ian 'e?e -- 'ta'ka'e?e -- 'e?e -- , 'e"rum + 397 + ,'ma?a"txi 'a'ua"ien + ,'por'ke 'u'?kah"na?ar 'pehk"?pir + ,'ke"ha?ax "uar 'u 'num"se?e 'noh"?kin 'ia"ha?a + 400 + ,'tu "no?or 'iuh"?tsu?u?p + 'lo'ke?e -- ,'a"ian + ,'u '?ka"ni "tua?a '?ka?a"pu?u 'pu"ta + "ehs 'to 'a?an'?txak -- .'a?an'?txak"nu?ut 'e"rum + 406 + ,'i'hai"mei 'gra'iuh"?tsu?u?p + ,"uar 'u'pu"ta '?a'?ko"toi + ,"es 'to'a'la"sie 'te + 'e?e -- . "o 'tro"di 'ia +

33. Offering to the Earth Spirit

411 + ,'en"ton 'ses + 'ie?e'txum"pi?i 'xe?e — ,"ua 'ra'txa'mes"na 'ia"ha?a 'ia"?katx + ,"kon 'da'ix"to 'a'?ka?a"pa + 'a?a -- ,'txe?e "na 'e'?kah'pes"iah + ,'en"ton 'ses 'a'?keh"txa + 'e?e — 'tu"no?or 'e?e -- ,'ah"tso?o + 'e?e -- 'lo'ke?e — ,'txa'mes"no?p 'ia"ha?a + ,'a'?keh 'txa?a"xin + 'tia?a"ua 'ra?a -- ,'a'txe?e"ne?e 'ko"si 'na + .'tia?a'?pu"?tur 'i'xik"tak + . "tua?a 'u'ius"to?o?p + 429 + 'i?i -- 'a"ka?ai 'u'go"rio?p 'e?e — .'u"txo?p 'e'ta"mal + 432 + ,'ie?e'ta"mal 'ia"ha?a + 'kon'de?e -- ,"txe 'a?an'?txak"na 'u?ut'e"rum + ,"uix 'a'ta"?ka 'e 'ta"mal + ,'en"ton 'ses'a"ka?ai 'a'puh"ka + ,'ta "ka 'e"hen 'te'xe?e'sa'koh"po?o?p 'ia"ha?a 'ta 'noh"?kin + 'a"ka?ai 'ah -- .'ah'?ku"na 'u'?ku "xo?p +

440 + ,'i'kon'da'ix"to + ,'a'?ka?a"pa 'tu "no?or 'e'puk'ma"iah 'ia"ha?a + 'en -- ,'en"ton 'ses'a'lo"?koi + ,'e'ui"nik 'xe?e"uar 'a'?kah 'pes"ian + .'a'lo"?koi 'a?a"xin 'tu?u'io"tot + 446 + ,'a?ah'?ku"na + ,'iŋ"gohr "?puhr 'u"sa?a + ,'tua?a'u'?ke"txa?a "xin 'tu?u'io"tot + ,'iah '?ku"na + .'iŋ"koh '?tor"ti?i 'ia?a"?katx + .'u '?ke"txa?a "xin + ,"i?i + .'ah'?ku"na 'e'ta"mal + "tua?a -- ."tua?a 'u'?ke"txa?a "xin + .'tu?u 'io"tot + 457 + ,"por 'ke"txe 'ke?e + 'e?e -- ,"ko 'txa'u'?kah"na?ar 'pehk"?pir + 'i'ah'?ku"na "mei 'gra'tu"no?or 'lo'ke?e -- .'e"ua 'ra'tur '?pa"na 'ia"ha?a + 462 + ,'ha?ax"to '?e"ra + , 'ta"ma 'e'lu'ga"ro?p + "ti?i 'ne'u'na?a"ta 'u?u — 'a'noh'?ki"ni 'ta'ma'u?u -- .'u'ua?a"ri?p 'u 'io"tot +

33. Offering to the Earth Spirit

1 There is a celebration held in the place where I live, 6 and not only in the place where I live -- in all the villages they hold that celebration.

17 On the fifteenth of January, when people are coming home from the celebration in Esquipulas, there are some who make an offering at the support of the house where they live, on the very afternoon when they come back from the celebration; they begin to grind the *chilate*; they grind until it gets to be seven or eight o'clock.

50 When the *chilate* has been prepared, and completely mixed with water, they begin to carry it to the arbor, to where the arbor stands. 59 There are some who put out as many as fifty bowls, some thirty, some twenty-five, some forty -- but so they put them out. 67 When they begin to carry that *chilate*, it is stood in front of the cross where the arbor is, lined up. 74 When the large bowls which -- the sweetened *chilate* -- the bread is thrown in on top, and the chocolate which we call cacao. 89 And then come two little gourds, alike, with neither sweetening nor bread. 95 Those two gourds they say are for the angels. 101 Because they say that the angels do not drink much. 105 One large bowl is set down, which holds a lot of *chilate*, and that bowl, when -- 114 then everything in the arbor is ready.

118 When all the *chilate* has been set out, and the legs of the tom and hen turkeys have been tied, and the chickens, and everything is ready, then they begin, some who were invited to conduct that offering, begin to pray. 142 They go on praying until it gets to be twelve midnight. 146 Because he keeps on praying, sit-

ting there, because that prayer-sayer was especially invited. 153 By the giver of the celebration. 154 But some who themselves know how to pray do not invite another. 160 But if the giver of the celebration does not know how to pray, he invites another of those who know. 166 And that prayer-sayer, when he is there praying, he speaks to what they say is -- the spirit of -- the earth.

177 He speaks like this: 179 "Our Holy Mother, 181 where you were left by Our Master God, who is living in the sky, 186 and you, He left you, 188 and we are living here, 190 we -- press you. 192 We are doing everything 193 to You. 195 You see us sinning. 198 We are sinful; you see everything we do. 200 But do not let you -- do not let your patience end. 202 You see us; bless us, do not turn your face from us. 205 Put your blessing upon us, and today, we human beings are bringing you to mind with our poultry, where we raise it. 217 And we want you to bless us; do not let disease fall on our children and on us, on all our poultry which we put out. 226 We bring it here, our poultry; it is your payment, and with it we entreat you. 232 Look on us with open eyes, and give to us what we eat with open hands."

237 That man sits praying. 240 His prayer is long. 242 He asks that disease not enter, 244 he asks that the chickens not die, 245 he asks that the children not die, that no disease fall on the house, 248 because they say that is what the payment is for, with the incense, the turkeys, and the chickens. 255 They say that it is the payment so that he does not let disease enter and fall on the house.

259 When the praying is finished, then

ting there, because that prayer-sayer was especially invited. 153 By the giver of the celebration. 154 But some who themselves know how to pray do not invite another. 160 But if the giver of the celebration does not know how to pray, he invites another of those who know. 166 And that prayer-sayer, when he is there praying, he speaks to what they say is -- the spirit of -- the earth.

177 He speaks like this: 179 "Our Holy Mother, 181 where you were left by Our Master God, who is living in the sky, 186 and you, He left you, 188 and we are living here, 190 we -- press you. 192 We are doing everything 193 to You. 195 You see us sinning. 198 We are sinful; you see everything we do. 200 But do not let you -- do not let your patience end. 202 You see us; bless us, do not turn your face from us. 205 Put your blessing upon us, and today, we human beings are bringing you to mind with our poultry, where we raise it. 217 And we want you to bless us; do not let disease fall on our children and on us, on all our poultry which we put out. 226 We bring it here, our poultry; it is your payment, and with it we entreat you. 232 Look on us with open eyes, and give to us what we eat with open hands."

237 That man sits praying. 240 His prayer is long. 242 He asks that disease not enter, 244 he asks that the chickens not die, 245 he asks that the children not die, that no disease fall on the house, 248 because they say that is what the payment is for, with the incense, the turkeys, and the chickens. 255 They say that it is the payment so that he does not let disease enter and fall on the house.

259 When the praying is finished, then

they begin to go out to the nearby paths with coals and the censer. 268 They walk along censing the path, carrying each a gourd of *chilate*; they pour it on the paths, 274 and they carry a few coals with the incense to pour out in the holes where they dug them. 281 Because those holes they dug just as the sun was setting. 286 They began to go to dig the holes in the nearby paths. 288 One is dug for the *chilate* to be put in, and one is dug for the coals to be put in where the incense is to be burned.

294 And they say that those little holes which -- the *chilate* is poured in and where the coals are placed with the incense, they say it is like an enclosure, 300 so that the master of disease does not pass, or any spirit who -- wants to enter the house, but they say that the -- *chilate* and the incense are like -- they are placed like a fence so that nothing may pass inside. 317 And the four corners of the paths they walk, pouring *chilate* in them and the incense on the coals. 325 They say it is like a fence which encloses the house within itself, so that disease does not enter. 328 And when.

329 But the -- place which is most -- important, is where the arbor stands. 336 Because there stands a cross which is planted on purpose by them. 342 And at the foot of that cross there they pour the *chilate* and cut the throats of the chickens, the tom turkey and the hen turkey. 349 And they pour out a whole bowl of *chilate* which they call white *chilate*. 356 And the two small gourds they say are for the angels they pour out there at the foot of that cross. 362 And then when all is finished, they begin to offer the *chilate* which is stood there by them, the *chilate* which is made with sugar and bread on top; they begin to give it to the

people.

376 When that sharing is finished, of the <u>chilate</u> with the people, there are some who go home and some who remain. 384 They sit down, because they do not sleep, because the man who was invited to conduct -- or -- who is praying to the earth, 397 he does not sleep, because he was invited on purpose to conduct that celebration. 400 All the incense which there is has to be all burned up, until it gets light on the earth. 406 And if there is much incense, he burns it until seven o'clock the next day.

411 Then the turkey which is being killed and the chicken, when the praying is finished, then it is carried, all the tom turkeys which were killed are carried over to where the -- they say is the kitchen, where it is full of women, so it will be prepared. 429 And they begin to pack -- they make tamales. 432 And those tamales when it grows light on the earth, the tamales are just cooked; then they begin to be distributed to the people who stayed up there for the celebration; they are given them to eat.

440 Then, when all that distribution is finished, then the man who was praying goes out and goes to his house. 446 He is given a jug of <u>chilate</u> to carry to his house and he is given a whole chicken to carry away, and he is given tamales to carry to -- to carry to his house. 457 Because they say that since he was invited especially, he is given a lot of everything that was put out. 462 Thus, in the places, there are some who know how to celebrate in the -- house place.

34. Birth of the Sun

1 + ,'o'tron"te?e 'noh"?kin 'a'txe?e"na +
.'ta'ma'el"do 'se'de"mar 'so + 3 + ,"txe 'ke?e
'ta'me?e"di 'ia'ia"ha?a + ,'e'u'kux"na?ar 'e
"?kin + .'xe?e'u'han'?txak'ne"son "to?or 'e"rum
+ 6 + ,"txe 'ke?e"?kin 'ia"ha?a + .'ma"ha?ax
'in'te?e"ra 'u'?ka"?pa?a + 8 + ,'xe?e're"mas
'na?a'tam"?pir 'u'me'ne"hen 'te + ,'tu"ru 'ta"ma
+ ."he 'su"kris 'to + 11 + ,"txe 'ke"kon 'da
"uar 'a?an'?txak"na + ,'u'?ka"?pa?a + ."ni 'nio
're'den"tor 'del"mun 'do + 14 + ,'e?en"te?e
'?ka"?pa?a + ."ni 'nio'de'pes"te 'ho + 16 + ,
'e?en"te?e '?ka"?pa?a + .'saŋ'gre"go 'rio'ah
'?tsa?p'tes"iah + 18 + ,'e?en"te?e '?ka"?pa?a
+ .'san'an"to 'nio'de'hus"ti 'sia + 20 + ,
'e?en"te?e + ."ni 'nio'de'kus"to 'dio + 22 + ,
'e?en"te?e + ."ni 'nio'de're"hu 'hio + 24 + ,
'?en"te?e + ."ni 'nio'san'pas"kual + 26 + ,
'e?en"te?e + ."ni 'nio'de'so"kor 'ro + 28 +
'e?en"te?e + ."ni 'nio"kre 'a"dor + 30 + .
txe?e"no?p 'ke?e + ,'a"ka 'da"o 'ra + !.'in'tia
"?txix 'u'?ka"?pa?a +

33 + ,'e"lu 'na + ,'tu"ru 'u'?ka"?pa?a 'u
'me'ne"ro?p + .'ta'ma"rei 'na'san'ta'ma"ri 'a +
36 + ,'e?en"te?e + ."rei 'na'pie"dad + 38 + ,
'e?en"te?e + ."rei 'na'ka'ri"dad + 40 + ,'e?en
"te?e + .'e"rei 'na'de'so"kor 'ro + 42 + ."rei
'na'de'hus"ti 'sia + ."rei 'na'de'kus"to 'dio +
44 + ."por 'ke"txe 'ke?e + ,'e"lu 'na + .'ix
'ka?ar"?pir 'tua?a'e'saŋ'gre"go 'rio +

47 + ,'txe?e"no?p 'ke"kon 'da'ka'txa"mai +
,"no?on 'e'ui'ni"kon + ,'txe?e"no?p 'ke?e"kon
'da'ka'?ko"toi 'tia?a'tu"ru 'e"dios + ,"txe
'ke?e"ha?ax 'e"rei 'na'a?a"?tso 'ta'ma"ron + .
"no?on 'e'ui'ni"kon + 52 + ,'ie?e'i'xik"tak +
.'a?ah"?tso?o?p 'u"men 'e"he 'su"kris 'to + 54
+ .'txe?e"no?p + ,'ke"kon 'da'a'?ka?a"pa 'a?ah
"?tsa + .'a'iah"ra 'ta"?kahk + .'xe'?a?a'ro?p"na
"pur 'ga"to 'rio + ,"es 'to"ke?e + ,'a'?tsak"ta

34. Birth of the Sun

"?a 'nio + .'ko"txe?e 'txa"men +

61 + ,"kon 'da'?ka?a"pi?ix 'u'to"ii 'tu "no?or 'u'ma'?pam'?pa"nir + ,'en"ton 'ses + .'a '?ko"toi 'e"?aŋ 'he"lo?p + ,'a'?txuh"ia?a 'lo "?koi + .'tu?u"ia?am 'e"?kahk + .'tua?a'a'tur "uan 'ta"ka 'e"dios + 67 + ,"por 'ke"txe 'ke?e + ,'e"?kahk 'ia"ha?a + .'tur'?pa"?pir 'u"men 'e "dios + ,'ke?e"ha?ax + ,'u'pu"ta + ,"i?i + ,'u 'po"ki 'tu"no?or 'ma'?pam'?pa"nir + .'lo'ke?e'a "ian 'ta'ma"ron + 75 + ."txe 'ke?e'ak'ta"?pir 'u"men 'e"dios + ,'ke?e"ha?ax 'e'lu"gar 'tia?a'a 'tua?am"pa 'tu"no?or 'ma'?pam'?pa"nir + ,'xe?e'a 'txe?em"pa 'a"ni + ."to?or 'e"rum + 79 + ,'po "re 'so'e"hen 'te + ,'a'?kah"pa 'a'?kah"pa + .'a '?kah'pes'ia"no?p "tu?ut + 82 + ."txe 'ke?e "tua?a 'ma?a"txi 'a?ah"?tso?o?p "mei 'gra + . "kon 'da'a'txa"mo?o?p +

84 + ,'ta"rix 'e"tiem 'po + ,"tie?e 'ne'ui 'ni'ko"?pix + ,'eh"?kar 'eh"?kar + .'a'?kah'pes 'ia"no?p + 88 + ,"naht '?ka"ni 'a?an'?txak"na + ,'a?atx"pa 'ta"ka + ."tu?ut 'u'?txak"tio?o?p + 91 + ,'a?a"xin + .'a'ko'tua"no?p 'tu?u"pot 'o "tot + 93 + ,'u'?tsah"?pes 'u'kan"de?e "lo?p + .'a"ka?ai 'a'?kah'?pe'sia"no?p "tu?ut + 95 + , 'por'ke?e'txe?e"no?p 'a"ni + .'ke"ha?ax 'e'iu 'mar"?pir 'ta'ma'tu"no?or 'lo'ke?e'a"ian + 97 + ,'?pan"to .'es"to?o 'ko"ne?er +

99 + ,'po"re 'so + ,'ta"ma 'el"do 'se'de "mar 'so + ."mei 'gra"ti?i 'ne'u"txe 'e'noh"?kin 'ia"ha?a + 102 + ,'u'pu"ta 'e"kue 'te + ,'u 'tur"?po?o?p 'e'kan"de 'la + ,'iuh"?tsu?u?p + , 'e"sa?a + .'u'xu"rio?o?p 'u"nu?u?k 'e'txum"pi?i +

107 + ,'xo?e'kai"to + ,'u?um"?pi 'u'kon"ta "ho?p + ,'lo'ke?e'u'?kah"tio?p 'a"ni + ,'i'tu "no?or 'lo'ke?e'iŋ'gui"ra 'u"txo?p + ,'kon'da

34. Birth of the Sun

"uar 'a'?kah'?pe 'sia"no?p + ."ha?ax 'e'?ka "?po?o?p 'i"ra + .'ko"txiatx 'ma?a"txix 'tu"ro?p + 114 + ,"hue 'lis'gon"sa 'les + 115 + ,'e 'da"ma 'sio"lo 'pes + 116 + ,'e"krus "su 'txe 'te + 117 + ,'e'san"tia 'go'de"ro 'sa + 118 + ,'na"kle 'to'ra"mi 'res + 119 + ,"pe 'dro'mo "ra 'les + 120 + 'fe'li"sia 'na"su 'txe'te + 121 + .'nar"si 'so"al 'ba'res +

34. Birth of the Sun

1 Another festival is held on the twelfth of March. 3 They say that on that day is the birth of the sun which illuminates us on earth. 6 They say that the sun has not just one name. 8 The one which is best known by people continues to be Jesus Christ. 11 They say that when it is just getting light its name is Child Redeemer of the World. 14 One name is San Gregorio the Illuminator. 18 One name is San Antonio of Judgement. 20 One name is Child Guardian. 22 One is Child Refuge. 24 One is Child San Pascual. 26 One is Child Succor. 28 One is Child Creator. 30 They say that at each hour, one of these is its name.

33 The moon's name given by them is Queen Santa Maria. 36 One is Queen Piety. 38 One is Queen Charity. 40 One is Queen Succor. 42 Queen of Judgement, Queen Guardian. 44 Because they say that the moon is married to San Gregorio.

47 They say that when we die, we men, they say that it is the Queen who whips us, we who are men. 52 And the women are lashed by Jesus Christ. 54 They say that when the whipping is finished they are thrown into the fire which is called Purgatory until a year has passed since death.

61 When they have finished paying for all their sins, then the Angels come and pick them from the midst of the fire, so they can be with God. 67 Because they say that that fire is set by God, and that it burns and cleanses all the sins which we have. 75 They say it is left by God; it is the place where all sins are paid for which were committed while on earth. 79 That is why they pray and pray, praying to Him. 82 They say that it is so they will not be whipped much when they die.

34. Birth of the Sun

84 Long ago, those who were already grown men prayed day after day. 88 Long before it began to grow light they rose from their beds 91 and went to kneel behind the house. 93 They lit candles, and began to pray to Him. 95 Because they used to say that He is the master of all there is. 97 And so until today.

99 That is why on the twelfth of March there are many who perform that ceremony. They fire rockets, they set out candles, incense, and chilate, and cut the throats of turkeys.

107 Those whose stories I heard, who used to tell it, and all that I saw doing it when they were praying, are these names here, since they are no longer alive: 114 Félix González, 115 Damasio López, 116 Cruz Súchete, 117 Santiago de Rosa, 118 Nacleto Ramírez, 119 Pedro Morales, 120 Feliciana Súchete, 121 and Narciso Álvarez.

35. Prayers to the Sun

1 + ,'e'?kah'?pes"iah 'xe'?a'txe?e"na 'ta 'ka'e"?kin + .'a'txe?e"na 'a'la"sin 'ko'de'la'ma "nia 'na + 3 + "ha?ax 'e"?o 'ra'xe?e"rer 'u '?kah"tio?p 'ta"kar + .'lo'ke?e'?ka"ni 'u'?kah "tio?p +

5 + .'u'ia?a"rio?p + .'ka'ta"ta?a 'dio"set + ,"ne?et 'ka'iu'ma"ret + .'tu?ut"?kin + 9 + . 'ah"?kin + .'ah"?kin + .'i'?tsa?a?p'tes"ian 'ti "ko?or + 12 + ,'meh"?kar 'ka'to"ii + ,'a'txoh '?pes"iah + .'lo'ke?e'a"txe 'ta'ka"ron + 15 + ,'tu"no?or 'iah"?kin + ."ma 'ko"txa 'tua?a'ka'to "ie?et +

17 + ,"pe 'ro'ka'na?a"ta + ,'ke?e'u"txu?u + ,"ia 'o'?po?k"na?ar "te?e + .'xe?e'txoh'?pes "?pir 'a"men "to?or 'e"rum + ,"no?on 'e'?pa "?ka?p 'e'ko'no"hon + ,'ka"txe 'tu'mim"?pir 'tua?a'ka"txe 'o'fre"ser "to?oit + ,'ko"txa 'in "te?e 'tua?a'ni"?pir + .'ta?a"?pa + 25 + ,'por 'ke?e"ne?et 'e"ra + .'a'txoh"?pes "to?or 'e"rum + 27 + .'i'ka'ua"ra?k 'tia?a"uar 'a'uah"?ko?on "to?or 'e"rum + 28 + ,'ko"ne?er 'i"ra + , 'tia?a'tu"ro?on + ,'ka'?tsin"?tsa + .'ta"ma 'ka "ual 'ma + 32 + ,'ta'ka'u'?ku"nir 'ka'ue"roh + .'tu"ro?on 'ka'pe"te 'ka"?pa "to?oit +

34 + ,'i'ra"non 'ko"ne?er + ,'pa'sar"hut + .'?txa"ma 'pa'sar"?ka?p + ,'lo'ke?e'tu"ru 'ka'me "ner + .'tu?u"tahn 'e'nues'tra"ma 'dre'san"ti 'si'ma + 39 + ,'i'ra"non + .'tia?a"uar 'ka'?ke "txe 'ka"?ka?p "to?oit + 41 + ,'ko"ne?er 'pa 'sar"?ka?p + ,'?ke"txe 'a'?ka?p'ti"ko?or + .'ta 'ka'tu"no?or 'a'iah"tsah +

44 + .'i"ra?a 'uak"to?on 'ka'?ka"xi 'tu?u "?ka?p 'e'mal"om 'bre + 45 + .'i'tu?u"?ka?p 'tu"no?or 'ah'na"ual 'ma'?pam"?pan + 46 + , 'hai'a"ian 'tia?a'tu"ru 'ka'pia?a"ro?p + .'u'iuh "ta 'u'xe"ror 'mu'si?i"?ko?p 'ti"ko?or + 48 +

35. Prayers to the Sun

,"pe 'ro"ne?et 'ta'ua"ret + .'tua?a'a'kor'pe"son
'ta'ma'tu?no?or 'xe"ror 'mu"si?ik 'tia?a'ua"tar
'ti"ko?or + 50 + ,'i"ra?a 'uak"ta 'a'?ke"?ko +
,'tia?a'tu"ro?on 'ma"kui?ir 'ko?o"tot + ,'ta'ka
'ia"ro?p 'ka'max"tak 'i'ta"ma 'ka'ua"ra?k + .
'tia?a"uar 'ka'?to"xi + 54 + ,'tu"no?or "muak
'tia?a'ua"tar 'ti"ko?or + .'uh'tan"txik 'tu?u
"?txu?ur 'mon"ta 'nia + .'tia?a"ma 'tu"?ka 'e
'?pa"?ka?p 'e'ko"noh +

57 + ,"no?on 'ma'ta'ua"ron + ,'tia?a'a"so
'te?e'kas"ti 'go + ,'ah'?ku"no?on 'u'to"?kor
"ko?oit + .'to"?kor 'ka'ue"roh + 61 + .'i'u
'?ke'?ko"ni?p "ko?ok + ,'u'?ke'?ko"ni?p 'ka
"?ka?p + ,'tia?a"uar 'a'ku?um"ian + .'e?ei'xim
"ian + 65 + ,'e'?pa"?ka?p 'e'ko"noh + .'i"ra
'a'?ka?a"pa 'a'pa"sen 'sia'ta'ka"ron + 67 + ,
"?txuh '?ku"non 'eh"?kar 'eh"?kar + 68 + ,'ta
'ka'tu"no?or 'a'?ku'ner"siah +

69 + ,'kon'da"uar 'a'pu"ru 'iuh"?tsu?u?p +
,'ie'kan"de 'la + .'u'?txuh"?kuo?p 'hai"uar 'a
'?ta"?pai 'u'?pu"?tsa?ar 'ti"txan + 72 + .'i'u
'ua"rar 'e"?kahk 'ta'me?e'kan"de 'la + 73 + ,
'i"hai 'e'kan"de 'la"uar 'o?oi"?ki + ,'o?o"uar
'a'hu?u"txa "mei 'gra + ,'txe?e"no?p 'ke?e + .
'ma?a"txi 'uar'o?o?p"na 'tu"?ka "ua 'ru'?kah
"tio?p + 77 + .'o'ke?e'a"ian 'txi'?ka"ni 'a
'txa"mai 'ta'me?e'o"tot +

78 + ,'en"ton 'ses + ,'u'si?ik"?po?p 'in
"te?e 'ah"?kin + .'tua?a'u'?ki"ni 'u'ui"ra + ,
'tu"?ka '?ka"ni 'a'nu"mui + .'ta'mio?o"tot + 83
+ ,'hai"ma + .'a?a"xo?p 'tua?a"ti?in 'a"ian 'u
"nai 'pe + ,'tua?a'u"txe 'a'de'bi"nar + .'lo
'ke?e'a?a"xi 'a'nu"mui 'ta'mi'o"tot + 87 + ,
'hai'txek"ta '?ka"ni 'a'txa"mai + ,'en"ton 'ses
'a"ka?ai + .'ta'ka'e'pu"rut 'kan"de 'la + .'eh
"?kar 'eh"?kar +

35. Prayers to the Sun

1 The prayer which they say to the sun
they say at five o'clock in the morning. 3
That is the time they can pray to it for what-
ever they want to pray for.

5 They say to it, "You are God our Father.
You are our master in the sky. 9 Sun, Sun, you
shed your light on us. 12 Never can we pay for
your blessings which you give to us. 15 Every-
thing is the Sun; there is no way we can pay
you.

17 But we know that with the sap of the
copal tree which was blessed by you on the
earth, we human beings make money for offering
to you, as a payment to you. 25 Because you
can bless the earth. 27 And our livestock
where it is, you give to us on earth. 28 Today
when we are alive, we feel sympathy in our
hearts. 32 With humble expressions, we sit
bowed down before you.

34 Look at us with open eyes, take with o-
pen hands what is set down by us on the top of
our Holy Mother. 39 Look at us when we hold
out our hands to you. 41 Today, with open
hand, hold out your hand to us with all your
love.

44 Do not let us fall into the hands of
the Evil One, 45 and into the hands of all the
evil spirits. 46 If there is one such where
our companions are, he blows his blighting
breath over us. 48 But you have the power to
protect us from every blighting breath which
comes over us. 50 Do not let it harden, where
we live in our houses, with our little children
and with our livestock where we are raising
them. 54 Every disease which comes over us,
blow away to where thc mountains lie, where

there are no human beings.

57 We can not stand the lash of punishment. Give us a healthy appearance, a healthy expression. 61 And toughness in our legs, toughness in our arms, where human beings are forming in eggs, are forming in seeds. 65 Do not let your patience with us human beings end. 67 Watch over us day after day 68 with all your compassion".

69 When the incense was burning, and the candles, they watched to see if their smoke was rising to the sky, and 72 the beam of light of the candle. 73 And if the candle was weeping or leaving many threads of wax, they said that what he was praying for was not being heard, 77 or that there was someone who was to die in the house.

78 Then, they sought a diviner to divine and see what was to happen in the house. 83 If not, they went for one who had playing cards so as to divine what was going to happen in the house. 87 If it appeared that he was to die, then they began to burn candles, day after day.

36. Holy Week

1 + ,'e?en"te?e 'noh"?kin + ,'a'nu"mui 'ta
'me?e'a"bril + .'xe?e'a'ro?p"na 'se"ma 'na"san
'ta + 4 + ,"mei 'ra"hen 'te'a?a"xin 'o'tro
"niahr + .'ta'noh"?kin 'es'ki"pu 'la + 6 + ,
"ti?i 'ne'ma?a"txi?i "xin 'ta'ma'?e"ne 'ro + .
'ha?ax"to 'a?a"xin 'ta'ma'e'a"bril + 8 + ,'a
'lo"?koi 'ta'u'io"tot 'ta'me?e"di 'ia"mar 'tes +
,'a'?ko'to"io?p "mier 'ko'les + ."tua?a 'ia?a'tu
"ro?o?p +

11 + ."hue 'bes'a'la"so 'txo + .'a'?keh
"txa 'a'mah"ka 'e'na'sa"re 'no + 'ta'man"te?e 'o
"tot + .'nah"tir 'ta'ma'u"ti?i 'e'txi"nam + 15
+ ,'io?o"tot 'ia"ha?a + 'tu"ni 'ta'ma"kar 'sel +
17 + ."ia 'u'ma"kio?o?p 'u'ua"?po?o?p +

18 + ,"ha?a 'xe"ra 'e"?o 'ra'ia"ha?a + ,
"tia?a 'u'ma"kio?o?p 'e'na'sa"re 'no + ,"txe
'ke?e + .'a'mak"?tsa 'e"glo 'ria + 22 + ,"ia
'ma"kar "ua?ar + 'a?a"xi 'tu"no?or 'e"tar 'de +
,"es 'to"o 'tro"di 'ia + .'ta'me?e"di 'ia"bier
'nes'u'lo?k"sio?p 'u'xan'tah're"so?p + .'ta'ma
'tu"no?or 'e"kaa "io?p 'te?e'txi"nam +

27 + ,'a'?kai"na 'u"me 'ne?e"pa 'gre + .
'tia?a"uar 'a'xan'tah'res"na 'ta"ka 'ie + 29 +
.'a?a'ro?p"na + ."bur 'ro + .'ka"ba 'io + .'o're
"hon + ,"por 'ke?e"txe 'ke"ha?ax + .'u'txo"ni 'u
'ta"ta?a + 35 + ,'i'tu?u"pat + ,'ua"tar + .'ux
"te?e 'max"tak + 38 + "uar 'u'xe"?kio?o?p 'ta
'ka'e?e -- .'e'ha"rar 'xe?e'u'?ke"txo?p + .'?tsa
"par 'e"kla 'bo'u'me'ne"ro?p 'ta'mu?u"hor 'e'ha
"rar + 41 + ,"uar 'a'xa"no?p + .'i"uar 'u'xe
"?kio?o?p 'u'?pa"ker 'u"pat 'e'na'sa"re 'no +

43 + ,'i"tia?a 'a'?ko"to?o?p + ,"tia?a
"tua?a 'u'ua"?puo?o?p 'e?ei"ri + .'ua"tar 'in
'te?e'ui"nik 'ta'kan"te?e 'es"poŋ 'ha'tu?u"?ka?p
+ 46 + ,'u'?pu"ri 'ta'ma"ian 'ie"li 'na + .'u
'?txu"?pa 'tu?u"ieh 'e'na'sa"re 'no + 48 + ,

36. Holy Week

"ehs 'to'ke?e"?pan + 'u'?ke"txo?p + .'a'?ko"toi 'ta'me?e'o"tot 'xe?e'txe?e"no?p "kar 'sel + 51

+ ,'i'hi"?tir 'u"na?a?k 'u"me 'ne"ro?p + .'ta'ma 'e"la 'so +

53 + ,'i'ta'kan"te?e "krus + "to?or 'u'keh "re?p + 55 + 'i?i — ,'ta're"re?e "di 'ia'ia "ha?a + ,'a'?keh"txa 'e'he"sus 'na'sa"re 'no + 58 + ,'xe?e"ha?ax 'e"o 'ra'a'las"sie 'te + . 'kon'da?a'mah"ka 'i"glo 'ria + 60 + ,'ta'me?e "di 'ia'ia"ha?a + ."ma 'mah"txi?i 'e"rer 'a'pat "na + 62 + ."nien 'tua?a"ti + 63 + ."nien 'tu?u'mo"ri 'u"si?i + 64 + .'txe?e"no?p + ,'ke 'u'ta"krio?p 'e"maa "lo?o?p + .'a'txam"san +

67 + ,'po"re 'so + ,"ti?i 'ne'?kan"to + , 'a?a"ti + ,'i'?kan"to 'u'mo"ri 'u"si?i + ,'a?a "xin + .'ak'?par"to + .'u'mo"ri 'u"si?i + 74 + .'e'rer"to 'a?a"ti + 75 + ,'kon'da'u'iu "?pio?o?p + ,'a?ah'kes"na 'e'kam"pa 'na'te?e'txi "nam + .'txe?e"no?p 'ke?e'ua"rix 'a'mah"ka 'i "glo 'ria +

78 + ,'e"?o 'ra'ia"ha?a + 'ma'mah"txi?i 'e "rer 'a'pat"na + 'nien'e"rer 'a?a"ti + 81 + , 'por'ke?e'txe?e"no?p + ,'ke"hai 'a?a"tio?p + ,'a 'mak"?tsa 'u'txi'ki"no?p + ."por 'ke?e'ma"kar 'i "glo 'ria + 85 + ,'u'koh"ko?o?p + 'es'to"o 'tro"di 'ia + .'ta'ma'e"di 'ia"sa 'ba'do +

88 + .'a'?ko"toi 'e"di 'ia"bier 'nes + 89 + ,'ta'me?e"di 'ia"bier 'nes + 'a'?txu?u?p"na 'e "san 'to'en"tier 'ro + .'xe?e'txe?e"no?p 'san'ma "nuel 'de'me"si 'ias +

92 + ,"kon 'da'a'?ko"toi 'a'la"so 'txo + , 'u'lo?k"sio?p 'u'xan'tah're"so?p + .'ta"ka 'ie + 95 + ,'u'?ke"txe 'u'?txu"?po?o?p + ."to?or 'e?en"te?e 'san"tar + 97 + .'u'koh"ko?p 'a'?ko

36. Holy Week

"toi 'a'las"kua 'tro + 98 + ,'u'iem"sio?p +
"tu?ut 'e"krus + .'u'?pi"tio?p 'a?a"xin 'u'ua
"?po?p 'ta'i"gle 'sia +

101 + ,'a'las"tres 'de'la"tar 'de + ,'a'lo
"?koi 'txa?a"te?e "bir 'hen + ,'i?i + .'ia?a"pos
'to"lo?p + 105 + ,'a'?pih"ta 'a?a"xo?p 'ta'pa
"rro 'kia + .'tia?a"?txa?ar 'e'san'man"uel +
107 + ,'iix"to 'ia"ha?a + ,'san'ta"ro?p + 109
+ .'a?a"xi 'e"tar 'de + 110 + ,'a'la"siŋ 'ko
'de'la"tar 'de + .'a'lo'?kes"na 'o'tron"iahr +
.'e'san"man"uel + 'ie?e"bir 'he"no?p 'e?e'a"pos
'to"lo?p + 114 + ,'in'te?e"ra 'a'lo"?kuo?p + ,
'a'?pih"ta?a 'xi"no?p + .'u'?ku"nir 'u'?ku"nir +

117 + ,"uar 'u"txo?p 're"sar "tu?ur + ,'a
"ka 'da'o"tot 'ta"ka 'ie + ,'a'dor"na 'do'u"ti?i
'e"puer 'ta + .'ta"ka 'u'io"por 'e'tah"te?e +
121 + .'i"ua?ar 'e"me 'sa'u"me 'ne"ro?p + 122
+ ,'ia'?ko"toi 'a'ua?a?p"na 'e'dio"so?p 'ia"ha?a
+ .'xe?e"uar 'a'?pih"ta 'a?a"xo?p + 124 + .'a
'?ko"toi 'es'ta?a'las"do 'se'de'la"no 'txe +
125 + ,'o?o'se"no?o?p + .'ma"kui?ir 'e'san"tua
'rio +

127 + ,'kon'da"uar 'o?o'se"na + ,'ta'me?e
'i"gle 'sia + .'u'mo'roh"sc 'u"?pa 'e"hen 'te +
130 + .'u"txo?p 're"sar + 131 + .'a"ian 'in
'te?e'kos"tum 'bre'u'na?a"to?o?p + 132 + ,'a
"ian "ti?i 'ne'u'ta"res 'e"nar 'xe?e"?txi?i
"?txu?ut + ,'tua?a'u'luk"?pa 'tu?u"?ka?p 'e"krus
+ .'tia?a"?txu?ur 'e'san'man"uel + 135 + ,
"ti?in 'u'ta"res 'u"?txum + ,'u'si?ik"?pa + .
'xe?e'xo'io"ioh 'u"nu?u?k + 138 + .'u'?txu"?pa
'tu?u'ieh"?tser 'tia?a'ka"txar "?txu?ur + 139
+ ."ti?in 'u'ta"res "ku?um 'u'lu"?pa "tu?ut +
140 + ,"por 'ke?e"txe 'ke"ha?ax 'iu'mar"?pir +
.'ta'ma'tu"no?or 'lo'ke?e'a"ian +

142 + ,'po"re 'so'e"hen 'te + ,"kon 'da

36. Holy Week

"uar 'a'?txa"muo?p + .'u'ke"te 'u'na"ro?p "ti?i 'ne'ga'la"nik 'sak"sak "u?ut + ,"ti?i 'ne'iax "nar + ."ti?in 'e'txak"nar + 147 + ."por 'ke "txe 'ke?e"ha?ax 'u'?txi"?txer 'e"he 'su"kri 'stu +

148 + ,'por'ke?e"txe?e "no?p 'ke?e'ta'ma'u '?txi"?txer 'e"he 'su"kri 'sto + ,'txek"ta 'tu "no?or "?pu?ur + ,"nar + ,"?txum + ,'si"?ka?p + .'ke"ne?e + 154 + ,"por 'ke?e"txe 'ke?e + ,'e "dia 'blo + ,'u'tah"ui 'u"?pa 'ta'ma'in"te?e 'di 'ia + .'ta'ka'e"he 'su"kri 'sto + 158 + .'u 'ia?a"re 'e"he 'su"kris 'to + .'ka"txi?ik 'pro "bar 'ka"?pa + 160 + ,'ka'ui"ra "txi "mas + . 'im"?puts 'u'?txi"?txer +

162 + ."txe 'ke'u'xu"ri 'u"?pa 'e"dia 'blo + 163 + ,'i'ta'mu?u'?txi"?txer 'e"dia 'blo + . "ia 'lo"?koi 'tu"no?or 'a'ni"mal 'xe?e"ma '?pam "?pan + ,"txan + ,'ma'na"kutx + ,"huh + ,'u "?pi?i + .'ah"pat + 170 + ,'i'ha?ax"to + ,'u '?txi"?txer 'e"kris 'to + 172 + "ia 'lo"?koi + ,'e'hi"nah + ,"?pu?ur + ,'si"?ka?p + ."?txum +

177 + ,'po'res"to + ,'e"hen 'te + .'a'?ku '?pe'sia"no?p 'es'to'ko"ne?er + 180 + ,"por 'ke?e"?pan 'a"ni + .'a'?ku'?pes"ian 'e'o"nia?aŋ "hen 'te + .'ta"rix 'e"tiem 'po + 183 + ,"pe 'ro'in'te?e"to 'noh"?kin + ,'u"txo?p 'in"so 'lo 'ta'ka'uh"?tsu?u?p + ,'kan"de 'la + ."sa?a + 187 + ,'ta"ma 'e'noh'?ki"no?p 'ia"ha?a + , "tia?a "uar 'a'io?o"pa 'e"hen 'te'es'ki"pu 'la + ,'ko"ra 'ko"ra + ,'a'mo'rok"na 'a'xa"no?o?p + , 'u'txo?p're"sar + .'ta'mio?o'to"to?p + 193 + , 'i'ko"ra 'ko"ra + ,'a'hi?i?k"na 'e'ui'tsi"ro?p + ,'u"men 'e"sian "kue 'te + ,'e"bom 'ba + .'tia?a "uar + 'a'uit'?kes"na + .'ta"ma 'e'al'de?e"io?p +

200 + ,'ha?a"xo?p 'txe?e"no?p 'ke?e'pro"me

36. Holy Week

'sa + ,'u'txo?p'ta'ka'e'mi'la"gro 'so + ,'tua?a 'a?ah'?ku"no?p 'tu"?ki?k 'tu"?ki?k + .'xe?e'u '?kah"tio?p + 204 + "txe 'ke?e + ."tua?a 'a?ah '?ka"re "u?ut 'u'io'to"to?p + 206 + .'po"re 'so'u'tu'ru"?po?p 'tu"?ki?k "xix +

36. Holy Week

1 One celebration happens in April, which
is called Holy Week. 4 Many people go again to
Esquipulas. 6 Anyone who didn't go in January
goes then in April. 8 Leaving the house on a
Tuesday, he arrives on Wednesday, so as to be
there.

11 Thursday at eight o'clock the Nazarene
is carried and shut away in a house far out on
the edge of town. 15 That house serves as a
prison. 17 There they stand him and shut him
away.

18 At that time, when they shut away the
Nazarene they say that the Glory is shut away.
22 There it stays shut away during the whole
evening and until the next day. On Friday they
take him out at eight o'clock. They take him
out and parade him around on all the streets of
the town.

27 He is scolded by the priest when he is
being paraded around. 29 He is called 'Burro!
Horse! Long-Ear!', because they say that he
sold his father. 35 And behind him come three
boys. 38 They are poking him with canes which
they carry, with nails stuck by them in the ends
of the canes. 41 They are walking and poking
the backbone of the Nazarene.

43 And when they reach a place where they
stand him to rest, a man comes with a sponge in
his hand; 46 he moistens it with dye and sus-
pends it at the mouth of the Nazarene. 48 So
they carry him until they reach the house which
is called the prison. 51 And his torso is
bound by them with rope, and with a cross on his
back.

53 And when that day is here, when Jesus

Nazarene is carried, 58 that is the time, at
seven o'clock, when the Glory is shut away. 60
On that day nobody can work, 62 nor bathe, 63
nor gather firewood. 64 They say those who do
help the evil ones kill.

67 That is why whoever wants to bathe and
wants to gather firewood, in the evening they
gather firewood. 74 Then they can bathe. 75
When they hear the sounding of the bell in the
town, they say that the Glory is already being
shut away.

78 At that time nobody can work, nor can
he bathe, 81 because they say that if he
bathes, his ears are plugged up, because the
Glory is shut away. 85 They wait until the
next day, on Saturday.

88 Friday comes. 89 On Friday, the Holy
Corpse, which they call _San Manuel de Mesías_ is
crucified.

92 When it gets to be eight o'clock, they
take him out and parade him in the street. 95
They carry him and crucify him on a cross. 97
They wait until it gets to be four o'clock. 98
They take him down from the cross and carry him
on their shoulders to stand him in the church.

101 At three o'clock in the afternoon, two
Virgins leave, and Apostles. 105 They are car-
ried along to the parish, where San Manuel lies.
107 And that is the way they spend 109 the
duration of the afternoon, 110 until five o'-
clock in the afternoon, when San Manuel is taken
out again, and the Virgins and Apostles. 114
All together they go out, being carried along on
shoulders, humbly, humbly.

36. Holy Week

117 They say prayers in front of them at every house on the street whose doorway is decorated with pine branches. 121 And a table was placed by them. 122 And they come and those Gods which they are carrying around are stood up. 124 It comes to be twelve o'clock at night 125 when they enter inside the sanctuary.

127 When he is put back into the church, the people gather themselves into a group. 130 They pray. 131 There is a custom they believe in. 132 There are some who bring corn whose grains are blood red, so as to hang them on the arms of the cross where San Manuel hangs. 135 Others bring squash, looking for one with a curled neck. 138 He hangs it beside where he is tied, hanging. 139 Another brings dough which he dips out in front of him, 140 because they say that he is the master of all that is.

142 That is why people, when they are dying, save their corn which has beautiful grains. They look for those with beautiful white grains, with black corn, with red corn. 147 Because they say that that is the blood of Jesus Christ.

148 Because, they say that with the blood of Jesus Christ there appeared all the beans, corn, squash, sugar-cane, and bananas. 154 Because they say that the devil met Jesus Christ one day. 158 He said to Jesus Christ, "Let us perform a test. 160 We will see whose blood is better."

162 They say that the devil cut himself. 163 And from the blood of the devil there came out all the animals which are evil: snakes, poisonous lizards, iguanas, worms, lizards. 170 And then, the blood of Christ. 172 There came

36. Holy Week

seedlings, beans, sugar-cane, squash.

177 That is why people believe until today. 180 Because so the old-timers used to believe, a long time ago. 183 But in each celebration they always use incense, candles, and _chilate_. 187 In that celebration, when people are coming home from Esquipulas all around, grouping together they walk along praying to the houses. 193 And all around the peaks thunder with the many rockets and bombs where they are bursting in the villages.

200 And they say that is a promise they make with the _Milagroso_, so that he will give them everything they ask for. 204 They say that so there will be abundance in the house. 206 That is why they put out all those things.

37. Exorcism of the Xiximai

1 + .'u'lo'?kes'ia"hir 'e'xi'xi"mai +

2 + ,'a"ian 'in"te?e 'noh"?kin + .'a'txe?e "na 'ta'me?e"hu 'lio + 4 + ."pe 'ro'txe?e"no?p 'mu"kur 'noh"?kin + 5 + .'ma?a'txu?u'?ka"nio?p 'tua?a'a'mo'roh"?ki 'e"hen 'te + 6 + ,"por 'ke?e'ma"ha?ax "mei 'gra + .'tu"?ka 'a'tur'?pa "na + 8 + ,'a"hrer 'ta'ka'in'te?e"bar 'ko"sa?a + ,'i"bein 'te"sin 'ko"bam 'ba'uh"?tsu?u?p + , 'txa?a"gohr "ma?a?k "sa?a + ,'u'?txa"?puo?p 'iŋ "koht 'no"xi?i "pa?a + 12 + ,'u'po"?tsio?o?p 'ta'me?e"sa?a 'u'ua"?puo?p 'ta'mu?ut'e"txa?a + . 'tia?a'a'txe?e"na 'e"hu?utx +

14 + ,'en"ton 'ses + ,'a"ka?ai 'u'?pu "?tso?o?p 'tu"no?or "u?ut 'e"txa?a 'u'ti?i'e "?kahk + ,"o?or 'e'?txuh'?pe"no?p + ,'e'?peh "to?p + ,'e'bar"ko?o?p + ,'e'?pu"hro?p + 20 + ,'u'?pu"?tso?p "u?ut 'e"te?e + ,'tia?a"uar 'u'na "ro?p + .'tu"no?or 'u"pat 'io?o"tot 'a'xa"na 'u '?pu"?tso?p + 23 + ,'u'mo'roh"sio?p 'tu"no?or 'e'max"tak + ,'tu"no?or 'lo'ke?e'tu"ro?p 'ta 'mio?o"tot +

25 + ,"kon 'da'a'?ka?a"pa + ,'a'?pu'?tsa?a "na 'tu"no?or 'u"pa 'tio?o"tot + .'u'?pu "?tso?o?p 'tu"no?or 'u'ko'ror"te?eir 'u'na"ro?p + 28 + ,'tui?ix"to 'a'lo'?kes"na 'e'xi'xi"mai 'ma"kui?ir 'io?o"tot + ,'a'lo"?koi 'e'i"xik + . 'pa'kax"pat 'pa'kax"pat + 31 + .'e'ui"nik "ua 'ru'?pu"?tsa?a 'u"nu?u?k 'u"iok 'e'i"xik + 32 + ,'ko"ra 'ko"ra 'u'iuh"mu 'e're'sen"sa 'rio'ta 'ma'u"tie?e "?pi?ir + .'tia?a"uar 'a?a"xin 'e'i "xik 'pa'kax"pat + 34 + ,'txe?e"no?p 'ke?ei "xik 'ia"ha?a + ."ko 'mo'ke"ha?ax 'e'xi'xi"mai + 36 + ,"uar 'a'lo'?kes"na + .'ma"kui?ir 'io?o "tot + 38 + ."ua 'ra'?kai"na + 39 + .'a'?keh "txa 'a'lo"?koi +

40 + ."txe "tua?a + ."do 'nian'te'se"sa

37. Exorcism of the Xiximai

'ria + ."rei 'an'te'se"sa 'rio + ."ni 'nian'te
'se"sa 'rio + .'ni'nian'te'se"sa 'ria + 45 + ,
'ko"ne?er 'tia?a"uar + .'in'to"io?ox + 47 + .
'txo"ki?ik 'ak'ta"nik 'nio?o"tot + ,'tia?a'tu
"ro?ox + ,"uar 'i'sah"?pes 'tu"?ka 'iŋ'?ku"xi +
.'ta'nio?o"tot 'ta'ka'ni'max"tak + 51 + ,
"no?ox 'ma?a"txi?i 'na?a"ta + .'ko"?pa 'ko?o"ier
+ 53 + ,"uar 'in'tah"ui + .'ta'ma'mi'pat"na?ar
+ 55 + .'i"no?ox '?pan"iu?ut 'e"ra + 56 + ,
'tu"ro?ox "ua 'ri'sah"?pes + .'ma"kui?ir 'nio?o
"tot + 58 + ,'i"men 'ta"ka + ,"uar 'u'katx'na
"?ki 'ui?i"nar 'ni'max"tak + ."tu?ut 'nio?o"tot
+ 61 + ,"pe 'ro'ko"ne?er + .'iŋ'guah"ko?ox 'i
'tua?a'ni"?pir 'i'lo"?ker + 63 + .'in"txo?ox
'u'ien"tar 'ta"ma 'u'?ka"?pa?a 'e"?ah 'ti'txa
"ner 'dio"so?p + 64 + ,"uar 'o?oh"ron + ,'i
"uar 'u'?pu"?tsa?a "u?ut 'e"?pi?ir + .'tia?a"uar
'a?a"xin 'e'i"xik +

67 + ,'u'ia?a"re + .'e'xi'xi"mai + 69 +
."ha?ax 'e"ra 'a'tua?a'ni"?pir 'a'lo"?ker + 70
+ ."do 'nian'te'se"sa 'ria + ,'ko"ne?er 'ix'ket
"pa + .'tu?u"?ka?p 'e"?aŋ 'he"lo?p + ,'tu?u'?ka
"?po?p "tui?ix 'ket"pa + ,'a"pun 'te"ra 'ia + .
'a"pun 'te'sen"te 'io + 76 + ,'tia?a'tu"ro?ox
+ ,'ua"rix 'sah'?pe"sian + .'ta"ma 'e'lu'ga"ro?p
+ 79 + ,"pe 'ro'e"?aŋ 'hel'saŋ'ga"briel + ,'e
"?aŋ 'hel"san 'to'to"mas + ,'e"saŋ 'mi"gel 'ar
"kaŋ 'hel + ,'tia?a"uar 'ka'?kah"pes 'i'?ka
"?pa?a + .'tu?u"hor 'iah'bia?a"ro?p 'i"ra + 84
+ .'ko"ne?er 'tia?a"uar 'in'tur"?pa 'ti?i"?ka?p
+ .'txe"nik 'u'ien"tar + ,'a"pun 'te"ra 'ia + .
'a"pun 'te'sen"te 'io + 88 + ,"txik '?ke"?kok
'ta"ma 'u"?txu?ur 'e'noh'mon"ta 'nia + .'e"iax
'mon"ta 'nia +

90 + ,"iix 'to"nik 'a'?ke"?ko + ,'tia?a'ga
"lan 'a'iax'mu"hri + .'e'lu"gar + 93 + ,'iix
"to 'a"ian + ,'e?en'txu?u"ren 'ia"rum + .'e?en
'txu?u"ren "?txa?an + 96 + ,'ko'txa'iix"to +

37. Exorcism of the Xiximai

'xe?e'a?ah'?ka"re + ,'tu"no?or 'ah'?kuh"xa?ar + ,'iix'to"nik + ,'a'ui?i"ri + ,'e"do 'nia'se"sa 'ria + .'i'?e"rei 'se"sa 'rio + 103 + ,'ta"ma 'u'?ka"?pa?a 'tu"no?or 'e"?aŋ 'he"lo?p + .'iŋ 'guah'ne"sox 'ix'lo"?koi "tu?ut 'nio?o"tot + 105 + ,'tia?a'tu"ru + .'tsah"tix "u?ut + 107 + ,'tsah"tix 'u'ie"roh + .'tia?a'tu"ro?ox +

109 + ,"uar 'ix'sah'?pe"sian + ,'ta'ma "u?ut 'u'io"tot + ,'i'ta"ma 'tu"no?or 'e'lu'ga "ro?p + ."tuam 'e'pa"?ka?p 'e'ko"noh "to?or 'e "rum + ,"do 'nia'se"sa 'ria + .'an'ta'se"dor + , "don 'se"sa 'rio + .'an'ta'se"dor + ."ni 'nio'se "sa 'rio + ."ni 'nia'se"sa 'ria + 119 + ,'i'ra "nik 'i"?pi?ir + ,'ta"ma 'e'?ix"ner "?kin + ,'ta "ma 'e"noh 'mon"ta 'nia + ,'e'noh'ui'tsi"ro?p + 123 + ,'iix"to '?ke'?kue?e"nik + .'tu"no?or 'e "tiem 'po + 125 + ,'por'ke"ma 'ta'ua"ron + .'i "ma 'ko'?pa'ka'ba"lor + .'tua?a'ka'ue?e"sio?ox + 128 + ,'por'ke"no?ox + .'na'ual"?pir 'i'xam "?par + 130 + ."ma 'txe"ker 'ko'txa'ix'ha"mi "tuam 'e'pa"?ka?p 'e'ko"noh + 131 + ,"pe 'ro 'ka'tur"?po?ox + .'tu?u"?ka?p 'e'na'ual"?pir 'dio"so?p + 133 + ,'e'o'hro"ner 'i"ra + . "ha?ax 'i'uah"nes 'ni"?pir 'u'suh"ti?i?p 'i'xam "?par +

135 + ,'en"ton 'ses + ,'e'?i"xik 'a'sut"pa + .'tu?u'poh'pi"rar +

37. Exorcism of the Xiximai

1 The removal of the Xiximai.

2 There is a ceremony performed in July. 4 But they say it is a secret ceremony. 5 They do not want people to gather. 6 Because not much is set out: 8 only a bowl of *chilate* and twenty-five discs of incense, and two balls of *chilate*-paste; and they lay down a large tortilla. 12 They dunk them in the *chilate* standing on the quern where the grinding is done.

14 Then they begin to cense the whole surface of the quern, the fireside, over the stone supports, the pots, the bowls, and the jugs. 20 They cense the logs where the corn is, and all around the back of the house they go censing. 23 They gather up all the children, everything which is in the house.

25 When all the back of the house has been completely censed, they cense all the corncribs. 28 Then, so that the *xiximai* in the house will go out, the woman goes out, walking backwards. 31 The man is censing the ankles of the woman, swinging the censer all around the edge of the path where the woman is walking backwards. 34 They say that that woman, it is as if she were the *xiximai*. 36 It is being ejected from the inside of the house. 38 It is being scolded. 39 It is carried out.

40 It is told: "Lady Ancestor! King Ancestor! Boy Ancestor! Girl Ancestor! 45 Today, when I am paying you, 47 abandon my house where you live. You are using up what I eat in my house with my children. 51 You do not know how much fatigue 53 I find in my work. 55 And you appear the same; 56 you are still using up everything inside my house. 58 By you alone, hunger is binding the bellies of my

children at my house. 61 But today I give you your payment, your leave. 63 I make you flee with the name of the gods above." 64 He is talking and censing the path where the woman is walking.

67 He says to the <u>xiximai</u>: 69 "This is your payment, your leave, 70 Lady Ancestor, today you remain in the hands of the angels, you remain in the hands of Lightning-Aimer, Thunder-Aimer. 76 Where you stay, you are using up e-verything in the place. 79 But the angel San Gabriel, the angel Santo Tomas, archangel San Miguel, when we are invoking your names, over the heads of those eaters. 84 Today when I am placing them in your hands, make them flee, Light-Aimer, Thunder-Aimer, 88 let them go take shape in the great mountains, the green mountains.

90 And if they do not take shape where it is good and green, 93 then let them collapse to the ground, collapse flat. 96 Since if there is abundance, they eat everything, and if there is not they are hungry, the Lady Ancestor, the King Ancestor. 103 In the name of all the angels, I chase you out of my house. 105 Where I am, your appearance is already gone. 107 Your expression is already gone, where you dwell.

109 You are using up everything in their houses and in all the places among the human be-ings on earth, Lady Ancestor, Predecessor, Lord Ancestor, Predecessor, Boy Ancestor, Girl Ances-tor. 119 See your road toward the sunset, in the great mountains, the great peaks. 123 There take shape for all time, 125 because we cannot endure you, and we can not stand to feed you, 128 because you go as spirits, 130 you

do not appear and mingle with the human beings.
131 But we place you in the hands of the spirit
gods. 133 This speech is to put you to flight,
retracing your steps."

135 Then the woman returns to her hearth.

38. Corncrib Offering

1 + .'u'li'mos"nir 'u'ko'ror"te?eir 'e "nar +

2 + ,'e"hen 'te + ,'kon'da"uar 'a'pe?ets 'na"rio?p + ,'u"txo?p 'a'kos'tum"brar 'u'pu "to?o?p 'iuh"?tsu?u?p + ,'u'xu"rio?p 'u"nu?u '?kia"?katx + .'u'uo"txo?p 'in'te?e"bar 'ko"sa?a + .'tia?a'u"txo?p 'u'ko'ror"te?eir 'e"nar + 8 + ,'e'li"mos 'na'ia"ha?a + ,'a'txe?e"na + ,'kon 'da"tui?ix 'e'pe?ets"nar + ,'e"di 'ia'tia?a'a 'txe?e"na 'e'li"mos 'na'ia"ha?a + ."o 'tro"di 'ia"tix 'e'pe?ets"nar +

13 + ,'tu?u"hor + ,'u'?txe"nar 'e"sa?a + , 'e"?txi?itx + ,'u'?tis"sio?p "u?ut 'e"te?e + . 'tua?a'u'pe"?tsio?p 'e"nar 'ta"mar + 18 + , "kon 'da'a"ka?ai + .'u'tso"ru?u "?po?o?p 'e"nar 'ta"mu?ut 'e"te?e + 20 + ,'u'?txa"?puo?p 'in "te?en "te?e "lib 'ra'uh"?tsu?u?p + ,'ta'ma"kua 'tre'rer"ti?i + .'u'ies"ki?i "nir 'u'ko'ror "te?eir 'e"nar + 23 + ,"txe 'ke?e'iuh"?tsu?u?p 'ia"ha?a + ."ha?ax 'tu?u"?pir "tua?a 'u"me?ein 'e"nar + .'tua?a'ma"ha?ax 'sah'?pes"?pir 'ta"ka '?a'?ka?a"pa +

26 + ,"kon 'da'u'pe'?tsio"?pix '?ta"?pai + ,"to?or 'u"na?a '?kio?o"tot + ,'a'sut"pa + ,'u '?txa"?puo?o?p 'in'te?en"te?e 'ma"sor 'ka'uh "?tsu?u?p + ,'ta'ma"kua 'tre'rer"ti?i + .'u'ies "ki?i "nir "o?or 'e"nar + 32 + ,'iuh"?tsu?u?p 'xe?e'pa?a?k"?pir 'ko'txe?e'tu"min + .'a'pu'rut "na 'tua?a'?ta"?pai 'u'?pu"?tsa?ar 'tu?ut"?kin + ,"ha?ax 'ko'txe?e'tua?a'ni"?pir + ,'tua?a'e'dio "so?p 'ti"txan + .'i'ko'txe?e'tua?a'ni"?pir 'tua?a'u'na'ua"lir 'e"rum +

37 + ,'po"re 'so + 'u'tu'ru"?po?p 'e"sa?a 'ta"ma 'e?e — .'u'ko'ror"te?eir 'e"nar + , 'tua?a'a'me?ei"ni + .'u'na'ua"lir 'e'ik"?pen 'ia "ha?a + 42 + ,"por 'ke"txe 'ke?e'u'na'ua"lir

38. Corncrib Offering

'e"rum + .'u'iet'o'hro"ner 'e'dio"so?p 'ti"txan + .'tua?a'ma?a"txi 'o?o"txoi 'e'xi'xi"mai 'ta 'me?e'o"tot +

45 + ,'e"krus 'xe?e'a'?kam'pes"na + ,"kon 'da'a'xu"hra 'u"nu?u?k 'e'txum"pi?i 'o'?a"?katx + ,'ie?e"sa?a + ,"kon 'da'?a'?ka?a"pa 'e'pe?ets "nar + .'a'?ta"?pes "na?a 'ua?a?p"na "to?or 'e "nar 'ti"txan + 50 + .'xe?e'pe?ets"?pir "nar + 51 + ."ia "ua?ar + ."es 'to'ke'?a'?ka?a"pa 'e "nar 'ia"ha?a + 53 + .'a'?ta'?pes"na 'u"li?i "brir 'iuh"?tsu?u?p 'ia"ha?a + .'ie?e"krus +

55 + ."ia '?ta'?pes"?pir "es 'to'ke?e"ma 'a'?ko"toi 'e"?a 'nio + .'xe?e"tua?a 'u'?kam'pe "so?p 'o'tron"iahr + 57 + ,'por'ke?e'uh "?tsu?u?p 'ia"ha?a + ."ha?ax 'me?eim"?pir + . 'tua?a'u"me?ein 'e"nar +

38. Corncrib Offering

1 The corncrib offering.

2 People, when they are stacking corn, customarily burn incense, cut the throats of chickens, and pour out a bowl of *chilate* where they make the corncrib. 8 That offering is made when the corn stacking time has come: the day when that offering is made is the day before the corn stacking.

13 On top of the holes for the *chilate* and the blood they lay out the sticks on which to stack the corn. 18 When it begins, they lay out the ears of corn side by side on the sticks. 20 They lay down a pound of incense in each of the four corners of the corncrib. 23 It is said that that incense is the mother of the spirit of the corn, so it will not be completely used up.

26 When they have been stacked up, rising above the sides of the house, they again lay down an ear of incense at each corner on the corn. 32 The incense which is molded like money, is burned so that the smoke rises into the sky: it is like a payment to the gods above, and like a payment to the Spirit of the Earth.

37 That is why they put out the *chilate* in the corncrib, so that the Spirit of that vegetable will be animated. 42 Because they say that the Spirit of the Earth is a companion in speech of the gods above, so that the *Xiximai* will not enter the house.

45 The cross which is used, when the throat of the turkey or chicken is cut, and the *chilate* [is poured], when the stacking of the corn is finished, is lifted and stood on the corn on top. 50 That is, the stacked corn. 51

38. Corncrib Offering

There it stands, until that corn is finished.
53 The pounds of incense are lifted up, and the
cross.

55 They are lifted up until a year has
come around, when they are used another time.
57 Because that incense is the animator of the
Spirit of the Corn.

39. Celebration in the Cornfield

1 + ,"pe 'ro'a"ian + 'o'tron"te?e -- ,'noh
"?kin 'a'txe?e"na + .'ta'mu"iok 'e'txo"ro?p + 5
+ ,'xe?e'noh"?kin + ,'a'txe?e"na 'ta'mu"iok 'e
'txo"ro?p + "ha?ax 'e?e -- ,'e"mes + .'de'a"gos
'to + 10 + "kuan 'do"uar 'a?a -- ,'tu"ruan 'tu
"no?or + ,'e'na"ro?p + .'ua"rix 'a'?ka"na + 14
+ 'en -- ,'a"ka?ai 'a'txe?e"na 'e'noh'?ki"no?p
'ia"ha?a + ,"txe 'ke?e"uar 'a'tua?a"na + "e?e --
,'u'na'ua"lir + 'e?e -- ,'e"rum +

21 + 'i"ti?i 'ne?e -- .'u'na?a"ta 'u"txe +
,'e'noh"?kin 'ia"ha?a 'ta'?u"iok 'u"txor + 'e?e
-- 'ta'me?e -- ,'a"gos 'to + 'kon'du'ui"ra 'ke?e
-- ,'a'?ka"ni?ix 'u"nar + ,'u"txe 'man"dar +
'a?a -- ,'a'txe?e"na 'e"sa?a + 32 + 'i?i -- ,
'u'tur"?pa 'iuh"?tsu?u?p + ,'u'pa"?ki + 'ko
"txe?e -- 'e?e -- 'e?e -- 'e'tu"min + ,'u'?ke
"txa?a "xin + .'tu"iok 'u"txor + 41 + 'e?e --
,'txum"pi?i + ,'a"?katx + 'u'ku"txa?a 'a'?kot --
,'a'?ko"tuo?p + ,'ma"kuir 'e"txor + 'e?e -- .'u
'xu"nio?p 'e"?kahk + 49 + ,"tua?a 'e?em"pa
"u?ut 'e"?kahk + ,'a"ka?ai + 'e?e -- ,'a"?kah
'pes"ian + ,"ti?i 'ne'tua?a'?kah'pes"ian + 54
+ 'i?i -- ,"?e 'kan"de 'la + .'tu"ru '?u'me"ner
+ 57 + .'u'tur"?pa 'u'?ka"?pa?a +

58 + ."txe + 59 + 'e?e -- .'nues"tra "ma
'dre'san"ti 'si'ma + 61 + ,'ko"ne?er + ,'tia?a
"uar 'ka'io?o"pa + ,'ka"toh 'ti?i'ie"set + 64
+ ,"?i + ,"uar + ,'ka'?kah"?pue?et + 'ta"ka +
'ka?a -- ,'ka'ua"ra?k + ,'i'ta"ka + ,'u"txu?u 'e
"te?e + ,"tia?a 'txoh'?pes"?pir + ,'u"men + 'e
'ka'iu"mar "dios + ,'ke'?ak'ta"?pir 'ta"mar +
"tua?a -- ,'ka'to"ie?et + ,'i'ta"ra + ,"uar 'ka
'ta"res + 80 + ,'ko"ne?er '?txa"ma + 'pa'sar
"?ka?p + .'i"ra?a 'ui"ra 'su'tur"hut + 83 +
'ie?e -- 'ko"txa?a -- ,"ne?et + ,"uar + ,'a'uah
"?kuo?on + .'tu"?ka 'ka'?ku"xi + 89 + ,'i'ta
"ra + "uar 'ka'io?o"pa + 'ka'tur"?pa "to?oit + .
'lo'ke?e"no?on 'ka'?kam"pes 'ma"kui?ir 'ko?o

39. Celebration in the Cornfield

"tot +

93 + ,'kon'da'ix"to + ,'?ka?a"pi?ix 'e '?kah'pes"iah 'ia"ha?a + ,'en"ton 'ses'a"ka?ai + 'u'pu"kio?p 'e"sa?a 'lo'ke?e -- ,'e'tu"ru?u 'me 'ne"ro?p + ,"pe 'ro'as"ta?a '?ka?a"pa + .'u'xu "rio?p 'u"nu?u?k 'e'txum"pi?i + 100 + .'por "ke?e + ,'u'io"rio?p + 'e?e -- .'ux"te?e 'e "?txen + 104 + ,'in"te?e 'tua?a'u'io'ri?i -- 'u'ia"rio?p 'e"sa?a 'ta"mar + 'ii?in'te?e"tua?a 'u'iar"io?p 'u'?txi"?txer 'e?e -- 'e?e -- ,'txum "pi?i 'ia"?katx + ,'iin"te?e + ,'tua?a'u'tu'ru "?po?p + ."u?ut 'e"?kahk 'ta"mar + 112 + ,'iin "te?e "?peht + ,'u'ua"?puo?p + ,"tua?a 'u'ia "rio?p 'iuh"?tsu?u?p + 'e?e -- ,'por"li 'bra + 'e?e -- 'o'hai -- ,"bam 'ba"?pir + .'ia"ia 'tu?u 'tsu'?po?o?p 'ta"mar + 121 + ,'i'ma?a"txi + , 'ua"to?p 'tu?u'io'to"to?p + .'ehs"to 'ke"ma?a '?ka?a"pa?a 'pu"rui 'tu"no?or 'iuh"?tsu?u?p 'ia "ha?a + 'lo'ke?e -- 'e?e -- 'u'?ke -- ,'u'?ke "txo?p 'a?a"xin +

128 + ."pe 'ro"kon 'da'?ka?a"pi?ix + .'xuh "ra 'u"nu?u?k + 'e?e -- .'txum"pi?i 'a"?katx + , 'i'tuh"?ki?ix 'e"sa?a 'ia"ha?a + ,'en"ton 'ses + 'lok -- ,'ke?e'a'ket"pa + .'ah'?ku"na 'u'iu"?txi 'e"hen 'te'xe?e'a'?ko"toi 'u'ui"ro?p 'e'noh"?kin + 137 + "por 'ke?e -- 'ko'txe?e"hen 'te'u'na?a "ti?ix 'ke?e -- 'a"ian 'e'noh"?kin "guar 'a'lu 'mes"na 'tu?u"iok "txor + ,'a'mo'roh"?kio?p + . 'u'ui"ro?p + '?ka"nui?i -- .'tua?a'u'ui"?txuo?p 'e"sa?a +

144 + ,'kon'dix"to + 'a'?ka?a"pa 'e?e -- , 'e'puk'ma"iah 'ia"ha?a 'ta'ke?e"sa?a + 'en"ton 'ses + ,"tie?e 'ne'?ka'na?a"xin 'tu?u'io"tot + . 'a?a"xin + 150 + ."pe 'ro + .'xe?e"uar 'a'?kah 'pes"ian + ,'i'iah"ium 'iok"txor + ,'ma?a"txi 'ua"tar 'tu?u'io"tot + 'es'to'ka"ma '?kot -- 'a '?ka -- ,'a'?ka?a"pa?a 'pu"rui 'tu"no?or 'iuh

39. Celebration in the Cornfield

"?tsu?u?p + 157 + ,'en"ton 'ses + 'u'a?a?k -- ,'u'ku"txi 'u"?puhr 'o'tro"niahr + 'e?e -- ,'u "tar + "pe 'ro'e?e -- ,'txum"pi?i + 'e'?o?o -- 'a"?katx + ,'a'?ka?a'pa'ta"kix + ,'a'xuh"tu?u "nu?u?k + ,'e?e'?pet"na?a "xin 'ta'mo?o"tot + "tua?a -- 'a?a -- ,'o?os'ta"na + .'ia?a'txe?e"na 'e'ta"mal 'ta"mar +

173 + .'kon'de"txe + 'a?a -- ,'a'io?o"pa + 'i'iah"ium 'u?u -- ,'u'iok"txor + 'e?e -- "?ah '?kah'pes"iah + .'u"rix 'a'tur"uan 'e'ta"mal + . 'tua?a'u'?ku"xio?p + 182 + .'por'ke?e -- "txe 'ke?e + 'e'iah'e?e -- ,'e'noh"?kin 'ia"ha?a + , 'u'tua?a'ni"?pir + 'e?e -- ,'e"rum + 'lo"ke?e -- ,"uar + 'a?a -- .'u'iah"?ku 'e"nar + 193 + ,'i 'po"re 'so + 'u?u -- ,'ha?a"xo?p + 'ma?a"txi 'u?u -- 'ma?a"txi 'e"rer 'a?a -- ,'pat"no?p + , "?pan 'ta"ka + ,'u"txu?u 'u'hi'na"ho?p + 'si"no 'ke?e -- 'u'to"io?p 'e?e -- 'e?e -- 'e?e -- .'e "rum + "tua?a 'ma?a"txi 'a'xer"ua?a -- ,'e'xe'ro "ri + 'e?e -- ,'e"nar + "tua?a 'ma?a"txi 'a?a -- 'a?a -- .'a'sat"pa + 213 + 'i"tua?a -- .'a'lo "?koi "mei 'gra'u'na"ro?p +

215 + ,'i'po"re 'so"txe 'ke?e + ,'u'to "io?p 'e"rum + "tu?ah '?ku"no?o?p "mei 'gra + . 'u'na"ro?p + 219 + ,'ha?ax"to 'e"ra + .'e'noh "?kin 'xe?e'a'txe?e"na +

39. Celebration in the Cornfield

1 But there is another celebration, performed in the cornfield. 5 This celebration performed in the cornfield is in the month of August. 10 When all the ears of corn are turning yellow, 14 then -- that celebration is begun; they say it is payment to the spirit of the earth.

21 And whoever knows how to perform that celebration in the cornfield in August, when he sees that the corn is already yellowing, he orders that the *chilate* be made. 32 And he puts out the incense molded like -- money, and carries it into the cornfield. 41 The turkeys and chickens he carries out on his back; when they arrive in the field, they light a fire, 49 so that coals will fall from it; he who is to pray begins praying. 54 The candles are placed by him. 57 They are given names.

58 He says, 59 "Our Holy Mother, 61 today we are coming to implore you and to bring to your mind, with our poultry and with the sap of the trees which were blessed by Our Lord God who left it for us to pay you, and here we are bringing it; 80 take it now with open hand, do not look with averted face. 83 And -- as you are giving us what we eat, 89 here we are coming to put before you what we use in our houses."

93 When that prayer has been finished, then they begin to give the *chilate* which was put out by them, but not until they have finished cutting the throats of the turkeys. 100 Because they have dug three holes. 104 One is to dig -- to pour the *chilate* in, and one is to pour the blood -- of the turkeys and chickens in, and one is to lay the coals in. 112 They set a dish to pour the incense in -- by the

39. Celebration in the Cornfield

pound, or if it is in discs, there they pile it up. 121 And they do not go back to their houses until all that incense has burned up, which they carried.

128 But when they have finished cutting the throats of the turkeys and chickens and given out that chilate, then what remains is given to drink to the people who came to see the celebration. 137 Because since people know that there is a celebration they pass by the cornfield and gather together to see and to drink the chilate.

144 When that distribution of chilate is finished, then whoever wants to go to his house goes. 150 But he who is praying, and the owner of the cornfield do not come back to their houses until they have finished burning all the incense. 157 Then they carry the jugs another time, but the -- turkeys and chickens have finished having their throats cut, and are sent along to the house to be prepared and for tamales to be made from them.

173 Then they say the owner of the cornfield and the prayer-sayer come to sit down to tamales to eat them. 182 Because they say that that celebration is the payment of the earth which gives the corn. 193 And because of that, they can not -- work just like that, planting their fields; rather they pay the earth so it will not blight the -- corn, so it will not -- be destroyed. 213 And so many ears of corn will come out.

215 And that is why they say that they pay the earth, so they will be given many ears of corn. 219 That is the celebration which is performed.

40. Celebration of the Cane Press

1 + ,'u'noh'?ki"nar 'e'tra"pitx 'a'txe?e
"na + ."kon 'da'?ka"nix 'a'txe?e"na 'e'sum'si
"?ka?a?p + 3 + ,'e'noh"?kin 'ia"ha?a 'a'txe?e
"na + ,'ta"ka 'iŋ"koht 'ah"tso?o + ,'i'txa?a
"koht 'a"?katx + ,'iŋ"koht 'u"tu?u 'e'txum"pi?i
'ko"txia?atx 'a'txe?e"na + .'tu?u"iok "txor + 8
+ .'?pa'nix"to 'ta"ka 'e'tra"pitx + 9 + ,'a'tu
'ru'?pa"na 'iuh"?tsu?u?p + .'ie"?pe?e 'tra"pitx
+ 11 + .'a'txe?e"na?a 'dor"nar 'txa?a"te?e
"krus 'ta"ma 'e"?kom + ,'a'ua?a?p"na 'ta"mu?ut
'e'tra"pitx + ,'e"sa?a 'a'ua?a?p"na 'ta"rum + .
'xe?e"tua?a 'o?o?tx"na + 15 + ,"pe 'ro'xe?e
"tua?a 'e"?aŋ 'he"lo?p + .'a'ua?a?p"na 'ta"mu?ut
'e'tra"pitx +

17 + ,"kon 'da?a'?ka?a"pa 'e'?kah'pes"iah
+ ,'e"sa?a 'xe?e'tua?a'e"?aŋ 'he"lo?p + .'o?oh
"txa 'ta"mo?or 'e'tra"pitx + 20 + ,'i"xe?e
'tua?a + 'a'ia"hra 'ta"?txen + ,'nah"tir 'u"pat
'e'tra"pitx 'a'io"hra 'e"?txen + .'o?oh"txa 'e
"sa?a 'ta"mar + 24 + .'ma?a"txi 'a'ia"hra
'tu?u'ua"ri?p 'e'tra"pitx + ,'por"ke?e + ,'a'pa
'?txar"na 'u"me 'ne"hen 'te + .'tia?a'a?a'ua
"no?p 'ta'ka'e'?ah'ne"siah 'ua"kax + ."kon 'da
'uar'u'su'tro?o?p'e'tra"pitx +

29 + ,'ta'rix"to + ,'me?e"rer 'u'uo"?txo?p
'ie"?pe?e 'tra"pitx + ,'nien"ha?ax 'u'?txi"?txer
'e'txum"pi?i + ,'nien'u'?txi"?txer 'ia?a"?katx +
33 + .'nah"tir 'a'iah"ra + 34 + ,'i'ha?ax"to
+ ,'xe?e'tua?a'e"?aŋ 'he"lo?p + 'txa?a"te?e
"rutx + ,'a"sihts 'ha?a"na + .'ta'ma'tu"no?or
"u?ut 'e'tra"pitx + ,'i'ta"ma 'tu"no?or 'lo'ke?e
'a'?kam'pes"na + .'ta'me?e'sum'si"?ka?p +

41 + 'u'?pu"?tso?o?p 'ta'ka'iuh"?tsu?u?p +
42 + ,'e'pa?a?k"?pir 'uh"?tsu?u?p + .'u'pu
"to?o?p 'ie'?pe?e'tra"pitx + 44 + ,'u'?pu
"?tso?o?p 'tu"no?or "o?or 'e"?or 'no + ,'e'?peh
"to?p + ,'u'uahr"ni?i?p 'e"txa?ap + ,'i'tu"no?or

40. Celebration of the Cane Press

'e'ior'?pir "tio?o?p + .'xe?e'u'mool"dir 'e
"txa?ap +

49 + ,'e'noh"?kin 'ia"ha?a + ,'a'txe?e"na
'tua?a'a'?po"ro 'e"txa?ap + ,'i'tua?a"ma 'tu
"?ka?a 'u'num"se 'u"?po?o?p + .'ta'ka'e'tra"pitx
+ 53 + ,"txe 'ke?e'tua?a'ma?a"txi 'o?o"txoi 'e
'mal"?om 'bre + ,'tu?u'ha"mo?p + 55 + .'i
'tua?a'ma?a"txi 'a'pu"rui 'e"txa?ap + 56 + ,'e
'uh"?tsu?u?p + ,"ha?ax 'u'tua?a'ni"?pir 'e'?aŋ
'he"lo?p + ,'i'tu"no?or 'ah'ti'txa"ner 'dio"so?p
+ ,'ko'txe?e"?aŋ 'he"lo?p + .'i'tua?a'u'na'ua
"lir 'e"rum +

61 + ,'po"re 'so'a'xuh"ra 'u"nu?u '?ke
'txum"pi?i + .'ia?a"?katx + 63 + ,'por'ke?e
'ha?a"xo?p 'txe?e"no?p 'e'ka"tu?u "mun 'do + .'u
"iet 'oh'ro"ner 'e'dio"so?p 'ti"txan + 65 + ,
'i"ha?ax 'a'?kaht'ma"ian 'ta'ma"ron + ,'ta'ka'e
'?ah'ti'txa"ner 'dio"so?p + .'ta"ma 'tu"no?or
'lo'ke?e'?ka"ni 'ka'num"se 'ka"?pa + ,'xe?e
"no?on + ."o?or 'u'ru"mir 'pa'?ka?a"?pon + 70
+ ."pe 'ro"ha?ax 'a'?ke'?koh"sian 'ta'ma"ron +
71 + ,'ma?a"txi 'u'iak"ta 'tu'?ki?k"xix 'na'ua
"lir 'ah'ma'?pam"?pan + .'ta'ma"ron +

73 + .'i'po"re 'so'tu"no?or 'e"hen 'te +
'a'noh'?ki"ni 'ta"ka 'u'na'ua"lir 'e"rum + ,'tu
"no?or "ti?i 'ne'a"ian 'u'te?e"rar 'u'ka"fe + ,
"ti?in 'a"ian 'u'si"?ka?a?p + ,"ti?in 'a"ian 'u
"pohp + .'a'noh'?ki"nio?p 'ma"kui?ir + 79 + ,
'u'?ke"txio?p 'e'txum"pi?i + ,'u'ia"?katx + ,
'iuh"?tsu?u?p + ,'?i'?e"sa?a + .'tua?a'u'uo
"txo?p 'ma"kui?ir 'u'poh"po?p + 84 + ,"por
'ke?e'ha?a"xo?p 'txe?e"no?p 'e'txum"pi?i 'ia
"?katx + ,"ha?ax 'in"te?e 'ua'ra"?pir + .'ko
'txe?e'tua?a'ni"?pir + .'tua?a'u'na'ua"lir 'e
"rum + 88 + ,'ke?e'e"?txi?itx 'ia"ha?a 'tue?e
'txum"pio?o?p + ,'ia?a"?katx + 'na'ual"?pir
'ha?a"xo?p 'u'nu"?tio?p + 91 + ,'ke"ha?ax 'in

40. Celebration of the Cane Press

"te?e 'a'li"men 'to + .'tua?a'u'na'ua"lir 'e"rum + 93 + .'i'ke?e'ta"mar 'a?ah'?ku"no?o?p 'u'ko 'see"txo?p + ,"nar + ,"?pu?ur + ,"?txum + , "tua?a 'a'?ka?a"uan 'u'ka"huio?p + .'i'tua?a'a "?txi?i 'u'poh"po?p + 99 + ,'tua?a'ma?a"txi 'a 'xe'ro"ri 'u'na"ro?p + .'i"tua?a 'ma?a"txi 'a'ua 'hra"mi 'u'?pu?u"ro?p + 101 + .'tua?a'a'?tox "pa 'u'ia'ra"?ko?p +

102 + ,'po'res"to + .'tu"no?or 'e"hen 'te + ,'u"txa?a 'kos'tum"brar + ,'u'xu"ri 'u"nu?u '?ke'txum"pi?i + ,'ia?a"?katx + .'ta'ma'?e"rum + ,'por'ke?e'u'na?a"to?p 'ke?e'ta"mar + ,'ua"tar 'e'txoh'?pe"siah 'ta'ma'?e'ko"see "txo?p + .'lo 'ke?e'u'?pa"kio?p + 111 + ,"por 'ke?e'txe?e "no?p 'ke?e + ,'u'na'ua"lir 'e"rum + ,"ha?ax 'me "?ker 'u'me"ner 'u"me?ein 'tu"no?or 'pa?a?k'?pa "hria?ar + .'lo'ke?e'a"ian +

40. Celebration of the Cane Press

1 The celebration of the cane press is held when the cane-wringing is about to be done. 3 That ceremony is performed with one tom turkey, two chickens, and one hen turkey, just as it is done in the cornfield. 8 So also with the press. 9 The incense is placed underneath the press. 11 Two crosses are adorned with *conte* leaves, and stood on the press; the *chilate* which is to be drunk is placed on the ground. 15 But that which is for the angels is placed on the press.

17 When the praying is completed, the *chilate* which is for the angels is poured over the press, and that which is for pouring into the hole; far behind the press the hole is dug, and the *chilate* poured into it. 24 It is not poured out on the press-site, because that is walked on by the people while they are standing around the oxen-run, when they are turning the press.

29 Hence they can not pour it out underneath the press, nor the blood of the turkeys, nor the blood of the chickens. 33 It is poured out far away. 34 And then the two bowls which are for the angels are sprinkled all over the outside of the press and on everything which is used for the cane-wringing.

41 They cense with the incense. 42 The molded incense they burn under the press; 44 they cense all over the fireplace, the pots, the syrup-collectors, and all the dug-out boards which are the sugar molds.

49 That celebration is held so that the syrup will be abundant and so that nothing will happen to them with the press. 53 They say it is so the Evil Man will not enter among them 55 and so the sugar will not burn. 56 The in-

cense, that is the payment of the angels and all
the gods above like the angels, and for the spi-
rit of the earth.

61 That is why the turkey's throat is cut,
and the chicken's, 63 because they say that
our Mother Earth is the companion in speech of
the gods above. 65 And she intercedes on our
behalf with the gods above concerning everything
which we want to have happen to us, we who are
the inhabitants of the surface of the earth. 70
But she is tough on our behalf, and does not
leave every sort of evil spirit with us.

73 And that is why everybody celebrates
the spirit of the earth; everyone who has his
coffee trees, who has his cane, who has his
rushes, celebrates inside. 79 They carry the
turkeys, the chickens, the incense, and the
chilate so as to pour it in among the rushes.
84 Because they say that the turkeys and chi-
ckens are an offering, like a payment for the
spirit of the earth. 88 That that blood of the
turkeys and chickens, as spirits they join toge-
ther, that it is a food for the spirit of the
earth, 93 and that by means of it they are gi-
ven their harvests: corn, beans, squash, and
that the coffee bears fruit, and the rushes
grow; 99 that their corn is not blighted, and
that their beans are not eaten up, 101 and
that their poultry is raised.

102 Therefore, all the people are accus-
tomed to cutting the throats of turkeys and chi-
ckens, on the ground, because they think that by
it, mercy will come to the harvest that they
planted. 111 Because they say that by the spi-
rit of the earth is embraced the ghost of all
the cultivated plants that there are.

GROUP VI

NOTES

31. Esquipulas

31.4 Esquipulas has been a major pilgrimage site for centuries, at least since the present town was founded ca. 1560 near a preconquest site. The Black Christ was purchased by the town and set in place in 1594; the present 'Milagroso' is a bronze replica of the original dark-brown wooden statue.

31.7 'Reground tortillas' are made from a paste of ground up tortillas. They do not harden as fast as those made from fresh dough.

31.15 A raw tortilla patty rolled around a mixture of beans and pumpkin seeds. The trunk or middle, naa?k, is filled, ?pu?t. The tube is wrapped in several layers of cane leaves, and boiled.

31.16 Pinol 'ground parched corn' is made from toasted whole kernels. It is carried as a dry meal, and added to hot or cold water before being eaten.

31.17-20 One reason for carrying a complete food supply for the trip is perhaps the ruinous prices charged in Esquipulas during the pilgrimage season.

31.20-23 These candles are carried to Esquipulas and back to the pilgrims' homes. One is bought each year for each of the two to four crosses of the household altar, where they are kept, in principle, forever. They are only burned 'in case of need'. These are the candles which are passed over the members of the household (see below, 31.438).

31.28 The trail crosses the Río San Juan about 4 km. south of Olopa.

31.45 This stream flows through the center of Esquipulas, from the W, where it is called the Chantiago, to the E, where it is called the Zepoctún. There is a plain on the E side of

31. Esquipulas

town where the pilgrims probably camp.

31.74 A small chapel was built in Esquipulas in 1578, and housed the 'Milagroso' until the present basilica was built, between 1734 and 1758.

31.76 There is no lake near Esquipulas. It seems likely that one is required for theological reasons, since lakes and seas are inhabited by the important divinities (see below, 31. 90-92).

31.95 Compare u&-uai-i 'he lays it down flat', a-uai-an 'he sleeps', and a-uai-?ka 'he dreams', with a 'middle' suffix. The form in the text is a 'factitive-causative' of this, with a na suffix: the old woman was caused to have a dream.

31.99-113 These phrases summarize the preparations for any of the important ceremonies, but note that neither crosses nor candles are mentioned.

31.157-168 There may be some substance to this episode. González remembers that there was a well within the church beside the Black Christ and that it had to be closed because children kept falling into it. If there is abundant ground water under the church, its construction might have been hindered in roughly the way the text describes.

31.208 Compare the angels compelled to hold the cornerposts of the world, in text 26.

31.223-224 From González' description, the sign of the mason's fall appears to be a plaque set in the outside wall of the basilica.

31. Esquipulas

31.240-244 The wire leading from a lightening-rod into the ground in front of the basilica is thought to be tied around the serpent's neck under the ground, and to hold him quietly in place.

31.259 The flagstones slip apart, and the person falls through into the lake below; thus, the flagstones empty, or free themselves. See below, 31.294.

31.263 That is, a person whose motives are not pure, or whose devotion is not single-minded.

31.272 Although the primary sense of tauar (tau-ar?) seems to be 'power' or 'authority', it is also used for physical power: m-ix ?ke?k-o-?k-en tuaa or ma-atxi vn&-tauar-i tuaa, both 'I can't resist him any more' (in a physical way).

31.294 Note that this form, a-ha?p-?tsa is the same one used above, in 31.259, of the flagstones. This root, not to be confused with hap 'open', has a number of interesting uses: ha?p-vr e-?puhr 'the jug is empty', u&-ha?p-i /'u'ua "?pi/ 'he empties it', and ma ha?p-vr-en 'I'm not free', thus 'I'm busy'.

31.309-310 The roadside cross in Wisdom (1940, facing 421) is still standing on the road to Olopa; it is one of the ones serving as indicated in the text.

31.311-324 Their fatigue is said to be transferred to the boughs, which are then left behind at the shrines.

31.327-330 Although it is not entirely clear, it seems likely that the offering to the Earth Spirit takes place when a pilgrim returns. Thus, when González speaks of January 15 as the date of the offering, he is assuming that the pilgrim leaves for Esquipulas on January 11.

31.373 The cross carried out by the women represents San Manuel, the Christ figure and the patron of corn and beans.

31.391 The returning pilgrims do not enter their homes before the prayer-sayer begins his rituals. Often he performs several of these on the same day, and the pilgrims wait on the trails until their turn comes.

31.423-426 The altar for this ceremony is placed against the wall opposite the door of the sleeping house. It is a flat platform of sticks resting on forked corner-posts with a horizontal stick at the back for the crosses to lean on. This platform supports an incense burner, the candles bought at Olopa and shown to the Pastora there, and two to four crosses, each named for and representing a saint. The favored names for these crosses, with their attributes as González explained them, are San Manuel (Christ), the patron of corn and beans, San Miguel (the Young Angel), who brought corn and beans to heaven, Santo Tomás and San Rafael, who bring rain, and San Antonio, the god of fire.

31.495 This ceremony is taken up in text 32. It is clear that the pilgrimage to Esquipulas is a preliminary part of the cycle of New Year ceremonies.

32. Preparations for the Limosna

32.4-25 This arbor is a small-scale house, whose roof construction matches that of the sleeping houses of traditional design. These are not usually thatched with banana leaves, however. The chief difference between this mode of construction and those pictured in Wisdom (1940:122) is the use of _txuhp_ 'tripods' resting on the side plates at either end to support the ridge pole.

32.28-29 The diagram of the sleeping house, arbor, and lot in Figure 1A is only hypothetical. The entrance to the arbor always faces the sleeping house, however, and the foliated cross is placed against the right-hand wall.

32.32 The tree that is planted as a cross is the _txakahr_, Spanish _palo jiote_, which Wisdom (1940:476) identifies as _Bursera simaruba_ (L.) It stands at the center rear of the area used as the altar, just as conventional crosses do in other ceremonies. See Figure 1B.

32.48 A man's child is his _unen_; a woman's is her _ar_. The distinction of sex of senior (rather than of kinsman) recurs in the sibling terms.

32.53 The _palangana_ or _convento_ is the altar or table (it is sometimes called the _mesa_) of the Earth Spirit. It is not a literal table, however, but rather the small plot of ground under the arbor, containing the holes and the furniture, and covered with banana leaves. These arrangements are also discussed in text 33.

32.63-64 It is in this sense that the offering area is a 'table'.

32.95-96 The head of the house is also a participant. He pours the _chilate_ into its hole

32. Preparations for the Limosna

for example.

32.105-110 It is explained in text 40 that the blood of the fowl is food for the Earth Spirit.

33. Offering to the Earth Spirit

33.18 This assumes that the celebrants went to Esquipulas in the second wave of pilgrims. The ceremony is held whenever the pilgrims return.

33.25 The support or base of the house is its plot of level ground, often made by cutting and filling on a slope.

33.31-32 Literally, the many womenfolk fill [the kitchen].

33.264 These trails lead from larger trails to houses. Since Chorti settlements have no center, the main trails (<u>?piir</u>) meander and branch rather than ending in a square or forming a grid.

33.273-280 A pair of holes is dug on the right-hand side of each trail (facing outward from the house); one is for <u>chilate</u>, the other for coals and incense. See Figure 1B.

33.319-320 Only in principle are there four access paths leading to each house, but the principle is an ancient one. See, for example, Michael Coe 1965.

34. Birth of the Sun

34.1-4 Wisdom (1940:445 n20) mentions a festival by this name held on May 11-15 or so, but says nothing about it.

34.5 The sun has not yet risen, but its beams push away the dark, like the beam of a man's flashlight.

34.6-7 The names of the sun were given in a fixed order by Damasio López, whose usage González is following here, but González knows only that the Redemptor comes first, before the actual sunrise.

34.15 González has a folk etymology for this form, from Spanish prestar.

34.17 Whereas han?txak-na has the sense merely of being illuminated, ?tsa?p 'blink' has the additional sense here, with the resultative suffix, of giving off a reflection. The light is less intense than with hih?p 'flash', as of lightning or a mirror in the sun.

34.25 Venus as Morning Star is also called San Pascual.

34.33-46 I do not know if these names refer to phases of the moon or to its diurnal motions.

34.59 Compare text 21.

34.64 The root is ?txui 'lift up'. Compare a-?txui-i 'he lifts', u&-?txui-i 'he baptizes, lifts it', a-?txui-ma 'he baptizes'. This is the root used to describe the way a hawk flies away with its prey.

34.114 Félix González was the maternal grandfather of Isidro González.

34.115 Damasio López (ca. 1880-1949) was also mentioned as González' source for the medical ceremonies.

34. Birth of the Sun

34.120 Feliciana Súchete is the paternal grandmother of Isidro González.

34.121 Narciso Álvarez (ca. 1913-1953) was the leading pupil of Damasio López. He was the husband of a younger sister of González' father.

35. Prayers to the Sun

35.2 This prayer was said as often as every day, rather than on a specific date.

36. Holy Week

36.11 This pilgrimage is timed so as to reach Esquipulas by Thursday of Holy Week, so as to see the confinement of the *Nazareno*. The same ceremony is performed on a smaller scale in Jocotan.

36.12-13 An arbor (*ramada*) used to be built at the edge of town for this purpose, but a small chapel is now used. The saint confined there is Jesús Nazareno, the son of the real Christ, San Manuel.

36.21 The *gloria* is explained as the place where God lives.

36.34 That is, he sold San Manuel.

36.148-176 Compare text 23.

37. Exorcism of the Xiximai

37.1 González reports that this ceremony, held at the end of July, is seldom performed now.

38. Corncrib Offering

38.1 This ceremony is performed at the end of December. It is held in the corncrib, a house like a sleeping house, whose size depends on the amount of corn usually harvested. The corncribs are rectangular structures of sticks inside the house (u&-otot-ir nar). See Figure 2 for the arrangement.

38.14-15 These holes are dug near the wall opposite the door.

38.16-19 The ears are stacked in pairs of rows, on sticks which keep them off the ground, side by side, with the small ends of the ears toward those of the next row and overlapping them.

38.20 The incense is molded to resemble an ear of corn, in a single block.

39. Celebration in the Cornfield

39.1-4 This festival apparently corresponds to the first fruits festival mentioned in Wisdom (1940:445), but is quite different.

39.13 It is difficult to say whether this form and the root ?kan 'yellow' should be treated as homonyms or two senses of the same element.

39.23 The txor is the entire milpa, field, plants, and whatever furniture or fittings go into it. The field itself is u&-ok e-txor 'the foot of the milpa'.

39.59-92 Note the similarity to the other prayers to the Earth Spirit (in text 32, 40).

40. Celebration of the Cane Press

40.1 The cane press is turned by oxen that pull a sweep to drive a vertical wooden roller, which in turn drives a wooden roller on either side through a set of wooden gears.

40.2 The root sum in this compound refers to a wringing action; it is also used for wringing water out of clothing.

40.7 See text 39.

40.47 The root is ior 'dig, drill': u&-ior-i e-?txen 'he digs a hole', a-ior-uan or a-ior-on 'it digs' (of the instrument).

40.52 Since the workmen usually drink throughout this job, and since cane is fed by hand into the rollers, there are many serious injuries.

FIGURE 1A: The House Lot

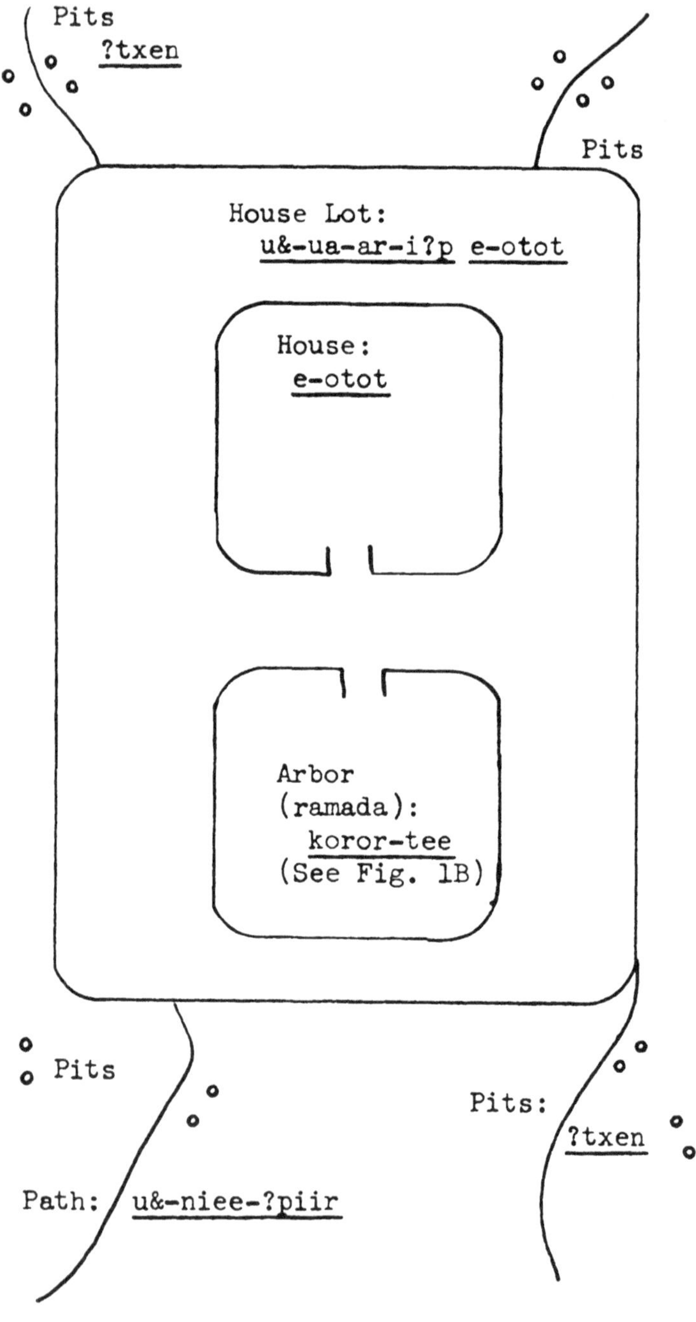

FIGURE 1B: The Arbor and Altar

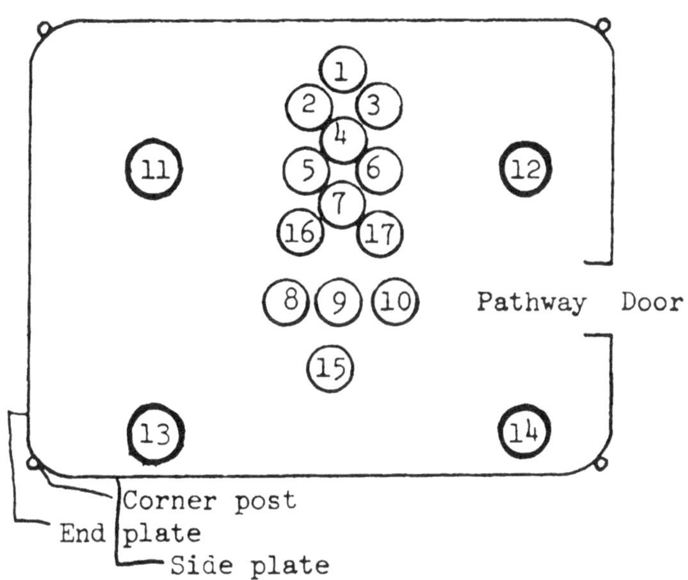

1 Living cross (palo jiote tree)
2 Pit for blood
3 Pit for <u>chilate</u>
4 Bowl of coals
5 Cross with <u>conte</u>
6 Cross with <u>conte</u>
7 Large bowl of unsweetened <u>chilate</u>: <u>saksa?a</u>
8 Large candle with <u>conte</u>
9 Small candle
10 Large candle with <u>conte</u>
11 <u>Bambas</u> of copal
12 Ears of copal
13 Two turkeys, tied
14 Two chickens, tied
15 Padrino
16 Small bowls for angels
17 Unsweetened <u>chilate</u>

FIGURE 2A: The Corncrib

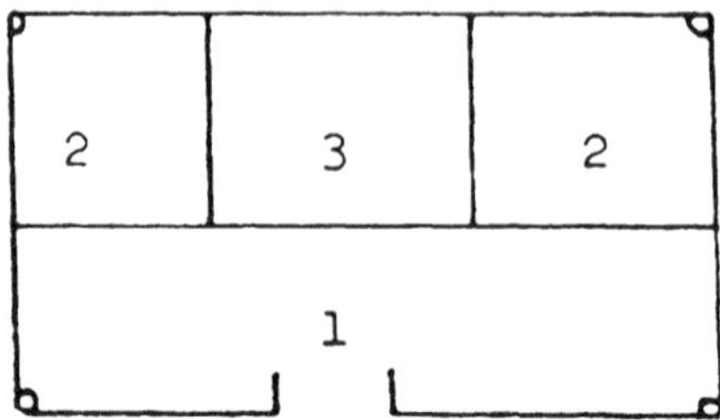

1 Interior of corn house
2 Corncribs
3 Area of offering

FIGURE 2B: Area of Offering

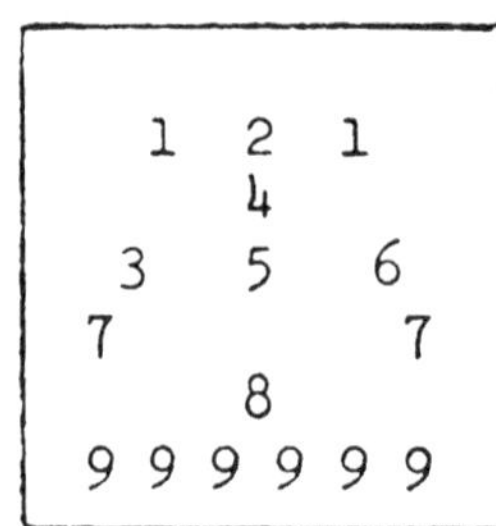

1 Large candles
2 Cross
3 Pit for blood
4 Small candle
5 Bowl for coals
6 Hole for _chilate_
7 Small bowls for angels
8 Large bowl of _chilate_
9 Bowls of sweet _chilate_, number not fixed

Bibliography

Leonard Bloomfield. 1939. 'Menomini morphophonemics', TCLP 8.

Michael D. Coe. 1965. 'A model of ancient community structure in the Maya Lowlands', SWJA 21:97-114.

Dirección General de Cartografía. 1961. Diccionario Geográfico de Guatemala. Guatemala.

John Fought. 1967. Chorti (Mayan) phonology, morphophonemics, and morphology. Yale University Dissertation.

John Fought. 1969. 'Chorti (Mayan) Ceremonial Organization', AA 71:472-6.

Rafael Girard. 1949, 1958. Los Chorti ante el problema Maya. Mexico.

Rafael Girard. 1962. Los Mayas eternos. Mexico.

Rafael Girard. 1966. Los Mayas. Mexico.

Charles F. Hockett. 1961. 'Linguistic elements and their relations', Lg. 37:29-53.

Floyd G. Lounsbury. 1953. Oneida verb morphology. Yale University Publications in Anthropology, 48.

Ernest Noyes and Oliver LaFarge. 1932-33. Correspondence. Chol Studies III. Ms. in Peabody Museum Library, Harvard University.

Ernest Noyes. 1957. Grammar and lexicon of Black Carib and lexicon of Cholti and Chorti. University of Chicago, Microfilm Collection of Manuscripts on Middle American Cultural Anthropology, No. 39.

Helen Oakley. 1966. 'Chorti', in Marvin Mayers, ed., The Languages of Guatemala. The Hague, Janua Linguarum, series practica, 23:235-50.

France Scholes and Ralph Roys. 1948. The Maya Chontal Indians of Acalan-Tixchel. Carnegie Institution, Washington.

Bibliography, cont.

Charles Wisdom. 1940. The Chorti Indians of Guatemala. Chicago.

Charles Wisdom. 1950. Materials on the Chorti language. University of Chicago, Microfilm Collection of Manuscript Materials on American Indian Cultural Anthropology, No. 28.

Appendix

INDEX OF MOTIFS AND TALE TYPES

Gerald E. Parsons, Jr.

with

Margaret J. Bouslough

Appendix: The Sources of the Texts

All the texts in this collection were spoken by Sr. Isidro González. Most were tape recorded:

Reel 07, 7 August 1964, Chiquimula.
Reel 15, October 1964, New Haven.
Reel 38, January 1967, New Haven.
Reel 39, 24 January 1967, New Haven.
Reel 42, 28 February 1967, New Haven.

There are three texts (and miscellaneous material) on reel 07, 21 on reel 15, three on reel 38, one on reel 39, and two on reel 42. Some of these texts were omitted from this collection: 15/04, the Basilisk, because it will appear elsewhere, 15/15, a long anthology of fable episodes, because it is too long and repetitive for inclusion here, and D 13, a cornfield ceremony, because it is incomplete.

Between January and June 1967, in New Haven, González dictated fourteen texts; later a fifteenth (D 15) was produced by combining related portions of the fifth and eleventh of the series.

In the following table, the position of a tape-recorded text on the reel is shown by the number following the solidus. The date of recording follows. In the case of dictations this date shows when _my_ first transcription was completed; González used notes he had prepared in advance.

Text Sources and Dates

Text	Source	Date
1	15/05	10/64
2	15/07	10/64
3	15/06	10/64
4	15/09	10/64
5	15/08	10/64
6	15/01	10/64
7	15/02	10/64
8	07/02	7/8/64
9	07/01	7/8/64
10	15/03	10/64
11	15/16	10/64
12	38/03	1/67
13	42/02	28/2/67
14	15/13	10/64
15	15/14	10/64
16	15/19	10/64
17	15/20	10/64
18	15/21	10/64
19	D5	28/2/67
20	D6	14/3/67
21	15/11	10/64
22	15/12	10/64
23	15/18	10/64
24	D14	13/6/67
25	15/10	10/64
26	42/01	28/2/67
27	D11	30/5/67
28	39/01	24/1/67
29	D12	7/6/67
30	D15	30/5/67
31	D1	31/1/67
32	D7	24/3/67
33	38/01	1/67
34	D2	22/2/67
35	D4	25/2/67
36	D3	23/2/67
37	D8	17/5/67
38	D9	17/5/67
39	38/02	1/67
40	D10	20/5/67

Most readers of the preceding tales probably wonder how much of a given story could be attributed to the contemporary culture of inland Guatemala, how much to that of Colonial Spain, and how much to that of the ancient Maya. Such questions of origin and distribution hark back to the early Nineteenth Century, a time when the study of language and the study of verbal art were more closely integrated than they are at present. It was believed, in those early decades of the 1800's, that there were patterns _in_ language (words and sounds) and patterns _of_ language (folktales), and that the historical reconstruction of either would lead the researcher ultimately back to Mother India. The classic figure of such research is Jacob Grimm, who is remembered both for his _Kinder- und Hausmärchen_ and his laws of sound change. Grimm's laws formalized the relationship between European languages and Sanskrit and in the process demonstrated the power of the comparative method in historical linguistics. Since that time, although the study of language and the study of verbal art have been drifting apart, there is also a comparative method employed in the study of folk narrative. Though it owes much to the work of Grimm, and its aims are the perfectly straightforward ones of tracing the history of particular folktales, the comparative method of the folklorist differs in a number of respects from that of the historical linguist.

In the first place, several tools have been fashioned especially for the folklorist's trade. These are: _The Types of the Folktale_ by Antti Aarne and Stith Thompson (1928) and _The Motif-Index of Folk Literature_ (1955) also by Thompson. The first of these provides index numbers for the many stories which recur in oral tradition as whole story units. The second work provides a catalogue of what Thompson describes as "the smallest units of a narration capable of persisting in oral tradition," that is, motifs. The six weighty volumes of motifs represent a monumental scholarly effort which Thompson says he felt called to undertake because: "Outside of Europe, Aarne's index [of tale types] is of little use. In the remoter parts of the world, whither any adequate study must lead us, the European tale-types are applicable to very few stories. Yet there is much common matter in the folk-literature of the world. The similarities consist not so often in complete tales as in simple motifs. Accordingly, if an attempt is made to reduce the traditional narrative material of the whole earth to order (as, for example the scientists have done with the world-wide phenomena of biology), it must be by means of a classification of single motifs -- those details out of which full-fledged narratives are composed."[1]

Beyond this unique scholarly equipment, there lie some other features of type and motif classification which set it apart from the comparative method familiar to the linguist. While comparative studies in linguistics have been concerned with the systematic correspondences, whether similarities or differences, between a language and its supposed relatives, the relationship between folktales has been figured on similarities alone. A corollary to this point is that the folklore indexing system does not take account of the interrelationship of tale types and motifs with other types and motifs that may be found in the same culture, or in the repertory of the same informant. Efforts to discover such units of analysis are now being pressed in the structuralist movement in folklore studies and some promising developments have appeared. None of these developments, however, is reflected in the following classifications of the Chorti tales. The lists of tale types and motifs which follow conform to the traditional standards of Aarne-Thompson processing. They are purely and simply catalogues of literary forms, independent of their social and psychological connotations, which have occurred both in the stories of Isidro González and in the stories of other narrators throughout the world.

To what uses, then, may these classifications be put? The classic employment for types and motifs is, as has been indicated, in unravelling the historical and geographical meanderings of a single folktale back to its point of origin and its putative original form. This involves a comparison of all known texts of the story from both printed and oral sources; the index numbers provide a guide in locating these texts. A second, and perhaps growing use of the two indexes is to scan collections of stories quickly for references to certain story situations that interest the researcher. In this light, the many appendices of motifs and tale-types within the folklore literature may be seen as an adjunct to the Human Relations Area File, useful in cross-cultural studies of the fictional expression of social and cultural affairs. This appendix does not, of course, offer any conclusions regarding either the history of the tales or their comparison to the tales of other people.

One example in which the universal character of human experience undermines an "obvious" judgement about Chorti culture may suffice to demonstrate the subtlety required if such comparisons are to be valid. In story #16, "The Henpecked Husband," the protagonist is made to drink a potion of ant and scorpion stingers, so as to restore manliness with respect to his overbearing and philandering wife. Nothing seems at first glance more foreign; yet _Mackenzie's Five Thousand Receipts_, published in Philadelphia in 1831, contains the following: "Take of ants, one pound, boiling water, four pounds. Infuse for three hours press out the liquid and steam... for impotency."[2] This is certainly close enough to serve as a caution against easy generalizations.

In the following classification, I have departed from the normal canons of tale typing and motifing in two regards: 1) I have supplied motif numbers for some accounts which were not, strictly speaking, stories. This was done because the tales of the Chorti have not been analyzed before and it seemed that identification of potential motifs might add to the usefullness of the work. 2) I have introduced a new symbol as a qualifier of the index numbers: ? before a number means that the feature of the story in this collection resembles a feature found in the international tales, but that the similarity is not so close as to suggest a genetic relationship. A scholar working with a motif or type so indicated would want to know about this reference, but he might also want to exclude it from his final analysis. The asterisk which appears in front of many numbers is Thompson's standard symbol for a motif or type which has been discovered in the present work and which should be included in the sequence the next time the indices are edited.

FOOTNOTES

[1]Thompson, Stith. 1955. Motif index of folk literature. Bloomington, Indiana: Indiana University Press, 10.

[2]Smith, Elmer, ed. 1968. Early American home remedies. 'Mackenzie's five thousand receipts (by an American Physician)'. Lebanon, Pa.: Applied Arts Publishers, 11.

INDEX OF TALE TYPES

From Antti Aarne and Stith Thompson, The types of the folktale, Helsinki 1961.

INDEX OF MOTIFS: BY TALE

From Stith Thompson, Motif-Index of Folk Literature (6 vols.; Bloomington, Indiana, 1955-58).

1. The Sesimite

F531.1.3.2 Giant with heels in front. F531.6.2.1 Giants live in mountains or caves. @F531.6.2.2.3 Giant's home beneath waterfall. F531.6.7.1.1 Giants have animals (dogs, etc.) F942 Man sinks into earth. F949.1 Animal sinks into earth. G308.2 Water monster. G334 Ogre keeps human prisoners. G336 Ogre draws victims under water. G402 Pursuit of animal leads to ogre's house. G401 Children wander into ogre's house. G420 Capture by ogre. *G427 Ogre releases youth who trespasses. G610 Theft from ogre.

2. The Serpent

A1145.1 Earthquakes from movement of subterranean monster. A2145.0.1 Origin of horned serpent. A2496.2 Copulation of serpents. B91.3 Horned snake. B91.6 Serpent causes flood. *B91.8 Mythical serpent lives in mountain. B103.0.4 Gold-producing serpent. B115.0.1 Treasure-producing serpent's horn. *B115.3.1 Serpent with money in tail. B875.1 Giant serpent. @D1029.2.3 Magic snake tail. E714.2 The serpent dies.

3. The Landslide

A991 Origin of villages. A1145.1 Earthquakes from movement of subterranean monster. *B91.8 Mythical serpent lives in mountain. *F948.6 City is buried under mud. F962 Extraordinary precipitation. @F969.4 Extraordinary earthquake. M301.2 Old woman as prophet. M340.6 Prophecy of great misfortune. *M359.11 Prophecy of landslide. M370 Vain attempts to escape fulfillment of prophecy. N511.1 Treasure buried by men.

4. Stuckhorn

A930.1.1 Snake as creator of rivers and lakes. *A977.5.5 Rock formed by broken horn of serpent. A2496.2 Copulation of serpents. B91.3 Horned snake. *B91.5.3 Sea is full of snakes. B875.1 Giant serpent.

5. The Man and the Serpent

@A1029.1 Marvelous tree survives deluge. B103.0.4 Gold-producing serpent. @B108.1 Serpent as patron of wealth. @B112 Treasure-producing serpent's crown. B115.3 Animal with tail of plenty. D475.2 Transformation: object to money. @D1029.2.3 Magic snake tail. D1295 Magic incense. E714.2 The serpent dies. @F969.4.1 Rumble in earth attends slaying of giant serpent. R311 Tree refuge. Z71.1 Formulistic number: three.

6. The Toad and the Hawk

A2214 Animal characteristics from dropping ancient animal from air. *A2214.7 Ancient toad's jump down from heaven accounts for flat body. J512 Animal should not try to change his nature. *J512.16 Toad tries to fly back from heaven like falcon, but is smashed flat. J2413 Foolish imitation by an animal. L421 Attempt to fly to heaven punished.

7. The Toad

*A2212.3.1 Toads' eyes bulge out from shame of the ancient animal. B211.7.2 Speaking toad. *B214.1.7 Singing toad. *J2413.10 Toad tries to sing like a human but shamed by derisive response.

8. The Raccoon

A1835 Creation of raccoon (from p. 252). *A2261.7 Raccoon has feet, hands and other characteristics left over from time when he could shift back to man's form. B600.2 Animal husband provides characteristic animal food. *D599.1 Transformation: man to animal by crawling between wife's legs. D620 Periodic transformation. D621.1.1 Man by day, animal by night. *D657.4 Transformation in order to steal poultry. *D1745.3 Magic power lost when wives refuse to participate in ritual. OG211.2 .8 Witch as raccoon. OG229.1.1 Witch who is out of skin is prevented from re-entering it when person salts or peppers skin. T111 Marriage of mortal and supernatural being. *T111.7 Marriage of mortal wives and raccoon-spirit husbands.

9. The Coyote

A1834.1 Creation of coyotes. *A1834.2 Creation of coyotes from children transformed after eating new corn. C512 Tabu: plucking ear of grain. *C512.1 Tabu: plucking (and eating) green corn. C962 Transformation to animal for breaking tabu. *Q551.3.2.8 Punishment: children transformed to coyotes for eating new corn.

10. The Armadillo

A285.1 Lightning weapon of gods. A287 Rain god. A1141.4 Lightning as god's whip. A1715 Animals from men transformed from discourtesy to God (Jesus). A1897 Creation of armadillo. A2231 Animal characteristics punishment for impiety. *A2261.8 Armadillo continues to dig earth in rain as when he was a man. *A 2312.4 Origin of armadillo's shell. *A2356.2 .14 Why armadillo has back of bone. A2445 Animal given certain privilege. *A2445.6 Armadillo views his shell as protection against rain and dogs. C962 Transformation to animal for breaking tabu. D100 Transformation man to animal. Q221.3 Blasphemy punished.

11. The Turkeys
A2281 Enmity between animals from original quarrel. *B282.23 Wedding of turkeys.

12. The Buzzard
*A2212 Animal characteristics from great anger of ancient animal. A2435.4.5.1 Carrion as food of vultures. *A2458 Animal's occupation: why buzzard is a mason. J2413 Foolish imitation in animal, tries to go beyond his powers.

13. The Ants
@A2601 Origin of plants: creator sends down insects who plant them. *A2610.1 Creation of corn by transformation of ants. A2685.1 Origin of corn.

14. Indians and Ladinos
@A60 Marplot at creation. *A548 Culture hero (king) refuses God's gifts of clothes, etc. to his people. A661 Heaven: a blissful upper world. A1345 Origin of hunger. A1437 Origin of clothing. @A1610.5 Different tribes result from choice of things sun offers people. *A1683 .6 Why country people wear few clothes and shoes and suffer from poverty. J2052 God's mercy contrasted with man's short-sightedness. Q172 Reward: admission to heaven. Q281 Ingratitude punished. V311 Belief in life to come.

15. The Parent's Curse
D1792 Magic results from curse. *H1599 Test of one's power to bestow a curse: discoloring a loaf of bread. M411.1 Curse by parent. *M419 Test of the potency of one's curse: yellowing of loaf of bread. @Q588 Ungrateful son punished by having son equally ungrateful.

16. The Henpecked Husband
@D555 Transformation by drinking. D1040

Magic drink. D1242.2 Magic potion. D1358 Magic object makes person courageous. *D1358.1.3 Drinking poison of insects makes man courageous. D1782 Sympathetic magic. D1793 Characteristics of animal acquired by eating it. Q241 Adultery punished. Q330 Overweening punished. Q410 Death as punishment. Q411.0.1 Husband kills returning adulteress. Q411.0.2 Husband kills wife and paramour. Q458.0.1 Flogging as punishment for adultery. @T251.2 Taming the shrew. T251.8 Shrewish wife gives husband heating [sic] every morning. T251.10 Wife beats her husband and eats up everything he earns. T252 The overbearing wife. T256.3 Quarrelsome wife reproved by good whipping. T 481 Adultery. *W19 Unmanly husband gains courage.

17. The Henpecked Salesman

J2342 Husband refuses to believe in wife's infidelity. K811 Victim lured into house and killed. K1550 Husband outwits wife and paramour. K1551 Husband returns and secretly spies on adulteress and lovers. K2151 The corpse handed around. Q411.0.1.1 Adulterer killed. Q411.0.2 Husband kills wife and paramour. Q241 Adultery punished. T481 Adultery.

18. The Travelling Man

K811 Victim lured into house and killed. K1550 Husband outwits wife and paramour. Q241 Adultery punished. Q411.0.1.1 Adulterer killed. Q478.1 The eaten heart [etc.]. @S183.1 Person forced to eat hearts (flesh) of relatives (drink blood). T251.2 Taming the shrew. T251 Shrewish wife. T481 Adultery. *W19 Unmanly husband gains courage.

19. Belief in Diviners

A478 God of disease. A651 Hierarchy of worlds. A659.2 Big lake underneath the earth. A671 Hell, lower world of torment. A1337.0.3

Disease caused by witchcraft. A1337.0.5 Disease as punishment. A1337.8 Origin of illness from fire and cold. D1311.6.4 Divination by stars. D1712 Soothsayer (diviner, oracle, etc.) D1712.1 Soothsayer at work by various methods of divination. F402.1.5 Demon causes disease. F493.1 Spirits of various kinds of disease.

20. Curing

A1337.0.5 Disease as punishment. A1337.8 Origin of illness from fire and cold. @D1712 Soothsayer (diviner, oracle, etc.). @D1766.1 Magic results produced by prayer. D1766.7.1.1 Evil spirits conjured away in name of deity. F402.1.5 Demons cause disease. F493.1 Spirits of various kinds of disease.

21. The Funeral Ceremony

E300 Friendly return from the dead. E321 Dead husband's friendly return. *E328 Return of the dead on anniversary of death (weekly, yearly, etc.). @E384 Ghost summoned by music. *E386.6 Ghost summoned by inviting spirit to join the dance. E433.2 Possessions buried with the dead. E433.3 Animals sacrificed so the dead have food on way to other world. @E493 Dead men dance. E541.1 Food placed for returning souls of the dead. E721 Soul journeys from the body. V65.2 Drinking festival in memory of dead. V68 Preparation for burial.

22. Tsikin: The Day of the Dead

D1812.0.15 [sic; should be D1812.5.0.15] Weather signs. *D1812.5.0.15.1 Drizzle during feast of the dead means souls are returning. E300 Friendly return from the dead. *E384.4 Ghosts summoned by ringing of bell. E386.3 Ghosts summoned by calling them by name. E421.1 Invisible ghosts. E541.1 Food placed out for returning souls of the dead. E587.2 Ghosts walk on Halloween. E742.1 Soul as a taper (candle). V65.2 Drinking festival in memory of dead. ©V70.5 Festival of Samhain.

23. The Devil

*D457.1.3 Transformation: blood to wine. D1001 Magic spittle. D1720.1.1 Devil gives man power of wishing. G303.3.1 The devil appears in human form. G303.3.1.1 The devil as large strong man. G303.4.8.13 The devil is invisible. G303.6.1.2 Devil comes when called upon. G303.6.2.1 Devil appears invisible among dancers. G303.9.4.7 Devil tempts girl. ©G303 .16.8 Devil leaves at mention of God's name. M210 Bargain with the devil. M211 Man sells soul to devil. M217 Devil bargains to help man win woman. V70.5 Festival of Samhain.

24. Exorcising Disease

A651 Hierarchy of worlds. A671 Hell, lower world of torment. A1337.0.3 Disease caused by witchcraft. ©D113.1.1 Werewolf. D17 12 Soothsayer (diviner, oracle, etc.). D1712.1 Soothsayer at work by various methods of divination. D1766.7.1.1 Evil spirits conjured away in name of deity. F402.1.5 Demons cause disease. F493.1 Spirits of various kinds of disease. G303 Devil. V12.10 Incense as sacrifice.

25. What the World Used to be Like

A63 Succession of creations and cataclysms. A151 Home of the gods. A856.2 Ground previously all wet dries up. A922 Ocean made from blood. A930 Origin of streams. A960 Origin of mountains. A970 Origin of rocks and stones. A1010 Deluge. Inundation of whole world or section. F510.1 Monstrous races. F 512.2 Person with many eyes. F512.4 Person with eyes in back of head. F531 Giant. *F531 .6.2.7 Giants live in a land across the sea. F931.4 Extraordinary behavior of waves. *F989 .25 Animals come out of the sea to attack city.

G11.18 Cannibal tribe. Z71.1.9 Three seas surrounding the earth.

26. Earth, Sky, and Water

A50 Conflict of good and evil creators. A 60 Marplot at creation. A101 Supreme God. A 106 Opposition of good and evil gods. A151.1 Home of gods on high mountain. A220 Sun-god. A285.1 Lightning, weapon of the gods. A520 Gods as culture heros. A525 Good and bad culture heros. A530.1 Culture hero completes work of creator. A651 Hierarchy of worlds. *A 657.3 Sky and earth sealed at outer reaches of the sea of tar. A659.2 Big lake under earth. A662 Upper world (heaven) as a mountain. *A665 .7 Sacred wind supports sky. A671 Hell, lower world of torment. A671.0.2.1 Fire in hell. *A 671.2.1 Damned souls of murderers shown the blood, or heads, of their victims in hell. *A 702.3.2 Movement of earth around sun through sky. *A702.4 Sky as instep of God's foot. A 722.10 Sun and moon remain half their time in underworld. A731 Sun as king of sky and earth. A800 Creation of the earth. A810 Primeval water, everything covered by. A814.2 Earth [formed] from sand thrown on primeval water. A841 World columns [four]. *A872.2 Four seas encircle world. A1010 Deluge, inundation of whole world or section. A1015.1 Flood [caused by] conflict of the gods. A1058 End of world when culture hero removes one of the world-props. A 1110 Establishment of present order: waters. *A1119.4 Four part division of the sea under the earth. *A1124 Sacred, high altitude wind and profane low altitude wind protect earth from sun's heat. A1711 [Creation of] animals from transformation after the world calamity. A1715 Animals from transformed man. A1750 Animals created through opposition of devil to God. D 170 Transformation: man to fish. E752 Lost souls. E755.2.4.1 Hell fires kindled according to sins of sinners. E755.3 Souls in purgatory.

Q560.3 Sinners endure hell's tortures one year. *Z71.2.9 Four seas surrounding earth. *Z71.5.9 Formulistic number: eight.

27. Signs of the Rainy Season

A1127.1 Effect of the four winds on weather.

28. Rainmaking

A101 Supreme God. A1130.1 [Angel] set over clouds, winds, rains. B1.1 Angels of animals. B177.1 Magic toad. B311 Congenital helpful animal. D857 Magic object born with hero. D1542.1 Magic object produces rain. D2141.1 Storm magically stilled. D2143.1 Rain produced by magic. D2143.1.3 Rain produced by prayer. @D2143.2 Drought produced by magic. T554.8.1 Woman gives birth to toad. V12.9 Libations. V17.4 Sacrifice [to deity] for good weather.

29. Astronomy

A101 Supreme God. A121 Stars as deities. A121.1 Moon as deity. A737.1 Eclipse caused by monster devouring sun or moon. F961 Extraordinary behavior of heavenly bodies.

30. Other Signs of the Weather

@A735.1 Moon tied to sun so that when sun sinks moon is dragged up to light earth.

31. New Years in Esquipulas

A101 Supreme God. A531 Culture hero (demigod) overcomes monsters. A1072.3 Fettered monster as snake. A1544 Origin of idol. A1573.1.1 Heretics swallowed by earth. D2192 Work of day magically overthrown by night. F420.1.3.9 Water spirit as snake. F420.1.3.9.1 Water spirit snake recoils at mention of God's name. F968.2 Lake thunders like the sky. M301.2 Old woman as prophet. Q220 Impiety punished. S261 [Human] foundation sacrifice. V1.11

Worship of idol. V11.7.1 Sacrifice to serpent. V12.4 Animals as sacrifice. V17.0.1 Sacrifice to deity to gain favors. V17.8 Sacrifice at edification of temple. V59 Prayers answered. V 85 Religious pilgrimages. V111.3 Place where church is to be built miraculously indicated. V 530 Pilgrimages. Z71.5.9 Formulistic number: eight.

32. Preparations for the Limosna

V12.4 Animals as sacrifice. V12.9 Libations. V12.10 Incense as sacrifice. V17.0.1 Sacrifice to deity to gain favors.

33. Offering to the Earth Spirit

V12.4 Animals as sacrifice. V12.9 Libations. V12.10 Incense as sacrifice. V17.0.1 Sacrifice to deity to gain favors.

34. The Birth of the Sun

A139.1 Gods (supernatural beings) have many names. A220 Sun-god. A240.1 Moon goddess. E755.3 Souls in purgatory. Q560.3 Sinners endure hell's tortures for one year. V17.0.1 Sacrifice to deity to gain favors.

35. Prayers to the Sun

A101 Supreme God. A220 Sun-god. D1712.1 Soothsayer at work by various methods of divination. *D1712.4 Soothsayer divines by means of cards. *F1061.5 Guttering flame of prayer candle an omen that the deity denies the request. V19.1 Rising smoke as sign of acceptance of sacrifice.

36. Holy Week in Esquipulas

@A1551 The devil's animals and goods. *A1751.2 Blood of Christ yields useful plants, blood of Satan yields harmful creatures. C58 Tabu: profaning sacred day. C721.1 Tabu: bathing during a certain time. V17.0.1 Sacrifice to deity to gain favors. V85 Religious pilgrimages. V113 Shrines. V530 Pilgrimages.

37. The Exorcism of the Xiximai

D1766.7.1 Evil spirits conjured away in name of deity. D2176 Exorcising by magic. D2 176.3.2 Evil spirit exorcised by religious ceremony. E220 Dead relative's malevolent return. E281 Ghosts haunt house. E433 Ghosts placated through sacrifices. E437.1 Revenants banished to glaciers and uninhabited places. F4 05 Means of combatting spirits.

38. Corncrib Offering

V12.4 Animals as sacrifice. V12.9 Libations. V12.10 Incense as sacrifice. V17.1 Sacrifice for a good year, crops.

39. A Celebration in the Cornfield

V12.4 Animals as sacrifice. V12.9 Libations. V12.10 Incense as sacrifice. V17.1 Sacrifice for a good year, crops.

40. The Celebration of the Cane Press

A400.1 Goddess of the earth. V1.6.1 Worship of earth. V12.4 Animals as sacrifice. V1 2.9 Libations. V17.1 Sacrifice for a good year, crops.

INDEX OF MOTIFS: BY CATEGORY

A. Mythological Motifs

Motif Number: Motif Category: Tale Number(s)

A50 Conflict of good and evil creators 26
A60 Marplot at creation 26
@A60 Marplot at creation 14
A63 Succession of creations and cataclysms 25
A101 Supreme God 26, 28, 29, 31, 35
A106 Opposition of good and evil gods 26
A121 Stars as deities 29
A121.1 Moon as deity 29
A139.1 Gods (supernatural beings) have many names 34
A151 Home of the gods 25
A151.1 Home of gods on high mountain 26
A220 Sun-god 26, 34, 35
A240.1 Moon goddess 34
A285.1 Lightning, weapon of the gods 10, 26
A287 Rain god 10
A400.1 Goddess of the earth 40
A478 God of disease 19
A520 Gods as culture heros 26
A525 Good and bad culture heros 26
A530.1 Culture hero completes work of creator 26
A531 Culture hero (demigod) overcomes monsters 31
*A548 Culture hero (king) refuses God's gifts of clothes, etc. to his people 14
A651 Hierarchy of worlds 19, 24, 26
*A657.3 Sky and earth sealed at outer reaches of the sea of tar 26
A659.2 Big lake underneath the earth 19, 26
A661 Heaven: a blissful upper world 14
A662 Upper world (heaven) as a mountain 26
*A665.7 Sacred wind supports sky 26
A671 Hell, lower world of torment 19, 24, 26
A671.0.2.1 Fire in Hell 26

Motif Number: Motif Category: Tale Number(s)

*A671.2.1 Damned souls of murderers shown the blood, or heads, of their victims in hell 26
*A702.3.2 Movement of earth around sun through sky 26
*A702.4 Sky as instep of God's foot 26
A722.10 Sun and moon remain half their time in underworld 26
A731 Sun as king of sky and earth 26
@A735.1 Moon tied to sun so that when sun sinks moon is dragged up to light earth 30
A737.1 Eclipse caused by monster devouring sun or moon 29
A800 Creation of the earth 26
A810 Primeval water, everything covered by 26
A814.2 Earth [formed] from sand thrown on primeval water 26
A841 World columns [four] 26
A856.2 Ground previously all wet dries up 25
*A872.2 Four seas encircle world 26
A922 Ocean made from blood 25
A930 Origin of streams 25
A930.1.1 Snake as creator of rivers and lakes 4
A960 Origin of mountains 25
A970 Origin of rocks and stones 25
*A977.5.5 Rock formed by broken horn of serpent 4
A991 Origin of villages 3
A1010 Deluge; inundation of whole world or section 25, 26
A1015.1 Flood [caused by] conflict of the gods 26
@A1029.1 Marvelous tree survives deluge 5
A1058 End of world when culture hero removes one of the world-props 26
A1072.3 Fettered monster as snake 31
A1110 Establishment of present order: waters 26

Motif Number: Motif Category: Tale Number(s)

*A1119.4 Four part division of the sea under the earth 26
*A1124 Sacred, high altitude wind and profane low altitude wind protect earth from sun's heat 26
A1127.1 Effect of the four winds on weather 27
A1130.1 [Angel] set over clouds, winds, rains 28
A1141.4 Lightning as God's whip 10
A1145.1 Earthquakes from movement of subterranean monster 2, 3
A1337.0.3 Disease caused by witchcraft 19, 24
A1337.0.5 Disease as punishment 19, 20
A1337.8 Origin of illness from fire and cold 19, 20
A1345 Origin of hunger 14
A1437 Origin of clothing 14
A1544 Origin of idol 31
@A1551 The devils' animals and goods 36
A1573.1.1 Heretics swallowed by earth 31
@A1610.5 Different tribes result from choice of things sun offers people 14
*A1683.6 Why country people wear few clothes and shoes and suffer from poverty 14
A1711 [Creation of] animals from transformation after the world calamity 26
A1715 Animals from transformed men 10, 26
A1750 Animals created through opposition of devil to God 26
*A1751.2 Blood of Christ yields useful plants, blood of Satan yields harmful creatures 36
A1834.1 Creation of coyotes 9
*A1834.2 Creation of coyotes from children transformed after eating new corn 9
A1835 Creation of raccoon 8
A1897 Creation of armadillo 10
A2145.0.1 Origin of horned serpent 2

Motif Number: Motif Category: Tale Number(s)

*A2212 Animal characteristics from great anger of ancient animal 12
*A2212.3.1 Toads' eyes bulge out from shame of the ancient animal 7
A2214 Animal characteristics from dropping ancient animal from air 6
*A2214.7 Ancient toad's jump down from heaven accounts for flat body 6
A2231 Animal characteristics punishment for impiety 10
*A2261.7 Raccoon has feet, hands and other characteristics left over from time when he could shift back to man's form 8
*A2261.8 Armadillo continues to dig earth in rain as when he was a man 10
A2281 Enmity between animals from original quarrel 11
*A2312.4 Origin of armadillo's shell 10
*A2356.2.14 Why armadillo has back of bone 10
A2435.4.5.1 Carrion as food of vultures 12
A2445 Animal given certain privilege 10
*A2445.6 Armadillo views his shell as protection against rain and dogs 10
*A2458 Animal's occupation: why buzzard is a mason 12
A2496.2 Copulation of serpents 2, 4
©A2601 Origin of plants: creator sends down insects who plant them 13
*A2610.1 Creation of corn by transformation of ants 13
A2685.1 Origin of corn 13

B. Animals

B1.1 Angels of animals 28
B91.3 Horned snake 2, 4
*B91.5.3 Sea is full of snakes 4
B91.6 Serpent causes flood 2

Motif Number: Motif Category: Tale Number(s)

*B91.8 Mythical serpent lives in mountain 2, 3
B103.0.4 Gold-producing serpent 2, 5
B108.1 Serpent as patron of wealth 5
@B112 Treasure-producing serpent's crown 5
B115.0.1 Treasure-producing serpent's hown 2
B115.3 Animal with tail of plenty 5
*B115.3.1 Serpent with money in tail 2
B177.1 Magic toad 28
B211.7.2 Speaking toad 7
*B214.1.7 Singing toad 7
*B282.23 Wedding of turkeys 11
B311 Congenital helpful animal 28
B600.2 Animal husband provides characteristic animal food 8
B875.1 Giant serpent 2, 4

C. Tabu

C58 Tabu: profaning sacred day 36
C512 Tabu: plucking ear of grain 9
*C512.1 Tabu: plucking (and eating) green corn 9
C721.1 Tabu: bathing during a certain time 36
C962 Transformation to animal for breaking tabu 9, 10

D. Magic

D100 Transformation: man to animal 10
@D113.1.1 Werewolf 24
D170 Transformation: man to fish 26
*D457.1.3 Transformation: blood to wine 23
D475.2 Transformation: object to money 5
@D555 Transformation by drinking 16
*D599.1 Transformation: man to animal by crawling between wife's legs 8
D620 Periodic transformation 8

Motif Number: Motif Category: Tale Number(s)

D621.1.1 Man by day, animal by night 8
*D657.4 Transformation in order to steal poultry 8
D857 Magic object born with hero 28
D1001 Magic spittle 23
@D1029.2.3 Magic snake tail 2, 5
D1040 Magic drink 16
D1242.2 Magic potion 16
D1295 Magic incense 5
D1311.6.4 Divination by stars 19
D1358 Magic object makes person courageous 16
*D1358.1.3 Drinking poison of insects makes man courageous 16
D1542.1 Magic object produces rain 28
D1712 Soothsayer (diviner, oracle, etc.) 19, 24
@D1712 Soothsayer (diviner, oracle, etc.) 20
D1712.1 Soothsayer at work by various methods of divination 19, 24, 35
*D1712.4 Soothsayer divines by means of cards 35
D1720.1.1 Devil gives man power of wishing 23
*D1745.3 Magic power lost when wives refuse to participate in ritual 8
@D1766.1 Magic results produced by prayer 20
D1766.7.1 Evil spirits conjured away in name of deity 37
D1766.7.1.1 Evil spirits conjured away in name of deity 20, 24
D1782 Sympathetic magic 16
D1792 Magic results from curse 15
D1793 Characteristics of animal acquired by eating it 16
D1812.0.15 [sic: should be D1812.5.0.15] Weather signs 22
*D1812.5.0.15.1 Drizzle during feast of the dead means souls are returning 22
D2176 Exorcising by magic 37
@D2176.3.2 Evil spirit exorcised by religious ceremony 37

Motif Number: Motif Category: Tale Number(s)

D2141.1 Storm magically stilled 28
D2143.1 Rain produced by magic 28
D2143.1.3 Rain produced by prayer 28
@D2143.2 Drought produced by magic 28
D2192 Work of day magically overthrown by night 31

E. The Dead

E220 Dead relative's malevolent return 37
E281 Ghosts haunt house 37
E300 Friendly return from the dead 21, 22
E321 Dead husband's friendly return 21
*E328 Return of the dead on anniversary of death (weekly, yearly, etc.) 21
@E384 Ghost summoned by music 21
*E384.4 Ghosts summoned by ringing of bell 22
E386.3 Ghosts summoned by calling them by name 22
*E386.6 Ghost summoned by inviting spirit to join the dance 21
E421.1 Invisible ghosts 22
E433 Ghosts placated through sacrifices 37
E433.2 Possessions buried with the dead 21
E433.3 Animals sacrificed so the dead have food on way to other world 21
E437.1 Revenants banished to glaciers and uninhabited places 37
@E493 Dead men dance 21
E541.1 Food placed for returning souls of the dead 21, 22
E587.2 Ghosts walk on Halloween 22
E714.2 The serpent dies 2, 5
E721 Soul journeys from the body 21
E742.1 Soul as a taper (candle) 22
E752 Lost souls 26
E755.2.4.1 Hell fires kindled according to sins of sinners 26
E755.3 Souls in purgatory 26, 34

Motif Number: Motif Category: Tale Number(s)

F. Marvels

F402.1.5 Demon causes disease 19, 20, 24
F405 Means of combatting spirits 37
F420.1.3.9 Water spirit as snake 31
F420.1.3.9.1 Water spirit snake recoils at mention of God's name 31
F493.1 Spirits of various kinds of disease 19, 20, 24
F510.1 Monstrous races 25
F512.2 Person with many eyes 25
F512.4 Person with eyes in back of head 25
F531 Giant 25
F531.1.3.2 Giant with heels in front 1
F531.6.2.1 Giants live in mountains or caves 1
@F531.6.2.2.3 Giant's home beneath waterfall 1
*F531.6.2.7 Giants live in a land across the sea 25
F531.6.7.1.1 Giants have animals (dogs, etc.) 1
F931.4 Extraordinary behavior of waves 25
F942 Man sinks into earth 1
*F948.6 City is buried under mud 3
F949.1 Animal sinks into earth 1
F961 Extraordinary behavior of heavenly bodies 29
F962 Extraordinary precipitation 3
F968.2 Lake thunders like the sky 31
@F969.4 Extraordinary earthquake 3
*F989.25 Animals come out of the sea to attack city 25
@F969.4.1 Rumble in earth attends slaying of giant serpent 5
*F1061.5 Guttering flame of prayer candle an omen that the deity denies the request 35

G. Ogres

G11.18 Cannibal tribe 25
@G211.2.8 Witch as raccoon 8

Motif Number: Motif Category: Tale Number(s)

@G229.1.1 Witch who is out of skin is prevented from re-entering it when person salts or peppers skin 8
G303 Devil 24
G303.3.1 Devil [appears] in human form 23
G303.3.1.1 The devil as large, strong man 23
G303.4.8.13 The devil is invisible 23
G303.6.1.2 Devil comes when called upon 23
G303.6.2.1 Devil appears invisible among dancers 23
G303.9.4.7 Devil tempts girl 23
@G303.16.8 Devil leaves at mention of God's name 23
G308.2 Water monster 1
G334 Ogre keeps human prisoners 1
G336 Ogre draws victims under water 1
G401 Children wander into ogre's house 1
G402 Pursuit of animal leads to ogre's house 1
G420 Capture by ogre 1
*G427 Ogre releases youth who trespasses 1
G610 Theft from ogre 1

H. Tests

*H1599 Test of one's power to bestow a curse: discoloring a loaf of bread 15

J. The Wise and the Foolish

J512 Animal should not try to change his nature 6
*J512.16 Toad tries to fly back from heaven like falcon, but is smashed flat 6
J2052 God's mercy contrasted with man's shortsightedness 14
J2342 Husband refuses to believe in wife's infidelity 17
J2413 Foolish imitation by an animal 6, 12

Motif Number: Motif Category: Tale Number(s)

*J2413.10 Toad tries to sing like a human but is shamed by derisive response 7

K. Deceptions

K811 Victim lured into house and killed 17, 18

K1550 Husband outwits wife and paramour 17, 18

K1551 Husband returns and secretly spies on adultress and lovers 17

K2151 The corpse handed around 17

L. Reversal of Fortune

L421 Attempt to fly to heaven punished 6

M. Ordaining the Future

M210 Bargain with the devil 23

M211 Man sells soul to devil 23

M217 Devil bargains to help man win woman 23

M301.2 Old woman as prophet 3, 31

M340.6 Prophecy of great misfortune 3

*M359.11 Prophecy of landslide 3

M370 Vain attempts to escape fulfillment of prophecy 3

M411.1 Curse by parent 15

*M419 Test of the potency of one's curse: yellowing of loaf of bread 15

N. Chance and Fate

N511.1 Treasure buried by men 3

Motif Number: Motif Category: Tale Number(s)

Q. Rewards and Punishments

Q172 Reward: admission to heaven 14
Q220 Impiety punished 31
Q221.3 Blasphemy punished 10
Q241 Adultery punished 16, 17, 18
Q281 Ingratitude punished 14
Q330 Overweening punished 16
Q410 Death as punishment 16
Q411.0.1 Husband kills returning adulteress 16
Q411.0.1.1 Adulterer killed 17, 18
Q411.0.2 Husband kills wife and paramour 16, 17
Q458.0.1 Flogging as punishment for adultery 16
Q478.1 The eaten heart [etc.] 18
*Q551.3.2.8 Punishment: children transformed to coyotes for eating new corn 9
Q560.3 Sinners endure hell's tortures one year 26, 34
@Q588 Ungrateful son punished by having son equally ungrateful 15

R. Captives and Fugitives

R311 Tree refuge 5

S. Unnatural Cruelty

@S183.1 Person forced to eat hearts (flesh) of relatives (drink blood) 18
S261 [Human] foundation sacrifice 31

T. Sex

T111 Marriage of mortal and supernatural being 8

Motif Number: Motif Category: Tale Number(s)

*T111.7 Marriage of mortal wives and raccoon-spirit husbands 8
T251 Shrewish wife 18
@T251.2 Taming the shrew 16, 18
T251.8 Shrewish wife gives husband heating [sic] every morning 16
T251.10 Wife beats her husband and eats up everything he earns 16
T252 The overbearing wife 16
@T256.3 Quarrelsome wife reproved by good whipping 16
T481 Adultery 16, 17, 18
T554.8.1 Woman gives birth to toad 28

V. Religion

V1.6.1 Worship of earth 40
V1.11 Worship of idol 31
V11.7.1 Sacrifice to serpent 31
V12.4 Animals as sacrifice 31, 32, 33, 38, 39, 40
V12.9 Libations 28, 32, 33, 38, 39, 40
V12.10 Incense as sacrifice 24, 32, 33, 38, 39
V17.0.1 Sacrifice to deity to gain favors 31, 32, 33, 34, 36
V17.1 Sacrifice for a good year, crops 38, 39, 40
V17.4 Sacrifice [to deity] for good weather 28
V17.8 Sacrifice at edification of temple 31
V19.1 Rising smoke as sign of acceptance of sacrifice 35
V59 Prayers answered 31
V65.2 Drinking festival in memory of dead 21, 22
V68 Preparation for burial 21
@V70.5 Festival of Samhain 22, 23
V85 Religious pilgrimages 31, 36

Motif Number: Motif Category: Tale Number(s)

V111.3 Place where church is to be built miraculously indicated 31
V113 Shrines 36
V311 Belief in life to come 14
V530 Pilgrimages 31, 36

W. Traits of Character

*W19 Unmanly husband gains courage 16, 18

Z. Miscellaneous Groups of Motifs

Z71.1 Formulistic number: three 5
Z71.1.9 Three seas surrounding the earth 25
*Z71.2.9 Four seas surrounding earth 26
*Z71.5.9 Formulistic number: eight 26, 31

www.ingramcontent.com/pod-product-compliance
Lightning Source LLC
Chambersburg PA
CBHW060640310726
48982CB00003B/827
9780812276671